NMC

Security Supervision and Management

Security Supervision and Management

Theory and Practice of Asset Protection

Fourth Edition

International Foundation for Protection Officers

Edited by

Sandi J. Davies

Christopher A. Hertig

Brion P. Gilbride

AMSTERDAM • BOSTON • HEIDELBERG • LONDON
NEW YORK • OXFORD • PARIS • SAN DIEGO
SAN FRANCISCO • SINGAPORE • SYDNEY • TOKYO

Butterworth-Heinemann is an imprint of Elsevier

ELSEVIER

BH

Butterworth-Heinemann is an imprint of Elsevier
The Boulevard, Langford Lane, Kidlington, Oxford OX5 1GB, UK
225 Wyman Street, Waltham, MA 02451, USA

First edition 1995
Second edition 1999
Third edition 2008
Fourth edition 2015

ISBN: 978-0-12-800113-4

British Library Cataloguing-in-Publication Data
A catalogue record for this book is available from the British Library

Library of Congress Cataloging-in-Publication Data
A catalog record for this book is available from the Library of Congress

For information on all Butterworth-Heinemann publications
visit our website at http://store.elsevier.com

www.elsevier.com • www.bookaid.org

Dedication

I fondly dedicate my contributions to this book to the loyal supporters of the International Foundation for Protection Officers (IFPO). For more then 25 years, the IFPO has been offering professional development opportunities to individuals in the security industry that has directly and favorably impacted their careers. To all of those who have contributed to the success of this Foundation and of course this project, I thank you!

On a more personal note, I want to thank Douglas D. Schumann for his patience, understanding, and support over the course of this project. He kept me laughing and smiling during this sometimes difficult and challenging journey! With all my love...

—Sandi J. Davies

First and foremost, I want to dedicate my contribution to this book to my wife and children. It was with their love and support that I was able to participate in this most worthwhile endeavor.

Secondly, I want to thank my co-authors Sandi and Chris for granting me the honor and privilege of sitting at the table with them to develop the best edition yet!

—Brion P. Gilbride, CPP, CSSM, CPO

To the "forgotten soldiers" in my life: the women who supported my writing and teaching. My wife Carla, who started me writing and is forever by my side. My friend Jackie. My mother Betty and grandmother Violet, who taught me and gave me so many things. And Cynthia, who helped when it was needed.

And to those I taught and helped along the way. They gave me back more than they will ever know.

—Christopher A. Hertig, CPP, CPOI

Contents

Unit I: Foundations

Unit II: Basics of Supervision

Unit III

Part 1: Human Resource Management

Part 2: Security-Related Business Functions

Unit IV: Technology in Security

Unit VII: Current Issues in Security

List of Authors and Contributors

Authors

Fern Abbott

Brian D. Baker, MA, CPP, PCI, CPOI

Daniel R. Baker

Tucker Beecher

Inge Sebyan Black, BA, CPP, CFE, CPOI

John T. Brobst Jr., CSSM, CPO

Paul A. Caron, BS

Jeffrey L. Colorossi, M.Sc, CISM, CISSP, CHFI

Tom M. Conley, MA, CPP, CPOI, CPO

Dr. Gerald D. Curry

Dr. Michael Dannecker, MPA, CSSM, CPO

Whitney DeCamp, Ph.D.

James A. DeMeo, MS

Bruce W. Dobbins, CPP, CPOI

Dr. Ona Ekhomu, CFE, CPP

Erik D. Erikson, CPO, CPOI

Lawrence J. Fennelly, CPOI, CSSM, HLS-III

Eric L. Garwood, CPP, CPO, CSS

Brion P. Gilbride, CPP, CSSM, CPO

Col. K.C. Goswami, CPOI

David N. Halcovitch, BA, CAS, CPOI

Kevin Herskovitz, MS

Christopher A. Hertig, CPP, CPOI

Christopher Innace, CPO

Glen Kitteringham, MS, CPP, CSSM, CPO

Dr. Bryan Kling, CPO

James J. Leflar Jr., MA, CPP, CBCP, MBCI

Gary Lyons, BA, CPO, CSSM, CPP

Robert A. Metscher, MBA, CPP, CISSP, CFE

Matthew J. Millsaps, BS, P-C, CPO

Ronald R. Minion, CPP, CPOI, CPO

Eloy L. Nunez, Ph.D

Patricia A. O'Donoghue

H.D.G.T. Oey

Kevin E. Palacios, M.Sc., CPP, PSP, CPOI

Marianna Perry, MS, CPP

Kevin E. Peterson, CPP, CPOI, CIPM II

David L. Ray, BA, LL.B

Andrew R. Reitnauer, MSFE, CLPE, CSCSA, CPO

Randy W. Rowett, CSSM, CPO

Jeffrey A. Slotnick, CPP, PSP

Larry Steele, MA, MA-TH, CPO

Matt Stiehm, Ph.D.

Charles T. Thibodeau, M.Ed., CPP, CSSM, CPOI

Franklin R. Timmons, CPP, CPOI

Ann Y. Trinca, Esq., CPP, CSSM, CPOI

Ernest G. Vendrell, Ph.D., CEM, CPP, CPO

Mavis Vet, CSSM, CPO

Ted Wade, MA

Scott A. Watson, MCJ, M.Ed., CPP, CFE

Eric Webb

Contributors

Eric Stauffer, CPO

James Drymiller, CPP

Alice Grime

David Foldi, CPP, CPOI

Author and contributor profiles can be found on the IFPO website: www.ifpo.org

Foreword

Marianna Perry and Lawrence J. Fennelly

Times have changed!

The baby boomers are retiring. The face of security is changing. Research is being done to advance the security profession to provide the highest level of protection while at the same time increasing the bottom-line profitability of the organization.

College courses are changing—going forward, the combination of business as a major field of study, and security or information technology as a minor, will be the new norm. This change is being implemented to prepare security professionals to properly protect corporate assets.

The new "buzz words" from 2015 to 2020 will be:

1. What kind of *skill set* does the candidate/officer have?
2. What *certifications and specialization* does the candidate/officer have?
3. Both *physical and informational security* will be merging with the move toward certifications.
4. *Career pathways* will be used by way of *internships*.
5. Your *certification* will be the bar for testing qualifications.
6. Education for a career in security is being *redesigned*. Are you ready?

Plan for the future now!

This is, in our opinion, a one-of-a-kind text that has been specifically written and offered to readers: the supervisor or manager, as well as the aspiring protection officer or university student. There is no substitute for experience, but this goes a long way in preparing the readers (participants) for their journey on the management career path and certifications. When we were both supervisors, there was no text and very little additional training provided for supervisors.

We salute all of the many contributors who assisted in putting the text together and sharing their expertise to make the path easier to attain supervisory skills and abilities. During the past 5 years, a lot has changed both nationally and internationally. Homeland security has developed and terrorism remains an ever evolving threat. Organized retail crime, identity theft/information loss, and natural disasters also continue to be major concerns of protection professionals. The top 10 crime threat problems according to a Securitas 2012 survey of Fortune 1000 companies are: cyber/communications security, workplace violence prevention, business continuity, employee selection/screening, property crime (e.g., external theft, vandalism), general employee theft, crisis management and response, unethical business conduct, litigation for inadequate security, and identity theft.

Consequently, the education and training provided must meet these threats. Supervisors and managers must be well versed in these topics and must inspire their subordinates to acquire more education, training, and experience. They must continually emphasize professional growth and development of the individual officer, agent, or investigator. Organizational development occurs when substantial numbers of the protection organization have undergone professional development experiences.

Introduction

Sandi J. Davies, Christopher A. Hertig, and Brion P. Gilbride

Sandi J. Davies, Co-editor

Sandi began her career in contract security in 1980 with a primary focus on personnel administration. She became deeply involved in training and was instrumental in developing security officer training programs for a major national guard company. Her interest in security training grew, and in 1988 she joined the newly formed International Foundation for Protection Officers (IFPO) as an administrative assistant. In 1991, she was named executive director of the IFPO and has been a driving force in Foundation program development worldwide and administration ever since. Sandi is a long-time member of ASIS International, having served in various executive positions at the chapter level. Sandi is also a member and former chair of the ASIS International Security Services Council and a member of the Women in Security Council.

Christopher A. Hertig, CPP, CPOI, Co-editor

Chris began his career in 1975 as a part-time student aide in the Security Department during his junior year in college. He has worked as a security officer and supervisor in various settings. He also did some investigative work and was a park police officer. In 1980, he became a Nuclear Security Training Administrator, where he developed instructional materials and taught security personnel. In late 1982, he met a young woman named Carla who inspired him to continue his graduate education and write for publication. He subsequently began writing and has published hundreds of articles, reviews, chapters, and books.

In 1984, he married Carla, completed his master's degree, and joined the Behavioral Sciences Department at York College of Pennsylvania. Chris has been active on the ASIS International Academic Programs Council. He is a member of the Board of Directors for the IFPO and has worked with the National Partnership for Careers in Law, Public Safety, Corrections, and Security. He has held instructor credentials in a number of subjects and is both a Certified Protection Professional (CPP) and Certified Protection Officer Instructor (CPOI).

Brion P. Gilbride, CPP, CSSM, CPO, Co-editor

Brion began his career in 1996 as a part-time campus security officer. He worked as a security officer and first-line supervisor in campus security and industrial security, earning his Certified Protection Officer (CPO) and Certified in Security Supervision and Management (CSSM) credentials. Brion began his law enforcement career in 2001 as an Inspector with the US Customs Service (now US Customs & Border Protection). He served as a Customs and Border Protection Officer in the land, air, and sea environments prior to promotion to Supervisory Customs & Border Protection Officer in 2007. From there, he transitioned into program management in 2009 at the regional level and in 2011 at the national (headquarters) level, specializing in insider threat analysis and deep-dive analytics. In 2013, Brion was awarded the CBP Commissioner's Unit Citation for his analytic work. He completed his undergraduate education at York College of Pennsylvania in 1999 and his graduate education at American Public University in 2008. In 2012, he joined ASIS International and earned his Certified Protection Professional (CPP) designation. Brion served as a member of the ASIS Supply Chain and Transportation Security Council from 2013–2014 and prepared their monthly Council Newsletter. He has written articles for Security Management magazine as well as chapters in IFPO's *Professional Protection Officer* and *Security Supervision and Management* texts.

Security Supervision and Management Text

Demand for the Security Supervision and Management Program, which was developed in 1990 by the International Foundation for Protection Officers (IFPO), has continued to grow. As new components were added to the program, a more current, relevant course text had to be developed. Commensurate with this demand was the need for college and university courses in security, asset protection, homeland security, and emergency management. The need to provide additional web support for the book was also apparent.

The IFPO embarked on the task of completing a new text to fulfill these needs and engaged a team of professionals to contribute to this effort. The result was the forming of an alliance between the IFPO/Butterworth-Heinemann and some of the industry's leading security supervisors, authors, educators, researchers, and consultants, who collectively contributed to the production of this text.

The book for security leaders is here. It serves participants in the Security Supervision and Management Program as well as students in other Foundation programs (visit ifpo.org). It also provides graduate and upper level undergraduate professors with an extremely useful companion text. *Security Supervision: Theory and Practice of Asset Protection* provides a broad foundation of knowledge, making it an ideal course text as well as a valued reference for protection practitioners and students alike.

Security Supervision and Management Program Objectives

To facilitate the academic and professional development of security professionals who aspire to enhance their leadership skills.

To deliver a functional supervisory/management instructional program developed to heighten each candidate's ability to master the techniques of security personnel management.

To provide a meaningful accreditation that will lend professional recognition to those candidates who exhibit the knowledge and skills required to be Certified in Security Supervision and Management (CSSM).

History of the Program

The International Foundation for Protection Officers was founded in 1988. A dedicated group of well-known senior members of the international security community set out to develop a nonprofit organization that would address the professional training and certification needs of security officers and first-line supervisors.

Through the commitment and vision of these industry leaders, the IFPO was formed. The Foundation's first and foremost undertaking was to develop the Certified Protection Officer (CPO) Program. Since the inception of the program, thousands of officers have earned their

CPO accreditation, now the recognized designation for professional officers employed by proprietary and contract security forces worldwide.

As the IFPO grew, so did the need for Foundation leadership in addressing the professional development requirements of members of the security industry. Security officers earned seniority and often assumed leadership roles within their respective security organizations. The IFPO recognized that there had to be a learning progression, a better defined professional development/career path. The Board of Directors and Foundation administrators subsequently developed the Security Supervisor Program and Certified Security Supervisor (CSS) designation. In 2004, the IFPO Board of Directors elected to rename the program and it evolved into the Security Supervision and Management Program and Certified in Security Supervision and Management (CSSM). This title change better reflects the content and emphasis of the program materials.

Security Supervision and Management Program Logistics

In addition to complete review of the program curriculum contained in this book additional learning support for students and instructors is available at ifpo.org.

To complete the Security Supervision and Management Program, each candidate must successfully achieve a score of no less than 70% on the final examination. Once the applicant has successfully completed this process, he or she would be awarded a certificate of completion for the Security Supervision and Management Program.

The candidate may then may elect to proceed with the Certified in Security Supervision and Management (CSSM) Program if he or she qualifies. Candidates enrolling into this program must have 18 months of full-time security experience with a minimum of 6 months at the supervisory or managerial level. Part-time experience may be used to fulfill this requirement at a 2:1 ratio. Experience submitted must be where the primary job duties are asset protection.

The CSSM program candidates are required to select and analyze a series of workplace scenarios that describe on-the-job conditions which are frequently encountered by the working security supervisor and/or manager. Each situation demands immediate leadership action. Candidates must describe in detail the appropriate actions recommended to bring the matter to a successful conclusion. The corrective measures employed by the supervisor or manager must be supported from the contents of the course text.

Candidates seeking the CSSM accreditation must submit an affidavit in the prescribed form, declaring that the written portion of the program is authored entirely by the applicant seeking accreditation.

The CSSM certification committee will review the scenarios and application along with the candidate's complete file to determine eligibility for the certification.

Conclusion

The Foundation has developed an important relationship with Butterworth–Heinemann (BH), who have responded positively to the need to recognize the working security professional as well as those studying asset protection in colleges and universities. Without the continued support of BH, it would be difficult for the IFPO to exercise its mandate of providing professional development opportunities to the rapidly expanding security industry.

Protection Officer Code of Ethics

The Protection Officer shall:

1. Respond to an employer's professional needs
2. Exhibit exemplary conduct
3. Protect confidential information
4. Maintain a safe and secure workplace
5. Dress to create professionalism
6. Enforce all lawful rules and regulations
7. Encourage liaison with public officers
8. Develop good rapport within the profession
9. Strive to attain professional competence
10. Encourage high standards of officer ethics

Protection Officer Code of Ethics

Today, business and the public expect a great deal from the uniformed security officer. In the past, there has been far too little attention paid to the ethical aspects of the profession. There has to be solid guidelines that each officer knows and understands. More importantly, it is essential that each manager and supervisor performs his or her duties in a manner what will reflect honesty, integrity, and professionalism.

Every training program should address the need for professional conduct on and off duty. Line officers must exhibit a willingness to gain professional competency and adhere to a strict code of ethics that must include the following.

Loyalty

The officer must be loyal to the employer, the client, and the public. The officer must have a complete and thorough understanding of all of the regulations and procedures that are necessary to protect people and assets on or in relation to the facility they are assigned to protect.

Exemplary Conduct

The officer is under constant scrutiny by everyone in work and public places. Hence, it is essential that he or she exhibits exemplary conduct at all times. Maturity and professionalism are the key words to guide all officers.

Confidentiality

Each officer is charged with the responsibility of working in the interests of his or her employer. Providing protection means that the officer will encounter confidential information which must be carefully guarded and never compromised.

Safety and Security

The foremost responsibility of all officers is to ensure that the facility is protected—safe and secure for all persons with lawful access. The officer must fully understand all necessary procedures to eliminate or control security and safety risks.

Deportment

Each officer must dress in an immaculate manner. Crisp, sharp, clean, and polished are the indicators that point to a professional officer that will execute his or her protection obligations in a proficient manner and will be a credit to the profession.

Law Enforcement Liaison

It is the responsibility of each officer to make every effort to encourage and enhance positive relations with members of public law enforcement. Seek assistance when a genuine need exists and offer assistance whenever possible.

Strive to Learn

To become professionally competent, each officer must constantly strive to be knowledgeable about his or her chosen career. How to protect people, assets, and information must always be a learning priority for every officer.

Develop Rapport

It is necessary to be constantly aware of the image that our profession projects. All officers can enhance the image of the industry, their employer, and themselves. Recognize and respect peers and security leaders throughout the industry.

Honesty

By virtue of the duties and responsibilities of all officers, honest behavior is absolutely essential at all times. Each officer occupies a position of trust that must not be violated. Dishonesty can never be tolerated by the security profession.

Prejudice

The job of protecting means that the officer must impose restrictions on people that frequent the security workplace. All human beings must be treated equally, with dignity and respect, regardless of color, race, religion, or political beliefs.

Self-Discipline

With the position of trust comes the responsibility to diligently protect life and property. These duties can only be discharged effectively when the officer understands the gravity of his or her position. Self-discipline means trying harder and caring more.

Conclusion

The job of protecting life and property focuses much attention on the individual security officer. Hence, it is essential to be aware of the need for professional conduct at all times. By strictly adhering to each section in this code of ethics, it may be expected that we as individuals and the industry as a whole will enjoy a good reputation and gain even more acceptance from the public as well as private and government corporations. You as the individual officer must be a principal in this process.

Foundations

1

What is Asset Protection?

Robert A. Metscher

What is *asset protection*? For that matter, what is security or safety, accounting, information systems, sales, or transportation? All too often, the definition of an organizational function is obvious to each individual, right up until it must be defined. This problem is representative of the famous comment by U.S. Supreme Court Justice Potter Stewart: "I know it when I see it." In many instances, it may not be necessary to declare, with any certainty, what asset protection is (or is not) if an organization simply allows it to develop organically from operational practices. As easy as it may be for an organization's management to sidestep defining it, there are few things more embarrassing to a practitioner than being unable to clearly answer what it is they do. Thus, organizations and professionals around the world ought to be capable of stating, with some clarity, what asset protection, security, and safety are and what they do. Moreover, it is a professional's role to contribute the best information to assist organizational leaders with their decisions.

The field of endeavor associated with protecting people and things from harm operates under several different titles. The most common—and historical—are *security and safety*. Other names, such as loss prevention, resource protection, loss control, and asset protection, may also be found in various organizations. For simplicity, this chapter uses the term *asset protection* to encompass all of these names. To better describe what asset protection is, one must first define the terms *safety* and *security*, and clarify the relationship between the two.

The delineation of safety and security is a sometimes hotly contested point. These fields are without a doubt related, yet they each have specific concerns that separate them. The lack of a clear, delineating definition for each term may cause turf issues among organizational managers. Much like within project management, where a poorly defined scope for the project can result in "mission creep," the same can occur when refining the role definition of an organization's safety and security programs. This is much less of a concern when both functional groups report to the same executive. However, in developing groups and larger organizations, these functions may operate entirely independently of each other, or there may be multiple separate entities filling these roles. Thus, friction may develop without a clear delineation of roles. Worse yet, turning to the dictionary for guidance in separating the roles of safety and security seems to be futile.

Merriam-Webster defines *safety* as "freedom from harm or danger: the state of being safe."[1] Dictionary.com defines *safety* a little differently, as "the state of being safe; freedom from the occurrence or risk of injury, danger, or loss."[2] Both definitions reference freedom from danger, whereas one references freedom from harm and the other references

Security Supervision and Management. http://dx.doi.org/10.1016/B978-0-12-800113-4.00001-8

freedom from occurrence, or risk of injury or loss. Merriam-Webster's definition appears to refer only to people, while Dictionary.com includes property by use of the term "loss."

Merriam-Webster defines *security* as "the state of being protected or safe from harm."[3] This is very similar to Merriam-Webster's definition of safety. Dictionary.com defines *security* as "freedom from danger, risk, et cetera; safety."[4] This is different from Dictionary.com's definition of safety, but their definition of security includes the word *safety*.

Although both safety and security appear to concern protecting people from harm—and the dictionary definitions of both are synonymous—it is necessary to find clarification elsewhere. It is possible to recognize that both safety and security relate to events resulting in some sort of loss to an organization. Whether this is in the form of harm to a person or animal, damage to equipment, or means of production, organizational reputation, or financial instruments, the commonality is that a loss event occurs in some fashion. The most apparent separation between safety and security relates to the circumstances surrounding the causes of a loss event. Safety is often associated with accident prevention. Accidents can be characterized by a confluence of conditions in the immediate environment and human behaviors, leading to an event resulting in harm, near harm, or damage.

A key component of an accident is the unexpectedness of the event by those involved. That is, none of the individuals associated with the event took intentional steps or made preparations to ensure that it happened. Consider the following definitions for *accident*. Merriam-Webster defines it as "a sudden event (such as a crash) that is not planned or intended and that causes damage or injury."[5] Dictionary.com defines an accident as "an undesirable or unfortunate happening that occurs unintentionally and usually results in harm, injury, damage, or loss; casualty; mishap: 'automobile accidents'."[6]

By these definitions, an accident lacks intent. The event may be directly caused by the inaction of a person or through their negligence, or it could be the result of some other failure within an environment. When intent is introduced, the same event often shifts into other defined categories, such as assault, sabotage, theft, and fraud. Intent is generally a human aspect of the event—the intent to gain personally, to harm another person, or to harm the company. A person intends that a series of events will occur by their actions.

Mission

The mission of asset protection entities (including the roles of safety and security) is an organizational management function responsible for preserving management's capacity for achieving their purpose by defending the organization, its assets, and its relationships from non-market-based threats. It is the role of more traditional organizational functions such as operations, marketing, and finance to addressing true market-based threats. These may include changes in consumer demand, product or service quality, or financial market performance. Consequently, asset protection is the application of risk management methodologies through policies, procedures, and practices to ensure that any non-market-based unwanted outcomes are within the organization's risk appetite. That is, asset protection works to implement and manage activities that strive to keep the unwanted results of loss events within the expectations defined by organizational management.

Understanding what asset protection is, and what those engaging in it seek to accomplish, paints a fairly broad picture. It can become a nearly overwhelming topic if it is discussed without some sort of framework. To segment that discussion, consider that asset protection may be viewed as a function, a duty or task, a job, and a discipline of study. Each of these may be addressed individually and used as a tool for sorting through the myriad of activities an organization may engage in, both by design and by happenstance, to protect itself from harm.

Asset protection is an organizational function in that each organization must engage in protective activities to some degree. The purpose of organizational management is to maximize the wealth of the owners, and one part of this purpose is the protection of existing assets. An organization that fails to engage in asset protection activities will likely suffer losses from a variety of sources. Consider the various industrial accidents that have occurred in recent years and the range of crimes that targeted businesses and other organizations.

Asset protection is also represented as a duty or a task. There may be tasks or duties relating to asset protection assigned throughout an organization. Individuals within an organization may have duties or tasks that serve to protect the organization. Something as simple as a policy requiring that a person ensure doors are secured or locked behind them demonstrates an asset protection duty each employee would be expected to perform. Other similar duties might be driven by policies for picking up loose items on floors, maintaining a desk devoid of sensitive data when unattended (empty desk policy), or reporting suspicious activity.

Asset protection is most often associated with a job that an individual is employed to perform. Ideally, these positions are staffed either by professionals or those with professional aspirations. A quick look around the United States offers some indication as to the common perception of what constitutes security. In some instances, an organization might employ a person in a security job with little or no formal training and education.

Asset protection has also evolved into a discipline of study around the world. Safety efforts and studies have grown in the last century in relation to the prevention of industrial accidents and injuries, as well as in response to government regulations (e.g., US Occupational Safety and Health Administration, US Mine Safety and Health Administration). Security academic studies around the world are fragmented; contemporary industry traces its roots to the industrial security programs of the World War II era, and with significant visible growth since the events of September 11, 2001. Some of the terminology has also changed, while the programs remain the same; for example, "homeland security" has become the catch-all for what used to be security, safety, or emergency management programs. This change is logical when one considers that the actual US Department of Homeland Security itself is responsible for all of these things as well as some others.

Even with a limited amount of academic commitment, a body of knowledge has been preserved and developed through professional and trade organizations. Organizations such as ASIS International (formerly the American Society for Industrial Security), the Security Industry Association, and the International Foundation for Protection Officers have worked for decades to credential individuals who have mastered some or all of this body of knowledge. Newer organizations have emerged to assist in formalizing the prevention and response to threats such as corporate fraud (e.g., Association of Certified Fraud Examiners) and information systems security (e.g., International Information Systems Security Certification Consortium, SANS Institute), among many others.

Given that asset protection is concerned with avoiding and mitigating losses, the range of opportunities for loss drives a number of security and safety specialties. Within security, there are areas such as personnel security, physical security, information asset security, supply chain security, retail security, pharmaceutical security, private investigations, corporate security, and information systems security—to name a few. The same can be found within safety as well.

Individuals working within the asset protection field can gain exposure to some or all of these areas. Furthermore, opportunities for specialization may influence the development of specific career paths in addition to becoming a generalist. The degree to which any one expertise is needed by an organization is determined by the nature of operations and corresponding activities. The process for determining this need is often referred to as *risk assessment*. Risk assessment represents a comprehensive review of an organization's activities, the assets it possesses, countermeasures currently in place to protect those activities and assets, and the degree to which an adversary might desire to harm or steal those assets.

Further tools exist and are used by the asset protection professional to assist in determining the need for risk reduction efforts, adversary capabilities, and the ongoing execution of protection efforts. These tools include threat assessment, vulnerability assessment, and security surveys, among others. In addition to these, another approach is sometimes used to test the effectiveness of protection efforts. These efforts are sometimes referred to as a red team, a tiger team, or penetration testing. Red teams play the role of an adversary and attempt to defeat the current countermeasures to accomplish some nefarious mission. Whether it is to steal a valued physical asset, obtain a chemical formula, or breach an information system, red teams can help gauge the sufficiency of current protection efforts and also identify vulnerabilities. These exercises can be conducted as a tabletop exercise or in a laboratory environment to avoid inadvertently disrupting any real-world protection efforts.

Nature of the Asset Protection Professional

A wide variety of individuals are drawn to work in the asset protection field. Regardless of the individual or their reasons for seeking asset protection work, there are a number of expectations required in their performance and behavior. It is essential that anyone providing asset protection services have the highest level of integrity. The asset protection practitioner is often called upon to provide information that must be accurate and organized. This information may be used in legal, quasi-legal, or employment proceedings. As a result, their verbal and written statements must be trustworthy, and the consumers of those statements must be confident that the information is accurate. There are many other traits that are considered important, but at their foundation is the honesty and integrity of the practitioner, serving not only to demonstrate their professionalism but also that of their peers.

Asset protection professionals occupy a unique space in an organizational environment. Typically, their activities do not contribute directly to productivity. Their value is derived from preventing unwanted events, identifying those involved in ongoing loss, or engaged in noncompliant or otherwise dishonest activities. The asset protection professional is, in many ways, analogous to a sheepdog, as they seek to identify those individuals (wolves) that would do harm to the organization (flock) while protecting and shielding those within the organization (sheep). Taking this analogy one step further, the sheepdog must never turn or "show their teeth" to those they protect. In other words, an asset protection professional must operate above reproach—never engaging in dishonest activity or inappropriately challenging or usurping organizational leadership. In the unfortunate circumstance when an asset protection professional does stray, the response must be swift and the severity of punishment severe.

Working within a field that often provides considerable access to company assets, the authority to affect coworkers' employment, and considerable discretion in the execution of their duties, asset protection professionals must display strong character. Such a high level of trust lends itself to abuse by an immature or petty individual. An asset protection team with a member that engages in such abuse will have to expend considerable effort and time to repair the damaged trust—if it even can be repaired. It is for this reason that a swift response and severe discipline is necessary to minimize the damage caused.

Due to their unique role in an organization, asset protection professionals will likely encounter information that is sensitive to the organization and/or to the persons working in and for the organization. In these situations, a person of mature character is needed to exercise good judgment and discretion. Few in an organization appreciate the "office gossiper"; should a security or safety team member take on that role, it will become far more potent due to the access inherent in the asset protection professional's position. Information pertinent to asset protection efforts should be reported through appropriate channels in a timely fashion. It is imperative that an asset protection professional not offer any promises of confidentiality beyond those of personal courtesy, as their communications are typically not covered by laws related to protected communications.

Asset protection may be considered from a number of different perspectives. It can be found as a function, a duty, a job, and a field of study. It is an essential part of any organization because it strives to avoid and mitigate potential losses outside of routine market or operational environments. It represents the practical application of risk management methodologies to ensure loss events are within organizational expectations, and it affects nearly every aspect of an organization's activities. Such a field of endeavor requires a practitioner of strong character and moral demeanor.

Refer website http://www.ifpo.org for further information

End Notes

1. Safety. Merriam-Webster Dictionary accessed January 11, 2015. Available: http://www.merriam-webster.com/dictionary/safety.
2. Safety. Dictionary.com accessed January 11, 2015. Available: http://dictionary.reference.com/browse/safety.
3. Security. Merriam-Webster Dictionary accessed January 11, 2015. Available: http://www.merriam-webster.com/dictionary/security. Available: http://dictionary.reference.com/browse/safety.
4. Security. Dictionary.com accessed January 11, 2015. Available: http://dictionary.reference.com/browse/security.
5. Accident. Merriam-Webster Dictionary accessed January 11, 2015. Available: http://www.merriam-webster.com/dictionary/accident.
6. Accident. Dictionary.com accessed January 11, 2015. Available: http://dictionary.reference.com/browse/accident.

2

Legal Aspects of Security

Christopher A. Hertig, David L. Ray

Introduction

Protection professionals work within a complex array of legal standards. Their daily function requires that they be knowledgeable of laws governing the employment relationships present in the workplace, civil and criminal laws, standards of practice, as well as a myriad of other government regulations. Added to this mixture is the burgeoning repertoire of professional standards enacted by such entities as ASIS International or local- and country-based associations related to the industry, as well as policies and codes of conduct that may be required by their employer or clients.

Unfortunately, traditional texts on legal aspects often focus on criminal law and civil liability, with limited coverage of administrative or regulatory law. Almost no attention is paid to the complex spectrum of employment law. This chapter provides a brief introduction to various legal aspects about which protection supervisors must be knowledgeable. Readers are encouraged to increase their knowledge and understanding of these areas by studying laws and regulations for their own jurisdiction and obtaining advice from competent legal counsel.

Historical Perspectives

The Roman Empire was the first to develop a system of written laws. They brought those laws to the nations that they conquered, and over time these laws evolved into individual country codes, such as the French Civil Code. The common law system developed in England during feudal times; eventually, a doctrine of precedent developed to assist courts and decision makers in ensuring consistency in the application of laws.

After the Battle of Hastings, William the Conqueror set up a system of courts and judges in England that essentially combined the French civil code with the common law system of justice. Today, that civil law system remains both in Europe as well as those jurisdictions that were settled by European countries, such as the English system of justice used in North America and other countries that England settled during the development of trade routes. Many countries have hybrid legal systems because of their history and relationship with Europe. For example, South African laws are based on a civil law system from the Dutch, a common law system inherited from the British, and laws based on customs inherited from the indigenous people. Jurisdictions such as Quebec, Louisiana, and

California also have some elements of civil law systems acquired from the French or Spanish settlers.

Key Terms and Concepts

Action or civil proceedings: A formal legal proceeding by one party against another. A cause of action is the right of one party to institute a legal proceeding. Actionable, means furnishing legal grounds for an action. In common law jurisdictions these actions may be in intentional torts, negligence, or breach of contract.

Agent: An individual authorized to act for or in place of another (principal) who represents that person.

Burden of proof: The duty placed on a party to prove or disprove a disputed fact. The burden of proof varies between different legal processes. For example:

- Prima facie: At first sight, the evidence is sufficient on its face to establish proof. The amount of evidence necessary supports the fact at issue without rebuttal by the opposing party. Prima facie evidence is the test used in those jurisdictions that have preliminary hearings to bind a case over to trial in criminal cases. It is enough to send a case to trial but not enough to convict.
- Balance of probabilities: The standard for civil decisions in Canada and the United Kingdom; and arbitration awards other than dishonesty cases in Canada. In the United States, it is considered equivalent to preponderance of evidence (see below).
- Preponderance of evidence: The majority or greater weight of evidence; more probable than not. The standard used for grand jury indictments and family court issues in the United States, as well as arbitration proceedings for dishonesty in Canada.
- Clear and convincing evidence: Highly and substantially more probable to be the truth than not. More than a preponderance of evidence but less than beyond a reasonable doubt. It is often used in labor arbitrations.
- Beyond a reasonable doubt: Fully satisfied; entirely convinced to a moral certainty. Reasonable doubt is the degree of doubt that would cause a prudent person to hesitate in acting on matters of great import to them. This is the standard of proof necessary in most criminal cases.

Evidence may be "direct" when it comes by way of one or more of the five senses, such as when a witness sees the accused pick up a brick and throw it through a window. Circumstantial evidence comes from inference. For example, a witness saw the accused with a brick in his hand and, a few seconds later, a window was smashed with a brick. No one saw the accused throw the brick, but the evidence may still be admissible as the inference is that the accused smashed the window.

Certiorari: A writ issued by an appeals court to a lower court (court of first instance, lower court, trial court) requiring that the lower court produce records of a particular case. Certiorari is used to inspect the lower court's actions in order to uncover irregularities.

"Color of law": An assessment of whether a government agent acted within lawful authority, such as whether a police office did or did not have lawful authority to make an arrest.

Contract: An agreement containing a promise or set of promises, the breach of which is actionable. Contracts can be either expressed (manifested in written or spoken words) or implied (shown by actions rather than words). Contracts consist of several key parts, and is:

- An agreement to do or not do a certain thing
- Between legally competent parties (consulting adults)
- Based on genuine consent of the parties
- Supported by consideration (profit or benefit accruing to each party)
- Made for a lawful objective, not in violation of public policy
- In the form required by law

Actus reus: The actual, overt act of committing the offense. For example, to prove the offense of theft, the prosecution must prove that the accused moved the item or caused it to be moved (actus reus) and that the accused intended to steal the item (mens rea).

Absolute liability: Criminal responsibility irrespective of fault and only the actus reus need be proved. Absolute liability exists in some criminal offenses and often in environmental offenses. For example, the prosecutor, in proving that the accused drove a motor vehicle while impaired by alcohol or drugs, may not need to show that the accused did so with intent or mens rea.

Evidence: Proof of a fact at issue. Any testimony, writings, exhibits, physical objects, etc., that may help prove the existence or nonexistence of a fact.

Hearsay: Evidence that the witness heard from someone else and is not admissible in most circumstances (although there are a few exceptions). A confession from an accused individual is technically hearsay but may be admissible in court. Other exceptions to the general rule, excluding hearsay, may include evidence from an expert, business or banking documents, and affidavits and depositions.

Mens rea: The guilty mind or intention to commit the offense. Generally, in a criminal matter, the prosecution must establish mens rea and actus reus to prove that a criminal offense took place.

Negligence: Negligence can fall under civil and/or criminal law. To prove negligence in a civil context, the plaintiff must show that there was a breach of a duty owed by the defendant that caused harm to the plaintiff. In the criminal context, the prosecution must prove that the defendant was negligent to the standard specified by the statute and cause harm or death to another.

Probable cause: Also known as "reasonable cause"; a low standard of proof but enough evidence for a belief in the alleged facts. An apparent state of facts is found after a reasonable inquiry. Circumstances are sufficient in themselves to warrant a reasonable person believing the accused to be guilty. The necessary evidence is used for arrest, search, or the issuance of an arrest or search warrant. Probable cause is also necessary to defend against suits for false arrest.

Reasonable suspicion: The degree of facts and circumstances necessary to make a prudent and cautious person believe that criminal activity is occurring. Reasonable suspicion must be based on articulable facts and circumstances.

Recovery: An action or award by court for an amount of legal entitlement. The recovery may be for an amount due as a result of assault, false imprisonment, false arrest, malicious prosecution, wrongful death, or damages for breach of contract.

Statute of limitations: The time limit within which a plaintiff must initiate a civil procedure or the prosecution must initiate charges in a criminal matter.

Strict liability: These statutory offenses may contain terms such as "without reasonable grounds" or "without good reason," which puts an onus on the accused defendant to provide a reasonable defense.

Summary judgment: A decision rendered by a court when there is no dispute as to the facts of a case and there is only a question of law to be addressed. Summary judgments allow the expeditious handling of civil complaints whereby one party believes it will prevail as a matter of law.

Arrest and Detention

Arrest: Depriving a person of liberty by legal authority in order that they may answer to a criminal charge. Generally, a citizen's arrest can be performed for the following reasons, which vary considerably from jurisdiction to jurisdiction:

- Commission of a serious criminal offense (felony, indictable offense, etc.)
- Serious criminal offense committed in an arrestor's presence
- Serious criminal offense witnessed by arrestor
- Breach of the peace resulting from a criminal offense being committed

Some jurisdictions provide for powers of arrest by property owners or people authorized by property owners where they see a criminal offense committed on or in relation to the property. In many jurisdictions, the citizen's arrest provision only apply where the suspect is being pursued by the police.

Detention: Detention is the act of temporarily stopping someone's freedom of movement. The power to detain will vary from jurisdiction to jurisdiction, but there may be authority to detain to protect the officer or others from an assault, to stop a trespasser, or to recover merchandise or other evidence under what is commonly known as "shopkeeper's privilege." Detention could result in arrest, but is generally not performed with the intent of bringing someone before a court. Detention should not involve the use of force except in exigent circumstances.

Arrest or detention procedures: Where security professionals are granted the legal authority to arrest or detain, they should comply with the following procedures:

- Identify oneself as a security officer, loss prevention agent, etc.
- Notify the arrestee of the purpose of the arrest.

- Be certain to use only reasonable or necessary force in the course of the arrest.
- Where search is authorized, ensure that the search is appropriate to the circumstances.
- Do not keep the person in custody any longer than is necessary.
- The police should be notified as soon after the arrest as possible and the arrestee should be delivered to the police without delay.

Juveniles or young offenders: Juveniles or young offenders being arrested or detained give rise to special problems and requirements. Many jurisdictions have complicated and changing rules concerning juveniles and young offenders. The protection officer should be aware of local statutory requirements when taking a juvenile into custody:

- The age of majority for that jurisdiction
- What authorities need to be notified—police, juvenile probation, truant officers?
- Notification to parents or guardians
- Release procedures to parents or guardians for various levels of offenses and different statutes
- Ages at which children can be charged with an offense

Regardless of whether the situation involves an arrest or a detention, the steps below should be part of the arrest or detention process:

- There should be a written policy on arrests and/or detentions based on existing laws that contains specific procedures, post orders, etc.
- Supervisors must know the policy and be familiar with operating procedures of responding law enforcement agencies.
- Notify police as soon as possible in those cases requiring their assistance: where the detainee is violent, and/or where criminal charges may be brought against someone.
- Record the times of calls to the police, the result of those calls, arrival times, and numbers and names of responding police officers. If emergency medical services (EMS) are notified, record those times and results as well.
- Use effective and legally correct (truthful, accurate) verbalization when detaining.
- Tell the detainee what is transpiring but no more than is necessary. Provide a basic explanation, but do not engage in protracted dialogue about the reason, the officer's authority, etc. The less said, the better.
- Be as polite and considerate as possible to the detainee. Address them only by name and make no offhand remarks or comments. Remember the adage that "respect begets respect."
- Avoid physical contact, and document in detail any and all physical contact that occurs.
- Those effecting and controlling the detainee should be the same gender if possible.
- If a search is authorized, it should be conducted in an appropriate manner: visual scan, cursory search for weapons, consent search of purse, etc. Employer policies will dictate the type and nature of the search.
- Restrain the detainee in an appropriate manner; have them sit with hands in view, handcuffed, with four-position restraints, etc.
- Separate detainees from each other.

It is imperative that the approach and contact be made in the safest manner possible given the circumstances and location. Once the decision is made to arrest or detain, there are additional steps regarding where to hold the detainee, how to treat them, and how to obtain information from them.

- Assess the detainee and environment for safety. Avoid areas with glass, access to weapons, hazardous materials, or the inability to secure or control the area before initiating the contact. Entities that detain someone may be held liable for any harm that comes to the detainee (or others) as a result of the detention.
- Detain in a private, quiet, and secluded place when possible, such as an office environment. This will help to mitigate tension between the security officer(s) and the detainee. A private setting helps preclude any embarrassment the detainee may feel and also mitigate defamation or false arrest allegations.
- Understand the relationship of the detainee to your employer as much as possible. An employee sometimes may be treated differently than a member of the public as they are compensated for their time via an established business relationship. They may have contractual obligations regarding the answering of questions as well.
- If appropriate, question detainees for basic information and record their statements. Ask their names, purpose for being in the area, their identification cards, etc. This is basic information rather than an interrogation with the intent of obtaining statements or suggesting guilt by the detainee. If the detainee freely offers information or statements, do not interrupt; merely record what they have stated.
- Document the detention completely, being sure to include all statements, admissions, threats, etc.

Interrogation

Interrogation, or focused interviewing, is often performed by protection professionals. Sometimes this is done as part of an investigation and as a planned activity; sometimes it is spontaneous, such as when catching someone in the act of committing an offense. Regardless, interviews must be held free from duress and coercion of the subject. The resulting admission, statement, or confession must be valid and the results must be acceptable in court. The following cases address interrogation by private security personnel.

Most jurisdictions have requirements for some kind of warning to be given to the subject prior to any interrogation. In the United States, this is known as the Miranda warning (after the Supreme Court case that established the Miranda rights); in Canada, the warning is based on the Charter of Rights and Freedoms. These warnings ensure that the accused understands their rights and that their response may be admissible in a court of law. Generally, requirements will include notice to the accused that:

- They have the right to remain silent; to not answer questions.
- Whatever they do say may be used against them in any subsequent proceeding.

- They have the right to have an attorney present during questioning.
- They will be provided a lawyer if they cannot afford one.

Interrogation may only proceed after the suspect makes a "knowing and intelligent waiver" of his or her rights, and this must be in writing!

Generally, security personnel operating free and clear of government direction or control, are not obligated to give warnings in most jurisdictions. Security personnel acting in furtherance of a government interest may be subject to requirements to provide a warning or caution as well as all other constitutional protection. Requirements may vary from one jurisdiction to another on whether an individual has a right to representation.

Key Points on Interrogation

- The interrogator must be thoroughly aware of the facts and information surrounding the particular case.
- Conduct the interrogation in a private setting. There may be another investigator, supervisor, union representative, or same-sex witness present, but privacy is the key element. Any person in the room should have a legitimate interest in the case. They must be there for a reason!
- Be as nonaccusatory as possible.
- Make no promises that cannot be kept, such as promising not to prosecute criminally if restitution is made.
- Keep statement preambles short—a few words to the effect that the statement is "free and voluntary" are sufficient.
- With procedural violation statements, be sure to highlight sufficient biographical and work history data to indicate the employee's level of training and experience so that they are accurately depicted.
- Make sure that the statement is given free of duress and is in the subject's own words.
- It may be advisable for the investigator to write the statement with the subject; in this way, words and phrases that establish the key elements of culpability can be put into the statement.
- Be aware of—and scrupulously follow—any laws regarding juveniles. Generally, this means having the parents or guardians involved. Giving the parents/guardians time alone with the juvenile beforehand and then starting the interview may be the appropriate course of action.

Search and Seizure

Search and seizure by private persons is not normally controlled by constitutional rights. Exceptions would be where a governmental interest or instigation was present or where evidence of the search is later being presented in criminal court. If government agents are directing the investigation, then it is a governmental activity. Questions arise in those instances where there is government involvement but not specific direction. In many jurisdictions, a search of a suspect for weapons (frisk, pat down) can be performed by security personnel just as it can be by police who have reasonable suspicion to believe that criminal activity is afoot and that their personal safety, or the safety of others, is at stake.

Similarly, property owners can perform searches of persons entering or remaining on their property. These searches should be for specific, lawful purposes (combating the introduction of weapons or explosives or the theft of materials or equipment), and should be written into policy with specific procedures developed for their implementation. There should be notices posted regarding the search requirement. If the workplace is unionized, the management's right to search should be incorporated into any collective bargaining agreement. The following example might be appropriate for a museum or similar type of facility.

NOTICE: All bags must be checked. Receipts will be issued. Purses, briefcases, and other similar items are subject to search.

Additionally, the use of consent forms is suggested. If people are to be given a hands-on search, they should sign a form giving their consent, which can be signed at the point of entry. Such forms can also include an acknowledgment of the rules for entering and remaining on the property. At a nuclear facility or research center, escort procedures would apply. Public events where people come into contact with high-profile individuals and celebrities would also use consent forms containing an outline of entry rules.

Searches by private protection officers are overshadowed by the specter of civil liability. Tort actions for invasion of privacy, assault, battery, false arrest, false imprisonment, or negligent infliction of emotional distress can result from improper searches. Consent should always be obtained except in emergency situations or where an arrest is being made: if someone is assaultive, they need to be searched for weapons. In some jurisdictions, a person may have the right to refuse a search even after signing a consent form; the only alternative of the employer or property owner may be to refuse entry to that person in the future or termination for refusal to follow a company policy if they are an employee.

Once consent is obtained (or, in the case of an employment contract or collective bargaining agreement, implied) and a search is to be conducted, there are a number of things to keep in mind. Security staff must be aware of company policy on conducting searches and must follow it. If the policy is not followed, the actions the security staff does take, may be construed as a "past practice" and in the courtroom that will not be advantageous to the company defending against a suit.

The most important objective is: what is being searched for? Whether it is stolen property, merchandise, narcotics, weapons, or any other item, what is being searched for must be clearly articulated, whether via signage or by verbal explanation from the officer(s) conducting the search. Searches should be done in a private area to the extent as safely possible. Curtains or dividers that section off a space to conduct the search out of public view are usually sufficient. The security officer conducting the search should be of the same gender as the person being searched; this helps protect against accusations of sexual harassment or sexual assault. The person witnessing the search may be of either gender. In the rare situation where a male security officer must search a female subject, ensure that there is a witness present; if possible, it should be a female witness. Keep in mind also that the witness to a search does not have to be a fellow security officer (although it should be). Finally, all actions taken during the search—areas searched, the item searched for, the start and stop times of the search, the names and contact information of any witnesses, what items were found (if any), the disposition of those items, and the location in which the search was conducted—should be documented in any report on the situation.

Considerations Regarding the Use of Force

The lawful and safe use of force is critical to any security operation. Private security personnel may encounter aggressive and potentially violent individuals in shopping centers, theaters, restaurants, amusement parks, gated communities, or other locations. As there is more privatization of protective services in courthouses, municipal buildings, public parks, municipal garages, housing projects, and other public areas, the potential need for the use of force increases.

A Use of Force Continuum was developed by Dr. Kevin Parsons and is a guide to using only the degree of force necessary to accomplish the immediate purpose for its employment. Other continuums have been developed by PPCT Management Systems, Larry Smith Enterprises, the Federal Law Enforcement Training Center, Calibre Press, and others. All consist of a series of logical steps toward escalating the level of force used against an assailant. Officer presence would be followed by verbal controls, which would be followed by soft empty hand control. After this would be striking with the hands, impact weapons, and, finally, deadly force. Note that there are differences of opinion among the experts regarding these continuums. Also note that the particular circumstances involving the use of force vary from situation to situation. An untrained officer using a lateral vascular neck restraint is a far cry from a trained and proficient individual employing that same technique.

Deadly force is force that is readily capable of causing death or serious bodily injury. Deadly force can never be used if the possibility exists that one can retreat without injury to themselves or others. Serious bodily injury is injury that creates a substantial risk of death or results in permanent disfigurement, or the protracted loss of use of any bodily member or organ. Sometimes this is called great or grievous bodily harm.

Evaluating the Use of Force

The following are some basic standards that courts use to evaluate the use of force by police and security personnel based on the definition of assault. The officer must be under assault to use force.

- Ability: does the assailant have the ability to cause bodily harm to the officer or someone he or she has a duty to protect?
- Manifest intent: has the assailant shown, by his/her actions, an intent to harm the officer?
- Imminent jeopardy: does the officer or others whom the officer has a duty to protect feel threatened, fearful or in fear of serious harm based on the assailants show of intent to act? *Right here and right now?*

- Consider alternatives: is the officer precluded from using force by taking some alternative action such as verbal persuasion, hard verbal commands, retreating, or the use of a lesser degree of force? As most encounters do not call for the use of force, some use of supportive communications should be considered:
  - Honor the subject's personal space.
  - Introduce yourself.
  - Employ active listening techniques.
  - Use "we" rather than "you," avoiding words that tend to be accusatory and inflammatory.
  - Have the subject sit down.
  - Offer the subject something to drink.
  - Ask open-ended questions that require some explanation by the subject.
  - Use paraphrasing and reflection to clarify what the subject says.
  - Be aware of one's fears and prejudices.

Some questions the officer can address to determine what, if any, force to employ in a given situation are:

- Is the officer in imminent physical jeopardy?
- Is someone that the officer has a duty to protect in imminent physical jeopardy?
- Is the mission in jeopardy—preventing trespass, protecting assets from destruction, preventing theft, maintaining order, preventing escape?
- Is there an alternative—persuasion, "hard" verbal techniques such as screaming, retreat, and subsequent criminal or civil redress—to using force?
- How will the officer's actions be considered by others—supervisors, police, courts, the public/community—who may evaluate them?
- Preclusion—if the officer has no alternative than the use of force and it is the only last resort, then the circumstances may preclude all other options.

Specific Circumstances

Some jurisdictions have statutes that enable private persons to use force in specific situations, such as mental health circumstances, at schools where required by law to maintain order, where persons are assembled, etc. These statutes create both a legal justification for the use of force and a professional obligation, which must not to be taken lightly. Officers should become familiar with the applicable local laws.

Post-event Actions

Much of the legal and public/community relations difficulties associated with the use of force, occur after the incident. Unprofessional behavior after an encounter with an aggressor can sway the verdict in both the legal system and the "court of public opinion." This is sometimes true even if the use of force was appropriate. For this reason, extreme care must be taken following a use of force encounter. Complete documentation of the incident and control of statements and media coverage is crucial! At a minimum, the following should be recorded in use of force situations:

- Complete, professional description of subject's aggressive behavior. This includes verbal and nonverbal behavior. It must include all behaviors that lead to the employment of force against the subject.
- Complete, professional description of officers' actions to control the subject.
- All witnesses and points of contacts, such as home and work phone numbers, email, addresses, etc.
- Listing of all persons who assisted and responded to the incident. Often, witnesses recall seeing a large number of security and/or police officers at the scene of a fight. The perception is that a large number of officers were using force against the subject. In fact, most of the "uniforms" present have arrived after the incident is over. Unfortunately, witnesses—and cameras—see a lone subject being overwhelmed by "an army" of officers. Care should be taken to specify the arrival time of each officer as best as can be done. Obviously, a video of an event provides a record and the chance to examine what occurred (this may be a sound argument for installing surveillance cameras in certain locations).
- Description of medical care given. Note that the officer has a duty to provide medical care to an assailant. Information on ambulance response time, hospital care, and any and all medical care should be noted. If medical care is offered and refused, this should also be noted.
- Chronological detail of facts, leading up to the most aggressive actions by the subject. This will "walk the reader" through the scenario so that he or she can completely understand it. Note that a good report is one that enables the reader to feel almost as if they were at the scene of the incident.
- Factual agreement between all accounts is needed!

Media and public statements should be minimized. Statements to the media should only be given by a designated media representative. These persons should be briefed as soon as practicable. Any statements by the officer should not be given to anyone except his or her supervisor and/or legal representative. Beware of electronic communications— once the email or Tweet is sent, it cannot be unsent and may cause irreparable damage!

Civil Liability

Civil law affects protective forces every day. The potential liability of being sued means having to pay legal fees and spend an extensive amount of man-hours on the case. Therefore, circumstances that could create lawsuits should be identified and avoided. Should a civil action make it to court (out-of-court settlements are usually agreed to by the defendant in most cases) and the plaintiff prevails, the potential of having to pay the plaintiff's legal fees, compensatory damages, and possible punitive damages raises the stakes that much further.

Intentional Torts

Assault

An assault is an intentional act causing an imminent fear of offensive contact. In order for the assault to be complete, there need not necessarily be contact; a threat with fear of physical harm may be sufficient for the plaintiff to be successful.

Battery

Battery is generally defined as unconsented, unlawful touching. No fear of touching is necessary; any degree of physical contact can be battery. Battery may also include causing contact with the person by his or her clothing, such as knocking off someone's hat or spitting.

False Arrest

The unlawful restraint of another person.

False Imprisonment

An act that completely confines a plaintiff within fixed boundaries. It requires intent to confine. Defendant was responsible for or caused the confinement. Plaintiff was aware and knowledgeable of the confinement or was harmed by it.

Defamation

Defamation consists of false accusations that cause injury to another's reputation, whether written (libel) or spoken (slander). Accusing someone of committing of a crime is defamation per se.

Invasion of Privacy

This is an unlawful, unreasonable intrusion on another's physical or mental privacy. The uncontested publication of a private fact to a third party is considered an invasion of privacy.

Malicious Prosecution

This is the act of pursuing groundless or malicious criminal charges against another person. The key identifier is lack of probable cause. Any criminal proceeding will terminate in favor of the defendant.

Negligent or Malicious Infliction of Emotional Distress or Mental Suffering

This includes any act that is deemed extreme or outrageous and intended to cause another severe emotional distress by the defendant. Some feel that the distress may need to be caused by physical contact. This tort generally cannot stand alone; there will be another tort action underlying it, such as an assault, defamation, or false arrest. This tort does, however, provide an additional avenue of recovery. To be successful, the plaintiff must prove through evidence (medical or otherwise) that there were damages inflicted as a result of the distress.

Conversion

Conversion is the wrongful appropriation of property of another that has the effect of depriving the owner of that property for an indefinite time. Altering or otherwise exercising control over the property of another, so that the owner's rights are excluded, also constitutes conversion. Conversion is the civil aspect of theft.

Wrongful Discharge or Termination

This tort can be inflicted on an at-will employee (plaintiff) alleging that the employer discharged the employee in violation of a law or a contractual right or agreement. The employment at-will protection of the defendant is reduced or eliminated by the following factors:

- Contractual relationships: violation of the terms of the agreement by the employer enables the employee to sue for wrongful termination. The employer has an affirmative defense if the plaintiff breached the contractual relationship and termination was on that basis.
- Public policy: protection against discriminatory practices or whistleblower protection statutes. An example of this may be an employee in a safety-regulated workplace lodging a complaint concerning a safety violation.
- An implied employment contract where promises were made to the employee ("You'll always have a job here as long as you want one").
- An implied covenant of good faith in which the employer must behave honestly and conscientiously. If trickery, deceit, or duress is applied to the employee, there may be grounds for a wrongful termination action against the employer.

In some cases, actions for emotional stress are filed due to the loss of the job, status, and income. Depending on the jurisdiction, these charges can add substantially to the amount recovered by the plaintiff and can increase the inclination of the defendant to settle.

Negligence

Negligence is failing to prevent loss/harm/injury when there was a duty owed to the plaintiff and reasonable and due care would have prevented the injury or damages from occurring. Negligence actions can easily be lodged against an organization. In some cases, managers can be held personally liable for their negligence. In essence, negligence consists of five elements:

- The existence of a duty as established via law or contract.
- A failure to perform that duty.
- Harm or injury to a party to whom the duty was owed.
- The harm was reasonably foreseeable.
- The harm was caused by the failure to perform the duty.

Negligence suits are based on the principle of respondeat superior ("let the master answer"), meaning that employers can be held liable for actions of their employees committed within the scope of employment. Scope of employment is generally defined by:

- Time: was the employee on-duty when the action occurred?
- Place: was the employee on employer's property at time of offense?
- Purpose: was the act committed in furtherance of the employer's interests?

Negligence suits can be filed for a variety of reasons. Suits filed for failing to take reasonable and due care to prevent a foreseeable injury that the employer had a duty to prevent might occur in any of the following situations:

- Selection: hiring someone without properly screening them and placing them in a position of trust. Maintenance employees with keys to all facilities, cashiers or accountants with access to significant amounts of cash, instructional aides with access to children, or information technology (IT) specialists with access to sensitive data, must all be properly vetted and screened for criminal history or prior behavior that might make hiring such individuals a risk.
- Retention: continuing the employment of someone with whom the defendant knows or should have known has dangerous proclivities.
- Entrustment: entrusting a dangerous item to another when the employer knew (or should have known) the individual would use it in such a way as to cause harm to others. Examples might include giving a delivery driver with a history of alcoholism the keys to a delivery truck, or arming a security officer with a history of reckless behavior that involved weapons or use of force.
- Supervision: not properly supervising personnel in situations where someone suffers injury due to the failure. This could include an inadequate span of control or an absence of supervisory checks.
- Instruction: failing to properly direct a subordinate so that a third party or the subordinate suffers harm.
- Training: failing to properly train someone to perform their job duties with the result that an injury is caused.

Independent Contractors

These are individuals that perform work for a principal (their client) but the principal does not directly control them. The principal is not vicariously liable for the acts of an independent contractor, except in the following circumstances:

- The activity being carried out is inherently dangerous.
- The activity is personal in nature and thus nondelegable—safety and security functions are often found by courts to be nondelegable.
- Ratification of the act by the principal occurs (e.g., the contractor undertakes an act that is negligent but the principal later supports the actions of the contractor).

Section 1983 and 1985 Actions (US)

Title 42, Section 1983 of the US Code provides for civil redress in federal court for people whose Fourth Amendment rights are infringed on by those acting under color of law. Section 1983 provides an additional remedy for tortious conduct within the federal court system.

A few key points concerning Section 1983 actions are:

- The defendant must be acting under color of law.
- Private corporations cannot be held vicariously liable for the actions of employees.
- Private party defendants cannot assert qualified immunity defenses to suits as can publicly employed police officers.
- Private corporations can be held liable for attorneys' fees in Section 1983 suits if they employ a public (off-duty) officer.

Section 1983 actions will probably escalate with increasing privatization and closer relations between police and security organizations. Additionally, criminal penalties may be imposed in certain circumstances for civil rights violations. Title 18, United States Code, Section 242, provides for criminal prosecution for anyone who, under color of law, statute, ordinance, regulation or custom, willfully subjects an inhabitant of any State, Territory, or the District of Columbia to the deprivation of any rights, privileges, or immunities secured or protected by the Constitution of the United States, or to different punishments, pains, or penalties, on account of such an inhabitant being an alien, or by reason of his color or race, than are prescribed for the punishment of citizens, shall be fined not more than $1000 or imprisoned not more than one year, or both. If bodily injury results, they may be subject to 10 years imprisonment. If death occurs they may be subject to any term of years or for life.

Title 42, Section 1985 of the US Code provides for recovery by plaintiffs where a conspiracy exists to deprive someone of their rights, privileges, and immunities secured by the Constitution and laws of the United States. Two or more persons planning to deprive someone of their rights may be prosecuted under Section 1985. With the increased use of investigative task forces and closer cooperation in the investigative and intelligence arenas, the potential for 1985 actions has also increased.

Bottom Line: Governmental authority creates legal complexity.

Strict Liability

Strict liability is applied in cases where there is no intent to cause harm or injury; the act itself is ultrahazardous; it is dangerous enough to cause unconditional or absolute liability. In these cases, guilt may be established when the actus reus is proved without having to establish the mens rea or guilty mind. Activities that qualify for strict liability include:

- Certain criminal offenses, such as driving while impaired: the prosecutor need not show that the accused intentionally drove a vehicle knowing they were impaired, only that they were impaired at the time of driving the vehicle.
- Keeping wild animals.
- Using explosives.

- Certain cases involving firearms.
- Environmental offenses.
- "Certificates of authority" issued by government agencies to private entities may also create absolute liability, at least in the United States.

Criminal Law and Criminal Liability

Criminal law is of obvious importance to protection professionals who deal with a limited set of behaviors (crimes) within their respective work environments. Security personnel must be knowledgeable of these offenses. They must know the elements of each and must understand how to document and articulate those elements when called upon to do so. Aside from the obvious benefit this knowledge has in terms of job proficiency, it is also essential for avoiding liability and preserving good relations with law enforcement and local district attorneys. Police should be called to make valid, "solid" arrests. The security officer should know the elements of the offense in question to make the police officers' jobs easier.

At times, understanding the elements of criminal law and how to identify them is complicated by the enactment of new laws. Sometimes, new laws are written and police are uncomfortable enforcing them. Protection professionals should attempt to learn as much as possible about the new laws. They may have to seek legal advice to understand the nuances behind the new legislation. They should also be knowledgeable of other offenses that tend to occur in conjunction with a particular offense. Examples of these would be indecent or sexual assault in cases of rape, receiving stolen property in cases of robbery or burglary (the perpetrator has stolen property on his or her person), and conspiracy in cases regarding controlled substances.

Trespassing

Statutes vary widely from jurisdiction to jurisdiction in relation to petty trespass or trespass to property legislation. Protection professionals should be aware of the terms of the legislation for their jurisdiction, especially the following:

- The definition of property and whether it applies to land, buildings, and publicly accessible structures such as public buildings and shopping centers
- Whether there is a requirement for the owner or person authorized to ask the trespasser to leave before charges can be filed, and in what form that request must take
- Powers of the owner or person authorized by the owner to detain or arrest
- Posting in a manner prescribed by law
- Fencing or enclosure manifestly designed to exclude intruders
- Affirmative defenses to trespassing charge

Dealing with Trespassers

Protection officers are often called on to evict persons from the property they are hired to protect. Performing this function can involve a host of difficulties that are generally not foreseen by property managers. Property/facility managers simply desire a certain "culture" or ambience within the boundaries of the facility or property. They leave the details to the protection officers as to how to be the "preservers of the corporate culture." Such a role is complex and challenging. How effectively the protection officer can secure the property he or she is employed to protect will determine the degree of legal, operational, and safety problems that are confronted. For this reason evicting trespassers should be done professionally. Below is a list of recommended practices for controlling trespass to property:

- A polite request to leave should be employed. This can be prefaced with an interview as to what the person is doing so as to better assess the situation. Have at least one backup officer as witness.
- Conduct the process in private as much as possible to preclude any acting-out behavior in front of an audience as well as to avoid exposure to defamation/ invasion of privacy actions. Some will leave upon request, and others will resist passively or even actively.
- Advise the individual of the legal consequences of his or her actions. Knowledge of the law serves to establish the officer's professionalism and authority; few persons will argue if the officer knows what he or she is doing.
- Use the phrases "private property" or " [company, college, hospital, etc.] property." Most people have a degree of respect for private property, realize they are on someone else's "turf," and comply with reasonable directions. Even chronic troublemakers are thrown off guard by the phrase "private property."
- Avoid invading the personal space of the evictee! A respectable distance must be maintained at all times. If the person is or may become violent, this distance should be a minimum of 10 feet. Take care not to corner the person when approaching them or going through a doorway. The latter scenario is a common cause of aggressive behavior when evicting someone from a room.
- Accompany the evictee all the way off the property so as to monitor and influence their behavior. Too much distance between security personnel and an evictee can make them feel unsupervised and rebellious. Acting-out behavior, such as shouting, cursing, and threatening, is likely to escalate and may incite problems from nearby crowds of people.
- Document the action in a daily log, etc. This lists the basic information regarding a routine eviction. Should there be a substantial problem or the person being evicted has been a problem in the past, a complete incident report should be prepared. Also include video, still shots, and/or audio documentation where available.
- Obtain police assistance if force must be used. Advise police if the person has been violent, threatening, or has caused prior disturbances.
- After the situation has been resolved, discuss with police and other parties how to improve on the process. Make sure that everyone can share perspectives on the process!

Eviction of trespassers is a challenging undertaking that must be professionally handled in order to ensure that civil rights, property rights, and the appropriate rules/culture/decorum are preserved. Management representatives—protection officers—who serve as the ambassadors of the organization can do no less.

Labor Law, Discipline, and Dismissal

As security personnel are the representatives of their employers, they serve as liaison between employees and management. There are certain legal and ethical standards governing the employee–employer relationship. Labor law encompasses statutory law (legislation), administrative or regulatory law, contract law, civil law, court decisions, and a smattering of criminal law. Unfortunately, labor law has traditionally been overlooked in texts and courses for protection officers.

Employment-at-Will

Absent of an express agreement to the contrary (e.g., a unionized work environment where the employment agreement is covered by a union–management agreement), either party may terminate the employment relationship. No cause must be shown to terminate the employment relationship. There may, however, be statutes that preclude an employer from terminating an employee without just cause. There are also some general exceptions to the employment-at-will doctrine, such as:

- Public policy: Generally one cannot hire or fire someone because they are on jury duty, pregnant, or have a disability that is not a bona fide occupational requirement for the job, etc. Persons filing complaints that would fit under a "whistleblower" statute also generally cannot be fired on that basis.
- Good faith: employers must treat employees in a fair, honest manner and practice natural justice.
- Implied contracts: promises made by employers must be adhered to. Promises can be made in job interviews, employee handbooks, memos, etc.

Labor relations statutes and, in some cases, criminal statutes may place requirements on employers that they not:

- Interfere with efforts of employees in the formation of a labor union
- Dominate a labor organization or contribute financial or other support to it
- Discriminate in hiring or tenure of employees for reason of union affiliation

Court Injunctions

Injunctive relief can be obtained from the courts in labor disputes, provided that the petitioner has complied with all lawful obligations and has taken reasonable steps to resolve the conflict through negotiation. In general, courts will issue restraining orders when they find the following:

- Unlawful acts have been either threatened or committed and will continue to be committed unless they are restrained by the court.
- Damage of a substantial, irreparable nature will be done to the complainant's property.
- The complainant will suffer greater injury by not having the order than the defendant will suffer by having it.
- The complainant does not have an adequate remedy at law (civil or criminal).
- Public authorities are unable or unwilling to protect the complainant's property.

Strike Surveillance

Protection professionals should also be familiar with jurisdictional requirements for surveillance and security during strikes. Legislation may place restrictions on video surveillance and courts, or labor relations tribunals may place restrictions on the placement and number of pickets during a strike.

Polygraph in the Work Site

The use of a polygraph in the course of workplace investigations is voluntary on the part of the employee, and some jurisdictions (e.g., the United States) place strict limitations its use. Polygraph results are usually not admissible in criminal or civil courts but may be used to initiate confessions from a suspect employee.

Discipline

- Most employers have policies on progressive discipline for employment offenses, but some serious offenses such as theft or fraud may lead directly to discharge.
- Decisions on the appropriate level of discipline are usually made by management in consultation with independent advice from human resources and/or legal counsel.
- Employee handbook and policies should be kept current so that employees are aware of the employer requirements and to support just cause terminations.

Dismissal/Removal

The dismissal or removal of an employee from company property is much like an eviction or a trespass warning. The same considerations apply—the security department has to take someone the company does not want on the property and arrange to remove them (or have them removed, as the case may be).

- Ensure that there are clear policies regarding terminable offenses.
- Ascertain and document that all employer policies have been followed leading up to the termination.

- Have a written termination notice that specifies all previous disciplinary problems the employer has encountered with the employee.
- Select a neutral location.
- Have a witness who does not talk, only listens.
- Be objective and a good listener; do not argue! Minimize attempts at reasoning with the to-be-terminated employee who is probably too emotional to be rational.
- Avoid giving notice at the end of a work day, prior to a holiday, or when the employee has just returned from vacation.

Legal Standards Regarding Privacy

Privacy is a large and growing issue. Databases can be misused, private information can be disseminated, and serious problems can plague individuals. Identity theft, as an example, can take 700h to correct once one has been victimized. There is a growing array of legal standards which protect the privacy of information. Some of these statutes require specific protection measures, some contain criminal sanctions. Protection professionals should be aware of the requirements for the gathering, use and disclosure of personal information during the implementation of security procedures such as video taping, and during the course of investigations.

Employee Background Investigations

As employee background investigations are commonly and increasingly being conducted; it is essential to do them in a lawful, ethical, and professional manner. Privacy, credit reporting, or criminal records reporting requirements may govern the conduct of employee background investigations. The following points are relevant to the conduct of background investigations in any jurisdiction:

- The investigation should be well rounded. It should examine various aspects of the applicants past that are job related. If available, criminal history should be checked on the applicant's home, work, commuting jurisdictions, and previous residences as they may have been convicted of crimes in any of those areas. A prior employment check and a reference check should always be done—and not just on references provided by the applicant.
- The investigation should comply with accepted standards. The ASIS guideline on background investigations is a good place to start.
- The investigation's depth and scope should be commensurate with the position being applied for. Background checks have levels of inquiry, which vary according to the sensitivity of the position for which the applicant is a candidate. A cashier position at a fast food restaurant may require local criminal history but not a motor vehicle check or civil records. A manager position may require a credit check, civil records, driving history, and developed references.

- Keep the investigation focused on employment-related issues. Do not stray off into a "witch hunt" or "fishing expedition" where non-job-related information is uncovered. All inquiries must have clearly defined business objectives. Work history and references should always be checked. An employee who walks to work does not need a motor vehicle bureau check. An employee who has no access to cash or financial transactions does not need a credit check.
- Never violate any applicable legal standards, in spirit as well as in letter.
- Notify applicants and obtain written consent before any inquiry is initiated. Even if not specifically required by law, gaining written consent sends a message to the applicant that the inquiry will be conducted in a serious manner. This also limits liability if an applicant claims the company violated his or her privacy.
- Utilize professional screening services if outsourcing. There are firms that specialize in background investigation.
- Verify all information of a derogatory nature before taking any adverse action. Database information should be verified against original documentation and/or supporting sources.

Trade Secrets

Trade secrets are formulas, patterns, processes, devices, or compilations of information that companies hold as part of their intellectual property. Should a competitor gain access to one or more of these trade secrets, that competitor would gain a huge advantage in the marketplace. A trade secret has continuous use in the operation of the business. Not all information used in business is a trade secret. Some factors used in determining whether information constitutes a trade secret are:

- To what extent is data known to the outside world?
- To what extent is data known by the employees?
- What protective measures have been taken to safeguard the data?
- What is the value of the information to the business and the competition?
- How much effort and money was spent in developing the data?
- How easily could this data be acquired legitimately by competitors?

Examples of a trade secret include a manufacturing process, a die pattern for a machine, customer lists, discount/rebate codes, or bookkeeping methods.

Administrative Law

Administrative agencies regulate both business and government so that rapid changes to a particular industry or segment can be effectively addressed. Administrative agencies have a tremendous impact on the day-to-day operations of a business—one that is substantially greater than that of the courts or legislatures. Agencies differ in their jurisdiction and authority. While most have some form of judicial review, some do not. Some agencies enforce their rules through an internal appellate process prior to external judicial review; others may have the courts or tribunals to enforce their orders. In general, administrative agencies have the following types of authority:

- Rule-making or quasi-legislative power as enumerated in the enabling statute that created the agency.
- Quasi-judicial. Agencies hold hearings that are not limited by the formal rules of evidence or procedure used in court. The hearings must follow due process, the agency's own rules and regulations, provisions of administrative procedures legislation.

Judicial review of an agency decision does occur, depending on the enabling statute that specifies the amount of authority that the agency has. Other factors include the impact of its rulings; those with minimal impact are unlikely to be appealed in court while those creating major financial burdens will be. Some factors that a court will examine on review are:

- Whether the agency was empowered to act as it did.
- Whether the agency followed statutory procedures or its own published procedures.
- Whether the agency acted in an arbitrary and capricious manner.
- Whether the record shows at least some facts on which the decision could rest.
- Whether the party requesting review (or relief) from an agency's decision have standing to make such a request.
- Whether all other administrative remedies were exhausted.

If permitted by statute, an agency can investigate and issue subpoenas for persons to testify at hearings and to produce documents. Subpoenas are enforced by the appropriate court via contempt citations, fines, and imprisonment. Agencies that deal in environmental protection, trade, labor relations, or occupational safety, for example, issue subpoenas.

Because administrative agencies can fine, suspend, or revoke licenses to operate, as well as sue, management is very concerned about compliance. Surviving an audit by a government inspector or investigator is important; learning an agency's rules, and the interpretation of them, is crucial to success for security managers.

Administrative Language

Administrative language is important for security managers to understand. When reading regulations, the meanings of the following key words may apply:

- "Shall": this may mean "must." Implies a requirement to do a certain thing.
- "Should": this may mean "recommended". Be wary; today's "shoulds" can become tomorrow's "shalls."
- "May": this means that the activity discussed is optional.

Audits and Agency Investigations

Being audited or investigated is a fact of life for most businesses and governmental units. Whether by a government agency, an insurance carrier, a professional accreditation body, or some other entity, the points listed below will likely apply.

- Maintain up-to-date documentation of the standards being audited.
- Understand the formal authority of the administrative organization.
- Assess probable areas of specific inquiry and ensure any necessary data is retrievable.
- Neatness/image is everything!
- Use the language of the entity.
- Educate all personnel in the organization about the process.
- Internalize the process: seek out suggestions from the administrative organization and develop internal audits.

Regulations Governing the Security Industry

There are various regulations that affect the security industry, mostly at the state or provincial level. Some regulation is at the federal level. In general, states and provinces tend to regulate the following classes of personnel:

- Armed security officers
- Contract security service firms
- Private investigators
- Alarm dealers and installers
- Locksmiths
- Polygraph operators
- Dog handlers

Regulations may include requirements for training of security personnel. These laws may require a certain number of hours of training in specified topics or may include in-service training requirements. Armed personnel must also undergo additional training related to carrying weapons and becoming qualified. States and provinces may change these requirements from time to time; however, federal governments are typically only involved in these matters if the federal government has contracted with a private company for security services.

There is a growing awareness on the part of the US Congress that private security personnel play a growing role in crime control. As the Department of Homeland Security matures, there are reports that indicate an awareness of the substantial role of private protection forces in securing key aspects of America's infrastructure. In Canada, the Canadian General Standards Board has established regulations for security officers. Sometimes such legislation serves not so much to regulate directly as symbolically: subsequent laws, standards, and practices follow the original regulations to a large extent. An example of this would be the Bank Protection Act in the United States. Currently, credit unions are not covered by the Act's provisions but nonetheless have adopted them. The Bank Protection Act has, in effect, established an industry standard within the financial services community.

Standards

Standards are of extreme importance in the arena of protective services. Created by the surrounding community, the security industry itself, insurance organizations such as Underwriter's Laboratories or Factory Mutual, or professional organizations, standards are necessary because they provide a recognized level of excellence. Standards are also fundamental to individual protective service careers, as compliance with standards is essential in certain industries.

Types of Standards

There are various types and sources for the promulgation of standards within the security industry. These can be broken down into the following categories:

Government-mandated standards: These are set by legislation and may include bank protection standards, licensing laws for private investigators, local ordinances on false alarms, or the securing of parking lots. This category also includes standards set by regulatory agencies, such as licensing requirements for security service firms, physical security plan requirements, or contingency plan mandates for power or nuclear plants. In some cases, government agencies specify requirements that security service firms must comply with. They may require certain screening and training procedures in requests for proposals dealing with providing security for government property. Note that municipal standards, such as robbery prevention measures in convenience stores or security practices at parking garages, may also be adopted.

Community standards: These are practices generally accepted within a geographical area. Examples would include the use of armed guards in shopping centers, closed-circuit television in the lobbies of hotels, or doormen in office buildings. Community standards are not necessarily documented or published; they may simply be the operational norm within an area.

Industry standards: These are generally accepted practices within an industry. These can be formally established through professional organizations, such as the National Burglar and Fire Alarm Association or ASIS International, or can simply be those practices commonly followed within the hotel, shopping center, or telecommunications industry. ISO standards can be thought of as industry standards regulating businesses conducting foreign commerce. The following are some of the standard-setting organizations in the security industry:

- ASIS International has developed a number of standards on such topics as security officer selection and training, information asset protection, business continuity, chief security officer (CSO), pre-employment background screening, and threat advisory system response.
- National Fire Protection Association (NFPA) has developed codes on fire and electricity, such as NFPA 730 Guide for Premises Security. NFPA 730 covers construction, protection, occupancy features, and practices designed to reduce security vulnerabilities

to life and property. Similarly, NFPA 731 Standard for the Installation of Electronic Premises Security Systems covers the application, location, installation, performance, testing, and maintenance of physical security systems and their components.

- International Association of Campus Law Enforcement Administrators (IACLEA): This organization provides accreditation services to college and university police, security, and public safety departments. The IACLEA accreditation standards are based on the Commission on Law Enforcement Accreditation (CALEA) where applicable.
- International Association of Healthcare Security and Safety (IAHSS) has developed training standards for healthcare security officers and supervisors, as well as other specifications for healthcare security.

Giving Depositions and Testifying in Legal and Quasi-Legal Proceedings

Security personnel are often required to testify in disciplinary hearings for their employers, preliminary or probable cause criminal hearings, criminal trials, civil trials, and hearings conducted by administrative agencies (unemployment, workers' compensation, labor arbitration). They are also often asked to give depositions in civil cases. Testimony in court for civil or criminal proceedings may include an examination-in-chief by the party calling the protection professional to submit evidence, and then cross-examination by the lawyer for the other party. Testimony is important for the following reasons:

- Effective testimony establishes professionalism, whereas ineffective testimony destroys credibility.
- The proficiency of testimony can be the determining factor in relationships with local police, clients, etc.
- Testimony in one proceeding can be used in another proceeding. Single incidents often are heard in a variety of hearings. A criminal trial's testimony could be used later in a civil proceeding, often to the detriment of the officer.

Regardless of the setting, the following points are key to being a successful testifier:

- Prepare by having all notes and evidence in good order.
- Have proof of corporate existence via a certified copy of the articles of incorporation.
- Be able to establish value of merchandise or extent of damage through a professional assessment. A store buyer, contractor's estimate, etc. should be brought to court.
- Meet with counsel.
- Keep answers short.
- Make eye contact with the trier of fact.
- Be polite, addressing everyone by "sir," "ma'am," or their proper title.
- Avoid absolutes, such as "always" and "never."
- Do not guess, speculate, or answer hypothetical questions.
- If unsure about a question, wait for an objection and a ruling on it.

Depositions

Depositions are often used in civil proceedings as part of the discovery process. They are usually given at an attorney's office after a notice to appear has been sent out to the person being deposed (deponent). Depositions are formal legal proceedings with court reporters and legal counsel present. Lists of questions are prepared in advance by attorneys and paralegals. Litigation assistants also take notes at the deposition. While the formal, legal reason for conducting depositions is to obtain testimony out of court, when having such testimony in court is impractical, there are several tactical reasons for depositions:

- To observe and assess the witness.
- To assess the recollection of the opposing witness when they are confronted with unexpected questions.
- To gauge the testimony of the witness and predict what will be said in a subsequent court appearance.
- To obtain testimony in writing for possible impeachment later.
- To identify witnesses known to the plaintiff or defendant.
- To require that documents be produced via a request for production.

Take the proceeding seriously. Do not be sarcastic or cocky; be very careful that the deposition is taken seriously—even if the setting is relaxed and informal.

Interrogatories

Interrogatories are sets of written questions submitted by one party in a case to the other as part of the discovery process. Interrogatories are usually given under oath, with the person answering them signing a sworn statement that they are true. Interrogatories are also submitted to a jury.

Emerging Trends

Developing licensing and regulation is a tedious and exasperating process that often only covers a segment of the industry. They tend to be minimal in terms of what they require. Once developed and enacted, there are further challenges when following through with the regulations. These issues gave rise to the development of the International Association of Security and Investigative Regulators (IASIR), which is a professional organization for regulatory personnel at the state and provincial level. Licensing is more prevalent in Canada and the United Kingdom because of the structure of their governments and the considerably fewer jurisdictions involved. This could change if highly publicized incidents involving security personnel occur, or more likely when jurisdictions realize that a significant revenue stream can be created via licensing fees.

Indirect regulation, such as those issued by the Payment Card Industry Security Standards Council on information protection in the retail and banking arenas, is growing steadily. Another example is the Joint Commission in healthcare. These have both direct and indirect relevance to security departments, depending upon the vertical and the individual organization. As a result of this movement, the security industry is largely unregulated by government but guided quite extensively by professional associations, insurance carriers, accrediting agencies, etc. *Compliance management* is an increasing concern and has developed into a specialty area of its own.

Having sworn security officers with arrest powers is also growing in some verticals, such as schools and colleges. While there is considerable legal complexity in this arrangement, it may be a necessity. If the property is large, has traffic control as a significant function, or if it is remotely located, a sworn department may be necessary. Access to intelligence and some training is often restricted to law enforcement agencies. An organization needs to look at all of these factors in making the transition from unsworn to sworn—or vice versa.

Intellectual property management, ever-expanding electronic communications, and an emphasis on enterprise risk management will all impact the legal concerns of security practitioners. Investigative activity is changing rapidly due to email, social networks, etc. So too is IT protection.

Refer website http://www.ifpo.org for further information

End Notes

1. Anderson R. A., Fox I., and Twomey D. P., *Business Law* (Cincinnati, OH: South Western, 1984).
2. Apo A. M., "Is it time for premises security standards?" *Security Management* 40, (1996): 4.
3. Bequai A., *Every Manager's Legal Guide to Hiring* (Homewood, IL: Dow-Jones-Irwin, 1990).
4. Black H. C., *Black's Law Dictionary* (St. Paul, MN: West, 1990).
5. Bullock J., Haddow G., Coppola D., Ergin E., Westerman L., and Yeletaysi S., *Introduction to Homeland Security* (Burlington, MA: Elsevier Butterworth-Heinemann, 2006).
6. Cohen D., "Giving notification where it's due," *Security Management* 42, (1998): 3.
7. Corley R. N. and Black R. L., *The Legal Environment of Business* (New York, NY: McGraw-Hill, 1973).
8. Curtis G. E. and McBride B. R., *Proactive Security Administration* (Upper Saddle River, NJ: Pearson Prentice Hall, 2005).
9. Garvey C., "Outsourcing background checks," *HR Magazine* 46, (2001): 3.
10. Givens B., *The Privacy Rights Handbook: How to Take Control of Your Personal Information* (New York, NY: Avon Books, 1997).
11. Hartman J. D., *Legal Guidelines for Covert Surveillance Operations in the Private Sector* (Stoneham, MA: Butterworth-Heinemann, 1993).
12. Hertig C. A., *Civil Liability for Security Personnel* (Bellingham, WA: International Foundation for Protection Officers, 1992).
13. Horan D. J., *The Retailer's Guide to Loss Prevention and Security* (Boca Raton, FL: CRC Press, 1996).
14. Inbau F. E., Farber B. J., and Arnold D. W., *Protective Security Law* (Newton, MA: Butterworth-Heinemann, 1996).

15. Klotter J. C., *Criminal Law* (Cincinnati, OH: Anderson, 1990).

16. Nadell B. J., "Timeliness of records now critical," *Security Management* 42, (1998): 3.

17. Nemeth C. P., *Protective Security and the Law* (Cincinnati, OH: Anderson, 1995).

18. Ortmeier P. J. *Security Management: An Introduction* (Upper Saddle River, NJ: Pearson Prentice Hall, 2005).

19. Schiff T. K., "Demystifying worker's comp calculations," *Security Management* 42, (1998): 3.

20. Thibodeau C. T. *Use of Force, Alternatives to the Use of Force, Legal Aspects of the Use of Force. A seminar by Q/A Systems & Consultants*, (Minneapolis, MN: August, 1995).

21. White A., "The Regulation Journey" Speech given at the Security Industry Authority Annual Conference, Manchester Central, (21st May 2009), (2009), http://www.bsia.co.uk/web_images/publications/The%20Regulation%20Journey.pdf. Retrieved January 1, 2015.

3

Theories of Crime and Criminal Behavior and Their Implications for Security

Whitney DeCamp

Humans have long struggled to understand the different behaviors of our own kind. Many people study various aspects of social behavior, such as how we eat, courtship rituals, and social hierarchy. Crime is certainly no different. It, like any other human behavior, has various possible causes, both obvious and subtle, that might sway an individual toward or away from criminal behavior. To at least partially explain such behavior, criminological theories offer social, biological, and psychological factors that can encourage or prevent involvement in crime.

A criminological theory is a scientific theory, which is, by definition, a series of falsifiable statements about relationships between two or more observable phenomena. Several parts of that definition require further explanation. First, the statements of a theory are causal statements, such as, "*X* causes *Y*." Typically, crime is the latter part of these statements in criminological theories, while social factors often represent the former part. Additionally, all scientific theories relate to observable phenomena, meaning that theories involve things we can measure. Finally, and importantly, a theory's statements must be falsifiable. The scientific method requires that we can test the validity of statements. For example, "lack of parental attachment causes crime" is testable because we have ways to observe the degree of attachment a child has to his or her mother and father, whereas "life causes crime" or "demonic influences cause crime" are statements that cannot be tested.

Ideally, a criminological theory will explain all four elements of crime: motivation, lack of control/constraint (a freedom from social or internal pressure to behave in an approved manner), opportunity, and ability (see Figure 3.1). Typically, it is too difficult to engage in rehabilitation to alter motivation and lack of control without a strong financial support system, and ability is rarely something that can be removed once it is present. Therefore, opportunity is of the greatest concern to individuals and small groups seeking to prevent crime.

Learning what causes crime has its own purpose to researchers seeking to develop and test these theories. However, the implications from theories represent a more practical

Security Supervision and Management. http://dx.doi.org/10.1016/B978-0-12-800113-4.00003-1

Parts of a Crime	Description
Motivation	A psychological drive that influences one's goals.
Lack of constraint	The absence of something that discourage behavior that goes against society's norms and rules.
Opportunity	A situation in which it is possible to commit a crime (the right place at the right time).
Ability	Familiarity with the techniques of certain crimes. Especially necessary for complicated crimes.

FIGURE 3.1 The four parts of crime.

reason for studying this complicated topic. By knowing what causes crime, it is possible to prevent it by removing its cause. These implications range from the relatively simple solutions (e.g., increasing punishment in order to deter, altering the environment to disrupt the process of the crime), to the socially achievable (e.g., social programs to teach better parenting practices), to more radical implications. For individuals in a managerial or supervisory position, the relatively simple solutions are the most feasible to implement and will be discussed to the greatest length in this chapter.

The Classical and Neoclassical Schools of Thought

General Deterrence

In 1764, Ceasare Beccaria published an essay called, *On Crimes and Punishments*.[1] The essay was largely motivated by the politics of Beccaria's day, as it gave specific outlines for the proper duties of legislature and judges in a demand for a fair and just system of punishment. Of greater interest to the birth of the criminological theory was Beccaria's description of what punishment should be. Beccaria based his statements about punishment on what we now call *hedonistic calculus*, which assumes that humankind is rational (capable of thinking about consequences before acting) and makes calculated decisions based on a pleasure-seeking and pain-avoiding motivation.

Stealing is an excellent example of hedonistic calculus; an individual will be motivated to steal something because owning it would more pleasurable than not. Buying the item would not be as pleasurable as stealing it, because giving up the money required for the purchase would be a pain approximately equal to the pleasure gained from the item. Stealing, on the other hand, would only result in a loss if the perpetrator is caught and punished. Therefore, the best way to prevent a theft is to keep punishment as certain as possible and more painful than the possible benefits of stealing.

Although this motivation is not always explicitly discussed, it is generally common sense for criminal justice practitioners. The way to maximize the effect of punishment is less clear but is where Beccaria's work is specific. Beccaria specified three goals for punishment: severity, celerity, and certainty. For punishment to be an effective deterrent, all three goals must be met. *Certainty* is, perhaps, the simplest of the three—based on the commonsense concept that the more likely the punishment is, the more fearful the potential offender will be that he or she will be caught. The public spectacle of punishment is an element of certainty that is often overlooked in today's criminal justice system; if people do not witness or hear of a punishment, they will not fear it. *Celerity*, also referred to as swiftness, is best defined through the length of time that occurs between the crime and the punishment. The quicker a punishment occurs after the crime, the more obvious it will be to the public that the two events are clearly related. *Severity* is a concept common in the modern criminal justice system. It is often the element of deterrence most easily influenced through legislation and therefore becomes the target of "get tough on crime" policies. However, according to Beccaria's essay, severity only needs to exceed the amount of damage inflicted upon society, and anything beyond that is superfluous. In other words, the severity of the punishment must be the amount necessary to make punishment more painful than the pleasure from the crime. Increasing severity once it has achieved this goal is no longer effective and only increases the burden on the criminal justice system given the cost of incarceration. Instead, certainty and celerity, while more difficult to increase, should become the focus for improving punishment's effectiveness in deterring crime.

It should be noted that two different deterrence theories are derived from Beccaria's work. *General deterrence theory* focuses on the public's willingness to commit crimes after witnessing or hearing of the punishment of an already existing criminal (see Figure 3.2). *Specific deterrence theory*, conversely, discusses the effects of punishment on the individual being punished (see Figure 3.3), but uses many of the same principles as the general deterrence theory. The corrections system currently used in the United States gives a great example of both forms of deterrence. First, it creates a specific deterrence because (in theory) offenders do not enjoy their stay in prison and will not want to perform actions that could result in another prison sentence. Second, citizens are aware of the unpleasantness of prisons and also wish to avoid spending time behind bars, thus creating a general deterrence.

Rational Choice Perspective

The classical theory of deterrence is a relatively simple model that often fails to explain all the elements of crime and criminality. Although no theory has perfected a formula for

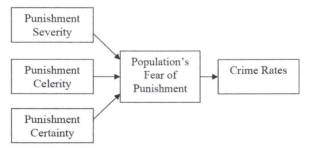

FIGURE 3.2 A graphical representation of general deterrence theory.

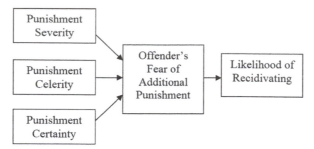

FIGURE 3.3 A graphical representation of specific deterrence theory.

explaining all the variances, the rational choice perspective is a clear step forward from Beccaria's work and with it began the neoclassical school of criminology.

Rational choice has existed in various forms throughout the last few decades. The earliest version usually identified is Becker's economic approach to crime from the late 1960s. However, the most often studied rational choice theory, and the one discussed here, was developed in 1985 by Clarke and Cornish.[2] The theory begins with the assumption that there is a purpose behind every crime (usually to the benefit of the offender). Furthermore, the criminal chooses to commit the crime based on his or her limited ability to weigh the benefits and risks involved. The term *limited* was specifically chosen to describe the criminal's ability to reason, not because of some mental deficiency on the part the offender, but rather because there is no way for a single person to know all the potential benefits and risks involved. Essentially, potential offenders always face uncertainty and therefore do not always make the best decisions.

The rational choice model includes three parts: initiation (leading up to the first offense), habituation (continued offending), and desistance (either becoming non-criminal or moving to a different crime). Focusing on each of these divisions is not practical for the topic of asset protection, but some of the variables provided in the model are of use. The variables include background factors (e.g., upbringing), current life circumstances (e.g., unemployed), and situational variables. The situational variables are of most interest here, as they are the most easily influenced by individuals outside of the potential offender's personal life, such as a security officer. For a better look at these situational variables, the routine activities theory provides a more in-depth focus on opportunity.

Routine Activity

Routine activity theory was developed in 1979 by Cohen and Felson.[3] Unlike most theories, routine activity theory focuses not on why people want to commit crimes, but rather on why crimes occur at specific places and times. This theory will be quite familiar to professionals in asset protection, as it is one of the more practical theories and compatible with common practices of the profession (target hardening, crime prevention through environmental design, situational crime prevention, etc.). Rather than focus on crime from the criminal's perspective, this theory places higher emphasis on what leads to victimization.

The main assertion of Cohen and Felson's routine activity theory is that crime is the function of a space–time convergence of: a motivated offender, a suitable target, and the lack of capable guardianship. In other words, a crime (theft) occurs when someone interested in stealing, notices that an accessible target is not being guarded. The authors' interest in the theory stems from an attempt to explain increased crime rates in the modern world. Specifically, an increase in property crime is the result of greater availability of targets and increased absence of guardianship. The original article primarily focused on family households to explain this change. In short, the modern world has left the family less likely to be home, while simultaneously increasing the amount of valuables kept inside the home. Ironically, the decline in crime rates since the theory's publication runs counter to the expectations that one would expect.

In the time since the theory originated, routine activity theory has been used to empirically describe and test many practices already in place in the asset protection profession. The guardianship concept has received much attention in subsequent research. Research has described capable guardians as police officers, security officers, store employees, or any person capable of defending his or her property. In addition, others have extended the original concept of guardianship to include nonhuman guardians, such as security cameras and alarm systems, as they increase the likelihood of a capable guardian arriving when a crime occurs. The quality of guardianship can also be a consideration based on appearance of professionalism, physical stature or the interactive closed-circuit television (CCTV) capabilities and ability to summon assistance quickly.

The suitable target is also a concept used for practical application of the theory. Research on routine activity theory has described the suitability of a target in numerous ways. However, most agree that the financial value, inertia (ease in moving the item), accessibility, and visibility of the target are all related to suitability in one way or another. The practical implication from this is target hardening, varies based on each target's usefulness. For example, an item for sale should generally be accessible and visible to potential customers. Doing so makes it inherently vulnerable to theft, however. Options might include attaching the item to the counter to prevent removal, with "live" merchandise secured separately that only sales associates may access, thus reducing the potential inertia of the item and increasing the guardianship of the live merchandise without truly reducing accessibility. In other situations, such as the counting of money in a vault, it may not be possible to change the accessibility or inertia. Instead, the level of guardianship is significantly increased, with all activity conducted by two persons (dual control), while everything is monitored and recorded by CCTV, and all funds are counted prior to the departure of the employees.

The Positivist School of Thought

Unlike the theories of the classical school of thought, which often assumes everyone is equally likely to become a criminal and it is because of the situation before them that causes them to choose to be criminal, the positivist theory focuses more on why some people are more prone to criminality than others. The positivist school of thought is often credited to Cesare Lombroso, whose book (*The Criminal Man [2011]*) is often cited as the earliest positivist theory.[4] Lombroso's main hypothesis was that a moderately-sized subset of criminals are atavistic, an evolutionary throwback to primitive man. Furthermore, the criminals Lombroso described had five or more physical abnormalities (large nose, large skull, increased body hair, etc.) and were a "born criminal." Although the theory has since been widely disregarded for being overly simplistic and discriminatory, it was still one of the first to go beyond describing criminality as a choice or a result of demonic activity.

Today, most positivist theories focus on various social factors that affect one's willingness to commit crime, but biology and psychology are also present. These theories are often more elaborate and offer complex solutions. As such, the conclusions are normally less practical for one person or business to implement. For this reason, these theories will receive less attention in this text. However, interested readers would do well to learn more about these complex theories using any one of the various sources referenced.

Social Disorganization

One of the oldest positivist theories still researched today, social disorganization, was the product of research in the 1920s by Clifford R. Shaw and Henry D. McKay.[5] The research primarily focused on the city of Chicago and the "concentric zones" that existed there. As a city slowly expands outward, each circular zone also expands by invading the next zone. While each zone has individual characteristics, the ones essential to social disorganization are the first and second zones. The first zone, the business district, is located in the center of the city; the second zone, the area with the poorest residents, exists around the first. The second zone is uniquely plagued with a series of invasions by both new immigrants and the expanding business district. The areas most affected by this change are called the *interstitial zone*. The rapid change creates social disorganization, which allows crime to occur.

More recent iterations of the theory are representative of present day cities. Sampson's social disorganization theory, *collective efficacy*, is the version most commonly used in current research.[6] The focus in Sampson's theory is on zones of transition in inner-city areas. People in these areas have high "residential mobility," which means they can easily move, yet they usually move to other areas within the zones of transition. In essence, these people are stuck in poor areas, but still move often. This creates a lack of collective efficacy because frequently moving residents cannot have mutual trust with neighbors. In other words, residents of inner-cities do not get to know their neighbors. This, combined with other factors such as structural disadvantage, explains the higher crime rates in certain areas of cities.

Social Learning Theories

Social learning theory, another long-studied theory, was developed and published in various stages between 1934 and 1947. Differential association, as the first social learning theory was later dubbed, was the work of Edwin Sutherland and, to a lesser extent, his co-author Donald Cressey.[7] The main hypothesis of differential association is that criminal behavior is learned. More specifically, "a person becomes delinquent because of an excess of definitions favorable to violation of law over definitions unfavorable to violation of law." In more common language, a person becomes a criminal when the majority of the ideas to which they are exposed are pro-crime. Although the theory and subsequent research goes beyond simply the number of criminals versus noncriminals (focusing on the frequency, duration, priority, and intensity of pro-criminal messages from friends and family), the main hypothesis nonetheless is that criminal behavior is learned from other people. Furthermore, people must learn three things from criminals to become criminals themselves: motive, attitude (a rationalization for breaking the law), and technique (skills for certain crimes).

Social learning theories, however, are not limited to differential association. Rather, more contemporary social learning theories have expanded upon Sutherland's work, spawning many variations. One of the more often cited social learning theories, from Burgess and Akers in 1966, includes more societal level concepts to explain how society as a whole contributes to delinquency and criminality as well.[8] For example, differential reinforcement explains how potential rewards and punishments that follow crimes can influence the potential offender and recidivists.

Techniques of Neutralization

Sometimes called drift theory, the techniques of neutralization from Sykes and Matza (1957) are used to explain how people, especially delinquents, can believe a crime is wrong, commit the crime, then still go on believing the crime is wrong but that they have done nothing wrong.[9] In other words, the techniques of neutralization are ways for offenders to rationalize their actions and essentially create an exception specifically tailored for their own actions. Figure 3.4 explains each of the techniques and example usages.

Strain Theories

Although strain theories date back to Durkheim, criminological theories using strain are more recent, relatively speaking. The first strain theory of crime, sometimes called

Techniques of Neutralization	Sample Usage
Denial of responsibility	It was an accident. It was not my fault.
Denial of injury	It did not hurt anyone. I was just borrowing it.
Denial of victim	He deserved it. His kind deserves it.
Condemnation of the condemners	The police are corrupt. That teacher plays favorites anyway. He would have done it too.
Appeals to higher loyalties	I was just following orders.

FIGURE 3.4 Techniques of neutralization.

"anomie" (not to be confused with Durkheim's concept for which this theory is based upon), was developed by Robert Merton in 1938.[10] According to the theory, Americans share two distinct beliefs. First, they want the American dream, that is, people want to be successful financially and live a middle- or upper-class lifestyle. Second, Americans live by a puritan work ethic—they believe hard work is the only way to become successful. Most of the time, people are *conformists* and achieve their goals using their work ethic. When people experience strain, which is a disjunction between their goals and means (meaning they cannot get what they want doing what they believe is right), they must respond in one of four ways. Firstly, they can *innovate* by rejecting the traditional means (by stealing or other profitable crimes). Secondly, they can turn to *ritualism* (continue working hard even though they know it will not improve their living conditions). Thirdly, they can become *retreatists* and turn to substance use or other forms of escapism. Finally, they can *rebel* and create new goals and means (typically rejecting capitalism altogether, sometimes forming micro-societies like communes). See Figure 3.5.

Another classic strain theory is *differential opportunity* from Cloward and Ohlin in 1960.[11] Similar to previous theories, Cloward and Ohlin believe that some youths fail to obtain the goals they want and look for alternatives. What alternative they choose, much like Merton's theory, varies. If illegitimate means for obtaining money exists (e.g., organized crime, fencing opportunities, etc.) and the youth has the skill necessary, he will join a "criminal" gang. If these opportunities do not exist, on the other hand, the youth may turn to a "conflict" gang that acts out in violence. Finally, if the youth fails in both criminal and conflict gangs, or if these types of gangs are incompatible with the

	Goal	Mean
Conformity	+	+
Innovation	+	−
Ritualism	−	+
Retreatism	−	−
Rebellion	+/−	+/−

FIGURE 3.5 Possible outcomes of strain.

youth's morality, a "retreatist subculture" involving drugs is a last resort for "double failures."

The most recent reiteration of strain theory, general strain theory, came in 1992 from Robert Agnew.[12] The flexibility and generality of the theory is both its strength and weakness. According to the theory, strain can be caused by one of two actions: the removal of positively valued stimuli or the presentation of negative stimuli. Essentially, people commit crimes when they lose something they like or when someone does something to them they do not like. This theory has been praised for its broadness, but it has also been criticized for not being specific enough. Current research is investigating which negative and positive stimuli have more powerful effects on crime.

Control Theories

Unlike most criminological theories, which focus on why someone becomes criminal, control theories focus on why some people do not. In essence, control theories examine the parts of society that act to prevent criminality. In some cases, this can involve the social ramifications of crime, but usually the factors studied are nonfinancial.

Although not the oldest control theory, Travis Hirschi's 1969 theory of social bonding is probably the most often discussed control theory.[13] According to this theory, there are four social factors that prevent delinquency: attachment, commitment, involvement, and belief. The first, attachment, refers to one's relationship with his or her parents and school. The greater that person's attachment is, the more likely he or she is to care about the disapproval that would result from criminality. The second element, commitment, is similar to classical theories in its focus on the negative results of crime. When someone has made an investment that would be lost due to crime (a *stake in conformity*), that person is less likely to risk losing the said investment. Unlike the classical theories, however, Hirschi allowed for this investment to be more than just money or freedom. The commitment can also include a career that could be lost or an education cut short.

The third concept that affects a social bond is involvement, which can include employment or other time-consuming activities. For involvement, the idea is not that these activities produce pro-social attitudes, but rather that a potential criminal without free time will not have the opportunity to commit a crime. It should be noted, however, that most research finds no significant effect from the involvement concept on crime. Finally, the belief element is fairly obvious; the belief that something is wrong will prevent the believer from turning to crime. Worthy of note in this theory, however, is that Hirschi posited that we live in a consensus-based society, meaning that everyone holds similar beliefs. What differs from person to person is the strength of the belief; the weaker the belief, the more willing someone is to act against their own belief.

Another control theory that should be addressed is the low self-control theory by Gottfredson and Hirschi from 1990.[14] It takes the elements discussed, both in Hirschi's earlier theory and other positivist theories, and further investigates what causes them. The main hypothesis is that poor childrearing is the root cause of all crime, as it results in low self-control. Additionally, they state that most or all of one's self-control is established before the age of eight and remains constant throughout one's life. Low self-control is currently one of the most heavily debated theories. There is currently a divide between the theorists who support it—those who believe it explains why a minority of people account for the majority of crime, and those who claim it fails to explain why most offending occurs during the teenage years if low self-control remains after that time.

Other Explanations of Criminality

For the most part, the theories discussed so far, are rooted in a *consensus paradigm*, which makes an assumption that crime is a deviant act that goes against society's beliefs. Conversely, a *conflict paradigm* theory explains crime as a normal function of certain groups. Theories within this paradigm are often called theories of critical criminology. The groups in these theories, however, have neither the power to create laws protecting their preferred actions, nor the ability to remove laws barring such actions. For example, a critical theory could explain violent behavior as a legitimate source of status for certain subcultures. White collar crime is one of the major strengths of conflict theories, as the lack of focus on white collar crimes in society is explained because people with power, who decide which laws to enforce, are usually the perpetrators of such crimes.

Sometimes considered a critical theory and other times listed separately, *Marxist theories* also explain crime differently than consensus theories. The major characteristic of Marxist theories that separates them from other critical theories is the focus on economic class. Unlike other conflict theories, which are more general in defining the groups involved, Marxist theories specify that the conflict is between the *bourgeois* upper class and the *proletarian* working class. According to the theories, the bourgeois own and control the means of production (businesses, factories, etc.) and keep all the money their workers earn, sans their paychecks, which only gives their workers enough to buy food and other necessities to stay alive and healthy enough to work.

Not all of the alternative explanations of crime are at odds with the consensus theories. In some cases, special theories exist for certain situations that are frequently compatible with a consensus perspective. *Feminist criminological theories*, for example, can help in explaining why female delinquency is increasing (equal treatment), although it has still not reached the prevalence of delinquency by males. They also contribute to explanations for why females are less likely in general to commit crimes. These explanations sometimes focus on physical differences (hormonal aggression, strength, etc.), but they often focus on social trends and the differential treatment of girls and boys during childhood (e.g., girls being taught to be passive rather than aggressive). Similarly, *life course theories* explain why teenage youth account for the majority of crime. These theories usually involve explaining the criminal tendencies as a function of the transition from childhood to adulthood due to the increased freedom without adult obligations (work, marriage, parenting, etc.).

Criminological Theories in the Real World

The criminological theories of today *theoretically* explain crime rather well. However, in the statistical analyses used to test the theories, there is a term that is a significant challenge to the theories: the error term. A theory is a series of falsifiable statements about relationships between two or more observable phenomena. Because true scientific theories are inherently falsifiable, they can and should be tested to determine their validity and reliability. When a theory is tested with real-world data, usually using survey data, a lot of crime goes unexplained. Using current statistical techniques, such as *regression* models using multiple controls or *structural equation modeling* (see Figure 3.6), a theory is generally considered a success if it can explain 10–20% of the variation in crime. Essentially, each theory explains only a small portion of crime. Even more elaborate models that combine theories, often called integrated theories, cannot explain everything. There are other obstacles as well. For example, researchers almost always find that delinquents are more likely than nondelinquents to report that their friends are also delinquent. Although this would be considered support for social learning theories, it does not really prove the theory. It could mean that delinquency is learned, but it could also mean that delinquents exaggerate their friends' criminality on surveys, or it could simply be proving that delinquents seek out other delinquents to have as friends.

Presently, theories find moderate support in empirical tests. No theory has been proven to be completely true, yet nearly all discussed here are true enough to be better than no theory at all. In the simplest of terms, criminological theories are far from perfect. There is still much to be explained and the theories we do have are each only small pieces of a very large puzzle, but knowing the basics is the first step to explaining the phenomenon of crime.

Procedure	Description
T-Test	Compares groups to see if there are significant differences. Example usage: to see if people who have read a pro-crime essay believe crime is more acceptable than those who have not read the essay.
Regression	Determines how much variance in a dependent variable (e.g., crime) is caused by changes in other measured variables. Example outcome: "attachment was the most powerful predictor of delinquency."
Structural Equation Modeling (SEM)	Similar to regression, but allows for more complex models that include multiple paths of causality. Example: *A* Causes *B* and *B & C* both cause *Y*. Explains and measures *mediating effects*.
Hierarchical Linear Modeling (HLM)	Controls for "nesting effects" in certain sampling techniques that result in multiple classes or other *clusters* being sampled. In other words, determines whether changes are due to individual differences, classroom level variables, school characteristics, or geographic region.

FIGURE 3.6 Common statistical procedures.

Appendix: Quick Reference Theory Matrix

Theory	Description
Deterrence Beccaria, 1764[15]	When punishment severity, celerity, and certainty are low, people will commit crimes because the punishment is less likely and less significant.
Rational Choice Clarke/Cornish, developed 1985[16]	People commit crimes because they believe it to be an easier and more beneficial option.
Routine Activity Cohen/Felson, 1979[17]	A crime occurs when a motivated offender and suitable target meet in time and space *if* a capable guardian is not present.
Social Disorganization Shaw/McKay[18]; Sampson Groves[19] research 1920s; 1980s	Crime occurs in areas where frequent moving occurs and where the city lack collective efficacy to enforce laws and promote other social programs.
Social Learning Theory Sutherland/Cressey[20]; Burgess/Akers[21] original publication 1947; 1966	Crime is learned through social interaction with criminals and people supportive of crime. The motive, attitudes, and techniques supportive of crime are transmitted primarily from family and friends. Society as a whole also contributes through rewards/punishments.
Techniques of Neutralization Sykes & Matza, 1957[22]	Explains how people with conforming beliefs can rationalize their actions through denial and shifting the blame.
Strain Merton[23]; Cloward/Ohlin[24] 1938; 1960	People turn to crime (for differing reasons depending on the theorist) when their chance of achieving their goal through convention means is blocked. Usually focuses on the lower class or middle class.
General Strain Agnew[25], 1992	Crime is the result of the removal of positively valued stimuli or the presentation of negative stimuli.
Social Bond Hirschi[26], 1969	Crime is prevented when a potential delinquent has attachment to parents or school, commitment to a convention way of life, involvement in noncriminal activities, and/or strong beliefs.
Low Self-control Gottfredson & Hirschi[27], 1990	Crime is prevented when someone has high self-control. People with low self-control are present-oriented and do not see future consequences. Poor childrearing causes low self-control.
Conflict/critical theories	The people in power use their power by creating laws that keep others, usually minorities or the lower class, in check.
Marxist theories	Similar to conflict but specifies that the parties involved are the *bourgeois* upper class and the *proletarian* working class, and that crime is the result of continued greed and selfishness.
Feminist theories	Theories that explain why female delinquency is increasing and why females are less likely in general to commit crimes.
Life-course theories	Theories that explain the desistance process and how crime is related to age.

Refer website http://www.ifpo.org for further information

End Notes

1. Beccaria, C., *On Crimes and Punishments* (1764).

2. Clarke, R.V., & Cornish, D.B., "Rational choice," in *Explaining Criminals and Crime: Essays in Contemporary Criminological Theory*, eds. Paternoster R., & Bachman R (Los Angeles: Roxbury, 2001), 23–42.

3. Cohen, L.E., & Felson, M., "Social change and crime rate trends: a routine activity approach," *American Sociological Review* 44, (1979): 588–608.

4. Lombroso, C., *The Criminal Man* (1911).

5. Shaw, C.R., & McKay, H.D., *Juvenile delinquency and urban areas* (Chicago: University of Chicago, 1942).

6. Sampson, R.J., Raudenbush, S.W., & Earls, F., "Neighborhoods and violent crime: a multilevel study of collective efficacy," *Science* 277, (1997): 918–924.

7. Sutherland, E.H., & Cressey, D.R., *Principles of criminology*, Sixth Edition, (1960).

8. Burgess, R.L., & Akers, R.L., "A differential association-reinforcement theory of criminal behavior," *Social Problems* 14, (1966): 128–147.

9. Sykes, G.M., & Matza, D., "Techniques of neutralization: a theory of delinquency," *American Sociological Review* 22, (1957): 664–670.

10. Merton, R.K., "Social structure and anomie," *American Sociological Review* 3, (1938).

11. Cloward, R.A., & Ohlin, L.E., *Delinquency and opportunity: A theory of delinquent gangs* (New York: Free Press, 1960).

12. Agnew, R., "Foundation for a general strain theory of crime and delinquency," *Criminology* 30, (1992): 47–87.

13. Hirschi, T., *The causes of delinquency* (Berkeley, CA: University of California, 1969).

14. Gottfredson, M.R., & Hirschi, T., *A general theory of crime* (Stanford, CA: Stanford University, 1990).

15. See note 1 above.

16. See note 2 above.

17. See note 3 above.

18. See note 5 above

19. See note 6 above.

20. See note 7 above.

21. See note 7 above.

22. See note 9 above.

23. See note 10 above.

24. See note 11 above.

25. See note 12 above.

26. See note 13 above.

27. See note 14 above.

4

Ethics, Integrity, and Professional Conduct

Larry Steele, Brion P. Gilbride, Christopher A. Hertig,
Lawrence J. Fennelly, Marianna Perry

This chapter is dedicated to Dr. Neal Trautman; the original author of this chapter in the second and third editions. Neal spent his working life in the service of others—protecting, teaching, and writing. He founded the Law Enforcement Television Network and played an instrumental role in various professional groups, such as the International Law Enforcement Educators and Trainers Association. He was also the founder of The National Institute of Ethics.

We miss him dearly. We remember him fondly. We walk in the path he showed us.

Introduction

Similar to law enforcement, the security profession provides employment for hundreds of thousands of individuals throughout the world. As with any profession, unfortunately, a very small minority of those individuals engage in unlawful or unethical conduct. These few violate the trust that their employers, as well as the public at large, have placed in them. This violation of trust hurts the security profession more than any specific unlawful acts that occur. As with other professions, such as law enforcement or education, security is only effective if there is trust between the protectors and the people they are charged with protecting. Because of the negative impact of individual unethical or unprofessional conduct on the security profession as a whole, two well-known security organizations, ASIS International and Interagency Security Commission (ISC)[2] have adopted a *Code of Ethics* as a condition of membership or affiliation to place emphasis on the importance of ethical business practices, personal integrity, and professional conduct for those individuals working in the security industry.

The security profession itself can be conducive to certain unlawful activities. To ensure the security of people, places, or assets, security managers and their subordinate staff must each be aware of potential threats or disruptions to that security. To mitigate these potential threats or disruptions, the security professional oftentimes needs access to locations, items, persons, or information that could be misused, damaged, or destroyed if not properly protected. The access that is given to protect is the same access that can be misused.

Definition of Ethics

Through the years, ethics had been defined by many different scholars. Lawrence and Weber defined **ethics** as "the concept of right and wrong conduct. It tells whether [a] behavior is moral or immoral and deals with fundamental human relationships."[1] In other words, do unto others as you would have them do unto you. Similarly, A.B. Carroll referred to ethics as the ability and desire to make moral or ethical judgments, implying that the decision maker is concerned with the "spirit of the law" rather than just the "letter of the law." Carroll indicated that the ethics used by the everyday person and a corporation are different because business ethics is a field of "special" ethics—that is, the review of the ethical practices of a very specific field of study instead of the ethics of a particular individual.[2] For the purpose of this chapter, we focus on business ethics, which may have been best summarized by M.G. Velasquez, who stated that **business ethics** "is a study of moral right and wrong, concentrating on moral standards as applied to business practices."[3]

Security professionals view ethics as the backbone of the entire security industry. Without ethical people, the security field would be doomed. Who wants to hire a security corporation to protect their employees, visitors, and assets if that security corporation cannot be trusted to take the right course of action pertaining to the client's wishes and demands? If a security officer assigned to a chemical plant does not take the position's responsibilities seriously, he or she can put millions of people in jeopardy. For example, suppose that Security Officer Thomas becomes too friendly with the truck drivers who are moving dangerous chemicals to and from the client's chemical plan. Officer Thomas is too complacent; he does not hold each driver and transaction to the management's expectations. Because of Officer Thomas's lack of ethics, dangerous chemicals are stolen from the plant, causing a breach of homeland security. In this case, being ethical means fulfilling the client's protocol, specifications, and requirements to the fullest of the employee's power— not taking shortcuts or the easy way out of doing more work.

Code of Ethics

More than 90 percent of corporations in the United States have some type of code of ethics.[4] The normal unspoken agreement among employees regarding what is and is not acceptable is called the **ethical climate**. The three main parts of the ethical climate, called the *ethical criteria*, are egoism (self-centeredness), benevolence (concern for others), and principle (respect for one's own integrity, group norms, and society's laws).[5]

The **ethical criteria** are used to describe how individuals, companies, and society as a whole approach moral dilemmas. For example, if a security manager has an affair with one of his or her subordinates and then gives that individual choice assignments and overtime, a moral dilemma has taken place; this can be examined using the ethical criteria. The security manager violated the *egoism* aspect of the ethical criteria as it relates to the company's code of ethics by indulging in an inappropriate relationship at work.

The security officer violated the *benevolence* aspect of the ethical criteria as it relates to the company's code of ethics by disregarding the other employees and only giving choice assignments and overtime to his or her boyfriend or girlfriend. This security manager also violates the *principle* aspect of the ethical criteria as it relates to the company's code of ethics by jeopardizing his or her own integrity and imposing on the company's social norms. Also, society's laws were violated if the subordinate was not actually working the overtime assignments and the manager knowingly falsified the pay records, in turn assisting in a theft of the employer's funds.

As you can see from this example, an unethical act can violate a company's code of conduct in different ways and on various levels.

Leadership Commitment for Change

The first step in preventing corruption is to attain leadership commitment for change. The worldview held by administration is crucial; administrators must show that they believe in the pursuit of ethics and the foundation they work for must demonstrate commitment that reflects these beliefs within its mission statement. A mission statement is a declaration of a company's, organization's, or individual's purpose—a summation of why it exists.

The mission statement should guide the actions of the company, organization, or person and should include the following:

- State the overall goal
- Provide a path
- Guide decision-making

According to Hill and Jones, a mission statement is "the framework or context within which the company's strategies are formulated."[6] A **mission statement** can be looked at as what the company, organization, or individual wants to do for the world. Ethics should be a vital part of the current mission statement. If a mission statement does not exist, then the starting place is clear. Although developing a mission statement is essential, how it is written is equally important. Do not develop it alone. Rather, it is always best to involve the entire company because ownership of the mission statement is more likely to result.

All aspects of the company should be guided by the mission statement, which in turn should have a clear ethical direction. Goals are then developed to guide all efforts toward achieving the mission, and objectives are written to assist in reaching each goal. Positive leadership will fuel self-esteem and remove obstacles to attain these goals.

Internal commitment for preventing corruption can be demonstrated by the following:

- Assisting in the development of the ethical aspects of a mission statement, goals, and objectives
- Participating in the organization's ethics in-service training
- Being an ethical model
- Ensuring that all employees are treated with respect and fairness

A Model for Establishing a Code of Ethics in a Major Private Security Company

When building a code of ethics, it is important to use all levels of the company in terms of viewpoints, ideals, and understanding. If an employer does not take into consideration the education levels, cultures, and environments from which their workers come, the code of ethics will be made in vain. If the employees do not understand their employer's code of ethics or it contradicts their own beliefs, the employees will not follow the code; this can cause a major disruption within the company's productive environment. The following list provides some objectives that should be taken into consideration when establishing a code of ethics[7]:

- Equality, opportunity, and empowerment
- Excellence and innovation
- Integrity
- Quality through continuous improvement
- Humane environment that allows for quality improvement
- Human rights
- Shared vision and identity
- Honesty, reliability, discipline, and loyalty
- Social responsibility
- Investment in human capital
- Leadership and vision from the top
- Professional and ethical business procedures
- Active and visible participation of top management
- Open and honest communication
- Involvement and commitment from all employees
- Comprehensible internal company/client philosophy
- Diversity

Training to Make Ethical Decisions

A parent does not have to teach a child to be bad. Children can and do get into all types of mischief and make bad decisions on their own. However, a parent should teach a child to do the right thing and to make good choices in life. In the same way, an employer needs to also teach employees the correct way to make ethical decisions. The training must begin with explaining the employer's code of ethics, rules and regulations, and standard operating procedures. After the employee understands what the employer expects in terms of the employee's behavior, the employer must instill a no-tolerance policy for rule violations. The employee must understand the implications for making unethical decisions and the penalties and repercussions that follow from their actions.

After the employee understands what will occur if he or she violates the code of ethics, the rules, or standard operating procedures, it is time to teach the employee about the importance of following the rules and regulations and what could take place in terms of injuries, lawsuits, and loss of revenue for the company if they are not followed. The next step in the employee's ethics training is to train the employee to do his or her job correctly, which reduces the need for the employee to make decisions—of which some may be unethical.

For example, suppose a loss prevention associate in a major distribution center was given empty perfume boxes after their contents had been stolen by an unknown warehouse employee. The loss prevention employee may become frustrated if he or she does not know how to correctly enter the theft information into a national loss prevention database. The employee may just throw the boxes in the dumpster without conducting an investigation, thus giving the offender a chance to steal more of the employer's assets.

This is a prime example of an employer not fulfilling its duty to effectively train employees to do their jobs correctly. The entire organization is affected because of lost profits. In turn, the employer may not have enough capital to hire more loss prevention associates, which in turn increases the workload of the loss prevention staff and hurts the department's morale. When the loss prevention department is overworked, some of the staff may decide to take shortcuts when conducting investigations. This starts a vicious cycle of theft and property loss, until the company goes bankrupt and no one has a job. When thefts are not investigated or reported, it gives the thieves more opportunity to steal and prevents the employer from filing a claim with its insurance company.

Integrity Issues Involving Time or Abuse of Office

Regardless of how many duties a supervisor or a manager holds, they are first and foremost a *leader*. It is the leader who demonstrates by his or her actions how to be ethical, how to maintain personal integrity, and how to remain professional in their conduct. It is the leader who demonstrates that the only way rules or regulations are effective is if they are followed. If the leader fails to demonstrate this, the security staff may also fail to act ethically, maintain personal integrity, or conduct themselves professionally. As a leader, the supervisor or manager must recognize the presence of integrity in subordinates because he or she will also be called upon from time to time to understand and anticipate situations where the integrity or ethics of a subordinate could be called into question.

A supervisor or manager has many things to deal with, both tactically in day-to-day operations as well as strategically over the course of a month, quarter, or year, *time*. Time encompasses a variety of issues, including work schedules, training, patrols, emergency response, report writing, and many other things. Work schedules are concerned with time and nothing else. Work schedules provide as much opportunity for security personnel to maintain their personal integrity as they provide opportunities for unethical conduct. Consider the following situations regarding time.

Situation 1: Security Officer Smith works at a manufacturing plant and is required to swipe his employee identification (ID) badge through a time clock in order to record his arrival and departure times as an hourly employee. Employees that forget their badges can also punch in their employee ID to record their time. Officer Smith, running late for work due to inclement weather, called a friend at the worksite and asked him to punch in Officer Smith's employee ID into the time clock. Officer Smith arrived approximately 15 min after the start of his scheduled shift and began patrolling. Officer Brown, monitoring the digital video system, saw Officer Smith's vehicle pulling into the lot and noticed that Smith was several minutes late, but said nothing. Officer Johnson, whose shift ended 15 min prior, was waiting near the employee entrance, wondering where her relief was; Officer Johnson could not relinquish her post until relief arrived. When Supervisor Shah reviewed the time-card records the next day, he saw Officer Smith worked his usual 8-h shift.

As a condition of employment, security officers are assigned to a particular 8-h shift. They are required to be on-duty at the start of the shift; they should have the necessary uniforms and equipment and have received any pass-down information from the officer(s) they are relieving. This is a common scenario in any job, not just security—consider how many parties are affected here and in what ways.

1. Officer Smith used another individual to punch his timecard so that he was credited for 15 minutes of pay to which he was not entitled.
2. The unnamed employee punched the timecard belonging to Officer Smith, enabling Officer Smith to be credited for the 15 min of pay to which he is not entitled.
3. Officer Brown could prove, by virtue of the video system, what time Officer Smith actually arrived for work, but he failed to report the incident.
4. Officer Johnson must now be paid 15 min of overtime, to which she would not have been entitled had Officer Smith reported to work on time.

Officer Smith and the unnamed employee acted in concert to falsely claim hours Officer Smith did not work but would still be compensated for, which is another way of saying Officer Smith stole that amount of pay from the company; Smith was not entitled to that money and claimed it regardless. The unnamed employee that swiped Officer Smith's timecard is complicit in that theft from the company as well because it was the actual swiping that allowed the transaction to occur. Officer Brown is also complicit in the theft because Officer Brown failed to report the actual arrival time based on the video evidence Brown observed. Officer Brown, Officer Smith, and the unnamed employee not only cost the company the money paid to Brown, but also cost the overtime money paid to Officer Johnson who had to stay and cover the duties Brown was not present to perform.

Situation 2: Deputy Security Chief Thornton comes in to work at 10:00 am each day. On a typical day, Deputy Thornton goes to lunch around 1:00 pm and returns at 2:30 pm. At 4:30 pm, Deputy Thornton goes home for the day. Administrative Assistant Ramirez works for the security department, and one of her duties is to submit the department's payroll to human resources every 2 weeks. Ramirez works from 9:00 am to 5:00 pm each day and sees that Deputy Thornton always arrives *after* Ramirez comes to work. When Ramirez reconciles the work schedules to the payroll hours, she notices that Deputy Thornton's schedule on paper is 9:00 am to 5:00 pm, like hers, with a 30-min unpaid lunch time. Ramirez has a sick child, so both she and her husband have had to miss work and spend a great deal of money on healthcare. She cannot afford to be out of work, especially in a poor economy. Consider how this scenario affects the parties involved.

1. Deputy Security Chief Thornton is not accurately reporting his time: reporting 1 h late each day, taking an additional hour for lunch, and leaving 30 min early.
2. Administrative Assistant Ramirez fails to report the unusual attendance activity, enabling Thornton to continue to claim time for which he was not on duty.
3. Factors beyond Ramirez's control may be influencing her failure to address the situation.

Taking the 2.5-h per day, and mutliplying it by 10 to account for the 2-week payroll period, equals 25 h each paycheck that Thornton is stealing from the company by failing to report late arrivals, early departures, and long lunches. That can quickly add up to significant time. Ramirez, based on this scenario, likely fails to report the activity out of fear that Thornton might seek retribution if the company fails to act. Although done for noble reasons, Ramirez sacrifices her integrity by failing to report the situation, even if she is morally correct for ensuring job security for the sake of her family.

Situation 3: At XYZ Security, there is a policy that facilities may be run at 50% of normal staffing levels on any government-recognized holiday. Employees who work are paid at double time, and those who do not work receive straight pay for the holiday. The policy further states that the granting of holiday time off is to be determined by seniority within the department. Officer Connelly requested to be granted holiday time off for Christmas, but he was notified that he could not have that day off because the available holiday slots were taken by officers with greater seniority. While talking to a coworker, Officer Connelly was told that if he called in sick, the company could not deny the leave. On Christmas day, when Officer Connelly was scheduled to work from 12:00 pm to 8:00 pm, he called in sick. Due to the sick call, Officer Ahmad was forced to stay on duty until a relief officer could be called in. Consider how this affects the parties involved.

1. Officer Connelly requested holiday time off, which was denied according to the stated policy.
2. Officer Connelly called in sick in order to take Christmas off outside of the holiday policy.

Officer Connelly at first attempted to follow the holiday policy by requesting the time off. When told there were no slots available and that he would have to work Christmas, Officer Connelly was probably upset about it. Instead of coming into work as he was supposed to, he called in sick. The resulting sick call forced XYZ Security to have at least one officer cover Officer Connelly's shift. Officer Connelly circumvented the holiday policy by claiming sick time, which was unfair to the rest of the officers, and forced one (or more) of his fellow officers to have to stay at work beyond their scheduled shift until a relief officer was available.

Situation 4: Officer Hamilton works at a concert venue in London as part of the in-house security team. Officer Hamilton is scheduled to work in the crowd at an upcoming concert, which sold out as soon as the tickets went on sale. Several weeks prior to the concert, Officer Hamilton requested vacation time that conflicted with the concert date.

Accordingly, management denied the vacation request. On the night of the concert, Officer Hamilton showed up for work. As the concert venue filled up and the show began, Officer Hamilton surreptitiously left the venue and went home. Due to the size of the concert and the sheer number of personnel, nobody realized that Officer Hamilton had left, and his departure time was assumed to be in line with the rest of the staff. Consider how this affects the parties involved.

1. Officer Hamilton requested vacation time off that conflicted with a previously scheduled event.
2. Officer Hamilton left his post during the concert without informing anyone.

Officer Hamilton at first attempted to follow policy and requested vacation time. Management denied the request, probably because they could not spare the staff for such a complex event. Officer Hamilton was probably upset about the denial. Having worked numerous events at this concert venue, Officer Hamilton realized that once the concert had actually begun, he could depart the venue unnoticed—any security staff that saw him would not realize anything was amiss. Officer Hamilton further concluded, from experience, that nobody would attempt to contact him via radio or telephone because the volume of the concert would prohibit it. Because Officer Hamilton left the venue without reporting to anyone, the company paid him for the full shift that he would have worked had he stayed. Officer Hamilton stole that money from the company by being absent without leave.

Another issue that security professionals must be aware of is best referred to as "abuse of office." Abuse of office occurs when a manager or executive, whether in the security professional's hierarchy or outside of it, engages in certain activities. The common denominators among activities that constitute abuse of office include the following:

- Exceeding a given or existing authority
- Assuming an authority that does not exist
- Assuming an authority granted to someone else, where that person is lower in the hierarchy or in a comparable position elsewhere in the company

Although some abuse of office involves time, as described above, there are other situations where abuse occurs. Instructing subordinates to improperly perform their duties is one common scenario—the motives for this could be well-intentioned, selfish, or even malicious. Another common situation involves instructing subordinates to do things indirectly related to their job, such as personal errands. Situations where employee files are manipulated to pass an audit, or where manager's family members are given jobs for which they do not show up or for which they are grossly unqualified, also might constitute abuse of office.

Situation 1: Mr. Agarwal is the son of the president of a contract security firm. One day, Mr. Agarwal is involved in a motor vehicle accident while operating a company vehicle, damaging the vehicle and injuring another employee, Mr. Simpson. This security firm has a well-established policy that any employee involved in a motor vehicle accident must be drug-tested. The results of that test are shared with human resources and the firm's insurance carrier. Knowing this, the president of the firm arranges to substitute clean urine for that of Mr. Agarwal prior to the test. The president also tells the human resources manager not to take any action and that Mr. Agarwal will be placed in a treatment program. The substituted urine goes to the laboratory and tests negative for any substances. Per policy, the reports are shared with human resources and the insurance carrier. Consider how this situation affects the parties involved.

1. Mr. Agarwal, while on duty, had a motor vehicle accident in which a company employee was injured and a company vehicle damaged.
2. Mr. Agarwal is believed to have a measurable amount of a controlled substance in his body at the time of the accident.
3. The president arranged for Mr. Agarwal's mandatory urine test to be falsified.
4. The president instructed the human resources manager to take no action against Mr. Agarwal.
5. As a result of this chain of events, false information was reported to human resources and to the firm's insurance carrier.

Mr. Agarwal could be a controlled substance abuser, have ingested the substance on-duty or off-duty, or have ingested the substance unintentionally, such as at a concert where others were using the substance. Mr. Agarwal may have been unaware that he would be drug-tested after the accident. Alternatively, he may have known that he would test positive, assumed his father (the president) could protect him, and therefore allowed events to run their course.

The president abused his position and authority with the company in multiple ways. First, he arranged for clean urine to be substituted for the drug test. In doing so, the president would have instructed someone to tamper with the tests. Second, the president interfered with the investigation of the incident by ordering the human resources manager to take no action. Were this any other employee, human resources would have received the results of the drug test and proceeded accordingly with action against the employee. The insurance carrier for the security company would have been notified of the clean drug test, and that insurance carrier would conceivably have paid the claims relating to the damaged vehicle and the injured employee, Mr. Simpson. The injured employee, unaware of the controlled substance issue, accepts workers' compensation and does not file suit against the company for hiring Mr. Agarwal or permitting him to operate a vehicle.

Situation 2: Maple Leaf Mall Corporation contracts their security operation to a firm called Canadian Security International (CSI). As a condition of the contract, Maple Leaf Mall Corp. conducts two audits annually on CSI's personnel files to ensure that background checks have been administered on all CSI employees that work at Maple Leaf Mall. The contract contains no provision for Maple Leaf Mall to pay for the background checks, so CSI is forced to pay for them. For convenience, Maple Leaf Mall Corp. always schedules the audits for the weeks of June 1st and December 1st of each year. CSI, for a variety of reasons, has high turnover among their security officer staff at the mall. To keep expenses down, CSI's managing director has ordered the human resources division not to submit background checks for any new employees until the months of May and November. The managing director's argument is that the audit files will always be up-to-date and CSI is not spending money conducting backgrounds on employees who will probably resign prior to the next audit. Consider the impact on the parties involved.

1. Maple Leaf Mall requires that the security contractor CSI conduct background checks on all employees. Maple Leaf Mall conducts two audits of the files each year to confirm that the background checks are being administered.
2. CSI, due to high turnover among the staff, spends considerable money on background checks for personnel whose files will never be audited because they do not stay with the company long enough.
3. To save money, CSI conducts all background checks necessary to reach full compliance in one batch a few weeks prior to each audit.

The managing director has reneged on the contract with Maple Leaf Mall by not adhering to the conditions. Maple Leaf Mall requires that all security staff working at their site to have background checks performed. The managing director's order to hold background checks until just before each audit means that any security personnel that works for CSI for 5-months or less are likely not to have a complete background check unless their hire date is near the audit date. If the Maple Leaf Mall auditor comes from a different office, that auditor may not be aware of CSI's personnel turnover issue and may miss the pattern of dates on which background checks are conducted. The managing director's order places Maple Leaf Mall customers and employees at risk when CSI uses personnel without proper background checks.

Situation 3: Shift Supervisor Foley, while supervising a shift of mall security officers at Maple Leaf Mall, discovers that a manager in the mall food court is having an affair with a food court employee and that some of their trysts have taken place on mall property. Supervisor Foley confronts the food court manager privately and suggests that the affair could go unnoticed if Foley's staff can eat for free when they are on duty. Otherwise, Foley hints that there are cameras throughout the mall and it is possible one or more of the trysts might have been captured on video. The food court manager agrees to this, and Foley tells his officers that there is a new policy allowing them to eat free while working their shift.

Consider the impact on the parties involved.

1. Supervisor Foley discovered a food court manager having sexual relations with an employee on the premises.
2. Supervisor Foley confronted the manager and obtained free food for the security officers in exchange for silence.
3. Supervisor Foley did not report the food court manager.
4. The food court manager did not report Supervisor Foley's activity.

Supervisor Foley, having gained knowledge of inappropriate activity on the part of the food court manager, abused his office by trading his silence for free food. Conversely, the food court manager impugned his integrity by not reporting Supervisor Foley for extorting him, possibly because such reporting could cost the food court manager his job. Supervisor Foley further abused his office by telling his subordinates that the free food at the food court was a policy change. This would lead the subordinates to think some arrangement had been worked out between Maple Leaf Mall and CSI—that to accept free food was permissible because the parties had an agreement.

When Security Becomes the Enemy

As important as it is for security supervisors and managers to recognize the many ways people act unethically or unprofessionally, it is equally important for supervisors and managers to be aware that, in some cases, people cross the line into acting illegally. The brief sampling of criminal acts perpetrated by security personnel described in this section cover a variety of disciplines. Some of the criminal activity is contingent on the access that a security job can provide, while others will be of a nature contingent on the authority that the security job can provide. Some criminal activity has no relationship to the security position whatsoever. The information presented in this sampling is intended to provide insight into security professionals who were able to engage in illegal activity, to show how they were caught, and what became of them, as well as to identify any potential indicators that might have flagged them prior to the illegal activity taking place.

Incident 1: Manager of Security Systems at a University

In April 2011, the manager of security systems for the Duke University Police Department was arrested and ultimately charged with 34 counts, mostly related to burglary. According to news reports, the break-ins occurred at various medical offices in Cary, NC as well as other nearby towns. Security systems were tampered with and exterior door locks popped off. Both drugs and cash were reportedly taken; police could not determine what happened to the drugs. The individual had worked for Duke University Police for 9-years, with prior stints at security contractors Securitas and Pinkerton. This individual served in the military at nearby Fort Bragg.[8] (Note: At the time of this writing, the case has yet to be resolved.)

A number of factors stand out here. First, this individual's security career spanned at least one decade, based on the 9-year tenure at Duke University and incorporating prior security and military experience. Barring other unreported activity, that is a reasonably well-established career; thus, it is likely the individual did not seek the job deliberately in order to commit crimes. Second, the individual tampered with security systems and was proficient at defeating exterior locks. He used the skills likely learned throughout his career to maintain such systems as his means of defeating them when he chose to commit the alleged burglaries. Third, drugs and cash were allegedly the objective; the individual's motive might stem from a recent addiction or financial problem.

How might Duke's supervisors or managers have addressed this situation? A background investigation, if it is assumed that the individual's performance in the military and with the contract security firms was free of controversy, probably would not have identified a substance abuse issue or a financial difficulty. As the individual was with Duke University for 9-years, the individual may have held non-managerial positions prior to becoming the manager of security systems. Either way, provided his work performance was adequate, a substance abuse issue or financial difficulty would probably have gone unnoticed. Due to the nature of working with security systems (and other information technology equipment), it is possible that this individual spent considerable time working alone.

Incident 2: Contract Security Guard at a Hospital

In June 2009, the U.S. Attorney for the Northern District of Texas indicted Jesse William McGraw for hacking into the computer systems of the Carrell Clinic, a hospital in Dallas, Texas. According to the press release from the US Attorney's Office, McGraw worked for a contract security firm providing security at the hospital. While working the night shift, McGraw hacked into computers controlling the heating, ventilation, and air conditioning systems, as well as computers containing patient information.[9] McGraw hacked into a total of 14 machines over a period of several months, and even posted a YouTube video showing himself hacking into one of the station nurses' computers. As part of his guilty plea, McGraw admitted being part of a group called the "Electronik Tribulation Army," which advocated breaking into computer systems and committing denial-of-service attacks by downloading "bot" software into hacked computers. For all of this, McGraw was sentenced to 110 months in prison.[10]

There are important factors that stand out in this case as well. By gaining employment with the contract security firm, McGraw was able to place himself on the overnight shift—generally not a popular shift, especially for employees with families. The overnight shift meant fewer employees, fewer patients, and therefore more opportunities to identify potential computers to hack into. By working for contract security, McGraw likely had access to areas that most hospital employees did not, including the rooms housing the information technology, routing and server equipment. Although the available information does not indicate whether McGraw went beyond the 14 computers he broke into, he may have had the capability if not the opportunity. By posting videos of his activities online, he explained to others what he did and how he was able to do it—this could have made it possible for those watching to engage in the same activity, possibly at the same location.

Unlike the first case, a background investigation might have flagged this individual. Talking to some of his former coworkers or associates might have revealed his fascination with hacking. A basic Google search might have returned results linking him to the "Electronik Tribulation Army" or something similar. Perhaps one or more of his YouTube videos may have been identified, particularly because Google owns YouTube. Asking McGraw to talk about his interests during his employment interview might have elicited something. A downside here is McGraw's relative youth—he was in his mid-twenties—which would not leave much of a pattern of previous employment.

Incident 3: Executive Protection

In May 2009, a woman and two children were found strangled to death in a home in southern Illinois. Shortly afterward, Christopher Coleman was arrested and charged with murder. Coleman was working for the security department of Joyce Meyer Ministries at the time.[11] As the case progressed through the courts, it was revealed that Coleman was hired as a security guard in 2000 and rose to become head of the department. Also revealed was that Coleman was carrying on an affair with a high-school friend of Coleman's murdered wife. Anonymous threats were made against the Coleman family for months prior to the murders and at the crime scene itself graffiti was found; police believed that Coleman made the threats and graffiti himself to throw suspicion off of him.[12] He was convicted in 2011. The family of his late wife filed a civil suit against Joyce Meyer Ministries, arguing that the ministry should have known what Coleman would do because he used his workplace computer and phone to make threats against his family.[13] The suit was dismissed, refiled, and dismissed a second time in 2013.[14]

Given Coleman's 9-year tenure before the murders, it is unlikely that pre-employment screening would have picked up on his behavior outside his marriage. However, interviews with Coleman's friends or former coworkers might have provided insight. Had such a screening occurred at the time of his last promotion, the outcome might possibly have been different. The revelation that he used company computers and phones to place the threats is a different matter. Periodic audits of his phone and computer usage might have revealed communications with the person he was having the affair with or shown the threats he was "anonymously" sending. In the absence of any real evidence, the only clue Joyce Meyer Ministries might have had was changes in Coleman's behavior.

Incident 4: Managing Director for Airport Security

On June 3, 2013, a Ghanaian citizen named Solomon Adelaquaye and three others (one Colombian and two Nigerians) were indicted in the Southern District of New York for conspiring to import heroin into the United States, among other charges. According to a press release from the US Drug Enforcement Administration, Adelaquaye was paid US $10,000 to "facilitate the movement of the heroin through the airport without detection."[15] At the time, Adelaquaye worked as the managing director for Sohin Security Company, which operated security at Kotoka International Airport in Accra, Ghana. According to a BBC report on the arrests, in one instance Adelaquaye told an undercover agent to give a laptop computer loaded with 1 kg of heroin to a specific person at the airport and that after the agent passed through security, the laptop would be given back to him. That agent paid Adelaquaye approximately US $6,000.[16] His case is working through the US court system as of this writing.

Based on the available information, it did not appear that Adelaquaye was buying or selling the narcotics; Adelaquaye accepted a bribe to ensure that the movement of the narcotics was not interfered with. Corruption is not unusual in Ghana, although it is less so than in neighboring countries.[17] Also interesting is that security at the international airport in the capital city of Ghana was not staffed by police or security forces, but by private security. It is probable that had airport security been operated by law enforcement or military personnel, the bribe to pass narcotics through the airport may not have been successful.

Incident 5: Contract Security Guard at a University

In February 1995, a 26-year-old security guard at Middlesex Community-Technical College was charged with the murder of a professor's wife. According to news reports, the victim went to the college to clean out her husband's office as he had just passed away. Approximately 3 h later, Todd McGrath, a security guard with Pinkerton Security and Investigations who was working at the campus, reported a shooting to the local police. A subsequent investigation tied shell casings found in a pair of boots seized from McGrath to the victim. McGrath had applied to the state of Connecticut in 1993 to register as a security guard and a cursory background check was clear of any improprieties. Students indicated they knew little of McGrath and "few even remembered seeing him around campus."[18] McGrath pled no contest to the murder and in 1996 was sentenced to 45 years in prison. A motive for the crime was never identified.[19] The victim's estate also filed a civil suit against Pinkerton that was settled before the trial concluded.[20]

McGrath's registration with the state of Connecticut went through 2-years prior to the murder with a clean background check, meaning he had no prior encounters with law enforcement. He was 26 years old at the time of the murder, meaning he was about 24 when his background check was done. McGrath had only been a legal adult for 6 years, which is not much time to generate a pattern. It is not known if McGrath had served in the military or attended college. In addition, the available information on the murder does not indicate what, if any, relationship there was between the McGrath and the victim or the victim's late husband.

It seems unusual that students at a small community college would have minimal awareness of a security guard that works a daytime shift; if he were patrolling or stationed in areas with student traffic, it is likely that people would have noticed or recognized him. The implication here is that McGrath may have stayed out of sight during his on-duty time, enabling him to learn where student or faculty traffic was prevalent.

Incident 6: Security and Facilities Manager in Manufacturing/Processing

In 2011, the security and facilities manager at Mountaire Farms in Millsboro, Delaware, Ronald F. Tate, was arrested and charged with 14 counts of second-degree rape, two counts of sexual extortion, three counts of unlawful sexual conduct, and one count of sexual harassment. The charges were based on the allegations of four females and occurred between 2010 and 2011, wherein he allegedly assaulted them inside his office or on Mountaire property.[21] Prior to working at Mountaire Farms, Tate was a Delaware State Trooper.[22] Tate pled no contest to fourth-degree rape, sexual extortion, and unlawful sexual contact. He was sentenced to 12 years in prison.[23]

Working at a farm large enough to have a security and facilities manager, it is likely that Mountaire Farms has a significant number of buildings spread over a wide geographical area. This would provide more opportunity for Tate to have uninterrupted alone time with a person than working in mall security or campus security, for example. Tate was a state trooper prior to his career with Mountaire Farms, so it was likely that he was in good physical shape. Depending on the relationship between security and human resources at Mountaire Farms, Tate may have been able to exercise significant influence over the employment relationship. Add up these factors and an environment existed where Tate probably saw he could compel the females to do his bidding, or where the females perceived that not submitting to Tate's advances would cause problems later on. This power imbalance was likely more behind the rape allegations rather than physical force, as the news reports on Tate's case did not indicate physical force took place. Section 770 of the Delaware Criminal Code defines fourth-degree rape, and the use of force is not an element of that crime; the lack of consent is the element.[24]

What Can the Security Professional Do About This?

For a security supervisor, the different options available depend on the situation. Sometimes performing a simple Google search on a name (provided it is not too common) can be effective. A strong audit function on company-issued communication devices might flag potentially inappropriate activities. Drug-testing can be effective if the appropriate policies are in place and they occur often enough. However, the unpredictable legal environment with regard to drugs both in the United States and around the world presents challenges to the security supervisor as well. Maintaining a culture of integrity; that is, ensuring employees do not succumb to corruption and that when something inappropriate happens in the workplace they will notify someone who can take action—a supervisor or manager. A supervisor cannot address a problem he or she is unaware of.

A Google search might bring back information on an individual that would indicate a potential problem. In the case of the hospital security guard who hacked into computers and made videos of it, had he published any of that under his own name it could potentially be found. However, a Google search may also present problems when so much on the Internet is inaccurate. The audit function of items issued to security personnel—cell/smart phones, laptops, credit cards, or expense accounts—can identify patterns indicative of illegal activity. Such audits are difficult to contest because the equipment is company property. Had the security manager from Joyce Meyer Ministries been monitored, the threats might have been revealed and investigated before he could commit his crimes. Although front-line security personnel do not often have such tools, supervisors and managers are more likely to have access to phones and computers. Many employers have drug testing policies, but it is not known how many fail to test an employee after their initial hiring screening. Granted, this is primarily a logistical problem; the more employees there are, the harder it is to screen them all without significant expense and lost productivity. Drugs, legal or not, affect performance and/or perception; security professionals, regardless of rank, must remain free of these substances. The presence of drugs may be indicative of other problems, particularly if access to high-value items or even the drugs themselves is part of the security professional's work.

Among the six cases discussed in this chapter, there were as many commonalities as there were differences in the cases. Encompassing proprietary and contract security, the disciplines discussed in these cases ranged from college/university security to transportation security to executive protection. There were young people with little usable background to older, established professionals on their second careers. There were people whose prior activity might have exposed them, and there were people with perfectly clean backgrounds or solid work records. Some had prior military or law enforcement experience. Security supervisors and managers must be vigilant: even though the majority of security professionals would never engage in such activities, the actions of a few taint the reputations of all.

Emerging Trends

The increasing pace of technological advancement has had, and will continue to have, an impact on ethical issues throughout the protective services industry. Information technology in particular has created potential ethical pitfalls that security professionals are still struggling to understand and to adapt to. An increasingly information-dependent economy empowers more people to have access to more information. Those in managerial, investigative, or protection positions have additional information at their disposal. This creates a duty to protect and manage such information in an ethical manner. This is a growing concern as information moves faster and faster courtesy of the Internet. Reputations (image or brand) are more valuable and vulnerable than ever before.

Profiting from the publication of private information regarding celebrities will continue to create an ethical lapse. Close protection agents or other security team members in the presence of celebrities or senior government officials must maintain confidentiality. Selling or releasing "inside stories" to the media is unethical; it breaks the trust inherent in protection work. Selling stories to media outlets may not be a criminal act, but it will almost certainly violate a contract or otherwise open up a host of civil liability issues. Similar issues apply to hotel surveillance cameras; their purpose is to monitor an area for safety or protection, not so that someone can profit from the dissemination of sensational or embarrassing celebrity footage.

Surveillance/Video Systems

Public surveillance systems have become the subject of ethical quandaries, even though the technology has been around for decades. The issue here is that technological advances, such as digital storage, video compression, and transmission of surveillance video via wireless or other over-the-air technology, have facilitated the release of video. Dissemination of video was much more difficult when it was on magnetic or videocassette tape and had to be manually transferred in order to physically move the footage from one location to another.

In the twenty-first century, the line between private and public knowledge with respect to surveillance systems is becoming increasingly blurred. Consider surveillance systems operated by private entities (retail stores, colleges) that face and record public streets. In addition, drones provide a mobile surveillance platform capable of collecting more footage at different angles over different distances. Military and law enforcement drone utilization continues to expand and their capabilities continue to evolve, as do commercial applications for this technology. The regulatory climate surrounding drones is further complicating the matter. In the United States, individual states are struggling with how to regulate drone usage along with the Federal Aviation Administration and US Congress.

Intelligence Gathering

Similar to the increased use of camera and drone surveillance systems, there are also growing numbers of intelligence-related positions both inside and outside governments. A growing proportion of those are with private companies doing contract work for government entities. The analytical tools being used in these positions are often developed by private companies and sold for both military/law enforcement *and* civilian use. The data that goes into these tools comes from both government and private databases. Private databases have expanded into the private collection and geolocation of vehicle license plates in a given location. The aggregating of public records on an individual that shows an address history, credit history, real estate transactions, criminal record activity, and other information, not only occurs but the sources of information used in the aggregation continues to increase.

For a private company, the collection, storage, and dissemination of information are analogous to what a government intelligence agency would do; it is the integrity of the intelligence management process by private entities that is vulnerable. Criminal and civil laws do apply in this arena, but the laws and regulations do not keep pace with innovations in intelligence collection and analysis. As with other security services, determining whether the contractor or the client is responsible—and accountable—for certain functions is not so simple. Add in subcontracting and the equation gets more complex. The economic need to outsource drives the practice but simultaneously gives rise to questions regarding chain of command, law, and ethics.

Misuse of other technologies, such as detection equipment, is also impacted by advances in information acquisition, storage, and transmission. Today's X-ray devices are more powerful and the associated software allows for greater image clarity, colors, and the ability to manipulate the image—a far cry from the days of X-ray film. As the image is saved and manipulated via computer software, it can therefore also be saved, downloaded, or transmitted. Accordingly, the loss of privacy for those being scanned is accelerated.

Other Considerations

As companies have become global in the scope of their operations, the need for protective personnel has increased dramatically. Some of the areas that companies now operate in, have different legal and ethical cultures. Some of these legal/ethical cultures see bribery as entirely legal and permissible—a way of doing business. The United States, for example, uses the Foreign Corrupt Practices Act to prevent American companies from engaging in bribery or accepting kickbacks, but some countries have legal systems that do not address this. That means the real defense against engaging in bribery comes from corporate, military, or government ethic regulations or codes of conduct.

In many jurisdictions, law enforcement officials are permitted to obtain outside employment. Given the skill set inherent in law enforcement, many of these officials will "moonlight" in protective service operations as guards, bouncers, executive protection specialists, or similar occupations. Ethical and even legal issues are common with outside employment. Prioritizing one's full-time employment with a part-time job can be challenging on many levels. Scheduling and getting enough rest are concerns, among others. Acting legally within both the primary and secondary employment relationship is important. However, the unspoken, unwritten allegiance that an officer has to either or both parties is an ethical issue.

Refer website http://www.ifpo.org for further information

End Notes

1. Anne T. Lawrence and J. Weber, *Business and Society: Stakeholders, Ethics, Public Policy*, Thirteenth Edition (New York, NY: McGraw Hill), 71.

2. Carroll A. B., "A Three-Dimensional Conceptual Model of Corporate Performance," *Academy of Management Review* 4, no. 4 (1991): 497.

3. Velasquez M. G., *Business Ethics: Cases and Concepts* (Prentice Hall, Engle Wood Cliffs, N.J.), 6.

4. Lawrence and Weber, p. 96.

5. Ibid.

6. Hill C. and Jones G., *Strategic Management: An Integrated Approach*, Eighth Revised Edition (Mason, OH: South-Western Educational Publishing), 11.

7. Kokt D., "A Model for Establishing a Quality Culture in a Major Private Security Company," *Total Quality Management & Business Excellence* 20, no. 8 (August 2009): 787–98. Business Source Complete.

8. Hartness E., *Ex-Duke Security Expert Charged In Medical Office Break-Ins* (Raleigh, NC: WRAL, April 8, 2001), accessed February 2, 2014. Available: http://www.wral.com/news/local/story/9409597/.

9. A., *Arlington Security Guard Arrested on Federal Charges for Hacking into Hospital's Computer System* (Dallas, TX: U.S. Attorney for the Northern District of Texas, June 30, 2009), accessed February 6, 2014. Available: http://www.fbi.gov/dallas/press-releases/2009/dl063009.htm.

10. *Former Security Guard, Who Hacked Into Hospital's Computer System, Is Sentenced to 110 Months in Federal Prison* (Dallas, TX: U.S. Attorney for the Northern District of Texas, March 18, 2011), accessed February 6, 2014. Available: http://www.justice.gov/usao/txn/PressRel11/mcgraw_jesse_sen_pr.html.

11. *Man Pleads Not Guilty in Slayings of Wife, Sons* (Atlanta, GA: CNN, May 19, 2009), accessed January 20, 2014. Available: http://www.cnn.com/2009/CRIME/05/19/illinois.slaying.arrests/index.html?eref=rss_latest.

12. Smith R., *Murder Suspect Chris Coleman Was 'Trustworthy' Said Mega-Church* (New York, CBS, August 10, 2009), accessed January 20, 2014. Available: http://www.cbsnews.com/news/murder-suspect-chris-coleman-was-trustworthy-said-mega-church/.

13. Scheffler J., *Joyce Meyer Televangelist's Bodyguard Found Guilty of Murder* (Cincinnati, OH: Examiner.com, June 2, 2011), accessed January 20, 2014. Available: http://www.examiner.com/article/joyce-meyer-televangelist-s-security-guard-found-guilty-of-murder.

14. Walker M. A., *Judge Dismisses Lawsuit against Joyce Meyer Ministries over Coleman Murders* (St. Louis, MO: St. Louis Post-Dispatch, February 20, 2013), accessed January 20, 2014. Available: http://www.stltoday.com/news/local/crime-and-courts/judge-dismisses-lawsuit-against-joyce-meyer-ministries-over-coleman-murders/article_f947afbd-1916-5b49-8149-5719ee438d75.html.

15. DEA Public Affairs, *DEA NEWS: International Drug Traffickers Charged in Manhattan Federal Court* (Washington, DC: U.S. Drug Enforcement Administration, June 3, 2013), accessed February 2, 2014. Available: http://www.justice.gov/dea/divisions/hq/2013/hq060313.shtml.

16. Author Unknown, *Ghana Ex-Airport Official Adelaquaye Faces US Drug Charges* (London, UK: BBC, June 5, 2013), accessed February 2, 2014. Available: http://www.bbc.co.uk/news/world-africa-22780761.

17. Author Unknown, *2013 Investment Climate Statement – Ghana* (Washington, DC: U.S. Department of State, April 2013), accessed February 14, 2014. Available: http://www.state.gov/e/eb/rls/othr/ics/2013/204648.htm.

18. Kranhold K., *Spent Shell Casings Tie Guard to Middletown Death* (Hartford, CT: The Hartford Courant, February 16, 1995), accessed February 6, 2014. Available: http://articles.courant.com/1995-02-16/news/9502160339_1_todd-mcgrath-mother-s-death-security-guard.

19. Poitras C., *McGrath Gets 45-Year Sentence in Srb Murder* (Hartford, CT: The Hartford Courant, August 29, 1996), accessed February 6, 2014. Available: http://articles.courant.com/1996-08-29/news/9608290341_1_security-guard-college-campus-emotion.

20. Author Unknown, *Pinkerton, Family Settle Civil Lawsuit* (Hartford, CT: The Hartford Courant, January 21, 1999), accessed February 6, 2014. Available: http://articles.courant.com/1999-01-21/news/9901210522_1_security-guard-settlement-college-campus.

21. Author Unknown, *Mountaire Security Manager Arrested in Connection with Alleged Rapes* (Georgetown, DE: The Sussex Countian, July 27, 2011), accessed February 16, 2014. Available: http://www.sussexcountian.com/article/20110727/NEWS/307279979?te.

22. Author Unknown, *12-Year Sentence for Sexual Offenses in Delaware* (Milton, DE: WBOC, October 27, 2012), accessed February 17, 2014. Available: http://www.wboc.com/story/19931243/12-year-sentence-for-sexual-offen.

23. Steele K., *Former Mountaire Security Guard Sentenced to 12 Yrs in Prison for Sex Charges* (Rehoboth Beach, DE: WGMD, October 26, 2012), accessed February 16, 2014. Available: http://wp.wgmd.com/?p=69936.

24. Delaware Criminal Code, Title 11, Chap. 5, Subchapter II, Sec. 770, *Rape in the fourth Degree; Class C Felony*, accessed February 17, 2014. Available: http://delcode.delaware.gov/title11/c005/sc02/index.shtml.

The Theories of Accident Causation

Whitney DeCamp, Kevin Herskovitz

"They're funny things, Accidents. You never have them till you're having them."
Eeyore (from A. A. Milne's Winnie The Pooh)

Accidents occur every day and, one way or another, will affect virtually everyone. During the year 2012, there were more than 2.8 million on-the-job nonfatal injuries in the United States.[1] That same year, there were also 4,628 on-the-job fatalities.[2] Note that other incidents, such as workplace violence, add to this data as well, although a vast majority are related to accidents. Further highlighting the impact of accidents are the costs absorbed by organizations. Cost considerations include workers' compensation case management; the use of paid time off, sick time, and short- and/or long-term disability; worker replacement costs (e.g., training of an employee to replace the injured worker); and the time and money spent investigating the accident with follow-up corrective actions, which can include policy and/or equipment changes or upgrades.

Even further expansion on the impact of accidents is the great number of accidents that do not result in injuries. In an early study of accidents, H. W. Heinrich found that for every serious injury, there were 29 minor injuries and 300 accidents resulting in close calls. At that rate, even assuming that all injuries (major or otherwise) are included in the official statistics, there would be an additional 42 million accidents that go unreported. Figure 5.1 demonstrates Heinrich's "Foundation of a Major Injury," sometimes also referred to as the Injury Pyramid.[3]

It's important to note that the Occupational Safety and Health Administration (OSHA)[4] uses the term *incident* to refer to these events, whereas the National Safety Council—and typically the general public as a whole—uses the term *accident*. These terms are essentially interchangeable, but for the purposes of this text, we will use *accident* as defined by the National Safety Council—an undesired event that results in personal injury or property damage. This definition implies two important points. First, accidents are unavoidable; the chance of one occurring will virtually always be present. Second, the chance of an accident occurring is a variable that can be changed. While it is impossible to prevent *all* accidents, it is possible to decrease their rate of occurrence.

Understanding the cause of such phenomena is key to decreasing the rate at which accidents occur. Determining the true root cause of each accident is the *only* way to formulate effective prevention strategies. Presented in this chapter are a few of the most common theories used to explain accidents. As with theories discussed in other chapters, these are not perfect and will not explain every accident in full detail. Rather, they provide

Security Supervision and Management. http://dx.doi.org/10.1016/B978-0-12-800113-4.00005-5

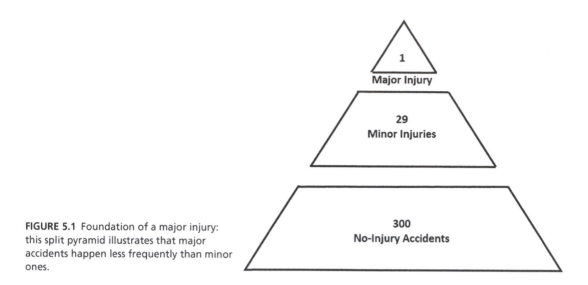

FIGURE 5.1 Foundation of a major injury: this split pyramid illustrates that major accidents happen less frequently than minor ones.

a nomothetic explanation that seeks to explain what usually happens and attempts to address the most common underlying causes.

Heinrich's Domino Theory

Heinrich's theory explains accidents using the analogy of dominoes falling over one another and creating a chain of events. Although this theory is not the most advanced or complex theory, it is especially noteworthy as one of the first scientific theories used to explain accidents. It is often still referenced today, seven decades later.

When dominoes fall over, each tips the next enough to push it over and continue the process until all the connected dominoes have fallen. However, if just a single domino is removed, the entire process ceases. Heinrich explains accident causation in the same way.

As you can see from Figure 5.2, Heinrich identified five stages of accident causation. The first stage, the social environment and ancestry, encompasses anything that may lead to producing undesirable traits in people. It is worth noting that Heinrich's inclusion of genetics and ancestry is very much a product of the time it was written. A modernized version of this theory would likely use the term *inherited behavior*, similar to how alcoholism and temperaments can be inherited. This stage of accident causation is quite similar to the s*ocial learning theories* discussed in the criminological theories chapter of this textbook.

The second stage, faults of a person, refers to personal characteristics that are conducive to accidents. For example, having a bad temper may lead to spontaneous outbursts and disregard for safety. Similarly, general recklessness can also be one of the manifestations of poor character. Ignorance, such as not knowing safety regulations or standard operating procedures, is also an example of this stage.

The third stage, an unsafe act or condition, is often the identifiable beginning of a specific incident. Unlike the first two stages, which affect the probability of accidents occurring, this stage is closer to the accident in terms of temporal proximity. This can include a

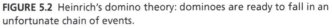

FIGURE 5.2 Heinrich's domino theory: dominoes are ready to fall in an unfortunate chain of events.

specific act that is unsafe, such as starting a machine without proper warning, or failing to perform appropriate preventive actions, such as using guardrails or other safety measures. In essence, this stage entails acts (or failures to act) that occasionally cause accidents.

The next stage, logically, is the accident itself. This, in and of itself, needs little explanation. It is simply when something occurs that is undesirable and not intended. The final stage, injury, is the unfortunate outcome of some accidents. Whether an injury occurs during an accident is often a matter of chance and not always the outcome. This relationship highlights the association (or links - relationship is repeated in sentence) between stages in terms of causality. An accident occurring is not a sufficient cause for an injury, but it is a necessary one. Similarly, the undesirable characteristics in the second stage do not always occur in poor environments, but they could not occur without such environments.

Given this necessary causality, the most important policy implication is to remove at least one of the dominoes, which can in turn lead to a healthy subculture through positive accident prevention training and seminars. An organization may not be able to weed out all of the people with undesirable characteristics, but it can have a procedure in place for dealing with accidents to minimize injury and loss.

Ferrell's Human Factor Model

Unlike Heinrich, who explained accidents as a single-chain reaction in vague terms, Ferrell's model incorporates multiple causes and is very specific about these causes.[5] Additionally, Ferrell defines accidents in terms of being the result of an error by an individual. As such, he explained his theory using the assumption that accidents are caused by one person.

Ferrell identified three general causes of accidents: overload, incompatibility, and improper activity. These are broad categories that contain several more specific causes. Improper activity is perhaps the simplest of the concepts, as it encompasses two straightforward sources of accidents. First, it is possible that the responsible person simply did not know any better. Alternatively, he or she may have known that an accident may result from an action, but deliberately chose to take that risk. The incompatibility cause is slightly more complex than improper activities. It encompasses both an incorrect response to a situation by an individual, as well as subtle environmental characteristics, such as a work station that is incorrectly sized.

The remaining cause, overload, is the most complex of Ferrell's causes. It can further be broken down into three subcategories. First, the emotional state of the individual accounts for part of an overload. These states include conditions such as unmotivated and agitated. Second, the capacity refers to the individual's physical and educational background. Physical fitness, training, and even genetics play a part of this. Situational factors, such as exposure to drugs and pollutants, as well as job-related stressors and pressures, also affect one's capacity. Finally, the load of the individual can also contribute to an overload. This includes the difficulty of the task, the negative or positive effects of the environment (noise, distractions, etc.), and even the danger level of the task. Separate from each other, overload, incompatibility, and improper activities can all cause a human error to occur, which can lead to an accident.

Petersen's Accident/Incident Model

Petersen's model is largely an expansion upon Ferrell's Human Factor Model.[6] The notion of an overload, caused by capacity, state, or load, is very similar to Ferrell's work. However, a few changes and refinements do exist. First, Petersen conceptualized the environmental aspect of incompatibility (work station design and displays/controls) as a different part of the model, calling them ergonomic traps. Additionally, Petersen also separated a decision to err from the overload cause. Furthermore, Petersen also specified separate reasons to choose to err. These reasons include a logical decision due to the situation (primarily for financial cost and temporal deadlines), an unconscious desire to err (psychological failings), and perceived low probability of an accident occurring. The latter of those reasons, the perception of low accident probability, can include both actual instances of an accident being extremely unlikely, as well as the natural inclination of a human to disregard his or her own mortality. This aspect of Petersen's model is akin to criminology's *rational choice perspective*, as it makes the same assumptions of human rationality and hedonistic calculus.

Another noteworthy contribution is Petersen's recognition that human error is only part of a larger model. A system failure— the inability of the organization to correct errors— was added as a possible mediator between errors and accidents. These failures have a range of possible occurrences. The failure of management to detect mistakes and a lack of training are but two examples of system failures. Even poor policy itself can lead to a systems failure that does not prevent an accident from occurring following a human error.

Systems Models

Most of the theories thus far discussed, focus on human errors and environmental flaws. A systems model theory, approaches the relationship between persons and their environments differently. Rather than the environment being full of hazards and a person being error prone, a system model view sees a harmony between man, machine, and environment. Under normal circumstances, the chances of an accident are very low. If someone or something disrupts this harmony, whether by changing one component or changing the relationship between the three, the probability of an accident occurring increases substantially.

Another aspect of the systems model is what is referred to as risk-taking. Whenever someone chooses to do something, there is an associated risk.[7] Smaller tasks and risks are often calculated on an unconscious level. For example, when one chooses to drive to work each morning, that person weighs the risks (slight chance of being in a car accident) and the benefits (making a living) and decides the benefits outweigh the risks. This hedonistic calculus, as with Petersen's model, is quite similar to the rational choice perspective. Just as potential criminals may weigh the risks of being caught, managers, safety specialists, and supervisors consider the chances of injury or financial loss. The decision to move forward with the task is only taken when it is decided that the potential benefits outweigh the potential loss. In a real life example of this type of risk taking behavior, Ford was once accused of deciding that the risks of releasing a defective vehicle (causing several fatalities that would result in wrongful deaths) were not enough to outweigh the benefit (not having to pay to fix all the defective vehicles) on the assembly line. While subsequent reports have shown that this accusation is false to a large extent[8], this particular case has often been cited as an example of the ethical and financial calculations of risk-taking.

Firenze[9] suggests considering five calculated risks and benefits:

1. Job requirements
2. The capabilities and limitations of the worker in relationship to his or her job
3. The potential gain upon succeeding
4. The potential consequences upon failure
5. The potential loss of not attempting the task

Additional information about these five factors becomes available through feedback after an initial attempt. In other words, a common task previously taken has well-known risks and benefits, while a new task often has more unknown factors.

Reason's Swiss Cheese Model

Perhaps the most popular systems theory on accident causation is James Reason's Swiss cheese model, originally proposed in 1990. According to this theory, every step in a process has the potential for failure.[10] Each layer of defense is represented by a slice of Swiss cheese, and the possible problems or failures in that defense are represented by the holes in the cheese. There are two types of failures that can occur: active and latent. Active failures are unsafe acts that directly contribute to an accident. Latent failure is a condition that exists that may lay dormant for a period of time until it leads to an accident. An example of a latent failure could be the lack of a policy describing how a given work task should be completed safely.

For an accident to occur, the holes have to line up—no layer of defense can catch the problem. If the holes do not line up, then the problem has been (present tense) caught and no accident occurs.

For example, the first layer could be the policy that addresses work needing completion. The next layer could be the personal protective equipment (PPE) required to be worn to complete the task. If the policy does not address the PPE or requires the wrong PPE, the problem passes that line of defense through the first hole. Choosing to not wear the PPE,

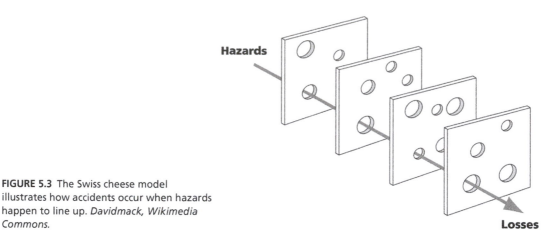

FIGURE 5.3 The Swiss cheese model illustrates how accidents occur when hazards happen to line up. *Davidmack, Wikimedia Commons.*

or wearing the wrong PPE as described in the policy, allows passage through the next hole. Assuming there are no additional layers of defense, these conditions will allow an accident to happen. Figure 5.3 illustrates this model. Despite successive layers of defense, small holes in each layer allow for some possibility that the defense will be ineffective. If the circumstances are right, these holes can align and allow an accident to occur.

The Integration of Theories and General Safety Program Implications

It is important to understand that each theory of accident causation does not explain every accident. Each theory explains only a portion of accidents, and all of these theories are incomplete as evidenced by the number of published works countering each theory. **It is therefore important to recognize that true accident prevention—the reduction of the probability of accidents—can only occur when all possible causes are addressed**. Focusing on only one or two theories is simply not enough. Furthermore, there are numerous theories not even briefly discussed in this chapter. Safety specialists and individuals with related duties are highly encouraged to consult additional information about accident causation.

There are numerous program implications that can be derived even from the few theories discussed in this chapter. Many of these are common sense, as they are often-used practices. First, most theories and models agree that human error is always a possible cause of accidents. An effective strategy is to train employees carefully and continually. Better safety training and increased knowledge and awareness of possible dangers can only decrease the chance of an accident occurring.

Second, socialization and subculture are also a common thread in accident causation. This further underscores the need for regular training and safety programs. An unsafe employee not only increases the risk of causing an accident, he or she can also corrupt future staff and make the problem grow exponentially. A safety awareness program is a good example of how to approach this problem. Regular meetings and positive safety posters are some of the tactics that an awareness program can use. Keeping employees motivated to stay safe is another contributing factor to a successful safety program. The two-factor theory of motivation, also called the Motivator-Hygiene theory[11], suggests that employees should be exposed to motivators (positive rewards) and hygiene factors (routine parts of a job, such as a good working environment, that prevent dissatisfaction). Management should understand the importance of maintaining a positive subculture and be trained with intervention strategies for problem employees. Management buy-in into the safety program is also extremely important.

Third, the physical environment is also an important aspect of accident causation that must be addressed. In addition to obvious implications (guard rails, safety warnings, hardhats, etc.), the subtle relationships between man and the environment must also be considered. Ergonomic designs, often used to increase productivity, can also increase a worker's comfort. Stress and boredom can play a role in human error, so keeping agitators to a minimum using ergonomic designs may also be helpful.

Finally, do not rely solely on conventional thinking. Safety, like security, is often reactive in nature; being *proactive* and using outside-the-box thinking can further a safety program substantially. Offering incentives and rewards to safety-oriented workers is a relatively new approach that, at minimum, gets attention. The status quo can also be challenged by simply asking if more can be done to keep employees safe. An important part of any program is a regular evaluation to make sure it is working. Statistical analyses of accident rates, surveys of individuals' perceptions of safety, and inspections by safety specialists are all examples of potential indicators of program effectiveness. Confirmation of the findings by using multiple indicators is important to validate findings. If possible, different programs should be implemented within different environments so that effectiveness (or lack thereof) can be compared. If a program is not working, ask how it could be better. If it is working, ask the same.

Emerging Trends

The main goal of any good safety program is to meet legal requirements and prevent accidents. However, because accidents can never be completely prevented, a secondary goal is to be prepared for the inevitable. In the aftermath of the terrorist attacks of September 11, 2001, interest in emergency management has heightened. However, such interest has largely overlooked individual accidents, especially on the small scale, in favor of terrorism and other acts of malicious or intentional harm.[12] In the wake of Hurricane Katrina, the focus of emergency management has at least partially included nonmalicious events. Where does this leave the safety specialist concerned with individual accidents and workplace safety?

Despite the lack of interest by the public and the media, accident prevention continues to be an important topic. Fiems and Hertig[13] noted that fines by OSHA have increased and are being imposed more liberally than in years past for violations of unsafe working conditions. Additionally, more states are legislating safety standards, and security organizations are placing more emphasis on providing both security and safety. Accident prevention increasingly rests with the individual organization.

Organizational economic situations may play a role in accident prevention as well. A fiscally healthy organization may not see the workers' compensation "bottom line" as a significant number, or they may see it as something out of their control. Struggling organizations do right by critically looking at every dollar spent, and focusing energy appropriately in controlling costs, especially considering the $58,000 cost of the average disabling workplace injury.[14] Not only can reducing accidents be a huge money saver, it can easily be argued that it is the right thing to do. A workforce that feels safe is better equipped—literally and figuratively—to be more productive as well.

Since Heinrich's Domino theory in 1936, knowledge about accident causation and its counterpart, accident prevention, has grown remarkably. What was once the only theory explaining accidents has served as the foundation of a discipline home to many theories, perspectives, and implications. This increase in knowledge, both among safety professionals and other individuals, has a substantial impact on safety in the modern world. Together with technological advances in safety and communication, accident causation theory and accident prevention are more advanced than ever, as at least partially evidenced by the 32% reduction in nonfatal injury and illness rates over the last 10 years.[15] Understanding and quantifying causation will lead us to a more scientific approach and greater cost-effective intervention strategies.

Refer website http://www.ifpo.org for further information

End Notes

1. Bureau of Labor Statistics, *Employer-Reported Workplace Injuries and Illnesses–2012* (2013). Retrieved from: http://www.bls.gov/iif/oshwc/osh/os/ostb3569.pdf.

2. Bureau of Labor Statistics, *Revisions to the 2012 Census of Fatal Occupational Injuries (CFOI) counts, April 2014* (2014). Retrieved from: http://stats.bls.gov/iif/oshwc/cfoi/cfoi_revised12.pdf.

3. Heinrich, H. W., *Industrial Accident Prevention*, Third Edition (New York: McGraw Hill, 1950), 24.

4. Occupational Safety & Health Administration (OSHA), *Accident/Incident Investigation* (n.d.). Retrieved from: https://www.osha.gov/SLTC/etools/safetyhealth/mod4_factsheets_accinvest.html.

5. Heinrich, H. W., Petersen, D., and Roos, N., *Industrial Accident Prevention* (New York: McGraw-Hill, 1980).

6. Ibid.

7. Firenze, R. J., *The Process of Hazard Control* (New York: Kendall/Hunt, 1978).

8. Schwartz, G. T., "The myth of the Ford Pinto case," *Rutgers Law Review* 43, (1991): 1013–1068.

9. See note 7.

10. Reason, J., *Human Error* (Cambridge: Cambridge University Press, 1990).

11. Herzberg, F., Mausner, B., and Snyderman, B. B., *The Motivation to Work* (New York: John Wiley, 1959).

12. Haddow, G. D. and Bullock, J. A., *Introduction to Emergency Management*, Second Edition (Oxford: Butterworth-Heinemann, 2006).

13. Fiems, R. A., and Hertig, C. A., *Protection Office Guidebook* (Naples, FL: International Foundation for Protection Officers, 2001).

14. National Safety Council, *Estimating the Costs of Unintentional Injuries* (2012). Retrieved from: http://www.nsc.org/news_resources/injury_and_death_statistics/pages/EstimatingtheCostsof UnintentionalInjuries.aspx.

15. Bureau of Labor Statistics (2013).

6

An Introduction to the Supply Chain

Brion P. Gilbride

Whether in transportation security, industrial security, cybersecurity, or retail security, the security supervisor will interact with at least one link of the supply chain. To better understand what this means, the security professional must understand what the supply chain is. Simply put, the supply chain is the journey an item takes from its manufacture to its final use. That item might be a final product ready for consumption by someone, or it might be just a simple part in a complex machine. A supply chain might be as short as from the oven to the tabletop, or it might stretch around the world twice.

What Is the Supply Chain?

As a security professional, the supply chain is an integral part of operations. A security supervisor at a manufacturing plant, for example, has multiple supply chains to be aware of. Parts manufactured elsewhere are brought into the plant. Security at the manufacturing plant is responsible for ensuring the security of the parts as they are offloaded, as well as for the conveyance and its operator(s) while on site. Security might be responsible for breaking the seal on the truck and logging it, validating the piece count, or confirming the weight of the shipment. Security has to be aware of any hazardous material issues involving the shipment, such as the use of a caustic chemical by a manufacturing plant to treat their product.

The same security supervisor may also be responsible for finished manufactured products leaving the plant. These products may be going directly to a customer via truck. They may be transported to a seaport by truck to be loaded onto ships. The sea container may be loaded at the manufacturing plant, or a partial shipment may be loaded by a freight forwarder somewhere else. From the time the conveyance (usually a commercial truck) leaves the plant with a certain amount of product, until the time the truck unloads the same amount of product at its destination, the security supervisor will need to know as much information as possible: How much product was put into the truck? How was the product secured in the trailer? Was it sealed? Was the count verified when it was loaded? Who authorized the truck to be released? Who owns the truck? Who employs the driver? Were background checks, or some other due diligence, done on the driver transporting the product? Who is authorized to accept the product at its destination? Will any discrepancies be reported back to the company? How? This is just a sampling of issues that might arise.

There can be as few as one link in a supply chain, with the ways in which product is transported, and by whom, being limited. Items can be shipped via road, rail, air, or sea. When produce is grown on a farm, harvested, and sold at a roadside stand in front of the farm, that is a supply chain—albeit a short one. In a more likely scenario, product parts are manufactured overseas, shipped to a third country for assembly, imported into the end-user country, moved by rail to a major city, and shipped by truck to the ultimate destination. Regardless of the length of the supply chain, a security professional is involved somewhere.

How Goods Move Through the Supply Chain

Once one understands what a supply chain is, the next step is to identify how goods move through the chain. The short answer is: by conveyance. A conveyance is anything that can move those goods from one place to another. A donkey and cart is a conveyance. A pickup truck is a conveyance. A container ship is a conveyance; so is an aircraft, a train, even a pipeline. The movement of goods through the supply chain may involve multiple conveyances. The security professional must understand conveyances—how to access them, search them, secure them, and even disable them, if necessary.

A supply chain concerns transportation and storage of finished or unfinished goods as they move from the point of manufacture to the place where they will ultimately be sold to the consumer. The way the goods can be moved depends on their size, shape, and weight:

- A 52-foot container loaded onto a commercial trailer can typically carry up to 60,000 pounds of dry goods.
- A freight train hauling 50 of those containers can carry 3,000,000 pounds of dry goods.
- A McDonnell-Douglas MD-11 commercial aircraft can carry 180,779 pounds.[1]

This list is by no means exhaustive. It does not include container ships, tankers, railroad tank cars, or a variety of other ways to convey items. Even so, the numbers listed above are good to know, even though they do not tell the whole story. An MD-11 might carry 180,779 pounds, but only items small enough to fit in the cargo hold of the aircraft can be carried. A commercial truck, on the other hand, could move items larger than the dimensions of the trailer in some circumstances (moving a prefabricated house, for example). A freight train has some size limitations but can carry far more weight on land than any other method.

Knowing what a supply chain is generally, as well as *how* the goods are moved from place to place, is a significant part of the puzzle. The location where the goods stay when they are not in transit is also important. Consider the earlier example in which product parts are manufactured overseas, shipped to a third country for assembly, imported into this country, moved by rail to a major city, and shipped by truck to the ultimate destination.

In this example, the chain begins at the factory where the parts are manufactured. Assume the item manufactured is a "widget" part. It takes 3 days of manufacturing to produce enough widget parts to fill a 52-foot commercial trailer. The trailer is driven by truck to a seaport to be loaded onto the M/V Widget Mover, a container ship bound from Chennai, India to London, United Kingdom via the Suez Canal; it takes a day for the trailer to be loaded aboard the ship, then the M/V Widget Mover departs the following day. So far,

5 days have passed, during which time the widgets have been manufactured, transported by truck to a seaport, and loaded onto a vessel, and the vessel begins transit. The journey is expected to take 30 days by sea. Upon arrival in the United Kingdom, the trailer full of widget parts has been in transit for 36 days. The widget parts are loaded aboard a train and transported to Edinburgh, Scotland, which takes 1 day. After 37 days and a journey from India to the United Kingdom, the widget parts are combined with other parts at the Edinburgh factory to create the widget. The widgets are then transported by lorry (truck) to various stores throughout the United Kingdom for sale to consumers.

Time and Cost versus Impacts

The objective for a company is to safely move as much product as possible in the shortest amount of time for the least amount of money. Time and cost are considerations; the supply chain must be flexible enough to accommodate this. The biggest impact to time and cost are mechanical, environmental, political, regulatory and/or human issues. In the previous example, had the widget parts been shipped via air rather than by sea, the transit time would have been drastically shortened; however, it may have been a great deal more expensive. There may be reasons the widget parts could not be shipped by air: perhaps the shipment was physically too large to move by aircraft; aviation regulations prohibit the shipping of widget parts; or the expense could not be justified because the final assembly plant had enough widget parts on hand to allow for the longer shipping time (which might have been cheaper for the company).

Mechanical

Mechanical problems are commonplace throughout the supply chain, regardless of the conveyances or storage methods. Trucks break down, trains derail, freezer units fail, and vessels hit reefs or become grounded, among a variety of other mechanical issues. Some mechanical problems can be avoided if equipment is used and maintained properly. If a truck breaks down, the goods can remain locked in the trailer while the truck is being repaired. If a train derails, the freight cars can be righted and the track repaired. If the vessel damages a propeller, the containers can be offloaded and trucked or shipped by rail to their destination or to another vessel that can take them the rest of the way. If the power goes out, generators can be used to keep the refrigerated trailers running until the power is restored. There are many kinds of mechanical issues that can impact the supply chain, and the impacts range from losing a few hours to losing entire shipments.

What do mechanical problems mean to the security supervisor? If the supervisor manages a staff that provides security to port facilities, it means there might be a disabled vessel for which security will have to be provided outside of the original assignment (so that other vessels arrive & depart timely). If a train derails, the security staff of the rail carrier might have to make arrangements to secure a site that could encompass thousands of feet of rail and right-of-way on either side while recovery operations and repairs are underway.

For the warehouse or freight forwarder, there might be no impact: one additional trac-tor/trailer locked in the yard until repairs are made or the truck is towed. Airports have a finite number of landing slots to allocate to air carriers, and rails can only have so many trains operating simultaneously. Vessels, depending on size, cannot use certain waterways or dock in certain ports.

Environmental

Environmental problems are also commonplace throughout the supply chain. Rain, snow, heat, and cold all play a role, as do hurricanes, typhoons, volcanic eruptions, earthquakes, and similar catastrophic events. Rain and snow tend to cause more vehicle accidents, meaning more delays in traffic when moving goods by car or truck. Ice makes driving with heavy trailer loads quite hazardous. Rain and snow sometimes cause tree limbs to fall from the weight, causing power lines to be damaged or rails to be blocked. Trains relying on electrical power (overhead catenary wires) would be delayed, just as they would be while the rails are cleared of debris. Or worse, the train hits a downed tree and cars derail as a result. A microburst might cause flash flooding or wash out a bridge. These are just normal weather patterns around the world.

Catastrophic events, although less common, are more disruptive. A hurricane devel-oping off the African coast means vessels might have to be rerouted around the storms, which span hundreds of miles. Aircraft may fly above a storm, and if a volcano erupts, the aircraft must divert around the ash, which also can extend for miles. A typhoon might cap-size smaller interisland cargo vessels, or cause the airport to be shut down until the storm and resulting cleanup have passed. This could cost a day or even a week for a shipment going out via aircraft. Earthquakes damage roadways and runways. If the earthquake hap-pens out to sea, it can generate a tsunami, like the one that smashed Japan in 2011. Any-thing near the coast where the tsunami hits—vessels, docks, support facilities, airports, aircraft, runways—may be destroyed or heavily damaged.

For the security supervisor, weather is a fact of life. Patrols occur on a 24/7 basis year-round. Precautions are taken for hurricanes, typhoons, and cyclones, likely in con-cert with safety or facilities/maintenance departments. Vehicles are properly equipped for the climate with snow tires, heavy-duty wiper blades, etc. Security departments may be the first responders to any power outage, flooding, or other damage. They might be called upon to enforce a plant shutdown order when employees are ordered to stay home. The security department might turn away arriving shipments until the facility is capable of safely accepting them. Security supervisors have to be cognizant of all of these things, as well as many others.

Political

Political issues, as far as the supply chain is concerned, is something of a catch-all term. Labor unrest, such as strikes, walkouts, or lockouts, is political in nature. A group of peo-ple want something from an organization and try to obtain that something by disrupting operations. Turmoil, such as the 2014 unrest involving Ukraine and Russia, can impact manufacturing, storage, and transport—any and every facet of the supply chain. Piracy, such as that which occurs off the Horn of Africa, is another consideration. The problem has subsided for the moment, but a number of ocean-going cargo ships have previously (needs adding as "the problem has subsided") been seized and held for ransom, regardless of what flag the vessel was flying.

Some shipping lines are hiring armed security for their vessels, whether on their own volition or because customers demand and pay for it. Some countries are entirely disinterested in armed security aboard vessels; some have developed regulatory schemes to manage this; and still others have seized vessels or detained personnel over the issue. Some airlines are government-owned or operated, which inserts politics directly into the transportation process. Some areas, particularly in eastern Africa, lack functioning governmental structures, meaning that moving goods through that region can be fraught with risk.

The best defense against political events impacting the supply chain is a good offense. Intelligence is the key. Security professionals must be aware of the political situation in certain regions in which their company's goods are manufactured or through which they are transshipped. Security professionals must continually update themselves on events in these areas, and where possible cultivate relationships with civilians and with government and law enforcement officials in those areas. If the security team has a good relationship with corporate leadership, the security supervisor must be prepared to develop and recommend mitigation or avoidance strategies to leadership. It is in these situations that security professionals can shine.

Regulatory

Regulatory issues are location-dependent. The United States offers excellent examples of this. The US Department of Transportation rules mandate that commercial truck drivers (generally) cannot drive for more than 11 h in a day, nor can they have a work day that is longer than 14 h. In terms of a week, the maximum average workweek a driver can have is 70 h; however, if a driver rests for 34 consecutive hours, he or she can drive over the 70-h limit.[2] The US Federal Aviation Administration mandates that during a 24-h period, a one-person flight crew can fly no more than 8 h and a two-person flight crew no more than 10 h.[3]

Leaving aside regulations that impact the people driving the trucks, flying the planes, or commanding the vessels, there are also a myriad of regulations that deal with the items being shipped. Hazardous material regulations can impact the packaging, storage, labeling, permit paperwork, or operator licensing requirements necessary to transport shipments. Agriculture or food and drug regulations can impact the packaging, storage, labeling, or permit paperwork necessary to transport shipments.

Different countries have different regulatory schemes; some countries do try to achieve a degree of consistency, but it is incumbent on the carrier to know and follow the regulations. These regulations have the effect of increasing the time and ultimately the costs of complying, while also ensuring the safety of the drivers, captains, pilots, crews, and the people whose homes and businesses they pass by, whether on land, sea, or in the air.

Human

Mechanical, environmental, political, and regulatory issues are subject to at least some prediction and mitigation. Humans are essential ingredients of the supply chain at every step—and they are the biggest threat to it as well. Humans get tired, they ignore the rules, they believe nothing bad will ever happen to them, and occasionally they use substances that they should not. The news is replete with stories of this nature:

When Air France Flight 447 crashed on June 1, 2009, into the waters off Brazil, it was partly blamed on errors made by the flight crew in response to a failure of an airspeed sensing system.[4]

On December 8, 2012, a pilot operating a Flight Express cargo plane from North Carolina to Tampa lost contact with air-traffic controllers. US Air Force jets searched for the pilot unsuccessfully before the pilot reestablished contact with controllers. Upon landing, he was tested and found to have a blood-alcohol content nearly seven times the legal limit. The pilot pled guilty to operating a plane under the influence of alcohol.[5]

On March 24, 1989, the M/V Exxon Valdez ran aground on Bligh Reef in the waters of Prince William Sound off the coast of Alaska, spilling 11,000,000 gallons of oil. The captain of the vessel was not at the helm at the time of the grounding; the third mate was at the wheel. The captain allegedly had consumed alcohol prior to the voyage, but a criminal trial on that basis found him innocent. The captain was convicted of negligent discharge of oil, and completed community service.[6]

On April 15, 1912, the R.M.S. Titanic sank after striking an iceberg off the coast of Newfoundland, Canada, killing over 1500 people. Among other issues, the lookouts saw the iceberg above the waterline and reported it in time for the Titanic to turn, but what they failed to see was the huge portion of the iceberg below the water, and it was that which the Titanic struck. This was compounded by a lack of lifeboats and by a disordered evacuation process.[7]

Humans also commit criminal acts, which are a significant threat to the supply chain as well. Theft, by both outsiders and insiders, is a constant security issue. Smuggling between international points in the supply chain is another issue—whether it is stowaways, narcotics, or other items.

Information Is Everything

Knowing what the supply chain is and how it can be impacted is important to any security supervisor. Once this knowledge has been processed, the security supervisor must then identify what steps can be taken to maintain supply chain security, as well as what steps can be taken to mitigate or minimize threats to that chain. As mentioned earlier, intelligence is the key. Intelligence is information. In terms of securing a supply chain, the security supervisor must first be aware of their location or role(s) within the supply chain. Depending on the chain, there may be security at the manufacturer, the airport/seaport, the freight forwarder or customs broker, the warehouse, and the mall receiving the shipment. In addition to the security entities, if the shipment is international, there will be law enforcement and regulatory interest as well. Most countries have a customs function, so shipments may be inspected on either arrival, departure, or both depending on the nature of the item.

Security supervisors must understand the threat that weather and/or natural disasters pose. They must maintain awareness of any developing storms, geological issues, or other phenomena. They must understand how heat, cold, wind, rain, snow, or hail impact the movement of trucks, trains, aircraft, or vessels, and must have an awareness of the political and regulatory environments that each shipment will be subject to. They must have an awareness of how the cargo is secured—whether it is palletized, in a case that can be sealed, has a radiofrequency identification chip, has a bolt seal, and other specifications. If the container does have a bolt seal, they need to know what the seal number is, who placed it there and when, and whether the integrity of the seal has been maintained. The supervisor needs to know the piece counts inside the container and be prepared to verify that information if necessary. They need to understand how bolt seals work, how to use global positioning system devices, and how to read log books, manifests, invoices, or consists.

In addition to all of that, the security supervisor needs to be fluent with the people involved in their supply chain. They need to know about the baggage handlers, the cart men, the drivers, the pilots, the shipping clerks, the traffic controllers, and their own security staff. They need to develop relationships with staff from the carriers that move their goods, with the customs officials that inspect them, with the motor safety officials who may or may not also be law enforcement, the emergency responders, the alarm technicians, the information technology staff, and the facilities staff. When necessary the supervisor must be as willing to share information as readily to those that request it.

Heavy are the shoulders that bear the supervisory rank—particularly those shoulders that are responsible for some part of the all-encompassing supply chain. There is a great deal of information out there—far more than was available 20 or 30 years ago. Therefore, the supervisor must understand his or her role and impact on the supply chain as soon, and as thoroughly, as possible. That is also why the supervisor must cultivate relationships with counterparts throughout this same supply chain. A layered defense involves coordination and cooperation.

Refer website http://www.ifpo.org for further information

End Notes

1. Brion Gilbride and Allan McDougall, *Links in the Chain: Vulnerabilities Between the Points* (Alexandria, VA: ASIS International, 2013), 3.
2. *Hours of Service* (Washington, DC: Federal Motor Carrier Safety Administration, Date Unknown), accessed October 13, 2014. Available: http://www.fmcsa.dot.gov/regulations/hours-of-service.
3. 14 CFR 91.1059 (2014).

7

Supervisory Characteristics and Expectations

Mavis Vet, Charles T. Thibodeau

Two things are essential for new supervisors to understand when they first enter the job: what makes a successful supervisor and what is expected of the supervisor.[1] The skill sets required to be a successful supervisor,[2] and to meet the employer's or client's expectations, are not always the same. To begin, a supervisor should understand the definition of the term *supervision*.

Supervision means overseeing the work of other employees. The National Labor Management Relations Act of 1947 (United States) was more specific, defining a supervisor as "any individual having authority, in the interest of the employer, to hire, transfer, suspend, lay off, recall, promote, discharge, assign, reward, or discipline other employees, or responsibility to direct them, or to adjust their grievances, or effectively recommend such action, if in connection with the foregoing the exercise of such authority is not of a merely routine or clerical nature, but requires the use of independent judgment."

Contract versus Proprietary

To properly understand the expectations of a supervisor, you first have to understand the two types of private security departments or companies; Contract and Proprietary.[3] Contract security officers do not perform their duties at the company that hires them. The contract company exists for the purpose of providing temporary workers for their clients. The contract company charges a client for the services rendered by the contract security officer at the client's facility. The contract company makes a profit from the business of providing clients with their contract employees for a fee.

Proprietary security companies are made up of security officers hired directly by the company to work exclusively for that company. These security officers are actually employees of the proprietary company and protect the property and their fellow employees. Proprietary security employees are restricted from working for companies other than the companies that hire them because, in most states, they are not licensed to be contracted security personnel.

These two types of companies differ in their management organizations. The contract companies maintain much more of a military bearing than the proprietary company. The proprietary company has a corporate profile of management. In a contract company, you are likely to find captains, lieutenants, sergeants, corporals, etc. In a proprietary company,

Security Supervision and Management. http://dx.doi.org/10.1016/B978-0-12-800113-4.00007-9

one will find a vice president of security, corporate security managers, security supervisors, etc. Setting aside the differences in types of business entities, both have the position of supervisor, and the materials in this chapter apply to both.

A typical company structure demonstrates how the levels of supervisors fit in. To examine this, one needs to understand the overall possible management titles of different security companies, including president/vice president, division heads, middle management, and supervisors. These four general headings are explained and contrasted as follows:

1. **The president/vice president level** is the executive level of the company. As such, those working at this level set the policy of the company regarding security operations. Within this expanded executive group, there may be many vice presidents, which are broken down into senior vice presidents and junior vice presidents. There may be general managers and corporate managers, and way down at the bottom, there will be front-line supervisors. Front-line supervision is sometimes broken into categories of directors, and department managers. Some security departments are large enough to have many levels of executive management that include several of these titles. Some proprietary retail chains, and some banks, have vice presidents of security. Some of the larger contract security companies have presidents, chief executive officers (CEOs), vice presidents, and other position titles as well.

2. **The division-head level** is where the policies are set out for a specific division of the company. However, most often policy setting is part of the overall corporate plan and not specifically a security contingent policy only. The security policies will be found in the employee manual, a copy of which each security employee should receive when they are hired. These policies can also be spelled out in a contract if there is a union. All terms and conditions for employment should be covered, including performance expectations for the front-line supervisors.

3. **The middle-management levels,** including general managers, corporate managers, etc., are the levels where procedures are set out for the next levels to follow. In the day-to-day operations, all terms and conditions of employment must be met, such as following all state and federal laws and administrative guidelines that apply to private security. In union-organized companies, middle management will communicate union-negotiated guidelines to assure the security employees are following union regulations agreed to by the company during the union negotiations. The middle manager is responsible for ensuring supervisors and security employees work effectively and develop their full potential for advancement. The more effectively they do their jobs, the less upper management has to be concerned with day-to-day operations.

4. **The supervisor level** is the closest link than all the above identified levels to the trenches, where all the security employees are working. The supervisor has to know and understand all the policies and procedures set out by the company. In contract security companies, the supervisor must know what each client expects to be done on their site. The successful supervisor will be the one who keeps his or her employees

informed as to what is expected from the employees and what the employees can expect from the supervisor.

In many companies, the supervisors will receive little or no cognitive training, and education will not be a criteria upon which the company determines who will be the supervisor. It is not uncommon for a company to recognize what appears to be leadership in an employee just because they come to work on time every day and appear to be a hard-working loyal company employee. When the need arises, they promote that employee into the supervisor position. That is, in many cases upper management will take the most effective and ambitious employee on the floor and promote him or her to a level of incompetence.

Promoting above the employee's level of competence is called the "Peter Principle." This has been the cause of failure of security departments to reach their goals. The Peter Principle[4] was first observed by Dr. Laurence J. Peter in 1968, and is based on the notion that employees rise to their level of incompetence and stay there. Over time, every position in the hierarchy will be filled by someone who is incompetent to carry out his or her new duties.

Thus, the supervisor who becomes a winner and is promoted to higher and higher levels of management—and ultimately to better wages and better benefits—is the supervisor who breaks out of the incompetence cap and learns how to be observed by others as the best supervisor in the company. That starts with pushing for training and education. If the company does not supply those things, then the supervisor should go out and get training at a local postsecondary college. There are supervisory courses available in every category all over the country, as well as online, so supervisors can complete these courses at their convenience.

The Promotion to Supervisor

A very simple definition of supervision would be the accomplishment of work tasks through the efforts of others. At this level of management, supervising versus doing the work alone is the key. When promoting someone to supervisor, unlike following the Peter Principle, human resources will look for certain characteristics in the candidates for the job—all of which lead to this one attribute "Can this candidate for supervisor get work done through the efforts of others or must they do it themselves.?"

The supervisors who are chosen will have characteristics that impress upper management enough to offer the promotion. Among others, those characteristics are likely to include the following:

1. **Job knowledge**: The supervisor candidate displays a standard of following the company policies, procedures, and training and is consistent in their job performance.
2. **Leadership**: The supervisor candidate is looked up to by their peers and is willing to pitch in and help others, even if that means going out of his or her way to help.

3. **Judgment**: The supervisor candidate consistently demonstrates good judgment when dealing with unexpected situations, deescalating potentially hostile issues, and responding well to emergency situations.

4. **Stability**: The supervisor candidate appears to be a level-headed decision maker, and dedicated to the establishment and maintenance of a stable and relatively predictable work environment. The candidate's work shows a consistency in applying proactive prevention strategies. When proactive prevention fails in his or her work history, the candidate consistently responds appropriately, following all protocols required for the proper response.

5. **Attitude**: The supervisor candidate shows an understanding and willingness to perform the job requirements of a supervisor, including training employees, supplying employees, directing employees with tasks that do not exceed an employee's skill set, and providing appropriate task performance follow-up and follow-through to assure that the employee successfully completes his or her work tasks. The supervisor candidate must be an "other-people centered" individual, dedicated to assuring that the employees, for whom they are responsible, meet their goals and succeed on the job.

Characteristics of a Good Supervisor[5]

1. Know Who Is in Charge.

Now that the employee has been promoted to supervisor, it is important for the new supervisor to realize who the boss is. Well, it is not the new supervisor. The supervisor is there to serve the employees—not the other way around. The winning supervisor will spend a lot of time finding an employee need and filling it, and getting the employee the tools and equipment they will need to do the best job. Make them successful with each task you give them. Involve them in goal setting. Give them praise when they do well and give them a reprimand when they fail. The supervisor who takes time to show employees he or she cares about them and their success will have employees that look forward to pleasing the supervisor and ultimately making the supervisor look good to upper management. Make supervision a win-win-win proposition for everyone involved.

2. Find Your Replacement.

Never be afraid of the employees showing leadership skills. The supervisor's job is secure, so they should never lock themselves in so tight that they cannot be promoted themselves. Identify those leaders in the employee pool, so when the time comes for the next promotion, the upper management will see that moving the supervisor to the next level will not break the continuity of the department. Find the best employees and support their advancement to the next level—even if that is your current job. There are two ways to get ahead in business: step on those below you to raise yourself up or have those under you push you to greater success. The choice is yours.

3. Lead by Example.

It is said that the best way to lead is from behind, but that never works. If a supervisor intends to be successful, he or she must get out front and lead by example. Hanging back to prevent making a mistake results in poor decision making and more mistakes than being out front. A supervisor who cannot make a decision is a poor supervisor. Ultimately, decision making is the primary job of the supervisor, or nothing gets done. Decisions have to be made all day long, and it takes a real leader to keep up with that demand. Employees who observe the supervisor making decisions will see strength, knowledge, and drive and will strive to equal or excel in those character traits themselves.

4. Give the Employees Slack.

Supervising an employee gives the employee the best opportunity to be creative. Give them the outline of what you expect, give them a clear picture of what a successful outcome will look like, then give them a time for completion of the task, but do not tell them how to accomplish the goal until they ask for more direction. Let them be creative so you have something to praise. Tell them there is nothing they can break that you cannot fix, so to be creative and figure out how to accomplish the goal. Also, the supervisor should communicate that he or she has an open-door policy for the employees and will provide anything they need to successfully complete the task at hand.

5. If It Isn't Broken, Don't Fix It.

Perfection is not always necessary. When the supervisor gives an employee a work directive, do not set the expectations so high that the employee fails. The supervisor's job is to make sure the employee is successful as often as possible. Sometimes that means the employee will not reach a level of success that the supervisor could do if they did it themselves. The question is, how much perfection will be enough? Where does the supervisor draw the line? The more realistic the supervisor is about perfection, the better the chance the employee will meet that expectation. When that level of perfection is hit, cut it off and give praise.

6. Catch the Employees Doing Things Right.

Did you ever notice that many supervisors never talk to employees unless the supervisor was complaining about something the employee did wrong? Did you ever have a boss who told you, "If you do not hear from me, that means everything is going alright." That supervision style is a set up. A much better strategy is to find employees doing things right and immediately praise them. Praising employee success begets more employee success.

7. Praise in Public, Reprimand in Private.

Never reprimand an employee in public. That is always the way to create resentment in an employee, and what goes around comes around. That employee will make the supervisor pay for such defamation. Supervisors are not hired to create dissension in the ranks. Supervisors are supposed to be part of the stability and predictability strategy. If a supervisor loses employee morale, it will take forever to get it back and the employees may never trust the supervisor again.

8. Include Employees in the Planning.

Goal setting is an important part of the planning stage of every supervisor's job. The supervisor should get all employees together for a short meeting to do planning. That could be an ongoing half-hour meeting every Friday. Although we do not recommend day-long planning sessions, we do recommend having a select group of employees assist with planning. The employees need to know they belong to a cohesive group that is dedicated to the success of the company goals.

9. Remain Friendly but Not Social.

The supervisor must be social but not too close. Employees must know their supervisor cares about their emotional needs at critical times in their lives. A supervisor may attend a funeral for an employee's close relative or the wedding of an employee if invited. However, a supervisor should not play softball on an employee's team, go to a bar with an employee, or attend an employee's bachelor party before the wedding. The supervisor is not the employee's friend, the supervisor is the employee's boss. Although bosses can be friendly, they should never become a best friend.

10. Know Maslow's Eight-Level Hierarchy of Needs.

Elsewhere in this book there is an in-depth explanation of Maslow's original five-level Hierarchy of Needs. In the 1990s, Maslow's five levels of hierarchy were expanded to eight levels. The value of this study for the new or experienced supervisor is that it gives an insight as to what targets the supervisor can identify, and what to work on to improve the chances of employee success on tasks.

How the Supervisor Supports Employee Success

1. **Biological needs and physiological needs:** Air, food, drink, shelter, warmth, sleep, etc. These very basic life-sustaining needs are related to the paycheck and how much money employees take home to feed themselves and their families. They are also related to the benefit package provided by the employer, including affordable healthcare to keep employees and their families healthy and safe from avoidable disease.
2. **Safety needs**: Protection from elements, by providing security, order, law, limits, stability, etc. This includes the safety and security made available in the workplace by the employer.
3. **Belongingness needs**: Work group inclusion, family, affection, relationships, etc. This is accomplished by the supervisor including the employee in goal setting at the department level.
4. **Esteem needs**: Self-esteem, achievement, mastery, independence, status, etc. This involves briefly praising an employee for accomplishing a time-dated goal-oriented task.

5. **Cognitive needs**: Knowledge, meaning, etc. This includes broad and specific training and education related to the type of employment. In private security, training is the key to success. In addition to post-secondary and undergraduate studies, there are many certifications available, such as the CSSM (Certified in Security Supervision and Management) awarded by the International Foundation for Protection Officers.

6. **Aesthetic needs**: Appreciation and pursuit of appearance, balance, form, etc. This includes the need for each security employee to project the proper demeanor and visual presence of authority while on the job.

7. **Self-actualization needs**: Realizing personal potential, self-fulfillment, personal growth and peak performance, etc. The smart supervisor of any department will set aside time to do career development with employees. Coaching employees to advance themselves is not only good for the employee, it is good for the department.

8. **Transcendence needs**: Helping others to achieve self-actualization. It is believed that selfless charity work is a form of personal growth-motivation. Private security is an other-people-centered profession, involving reaching out to help others. Although helping others is the primary purpose for doing this, it is always a positive experience for the employee.

The Impact of Poor Supervision

The overall result of poor supervision is low morale, poor quality work, high turnover, and a very unhappy client. Whether you are a supervisor in a proprietary or contractual security contingent, you have a few standards that must be met if the security operation is to be successful. The supervisor must assure their clients that the security officer working at their property, has the best guidance to perform the duties according to the client's requirements. It is the supervisor's responsibility to see that the officers have the proper equipment and the proper training in it's use. If there is any breakdown of this equipment, the supervisor should attend to the repair immediately.

Sites should be regularly checked to ensure the safety of the officers working there. Review the officers regularly to maintain the standards set by the company. Follow up on problems or complaints as soon as possible and submit a full report on how to correct them. Above all, professionalism must be maintained in all your dealings.

The supervisor who fails to perform any of the above directives will be considered a poor supervisor. If not corrected, this could lead to failure of the department's mission. In a contract security company, a poor supervisor certainly would fail the mandates set out in the contract with the client, and that contract could be lost. Therefore, it is important that we reject the Peter Principle method of picking supervisors, and when the wrong person is placed in that position, upper management must also take corrective action immediately. This applies to both proprietary and contract security contingents.

What Employees Expect from Supervisors

Everyone likes to hear they are doing a good job. Do not be afraid to tell someone they did well in dealing with a situation, no matter how big or small it was. As a supervisor, you must be aware of what all the employees in your command are doing. If officers need help, help them. Their problems may seem so small that they do not think they should bother asking for help.

Employees expect clear and concise communications. The proper information flow can clear up a lot of trouble before it starts. Everyone wants to feel they are involved with the company. Rumors can be very damaging to morale. Successful supervisors keep the lines of communication open by giving the employees the information they need to know and keeping them up to date on the major events going on in the company.

Employees look to the supervisor as someone they can go to for help. If an employee is not sure of the proper procedure to handle a situation or potential legal issue, they need someone to talk to, and the supervisor should be that person. If you are not sure of something, let them know you will find the proper answer for them, and get it. Always follow up on what you start.

Another aspect of being a supervisor is loyalty to the people working for you. Employees need to know that in their time of need you will "go to bat" for them. With this kind of relationship, employees become encouraged to take on more responsibility and develop in their job; they know that if something goes wrong, the supervisor will be supportive and help them through the situation.

One of the most important things that will concern an employee is tactful discipline. No one likes the embarrassment of being reprimanded in public. Everyone wants guidance and feedback on their performance. If you must be harsh with someone, try and offset it with how well the officer performs in general. Always try to give some good words with the bad. Remember, these officers reflect on your ability as a good supervisor.

Conclusions

Possibly, the most important cog in the wheel of any successful private security effort is the front-line supervisor. To say the very least, he or she certainly must be a multitasker. The supervisor fills the work day with planning, decision making, organizing, managing employees, and controlling both people and situations. With all these irons in the fire, the supervisor must find a way each day to accomplish individual strategic department and company objectives.

Consider just one of the supervisor's tasks—managing people. Depending on the size of the supervisor's span of control, there could be as many as two dozen employees in the supervisor's work group or team. To serve these employees, the supervisor must deal with motivation, follow up with delegations and follow through, participate with employees in goal setting and decision making, create and communicate job descriptions, coach and develop a skilled work force, praise employees who do well, and discipline employees who fail to meet minimal department standards.

Does it sound like supervisors have their hands full? They do! It is our hope that this introduction to supervision exposes some of the challenges that await anyone who might be career minded and wants to take the next step toward management. In addition, we hope that we have not just exposed the tremendous workload carried by a supervisor, but that supervisory activities carry with them real excitement and a sense of a huge accomplishment every day.

Expectations for the supervisor do not just come from the company they work for or the client they serve, but from the employees they supervise. Meeting everyone's expectations cannot only be demanding, it can be the exact exposure the supervisor needs to advance up the management chain to director of security, or higher. If that is your goal, then security supervision may be your ticket. Good luck, and we hope to see you at the top!

Refer website http://www.ifpo.org for further information

End Notes

1. United States, Department of Labor; Policy for Supervisor Training, Supervisor's Role and Responsibilities, http://www.dol.gov/elaws/asp/drugfree/drugs/supervisor/screen50.asp Circa 2010.

2. Ads By Google, The Qualities of a Good Supervisor, http://www.job-interview-site.com/what-makes-a-good-supervisor.html Circa 2010.

3. Ted Martin, eHow contributor, Proprietary Vs. Contract Security Companies, http://www.ehow.com/about_5516761_proprietary-vs-contract-security-companies.html Circa 2010.

4. Josh Clark, How the Peter Principle Works, http://money.howstuffworks.com/peter-principle.htm Circa 2012.

5. K. Blanchard & S. Johnson, The One Minute Manager, http://butler-bowdon.com/the-one-minute-manager © 1981.

8

Company Policy and Procedures: The Security Supervisor's Primer

John T. Brobst Jr.

How many times are the words *policies* and *procedures* heard during day-to-day activities? Someone may be quoting them, breaking them, or needing a new one for some problem or concern that has arisen. Unfortunately, many security departments run on an antiquated system of "that's how we've always done it" or "there's a memo here somewhere about that." The frontline security officer's duties have grown rapidly in today's society. Security professionals are no longer the "guy at the gate"; often times, he or she is the person responding to crimes in progress, lost children, chemical spills, and fires. A company or security department that does not have a written policy and procedure manual is doing itself and the people it protects a great disservice.

For security supervisors, policies become more than something that is enforced. Policies become an added facet of the job—tools that assist the managers, the employees, and the security department to function more efficiently. The focus of this chapter is to help the security manager understand exactly what policies, procedures, and rules are; how they can be written; and, finally, how they are applied and implemented during everyday activity.

What Are Policies, and How Do Procedures and Rules Influence Them?

Webster's dictionary defines *policy* as "a principle or course of action chosen to guide decision-making." For a security department, policy making involves a degree of thought and the ability to place those thoughts in a logical and easy-to-understand document. Policy sets a general outline for a task or idea for a problem or circumstance that an employee is likely to happen upon. For instance, a policy may state: "It is the policy of the Acme Company Security Department to conduct routine patrols of all company grounds and buildings to prevent criminal activity, to locate and report events such as fires, power outages, and safety hazards." This statement does not tell the security officer how to patrol, how frequently patrols are to be made, or even to whom to report power outages. It only shows that the security department will patrol the area and gives some reasons as to why they will patrol. Post orders and procedures take over where a policy stops. The procedure or post orders will tell the officer, for example, that patrols are to

Security Supervision and Management. http://dx.doi.org/10.1016/B978-0-12-800113-4.00008-0

be made a minimum of three times a shift and to whom to report safety hazards. Simply put, policies tell the security department *what* to do, whereas post orders and procedures tell the department *how* to do the policies required.

Policies can also spell out the stance a company or department takes regarding public and employee issues. For example, a policy may spell out what the minimum requirements are to be employed as a security officer in the facility or that the company is an equal opportunity employer.

Administrative policies are policies that address a situation that all employees of a facility should be aware of. For instance, a smoke-free workplace policy and an employee accident policy are policies that address actions to all company employees. The security supervisor usually does not write administrative policies, but he or she may be asked to provide input into their creation.

Departmental policies address situations or procedures that occur or are specific to a certain department. A departmental policy may be a job description, a call-in procedure, or a use-of-force policy. This type of policy is the one most commonly written by the security manager.

Procedures are often contained in policies to describe the steps taken to produce a desired result. Not all policies require procedures—for instance, a security policy might state that the department is an equal opportunity employer or list what the chain of command should be. Depending on the issue, a policy that includes procedures can become quite lengthy. If a lengthy policy becomes necessary, the author must ensure that such a policy is as thorough as it is complete. Procedures are more resolute in their function. They are meant to give systematic directions on the actions that are to be performed. The procedure is the most recognizable of all the parts of a policy. In fact, very few policies are written without some form of procedure being contained within it. A procedure often addresses day-to-day activities; for example, signing out a company vehicle, filing incident reports, and outlining steps to follow when calling in sick.

Rules serve a function only when they are made about very simple and clear activities. For example, "no smoking in the jet refueling area" is a very clear, understandable, and sane rule. "Patrol vehicle will be refueled at the end of the shift" and "all incident reports will be completed before going off duty" are more examples. Rules define exactly what employees have to do—no more, no less. However, the use of rules in policies can be a double-edged sword. Use them only when absolutely necessary. The overuse of rules tends to discourage the use of discretion and common sense by the officers and often results in them "only doing what I have to do" to get the job done. Not using rules results in mistakes and miscommunication.

In summary, policies state the guidelines and are relatively flexible. Procedures spell out steps needed in order to get to the goal, but are more strict. Rules are absolutely clear about what can and cannot be done, and they are most inflexible. Procedures and rules are generally components of policies; however, rules should only be used when necessary.

The proper utilization of procedures and rules in policy making, provides the manager with an excellent communication tool. Providing employees with current, up-to-date information about what should be done, and how to do it, encourages professionalism and pride in the department and the job function. Keeping this in mind, let us look at how to begin writing a policy and procedure manual.

Planning

A major task of the manager or supervisor is to create policies, procedures, and rules to address various subjects and situations that personnel may encounter while doing their day-to-day activities. In addition to drafting policy or procedure from scratch, security managers may also have to write policies and procedures that incorporate administrative policies or mission statements. If a policy manual or standard operating procedure (SOP) already exists, managers should periodically review all the policies, taking careful notes about what needs to be changed, deleted, or added. These changes should be discussed with senior management or corporate counsel prior to implementation.

When preparing to write a new policy, a few things should be addressed. First, is a policy necessary for the task at hand? For example, writing a policy requiring officers to lock the security office door when it is unoccupied is needless because it is an issue that can be addressed by general orientation.

List the goals that the policy is intended to achieve. A policy cannot be effective if it only reaches half of its expected purpose. How will staff follow the policy? Will this policy be an administrative policy affecting the entire facility? An administrative policy regarding package inspections would affect the entire population of the facility. What will the policy accomplish? Theft reduction for fear of being caught would be one outcome. Catching thieves in the act could be another. Supervisors should be realistic and remember that policies are only guidelines to assist the staff in solving problems or addressing specific situations.

Will the security policy impact other departments directly or indirectly? A policy changing the times an entrance is locked or opened can affect employees and the public. This change could impact deliveries to the entire facility or just one person. Be sure to consult the departments or persons affected to gain their input. Involving other staff gives the added benefit that the new policy will be followed because affected parties will feel as if they had something to do with its creation.

Creating a new policy manual will require involving administration, supervisory staff from other departments, and possibly legal counsel. Writing new policies really only involves one extra step—understanding what the policy will be about. New security policies should address general security matters as well as site-specific problems. Past events will dictate what policies and procedures might be necessary.

Finding a need for a policy is not difficult; every time a new job function or a new post is added, a policy should be implemented if the activity does not fall under an existing policy. The policy may have a general statement to show the stance the department takes on a particular subject, may list a procedure to follow, or have a rule that must be followed to

3. In the event non-security personnel utilize a marked vehicle, the Security Officer on duty will:

   a. Place "OUT OF SERVICE" cover on the roof mounted light bar.

   b. Place magnetic "OUT OF SERVICE" placards over the decals on the door panels.

   c. Remove any security equipment in the vehicle and secure it in the office.

4. All vehicle keys are to be maintained in the security office.

5. Unmarked security vehicles will not be used for personal use without the written authorization of the Company President or the Captain.

6. Marked vehicles shall be used for official security business only.

7. Gasoline will be obtained at the maintenance storage shed.

Note: This policy, as with all policies, is intended as a guideline and is subject to change at the Company's sole and reasonable discretion. Policies are not contracts or employment guarantees for any specific duration.

ORIGINAL IMPLEMENTATION DATE: 01/01/XX

ORIGINATING DEPARTMENT: Security

REVIEW DATE: 09/XX

REVIEWED: Capt. J. Jones Jr.

REVISED: 10/06/XX

CROSS REFERENCE:

FIGURE 8.1 Sample policy with procedure. Cont'd.

In addition to the disclaimer, include relevant information about the policy. This information would include but is not limited to:

1. Implementation date: when the policy came into effect
2. Originating department: who wrote it, or where the policy originated
3. Review date: date policy was last reviewed
4. Reviewed: who reviewed the policy on the review date
5. Revised: when the policy was last revised
6. Cross-reference: any policies or procedures that refer to or are referred from the policy

An individual facility's policies may include all, some, or none of the above listings. The various dates that list when things were done and who did them are tools that the manager

ACME COMPANY

SECURITY POLICY

COMPANY SECURITY ORIENTATION

Policy Number: 2001

Effective Date: 02/01/xx

Revised:

POLICY STATEMENT

It shall be the policy of the Acme Company Security Department to conduct a security orientation program for new employees. This program is given monthly as part of the general orientation program provided by the Human Resources Department. The following is a list of topics covered in the orientation:

1. Personal Safety

2. Security Assistance

3. Identification Badges

4. Parking Control

5. Key Card System

6. Alarm Systems

7. Incident Reporting

8. Package Inspections

9. Crime Prevention

10. Additional Information as Required

NOTE: This policy, as with all policies, is intended as a guideline and is subject to change at the Company's sole and reasonable discretion. Policies are not contracts or employment guarantees for any specific duration.

ORIGINAL IMPLEMENTATION DATE: 02/01/XX

ORIGINATING DEPARTMENT: Security

REVIEW DATE:

REVIEWED:

REVISED:

CROSS REFERENCE:

FIGURE 8.2 Sample policy: policy only.

can use when reviewing policies for content, applicability, and timeliness. Any forms or paperwork required to comply with the new policy should also be included as exhibits or appendices to the policy itself.

The format in which policies are written is not as important as the information they contain. However, a clear and concise style for writing policy is important in that it enables the employee to obtain information in a timely and efficient manner, as well as helping the manager maintain the policy as an effective administrative tool.

Implementing Policies

Once the initial policy is written, it may need to go through an approval process until the final written form is produced, distributed, and implemented. Some facilities have a policy review board through which all policies and procedures pass through for approval. Others may allow the individual department heads to approve a policy, provided that it affects only that department.

Any time a policy is written or revised, a manager should have his or her director or administrator review the policy with a critical eye. This will assist in finding any problems or items that should be addressed in the policy. In addition, when the security policy affects another department or the entire facility, administration should be consulted and permitted to review the policy for any issues that may need to be resolved.

Once a policy has been written, approved, and printed, it becomes time to implement it. Making sure that the employees read, understand, and know where to find the policy is a concern all managers face when instituting a new policy or procedure. How a new policy or procedure is introduced may vary from department to department or company to company.

Some supervisors post the policy or give a copy to the individual employees and have the employees sign a sheet (Figure 8.3) stating that they have read and understand the policy. This sheet, once all the officers have signed it, is filed for the future in the event that a problem arises in which an officer states that he or she never received the policy. Attach a copy of the policy to the sign-off sheet to ensure that the employees read it. Use daily briefings or staff meetings to tell the officers about the new policy. If the policy is briefed verbally to the staff, they should still sign off on a sheet stating that they received and understood the policy.

Making sure that a policy is read company-wide is another matter entirely. Issue a memo with the new policy attached to the various department supervisors and have them share the policy with their employees. Although this is not a foolproof method, it will reach a majority of the employees. Send a general employee memo after the supervisor's memo, telling employees that a new policy has been placed into effect and attach a copy of it to the memo. With email, policies can be mass-distributed easily and an electronic audit trail can be devised to ensure all employees have received it.

If the new policy is an administrative or company-wide policy, both memos should state where the new policy will be placed and where the employees can find it.

TO: Security Officers

FROM: Captain J. Jones Jr.

DATE: 12/20/XX

SUBJECT: "*SECURITY VEHICLES*" Policy Number 1000 (Attached)

Please read the policy, initial, and date the form below. If you have any questions, please contact me.

I have read and understand Security Department Policy Number 1000- "Security Vehicles".

Initials	Date
1. JIB	12/21/xx
2. ILW	12/23/xx
3. HBH	12/23/xx

FIGURE 8.3 Employee information sheet.

Reviewing/Revising Policies

Unfortunately, policies and procedures are not eternal; duties are added, changed, and deleted. The security manager is responsible for updating the security policy manual to keep it current. Policy manuals should be reviewed and revised a minimum of once a year. This ensures that employees do not receive conflicting information from a new policy when an old one seems to be still in effect.

The easiest way to ensure that the manual is still effective is to update it throughout the year as topics and changes arise. However, it is sometimes difficult to catch every small change as it appears. Read each policy and take notes as to what needs to be changed or removed. Revise the policy and release it the same way a new policy would be released. Keep a copy of the original policy, as well as each individual revision to it, in the event that a question should arise in the future about past practice. For example, a lawsuit may be brought against the company for an assault on an employee that occurred 5 years before. The lawsuit states that security is responsible for patrolling the parking lot at the times when employees arrive and leave work after dark, and that the current policy states that officers are present at all the parking areas to ensure the safety of employees. However, on reviewing the policy in effect at the time, it is shown that the employees were responsible for calling security when they needed an escort to their cars.

When discontinuing a policy—for example, a monthly lighting survey was previously performed by security personnel but has now been taken over by the facilities department—the supervisor needs to inform the officers that the task is no longer part of their duties. A memo will serve the purpose of informing the officers and any other employees that need to be notified. The discontinued policy should be signed and dated as to when the policy was discontinued and filed for future reference.

The Security Policy and Procedure Manual

The security policy and procedure manual, sometimes known as SOP, should be as important to the employee for information as their uniform is for identifying them. The manual should be a place to look for guidance in problem situations and as a tool to help other employees with any security concerns they may have. It is the supervisor's job to ensure that this information is up to date, complete, and available.

As a manager, make sure that the officers and other department employees read and understand the manual. In addition to having the officers' initial and date any new policies that come into the department, they should also be required to read the entire policy manual and initial that they have read and understand it. This can be accomplished simply by having a sheet posted in the front of the manual with each of the officer's names on it. As they read the manual, they initial and date the sheet when completed; this should be done a minimum of once a year, and also for any other policy manuals affecting the department (administrative, fire and safety, etc.) to ensure that the staff is up to date on the information contained within them.

Online or digital policy and procedure manuals are commonly used and are easily accessible while on patrol or off-site. Many departments maintain a paper master policy manual and post their policies and procedures on the company intranet, online, or make them available in digital format for downloading onto computers and other mobile devices. Just as with a paper manual, revisions and annual updates must be completed and a record of the changes should also be reflected online as to when they were made.

Finally, review various policies (old and new) with your staff during training sessions, staff meetings, and daily briefings. Give a little seminar followed by a quiz. Document any sessions during which policy was reviewed and include a listing of the staff members in attendance. During employee evaluations, include a section on their knowledge of policy and procedures. All of these ideas are tools the manager can use to make sure that employees are aware of the policy manual and how to use it.

In conclusion, policies and procedures guide us, give us information, and are valuable tools that the employee and manager can use to benefit both the department and themselves. Writing policy may not be the most exciting task a supervisor performs, but it can be made simple. Planning, writing, implementing, and revising are the steps taken to make that procedure even easier. A well-kept, up-to-date, and professional-looking security policy manual will benefit more than just the department and its employees. It will benefit the company it protects as well.

Refer website http://www.ifpo.org for further information

9

Operational Supervision

David N. Halcovitch

Operational supervision in the security profession should be consistent and similar regardless of the organization or its geographical location. Although operational supervision may go by other names or other euphemisms, the term deals with the day-to-day management of security operations regardless of the environment. As stated more than 2000 years ago by a Chinese warrior-philosopher named Sun Tzu in the book called *The Art of War*, "Leadership is a matter of intelligence, trustworthiness, humaneness, courage and sternness."[1] This concept of leadership is just as true today.

The term *operational supervision* is defined in such a way as to separate it from what many people envision when they consider what a supervisor does. Although every organizational leadership role is important, the front-line or operational supervisor is paramount, no matter the size of organization that is being protected. The operational division of the organization is open in most cases 24/7 and 365 days a year and needs to be ready to respond to any and all issues. Those responsibilities, particularly during days and times when the facility is not open for routine business, fall upon the security function. The security professionals are often the only personnel at a facility when it is not open for business, meaning they deal with various unrelated issues that would normally be handled by other parts of the organization. It does not matter what the time of day or night—people depend on the security unit to do their job and more. How many times has a security officer received a call from someone who said, "I didn't know who else to call?" This is why security is one of the few entities within any organization that crosses paths with all aspects—units and people—from every level of the organization they protect and serve. It is important for a security guard/officer to have a good working knowledge of their organization, but it is the operational supervisor who must have a thorough understanding of all areas of the organization.

Let us define the terms *operational* and *supervision*. Webster's dictionary defines operational as "a set of actions for a particular purpose"[2] and supervision as "the act of overseeing".[3] Combined, these two words become *operational supervision*, which would refer to "overseeing a set of actions for a particular purpose." This is exactly what security professionals do—watch over the routine functioning and activities of an organization for the purpose of keeping the staff and facilities secure. Furthermore, this oversight ensures the safety of everyone who works at or visits a location, and protects all aspects of their assets.[4] In many organizations, the supervisor may be considered "management," but the purpose the supervisor truly serves, is to be the bridge between management and the front-line staff. The supervisor receives information from management on policy, processes, or procedures and ensures that the front-line security personnel carry them out. At the same time, the supervisor brings back information from front-line security personnel to management. The supervisor is himself or herself a two-way street, bringing account-ability from the managers to the front-line staff, and information from the front-line staff to the managers.

In most security organizations around the world, the security mandate can be described as four *P*s, as follows:

- Protection of life
- Protection of property and premises
- Prevention of loss and waste
- Prevention and determent of crime

A key attribute of any operational supervisor is to be a leader and fully understand the four *P*s. The supervisor must have the respect of his or her staff and be able to direct them with confidence throughout the challenges of the day. Security personnel are dependent on the supervisor to have the right answers, and more. Operational supervisors also have four other *P*s to understand: **processes, policies, procedures, and post orders**. The operational supervisor must understand both their own role, as well as the roles of every member of their staff, for each area of the organization that they deal with. In the daily routine of operational supervision, they will interact with both internal and external partners.

Relative Information of Faults and Attributes for an Operational Supervisor

Many words can be used to gain an understanding of what is required to be an operational supervisor. Relative information constitutes the *R* and *I* in the relative information of faults and attributes of the RIFA acronym. The term *relative information* is used to describe the positive attributes that an operational supervisor must possess to be successful in their duties. Conversely, the *F* in RIFA corresponds to the word *faults*, which is the negative side of the coin. The operational supervisor does not want to have faults that detract from their duties in any way. Consider Figure 9.1: only *R* or *I* words are used to describe attributes and faults. Review the 10 words on either side of the chart to describe these attributes or faults.

It is important to understand what attributes make a good operational supervisor. A study was conducted on new security officers in a large Gulf Cooperative Council (GCC) oil corporation. The new security officers' average age was 20 years old; they had little prior work experience and had completed high school (or its equivalent). The newly recruited security officers were all male, coming from various regions of the country in which they would be working. In this study, 100 of the new security officers were asked the following:

- What is the most important attribute you believe an operational supervisor should have to lead and be in charge of you?
- What do you not want to see from your operational supervisor when starting out in the new organization you have become part of?

Attributes	Faults
Integrity A person is honest and sincere in their daily life activities	**Inconsistent** A person who does not always behave the same way
Informative A person who will give the proper facts	**Incompetent** A person who does not do a particular job well or to an appropriate level or standard
Instructional A person who can inform you on how to do something correctly or properly	**Impatient** A person who is not willing to wait, when or where appropriate
Reliable A person who you can depend on	**Indecisive** A person who has a hard time making the appropriate decision
Responsive A person who has an answer, reply, or reaction to a situation or incident	**Inconsiderate** A person who is thoughtless to others
Resourceful A person who is creative and imaginative in dealing with a situation or incident through capable means, even though they could be hampered with limited resources	**Insensitive** A person who is heartless and uncaring to other people
Responsible A person who is mature, sensible, and dependable, in order to complete the task appropriately	**Inactive** A person who is not working at an appropriate level
Reactive A person who can respond appropriately to various situations or incidents	**Rigid** A person who is unbending or stringent in how they carry out their activities
Representative A person who can act on behalf of or be seen as the person who reflects the standards of the organization	**Rude** A person who is bad mannered or impolite towards others
Ready A person who is prepared for anything that can happen on their shift or in their daily responsibilities.	**Racist** A person who discriminates or is prejudiced against another person.*

OS, operational supervisor.

* This certainly speaks for itself as often security officers are from a diverse, multicultural background. A team has to function in a respectful way, even though in many countries there is human rights legislation to protect employees.

FIGURE 9.1 Positive attributes and negative faults.

The most important attributes identified were:

- The supervisor should be helpful.
- The supervisor should be knowledgeable.
- The supervisor should be understanding.

The reasoning behind these three attributes was that the new security officers were aware of their status as beginners. They wanted supervisors who kept this in mind (understanding). They wanted supervisors that would be able to answer their questions about the job. More importantly, they wanted supervisors that were willing to share knowledge without being asked (helpful and understanding).

In response to the second question, the new security officers did not want operational supervisors who were unfair, too firm or strict, or unknowledgeable. The reasoning behind this was that the new officers were sensitive to their age and lack of experience, and accordingly did not fully understand what would be expected of them. Knowing that they required time to learn, make mistakes, and learn from their mistakes, the new security officers wanted supervision that would be firm but not strict or unfair. They also recognized that they could not learn anything from supervisors who did not understand the job themselves.

The operational security supervisor position was also examined in the same large GCC oil corporation. A survey was conducted using 20 supervisors who had an average of 18 years' experience. Like the officers in the study, the supervisors came from various regions within the country in which they worked.

The following questions were asked of the supervisors:

- As a supervisor, what are the top three problems with the staff?
- What actions or measure did you take to stop, correct, or discipline the person causing the problem that was recognized by you as a supervisor?

The top three problems were:

- Being late/attendance
- Sleeping on the job
- Playing games or texting on mobile phones during work hours

The problem of attendance is not only related to new hires, but many long-term employees as well. In some cultures, punctuality is very important, whereas in others it is less so. Sleeping on the job is a common issue. In work locations with an arid climate, some believe that sleeping on the job occurs due to the heat. While others are sympathetic to this view, it should be noted that many of the security officers that the supervisors caught sleeping were working in climate-controlled areas. Mobile phones are a concern as more and more employees become attached to this mode of communication and entertainment. Nowadays, people use their mobile phones for entertainment and lifestyle purposes rather than to make and receive calls.

Having identified the issues, the supervisors answered how they handled the issues. The top three ways identified were:

- Speak to and warn the person
- Document the issues and take disciplinary action if warranted
- Remove the mobile phone from the workplace

These three responses are simple and adhere to progressive discipline. Progressive discipline refers to a style of addressing employee issues that begins at the lowest (least serious) level necessary to correct the behavior, and escalating through each step if the behavior is not corrected. Ultimately, it is the supervisor's responsibility to maintain order on their shift and ensure employees follow policy. The easiest way to regulate mobile phone usage is to not allow security staff to have access to mobile phones while the workplace. This causes tension, however, as some employers want their employee to have a personal mobile phone by which to contact that employee. This saves the employer the costs associated with providing a company-issued mobile phone. While it is true that security professionals require a communications capability of some kind, a mobile phone is generally not necessary as many security companies have portable radios.

The standard practice of "speak to and warn" an employee is only as good as the organization's rules regarding progressive discipline. If the rules in place are not consistently adhered to, then there is no reason to have the rules. As the operational supervisor, one must always observe the "three *F*s" when considering taking disciplinary action against an employee. When used successfully, the "three *F*s" concept—**fair, fast, and firm**—can enhance the respect for the operational supervisor as the employee recognizes that they will be treated fairly should any transgression of workplace rules occur.

In relation to discipline, organizations vary widely in how much or how little is used on their employees. In some cases where there may be collective bargaining agreements in place, there are written stipulations as to when and how someone will be disciplined and for what violations. The penalty or type of discipline may also be set in those agreements. On the opposite extreme, there may be no agreements or rules set out. Discipline is handed down by an individual in charge, who may or may not be schooled in human resources or employee motivation skills. This means that the person could be extremely strict, extremely lenient, or anywhere in between. It is difficult for a team to function under a regime that is either too strict or too lenient. Balance is the key.

To continue on the thought of the three *F*s (fair, fast, and firm), one needs two *C*s: **common sense and compassion**. Again, both of these attributes should be a normal requirement to be an operational supervisor. The commonsense side is extremely important when dealing with people who have had an issue or what would be considered a misconduct or breaking of a rule. The questions that need to be asked from the commonsense side are: Did this violation take place on purpose? Was it a mistake or simply poor training? The operational supervisor should be able to determine which of these aspects apply to the situation. If someone deliberately committed a violation or the violation was such that the person should have known that what they were doing was wrong, then that person should be punished. An example of this type of violation would be theft. Then there are those who have committed a violation but may not understand what they were doing was wrong. It was simply a mistake. This person should also be disciplined, but perhaps with more of a probationary-type of discipline. Finally, there is the individual who did something wrong but lacked the adequate training or knowledge to recognize that what was done was wrong. This type of misconduct should be held as a training issue, and most examples of this violation fall under failures to follow policy or procedure. The operational supervisor should be able to determine why the individual was not trained to the level required, and will then know what is required to get the person back on track and trained appropriately.

Although a lot has been said about discipline, in many cases it can be avoided if the policy, process, and post orders are clear and defined. They all should be written in a language that is understood and common to the people who are carry them out. Difficulties arise if policies, processes, or post orders are written or explained in English when the majority of those who have to understand them are not fluent in English. To correct this, either the written documents have to be translated into the necessary language(s) or the person explaining them has to be fluent in the necessary language(s). It is impossible to hold employees responsible for failure to follow policy when they cannot understand what is required of them.

In many organizations, the post order is a common way for the staff to be given their direction on what is required to do a particular task and how to perform it. Post orders are simply written instructions for the security officer to do a particular task at a specific location. It also may say when it needs to be done as well. These written instructions need to be very specific and clear for the security officer to know what is required of them. The key is that everyone should know in what way and how a specific task should be done, which will give consistency for the whole security staff doing it the same and proper way. It can act like a checklist for all of the steps that need to be taken to complete the task. If all of the steps are followed, this reduces mistakes, which should remove any requirement for discipline. In having good post orders, the operational supervisor should just need to tell their staff what a good job they are doing.

Post orders should be developed and written by those with sufficient writing skill to do so. Some post orders may be very technical and include legal language, whereas others might be as short as a sentence. An organization faced with developing new post orders, or updating existing ones, must ensure they meet any legal requirements while simultaneously being simple to understand. Topics for post orders include report writing, safety, emergency response, access control, and code-of-conduct responsibilities, to name a few.

A post order should be broken down into sections and subsections depending on how complicated the subject matter is. The sections should flow logically based on the steps involved. A post order on report writing, for example, should tell the reader when a report is required, what information should be collected, what follow up is needed in different circumstances, to whom the report is submitted for approval, and where and to whom the approved report is distributed.

Staff Sergeant Raymond Rikic of the Hamilton Police Service in Ontario, Canada, was interviewed on his viewpoint on operational supervision. He has 30 years of supervision experience within the organization with over 1200 members. When Rikic was asked what he felt were the important aspects, attributes, characteristics, or requirements of a good front-line operational supervisor, he described them as follows:

- A good listener
- Respectful
- Responsive to questions from subordinates
- Honest

- A good communicator
- Fair and consistent
- Able to request information when it is not known
- Avoids stereotypes
- Knowledgeable of policy, procedure, and/or contractual obligations
- Knowledgeable of the skills and abilities of subordinates
- Encourages and personally supports employee training and development

Rikic's conclusion was that "the payoff for being a good front-line operational supervisor is acquiring influence. You cannot neglect the needs of the member whom you rely on. It is all about give and take. If you give, you can take much more with the buy-in from the member. Supervisors will not generate loyalty without also developing good relationships with the members they supervise." This statement was from Staff Sergeant Rikic (Hamilton Police Service) in his interview when questioned about his thoughts on supervision.

Operational Briefing

Operational supervisors conduct briefings on a regular basis, if not every day and shift. The nature of the briefing depends on a number of variables, such as a facility's accessibility to the public, the threat level generally in the area, recent incidents, or the type of facility. Regardless of the nature of the security organization, operational briefings are the responsibility of the first-line (operational) supervisor. How often these briefings occur might be determined by company policy, they might be situational, or they might even be at the whim of managers and supervisors. They may also be formal or informal in nature. In many organizations, every shift begins with a briefing.

Consider the following points when preparing to deliver an operational briefing to subordinate security professionals. It is imperative that the supervisor conduct briefings in a professional and informative manner. Remember that the purpose of the briefing is to provide security officers with information that will assist them in their duties, alert them to a problem, alert them to be on the lookout for a particular person, and hopefully keep them safe.

- If there is an assigned time for the briefing, when feasible, do not start a briefing until all required personnel are present. When people walk in during your briefing, it will upset the flow or cause someone to miss an important piece of information. At times, however, available briefing time is limited and some staff may miss it; the supervisor must brief them afterward if necessary.
- Use simple language to avoid confusion. Be clear, as the language the supervisor speaks might not be a native language to some of the staff. Always repeat dates and times to ensure the audience understands.
- Stick to the original briefing and do not add or delete things as the briefing progresses. Stay on topic and emphasize important points. This is especially important if time is limited.

safety and security manager or director position. There are also directors of campus safety with colleges or public safety in cities.

Industrial hygiene is a specialty dealing with health issues within safety. Prevention of epidemics and pandemics falls within the rubric of industrial hygiene. These are obviously significant for naturally occurring airborne or bloodborne pathogens, such as mold or the human immunodeficiency virus. Certainly, the efforts of industrial hygienists to prevent and control disease in the workplace tie in with response to weapons of mass destruction of the biological or radiological variety.

A foundation of knowledge in safety then, can enable one to learn about other key areas. A solidly developed safety program will facilitate and support efforts to deal with related loss events. If the foundation is there, it is easier to adapt to fluid and varied risks.

Supervising Crisis Situations

Supervisors know that rarely does the client or their staff call upon protection staff, or associate with them in most cases, unless in times of need or safety problems. This lack of contact can sometimes produce negative feelings or even alienation, whereby protection staff feels as if they do not belong. Participation by security staff in local departments or facilities near the work area can assist in building rapport and provide protection staff with the opportunity to contribute to the safety of the area or community through positive proactive functions. This pays substantial dividends to all stakeholders over time.

Safety planning is essential and the supervisory role is to set forth the correct response in crisis situations and to organize crisis intervention. Supervisors must also recognize weaknesses and plan accordingly to achieve uniformity in critical areas.

No matter what type of crisis occurs, cooperation between protection staff and the public (employees, students, patients, residents, or the general public) can be achieved by the following four steps:

1. Arrange or participate in safety meetings between key protection staff and supervisors.
2. Coordinate crisis plans through public relations, human resources (HR), and other departments.
3. Provide leadership and monitor all meetings.
4. Test the results, and correct the areas needing more attention.

Each environment is unique and every organization has its own culture. This requires a tailored approach to organizational growth and development in the area of safety. When the correct formula for training is used, success will be achieved and a safety attitude will prevail.

Protection supervisors are tasked with a variety of functions relating to the safety of the general public, customers, and employees. Safety in the workplace requires that all personnel be trained in recognizing and rectifying problems before they occur. Examples of safety concerns where the supervisor is involved in training staff are: fire safety, industrial equipment protection and use, unsafe work practices, health-related matters (e.g., first aid, cardiopulmonary resuscitation [CPR]), sanitation, hazardous materials, employee

Theory	Socialization Flaws
Heinrich's domino theory	The "social environment" teaches unsafe methods. Unhealthy values and behaviors develop within the work group.
Farrell's human factor model	Improper activities are engaged in. These unsafe acts are performed because of simply not knowing any better or deliberate risk taking.
Peterson's accident/incident model	A logical decision to err is made. This can be due to financial costs or deadlines. Another reason can be the perceived low probability of an accident occurring.

FIGURE 10.1 Accident causation theories.

accidents and reduced injury plans, safety meetings, structural problems (which may cause injury or death), crime prevention, and many others.

Attitude plays a key part in the proper development of a safety program. Supervisors should be students of workplace socialization processes so that the correct attitude is developed. Some of the accident causation theories that discuss various aspects of workplace socialization are shown in Figure 10.1. Causation theories are described in more detail in a chapter five.

Safety Committee Meetings

The safety meeting is increasingly becoming a legislated and mandatory function in the workplace. Safety committee meetings should include representation from all sections or departments of a facility or organization. Naturally, security supervisors play a major role in participating in these meetings. Topics regularly covered in these meetings should include, but are not limited to, the following:

1. Recent number of accidents per calendar month/year
2. Number of employees injured/killed on the job
3. Causes of accidents—tripping, falling, improper storage of items, improper safety shoes, malfunctioning safety equipment, structural problems impacting work areas, slipping on wet floors, insufficient safety training for employees, etc.
4. Steps to accident correction
5. Illnesses caused by accidental or neglected industrial hazards
6. Hidden or indirect costs of accidents (staff losses, replacements, and training of new employees)
7. Follow-up to results and problems
8. Other areas for which the parent organization has given security responsibility, such as life safety (e.g., number and results of fire drills conducted last month/quarter).

As part of the safety development approach process, protection officers should participate in monthly inspections of facilities for accident prevention purposes. Conditions relating to health matters, such as unsanitary conditions and fire hazards, must also be reported. The security supervisor or manager then conveys these observations, with corrective actions taken, to the committee.

Safety Attitude Development: A Culture of Safety

Security supervisors are responsible for the safety education of their officers. There are many ways to begin this education process. For example, when an officer is first hired—either through the contract company or client organization—incorporate a film on safety into the orientation program. On site, the security supervisor should present appropriate safety training to all new security staff and other employees during the new hire orientation process. This orientation should be mandatory for all new staff.

It is not easy to develop or maintain a culture of safety, but by continually reinforcing key points in a positive fashion, it can be done. Some methods to help in this development can include the following:

1. Videos: There are many available on safety and prevention of accidents from leading safety organizations, and may be obtained at little or no charge. Films should be short and direct. Do not rely on films to completely convey the message—only use them to supplement and reinforce it.
2. Posters: Messages such as "Accidents cost jobs and lives" are available from industrial safety companies and safety supply outlets. The in-house development of job-specific safety posters can help bring a personal touch to the safety message.
3. Safety committee meetings: Crucial metrics should be reviewed, such as the amount of work hours lost due to illness or accident, amounts of workman's compensation claims before and after a safety initiative has been implemented, or the amount of man hours spent investigating vehicle accidents.
4. Communication: For any organization that has a newsletter, there should be a security supervisor or director willing to write regular articles regarding local safety matters. Short, stimulating, reader-friendly safety and crime prevention notes both inform and reinforce. Websites and blogs can be used to communicate a safety message. These types of media have tremendous potential in terms of linkage to other sites, e-mails, posters, etc. Enterprising supervisors can develop extensive instructional programs via this method.
5. Award programs: Recognize employees who have made a solid contribution to the protection department in the interests of the safety program. Certificates can be created for such a purpose. Patches on uniforms can also be utilized, as can stickers on vehicles, and other privileges such as preferred parking spaces. Be careful when monetizing the prizes or otherwise making them have hard value, as this type of incentive can have negative consequences. It may well drive down the proper reporting of incidents and accidents.
6. Guest speakers, seminars, and webinars: Attendees can learn from and appreciate these seminars. In the workplace, they enhance learning development and employee morale. It is important for the supervisor to follow up on the message of any special guest, as the message of the speaker should not be allowed to quickly be forgotten. Seminars/webinars can also target people outside of the workplace, such as family

members of employees. Secondary or college students may also be potential markets, as can groups of personnel that the organization wishes to recruit as employees. Providing an attractive certificate can be a powerful motivator for people to attend. A safety message can gets out to the surrounding community as part of a community relations program.

Making a list of potential means of communicating a safety message is a worthwhile exercise. It generally uncovers mediums that were unseen and that can be exploited to great advantage. Making a list of the topics on which safety messages can be developed is also worthwhile. In some cases, the topics will help address multiple issues and thus are time and cost-effective.

Examples of safety matters are as follows:

1. Fire safety
   - The organization's fire response plan
   - How to respond during a fire drill, adding tips on why it is important to close all doors, for example
   - Fire extinguisher usage (P.A.S.S.)
2. Industrial equipment protection and use
   - Areas where ear plugs are required to be worn
3. Health-related safety (including first aid and stocking of materials, etc.)
   - How to use an automated external defibrillator
   - How to report first aid incidents
4. Safe storage of hazardous materials and products
   - How oxygen and acetylene must be stored separately when not in use
5. Employee accidents and reduced injury plans
   - Focus on slip, trip, fall hazards: only walk on cleared walking surfaces during inclement/snowy weather; do not walk between cars.
6. Electrical hazards
   - Are space heaters being used appropriately and safety?
   - Are extension cords being used properly?
7. Structural problems (which may cause accidents or injury)
   - If a stairwell is under construction, advise staff to exit via another means in the event of an emergency
   - Ergonomic concerns caused by improper work station design and many others

Safety in the workplace or in a facility requires that site personnel be trained in recognition of potential problems before they occur. Prior planning is effective in prevention of accidents. The use of "constructive daydreaming" by officers on post or patrol duty can identify potential accident scenarios. Attitude also plays a key role in safety development. Unsafe acts or improper activities are a major causal factor in accidents. These may be caused by the person not knowing any better or deliberately choosing risky behavior. Learning to recognize safety hazards and correcting them before they become factors in an accident is important for security officers. Protection staff can assist by watching for hazards, such as the following:

1. Blocked fire exits
2. Improperly stocked shelves in cupboards or storage facilities
3. Fire cabinets with improper or missing equipment
4. Poor lighting in employee-traveled areas or in areas designated for use to exit during an emergency (where there is an exit sign, indicates a designated area)

Supervising Accident Scenes

The protection supervisor is responsible for the initial investigation, which includes accurate and complete reporting of an accident scene. Regardless of whether an injury has occurred or whether it was narrowly avoided, the area must be sealed off and an investigation conducted to determine the cause. A review must then be made after the report has been submitted. Remember the following 10 steps in supervising the reporting of accidents:

1. Seal off, isolate the area, and notify emergency personnel (fire, ambulance, police, etc.).
2. Minimize risks to victims or bystanders (from electrical wires down, fire, or gas leaks) and coordinate rescue, etc.
3. Treat victims for injuries (first aid/CPR).
4. Determine the cause—that is, carelessness, vehicle accident, etc. Identify all causal factors rather than simply focusing on the primary factor.
5. Coordinate report—names of victims and witnesses, addresses and complete points of contact; remarks made by victims; video of the scene; and liaison with emergency responders, police, and fire department.
6. Follow-up with results of victim treatment, etc. Assign trained safety investigators. Coordinate with HR, police and fire investigators.
7. Interview witnesses—take names, email and phone numbers, statements made. Have them provide a written statement if possible.
8. Final examination—determine if follow-up removed existing hazards from scene (to prevent a second incident).
9. Collect all information for presentation to safety committee and outside agencies.
10. Review matter with safety committee.

When a person commits himself or herself to the task of security, protection, or law enforcement work, there is an understanding that danger, through risks of injury or even death while performing the duties, may be encountered. Supervisors need to be aware of constant inherent dangers caused by risks such as fire, bombs, assaults, and domestic disturbances.

The security supervisor must be prepared for any eventuality and training must be coordinated for the protection of his or her staff. Training sessions need to be allowed to not only involve the physical response, but allow for the emotional response that can happen during and after an emergency. If applicable, include critical incident stress management (CISM) processes and programs during a drill or exercise. Many communities have CISM teams that can be deployed to sites to help deal with the emotional stress of being involved in a disaster. Similarly, an increasing number of employers have employee assistance programs, in which staff can reach out to seek various types of professional help—often at no cost to the employee. Stress-related factors can cause carelessness in decision making. Farrell's Human Factor Model refers to this as "overload," and accidents can result. Organizational safety or wellness programs should provide for the handling of stress and pressure on the job. The supervisor should be ultimately prepared to intervene if there is a risk of injury to officers or the public due to work/personal problems.

Another tactic the supervisor needs to be prepared for is to simply be available to address safety concerns of all types. These concerns can be created from any person or source. Even if the security supervisor is not equipped to deal with the concern that is raised, he or she must make sure that the concern is taken through the proper channels so that it does not go unaddressed. Peterson noted that a system failure by management to correct problems was a mediator between errors and accidents. Supervisors need to serve as "auditors" of safety systems who can detect flaws and take the appropriate action to correct them.

Enforcement of Safety Regulations

The security supervisor is part of the management team. It is therefore the supervisor's responsibility to monitor and ensure that all safety regulations are being maintained in compliance with policy. As Reason and his Swiss cheese theory of accident causation might say, keep the Swiss cheese from lining up and allowing an accident to happen.

When violations occur, investigations must be initiated and corrective action taken.

The types of safety regulations to enforce include the following:

1. Fire safety—excessive trash, papers, nonsmoking areas, blocked fire extinguishers, etc.
2. Malfunctioning or missing protective safety equipment—its abuse, or failing to wear appropriate devices.
3. Workers using unsafe practices—this action can lead to employee injury or injury to bystanders. Another example is staff going into risky areas without proper back up from officers. Supervisors should constantly reinforce the concept "not to make yourself the first victim."
4. Nonalert staff—part of the problem may be staff shortages causing fatigue due to extended hours. This is a risk situation. Extra-long hours diminish cognitive ability and concentration. Proper sleep, diet, and lifestyle assists in an alert staff. Frequent breaks can also help reduce inattention and the resultant errors in judgment, as can the removal of distractions (lights, noise) from the environment.

5. Health/sanitation—security officers should be instructed to report unhealthy practices relating to risk. An example is unsafe food handling. Food-related illnesses can cause extensive sickness within an environment. They also create negative publicity.

There are many other areas to be considered. One point of importance is the compliance factor. Security staff must enforce and also comply with existing policies and regulations. Security supervisors have a required duty to assist in monitoring compliance to safety matters.

One rule to remember is, "If you enforce the safety rule—do not violate it!" The entire security team's credibility is at stake.

TYPES OF CONDUCT/VIOLATIONS CAUSING ACCIDENTS
- Blocked fire exits or insufficient equipment
- Electrical problems
- Chemical storage (flammable) violations
- Improper lighting
- Lack of fire equipment
- Training insufficiencies—safety policies
- Employee carelessness
- Insufficient surveillance equipment
- Lack of awareness
- Ego errors or faults of a person, such as being bad tempered or reckless

NATURAL CAUSES OF ACCIDENTS
- Aircraft incidents
- Earthquakes
- Floods
- Wind damage
- Fires due to lightning
- Power outages—electrical

CORRECTIVE/PROACTIVE APPROACH
- Perform frequent inspections—measuring results
- Set up guidelines and policy retraining
- Ensure all equipment is present (and at least to minimum acceptable standards)
- Arrange security/safety awareness programs
- Provide first aid, CPR, and rescue training
- Coordinate with local authorities
- Ensure all mechanical equipment functions correctly
- Conduct annual retraining, and testing with safety programs
- Bring in experts in the field, such as instructors of safety programs
- Address crime prevention activities

Fire Safety Supervisory Functions

The following tips are useful for allowing protection supervisors to coordinate, develop, and maintain fire safety programs.

- Know types of fire extinguishers to be used. Do not rely on a specific department in a facility to handle situations entirely. Supervisors must train protection officers and facilitate professional liaison with government safety inspectors, law enforcement personnel, and other emergency responders. Therefore, a good supervisor will always learn and practice as much about fire safety as is required. Certain fire codes must always be maintained and knowledge of these codes is essential. Check with the local fire department or fire prevention company for courses and information pertaining to codes, prevention, and enforcement. Make certain that federal, state, and municipal/ local code compliance is maintained. Know that federal government agencies—most often the NFPA for issues related to fire safety—establish at least the basic guidelines. States or provinces may enact even stricter codes or regulations on certain issues. Additionally, some municipalities have their own code enforcement departments in which they can still further regulate certain life safety practices. The "authority having jurisdiction" is a term used in the Life Safety Code, and the security supervisor should know in what situations this "authority" is relevant.
- Coordinate plans for emergency response. Liaise with fire department and other emergency response personnel. Have a meeting with authorities at a nearby airport, sporting facility, or major business. Develop evacuation plans and, later, initiate and practice that plan to share shelter and aid with other organizations in the event of an emergency. If necessary, develop a *memorandum of understanding* (MOU) with critical business partners in the event of a major disaster. These MOUs are intended to be a reminder that facilities can share services, staff, and facilities if needed in the event of certain types of disasters. In the case of hospitals, for example, an MOU in place with the Red Cross can help ensure that a certain number of cots are provided to help care for patients if a wing of the hospital is damaged or destroyed by fire.
- Security personnel should be trained in types of fires, types of extinguishing materials, and causes of fires. Develop proposals for fire protection such as cameras, flame detectors, heat sensors, smoke detectors, and ionization detectors. Thermal imagers can help find "hotspots" in blind areas, such as within a wall, where a fire may have started but cannot otherwise be detected. This is useful for both fire safety and regular security duties.
- Introduce and use crash carts in every facility. Included should be oxygen, first aid kits, extinguishers, smoke masks, flashlights, and any other items required. Ensure all security staff and, if appropriate, relevant employees from other departments, are trained on their use.
- Organize inspections by protection staff on a monthly basis. Ensure areas of deficiency are addressed. Any facility or property will benefit from this proactive approach to fire safety.

Summary

Protection supervisors have key responsibilities for ensuring the success of safety programs. The following is a general, but not all-inclusive, list of pertinent duties.

1. Coordination at local command post of accident.
2. Policy formulation and awareness programs.
3. Reviewing accident statistics and taking corrective approaches to lower accident numbers.
4. Officer safety training and safe response practices.
5. Implementing first aid/CPR programs.
6. Investigation of actual and observed safety hazards through inspections.
7. Liaison with local authorities and businesses.
8. Ensuring all pertinent investigative material is available for local authorities, court, or insurance matters. Supervisors must be aware of company or organization regulations pertaining to reporting and command chain.
9. Maintain lists of on-call personnel to dispatch in the event of an emergency. Security staff must have personal phone numbers at the department for call-out purposes.
10. Arrange awards for outstanding safety contributions.
11. Organize and supervise awareness campaigns such as crime prevention, accident watch, safe driving, etc. Continually assess the level of awareness of the facility population and tailor the awareness campaigns to cover any identified gaps.

This chapter has provided a brief examination of safety. The emphasis is on observation, prevention, attitude, and approach to various problems and procedures. Throughout any organization, there are accidents that are tragic in nature. Some are caused by wrongful acts, such as crime or negligence. Many more are caused by weaknesses in observation, in reporting, and corrective action follow-through. Some accidents still happen because of improper attitude and approach to the situation. Any supervisor will need to play a highly active role in setting up the best protection program possible. Integrating safety inspections, crime prevention, equipment usage, committee involvement, employee participation, and safe work practices into the overall safety program is important. Each initiative contributes to the overall objective, and has some degree of overlap and carryover with other areas.

The protection supervisor is tasked with all these duties and more. Anyone who ever investigated accidents, and found that they were preventable, feels compelled to create an effective safety plan for the benefit of everyone. Be sure the Swiss cheese does not line up! The rewards for promoting safety are ongoing. We have all chosen to work in the protection field. Therefore, we must all strive to make things as safe as possible. That is our professional duty.

Emerging Trends

The field of safety is an ever-evolving profession in which there are always more regulations and requirements to be compliant; rarely are safety regulations reduced or eliminated.

That said, organizations will need to find creative ways to accomplish these tasks with the staff they already have in place. In other words, organizations are not likely to hire additional staff for every new regulation; they will simply assign compliance duties to an existing position. While usually that assignment goes to the individual handling safety, it often falls on the plate of the security supervisor or manager.

Other drives for increasing an organization's safety responsibilities include terrorism and adverse weather conditions. Protective planning for acts of violence often falls within the domain of safety. While this generally relates to in-house stakeholders, it may well include external entities. A common example of the latter is hospitals where first responders must go for clean up after a hazardous materials incident.

Preparation for snow storms, floods, earthquakes, and even volcanic eruptions also falls within the province of the safety department, in whole or in part. These loss events become more significant with large population density. They are of even greater concern when that population is elderly, disabled, or very young, as in the case of school children.

Searching job boards for open positions reveals that many companies are now recruiting for "safety/security officers" to accomplish much of what has been discussed in this chapter. Slowly but surely, the field of security is becoming blended in with safety and emergency management. Hotels, for instance, often want candidates to have a working knowledge of fire protection systems, such as how to perform regular system checks. Hospitals may ask security personnel to respond not only to emergencies, such as with physically acting out or aggressive patients, but to medical emergencies in which CPR may be needed. In many industries, security personnel are asked to be the first responders to fire situations. Not only does the officer need to know how to safely operate the extinguisher, but they need to know when it is time to stop fighting the fire and evacuate, how and where to evacuate, and yet still, be available to aid the fire department for any assistance they may require, such as elevator access.

Daily, more and more lives are being put in the hands of the protection officer, and therefore the supervisor—whether or not he or she is on duty. Taking that one step further, it has almost become the norm that one will have to change professions once or more during a working lifetime. As organizations' safety responsibilities have increased, so have the number of jobs dealing with safety, either exclusively or as part of the duties. Becoming knowledgeable about safety—whether as a protection officer, supervisor, or student—will make one much more marketable in the employment arena.

Refer website http://www.ifpo.org for further information

11

The Supervisor's Role in Improving Customer Service and Tenant Relations

Christopher A. Hertig, Brion P. Gilbride, Glen Kitteringham

The security supervisor is a key player in both establishing and maintaining an appropriate customer service orientation within the protection force. To better understand how the supervisor functions, we must first examine the role of the supervisor and then assess the development of an organizational philosophy.

The Role of the Supervisor

The supervisor is the physical manifestation of higher authority—the core of the philosophy of the organization—to subordinates. The supervisor is the link between management and line officers or loss prevention agents. He or she is the person that ensures compliance with policies and procedures. He or she ensures quality performance in the customer service area. It is the supervisor who is responsible for communication both within their chain from management to that of subordinate, as well as for communication with clients, landlords, tenants, law enforcement and emergency services, regulators, and almost anyone else that visits, works in, or transits through their facility.

The supervisor does all of these things because the supervisor is the first responder to any and all situations. This requires the supervisor to assume a variety of roles on the spot, with the two main roles being that of a diplomat or a mediator. Diplomacy is necessary to assist accident victims, support investigations, or address personnel issues. Diplomacy is necessary when there are competing interests involved in a situation. Subordinates, other supervisors, senior managers, customers, landlords, and/or government agencies, all have an interest in how situations are handled, and it is the supervisor who will often have to manage expectations for some or all of those different interests. In addition to being a diplomat, the supervisor will often function as a mediator. For differences between merchants and customers, employees in the same company, or outside employees and contractors, the security supervisors and officers will be called upon to adjudicate disagreements between people that cannot, for whatever reason, do it themselves.

Security Supervision and Management. http://dx.doi.org/10.1016/B978-0-12-800113-4.00011-0

Core Philosophy of Parent or Client Organization

To gain a firm foothold in public or customer relations, one must first understand what the philosophical foundations are within the parent or client organization. Each organization is different; they do not simply all want "to make money," as the uninformed may believe. Each organization may indeed want to make money but in its own manner. Each takes a different path. Some rely on innovations in technology. Some work on customer loyalty. Others focus on cost containment. Still others place great emphasis on ties to the community. Whichever guiding beliefs lie at the center of the organization, these must be firmly understood by those who wish to effectively represent that organization to customers. The security staff are the people most often seen (and often seen first) by people who work for the organization, provide support to the organization, patronize the organization, or use the organization's services. To best represent the organization, the security staff must be aware of the mission statement, guiding principles, and any other documents which lay out that philosophy.

The Key Questions

There are several important questions that can help the supervisor understand the importance of the customer service function. These questions help the supervisor to understand his or her role in the organization, the history of the organization, and how the policies and procedures used by the organization support the customer service aspect. Some of these questions have straightforward answers, while others require effort to understand. The answers to these questions vary from organization to organization.

1. What makes my employer and/or client unique from other organizations in the same field of endeavor?

A: Organizational philosophy is founded in the history of the organization. Each organization is established at some point and evolves over time. The original beliefs may be modified somewhat, or they may remain unchanged and be further cemented into the organizational culture. The supervisor must understand how this employer and organization differ from previous ones they might have worked for.

2. What is this history/organizational philosophy of my employer?

A: This is especially important for security providers. Some of them, such as Securitas (which acquired Pinkertons), have an illustrious history. One could probably develop a three-credit college course on the contributions of Alan Pinkerton. He was a prominent citizen who played a key role in the history of the United States and the development of investigative practice. Other firms may also have founders and principals who were industry pioneers. Each organization has a unique history that can illustrate important lessons.

Knowing this history helps to make each officer a more effective company representative. Unfortunately, this is often not capitalized upon as effectively as it could be.

Organizational philosophy is framed in the policies of the organization. Reading and understanding these policies is essential to comprehending the philosophy of the organization, as well as knowing what rules are to be enforced. The philosophy guides the policies, and the policies inform the procedures. When policies become unmoored from the organizational philosophy, the policies become a recipe for disaster.

3. What do the policies of my employer state?

A: Organizational philosophy is more precisely articulated in the procedures established by an organization. These specify the *what* and *how* of the policies. They state how the policy (philosophy) is executed. Consider a company policy on employees who are arrested for off-duty conduct. If the organizational philosophy emphasizes integrity, then company policy in this matter is likely to be strict and comprehensive. If the organizational philosophy emphasizes freedom, such that off-duty situations with no nexus to the workplace, so they are in effect ignored, then policy will probably be either lenient or perhaps even nonexistent. When policies are developed as responses to problems rather than as part of the organizational philosophy, disparities will likely be seen in the treatment of one situation versus another that will appear illogical to the independent observer.

4. What do the procedures explain?

A: Once policies and procedures are fully comprehended, it becomes necessary to examine the role of the security department in advancing the organizational philosophy. Upper management has delegated certain functions to the security department.

5. What is the role of the asset protection/security department in advancing that philosophy?

A: Efficient use of resources and organizational survival mandates that this question be addressed. Supervisors must ensure that their charges perform to the best of their ability. They must also work to achieve quality through adherence to recognized, guidelines, standards, or best practices. There are several steps to take toward this end. One step is to research the existence of guidelines, standards, etc. Another step is to conduct a job task analysis to determine roles and functions of officers. Once this is done, a clear picture emerges as to what officers can do and what their key competencies are. From there, recruitment, selection, training, and the remainder of the human resource management process can occur.

The Customer Service Role of Protection Officers

Protection officers, by virtue of their jobs, are often highly involved in public relations/customer service. At a seminar given some years ago, a security officer in attendance stated that "public relations are 90 percent of this job." It was interesting to note that the seminar

Job Title: Lounge Host
Organizational Unit: Asset Protection
Accountability: Security Shift Supervisor
Job Summary: To provide for a safe, enjoyable atmosphere for our guests.
Duties and Responsibilities:
- Greeting customers in the Lounge.
- Controlling access to Lounge.
- Maintaining an accurate customer count.
- Ensuring the safety of the Lounge and the surrounding area.
- Maintaining order in the Lounge.
- Ensuring compliance with Alcoholic Beverage Commission regulations.
- Customer assistance as appropriate.

Interaction: Lounge manager, Bartender
Prepared By: Director of Asset Protection
Approved By: Vice-President, Human Resources

FIGURE 11.1 Happy time Resorts.

was held at a manufacturing facility where public/customer contact is not as great as it would be in a shopping center, college campus, park, or office building. A study done in 1985 attempted to identify a generic security officer training curriculum. Part of the study involved a questionnaire sent to randomly selected security managers. The respondents were asked to rank which topics they felt were most important for a security curriculum to include. One respondent felt that public relations was the most critical area for a security officer to be proficient because an officer's interaction with others determined how a negative event was perceived; thus, no matter how bad a situation, an officer's public relations skills can be the critical factor in how bad the situation is perceived.

Some organizations, such as shopping centers, hotels, and amusement parks, use security personnel as customer service agents to a large extent. Sam's Club "greeters" serve to welcome a customer into the store while at the same time ensuring that they are members. In many hotels, a similar function is performed by protection officers in the hotel lobby. Lounges employ hosts to welcome customers and keep out troublemakers. The sample job description given in Figure 11.1 provides ample evidence of the customer service role for security personnel.

The supervisor's role in customer service is especially profound. When working at any venue—whether in a public forum like a university or a shopping center, or a private one like a manufacturing facility—when individuals have a problem with the actions of a security officer, they are going to ask to speak to a supervisor. These interactions can be quite stressful. The supervisor is already at a disadvantage in a way because the person requesting their intervention is already aggrieved, feels wronged, or in some other way objects to what the security officer has said or done. The supervisor's mission, at this point, is as follows: (1) find out what happened; (2) do not further agitate the person complaining; (3) determine, perhaps without specifically asking, what action the complainant wants the supervisor to take; and (4) send the complainant on his or her way with positive feelings about the supervisory interaction.

The supervisor accomplishes this multifaceted mission primarily by using *active listening*. Active listening is defined by the Conflict Research Consortium at the University of Colorado as "a structured form of listening and responding that focuses the attention on the speaker."[1] With this technique, the listener repeats the gist of what was said so that the speaker can confirm or enhance the understanding. In a typical conflict situation, the listener does not listen so much as assume what the speaker is saying, and the listener formulates a response before the speaker is done speaking. This is not conducive to either party understanding the other. The supervisor must listen to what a complainant has to say and confirm his or her understanding. This established understanding will enable a conversation to take place; the complainant will be validated and the supervisor can formulate a reasonable response based on facts rather than emotion. When successful, the complainant will see that the supervisor is attempting to understand what was said and should feel that their complaint is taken seriously. Active listening may calm the situation and make a successful (or at least not unsuccessful) resolution possible.

The Supervisor's Role in Tenant Relations

Solid working relationships with the tenants whose businesses or endeavors are part of the security department's worksite are essential for a variety of reasons. The supervisor must also be a diplomat and a mediator when dealing with nonpublic constituencies. If the security department oversees an office park, shopping mall, or university, for example, the department will interact regularly with representatives of the companies, businesses, professors, and all of the support staff those entities require to function. In all of the entities cited above, the responsibilities of the security department may overlap those of the individual entities; thus, from time to time, those responsibilities will often require clarification. Tenants can serve a number of valuable purposes within the security operation. The better the relationship between the security department and the tenants, the more value will be realized via cooperation.

The Force Multiplier

The tenants and their employees are the eyes and ears that are often in areas that cameras cannot see and can hear things that cameras cannot hear. Cultivating good relationships with these individuals means that when there is a problem or a potential problem, they will likely reach out to the security department and do so quickly. The security supervisor may not cultivate all of these relationships personally, but the security officers probably will in their day-to-day duties and the supervisor may still benefit. In addition, good relationships with customers or vendors/suppliers are encouraged, as they may also be aware of situations that the security department may not be, particularly concerning theft, fraudulent incidents, and similar matters.

The Enhancement to Physical Security Measures

Tenants and their employees can support the security function by virtue of basic safeguards. They can close and lock doors, secure valuables, have sufficient cash controls in place to deter/mitigate the possibility of theft, activate alarm systems or antitheft devices, and plenty of other basic steps. The entities that lock their doors save the security department from having to secure those locations. This is especially important because if the security staff is responding to an incident, it may be minutes or even hours before they can resume normal operations in some cases. A shop with a well-calibrated inventory control system will enable security staff to react quickly to a potential theft incident. A stadium that supports in-house security by requiring all potential employees and contractors to be vetted through security, means that employers and contract companies can be alerted to potential issues before an incident rather than after. Cultivating good relations will encourage tenants and their employees to be mindful of security generally and strengthen communication between tenants and security that benefits all involved.

Common Interests

One inherent advantage in the security department's quest to have a positive relationship with the employers and tenants operating within their worksite is that chaos is bad for business. Nobody wants to have criminals and other malefactors loitering in their facilities, damaging the property, stealing the inventory, harassing the customers and the employees, or just being generally disruptive. Customers will not shop where they do not feel safe and secure. Students (or their parents) will not spend thousands of dollars to attend school at a campus that is not safe, secure, or otherwise conducive to learning. Sports teams will not be able to fill their seats, especially at today's exorbitant prices, if the patrons are worried about the safety of their persons, belongings, or vehicles. One facet of developing positive relationships with tenants working under the security department's umbrella, is recognizing and working toward those common interests.

The Tenants and Landlords Have Responsibilities Too

Problems happen at every worksite, and the security department's primary role is to respond. Responding is the easy part. The hard part is determining who is responsible for addressing the problem to which the security team responds. The security supervisor, who typically will be either the first responder or has supervisory authority over the security officers who respond first, must know how to contact and obtain the cooperation of those who will ultimately rectify the situation. Does the worksite have multiple tenants? If so, who is responsible for repairs (e.g., the tenant, the site owner), and does it depend upon what needs repairing? The security supervisor may even have to intercede if repairs are critical, such as a water main break that floods a computer server room. Positive relationships with tenants will reduce the friction generated when a crisis occurs and uncertainty exists.

Challenges to Maintaining Good Relations

The Impact of Alcohol

The benefits and advantages of positive security/tenant relations cannot be discussed without also discussing the challenges to maintaining that positive relationship. One

of the biggest and most complex challenges is alcohol. Malls have restaurants and bars. Colleges and universities either have bars on campus or near the campus. Sporting venues often serve alcohol. Most people will drink in moderation. The very few people who get highly intoxicated at these venues are the ones at issue. These highly intoxicated patrons can create a legal nightmare, sometimes in spite of the best efforts of the security department to mitigate or prevent it.

If the venue that serves alcohol is on the property for which the security department is responsible, this presents some unique challenges. Inside the venue, alcohol generates business; the venue, like any other business, seeks profit. Therefore, they will serve as many people as they can for as long as they can. What happens when they stop serving and close for the night becomes the security department's problem until all of the people are out of the area that the security department covers. To further complicate matters, alcohol is frequently a factor in assaults and accusations of assault, both physical and sexual. For example, after a good Saturday night of business, a venue may close at the legally designated time. A few very intoxicated patrons may exit the venue and remain in the parking lot, the mall, or elsewhere on the property. Along with intoxicated individuals, potentially comes fights (assaults), urination in public, lewdness, driving under the influence (also known as impaired driving, DUI, DWI, and other names), and other offenses. These issues are difficult for security departments to deal with and are fraught with potential liability issues—but they must still be addressed.

Tenant relations are not improved when the security department has to notify local law enforcement of a fight where parties want to press charges, or of an alleged drunk driving accident, or worse, of an alleged sexual assault in a poorly lit part of the property. When local law enforcement becomes involved, often because the venue is a "problem establishment" that receives numerous calls for service, it could impact the operation of the venue itself. Some communities will revoke a liquor license for reasons such as these. Tension is created because the security department must ensure the safety of all guests, employees, and tenants while they also have a responsibility to report alleged crimes to the appropriate authorities. In many areas, if the security department cannot adequately respond, they too will be held liable in civil court if a suit is filed. With alcohol, the necessity of maintaining good relations with the tenant is once more made apparent. If the security department has good relations with the tenant serving the liquor, perhaps agreed notifications can be made about troublesome patrons, enabling a discreet response that addresses an intoxicated individual before the incident rather than afterward.

TENANT DISREGARD OR INCOMPATIBLE BUSINESS OPERATIONS

Although alcohol is a significant challenge, there are other challenges as well. Some tenants will feel that the presence of the security department suggests that a location has crime problems, rather than viewing security as a deterrent. As such, these tenants will not want security to patrol near their establishments or enforce shoplifting laws. Also, some tenants will sell or market items that, although legal, attract a criminal element. These might include shops with smell smoking paraphernalia (head shops); shops that sell knives, swords, and/or other weapons; or pawn shops. These locations also tend to attract the interest of law enforcement more often than other types of establishments. Unfortunately, the security supervisor cannot control who rents space in an office park or mall; therefore, security operations must be planned with these locations and/or clientele in mind. Developing a positive relationship with these tenants is mutually beneficial, but it may take more work to reach a good level of understanding. The tenant and security department together can ensure that customers of such locations can be just that, a customer. Better relations with security (and law enforcement) means that problem customers or suspicious activity can be addressed.

PHYSICAL ASPECTS

The physical design of a facility may lend itself to challenges. These issues, primarily related to safety, impact the security department's relationship with the tenant because, fairly or unfairly, the security department will be blamed for failing to prevent incidents should they occur. Poor lighting, trash, chipped paint on curbsides, faded crosswalks, dented/bent/missing signage, inadequate camera coverage in the parking lots or other common areas, and even poor traffic flow may be blamed on the security department. There is a theory, commonly referred to as "broken windows," which in part says that once a building or other structure begins to look like nobody takes care of it, people will act accordingly and also not take care of it. Crime increases in the immediate area because criminals believe, based on the lack of care or attention to the area, that they can (and frequently do) operate with impunity.

Therefore, poor lighting, trash, chipped paint, faded crosswalks, and missing signage tell people that nobody particularly cares about the area. The same message is sent if the security department is understaffed, cameras are visibly broken or damaged, security department vehicles look dented/damaged or have faded paint or damaged markings, or the security staff lacks or fails to wear proper uniforms. If criminals and other undesirable elements see this, they will congregate at that location because they will infer that it is safe for them to do so.

Remember, tenants do not see the managers or the owners of the facility, they see the security department. The security department must combat criminality themselves, or in cooperation with law enforcement. Aside from that, the security department must work with the departments responsible for maintenance, environmental services, and/or groundskeeping to help resolve lighting, traffic flow, and upkeep issues. Tenant relations are important here because the tenants can verify that such situations are occurring, and lessees may be able to leverage support that the security department is unable to access on its own.

MULTI-TENANT FACILITIES

In multi-tenant environments, there may be multiple security entities working in different parts of the overall location, whether it be an office tower, a sporting venue, hotel, or some other complex. The security inside the sporting venue might be proprietary and focused on crowd control, while the security outside may be contract and focused on traffic control and collecting parking fees. The security at the hotel might be proprietary, with them worried about loss/theft from customer rooms, while the bar inside the hotel might have a bouncer or two mainly worried about breaking up fights. Convention center security staff might be worried about controlling access to the event but not about what happens after patrons are admitted. The security department with overall responsibility for an entire site should be worried about all of these things, as well as others. Site supervisors must have some communication with all these individual entities; in a crisis, there will be no time to argue over roles, responsibilities, equipment, or anything else. A multitude of issues will require coordination and cooperation. These include, but are not limited to, interoperable communications; common radio codes/10-codes; procedures for activating police, fire, or ambulance services; responsibility for major facility issues, such as power failures or water main breaks.

Without solid tenant relations, even the simplest thing can turn into a nightmare. The only proven, tested way to have and develop solid tenant relations is communication.

The Solution: Communication

In tenant relations, just as in customer service, the key to success is communication. Different approaches will yield different results with different groups. Mass communication, such as a monthly newsletter or a digest on crime trends, security issues, and/or safety tips, can be tailored to an individual audience, whether it is customers, employees, tenants, or all three. Specific times of year, such as Christmas or Super Bowl Sunday, can be addressed in this manner as well. Other options include web postings and videos; the technology is limitless. A Twitter account, used wisely, can be used to send short, critical messages very quickly; other social media tools may perform this service as well or better than a mass e-mail could. These methods, however, do not lend themselves to the face-to-face relationships between a tenant and a security supervisor that will be critical.

Formal meetings where site management or ownership meets with tenants are a place to start. If the security department does not have a seat at that table as a representative of management or ownership, they will have to try to make changes. That may be a simple matter of requesting to attend, or it may be a significant matter of researching and justifying just how the security's presence will benefit the enterprise as a whole, and convincing the executives of its importance. If security wins a seat at that table, they should provide information to the group, particularly about events that impact the worksite as a whole as well as the tenants. This might be information on criminal activity, maintenance issues, upcoming events, traffic problems, or any other issue that the security department might provide in the way of support or request for support.

More important than a formal presence at periodic meetings, however, are interpersonal relationships. The security supervisor must be familiar with his or her counterpart(s) if they are present at the worksite, and with the store managers or their representatives on the individual work shifts when possible. The only way to become familiar with these people is to go out and meet them personally. The security supervisor must introduce themselves, offer assistance, provide a business card if available, and must return to reestablish contact on a semi-regular basis; if the supervisor cannot do that in person, he or she should encourage their security patrols to make those contacts.

Meetings and personal relationships are essential to sharing intelligence, coordinating emergency response, and providing mutual support—and are just good business practices generally. The same skill sets that the security supervisor needs to provide for good customer service, especially active listening, are the ones that the supervisor will use to maintain good relations with tenants and employees throughout their worksite. These skill sets should also be developed with subordinate officers because the supervisor can support good relations with customers and tenants via their security officers.

Refer website http://www.ifpo.org for further information

End Note

1. Author Unknown, *Active Listening* (Boulder, CO: University of Colorado, Conflict Research Consortium, 1998), accessed Nov 8, 2014. Available: http://www.colorado.edu/conflict/peace/treatment/activel. htm.

Supervising During Special Events

Christopher Innace, Christopher A. Hertig, James A. DeMeo

The role of a security supervisor is a challenging one, often requiring planning and communication with various entities. Special events such as rock concerts, athletic events, speeches, autograph sessions, political rallies, and stockholder meetings pose a unique set of challenges. There are many potential risks at special events of which security supervisors should be aware—the major one being violent crowds. The potential risks cannot be stressed enough. Crowds are capable of extensive violence and destruction, often unleashing their fury in an explosive manner. Effective crowd management is a major step in avoiding a disaster during special events.

Additionally, special events provide an opportunity for image enhancement, both for the protection entity and the parent/client organization. In some cases, projecting a positive image and relating well to visitors, customers, and the public at large is the sole reason for the existence of the parent/client or security organization at an event. With shopping centers, amusement parks, and stadiums all existing for the comfort and entertainment of patrons, the era of experiential marketing has raised the bar in terms of customer satisfaction. Supervisory personnel who wish to thrive in their professional careers need to exploit this opportunity to the greatest extent possible!

Assessment

There are many options to consider when assessing for crowd management. The security supervisor must work with the facility and venue manager to have an effective plan. Together, they should try to ascertain the characteristics of the crowd/audience due at a particular event. Assessing the size and nature of a crowd is important for a security supervisor. The size of a crowd can be determined by ticket sales, counting seats, etc. The nature of the crowd may be determined by the event itself. For example, if it is a football game, then crowds tend to be rowdy. One can estimate that alcohol will be a factor in escalating a persons' behavior in this type of crowd. If it is a gymnastics crowd, for example, then the crowd tends to be calmer and more relaxed.

"Flash mobs" have injected a new dimension into crowd management, including for environments like retail centers, where it may not have been previously considered. Flash mobs are crowds that quickly form through social media communications. Although a special event may not have flash mobs per se, there are situations where these can occur, taking the form of protests, demonstrations, or criminal assaults. "Wilding" occurs where large groups of youths assault people, steal items, and damage property. Efficient intelligence capabilities and procedures for rapid intervention are becoming increasingly important in the management of retail establishments, arenas, parties, and any environment where crowds may form.

A security supervisor should be aware of five different types of crowds:

- An *acquisitive crowd* is motivated by the desire to get something. They are concerned with their own interest in buying merchandise, getting an autograph, or shaking the hand of a celebrity. As long as their desires are met quickly and efficiently, they are easily managed.
- An *expressive crowd* usually occurs when crowd members express their feelings at a protest, demonstration, or convention. This type of crowd is usually well behaved but can easily become hostile if the proper causal factors are present.
- A *spectator crowd* usually gathers to watch an athletic event or some type of entertainment. A concern here is that emotions can change rapidly, especially during sporting events. Troublemakers must be spotted and dealt with early on and the crowd as a whole continually assessed as to their mood.
- A *hostile crowd* is motivated by feelings of hate and fear. This type of crowd is ready to fight for what they believe in. This usually occurs at strikes, riots, or political demonstrations. Obviously, plans must be made to immediately implement dispersal procedures.
- An *escape crowd* is a crowd that is trying to flee. This can occur due to an emergency situation, such as a fire or other sudden disaster. Escape crowds can also be created due to mismanagement by protection forces. Care must be taken to ensure that crowds do not become too large or confined. There must also be the ability for the crowd members to see and hear, especially those at the extreme front and rear. Quick, efficient, orderly evacuation routes must be established.

A security supervisor also should make note of the following five psychological factors of crowd members:

- *Security*—Some people may join a crowd because they feel safe due to the presence of many other people. For example, this may occur when a gang is threatening citizens and some of the citizens join the gang for security purposes.
- *Suggestion*—By joining a crowd, people accept ideas of the leader and forget about their own beliefs, values, morals, or basic common sense.
- *Novelty*—A person may enter a group to get away from his or her normal routine or regular duties. This person feels like he or she belongs to a new adventure. This is usually due to some influence from the crowd leader.
- *Loss of identity*—A person loses his or her sense of individuality, and individual accountability, by being in a crowd. People may believe that they can act with impunity and thus engage in deviant behaviors that they would not normally entertain.
- *Release of emotions*—In an emotionally-charged crowd, a person's faults (anger, hostility, etc.) can surface. This gives the crowd member a chance to do things that he or she normally would not do.

Pre-event intelligence can be used to better manage the crowd. Social network platforms are one method, but there are others, such as a simple email to members of a professional group. The example below uses the International Association and Campus Law Enforcement Administrators' (IACLEA) email list.

Access Control

Barriers play an important role as to who gets allowed onto the premises. Who gets in and where they can go requires decision making by the security supervisor and venue management. Criteria for spectators getting into the facility can include tickets and a guest list. Employees—and in some cases, visitors—are supplied with identification cards. These cards should have a recent photo of the employee, as well as the employee's name, job title and/or department, etc. The identification cards must be worn so that they are readily visible at all times. Protection against counterfeiting is another consideration in a card system, especially at high-priced entertainment facilities or functions where very important persons (VIPs) will be in attendance.

Other decisions depend on whether the facility has gates or doors that lock up the outside premises. The security supervisor must decide with facility/venue management when to open and close the facility for employees, performers, athletes, etc. Other barriers that must be checked constantly are entrances and exits. You should know how many are there and when they need to be locked or unlocked.

Communications

Communication is an integral component of preparing for a special event. All communication equipment should be tested prior to the event. The security supervisor should establish a method for security, venue management, and law enforcement agencies to be able to contact each other. This can be accomplished via radios equipped with multiple channels. Backup battery packs and spare radios are also essential to the security supervisor. Other communication equipment to be used should include enough telephones, cellular phones, intercompany phones, and "bell line" phones to handle the increased traffic required during emergencies. A public address system in the facility can be very useful, as well as portable public address systems ("bullhorns") and whistles. Think in terms of diversity and contingency when dealing with communications. Old and new systems can be used; systems can complement each other.

In many facilities, large video monitors are placed at strategic locations to provide entertainment, information, or emergency instructions to crowd members or employees. These monitors can keep the attention of crowd members focused in a positive manner, especially if there are periods of waiting. Spectators are entertained and not as easily aggravated by having to wait in line. This can easily be tied into the parent or client organization's marketing efforts by providing information on sales, promotions, upcoming events, etc.

Protection officers should have all of their lines of communication checked for both transmission and reception capabilities at the beginning of each shift. There should also be periodic checks to ensure that radio batteries are at proper strength and "dead zones" are avoided, etc. Officers should always think in terms of backup communications in case the primary method of communication is unusable for any reason. This should be stressed and reinforced at every opportunity.

Traffic Control

Traffic control is essential during special events, especially when there are emergencies. No emergency plan can succeed without effective traffic control systems in place. It is also important for the purpose of public relations because it is at this juncture that visitors first come into contact with representatives of the facility—the protection officers directing traffic.

Officers must possess the proper equipment when assigned to traffic control duty. A flashlight, radio, and whistle are necessary. Also, officers must dress according to the weather so that comfort is assured during long hours. For safety and public recognition purposes, officers should dress to be visible. Reflective body vests should be required so that both ease of recognition and officer safety are enhanced.

A traffic lane must be cleared in the case of a fire or other emergency situation. Being able to quickly remove persons (injured, evicted, arrested) is important. Being able to bring in fire equipment, vendor supplies, or additional personnel efficiently is also a key to successful event management. It is advantageous to be able to do this without crowd members seeing the ambulance, arrestee, additional personnel, etc. arriving or departing. Prudent security supervisors make sure that lanes of approach and exit are kept open.

Training of protection officers in proper traffic control procedures is essential. Initial and periodic refresher classes must be given to ensure proficiency. Improper procedures, such as incorrect hand signals, could lead to accidents, so training to prevent these behaviors, along with continuous supervisory assessment on the job, are essential. Checking the proficiency of officers and the appearance/image of traffic control points is an essential supervisory function. Finding deficiencies and correcting them before they blossom into serious problems is the key.

When officers direct traffic, signals should be simple and distinct. Appropriate sign placement is also essential to both manage traffic and project the proper image. Supervisors should address the traffic control function from a system's perspective. Each part of the traffic control system should act in concert with the whole. At the same time, there should be the capability for immediate change in traffic flow.

Emergency Medical Operations

The security officer should be trained in first aid. When dealing with a person who is sick or injured, first communicate with the patient if possible. Then, the officer should provide basic first aid if necessary. The next step is to call for assistance (911) and lastly to manage crowds and bystanders. The officer must stay with the patient until medically trained help arrives. The ratio of emergency medical technicians (EMTs) to visitors should be 1:750. Certified EMTs are essential for the purpose of emergency medical operations.

Provisions must also be made for ambulance service. In some facilities, patient transport can be accomplished via golf carts or similar types of patrol vehicles. In-house ambulances may also be used. In all situations, external ambulance capabilities must be assessed. Similarly, emergency room capabilities at local hospitals must be factored in, should there be mass casualties. In terms of active threat scenarios, combat medicine should be part of the emergency response program so that multiple casualties with extensive wounds can be treated.

Evacuation

In an indoor facility, a 6-foot "clear zone" around the inside of the perimeter must be maintained for evacuation purposes. Any equipment must be secure and out of the way in case a panic situation arises. The security supervisor does not want this to interfere with crowds heading toward the exits. For an outside event, plans must be made and discussed concerning evacuation routes.

In addition to routes, there must be areas in which evacuating crowd members can congregate. These areas must be large enough to accommodate and provide for the safety of everyone. There should also be consideration given to what crowd members do after evacuating, such as getting in their cars and leaving, or assembling and being advised where to go next.

Fixed Posts

Fixed posts manned by security personnel are a necessity for any special event. At every fixed post, post orders are a must. Post orders must be clear and understandable so a person unfamiliar with security concepts can comprehend the orders. Every security officer manning the post should know the objective or mission of the post. The location of the post should be included in the post order. Manning orders should also be included to stipulate when the post is operational, as well as what type (unarmed, armed, male, female, etc.) and how many personnel man it.

Any equipment used must be listed and tested regularly. When first manning the post, there should be a sign-in sheet logging the use of any equipment for the security officer to sign. Some equipment common to fixed posts are portable radios, flashlights, rain gear, fire extinguishers, and video monitors. There are also many other types of possible equipment that may be used, contingent upon the operational and emergency needs of that post. Also, duties must be specified in a post order. This includes area of responsibility and an establishment of a route for retreat, should hostile crowd actions necessitate this.

Assignment of Security Officer Posts

There are a myriad of different assignments at posts. Examples of post order can be checking identifications at an assigned area, checking tickets or baggage at a spectator entrance, and observing crowd behavior at a special event, strike, or the scene of a recent fire.

Examples of post locations for a sporting event include the following:

- Main door
- Locker room entrance/exit
- Hallways
- Spectator entrance/exit
- VIP entrance/exit
- Seating areas
- Media entrance/exit
- Parking lots
- Athlete entrance/exit
- Delivery entrance/exit

Pre-event Briefings

The security supervisors should have briefings before the security officers go to their posts. These meetings should be brief and explain/remind everyone of what is expected. They should be planned and structured, using a predesigned outline of what is to be covered. The supervisors should go over different responsibilities, objectives, and approaches. They should make sure that everyone has their proper uniforms on and is ready to meet the public. A review and check of equipment should be performed. The supervisors should make sure that officers know how to use everything and that each piece of equipment is functional. This is especially important with weapons and communications equipment.

It is most important for the security officer to ascertain exactly what is expected of them. Clearing up any questions they may have is an absolute necessity.

Talking to Crowds

Communicating with crowds properly may prevent problems from occurring. Unfortunately, in many instances, proper preparation has not been made to accomplish this. When addressing a crowd, there are some steps that a security supervisor, as well as his or her subordinates, should follow:

1. Think before saying something so that the message is clear and concise.
2. When trying to relay a message, first get the crowd's attention through sound (whistle or clap) or verbal message ("May I have your attention?").
3. Speak slowly and clearly.
4. Project voice to the farthest person but try not to yell.
5. Use eye contact to express authority. Be somewhat direct with eye contact.
6. Try to make eye contact with every person in the group.
7. Be calm and relaxed.
8. When directing a crowd to move on, do not make exceptions allowing anyone to remain.
9. Be firm and assertive.
10. Be polite.

Post-Event Briefing

Debriefing should always take place after the event. Here, the security supervisor goes over how everything took place. There should be an overall summary between the security supervisor and venue management. Comments and recommendations should be discussed and recorded.

Managing Personnel

Aside from the strictly supervisory aspect of human resources for crowd management, there are some very important components to managing personnel:

1. Selection
2. Recruitment
3. Applications/interviews
4. Testing/vetting
5. Training

These components are generic, whether using a regular security force, an on-call contract force, off-duty police, interns/apprentices, volunteers, etc.

Selection

The type of individual hired is a key managerial aspect in any job. It determines the level of performance expected. It is especially important for crowd management. As a security manager, the type of individual hired is one who is smart, calm but decisive, assertive, and with an ability to communicate precisely and professionally. Other personal skills should include being a team player, having a service attitude, and possessing a mature personality.

In some cases, security managers hire their personnel en masse for special events without doing the requisite testing, interviews, or training. Obviously, this is undesirable. Any individual who acts on behalf of their employer's interests during a special event becomes the legal and moral responsibility of the employer.

Recruitment

Recruitment is essential to acquiring efficient security officers. Recruitment establishes the parameters of the selection pool, and can be accomplished by a variety of approaches. A few that might be applicable to special event staffing are the following:

- Visiting different colleges: Recruit students majoring in criminal justice, security, public relations, emergency management, etc. Also, recruit students with customer service skills and previous security jobs.
- Advertising in newspapers, on websites, or through social media: This is a good method because it will get many applicants. However, it may attract people who want to work a short time before becoming a police officer.

- Email: Emailing security/directors at different facilities such as hospitals, universities, etc., can be an effective way to acquire qualified applicants, particularly for those agencies that only require periodic staffing.

Applications/Interviews

Applications must be studied carefully because job seekers tend to exaggerate. Some things to look for during the screening process include the following:

1. Indications of being clearly overqualified
2. Unexplained gaps in employment history
3. Gaps in residences
4. Indications of a lack of job stability
5. Inadequate references

When interviewing a prospective employee, yes or no questions should not asked—at least not during the initial phase of the interview—these types of questions do not require the interviewee to think on the spot and explain themselves clearly and concisely. Answer skills should be assessed during an interview because they are essential attributes for crowd management personnel to possess. While interviewing, answers to questions should be compared to the application and resume. The job candidate's verbal response, resume, and application form should all be correlate to each other.

Testing/Vetting

After the interview stage, certain specific tests are recommended. These tests may include psychological exams, drugs tests, etc. Background investigations should also be required, in accordance with applicable standards and guidelines. An applicant's criminal history is an area of concern to employers especially when an applicant is applying for security employment. Failure to effectively screen personnel who are in positions of trust and subsequently violate that trust can result in extensive civil litigation.

Training:

A Supervisor's Responsibility to the Employee

When dealing with crowds, it is important that security personnel be trained effectively to handle various situations quickly, efficiently, and safely. Many approaches can be taken to training. Essentially, what must be done is to ensure that all necessary competency areas are covered thoroughly. A job task analysis should be performed before initiating training to ensure that this occurs. Once this is done, a list of topics or competency areas can be constructed.

Sample training topics include the following:

- Crowd management
- Report writing
- Safety
- Patrol techniques
- Traffic control
- Bomb threats
- First aid
- Fire prevention/control
- Emergency planning
- Alarm systems
- Hazardous materials
- Improvised explosive devices
- VIP protection
- Hostage situations
- Defensive tactics
- Suicide prevention
- Public relations

Delivery of Instructions

The supervisor should keep the following in mind during training:

1. Be patient, keep the learner interested, find out learner's background, and prepare for instruction.
2. Determine what must be taught and decide how much to teach.
3. Maintain records of training in order to know how much has been taught and which person has been taught what by whom.

Orientation of New Officers

This phase of training tells each new employee what is expected of them and also what the employee expects (feedback). Orientation also provides an overview of job requirements and tasks.

On-the-Job Training Phase

In this phase, remember the following:

1. Explain and demonstrate the steps of each job.
2. Make sure employee comprehends!
3. Document training by completing forms to show all areas that have been covered and taught, and have them signed by the employee.

Equipment

Another integral aspect of a security officer's training is his or her knowledge of equipment. There is a wide variety of equipment that the security officer must be able to handle at any given moment. Flashlights, radios, and first-aid equipment are all indispensable to any security job. Metal detectors can be very important in helping to ensure that weapons do not enter the premises. Specific, documented instruction should be given on each piece of equipment to be used during both routine and emergency conditions.

Sports Security: An Emerging Aspect of Special Event Protection

Today's sports and entertainment industries are multibillion dollar enterprises. Make no mistake, sport marketers are paying close attention to where security fits within their operation's parameters and organization's structure. The proper and effective supervision of sporting events is a key component to any successful security operation. However, significant security challenges exist, which keep industry professionals constantly searching for better results. Risk mitigation and brand protection are two prevailing themes on which ownership groups are focusing. Some of the current challenges facing the sports event management security industry include the following:

1. The Need for Highly Trained Security Staff

The unfortunate reality is that most security personnel, especially those entrusted with providing protection at large stadiums and venues, are not properly compensated for their experience and services. Depending on whether the officer is part-time, full-time, and/or contracted by an outside agency, the potential for employee turnover can be somewhat higher than most ownership groups care to admit.

There is one rule of thumb in the sports security industry—the 1:250 rule—which generally states that for every 250 patrons, there should be 1 highly trained security staff member. Sports marketers do not always follow this rule because their goal may be more financial in nature. As the old expression goes, "If it ain't broke, don't fix it." However, this is where the real problems can potentially come to light. Security is not a reactionary discipline. To make an impact on safety, security procedures can be more effective when planned well in advance. Pre-event and post-event meetings are key components to any successful security operation's game plan. Security directors would be well served by taking the necessary steps to properly train, motivate, and educate their staff. Providing staff with the necessary skills, knowledge, equipment, and direction from management can make a monumental difference in their job performance while they are representing the parent or client organization.

The key is to have security staff ready to react efficiently and effectively in the event of a security breach. There is no substitute for training as this is an ongoing, continuing, active learning process. Training instills knowledge, which places the ownership group in the best position possible—a position of exercising control over the sporting environment. This can help reduce inherent liabilities and risks associated with the operation of such entities, while providing for a safe, enjoyable, and secure environment for sports patrons.

2. The Emergence of Drone Technologies

Major League Baseball has seen increased security challenges with the advent of drone technology. Drone "flyovers" at open baseball stadiums has caused great concern with how league officials and security personnel are addressing this challenge. Security protocols and procedures are constantly being tweaked to handle such scenarios. New threats will evolve with drones, along with new applications. For example, some college athletic programs use drones to film linesmen for proper stance and player position—a positive, productive use of drone technologies.

The use of drones for filming events, such as making marketing videos, etc. will only grow and develop over time. The positive and negative aspects of drones will have to be managed on several levels. Federal regulations, such as those from the US Federal Aviation Administration, play a role, as do regulations at other governmental organizations. Facility managers will also be involved in managing drone usage in some manner. Drones are a game changer for security at all facilities. Those that involve large groups of people congregating outdoors, such as at stadiums, are more acutely affected by the proliferation of drone technology. Protection professionals will need to continually educate their subordinates on drone security issues and countermeasures.

3. Information Sharing and Coordination with First Responders

The coordination of efforts with emergency management, fire departments, and law enforcement agencies is yet another key to mitigating inherent risks associated with operating sports venues. Security training and communication are integral to establishing strong relationships between law enforcement and venue personnel. The importance of tabletop exercises, dry runs, and simulation software, especially with respect to evacuations and fire drills within venues, cannot be underscored. "**Plan, test, review**" must be the mantra of sports security professionals.

Paying close attention to the ingress/egress, landscape, and the creation of a safe inner/outer perimeter by effectively controlling these areas, is essential for patron protection. Establishing direct, clear lines of communications with first responders should be a top priority in any security operations plan. Crisis plans need to be in place in the event of an emergency situation, such as for an active shooter, bomb threat, hostage/barricade, inclement weather, drone attack, earthquake, power outage, and cybersecurity attack, just to name a few. Knowing the location of the incident command post is essential information for security staff and first responders.

The public information officer (PIO) should be entrusted by ownership to be well versed in handling requests from the media, many of which can be at a stadium during an event. The PIO must keep the media fed at all times. This creates and maintains positive relations with the media and so lessens the impact when the defecation hits the air conditioning. The situation may unfold rapidly, and a well-prepared PIO should be immediately available.

4. The Impact of Social Media

Social media platforms are certainly prevalent in contemporary society. Facebook, Linke-dIn, Pinterest, Google Hangout, Skype, and YouTube are all aimed at rapid dissemination of information to the masses. From a security and safety standpoint, paying close attention to what is posted online can save lives. Any effective security program should have highly trained, tech-savvy personnel on hand to effectively monitor various platforms. This may be done internally or outsourced to a specialized firm.

The utilization of handheld technologies by fans is another area of concern. Each and every fan with a handheld device becomes a reporter. Security staff need to closely monitor all activities, especially prior to an event taking place. Knowing in advance where the potential challenges, threats, and vulnerabilities may come from places security personnel in a strong position to thwart these problems in advance. This can help security staff deter acts of civil disobedience and violence before they occur.

5. Brand Protection: Risk Mitigation and Patron Protection

If there is a negative situation at a venue, fans will shy away from spending their hard-earned dollars on attending events, concerts, shows, etc. Therefore, brand and subsequent consumer behavior could be adversely affected. From a marketing perspective, advertising dollars will disappear quite quickly, thus affecting profit margins. Security officials need not instill a sense of fear, but they should take every opportunity to heighten awareness by educating patrons to be more acutely aware of their physical surroundings. Fans can play a more active role in bolstering their safety by following the mantra of "see something, say something." Patrons need to effectively convey their concerns to security staff and guest services so that problems can be averted, prevented, or de-escalated.

Negligent actions are a serious source of loss. Stadiums and sports teams have lost multimillion dollar judgments for violence outbreaks. Staffing levels are key here. Inadequate security staffing has been cited as a contributing factor in court decisions favoring the plaintiffs. Fair wages, compensation, and proper training for security personnel go hand in hand with reducing employee turnover. Ownership groups, because of these unfortunate incidents, are paying closer attention to the importance of security as a spoke in the proverbial wheel within their respective business models.

Sports security is rapidly becoming a significant niche market within the sports and entertainment industries. Following the Boston Marathon bombing, the stakes could not be any higher with respect to properly protecting patrons at sporting venues and stadiums. Sport stadiums and venues are critical components of the economic infrastructure of many countries. They are also prime targets for terrorist groups, both domestic and international, looking to make an impact and get their message out.

The National Center for Spectator Sports, Safety, and Security (NCS4) has received funding from the US Department of Homeland Security and is affiliated with the University of Southern Mississippi. NCS4 is an outstanding group of committed security and safety professionals dedicated to the ongoing research, proper training, and career development of sports security professionals. They have developed a professional certification process for sports security professionals and also hold an annual conference.

Preparing for a special event is a considerable undertaking. Persons with supervisory responsibility who are involved in asset protection must approach this task in a serious manner. The supervisor should be detailed, thorough, and flexible in his or her approach. Continuous professional growth is strongly recommended. Constant checking of personnel performance is required. Nothing can be left to chance when providing protection at a special event.

Emerging Trends

Acting as a liaison between protective organizations has always been a key component of special event security. For example, the Super Bowl has more than 50 different organizations involved in protecting the event. America's oldest fair, the York Fair in Pennsylvania, has its own police force, deputy sheriffs, local police, contract security, district attorney's office investigators, and probation officers involved, as well as private investigators dealing with product counterfeiting and state safety inspectors for the rides. With the concern over terrorism driving increased participation by military and public law enforcement organizations, the coordination of efforts will become even more complex. An added factor is the rise in outsourced security functions, which is only likely to expand. Services will be provided to arenas, stadiums, concert halls, and museums that are not being provided today.

Weather is a major challenge in special events. Rapidly changing severe weather conditions make carefully developed plans a necessity. A layered approach to weather has several different sources for receiving weather reports and various people checking those sources. At the bottom of the system is the lone protection officer, who must check weather several times daily and be especially vigilant in the hours leading up to the event.

Legal and industry standards are evolving. Regulation of crowds of shoppers is moving forward, both within professional associations such as the National Retail Federation and in municipalities that are concerned with shoppers being crushed during sales promotions. So too is the regulation as to security providers. The days of unlicensed agencies providing security at special events are drawing to a close.

There is a nexus between retail loss prevention and special event security. Special events are often held in retail stores or shopping centers. These events may vary considerably, ranging from appearances by celebrities, to sales promotions, to classes given to customers. At the same time, many special event venues, such as stadiums, arenas, and concert halls, have retail operations within them. Professional educational programs need a retail component within them in order to be complete.

Special events present an ideal environment for problems to occur. The risks are many and the negative publicity potential is steadily increasing. For example, a corporation holding a Christmas party requires a security presence to maintain order and decorum, so they contract with a service provider. As a result, specialized contract security firms have emerged to fill this market niche. Staffing is often done with a corps of individuals who are supplemented with off-duty police, off-duty probation officers, and the like. Sometimes, staff is recruited from other security forces or athletic teams ("t-shirt security").

Training and professionalism are key components of special event security. There is a greater need for more training on even more topics than in the past. Also, there can be no shortcuts taken in regard to training, screening, or any other aspect of human resources simply because the protection staff is temporary. Training organizations, such as Smart Horizons, will play a role in providing the necessary coursework.

As employment opportunities grow in special event security, so must the approaches taken to secure that employment. Experience is key! Gaining that experience through internships, apprenticeships, part-time jobs, or summer employment is a necessity.

Working for organizations involved with special event security can be a great career builder, providing job experience, training, and networking opportunities. Research into both proprietary organizations and contract agencies is important for career planning purposes.

There has also been a growth in personal protection specialists (PPS) being used by celebrities and professional athletes. Having close protection while at autograph sessions and the like is now common. PPS is part and parcel of special event security; both specialties overlap in many instances. Fully understanding the relationship of PPS to protection at special events is crucial to both operational and career success. Coursework and experience in PPS is a logical component of career development in special event security. Commensurate with this is the growth in hospitality management and sports management programs at colleges and universities.

On the service provider side, event planning and event management has grown into having a very large presence on LinkedIn, through which they address the multifaceted needs of special event planners. Clearly, there is a growing emphasis on providing entertainment, hospitality, and superior service in both academia and the corporate world. This is largely reflective of the experiential marketing era, where giving the customer the best experience possible is the primary goal.

Special event security will continue to grow and develop. There will be more career opportunities available for the highly motivated, and those working in special event security will have be on their "A game."

Refer website http://www.ifpo.org for further information

Further Reading

1. Bishop P. C., "Crowd Control Management and Procedures," in *Protection Officer Training Manual*, eds. Davies S. J. and Minion R. R. (Boston: Butterworth-Heinemann, 1998).
2. Davies J. and Minion R.R., eds. *Protection Officer Training Manual* (Boston: Butterworth-Heinemann, 1998).

3. Estes D. S., "Supervision and Training," in *Security Supervisor Training Manual*, eds. Davies S. J. and Minion R. R. (Boston: Butterworth-Heinemann, 1995).

4. Hertig C.A., "Supervisor's Role in Training," in *Security Supervisor Training Manual*, eds. Davies S. J. and Minion R. R. (Boston: Butterworth-Heinemann, 1995).

5. Hertig C. A., "Keep Your Guards Posted," *Security Management*, (June 1985): 65–66.

6. Holm A. A., "Traffic Control Procedures," in *Protection Officer Training Manual*, eds. Davies S. J. and Minion R. R. (Boston: Butterworth-Heinemann, 1998).

7. Millsaps M. J., *The F.A.S.T. Approach. Protection News* (Spring, 1998).

8. Poulin K. C., *Special Events: Avoiding the Disaster* (Florida: International Foundation for Protection Officers, 1992).

9. Purpura P., *Security and Loss Prevention* (Boston: Butterworth-Heinemann, 1991).

10. Tyo K., "Olympic Security: A Crowd Management Interview," *Crowd Management*, (1996, January–March): 6–11.

11. Sherwood C.W., "Security Management for a Major Event," *Security Management*, (August 1998): 9–16.

12. Task Force on Crowd Control and Safety, *Crowd management: Report on the Task Force on Crowd Control and Safety* (September 29, 1998). http://www.crowdsafe.com.

13. Diane Ritchey, *Balancing Security and the Fan Experience in Sports Security Entertaining the public is a unique animal* (July 1, 2014): Retrieved November 9, 2014. http://www.securitymagazine.com/articles/85610-balancing-security-and-the-fan-experience-in-sports-security?v=preview.

14. Andrew Brandt C, *Drones Causing Chaos at Sporting Events Worldwide* (October 2014): Retrieved November 8, 2014. http://www.athleticbusiness.com/event-security/drones-security.html?topic=6,400&eid=244063953&bid=947325.

13

Training and Development: A Primer for Protection Professionals

Christopher A. Hertig, Daniel R. Baker, Charles T. Thibodeau,
Ted Wade, Fern Abbott

Defining Training

Implementing productive learning programs is a responsibility shared by security managers, supervisors, training instructors, and faculty at educational institutions. To achieve this is not a simple undertaking. "Learning never stops" is an appropriate motto for those involved in the design and delivery of instructional programs related to security and asset protection. This chapter will address the major strategies, tactics, and challenges faced within the instructional field. It will primarily be from the perspective of the training instructor or security supervisor.

When people think of training, they envision teaching or instruction. They think of lectures, videos, training exercises, "showing a new employee the ropes," and quizzes or tests. Generally speaking, most view training in a very limited manner, by one of its segments or components, instead of the total process that it is.

Sometimes people equate training with classes held on a particular topic; in other cases, they think of it as learning and practicing a particular skill. While all of these activities are indeed training, they are merely components of the training process. Training can be thought of as a learning process where someone is taught a skill or knowledge that enables him or her to perform a job function. It incorporates various teaching and learning methods, and involves significant amounts of practice. In addition, training is always tested or validated in some manner.

Most people believe that a single well-intentioned learning episode will have a significant impact on job performance because they want to believe it, but the common mistake of believing that learning has occurred due to a single learning experience (a class, a meeting, an orientation session, etc.) should be avoided. The astute trainer/supervisor/manager knows that job performance improvement requires not only effort, but repeated and continual reinforcement, such as periodic in-service instruction, recertification, drills or scenarios, individual reading or research, and attending classes on the topic. The more separate, yet integrated, the learning episodes are, the greater is the likelihood that learning has occurred. The effective supervisor should know how to integrate training activities into a comprehensive learning system. By doing this, positive changes in job behavior are far more likely to result.

Security Supervision and Management. http://dx.doi.org/10.1016/B978-0-12-800113-4.00013-4

Benefits of Training

The benefits of training must be examined prior to embarking on an expensive, time-consuming training and development process. To ensure the greatest return on instructional dollars, both the benefits and costs must be understood. Some of the beneficial effects of training are as follows:

- Increased job efficiency when specific job tasks are performed better and faster, thereby reducing manpower costs.
- Improved relations between employees and management, as the employee better understands management perspective—a crucial element in security operations. Communication and teamwork are enhanced when personnel participate in a common learning experience. This also enhances professional identity among protection officers, who see positive growth within themselves.[1]
- Pride and job satisfaction; having successfully completed a training assignment.
- Increased loyalty to the employer, who has shown an interest in employees by training them.
- Decreased turnover, as there are fewer situations that make the officers feel uncomfortable and incompetent. This is a crucial point for younger personnel, who may be easily discouraged by failures.
- Fewer mistakes and fewer accidents.
- Improved discretionary judgment, with better decisions being made by personnel.
- Protection from allegations that management is negligent in preparing personnel to do their jobs.

Three Domains of Learning

It is important to realize that there are three domains of training: cognitive, psychomotor, and affective. A balanced training program will contain all three. The cognitive training domain is most often taught in a classroom prior to the officer being assigned to a post; this is usually known as pre-assignment training.

- **Cognitive learning** is the mental action or process of acquiring knowledge and understanding through thought, experience, and the senses. It is usually presented using lectures, demonstrations, video, illustrations, readings, tutorial examinations, and homework.
- **Psychomotor learning** is the hands-on part of the training process. It is often taught at the job site and consists of such things as facility orientation, patrol techniques, equipment training, emergency response, defensive tactics, and interviewing.
- **Affective domain learning** covers work values and professional attitudes. The danger here is that values are automatically and inadvertently being taught by everyone, all the time. The way people dress, their mannerisms, their statements about race, religion, sex—everything they say or do is constantly being communicated.

The audience, comprised of those that are communicated with (as well as uninvited listeners) are subjected to and influenced by values and attitudes whether they want to be or not, especially if the listener has great respect for the teachers, instructors, or trainers.

It is important for the instructor to be aware of effective training and to include some specific work-related values and attitudes in both the cognitive and psychomotor lesson plans. The way these values and attitudes are delivered is different from the cognitive and psychomotor training. Values and attitudes are not taught as separate subjects but are linked to the other two types of learning. Trainers must be prepared to inject the appropriate value or attitude whenever the opportunity presents itself. They must ensure that nothing in the instructional experience detracts from or contradicts these standards. Finally, the trainer should model the values, attitudes, and ethical standards being taught.

Learning over Time

- *Short-term learning* is a positive change in knowledge, skill, ability or attitude.
- *Retention* is the degree to which the knowledge, skill, or attitude is maintained over time.
- *Transfer* is how effectively the knowledge, skill, or attitude is put to use in the work environment. It is what educational and training programs strive for.
- *Reinforcement* of learning is most likely to increase retention and transfer. Reinforcement can come from planned instructionaltactics such as drills, refresher training, etc. It can also come from workplace socialization—the process of learning values, attitudes, and methods of job performance fromco-workers and supervisors.

All components of the employee's learning must be carefully assessed, planned and coordinated. Each learning episode (class, reading, work experience, pre-shift briefing, etc.) must be coordinated toward fulfilling the overall training objectives. For this reason, the training program must have a designated administrator or coordinator.

Determining Training Needs

Determining what areas security personnel need training in is the key to successful, cost-effective training. Training is wasted if it is used to solve problems that training cannot correct, such as *inadequate equipment, inadequate resources, or inappropriate job design.* Training cannot, by itself, serve to motivate personnel, nor can it solve other problems unrelated to the development of knowledge, skills, or abilities. To accurately assess training needs, it is first necessary to review the situation at hand. This will identify problems, causes, and possible approaches to addressing the situation without plunging into an expensive, time-consuming training endeavor. Some simple questions to ask in this regard are as follows:

- What is the job performance problem?
- Is the problem a result of inadequate skill or knowledge on the part of security personnel?
- Can the lack of knowledge or skill deficiency be corrected?

- Can the lack of knowledge or skill deficiency be corrected without adding new training or retraining staff on existing subjects?
- After exhausting options other than training or retraining, does the problem still exist?

Once the problem is identified (or problems, if more than one) and all other answers to the above questions are ruled out, training is the answer that remains. This leads to a new question: how does a security department develop a training program?

FOOD FOR THOUGHT

There is a high rate of turnover by contract security personnel at a client's site. Absenteeism is also a problem. Training is minimal, as officers are not there long enough to complete anything other than a 4-Hour orientation program. The client is considering changing security service firms. How should addressing this problem proceed from the standpoint of the supervisor in charge of the account?

Initiating Curriculum Design

The first step for designing a curriculum requires that a determination be made regarding what the organization desires the students to be able to accomplish once the training is completed. This design step forces the designer to know exactly what must be taught. It also incorporates all the tasks within a duty to be viewed from the job as a whole. For example, the unit of instruction might be "Provide Entry Control" within a course entitled *Foundations of Security Practices*. All of the tasks or units of training for the course come from a comprehensive job description. In developing specific curriculum, the designer uses all of the learning domains: the cognitive domain for theory and general knowledge; psychomotor domain for demonstrated skills requiring use of the hands in performing tasks; and the affective domain for interpersonal, intrapersonal, or value-oriented skills. The instructional goal may be derived from the following:

- A listing of overall goals of the school, course, or unit of study.
- A needs assessment: what really needs to be taught; the gap between what is being done and what must be done on the job.
- Practical experience: the commonsense approach to curriculum development. An external view may be insightful at this juncture.
- Analyzing how the job is already being accomplished. Job task analysis, surveys of job incumbents, review of reports, video, logs, etc.

Instructional Analysis

The next step for designing curriculum is conducting an instructional analysis. This is the process that happens after identifying the instructional goal. To accomplish it, one needs to know what type of learning is required on the part of the student. It requires the curriculum designer to perform a comprehensive analysis to accomplish the following:

- Identify subordinate skills that must be learned.
- Determine subordinate procedural steps that must be followed to learn a particular process, skill, ability, or performance.
- Create a chart or diagram that depicts required skills and shows relationships among them.

Identify Entry Behavior Characteristics

Next, the entry behaviors and characteristics that will be required of those participating in the training program must be identified. Every course of instruction has a minimum level of competency that must be met. For security, it is normal to require the applicant to be at least 18 years old, have no history of alcohol or drug abuse, and have no felony convictions. These are all entry-level behaviors or characteristics required for employment. But more than these, security applicants should be able to read and write in the language used within the company, exercise sound judgment, communicate effectively, and demonstrate the ability to control their emotions under stress. These entry-level behaviors and characteristics are normally required to enter a program and successfully complete it.

Entry-level behaviors and characteristics are not simply a listing of what the student can do; they also specify what is required of the student to participate in the learning process. These required behaviors and characteristics identify particular characteristic of the student that may be important to consider in the design of a specific curriculum.

Writing Performance Objectives

One cannot have a curriculum that has no performance objective. A performance objective tells the trainer and the trainee what will be expected of them. Written performance objectives are based on the instructional analysis, incorporation of specific entry behaviors and characteristics, and are specific statements of what the learner will be able to do upon completion of the course of study, unit of instruction, or task training. All written performance objectives should identify the following:

- The knowledge, abilities, or skills to be learned and the task to be accomplished.
- The conditions under which the knowledge, ability, or skill must be performed, and what will be provided to the student to complete the action required.
- The criteria or standards for successful performance.

An example of a written performance objective would be, "Upon completion of this chapter each security supervisor taking participation will be provided with a pencil, paper, and a desk, and write one performance objective for a psychomotor task to the satisfaction of the test examiner." The performance objective has a clear statement of the knowledge, ability, or skill that has to be mastered: "write one performance objective." It has two clearly stated conditions: "Upon completion of this course of study" and "provided pencil, paper, and a desk." Finally, it has a measurement statement: "to the satisfaction of the test examiner." The standard for successful performance could be "without error," or "a score of 85%," or "list six out of 10 approaches to curriculum design," etc. Simply put, it must have a statement that the students can use to know exactly how they will be evaluated.

Develop Performance Objective Test Criteria

Once the performance objectives have been identified, they must be validated. Validating is best accomplished by creating a performance-referenced test, based only on the performance objectives specified in curriculum development. To that end, the performance-referenced test is written before any lesson plans or reference materials are used in a course of study or training program. It is the formal evaluation instrument that will be used to measure the learner's accomplishment of the specified requirements for successful completion of the competency.

If the performance objective says the learner will write, the performance test question will require writing. Using the previously stated performance objective, the test question will be a statement: "Write a performance objective for a psychomotor skill." The directions for the accomplishment of this test item might be, "You will be provided with a pencil or pen, paper, a desk, and time to accomplish the task; each student will write a performance objective for a psychomotor skill to the test examiner's satisfaction." The test examiner then must be a subject-matter expert in the construction and evaluation of performance objectives. This will ensure that the measurement standard is objective and not subjective.

Implement an Instructional Strategy

Once a curriculum has been developed and the means to validate it are present (the tests), the final step is to identify the means by which the training will be delivered. The curriculum developer(s) must begin to make choices on the instructional style or strategy that will be used to facilitate learning. There are four primary strategies that can be used in curriculum development:

1. **Instructor-centered learning.** The instructor provides the information to the student and evaluates performance. This is personnel intensive and normally occurs in a lockstep model (every learner learns at the same rate). It does not account for learner differences.
2. **Individual-centered learning.** A plan is developed between the learner and the instructor (supervisor, manager, faculty member) on what is to be learned, how long the student will take to accomplish the learning, to what level the learning will be measured, and how. This is most effective with self-motivated individuals.
3. **Interactively centered learning.** The learner interacts with the environment by verbalizing learning, participating in discussion groups, or demonstrating competencies. This method of curriculum design incorporates case studies, panel discussions, and real-time demonstrations in the learning activities.

4. **Experiential-centered learning.** A process that incorporates cognitive, psychomotor, and affective learning in field or clinical settings. The experiential approach places the student on the job while at the same time requiring ancillary learning by study, drill and practice, and evaluation. Experiential learning is considered the best type of learning because it marries theory with practice. Internships, work study, apprenticeships, and projects or drills are all experiential learning.

In determining the instruction style or strategy to be used in the development of curriculum, the security educator utilizes each of the previous steps. The educator develops a timetable for all pre-instructional activities that must be accomplished, selects the method or methods in which the material to be mastered will be presented, designates methods to test and identify testing material needs, and determines how student feedback will be gathered.

Types of Training

Lectures are often used as an instructional technique. They can be effective or ineffective, depending upon the circumstances, such as the presentation topic, enthusiasm of the instructor, whether the lecture is supplemented with video, etc. Trainers must bear in mind that adults do not like to be lectured; they must instead be informed and stimulated. It is also worth note that attention spans are very limited, possibly due to all the high-stimulation digital media and electronic devices, etc. that people have become accustomed to. The following are a few things to remember to keep lectures effective:

- Keep lectures as short and to the point as possible.
- Lecture to establish a common base of knowledge when this base does not exist. Pre-instructional assessments can aid with this.
- Use visuals as much as possible, as most people are visual learners—video clips are good in this regard. Such clips should be short (not more than 10 min). TED Talks are a good model to follow as they are visual, fast paced, and stimulating.
- Use lectures to assess the learners, what they know, and how they feel about certain topics. Adults like to discuss their opinions.
- Only use lectures to make two or three points at a time; more information causes overload and learners blank out the learning.
- Reinforce lectures with active learning such as scenario exercises, discussions, and short tests. This changes the pace and requires application of the material being taught.
- Organize the lecture using the same format as a letter: an introduction, main body, and closing that reiterates key points. A simple way of remembering this in an instructional setting is:
  - Tell them what you are going to tell them.
  - Tell them.
  - Tell them what you told them.

Demonstration is an essential instructional technique for teaching proficiency areas, such as equipment use, interviewing, defensive tactics, firefighting, etc. To demonstrate effectively, the following points should be borne in mind:

- Explain what will be demonstrated beforehand.
- Make sure everyone can see.
- Make eye contact with everyone during the demonstration.
- Demonstrate the entire task so that visual learners can grasp what is to be done in a single demonstration.
- Use video if possible to ensure uniformity and documentation of the process to be demonstrated. Video also ensures that the whole class can see the procedure being performed.
- Have the class practice the skill at a slow, easy pace and then refine their proficiency.

Coaching or tutoring is also vital for supervisors because it is the essence of supervision. Coaching or tutoring can be done in a variety of situations on the job. A few ideas to be borne in mind include the following:

- Select the appropriate learning method (reading assignments, incident review, online course, research project, etc.) for the learner and for what is being taught.
- Be flexible and use multiple learning strategies; look for the opportunity to do so.
- Build on prior learning; however do not make assumptions about prior knowledge. Instructors cannot get frustrated if the trainee does not know what he or she is expected to know.
- Be patient. Not everyone learns at the same rate or in the same manner.

Role of Supervisory Personnel in Training

Orienting new employees, whether within the security department or other departments, is a function commonly performed by supervisors. This creates opportunities for security departments to teach new employees what is expected of them.[2] Orientation is an important part of that process. It combines the selection, training, and socialization aspects of the employment relationship. Supervisors should make the most of it by doing the following:

- Spread out the learning as much as possible. While the major block of instruction may best be covered in a single day, avoiding learner overload and building upon the initial session is essential.
- Instruct in the history and philosophy of the organization. *Effective socialization* of the employee over the long run is possible, when the officer has the foundation of knowledge to form understanding. An additional benefit may be that officers become a more positive representative for their organization and profession.
- Keep the sessions dynamic and ever-changing; use a variety of instructional techniques.
- Help the employee create a personal bond to people within the organization by introducing him or her to people such as mentors, supervisors, and upper-level

managers. Note that sometimes inviting upper-level managers to meet new employees can elevate the visibility of the security department.
- Prepare the new officer for orientation by informing him or her as to time, place, topics, and what to expect in terms of dress, deportment, and activities—reduce the amount of uncomfortable situations the new hire might be exposed to.

In many cases, supervisors are called upon to teach in-service classes. These can be brutal for both the teacher and students. While much of the information concerning overcoming resistance to training is relevant to in-service instruction, the following considerations are essential:

- Get feedback from the officers as to what they want to learn. Surveys of staff can provide some unique insight and prevent unnecessary effort and expense.
- Become an expert—do research and make it interesting by informing them of things they may not already know.
- Use different instructors—outside experts, personnel from other departments, and security officers.
- Keep the presentation moving with exercises and different activities. (This is especially important after lunch.)

On-the-job training (OJT) must be provided or overseen by security supervisors or managers, and it must be delivered in a professional manner via a mentor or field training officer (FTO) arrangement. OJT can be effective if it is structured and presented in a manner that is easy to understand, without oversimplifying or talking down to the employee. The mentor or FTO should have received specialized training, such as a train-the-trainer course, prior to delivering training. This ensures that the instructor is teaching in a professional manner and not simply misleading the learner with bad attitudes or habits. OJT must be a priority. It should be delivered in a structured, organized manner using the following techniques:

- Preface the learning by preceding the OJT with a classroom session and/or individual learning experience (e.g., a video) or relevant reading material (e.g., a training manual).
- Explain and demonstrate each job step.
- Demonstrate each job step while the employee explains the process.
- Have the employee demonstrate and explain each task.
- Document the training by having a form signed that lists all areas (procedures, equipment, and locations) that have been covered.
- Follow up the learning by having in-service sessions, drills, etc.

Job aids can be an effective method of reducing training costs while at the same time increasing job proficiency. Simply put, a job aid is an instruction or direction on how to do something. It can be a sign on a piece of equipment; it may be a procedural manual; it could be a sign or memo that serves as a reminder. Safety posters and posters reminding people of information security procedures are other examples of job aids. Whatever the form a job aid takes, there are several tips to remember about making them effective:

- Keep sentences short and to the point.
- List steps to be followed.
- Leave space around each sentence so that it is easy to read.
- Use a plain type style.
- The job aids should be accessible, convenient, and user friendly in every respect.

A mentoring program is where a senior employee guides and assists a new worker on the job. In the past, this involved merely pairing a new officer with a more senior one who "showed them the ropes." This approach often resulted in the new employee absorbing negative traits of the older worker. Mentoring is different because it is more structured. Mentoring should always involve special training and instruction for the mentor. A few things to bear in mind concerning mentoring programs are as follows:

- Select a mentor that the new employee should emulate.
- Provide the mentor with additional special training and education so that he or she may act as an effective coach.
- Introduce the new officer to the mentor at an early stage in the employment relationship, such as at orientation.
- Mentors should be easily approachable by trainees.
- Mentors must be good teachers who enjoy passing along their knowledge.
- Mentors should be able to give the new employee exposure within the organization.

Failing to Get It Right

Liability for failure to train may be imposed upon supervisors who have training as part of their responsibilities. Although liability exposure involving organizations and/or the individual supervisors who work for them is more common in settings where the security staff carry weapons, it is a potential risk at any time. As security personnel assume more tasks and have greater responsibility to the public, the potential for liability increases. Accordingly, along with adequate training, *practice* and *documentation* of that training are now essential. A less obvious but also common scenario involves potential liability for personnel who are not adequately instructed on how to use emergency equipment or who are expected to provide emergency services. A simple method of uncovering liability exposure in this area is to ask the following questions:

- What duty does the subordinate security staff owe to the employer, clients, visitors, etc.? What types of reasonably foreseeable emergencies do the protection officers respond to?
- What specific functions are they expected to perform during emergencies?
- What types of equipment/weapons can they be expected to use in emergencies?

Evaluation of Learning

The final stage in developing instructional programs is the evaluation process. There are two types of evaluations: *formative* and *normative*. Formative evaluations are conducted prior to testing the curriculum, and the first normative evaluation provides a baseline for further comparisons with follow-ups on students or classes. These evaluations are conducted constantly to ensure that the curriculum is accomplishing its goal (or goals) and keeps it current.

Formative evaluation is initiated upon completion of draft instructional materials. It may be accomplished in one of three ways: a one-to-one consultation with another subject-matter expert; evaluation by a small group of training professionals who specialize in the curriculum designed; field evaluations if the material is time critical or sensitive.

Normative evaluation is based on some level of acceptable standard. How many days, hours, or questions may be missed for the student to still pass or complete the course? Should the student be able to accomplish the task with no supervision, some supervision, or while closely supervised? What are the accepted tolerances? Must the task be accomplished without error or, as indicated, in some other manner? Normative evaluations should be objective and not subjective. When dealing with theory or cognitive material, there should be a written test. The demonstration of a skill requires application in a real work scenario and effective skills are evaluated when the learner models acceptable behaviors.

Both formative and normative evaluations are the first steps in redesigning a curriculum in the systems approach for designing a curriculum. They identify difficulties experienced by the learner, based on the successful or unsuccessful accomplishment of performance objectives. Formative and normative evaluations identify deficiencies in instruction and ultimately attest to the worth of the curriculum design. They are used to validate the effect, efficiency, and cost-effectiveness of the educational process. Formative evaluations are conducted best when someone outside the organization reviews all the material to measure suitability and the accomplishment of stated competency goals. Both evaluations should be based on quality, not quantity. Some simplified evaluation methods that can be implemented in either the formative or normative types of instruction include the following:

- Have learners evaluate the training via a predesigned form or by simply asking them to describe their perceptions regarding the program. However, filling out "happy sheets" usually only measures student happiness with the program rather than retention.
- Use an employee questionnaire before and after training that assesses the perception of employees regarding security force professionalism. This may provide a metric for the effectiveness of the program on the "public's" perception.
- Analyze incident frequency and severity before and after training to determine if training had a positive effect on how the officers handled incidents.
- Analyze incident handling times to see if the amount of time needed to respond to a problem decreased after training.
- Use off-the-shelf instructional programs that contain testing instruments. This can reduce or eliminate the complex, time-consuming task of designing tests. If the subject matter is generic in nature, off-the-shelf programs are generally cost-effective.

Another method of evaluating training is through the use of supervisory anecdotes. These are observations that supervisors make concerning job performance following a training program or session. Anecdotes are simple to use and must be done anyway to evaluate how the new employee is performing on the job. Instructors must not focus too much on anecdotes or "war stories"; however, an anecdote that relates specifically to the subject being taught is valuable as it provides a real-life example. A few things to bear in mind about supervisory anecdotes are:

- They must be completely objective and not tarnished by the opinions of other supervisors or preconceived notions of the supervisors making them.
- Supervisors should have substantial input into training design so that competition, jealousy, and general ill-will do not develop between trainers—who may not be supervisors—and the supervisors on staff.
- Use written questionnaires to evaluate so that all observations must be articulated clearly. The written questionnaires can evolve over time to collect key data and quantify it.

Testing for Learning Retention

The security supervisor may not be a certified classroom trainer, but he or she is clearly responsible for supervising on-the-job training for security officers and possibly also for selecting formal training courses. The security supervisor is responsible for ensuring that security officers attend formal training that is relevant, assures short-term learning from the classroom experience, and provides long-term retention of that learning.

Once the subject matter of the training has been selected (typically by corporate management or the training department), the security supervisor may be in a position to recommend a vendor or provider for the training. Because the subject matter has been predecided, the supervisor's choices are limited to the way in which the vendor guarantees that learning will take place and how long it will last. This discussion relates to one method for providing that assurance: an in-depth testing program.

To demonstrate that short-term learning has taken place, the individual must take a pretest and posttest on the subject matter and achieve more correct answers on the posttest than on the pretest. At the conclusion of the training, the security officer should be able to demonstrate sufficient short-term learning to indicate that the learning experience was worthwhile.

To demonstrate that long-term retention of the learning has taken place, the individual must take a posttest on the subject matter after a suitable period of time, say 6–12 months. More correct answers must be achieved than on the original pretest and almost as many correct answers as on the original posttest, with the implication being that sufficient learning took place during the training experience to have become internalized and available to be built upon with further training.

The in-depth testing program described above is not typical of most training programs because of the additional cost involved. This does not mean that the testing concept should be abandoned; it means that the security supervisor must demonstrate his or her ingenuity by establishing such a testing program on the job. Actually, this is not too difficult a chore for a good security supervisor who oversees an on-the-job training program.

Remember, the initial pretest and posttest are the same, but given at different times. To avoid the security officers becoming "test-aware", the security supervisor should consider an "observational" type of test, with a checklist containing all the activities that the security officer should be performing that directly relate to the training, and observe the extent to which those activities are being performed.

Training is essential if performance is to be enhanced to any appreciable degree. Unfortunately, the process of training is complex. It is, on its face, cost prohibitive if not implemented creatively and managed well. Regardless, there remain some common misperceptions involving the training of protection officers. Managed well, training dilemmas can be avoided or mitigated.

Challenges in Training

Although many security supervisors are enthusiastic about training, love to teach, and think of training in positive terms, there are sometimes problems involved in the design, development, and implementation of training that must be addressed. If not addressed, these problems may render training ineffective, serve to demoralize personnel, and may even cause budgetary problems.

Perhaps the worst (and most) dilemma that can befall training is that training just does not happen. This is both an obvious operational dilemma as well as an ethical lapse on the part of supervisors/managers, who have a duty to adequately train their subordinates. Budget restrictions are perhaps the most common problem in security officer training. Most organizations devote very few resources to training security personnel; some spend nothing at all. There are various approaches to take when addressing this problem:

- Hire personnel with as much training as possible. This does not ensure a properly trained protection force, but it may address the issue to some degree because highly trained people either have the specific job skills or can adapt.
- Attempt to have other departments within the organization provide instruction. This can include topics such as customer service, time management, safety, business writing, etc. These topics are certainly of value to security officers, and having officers attend internal training can be a very low-cost option. An additional benefit is the integration of the security department into the larger organization.
- Use distance education. Correspondence courses are one approach. While distance education (where the teacher and learner are distant from each other) is not cost-free, it consumes far less overhead such as overtime, travel, meals, and lodging costs, etc. It also bypasses the hurdle of scheduling a class and getting all officers into one class at the same time. This can be an even more important consideration when security officers or loss prevention agents are part-time, have work varying schedules, or are geographically dispersed.

Distance education encompasses several methods, from correspondence study to internet courses to having officers use video or audio tapes. Online learning communities can be established or joined. Staff members can communicate via e-mails. A very simple use of distance education is to have officers read policies and procedures on their own, and then answer questions developed by the supervisor on completion, by essay or fill-in-the-blank format. Such an approach eliminates costly classroom time spent going over mundane items that the can officer has access on his or her own. It can be incorporated into computerized instructional format or used in concert with audio or video tapes. The trainer should take care to reinforce and clarify the learning with person-to-person instruction (highlighting the training meetings, and reviewing with individual officers at their post, etc.) so as to ensure comprehension. Combining distance education with traditional classroom instruction can offer the best of both worlds. It can be used before or after a classroom session as a means of reinforcing lessons.

Online courses have grown in popularity throughout the contract and retail loss prevention sectors. Large security service firms and major retailers have been able to centralize training functions using web-based programs. These programs can be cost-effective and can be adjusted to various learning styles. Dynamic programs are more likely to capture the attention of contemporary learners, which in turn leads to reduced learning time. These are key factors in any training or educational endeavor. Additionally, the metrics within various programs are quite useful for keeping track of learning progress.

FOOD FOR THOUGHT

After suggesting that the security force be enrolled into the Certified Protection Officer program, a supervisor is told by his or her superior that the "correspondence study is a bunch of BS" What arguments could be used to persuade the manager? What facts and research are available to support the supervisor's arguments?

Tuition reimbursement can be used to empower people to improve their individual educational and/or training level. Many organizations have earmarked tuition assistance money, but unfortunately, many security departments have not taken advantage of it. While improving educational and/or training levels does not ensure a baseline foundation of knowledge, skill, or ability for the entire security force, it does help to promote professional development, which tends to pay for itself.

Finding the Time

Scheduling is a serious impediment to traditional training classes for security departments. To get everyone in the class, the session must be scheduled at least twice to compensate for officers on post, out sick, on vacation, newly hired officers, etc. The reality of security training is that unless *all* officers are trained *before* being assigned, there will always be gaps while unavailable staff members are rotated into a training class. Unfortunately, few supervisors/managers fully acknowledge this. Because of this failure, uniform and comprehensive training does not occur. There are a few approaches to overcoming this seemingly insurmountable dilemma:

- Distance education. This can be tailored to the individual learning style and pace, and because of its flexibility can be assigned around "down time" or in smaller chunks to accommodate the schedule.

- Give as much training as possible in the pre-assignment phase of the employee's training. This eliminates the hassle of attempting to schedule classes later on. It also reduces or eliminates uncomfortable situations that new officers are faced with, which can be a key cause of turnover. The downside is that too much pre-assignment training will overwhelm new staff.
- Require people to have certain training prior to being hired and/or to maintain certain levels of training throughout their tenure. Compensating the officers for doing this may be less expensive and troublesome than attempting to set up "master schedules" for all security force members.

Training should serve to create and improve job performance. Compliance with legal standards, while a necessity, is best thought of as a positive byproduct. Making compliance the primary goal of training is wasted training. The troops are not impressed, nor are many government inspectors.

FOOD FOR THOUGHT

A manager to whom the supervisor reports believes all the training that is necessary should be limited to that which is required by the state or province. He or she does not want any additional funds spent on training. What arguments could be advanced to persuade this individual that increased learning and development is beneficial?

Training Challenges

Training limited to compliance can be a problem in certain environments. This happens when training is completed solely to satisfy government requirements and therefore only to the minimum legal standard necessary. While legal mandates must be complied with, merely adhering to them is just not enough. Officers notice the halfhearted approach to training and behave accordingly—not only to training, but also to job performance. As a result, protection officers are demotivated to learn, and may block out future attempts to enhance their job capabilities.

Resistance by students is a significant problem facing those charged with training. In many cases, employees do not want to be in a particular training session or do not want to learn a new procedure. some methods of dealing with employee resistance to training include:

- Schedule training with minimal interference with the learner's life/schedule when possible.
- Recognize the experience, knowledge, and contributions each officer makes to the training experience. A genuine compliment can go a long way toward decreasing resistance to learning.
- Ask trainees what they want out of the training. Incorporate their needs in the design and implementation of training as much as possible. Training is not the

product of a single individual; it includes management, the public, as well as the trainees themselves. Good instructors understand this and involve all the stakeholders.

- Provide incentives. These depend upon the situation at hand. A list and photograph in the company newsletter is one low-cost way to reward students. Publicly presenting certificates and plaques is another. Providing meals and refreshments is also a nice gesture and is usually appreciated.
- Deal positively with students who challenge the instructor or content of the learning process. Sometimes these questions can be reflected back with a "How would you handle that?" Asking the class for their input is another strategy. However, sometimes having to the hostile questioner in a classroom setting that the question will be resolved over break—and following through on that promise—is necessary.

TRAINERS CAN BE CHALLENGING TOO

There are a variety of trainers that can complicate the training environment, whether intentionally or unintentionally. Some of them lack education, whereas others have too much. Others have unrealistic expectations of what training can do or do not understand what it cannot do.

Stuffed Shirts

These are security supervisors who obtain their positions due to their educational backgrounds. They have a degree but lack the experience or specific training to be competent. Accordingly, they often misunderstand the realistic applications of firefighting, handcuffing, crowd management, etc. While there is no background that is perfect, it is important to identify those weaknesses and work with them in a positive manner. Supervisors are not expected to be experts in everything, but they must be competent at all essential job tasks. They must also be humble enough (or confident enough) to ask for assistance from others. Supervisors should not hesitate to ask subordinates for assistance with a training problem, as they are often composed of people with diverse backgrounds (medics, firefighters, soldiers, polic officers, computer specialits, safety specialist, facilities technicians, etc.), and astute supervisors should use their talents.

The Definitional Dilemma

"The definitional dilemma" begins when managers do not truly understand what training is. They cannot adequately define training and consequently are unable to differentiate training from education or development. Those afflicted with the "dilemma" throw all three terms around interchangeably, ignorant of the fact that there are distinct differences between them. to avoid this trap, there should be a complete understanding of what "training," "education," and "development" means.

Training prepares the employee through the introduction of knowledge or the acquisition of skills or abilities to perform a specific job. Training focuses on "how to" do a job task, and involves practice, repetition, and skill development. The training process is designed to develop a specific job skill, such as driving, using a handgun or baton, patrolling specific points, or administering first aid. Training's focus is on task proficiency.

Education broadens one's perspective by increasing the employee's knowledge base. Education focuses on "why" a job task or duty is being performed. An employee who is educated may not necessarily be able to drive, shoot, patrol, or care for casualties, but should understand the concept of such things as stopping distance, friction, momentum, etc. The employee will be better able to make judgments about what constitutes safe driving, or be able to learn faster when in new training courses. At the managerial level, the employee will have a better idea on how to write driving policies and develop safe driving programs.

Development creates *growth* in the individual and the organization through the combination of training, education, and new opportunities. As the organization grows, so must the individual employee. When individual development is widespread throughout the organization, it becomes organizational development. Experience acts as a catalyst in the development process, bringing together the knowledge of education and the skill from training to make the employee a better performer. This is important because developing the proficiencies and strengths of current employees are significantly less expensive than hiring new ones. *Organizational development* also enables the organization to provide more and better services to both internal and external consumers.

Training, education, experience, and development are all separate entities that overlap one another. A smart manager understands this. Although related to one another, training, education, and experience are each a separate, distinct entity. Moreover, each entity has differing effects on performance. Training will have a readily identifiable, measurable impact on job performance (provided the training is properly given), whereas education will change attitudes and outlooks (affective domain). Task performance changes may not be as readily discernable with education.

The definitional dilemma often occurs when managers provide educational opportunities for their subordinates and think that the personnel have been "trained." Examples include having a guest speaker talk, or sending subordinates to seminars and conferences. These experiences educate but do not train. The dilemma hits when the manager expects the same performance changes with education as with training. The manager is disappointed that extensive performance improvement has not occurred when he sent his officers to a perceived "training session."

The Frog

"The Frog" is a nice fellow who really wants his officers to be well trained. The Frog does not see the complexities and problems inherent within the training process. He jumps into training without thinking through all of the logistical considerations:

- Training needs assessment.
- Training program development costs.

- Equipment and materials required.
- Scheduling and overtime considerations.
- Testing and validation methods.

The Frog enthusiastically jumps into training, then crawls out of it when logistical hurdles appear. Training is then abandoned for all practical purposes. Often, this occurs when a new manager takes over. In some security organizations, this has happened repeatedly over the years. The senior security officers have lived through several administrations that *intended* to have good, strong training programs. In all likelihood, they will outlast the current Frog. In these situations, expect that security officers will not to take training seriously.

The Panacea

Those who subscribe to this theory believe that training can solve any and all personnel performance problems. Unfortunately, job performance inadequacies can also be the result of people not being motivated to perform, being prevented from performing due to some impediment in the job design, or not knowing how to perform. Training can solve some performance problems, but the overwhelming majority of performance problems call for creative, no-nonsense supervision and management. Some steps that can be taken to more accurately diagnose the performance problem include the following:

- Describe the issue by writing a problem statement in specific terms.
- Conduct a job task analysis to ensure a clear picture of the total job environment.
- Determine the cause(s) of the problem by asking security officers and supervisors what they perceive to be the issue. Use their feedback to develop usable metrics.
- Determine if the problem can be addressed through increased knowledge, skill, or abilities.

Bad Medicine

"Bad Medicine" is the prescription of training for problems that the training cannot solve. There are two varieties of it—the first being the manager who uses training in a punitive manner. Training and discipline do not mix. training can, to some extent, be a motivator; however discipline is a demotivator and one cannot train demotivated people.

Bad Medicine hurts the organization by destroying the image of the training department by using training in cases where discipline would be appropriate. This leaves a bitter after-taste in the mouths of all involved and is certain to cause employees to view training in a punitive, negative light. Unfortunately, in some organizations, labor–management relations are allowed to deteriorate into such a state.

The second common manifestation of Bad Medicine relates to the individual who seeks out instruction in various topical areas and uses it for correcting personal deficiencies. It is not uncommon to find people who have taken innumerable classes and are not moving ahead in their careers. Some of these people have advanced degrees, certifications, etc. On paper they appear to be qualified, but they have a personal deficiency, personality trait, or lack of aptitude in a particular area.

The Assessment Ass

"The Assessment Ass" is not really serious about training. The Assessment Ass assesses and examines various training strategies, plans, and programs. Typically these are complex, sophisticated, and trendy ventures. The strategy, plan, or program that is being "assessed" may be very impressive but not viable. The Assessment Ass is either deliberately trying to mislead others or is simply too inept to realize that money does not grow on trees. Road-blocks that must be overcome include:

- Budgetary limitations
- Scheduling conflicts
- Availability of learning resources (equipment, software, instructors, etc.)

The Budget Buster

"The Budget Buster" is a manager who unintentionally (or intentionally) spends the entire training budget on one particular training program, generally put on by an outside consultant. In most cases, the outside consultant impresses management greatly. When the costs that manager failed to consider for this outside consultant are calculated, they wipe out whatever remained of the department's training budget.

Roleaids

The "Roleaids" manager fails to appreciate the following role(s) of the contemporary protection officer:

- Intelligence agent for management via the collection of information that management needs.
- Enforcement/compliance agent for management policies.
- Management representative through the enforcement of rules and providing of information and directions to visitors, employees, and customers.
- Legal consultant where the officer has a working knowledge of more areas of the law than any other member of the organization (labor law, administrative regulations such as the Occupational Safety and Health Administration (OSHA), criminal law, and civil liability standards).

The Roleaids manager thinks of security officers as "guards." Accordingly, he makes no effort to develop his subordinate officers. The officers are not socialized as adjunct members of the management team; they are not given the human and public relations training necessary to interact with others in a productive manner. Their interpersonal communication skills are not honed so that they can "sell" people on policy adherence. Writing skills are not developed to enable them to record information and observations. writing skills are not developed to enable them to record information and observations efficiently.

Mr./Ms. Unique

"Mr./Ms. Unique" resists purchasing off-the-shelf training programs because they are generic and not specific enough to his or her work environment. These people magnify the differences instead of linking the similarities between their organization and others. They create bias. Mr./Ms. Unique thinks that his or her problems are like no other; because no training "fits" their situation (in their minds), they do nothing regarding training. Mr. and/or Ms. Unique are very often convincing in their arguments, but they can be dealt with by assessing the following questions:

- What training program is currently in place?
- What training program is desirable in the near future?
- What would it cost in time and/or consulting fees to develop a tailored training program?
- How much budgetary support is available?
- What will be the results of failure to train personnel in the short run? The long run?

The Profiteer

"The Profiteer" is an unethical firm or individual who takes advantage of misinformed students and, in some cases, government grant monies. The Profiteer misrepresents instructional programs. Students are suckered out of their tuition monies with the promise of careers that are essentially unattainable or unrealistic. They use appealing advertising and sometimes exploit those paying the bill in states or provinces where training is mandated. They do not "tell the truth, the whole truth and nothing but the truth."

Emerging Trends

Online learning will continue to grow and develop, but not at the same pace in every industry or geographic area. It has numerous advantages and may be the only viable option in some settings. There are, however, instances where not all learners have access. There also are people who don't believe its effectiveness. While the "short answer" is that online learning will grow and grow, the two factors previously mentioned will curtail it. The correct answer is more complex, and it is further complicated by technologies such as Skype and NetMeeting, which are growing in popularity and availability. They have a place in some organizations, and this will increase over time.

Government-mandated training will grow, but history illustrates that it grows very, very slowly. It is only after significant media-grabbing tragedies that federal, state, or provincial governments are likely to enact legislation. What could change this is if governments see mandated training as a means of generating revenue. The licensing and training of security personnel can provide significant funds to government at all levels.

Conclusion

Supervisors and managers play a crucial role in the training process; in the final analysis, they are the ones who make training effective. By learning as much as possible about learning theory and delivery, supervisors can significantly enhance their contribution to officer performance. In doing so, they will expand their career potential and increase their value to the organization and to themselves. Training and development programs in contemporary protection organizations must be dynamic and multifaceted. While protection staff is the primary focus of developmental efforts, others may also be potential training recipients.

To fulfill this role and be a major contributor, protection supervisors must understand and be able to apply learning strategies. They must know what needs to be learned and how to best facilitate that learning, and become perpetual students of training and development. Protection supervisors must understand that learning never stops and should exploit every opportunity to see that it occurs.

Refer website http://www.ifpo.org for further information

End Notes

1. Ann Trinca, *Personal communication* (January 12, 2015).
2. Albrecht S, *Tough Training Topics: A Presenter's Survival Guide* (San Francisco, CA: John Wiley, 2006).

Human Resource Management

14

Recruitment and Retention of Security Personnel: Understanding and Meeting the Challenge

Christopher A. Hertig, Bryan Kling, Michael Dannecker

Introduction

Recruitment is where marketing the organization and employee selection come together. It is, ideally, a marriage of the two processes. An inherent difficulty with recruitment is that the process is initiated only when there is a need to hire new personnel. The recruitment effort at this point is behind schedule. Although an organization cannot advertise job openings it does not have, waiting to starting the process until after vacancies occur means that the employer is playing catch-up. A recruitment process whereby the employing organization is continuously reaching out to potential applicants is ideal. The artful marriage of personnel recruitment to a marketing campaign may provide this.

Within the security industry, such an arrangement must take place in both the macro- and micro-employment environments. Potential applicants must be aware of job and career potential as protection officers, loss prevention agents, investigators, supervisors, and directors. They must then know about specific job openings in particular organizations. There is obviously some degree of overlap between these, and it is important that real-life examples send a powerful message. It is also paramount to success that the proper image is projected—brand matters.

> *"The securing and training of proper persons is at the root of efficiency"*.
>
> **Sir Robert Peel**

Contemporary protection forces should take note of the above statement that is commonly attributed to Sir Robert Peel. Selection starts with recruitment. Targeting a specific type of individual and approaching them through the appropriate channels will help ensure that the new employee fits the job.

Traditional recruitment methods may not meet the demands of the future for those organizations wishing to hire security personnel. The other side of recruitment—retention—may not be met with yesterday's methods either. The labor pool may be shrinking because of demographic trends. The retirement of "baby boomers" is one

Security Supervision and Management. http://dx.doi.org/10.1016/B978-0-12-800113-4.00014-6

factor that may negatively affect retention. Recruitment may be hurt by fewer persons entering the job market. Demographic trends are important to monitor by those involved in recruitment. This corresponds with the traditional vagaries of labor markets, which vary significantly by geographic area. So too do the expectations of succeeding generations of employees. Finally, increased job demands in terms of technical expertise and public/end-user expectations require a new look at what type of person is needed and how best to attract and retain that person. Table 14.1 is a simplified menu of knowledge, skill, and ability areas. Specific job task analyses reveal considerably more detail.

In addition to these competencies, there is the necessity for in-depth knowledge and appreciation of the environment the officers are protecting. Effective socialization to the employer culture can be the difference between a present but isolated security function and an integrated, fully effective addition to an organization. This includes being educated about organizational structure, funding sources, operations, and cultures. Security officers must understand the retail business, school administrative structure, or nonprofit nature of the church, etc., in order to be effective.

Some appreciable time and effort must be spent in orientation. The orientation process should include exposure to all aspects of organizational operations. In addition to these "happy side effects" of socialization, this broad knowledge prepares the security officer to be in a position to recognize incorrect or unauthorized situations with respect to normal operations.

Recruitment

Recruitment efforts begin after a decision has been made to add to present staffing levels. There are two reasons this occurs:

- An expansion of the need for personnel. This is generally the addition of new line employees. It may, however, be the acquisition of supervisory staff, or managerial personnel. It may be temporary or permanent in nature. It can even encompass staffing operations that are new or creating entirely new positions within existing operations.
- Replacement of personnel who have departed. This may be caused by retirement, promotion, or regular attrition.

The next phase is to identify the ideal job candidate. This involves conducting a detailed job task analysis. All essential functions of the job must be identified. Typically, the human resources (HR) department of the organization will have a current job description on file and available for the position. This job description should be obtained and consulted regarding specific requirements of the position to be filled. The security functions of any organization are shaped by the needs of the larger entity. For example, because of the size and configuration of the facility or business operation, the security officer candidate may be required to walk long distances, climb ladders, or operate complex surveillance systems. These various features of the job will dictate the specific physical and mental requirements of the candidate.

Job duties should then be assessed in terms of the cultural fit that is expected of the new employee. After the "what" of the job has been laid out, it then becomes necessary to describe the "how" of the job.

Internal Recruitment

An employer's most valuable asset is its employees. Very often, there is no better place to recruit for an organization than from within. There are several ways employers can recruit from within, such as the following:

Bulletin: The simplest form of a job posting is by bulletin. Having an HR area where job/promotional opportunities exist can be a means for this bulletin to be displayed. A bulletin board of sorts can accomplish this need. These boards can be placed in areas, such as employee cafeterias, rest areas, and training rooms.

Interoffice mail: Sending all employees a memo is another way to recruit internally.

Electronic: If the employer is a mid- to large-size organization, it can use the intranet to post job openings/promotional opportunities. The intranet allows all employees access to this information. Additionally, it will allow employers to thwart any innuendo of hiding open positions. The same can be accomplished by use of an internal e-mail. In-house blogs may also be used.

Relational: During the course of normal interaction of security officers and other employees, the alert and friendly security officer typically forges sociable relationships with employees from all functions of the organization. This interaction provides an excellent recruitment opportunity for current and future job openings on the security team.

Skill inventories: These can be maintained so that when a particular competency is required, the employees possessing it can be quickly recruited. It may be both enlightening and useful to maintain a skills inventory for operational purposes in addition to its utility in recruitment efforts. Security departments often have a wide array of individuals with unique skills. This knowledge can aid in daily and emergency operations. It can also be used to enhance the image of the security department within the parent or client organization.

External Recruitment

Recruiting from outside the organization typically involves methods different from those that would be used for an internal recruitment. These methods might include the following:

Newspaper advertising: These have traditionally been used to recruit personnel over a wide area in a rapid manner. Newspaper advertisements may tend to reach those persons who are currently unemployed. In many cases, this is not the optimal target group. Newspaper advertisements should be seen as just that—"ads." They are representations of the organization and brand to a large segment of the general public. Within the general public are potential employees, clients, and customers. This recruitment tool may take longer to bear fruit than electronic options due to print cycle and distribution limits. However, this can be more efficient when using a newspaper's electronic and social media outlets.

Website advertising: Online advertising has the advantage of being "24/7" at low cost. For example, jobs may be advertised through Lpjobs.com or the career center on the International Foundation for Protection Officers' website. LPJobs.com is sponsored by *Loss Prevention* magazine and lists jobs in retail loss prevention throughout the United States. Listings are for loss prevention personnel at all levels. The use of website for recruiting will only continue to increase over time. Unfortunately, if potential applicants are unaware of the existence of the employer or industry, these advertisements will not be as effective as they could be. Outreach efforts by professional organizations such as ASIS International (American Society for Industrial Security) and the Partnership for Careers in Law, Public Safety, Corrections and Security are essential.

Micro-efforts by employers using websites allows for continuous advertising about the employing organization at a fixed cost. Effective programs have attractive sites that convey the culture and values of the employer. They are also linked to other sites. For example, USA contract service firms who are members of the National Association of Security Companies (NASCO) benefit from links to their own websites within the NASCO site.

Employee referral bonus programs: These programs offer incentives to employees to seek out prospective employees. Most programs offer monetary compensation and there are guidelines. These guidelines usually state that the new employees found must stay with the organization for a set amount of time. Benefits are twofold: the organization gains an employee who is more likely to want to be employed and the employee who recruited the new person gets compensation. Most important is that they acquire the right cultural fit between applicant and employer. Referral programs provide a human assessment so that this fit, which is crucial for protection staff, can be made.

Referrals are a good way to obtain applicants. Model employees are best prepared to find persons with characteristics similar to their own. Referrals can be done informally. Various methods of gaining referrals can be employed, such as developing a horizontal promotion scheme where certain designated persons are recruiters. Employee referral programs tend to wane over time.[1]

Bonuses may plateau over time with the numbers of personnel recruited remaining stable. In some cases, there may even be a drop in new hires. To revitalize a referral program, some employers in the high-tech arena have used additional rewards administered through a lottery system. Employees with successful referrals were able to put their names in a drawing each quarter for a 2-year lease on a Porsche. The result was that referrals doubled. The possibility of a car gave recruiting employees a visible reward that reinforced their ties to the company, in much the same manner as health insurance or a 401(k) retirement plan.[2] Security industry recruiters should look for reward programs that achieve similar objectives.

An additional means of enhancing referrals is through the use of social networks. Users can leverage personal relationships for referrals. Social networks may aid in recruiting as well as help with reference checks. The proper mix of technology and professionally trained recruiters may be very effective.

Posters: When placed in strategic locations designed for specific target markets (college students, women, active or reserve duty military, etc.), posters may bear fruit. Standard paper-size announcements that can be produced rapidly hold great potential. Having such a poster that can be quickly downloaded from an employer's website may provide recruiters with a useful tool. If such a form can be emailed to college faculty or recruiters in specific geographic locations, the recruitment process can move quite rapidly.

Professional recruiters: Professional recruiters, sometimes referred to as "head hunters," may be employed to locate candidates for managerial positions. These professional services typically charge a percentage of the starting salary of the candidate, which is paid by the hiring organization. They are effective if the professional recruiter has a good network of candidates and understands the position's requirements.

Billboards: Billboards may be an appropriate medium and should not be overlooked. Because billboards reach a wider audience, they should be considered as part of a general marketing effort by the organization, in addition to their employee recruitment processes. Advertising space may be donated to public entities as a public service and may be a potential tax deduction in the United States.

Presentations at job fairs, high schools, colleges, and military bases: Traditionally, the security industry has not done this to a large extent. It is more common to find public sector police and investigative agencies at job fairs than employers of private sector security personnel. One reason for this is the existence of recruitment officers and teams within public agencies. Having the designated recruiters, creates a need to send those recruiters out. The cost-effectiveness of this must be weighed, particularly during times when there are no job openings or when the target audience is not large. Private employers should consider having designated recruiters. This may help ensure the continuity of the recruitment effort. It could also serve as part of a horizontal promotion scheme: senior officers with certain training credentials would take on additional duties in recruitment. A change in job title or compensation could be part of such a program.

Recruitment stations or offices: These have been widely used by military recruiters, who have permanent offices. Temporary offices in shopping centers have also been used. Even if a full-time recruiter is on staff, an office is probably not appropriate for a security employer, although it may work for a very large one. It may also be cost-effective via some type of space sharing with another entity. Cooperative recruitment efforts, where several employers pool their resources together, may also make this a viable strategy.

Academy programs: Running a training academy on a "for-profit" basis and offering jobs to the top graduates holds some real promise. Contract security agencies in particular may be able to develop their own staff in a cost-effective manner while simultaneously taking advantage of a built-in recruitment tool.

Intern programs: For college students, internships may be used as a recruitment tool. While the main purpose of an internship is to provide an experiential learning opportunity to a student, marketing the organization to the student and the student's social contacts is a side benefit. Word of mouth works extensively as the college also takes on the role of recruiter. Generally, internships would be used for reaching out to and getting to know students to fill management positions. They hold great promise as developing future managers. The dearth of management trainee programs within the security industry may be addressed, in part, through the use of internship programs. Intern programs can also be used to recruit entry-level personnel. Offering a former student intern a summer job or a full-time position after graduation is certainly a possibility.

Older interns who are assessing new directions in their careers are being used increasingly within some industries. Baby boomers who have taken early retirement may want to begin a new career. Intern programs allow them to sample the new field. These individuals bring with them knowledge and experience. Such an approach may also be useful within the security industry. Military personnel nearing retirement may be submerged in the culture of a prospective employer.

Employers wishing to start intern programs should be very clear about the objectives they wish to achieve. They must develop goals and procedures. Working with ASIS, the International Foundation for Protection Officers (IFPO) and other organizations can aid in this process.

Extern programs: Externships consist of having a student "shadow" a job holder during the course of the workday. These may be used in secondary schools that teach protective service curricula or colleges that have criminal justice programs. Some schools have a requirement for doing a job shadow or ride-a-long, so employers may be able to exploit this opportunity quite readily. Schools that do not use externships may be persuaded to adopt them. Prospective students are attracted to programs with such practical components in their curriculums.

Coordinated recruitment: Security employers banding together to pool their recruitment efforts may be a major benefit, as pointed out in the following[3] description of the advantages this promotes within the realm of public policing:

- Creates the possibility of a more widespread recruitment effort.
- Enables justification for a more sophisticated advertising campaign.
- Provides an opportunity for recruitment and selection to be handled by professional personnel specialists.
- Applicants can take a single examination for several different police departments at one time.
- Potential candidates can be informed of vacancies throughout an entire state.
- Greater budgetary allocations can be given to the recruitment effort than if a single agency acted alone.
- Application procedures would become uniform for all participating agencies.

Policing agencies have adopted this model. It may be more attractive to them than it would be for security organizations due to the extensive selection costs associated with police officers. The concept does, however, have application to security organizations. Job fairs that occur in the United Kingdom and Canada allow both candidates and employers meet one another. Job fairs offer a rare opportunity for students to see "real-world" jobs and employers. Getting the major employment sectors together is important, including contract security, retail loss prevention, and informational technology security. A college or civic association could host the fair, and professional associations could play a leading role in organizing and marketing it.

Turnover Costs

Turnover is the number of personnel that remain in a job for one year. Positive turnover is few employees leaving the organization. Those who leave do so, leave because of retirement, family responsibilities, or promotion within the organization. Negative turnover is a high number of employees leaving a job position. Curtis and McBride[4] believe that negative turnover occurs when the rate exceeds 10% of the workforce. It is not unheard of in security departments for the rate to exceed 100%, typically within security service firms.

Turnover costs include the funds spent on recruiting, hiring, and training the new employee. While figures given for the cost of turnover vary widely, it is a reasonable estimate that the cost of hiring a new employee is 25% of his or her annual salary. This may, however, be too conservative a cost estimate in some situations.

Curtis and McBride[5] maintain that it takes one year for a security officer to be trained and learn the basic job functions. Obviously, this varies between different work environments. Moreover, the expanding duties of security officers require a lengthier time and a new view as to their role. More functions and added technology mandate this.

The largest factor may be cultural fit, especially with security staff who are "preservers of the organizational culture." Poor cultural fit for protection officers means failure at the job. It also is a significant cause of turnover, which usually occurs within the first 6 months or so. Staff quitting soon after employment may indicate that the recruitment message was inadequate in some way.

Another concern with high turnover is the loss of institutional memory. Organizations lacking people who have been involved in various approaches to problem-solving, cannot learn from their history. Experienced employees have an institutional memory—an important asset for any organization that seeks to sustain itself over time.

A cost that is difficult to quantify is the effect that droves of disgruntled former employees may have on the organization. This can take the form of negative advertising — "recruitment in reverse" by ex-security officers who disparage the organization. Such individuals are likely to reveal—and perhaps exaggerate—the organization's "dirty laundry." They will speak of the organization in negative terms and reach large numbers of people. It can also impact civil litigation when a plaintiff, alleging negligence, can find a number of ex-employees who hold feelings of animosity toward their former employer. Plaintiff's attorneys may then parade a group of them before the court so that the company's dirty laundry is aired. The organization is embarrassed at best or found negligent at worst.

Internal projections of a negative image may also occur. Security team members are typically in highly visible positions in the organization. High turnover in these key positions can lead to a general feeling of instability toward the organization's security function. Finally, the achievement of professional status is made impossible with high turnover. Professionals have a commitment to what they do. They do not jump around from job to job.

Absenteeism: A Precursor of Turnover?

High levels of absenteeism may be part of a turnover cycle. Employees—particularly those involved in fixed-post security functions—may be pressed to work extra hours in order to cover for absent coworkers. A 2006 survey of 300 HR executives, conducted by CCH, Inc. (a leading provider of human resources and employment law information), found the following major causes for absenteeism[6]: personal illness, 35%; family issues, 24%; personal needs, 18%; and deserving of more time off, 11%. A study conducted in northeastern Mexico on behalf of a contract security firm listed 17 causes for absenteeism. The leading causes of absenteeism in this survey were a short illness, personal time, holidays, lack of money for commuting, oversleeping, exhaustion because of work, laziness, and attending parties or social events.[7]

To control absenteeism, disciplinary action is taken by many employers; 90% of the firms surveyed by CCH did so. While discipline may play a role in controlling absenteeism, there are other measures that may be more effective. In the Mexican study, positive reinforcements were emphasized more than punitive ones. After implementing a series of measures designed to reduce absenteeism, the company's rate dropped from 16% to 10%. Measures included having the officers who missed work fill out a form detailing why they were absent, providing a lecture about absenteeism at orientation, and providing prizes and an annual bonus for security officers who missed work the least. The prizes were things that the officers' entire family could use, such as home appliances, movie tickets, and tickets to amusement parks. In addition to the drop in absenteeism, the reasons for missing work changed to personal time for visiting children's schools, conducting personal business, attending to legal issues, recuperating from short-term illness, and family issues such as caring for sick family members. Frivolous reasons for missing work were no longer major contributors.

De Los Santos[8] stressed the need to determine precisely what the causes of absenteeism are. In both the De Los Santos and CCH studies, the desire for more time off was a leading cause of unscheduled absenteeism. Sopelsa[9] noted that Americans have the least amount of vacation time in the developed world, averaging 13 days per year. The Japanese have 26, Canadians 25, and French 37. Examining vacation and other time off allocations is obviously important.

Keeping employees engaged and making them feel valuable is vital. Programs such as compressed workweeks and days, which enable an employee to leave early for a child's school function, are important to employees with children. These programs make employees feel as though they are valued by the employer. Increased productivity and loyalty result from their implementation.[10] In America, police departments and some security departments have adopted 12 hour shifts. This gives the officers more time off and makes planning personal time easier. Obviously, this must be balanced with overtime costs and alertness of personnel. It may also require employment agreements concerning secondary jobs, such as "moonlighting" that may easily lead to fatigue, stress, and bad judgment.

Retention Strategies

After recruitment, retaining employees is a significant component of organizational success. Much effort, time, and resources go into new employees. Keeping low attrition is very important to maintaining smooth day-to-day operations. Employee pay is probably the central issue as to why employees move on. Keeping salaries competitive should be a part of retention strategies. Salaries and salary structures should be analyzed by HR personnel (compensation specialists), who assess industry standards, inflation rates, and cost of living.

Realistic job previews are essential. The honesty and integrity of the recruitment effort carries into the retention arena. There is no point in having a "let's get them in the door and start them working" perspective because it only leads to decreased morale and subsequent absenteeism and turnover.

Realistic job previews can be administered via a video presentation of the workplace or through a personal discussion with a current job holder. Video footage can be placed on a website or network. It can also be distributed to college faculty to show to their classes. In-class videos can pique the interest of potential applicants while at the same time conveying an accurate depiction of the work environment, in just a few minutes of time.

Discussions with current job holders can provide the necessary personal touch that is expected by many of today's job seekers. Discussions can include such things as how decisions are made, how much authority employees have, and how people are held accountable.[11] Make the officers feel unique and special. Distinctive uniforms, job titles, and other symbols of membership in an exclusive group may help enhance *esprit de corps*. Some proprietary and contract companies provide the uniforms for personnel and even take care of the upkeep. The use of professional titles such as "protection officer" or "security agent" instead of "guard" is an additional approach. Another is through personality assessments. At the Wackenhut Institute, instructors used the Myers-Briggs Type Indicator (MBTI) tests to measure officers' personality traits. When the officers see that they are of a personality type that has organizational skills, are good practical problem solvers, and watchful and loyal, they begin to see themselves as different from the general population. They see that they have something unique that prepares them for a security career.[12]

Supervisors play a key role in maintaining employee morale and managing retention rates. A long-held management axiom that "line supervisors are the backbone of an organization" is quite valid. Supervisors are those to whom employees go to with complaints, concerns, and requests. Tulgan[13] found that the routine daily communication between supervisory managers and persons reporting directly to them has greater impact on productivity, quality, morale, and retention than any other single factor:

People don't quit their jobs; they quit their bosses.

Organizations must invest in identifying and promoting the best available persons they can as supervisors. The "care and feeding" of supervisors must also be given top priority. Investing in supervisory development programs seems to be a wise decision. Quality supervision has additional benefits. Top-notch supervisors may be good candidates for promotion to higher-level managerial positions. Quality supervision has also been a traditional selling point for contract security firms. These firms proclaim that their officers are the same as the rest of the industry, but that the quality of their supervision sets them apart from competitors.

Supervisors should have an open-door policy. Actively listening to employees is important, and arguably more so with the millennial generation. Open, honest communication encompasses both work-related and personal issues. Employment issues brought up by employees may provide clues to larger concerns. Personal issues may not be what the supervisors want to spend their time listening to, but they are important to the employee. Supervisors who believe that they are somehow above being a "shoulder to cry on" are sadly mistaken.

A good supervisor will take any and every opportunity to listen to subordinates. Being in settings comfortable to the employee and listening to their concerns with an open mind and an open heart will bring about the most motivation and loyalty from subordinates. Empathic listening is a cornerstone of effective supervision.

Increased compensation is key to recruitment and retention. Historically low pay was thought to be a problem in recruiting and retaining police personnel. As time went on, defined benefit pension packages and higher salaries came into place. Retention in most public police agencies, at least in North America, is not a major concern, largely due to excellent rates of pay. Providing monetary rewards relates to Frederick Taylor's scientific management theory, where workers were inspired to work harder for more money.

As wages have remained stagnant and living costs increased, compensation has become a significant source of stress for many employees. These employees may leave or stay but be less engaged and less productive. Obviously, this must be taken into account when setting wage rates and benefit packages.

Benefits are a key part of compensation, especially health insurance. In the United States, the affordability of health insurance is a major issue. The amount of money needed to pay for an individual's health insurance is approaching the amount necessary for rent! Organizations that have quality, health, and other benefit programs stand a better chance of retaining employees. Quality programs that are honestly presented by HR staff in a helpful manner are appreciated.

Another growing concern by employees is family care. Increasing numbers of people are taking care of elderly relatives or young children. Benefit programs must accommodate this or employee dissatisfaction will grow resulting in turnover.

Training is generally thought to be a key issue in employee retention. Employees see that a professionally delivered training effort reflects the value that the organization places on the officers and the jobs that they do. This is seen right away during the orientation training. Orientation is one of the fundamental early junctures in the employment relationship:

Trying to repair a damaged employee-employer relationship is very much like trying to change a tire on a moving car. The best solution for all involved is to make it right from the start. The investment of both care and energy in the selection, hiring, and orientation stages of employment sets the stage for a mutually profitable relationship.

Pre-assignment training is the next phase. Officers who have been prepared through pre-assignment training to handle a situation confronting them are less likely to be overwhelmed by that situation. This may be of particular importance when dealing with younger personnel who may expect lots of support from their employers. They want fast-paced, stimulating training that is useful to them.

One obvious problem is ascertaining the relative importance of training as a motivational tool. Organizations that spend time training their employees may also compensate them too well. There is evidence, however, from the West Manchester Mall in York, Pennsylvania, which suggests that training by itself without significant wage increases is a significant retention factor. The mall experienced an 85–90% reduction in security force turnover with only a 7–10% increase in wages. The training process designed by Director Randy Rice, CPOI, consisted of the following steps:

Pre-assignment phase. In this phase, pre-assignment training was given, including the Professional Security Training Network (PSTN) and Basic Security Officer Training Series (BSOTS). This provided a comprehensive introduction to the security officers' roles and functions. The series also aided in preparing officers for the Certified Protection Officer (CPO) designation.

The initial 90 days. Officers were assigned to a Field Training Officer who provided on-the-job instruction, coaching, and mentoring. The staff completed the PSTN Shopping Center Series concerning the specifics of shopping mall security. They also completed the Federal Emergency Management Agency "Emergency Response to Terrorism" course, along with regular monthly training on fire extinguishers, Oleoresin Capsicum Aerosol Training (OCAT), etc.

The first year. All officers completed the PSTN Supervisor Series. This was done due to the supervisory interface of security officers, who are in reality adjunct members of the management team. Such a role is highlighted during emergencies, when the officer is working alone in a closed facility, or during public/stakeholder interactions.

After 1 year. Officers completed the CPO process by taking the CPO Final Challenge Option.[14] Branham[15] maintains that keeping "Generation X" employees requires them to have some input into the training that they will receive. Letting them know that the employer will provide as much training as possible to develop new skills is important to them. This group is positively influenced by voluntary training, tuition reimbursement, and other programs. Contract security agencies have taken note of this and many, if not most, have an array of online career development opportunities.

Voluntary training has its roots in policing. Cleveland, Ohio, had a Forum Club in 1910 where police officers would gather on their own time and discuss police issues, sociology, and law.[16] Local ASIS chapters or other security organizations may do the same; perhaps via webinars. A local employer could host the webinar, which the ASIS chapter would purchase and charge admission for. This cuts learning costs and gives the chapter a revenue stream.

Training opportunities for police tactical teams and security forces at shopping malls and office complexes are common and growing as the concern with active threats increases. Reaching out to private-sector security personnel can extend the capabilities of the police force. Such an effort may also aid liaisons during investigations, emergencies, and public events, and as the different officers work together and get to know each other, a more positive relationship is developed.

Another approach to voluntary training is to hold weekend or evening classes that provide the officer or agent with a certificate and meal. Classes in executive protection, personal protective services, counterterrorism, and other popular subjects are likely to generate interest. The title is the "sizzle" and the content the "steak." As the old saying goes:

"You need to have the sizzle to sell the steak."

Executive protection would deal largely with manners, deportment, decorum, etc. Counterterrorism could teach search techniques, recognition of weapons of mass destruction and improvised explosive devices, etc. Such topics are important for routine operations and safety. Proper search of persons entering a secured facility, or recognition of dangerous chemicals, may be more routine uses of the subject matter.

Tuition reimbursement can be targeted toward those competencies that the employer values the most. It can also aid in organizational development without the enormous cost of employee wages during training. An assessment and ranking of the most desirable competencies would need to be done initially to ensure cost-effectiveness.

Scholarships can assume many forms. Supplying the tuition to a professional growth program for employees who meet certain criteria is one method. Employers can pay for approved training programs for employees who have a certain amount of service and positive performance reviews. There are many options to this, from emergency medical technician programs to the myriad of offerings given by professional organizations.

Bonuses are often a part of retention systems, particularly in retail. Annual bonuses or Christmas bonuses give employees something to look forward to and may deter them from leaving the organization. Bonuses can also be used at other junctures, contingent on organizational needs.

Seasonal employers, such as campgrounds, resorts, amusement parks, and retailers, can use bonuses to combat turnover during the busy season. Modest tuition assistance to college students who worked at an amusement park during the summer may be paid. This could be a small amount per hour that is paid in lump sum at the end of the season. Persons leaving before season's end would not get the bonus. Retaining college students may make good sense as the students will need a job after graduation and may be good candidates for advancement.

Stock options (profit sharing) should be drilled down as far as possible in the organization. Profit sharing signifies to employees that they are a part of the "team" and that they share in the rewards for successful operations. This is significant in security operations because protection officers are serving as representatives of management. Consequently, they should be made to feel as though they are a part of management. Unfortunately, security works when nothing happens. All too often, the only recognition security personnel receive is of a negative nature. Profit sharing, in whatever form it takes, is a positive stroke—something protection officers are in dire need of.

Retirement plans, such as 401(k), 403(b), and 457(b) plans, also signify to the employee that they are part of the organization. There are also options for enrolling employees in individual retirement accounts that employers may wish to explore. Once an employee sees their money beginning to grow, they feel more a part of the organization that brought them that good fortune.

Promotion possibilities, both within and outside of the security function, should be considered. Obviously, vertical (upward) and horizontal ("promotion in place") options are desirable. The chance to move outside of the security department may also be an option. While the security organization is losing an employee, it is gaining an advocate in another department. Having these avenues open may help to attract and retain certain candidates whose career aspirations are satisfied by these types of options.

Recognition helps to instill pride and confidence in an officer's ability, both in the officer and the organization. There are many ways to do this: continuous feeding to the internal newsletter about achievements of individual officers, "officer of the month" programs, annual awards ceremonies, letters of commendation, etc. Officers also may be recognized at local ASIS chapters. Many chapters have "security officer of the year" programs. The event can be publicized in local news media and business publications, giving recognition to the recipient of the award as well as the chapter. It may also be advisable to permit the officers to wear something different on their uniform. A CPO pin is commonly used for this purpose. The astute manager will look to public police and other security organizations for ideas on recognition. One example is the New York Police Department, which uses merit bars, similar to what military organizations wear. This has significant potential for motivation, recognition, and ultimately retention.

For newly hired security officers, early recognition of initial job accomplishments is the key to forming positive images of the employer. Early rewards, such as a "90-day celebration," are important to retaining younger employees who yearn for more instant gratification. This is a key point to motivating younger officers, who are probably averse to being told they have to "pay their dues" and put in a lengthy tenure in order to advance. Shorter milestones should be integrated within a retention program in order to address this demographic.

Emerging Trends

Industry growth due to data breaches, organized retail theft, and terrorism will continue. Information technology security, retail loss prevention, and contract agencies will continue as the largest sectors of job growth. Physical security is evolving as a career specialty and will continue to do so. All of this means that there will be more jobs and people needed to fill them.

At the managerial level, many firms are using "talent management" to describe their recruitment function. A senior talent acquisition specialist may be responsible for developing a strong pipeline of candidates through networking, direct sourcing, internet mining, and applicant tracking tools. They will interpret the organization's recruitment strategy, identify sources, and develop and execute recruiting plans so that the organization's staffing needs are met.

Staffing agencies have provided workers for security jobs in some instances. Employees have been hired from employment agencies directly into contract agencies. Obviously, there are questions of licensing regarding security officers, which may dissipate over time as regulation matures.

Closely related is the nexus between recruitment and selection. If employers are recruiting from the ranks of recent immigrants or young people, where conducting background investigations may be difficult, there are probably breakdowns in the vetting process. Where a person fishes determines what kind of fish are caught.

Outsourcing of some aspects of the recruitment and selection process continues to be popular. Unfortunately, there may be problems in complexity and accountability. What was checked by whom, etc. becomes more difficult to determine. The use of third-party vendors for selection and recruiting raises quality control issues. These need to be carefully weighed before a major crisis can erupt.

Online application processes that test for relevant job skills (bona fide occupational qualifications) have become standard. Applicants take simple math and reading comprehension tests as initial screening measures. This works well because it brings in a larger number of applicants. There are, however, some instances where the applicant has someone else take the tests for them. Online systems are easily audited so that compliance issues can be addressed. Their use will undoubtedly mature, but the right balance must be struck with the human element: a supervisor or HR interviewer plays a critical role in assessing the candidate. Automated systems cannot erode this function.

Social media provides a new way to recruit and screen candidates. This will continue to grow and develop, but care must be taken not to sacrifice quality for convenience. An added concern is that many young persons do not use the same social media that managers are familiar with. Referral of candidates is good for getting the cultural fit that is necessary. Millennials are particularly adept at seeing and understanding the cultural fit. Social media will increasingly be used in referral systems.

Job fairs may be used to recruit career-oriented protection officers. This holds great promise in some areas where there is a sufficient supply of job seekers and employers. Colleges and professional organizations can partner for job fairs so that officers can be recruited, associations become better known, and students meet and talk with professionals.

Increasing numbers of former military personnel has made it easier to recruit quality applicants in some instances. This is aligned with the trend for more professional security forces. "Premium service" in the contract sector, where the client demands a significantly better level of service, has grown over the last several decades and is now commonplace. Concerns with violence/terrorism are currently driving this trend because end users view their security officers more as immediate responders in crisis situations than "someone who calls the police." Violence has made the provision of security a whole new ball game.

Colleges have become more involved in career planning and career development. Schools are actively involved with the lifelong career needs of their students and alumni. This will escalate as competition for students increases between schools. There is fertile ground for collaborative relations with colleges by employers, which will be exploited more over time.

Secondary schools with protective services programs are a source for recruitment. This will also continue as these programs move away from a law enforcement orientation to one aligned with emergency medical, firefighting, and security, where the graduates have a reasonable chance of finding employment. There may also be some tie-in with programs run by secondary schools for adult learners. Coursework in security/crisis management can be inserted into these classes, thus providing an education/training/recruitment platform for relevant stakeholders.

Conclusion

Recruitment within the macroenvironment of sufficient numbers of qualified personnel will largely determine the future of the security industry. In addition, acquiring quality candidates will pave the way for the success or failure of an individual employer. The PROTECT acronym, which can be used in advertisements directed at potential applicants, may be tailored to suit the recruiting organization's individual needs, and should serve as a general guide as to what type of personnel is required in the security industry:

Prepared to handle problems and crises. Emotionally stable. Emotionally mature.
Reliable. Dependable. Is there when needed.
Objective and free of prejudice toward particular groups of people. Able to exercise discretion according to the expectations within a professional work environment.
Trustworthy. Able to be entrusted with high-value assets and information of a critical nature.
Enthusiastic in taking on new challenges, some of which may not be "security" in the strictest sense of the term.
Career oriented. Seeking to learn and grow within the security industry.
Team player. Willing to commit to others, aid them, and sacrifice for them in order to further organizational objectives.

Refer website http://www.ifpo.org for further information

End Notes

1. Berkshire J. C., *Social Network Recruiting* (Alexandria, VA: HR Magazine, April 1, 2005): vol. 50, pt. 6, accessed December 17, 2014. Available: http://www.shrm.org/publications/hrmagazine/editorialcontent/pages/0405berkshire.aspx.

2. Frase-Blunt M., *Driving Home Your Awards Program* (Alexandria, VA: HR Magazine, February 1, 2001): vol. 46, pt. 2, accessed December 17, 2014. Available: http://www.shrm.org/publications/hrmagazine/editorialcontent/0201/pages/0201hragn-awards.aspx.

3. Leonard V. A. and More H. W., *Police Organization and Management* (Mineola, NY: Foundation Press, 1978).

4. Curtis G. E. and McBride R. B., *Proactive Security Administration* (Saddle River, NJ: Pearson Prentice Hall, 2005).

5. Ibid.

6. Sopelsa B., *Cough, Cough Let's Head to the Beach: Employers Take Steps to Deal with Absenteeism* (York, PA: York Sunday News, November 26, 2006), pg. H1.

7. De Los Santos G., *Where Have All The Guards Gone?* (Alexandria, VA: Security Management, 2006): vol. 50, pt. 12, 38–42.

8. Ibid.

9. See note 6 above.

10. See note 6 above.

11. Brandon C., *Truth in Recruitment Branding* (Alexandria, VA: HR Magazine, 2005): vol. 50, pt. 11, accessed December 17, 2014. Available: http://www.shrm.org/publications/hrmagazine/editorialco ntent/pages/1105agenda_empstaff.aspx.

12. Goodboe M. E., *How to Turn Around Turnover* (Alexandria, VA: Security Management, 2002): vol. 46, pt. 11, 65–68.

13. Tulgan B., *Generational Shift: What We Saw at the Workplace Revolution* (New Haven, CT: Rainmaker Thinking, Inc., September 17, 2003).

14. Pero J., *Retention Through Training: A Success Story* (Location Unknown: Access Control & Security Systems, 2003): accessed October 15, 2006. Available: http//securitysolutions.com/mag/security_rete ntion_training_success/index.html.

15. Branham F., *Keeping the People Who Keep You in Business: 24 Ways to Hang On to Your Most Valuable Talent* (Saranac Lake, NY: AMACOM, November 1, 2000).

16. Wadman R. and Allison W. T., *To Protect and Serve: A History of Police in America* (Upper Saddle River, NJ: Pearson, 2004).

Further Reading

1. The Myth of Learning Styles Posted on December 19, 2014 by Ani Aharonian, http://www.skeptic.com/ insight/the-myth-of-learning-styles/. Retrieved January 29, 2015.

2. Albrecht S., *Tough Training Topics: A Presenter's Survival Guide* (San Francisco, CA: John Wiley, 2006).

3. Brockelsby L., "Good In-Service Training: The Chiefs Perspective." *The Police Chief* LII(11) (1986).

4. Bunting S. M., "Training Safety: A Supervisory Responsibility," in *Supervisory Survival*, ed. Nowicki E. (Powers Lake, WI: Performance Dimensions Publishing, 1993).

5. Ginny Field, "Supervisory Editing," in *Supervisory Survival*, ed. Nowicki E. (Powers Lake, WI: Performance Dimensions Publishing, 1993).

6. Frantzreb R. B., *Training and Development Yearbook* (Englewood Cliffs, NJ: Prentice-Hall, 1990).

7. Grossi D. M., "The Supervisor's Role in Officer Survival Training," in *Supervisory Survival* ed. Nowicki E. (Powers Lake, WI: Performance Dimensions Publishing, 1993).

8. Hertig C. A., *Avoiding Pitfalls in the Training Process* (Bellingham, WA: International Foundation for Protection Officers, 1993).

9. *International learning and talent development comparison survey 2011* (London, UK: Chartered Institute of Personnel and Development, August, 2011), http://www.shrm.org/Research/SurveyFindings/ Articles/Documents/CIPDandSHRMstudy.pdf. Retrieved December 23, 2014.

10. Holly Krenek, *You Have 8 Seconds to Make Your Event Count!* Posted in: Tips (November 12, 2014) http://www.eventmanagerblog.com/attendee-attention#kmIkTrfSQbAgiwmX.99, http://www.event managerblog.com/attendee-attention. Retrieved December 23, 2014.

11. Minor K. I., Snarr R. W., and Wells J. B., "Distance Learning: Examining New Directions and Challenges For Criminal Justice Educations," *ACJS TODAY* 16, no. 4 (1998).

12. Metzner R. "Training's Return On Investment: Don't Prove It, Find It," *Loss Prevention* 5, no. 6 (2006).

13. Mounts H. C., "Earn Your College Degree At Home," *Police and Security News* 13, no. 1 (1997).

14. Nadler L., *Developing Human Resources* (Houston, TX: Gulf, 1970).

15. Nichter D. A., "How MGM Grand Trains Security Officers, Supervisors, Managers," *Hotel/Motel Security and Safety Management* 15, no. 8 (1997).

16. Nilson C., *Training Program Workbook and Kit* (Englewood Cliffs, NJ: Prentice-Hall, 1989).

17. Roberts B. E., "Supervisory Liability," in *Supervisory Survival* ed. Nowicki E. (Powers Lake, WI: Performance Dimensions Publishing, 1993).

18. Sample J. A., "Police Performance Problems: Are They Training or Supervision Issues?" *The Police Chief* L(10) (1983).

19. Sennewald C. A., *Effective Security Management* (Stoneham, MA: Butterworth, 1985).

20. Siuru B., "NACHS—A One-Stop Shop for Homeland Security Information and Training," *Police & Security News* 23, no. 1 (2007).

21. Tyler K., "Training Revs Up," *HR Magazine* 50, no. 4 (2005).

22. Wanat J. A., Guy E. T., and Merrigan J. J., *Supervisory Techniques for the Security Professional* (Stoneham, MA: Butterworth-Heinemann, 1981).

23. Zemke R., Standke L., and Jones, P. *Designing and Delivering Cost-Effective Training—and Measuring the Results* (Minneapolis, MN: Lakewood Publications, 1981).

24. LaMotte , S. (2014, November 7) 5 Things Recruiters Don't Normally Share With Job Seekers http://www.foxbusiness.com/personal-finance/2014/11/07/5-things-recruiters-dont-normally-share-with-job-seekers/?intcmp=ob_homepage_personalfinance&intcmp=obnetwork. Retrieved November 10, 2014.

15

Career Development and Professional Growth for Security Professionals

Inge Sebyan Black, Christopher A. Hertig

Planning and implementing a career path is important for everyone. What a person does for a living determines their income, their self-image, their schedules, and perhaps even where they live. It affects every aspect of their professional lives. Perhaps more importantly, it affects almost every aspect of their personal lives. Career planning takes time and reflection. It takes research. It takes getting knocked around by the realities of professional life. Unfortunately, it is not easy as there is an abundance of misinformation coming from an abundance of sources, such as career advisors, books, friends, family members, and colleagues. One must vet this information to ensure accuracy as well as determine what value and utility it has.

In the protection business, there are numerous career paths to follow. Security has innumerable specialties/verticals, etc. Each of these should be assessed. After one or two are chosen (e.g., retail loss prevention or contract security), the career planner must be careful not to limit themselves to these areas. While having experience in multiple environments (office building, manufacturing, government, military, policing, parks, etc.) is important, it also prevents an employee from being "pigeon holed" into a certain area. One does not want to hear the following in an employment interview:

> *"I see by your resume that you have spent your entire career in bank security. As you know, we are a distribution center...."*

Other strategies are to keep oneself broad through higher education and professional certification. Both higher education and professional designation causes one to learn more than their immediate job requirements—to see the forest rather than a single tree. Both processes can also link to training, seminars, conferences, and other learning experiences. Both options also require a commitment of time and money, sometimes over the long term.

The Career Recipe

A foundational element of career planning and development is that careers are like recipes: they have various ingredients that must be combined in the proper proportions.

Security Supervision and Management. http://dx.doi.org/10.1016/B978-0-12-800113-4.00015-8

People with considerable experience but no higher education are limited as to where they can go with their career. The same is true for people who have a great deal of education but no experience. The former will probably top out and not be able to advance beyond a certain point. The latter will have trouble entering the field. Either way, their career path is cut short by a deficiency in one area. In basic terms, a "career recipe" consists of several key elements. While there are exceptions, in the overwhelming majority of cases a career candidate should have some of each of the following elements on his or her resume: education, training, experience, licensing, networking, and certification.

The Education Ingredient

Postsecondary education is essential to maximizing managerial performance. The military has commissioned officers and noncommissioned officers. The commissioned officers have degrees and are primarily middle (lieutenant, captain, major) or upper (colonel, general, commander, admiral) level managers. Noncommissioned officers are sergeants, corporals, and chief petty officers. They are primarily supervisory. This military organizational model makes sense and is duplicated more or less by nonmilitary organizations. Philosophy courses aid in critical thinking; languages aid in cultural awareness, etc.—precisely the skill sets that managers need. That said, getting a degree is difficult. Considerable self-discipline is necessary. It may make sense to complete a certificate or a 2-year associate degree before obtaining a bachelor's degree.

Another strategy is to take courses online. Doing so gives a person some degree of control over his or her schedule. It may be possible to complete a course (and degree) in a shorter amount of time than one would need for a traditional college or university. It must be said that many online programs require a lot of work and time, so the flexibility is not as great as one may think. One caution slowly diminishing, is that some unenlightened employers see online education as not being as rigorous as traditional university education. A perusal of profiles on social media suggests that a large number of people get their degree from a traditional college and then acquire a graduate degree through an online institution. As more and more traditional schools offer online opportunities, the concern of employers has lessened and should continue to do so.

Internships and apprenticeships are good career developers. While the security field does not have a large number of apprenticeships outside of technical areas, almost all colleges offer internships. These are marriages between academic and practical field work and are primarily completed at a sponsoring organization. Corporate security internships can be outstanding learning opportunities with the intern working on projects, conducting research, and performing at least some relevant job functions. Internships offer great learning opportunities and perhaps even on-the-job training. More importantly, they can open up a network. Some persons that serve as interns are later hired by their sponsoring organizations.

Education costs money—lots of money, and far too much in the view of many respected professionals. Some ways to make it more affordable are to take courses at community colleges where the tuition costs less. Seek out scholarships; colleges and professional organizations have information on this. Use tuition reimbursement programs offered by employers. Take full advantage of any free or discounted courses available—even if they do not lead to a degree they are still of value. Benefits received from the government or military to fund education is another option. Seek paid internships, perhaps at colleges where work can be done with the campus security department.

The Training Ingredient

Training on how to perform job functions is crucial for success. One must be able to perform all of the aspects of the job well, in order to supervise and manage others. One must be able to last long enough on the job in order to gain the necessary experience to advance. Proficiency in interviewing, managing people during crises, and enforcement, are critical skills for the security professional to have that *will not* be obtained via education alone. Employers need people who can deal with the public, manage problems, conduct investigations, and write reports. If educational programs do not provide these skills, they do not really provide professional development experiences.

The lack of adequate socialization that results from not having training can be an issue, especially for emergency or military-oriented training. Protection professionals must respond to a crisis. There is no time for discussion. People have to do what needs to be done and give or take orders. First aid, defensive tactics, and traffic control classes are oriented to provide the learner with some emergency/military orientation. This is necessary not only in terms of specific behaviors but also because of the commitment to service that protection professionals adhere to.

The Experience Ingredient

In some ways, experience is the best teacher. By doing something, one can learn it in a way that no other education or training approach can deliver. This is why professional certification requires experience. It is also why licenses often expect it, and some jobs demand a certain amount or type of experience. Managerial jobs will almost certainly require supervisory experience. Investigative jobs generally require experience as well. In some cases, investigators must be experienced in operations before they are hired on as investigators: one cannot investigate what one does not understand. If it is not required, astute career developers can leverage sector or vertical experience in order to obtain investigative, security, and/or supervisory positions. A summer spent working as a teller gives one some background in banking. A seasonal retail job that involves taking inventory may substantially aid one in moving into retail loss prevention/investigation or some type of auditing function.

It is common in many governmental agencies to require experience for investigative positions. Without military experience, one way to gain a foothold in those positions is through experience with retail loss prevention. Nearly every major store has at least one loss prevention agent; in larger stores, there will be a manager and a team of loss prevention staff. These jobs can be obtained on a part-time basis, especially around holidays.

In addition, the retail sector is the undisputed leader in terms of focused interviewing. Retail security personnel conduct interviews with suspected employee thieves more than in any other environment. This interviewing experience is critical, along with supply chain security, information and intelligence sharing, and liaison experience in retail loss prevention.

The Licensing Ingredient

Licenses issued by a government agency are required to perform certain functions, such as driving a vehicle, flying a plane, carrying a weapon, charging a fee for providing investigations, installing locks or security systems, and acting as a door supervisor. If one does not have a license, one cannot perform these functions. Possessing a license that is relevant to the job one applies for will stand out to an employer. If one does pursue licensure, such as for firearms or transportation of hazardous materials, it is important to keep abreast of licensing requirements as these change and can have a substantial effect upon one's career.

Networking and Organizations

Networking is essential to career development for various reasons. The obvious, most cited reason is to find employment. In order to get a job, one must first know of its existence. Most jobs are not advertised, or if they are advertised, they are unattainable: the job has already been filled, the posting is for employment law purposes only, there is too much competition to get the job, etc. Networking also aids in gaining contacts with people who can help solve problems or assist in research/intelligence. This enables one to succeed at a job—a key aspect for continued employment! Finally, networking helps keep one current as new developments are passed along the network.

There are various types of networks, and each network is different. Using various networks can work in one's favor—and the favor of others that they serve—and this is what they should aspire to achieve. There should be a mix of online and offline networks. Oftentimes, people make the mistake of relying too much on a single network. Externships or job shadowing can help develop a network. Part-time work can help develop a network. Keeping in touch with people that one meets or works with during externships or part-time work is also considered a network. The social and family networks are there—just by taking an inventory may help establish this. List the people in these networks and identify what jobs they have or have had. Identify their background and connections and talk to friends and family about their jobs, backgrounds, and connections.

Professional organizations are networks in and of themselves, and *they may be the most effective way to establish career networks*. The key is being a member—an active member—of one or more groups. An active member goes to meetings and participates in events or attends conferences and seminars. Conferences and seminars are excellent ways of meeting and keeping connected to true professionals. An inside perspective on various employment options can be obtained by speaking with people at a conference. Many organizations, regardless of type, have a presence on social media, and particularly on LinkedIn, which is intended for professionals to network with one another.

Civic organizations, such as Young Professionals, are commonly found in cities and provide local networking opportunities. Service organizations, such as the Lions Club or Rotary International, are also excellent networks with chapters throughout the world.

The Certification Ingredient: Milestones of Professionalism

Professional certification programs are established within each industry. The security industry has a wide array of professional certifications. Before the certification programs themselves are discussed, it is necessary to lay a foundation regarding what constitutes a "profession" and what a "professional" is.

Members of a profession are regarded as professionals. Professions generally have the following components:

- A recognized body of knowledge: This body of knowledge is unique to the profession. It can also include supportive knowledge shared with other fields.
- Advanced education and training: This is an extensive learning regimen undertaken only by members of the profession. It uses both theoretical and applied knowledge.
- An experiential component or apprenticeship of some sort: This can be an internship, apprenticeship, or required amount of time spent in the practice of the profession.
- Adherence to a code of ethics: Members of the profession share a consensus on what encompasses ethical conduct.
- Reputation as a professional organization or association: These professional entities facilitate the exchange of new research, legal standards, and methods of operation. It also creates and enforces ethical standards among members. Professional associations represent the profession to the public via lobbying efforts, news releases, websites, etc.
- Recognition by the public that it is a profession: Rigor, research, and exclusivity all help form the "product" that is marketed to the public. Public relations efforts, married with the passage of time, help the profession to gain acceptance.

Benefits of Professional Certification

Society at large benefits from professional certification processes in security. Security professionals who are certified receive recognition of that. Clients, employers, and end user (customers, visitors, tenants, patients, etc.) of the professional's services, see the certification and know that the holder has met a higher standard of expertise than someone without it. This is an important point because the public at large is increasingly dependent upon security professionals for their protection.

Employers, clients, and students or certified individuals also benefit. Employers can incorporate professionally certified employees into a vertical or horizontal promotional scheme, and they can market this externally via press releases to news media or industry-specific publications. This way, clients receive a substantial degree of assurance of professional competency. Having security service employees complete professional certification processes is an excellent means of quality assurance that can be written into a contract. In other settings, the client entities can assess how much contract companies support professional certification.

Taking time to become certified validates one's professional development and shows a commitment to self-improvement and adherence to increasingly high standards. Certification provides opportunities for personal growth and brings well-deserved recognition from peers and colleagues. Being professionally certified offers one an immense degree of personal accomplishment, for which it is impossible to put a price. Being professionally certified not only gives one an immense degree of accomplishment but will also make the individual stand out with the potential employer.

Preparing for professional certification is an incremental process whereby certification take time. One becomes designated after acquiring the knowledge and experience. One should not become intimidated by the extensive experience requirements mandated in certain programs. The appropriate perspective is to view this as a journey. Remember the old adage "The longest journey begins with the first step." Candidates should do what they can now to pave the way for acquiring certification later.

Gaining an initial designation and then progressing from there makes sense in terms of individual career development because the security industry lacks a distinct career ladder. However, certification can be combined with progressively more responsible jobs to create a career ladder. Security officers can become Certified Protection Officers. As they gain more experience, they can complete the Security Supervision and Management Program and step into a supervisory role. Once there, they can complete the process to become certified in Security Supervision and Management. After several more years of experience as a supervisor and eventually a manager, they can study for the Certified Protection Professional (CPP) designation and successfully take the CPP exam.

For information on security industry-related certifications, see the appendix.

Congratulations, You're Hired

Ultimately, all of this networking, training and certification should lead to a job commensurate with those efforts. Learning the organizational culture, people, and the roles and responsibilities will take time. Eventually, as experience is gained and relationships develop, one may someday decide that there are more opportunities out there. One thing that is not taught in schools, however, is how to take advantage of opportunities within the organization.

Getting Promoted

Part of career development is not just about the job one has at the moment, it is also about the next job via promotion. With that in mind, the following list will serve to guide the security professional into acquiring that promotion:

- Excel at current job tasks.
- Be visible. Work throughout the organization by way of special projects, committee membership, etc.

- Be reliable and responsible. This is critical to the protection and investigation business. It becomes even more so as one assumes greater responsibilities.
- Cultivate your own individual brand. Establish specialties. Develop your own unique expertise, contacts, and approaches to problem solving.
- Show real-world examples of leadership roles. Leadership experiences, in whatever way acquired, demonstrate that one can lead a team of people.
- Practice interviewing. There is no point in preparing for a career if one is going to fail in an interview. Students should leverage their school's career center. Asking help from knowledgeable relatives, friends, or associates is a good idea too.
- Prepare and practice an "elevator speech"—a 30-s communication designed to make essential points.
- Understand and use recruiters. Professional recruiters are often used to fill upper management positions. Recruiters are knowledgeable in interview strategies as well as the specialized verticals that they work in.
- Pay attention to details. Grammatical errors on resumes are noticed and can be a deciding factor when competing for a position. Have several people review the prepared resume (think "overlapping audit systems").
- Data driven results and data driven careers. Get familiar with data! Understanding how metrics can be used is a necessity in all market sectors. This will only grow over time.
- Project management experience is a definite career builder. Being able to operate independently, manage time frames, work with others, and communicate appropriately to different constituencies is key to executing a project. These interactions can help add to or develop networks.
- Be willing to move! Relocation will probably be a necessity at some points in one's career. However, this is a complex decision and all economic and family factors must be considered. Ascertaining the likelihood of having to move is something that should be done early in the career planning phase.

Moving On

Sometimes the best way to move up is to move out. It is important to carefully weigh all relevant factors before doing so. Once the decision is made, there are effective ways to leave while leaving a good impression. The incumbent should be as positive and productive as possible. What will be remembered is the time from the resignation to the last day at work, and unfortunately not the contributions made during the tenure. Advance notice should be given both in writing and in person. Giving adequate notice is professional. Waiting until the last moment or emailing a notice of resignation is not.

The only person who should be made aware of the resignation is the immediate supervisor by way of direct report. A private conversation with this supervisor should be accompanied with a very concise letter stating that another opportunity has arisen and that the time spent with the employer was appreciated. Be humble, positive, and polite. Prior to leaving, get all affairs, files, etc. in order. Demonstrate care, consideration, and concern with getting things accomplished and in proper order. Document properly all projects for the immediate supervisor. Leave a list of necessary contacts for the next person who will take the position. Be orderly, considerate, and professional.

Career Killers

There are some behaviors that will kill or seriously wound one's career. Most of these killers are behavioral, such as gossiping or whining. One fatal career wound is caused by failing to understand the job or organization to which one wants to belong. Understanding the career field and the employer is important. Most people do not realize the scope and nature of contract security, retail loss prevention, hospitality and casino security, or other subdisciplines within the security field. Researching employers is also critical because the culture, scope, and nature of an individual business must be understood. The duties of a casino security officer and an industrial security officer are similar but *not* the same, nor are they the same as a bank security officer, a campus security officer, or a loss prevention agent.

Behaviour can be an issue in the workplace. Two common behaviors that are not only career killers but also stifle a career are gossiping and complaining. Granted, people are human beings and they talk to one another and sometimes about one another. Sometimes people will talk about things they do not like. People who constantly talk about their coworkers, regardless of the veracity of their statements, eventually cause problems. One cornerstone of the security industry in most disciplines is the ability to be discrete. Those who gossip or badmouth others are not seen as discrete. With the prevalence of social media, these issues are now played out in writing, and live on with "The internet never forgets."

Sometimes it is what a person fails to do that causes his or her career to stagnate. Security professionals need to stay abreast of current events, technology, techniques, and tactics; educating oneself in these issues is an ongoing process. Failing to do this puts one at a disadvantage when seeking a promotion or a position with another entity. In a similar vein, when one becomes so comfortable in a particular position that development ceases, it can be problematic. In the end, management ultimately decides where and when someone works.

Emerging Trends

The security industry continues to grow and diversify. As a result, clients have been demanding better service from contract suppliers. Premium security services have shown significant growth in America. In the United Kingdom, a trend has occurred where contract agencies partner with other businesses and also provide services to government agencies. The United Kingdom has also seen some movement toward more licensing. Canada and the United States have seen a trend toward the regulation of both contract and proprietary security personnel, affecting several Canadian provinces and US states in doing so.

Retailers have instituted more training in the United States following significant lawsuits. Over the course of several decades, retailers have changed in terms of the activities they deal with. Today, retail loss prevention agents conduct internal investigations and actively fight organized retail crime, product counterfeiting, etc. Organized crime has caused some retailers to increase the size of their loss prevention departments. Large-scale fraud and massive customer data breaches will become major challenges to loss prevention professionals. These issues have spawned companies that now provide specialized intelligence, information technology security, background investigations, training, etc. These all create new career options, especially for the entrepreneurial individual.

Conclusion

Security supervisors have assumed more managerial roles in the last decade or so. While the job title may be "supervisor," much time is spent on managerial functions. At the same time, there is more interface with different departments, vendors, etc. The supervisor and the manager positions have morphed into more of a coordination role, where communication skills and emotional maturity are essential to success.

Refer website http://www.ifpo.org for further information

16

Orientation for Security Officers

Marianna Perry, Lawrence J. Fennelly

Introduction

Orientation begins prior to the effective date of employment, prior to communicating the corporate benefits package, and prior to introducing the new hire to organizational staff members. Orientation of new employees begins with the posting of a vacancy, the invitation to enter the employee screening process, and—most importantly—the interview itself.

When conducting interviews for one or two open positions, the goal should be to interview at least 10 applicants so there will be enough information to compare responses to the same questions. Look not only for education and professional certifications, but previous job experience and the number of years in the security industry, military, or customer service field.

The key to successful personnel selection means taking the time to hire the right person by performing all the steps in the process. Security has changed dramatically over the years. There now are designated budgets for security, similar to other management departments. Security is now considered to be a crucial member of the management team. Because the image of security has truly changed and become more professional, the security industry as a whole must continue to invest in future security personnel. This can only be accomplished by being dedicated to a thorough and well-defined hiring process supported by a comprehensive list of policies and procedures. Once that is in place, compliance with the process is critical.[1]

Those who choose a start career in security and related fields, such as law enforcement, communications, corrections, and emergency medical services, do not have the skills necessary to simply show up and perform the job in a proficient manner without training. These career fields have a basic training requirement, such as an academy or orientation training. Regardless of the size of the organization, one can expect some form of orientation and training. It is at this time that the scope of responsibility will be clarified. Basic training provides a foundation for job skills and responsibilities. However, it does not provide *all* the skills necessary to ensure candidates are ready to perform the duties required to do the job in a solo or proficient status. It is at this point that a field training officer (FTO) will take over the training of the newly hired officer.

Security Supervision and Management. http://dx.doi.org/10.1016/B978-0-12-800113-4.00016-X

Background Checks/Investigations

Because security is synonymous with trust, ensuring that a thorough background investigation is completed is a critical step in the hiring process. Conducting a thorough background investigation may involve the following:

- Criminal record check in a particular state or possibly nationwide
- Social security number verification
- Motor vehicle record validation
- Employment verification
- Credit report
- Fingerprinting for criminal background check (some states require fingerprinting on individuals specifically in the security profession)
- Drug testing

The Fair Credit Reporting Act governs all aspects of background checks.[2]

Technically speaking, the orientation of new employees begins when the applicant reports for their first day of employment. The mood should be light, the atmosphere comfortable, and the anticipation of beginning a new relationship (for both parties) one of enthusiasm rather than anxiety, paranoia, or distress. Taking appropriate measures during the marketing and selection process will help to set the foundation for a marriage between corporate objectives and an employee's desire for success.

What follows is a list of activities and/or topics that should help new staff become productive colleagues. Each organization should tailor this list to represent their unique business objectives and decide who in the organization will take responsibility for each item.

In this chapter, measures that should be considered prior to the selection process, as well as critical components that help in planning for a seamless transition for a new employee into the company, will be discussed. More importantly, the key review process that must be taken as part of an ongoing corporate orientation program, as well as performance measures, will be covered. These performance measures are integral to the orientation program because they allow the company to assess the effectiveness of the orientation program.

Pre-orientation

The basic rule of interviewing is to make a good first impression. Interviewees and new employees must remember this cliché, as their career paths may be determined on how they present themselves throughout the hiring process. The language used on company website and in advertisements to recruit new officers is important. The words that are used to describe the position are essentially "branding" the organization. It is essential that professionalism and integrity set the tone of the organization to attract the job applicant. The applicant will understand that they must display a professional attitude and appearance, not only be hired, but to "fit in" with the organization. They need to realize that all first impressions, especially the interview, are critical.

Although the applicant's first impression establishes a foundation for everything that follows during their interview process, the security supervisor must remember that the candidate is also forming an impression of the supervisor and the institution. With this in mind, supervisors must be cognizant of how they portray themselves, as well as the organization itself. How the supervisor communicates, both verbally and nonverbally, leaves a lasting impression in the mind of the applicant. It is critical to recognize this fact when advertising position vacancies, writing position descriptions, scheduling interviews, and meeting with the applicant for the first time. The organization depends on the supervisor to represent the organization's interests and to portray a positive image at all times.

Personal Appearance and Uniform Maintenance

Security officers are issued "wash and wear" or "dry clean only" uniforms and should be instructed on the proper care and maintenance of their uniforms. Discuss items such as shoes, socks, hats, and belts, as well as what the security officer should do if the uniform is in need of repair, replacement, or alterations.

Explain the company policy regarding acceptable hairstyles, including length and color, visible piercings, and tattoos. Keep in mind that reasonable accommodation may need to be made for religious beliefs or medical conditions.

Grooming and good personal hygiene are also important aspects of projecting a professional image. Emphasize that appearance, attitude, and actions reflect on the organization as a well as the individual security officer.

Within First Week of Arrival

If not completed on the first day, within the first week of employment, each new employee should be given a departmental orientation by the immediate supervisor. The orientation should cover the department's functions, organization, and goals. Information given to the employee will also include job responsibilities, annual review, performance evaluation standards and expectations, introduction to department members, tour of department, confidentiality, and emergency procedures.

It is important for the newly hired officer to be trained on the day shift in order to see how things function and where job responsibilities on their assigned shift fit into the overall operation of the site. All security officers need to be trained on the "front end" or the security desk/customer service desk. In this position, the security officer will learn how to respond to various situations and learn who to notify when there is a question or concern. When the recently hired security officer begins his or her on-the-job training with the site training officer, each step should be repeated again, and tours or "rounds" of the building completed, as it is important that the new security officer be given a thorough orientation of the site. This is best accomplished by a very capable and experienced FTO. For instance, if the lesson is on patrol procedures, the FTO should take the new officer to every location in the facility several times, until the new officer is familiar and aware of the various problems that have occurred in the past at each location. Emphasis must be placed on proper procedures for various situations that may occur. For example if there is an alarm at 2:00 am and the procedure is to notify four people, that is what must be done. It is important that post orders are followed for each and every incident or occurrence.

FTOs are similar to mentors in that they help to acclimatize the new hire to the job they will be doing. FTOs differ from mentors in that they may also be responsible for evaluating the probationary employee's job performance and making recommendations to improve performance. FTOs must be trained on how to instruct, as well as how to evaluate and supervise security officers.

Standardized FTO training helps reduce liability as it averts the following:

- Negligent hiring
- Negligent retention
- Negligent assignment
- Negligent entrustment
- Negligent training
- Negligent supervision
- Failure to direct
- Due process issues[3]

Training

Training topics, such as professionalism, ethics, confidentiality, limits of authority, use of force, drug and alcohol use, firearms and other weapons, workplace violence prevention, emergency response, harassment, and the company's social media policy, may be addressed during orientation and then again at each post or location.

In addition to company information and site-specific guidelines contained in the post orders, if the site or company has a designated Department of Homeland Security SAFETY Act certificate, additional training, such as on antiterrorism awareness, weapons of mass destruction, and Customs-Trade Partnership Against Terrorism, may be required by all security officers assigned to that particular site.

Additional training may be required by the Occupational Safety and Health Association or a state occupational safety and health program for those security officers assigned to a specific location or industry. This training may explain personal protective equipment, hazard communications, global harmonization systems training, fire extinguisher training, emergency response and preparedness, bloodborne pathogens, cardiopulmonary resuscitation, automated external defibrillator, and first aid training. Depending upon the industry-specific requirements, training in verbal de-escalation techniques or nonviolent physical crisis intervention may also be required. It is important to know what industry specific training is required.

If a security officer is assigned to a site where firearms, handcuffs, mace or pepper spray, nonlethal weapons, etc. are required as a condition of assignment, additional training will need to be conducted by a certified instructor in order to be in compliance with local, state, and federal laws. It is important that all aspects of training meet—and preferably exceed—industry standards. Certification may be required for specific training to acknowledge that the officer has reached a proficiency level through the training requirements. This training must be conducted by an instructor with certified credentials on the specific topic. Certification is not the same as licensing, and not all areas have licensing requirements.

Every security officer should receive training in human relations, in order to provide excellent customer service and effective communication techniques. Training should also include report writing, radio communications, and telephone etiquette.

Before a New Staff Member Arrives

New employee orientation should begin with ease and transition for both the employee and the organization. To make that connection, however, it is imperative that all facets of integration are used. With respect to the embracing of a new employee, current staff and the prospective newcomer should be aware of their roles as well as those that are complementary to them.

The new employee should review and become familiar with their job description. This job description should specifically explain how the officers need to perform within the organization. These job-specific instructions are called post orders. Post orders are basically a description of officer responsibilities as well as procedures to follow for a specific location. They should include control and planning tasks, and system-wide obligations. The direct authority over the employee should also be identified to prevent conflicts arising from uncertainty as to who makes the decisions for particular issues. The job description should also reflect the organization's expectations of employees regarding self-management responsibilities and should include temporary job assignments that may happen during employment.

Prior to a New Employee's First Day of Employment, It Is Recommended to Send the New Staff Member the Following Information:

- A welcome letter
- A job description, to be repeated in person
- Instructions for first day and week (e.g., review of policies and procedures)
- When, how, and where to arrive
- Who to contact and a direct telephone number
- Where to park and where not to park
- Uniform attire
- What to expect the first few days
- Explanation of on-the-job orientation/introduction to people, job, office, department, and the organization

- What to expect regarding meals, breaks, and time for personal business
- Initial work responsibilities and overtime rates/hours
- Required or recommended reading, such as publications created by the department
- A description of the work setting
- Any other advance material that would allow for a smooth transition for the new security officer and organization.

Consider the Following before Introducing the New Security Officer to Staff Members:

- Distribute an announcement to current staff
- Schedule time for all staff to meet the new employee; set up time for essential meetings with payroll, personnel, supervisor, etc.
- Communicate the new employees' role in the organization
- List the experience/value the security officer will bring to the institution
- Disseminate a photograph if possible
- Ask staff to make an effort to get to know the new security officer

Many organizations prefer to use an employee handbook. When this is the case, the security officer should sign a form to acknowledge receipt of the handbook. This handbook is helpful to the new employee as the written material can be reviewed when questions arise.

The Handbook May Include the Following Information:

- The mission of the organization and company values
- The working environment, outlining company policies on equal opportunity employment, discrimination, the Americans with Disabilities Act, harassment, drug and alcohol policies and testing, workplace violence, unsafe working conditions, and how to report issues in the workplace
- Professional development, including training and recognition programs in addition to how to communicate effectively
- Standards of conduct, which include ethics, guidelines, political activity, attendance, uniforms and appearance, post orders, equipment, communications, confidential information, conflicts of interest, nepotism, workplace relationships, dealing with the media, smoking, firearms policy, limits of authority, use of force, and vehicles
- Company employment policies , including classification, probationary period, transfers and promotions, hours of work and overtime, meals, salary, leaves of absence, the Family and Medical Leave Act, medical/personal/military/bereavement leave, and jury duty
- Benefits, including medical/dental/life/disability insurance programs, retirement, workers' compensation, and holidays/vacation/sick days
- Discipline and termination policies, including voluntary/involuntary termination and layoffs, discipline, and termination guidelines

First Day of Work

At the start of the first day, each new employee shall have a payroll and personnel orientation. The orientation is designed to help new employees better understand personnel policies and procedures. The session may last up to one hour and will review general payroll and personnel topics, such as meetings with the payroll/personnel team, pay rate and schedules, benefits, performance evaluation and standards, and holiday schedules.

Additional Checkpoints for the First Day Should Include the Following:

- Issue an employee identification. Nothing says "welcome to the team" like a new badge with your employee's photo, name, and corporate logo.
- Employee should meet with his or her supervisor (and others as appropriate) for office orientation, goals, and objectives.
- Review of primary activities.

Communicate policies, procedures, bulletins, pass-on logs, daily activity reports, and other governance documents, such as working hours, telephone techniques and etiquette, customer service, correspondence styles, staff meetings, budget and accountability, service culture, confidentiality, ethics, working with supervisors, colleagues, assistants, and/or volunteers.

Mentoring

Mentoring is a formal process in which mentors are trained and sometimes compensated for taking someone under their wing. Mentors are generally senior employees who can provide both an example to the new employee and address any concerns that they might have. Mentors are not supervisors. They perform no evaluative functions. They may represent management insofar as proper codes of conduct and performance are concerned, but they have no authority to discipline. A good mentor's objective is to see that the student advances within the profession and has the job knowledge to advance. Many times, a mentoring program will be used to prepare officers for promotional opportunities or positions with increased responsibility.

Report Writing

Professional report writing is difficult and it takes practice to develop this skill. Many people have never been taught how to properly write a report; some lack the literacy skills necessary and others simply do not want to write one. All of these obstruct the process and create problems for supervisors. The report must be completed by the end of shift, and it is important that the new officer understands this. It is important to stress the accuracy of all written reports.

Six Important Points for the Security Incident Report

Above all, the report should be clear and concise. A good report must answer and address these six basic questions:

1. **What?** What happened?
2. **Where?** Where is the exact location of the occurrence?
3. **Who?** The security officer here must address as many "who's" as possible: who made the call, who was notified and when, who was the cause of the incident, etc.
4. **When?** When were you notified? When did it happen?
5. **Why?** This involves judgment and opinion and may not be easily proven, but it may be very important in the judgment of guilt or liability.
6. **How?** How did it happen? Detail of the chain of events.

Role of the Security Officer

Uniforms demonstrate consistency and authority within an organization. Security/protection officers are often the first people that visitors to a facility or organization encounter; therefore, employers acknowledge the need for their officers to be professionally attired. However, security/protection officers should not rely only on their uniform to maintain a professional image; they must also ensure that every facet of their being serves to project a positive public image, including their demeanor and the manner in which they interact with people.

Uniforms not only allow a protection officer to obtain the respect of the community but also provide a foundation for a protection/security officer's self-respect. According to Sennewald: "Issuing or permitting the use of shabby uniforms … takes away from (an employee's) sense of pride. High standards for uniforms, on the other hand, automatically instill self-pride, and hence, self-respect."[4]

Other Points to Consider

It can be advantageous to assign a "partner" to a new security officer, preferably a peer, to whom the new employee can ask any questions without fear of reprisal. A colleague who is relatively new to the organization might be the best choice because they have a fresh perspective and are familiar with questions a new staff member might have. If a partner is not assigned, someone else should cover these topics with the new staff member.

Keep in mind that overwhelming the employee can have the same effect as doing nothing at all.

The Immediate Supervisor Should Address and Readdress All of the Following Key Components during the First Week:

- Ensure that the employee's work area is set up.
- Check in frequently to clarify expectations and answer questions that the employee may have.

- Request that colleagues should also check in to answer questions and offer support.
- Ensure that the "partner," mentor, or field training officer is checking in daily to answer questions and offer support.

The New Protection/Security Officer Should Meet with the Department's Business Manager and/or Payroll Personnel to Cover, As Appropriate, the Following:

- Time cards
- Vacation/sick/personal leave policies
- Keys
- Access to the office on nights and weekends
- Telephone: access code, personal calls, paying for personal long-distance calls
- E-mail address and access to the system
- Parking stamps, parking permits
- Travel and reimbursement (if the security officer will be traveling)
- Company credit card (if issued)
- Telephone credit card use (if issued)
- Cellular phones, pagers, and personal digital assistants
- Company vehicle policies
- Learning about and submit benefits applications (health and life insurance, retirement, etc.)
- Receiving company identification (highly recommended on first day)
- Obtaining company parking permit (if appropriate)
- Meeting with management information systems personnel for computer assistance, network access, and explanation of hardware (turning on, backing up, printing, etc.), software (word processing, data processing, emailing, etc.), and overview of policies and procedures, including confidentiality and piracy. After an assessment of computer proficiency, training may be scheduled if necessary
- Touring the building and immediate area

Within 6 Months of Starting:

The following should be completed within 6 months of a new employee's starting date, or in be part of the regular routine:

- Meeting of key people and offices within the company
- Meeting on a regular basis with supervisor to discuss issues and review job description, expectations, and performance
- Checking of "partner"/mentor on a regular basis to answer questions and offer support
- Attending the company's new staff orientation (for an overview of company people, departments, policies, and procedure), and taking a tour of the company facilities
- Performance measures and program evaluation, as part of 90-day and 180-day reviews

Orientation is a critical juncture in socializing the new employee. It marries recruitment, training, supervision, organizational attitudes, and personal characteristics into one consolidated impression. Due to the significant importance of first impressions, the reality of present-day security force training, and the critical element of understanding of the organizational culture by protection officers, orientation must be carefully programmed and regularly evaluated for effectiveness.

Implementing a review of any success should be part of every professional's personal assessment. As all professionals should effectively pursue opportunities to continuously improve, so should the image of the organization. While self-evaluation is highly recommended, all recruiters, mentors, managers, and staff should regularly evaluate their orientation programs for both success and opportunities for improvement.

Conclusion

Field training officers and mentors have been identified as being an integral part of the operation. Why? Consider the professionalism and image of the department. If the quality of a report is poor, then retraining might be required. If calls for service are not addressed properly, again retraining might be required. If retraining fails to correct the problem, it may be that the security officer is not a good fit for the organization. Give the officer the chance to improve.

Refer website http://www.ifpo.org for further information

End Notes

1. Black, Inge Sebyan, "Security Personnel Selection," in Davies, Sandi & Hertig, Christopher A., ed., *Security Supervision & Management: Theory and Practice of Asset Protection* (New York, NY: Elsevier, 2008), 63–66.

2. Black, Inge Sebyan.

3. Author Unknown, *National Association of Field Training Officers* (Peoria, AZ: National Association of Field Training Officers, 2013), accessed April 29, 2014. Available: http://ww.nafto.org.

4. Sennewald, Charles, *Effective Security Management* (New York, NY: Butterworth Heinemann, 1985), 66.

17

Time and Stress Management

Charles T. Thibodeau, Eric L. Garwood

A lack of adequate time management causes stress and can destroy a career. Stress left unmanaged can cause illness or death. In addition, it can really mess up your day! Because of the seriousness of this topic, this chapter is designed to assist us all with slowing down a little, chilling out, planning our work, and working our plan.

Time management and stress are topics that are very closely related. Just think of the last time you were late for a meeting and racing down the highway trying to get there by 10:00 am with only 3 minutes to go—but you were still 10 miles from your destination. If you had only left 15 minutes earlier, you could have had a stress-free ride to the meeting. This is a very typical stress caused by poor time management. How many other stressors do you have in your life that can be related to time management? Think about it. Is it possible that this is the result of road rage?

The interesting thing about time management and stress is that these two issues are sometimes linked. That is, poor time management may be caused by stress, and stress in turn may be caused by poor time management! The fact that we do not manage our time very well could be a cause of the stress that interferes with us managing our time properly. A person under pressure to meet a deadline generally experiences stress. When that stress peaks, a person may feel that time management is just getting in the way and abandons any hint of managing his or her time. On the other hand, if that same person starts the day under tremendous pressure, he or she may abandon the time it will take to plan out the day and become focused on meeting a single objective. Setting aside planning in the form of time management for one day may seem to accomplish one objective, but what about the rest of the time for that day?

When Is the Best Time for Planning Your Work?

Each day should not start with planning what to do. That should have already been done at the end of the previous day. Before ending any day, whether you are at your office desk or in your den at home, be sure that you spend some quiet time planning the next day. Go over your notes and upcoming calendar of events and have a solid plan for each day before you go to work. Keep in mind anything in the immediate future and what is coming your way just around the corner. You may not have an urgent deadline, but do you have a deadline coming in three weeks? Although this time may seem to be a long way off, it will be tomorrow's crisis sooner than you think. You may want to chip away at that long-range deadline a little each day. That way, when the deadline is just days away, you have the work almost finished.

Planning your time is a never-ending job. It is a balancing act between being able to deflect interruptions and being flexible enough to change when a true emergency happens. You must keep a calendar and notepad with you at all times so that you can update your plans periodically throughout the day. That way you can keep track of important business, projects, and deadlines. The idea of having something to write on and write with at all times is very similar to what we teach our security officers regarding field notes. We should follow our own advice.

The best time for planning is the evening before the next day's work. Find a quiet time and build a master plan for the next day or next week. By planning ahead for the next day, week, or even month, you can relax and not worry about forgetting something. This avoids reluctantly make adjustments to the master plan throughout the day as circumstances dictate. If some major event happens to throw your plan off, do not throw your hands up in defeat—get back on your plan as quickly as possible. Treat your master plan like a road map in which you took an unexpected detour and are now back on your mapped-out route.

Protecting the Master Plan

Time management becomes ineffective most often when we fail to plan, but there are also forces in our work environment that attempt to sabotage our master plan. At some point, those external forces sabotaging the supervisor's efforts to stay on track, must be defeated in order for the master plan to be followed. This can only occur if there is a plan to begin with. The word *management* in time management means controlling the requests for time. Time management control should include doing the following:

1. Handling the politically charged torpedoes as soon as possible.
2. Accommodating any time thievery that will help with personal or professional advancement.
3. Sidestepping requests by handling them through delegation to subordinates or scheduling the request for a later time.
4. Flat-out refusing to take precious time to be involved with other requests.

You know that time management saboteurs will be out there, so a part of time management planning includes planning how to say no to others graciously and who also want your immediate attention.

We recognize that you need to be flexible in the administration of your master plan, but never take your eye off the goal. You will want to become really possessive of your time management plan. Do not let anything or anyone take that away from you. The plan is always in your hands when it comes to spending supervisory time. Spend it wisely. Good time management means reduced stress on the job for you and everyone else affected by you and your decisions.

Routine Meetings

Although routine meetings are a necessity from time to time, the biggest drain on time management is time spent in those meetings. Meetings mean that people stop producing and meet at a place where they sit around and talk. There are some supervisors and managers who spend all their time going from one meeting to another. Trite but true is the saying "When it is all said and done, there is much more said than done."

Call a meeting only when it is absolutely necessary; keep the meeting time down to a minimum; always have a meeting agenda and stay on track; never serve refreshments; move the speakers along quickly; and dismiss the participants as soon as possible so that they can get back to the important jobs they were hired to perform. Do not allow the meeting to turn into a social gathering or a party. Keep it business oriented. It is a good idea to avoid calling meetings if other means of communications are available, such as email. If an actual meeting is necessary, use web conferencing and online meeting tools (e.g., GoToMeeting.Com) whenever possible. Use the other forms of communication when your physical presence is not absolutely necessary.

Remember the two important meetings that you will *not* want to miss: attend all politically charged meetings and meetings that will help your future advancement in the company. Other important meetings you should attend include job-related instruction and business planning meetings, professional license and certification credits training, and professional association meetings. Additional important meetings should be decided by the totality of the circumstances. Be sure to attend continuing training classes for professional certification or other mandatory training classes.

Politically Charged Meetings

From time to time, anyone in authority—from the supervisor to the president of the company—comes under scrutiny for decisions they have made. You must be observant of these occasions and defend your decisions in order to help others understand your rationale. You must be prepared to win support for the positions you take in your decisions. As you become more successful, you become a bigger target for those who get ahead by taking other people down. Corporate politics is serious business, so take it seriously.

Politically charged meetings are meetings where your position in the company may be threatened if you are not there. For instance, it may be seen as a point of embarrassment for your boss if you fail to show up at a meeting when he or she requested your presence. If you could get fired for missing a meeting, then definitely attend that meeting. If a meeting will result in exposure to individuals in the company who can make a positive difference in your future, you should attend that meeting as well.

Meeting Deadlines

Deadlines can be time management killers. Be sure when you promise to deliver something that you "promise long and deliver short." That is, if you think you can get a project done by

Wednesday, always promise it for Friday of that same week. When you come in early with a project, you create a euphoric response from your client. It is a stress reliever for the client, who does not have to worry about a deadline, especially with a critical time-sensitive commitment. Of course, just barely meeting the deadline on time might be acceptable, but finishing the project early is so much better! In addition, when you give yourself a cushion of time for delivery, you are being proactively preventative by taking into consideration unforeseen problems that could prevent your success of meeting that deadline.

Overextending your abilities can also be a time killer. The longer you struggle to complete an impossible task, the more time you waste. Never be afraid to admit that you do not have the skills and competence to accomplish something you are asked to do. None of us want to do this, but reality says that you cannot sacrifice the entire time management plan because your ego will not allow you to admit that you are not up to a specific task. Good time management requires you to know your skills and competencies, as well as having the ability to be honest with yourself and others regarding those things you cannot do. This prevents you from getting all bent out of shape with performance stress. Work toward reducing that list of "can't-do's"—you may not have a job if that list gets too long.

Prioritizing Your Work

Failure to prioritize is another time management problem. When planning your day, you need to be able to prioritize what it is you will be doing. See Table 17.1[1] for a simple time management form. You may want to set up a scale of first priority, second priority, and third priority (A, B, and C, respectively) with regard to what you will be doing the next day on the job. Those listed under the first priority (A) column should become an absolute imperative that must be accomplished before going home, including emergency response, meeting deadlines on deadline day, and satisfying politically charged issues.

In the second priority (B) column, you will include items that are day-to-day care needs, such as checking progress on delegated work, writing a portion of a long-term project, researching products you have been requested to purchase, maintaining databases, interviewing prospective employees, and other prescribed duties you are supposed to do

Table 17.1 Simple Time Management Form

Date/Time	First Priority (A)	Second Priority (B)	Third Priority (C)
8:00 am			
9:00 am			
10:00 am			
11:00 am			
12:00 pm			
1:00 pm			
2:00 pm			
3:00 pm			
4:00 pm			

with a high time priority. In the third priority (C) column, you will put the least important tasks—items that have no consequences if they do not get done that day; you can accomplish them the next day or even the next week if need be.

It may be nice to have some free time written into the C column for reading, researching, and professional development. That is a great stress-breaking strategy. In any event, having prioritized your tasks for the day will help you stay on track. You may lose part of your B column tasks and all of your C column tasks to the time management saboteurs, but you are not going home until you have completed your highest priority tasks. Prioritizing will provide a clear view of which tasks to refuse to deviate from when someone asks for some of your time. If the only items you accomplish are the A column tasks, you will have reduced your highest stress issues for that day. Then, your B column tasks can become your highest priority for tomorrow.

The Demon Phone and Social Media

Phone calling is almost archaic today with the advent of electronic communication, such as email, texting, and social media (e.g., Facebook). It seems like a new form of social media pops up every day. The advantage of electronic communications is that you can look at them when you have time. The disadvantage is that something urgent might not be seen for hours or even days. Nevertheless, these forms of communication can be some of the biggest time wasters ever—at least a phone call has a definite ending. However, phone interruptions can be a serious threat to your time management plan. Remember also that all forms of social media pose a high risk to sensitive data. Data cannot be secured on social media, so do not put company business there.

You can master your demon phone best if you have the right equipment. Caller identification is a must. Call forwarding and a good messaging system are also essentials. A sharp administrative assistant is a great barrier to unnecessary phone calls. When you do take a call, discipline yourself to stick to the topic of the phone call and end the call as quickly as possible so that you can get back to the tasks at hand. Your employer will appreciate that and you will reduce your stress level.

Delegation Skills That Lead to Success

Failure to delegate is a time waster. You are a supervisor because you are good at getting things done through the efforts of other people. Delegation of work tasks is actually a motivator. According to Abraham Maslow, the founder of humanistic psychology, employees need recognition and a feeling of belonging. By delegating important work to your subordinates, you will not only challenge them, you will be communicating that you value their skills and expertise—a form of recognition. In addition, you will be buying time to use on work that subordinates are not qualified or skilled enough to complete, you will motivate your subordinates, get more work done than you could all by yourself, and reduce stress through control of time management.

Dealing with Stress That Is Not Work Related

To survive in this world of ever-growing stress, we all must develop coping mechanisms. To accomplish this, we must start with a healthy lifestyle based on good values and attitudes. For some of us, that will be a big task because values and attitudes begin to develop very early in life. Our personality, which has a lot of influence on our values and attitudes, is said to be set by age six. In some cases then, it will take a personality change to acquire appropriate values and attitudes.

Our basic personality as well as our values and attitudes may lead us in all the wrong directions to reduce stress. Thus, if we really want a life-changing experience in these areas, it will be necessary for us to take a realistic personal inventory of all external stressors that negatively impact us to directly confront them. Seek education on how to enhance you people serving people skills. Strive every day to be other-people-centered and not so much self-centered. Your work as a supervisor is all about your subordinates and the clients you are serving, and not so much about you.

Handling Fears in Your Professional Life

It may be a good idea to make a list of all your fears regarding external stress components, such as fear of physical confrontation, public speaking, criticism, love disconnects, not belonging, not measuring up, not having a life plan, and just feeling disconnected from society. Rather than dodging these fears and hiding from them, it may be better to directly confront them until you lose your fear of them. Some terrific ways of fighting off and reconciling fears are joining a health club and working out on a regular basis, volunteering at a hospital to help others, becoming a tutor after school to help kids with reading difficulties, participating in an online community to meet people and have fun, getting 6–8 hrs of sleep every night, taking up bike riding, improving your diet, and losing weight, among countless other activities.

The idea here is to get active in the very things you fear. For instance, if you are afraid of public speaking, then take a Dale Carnegie course and become a public speaker. If you are afraid of crowds, heights, water, or anything else, then indulge in activities that bring you into direct contact with those fears. Force yourself to participate in those things you are afraid of. The more you expose yourself to performing in those character-weak spots, the stronger you will become. Soon you will be a good public speaker, swimmer, mountain climber, etc., and not have to fear the things that are holding you back.

The worst part of this kind of stress is what you become when you are doing nothing to fight it. As human beings, we cannot allow stress to control us; we must take control of it. Some of us quit smoking, quit drinking, clean up our language, and do as many other personal improvement activities that we can think of. We must take care of ourselves and raise our self-esteem before we can be an effective supervisor. You can do all of these things without expensive therapy. Stress is directly related to your physical and mental conditioning. In the end, we can be just about as stress free as we want to be.

Follow up and Follow through

Never leave a work task or project unsupervised for any reason. That is, be in control of the outcome of every work task that you delegate to an employee in your charge. Like the famous quote by President Harry S. Truman "The buck stops here." Ultimately, no matter who does the work, you are responsible for the positive or negative outcome.

You can accomplish excellent oversight on delegated work tasks by building in reporting stopgaps in the work direction. You can do this by requiring a progress report on where your employee is in the process of completion once a week, such as a Tuesday morning by 10:00 am. This should be done every Tuesday during the life span of the project or work task.

If you want to inject a shot of adrenaline into the personnel for whom you are responsible personally show up at the project site or work site to inspect their work in progress. Comment only on positive observations. Never let the employees feel that your onsite supervision is for punitive evidence gathering.

Site visits are for no other reason than to be available to the employee for help, or for something such as giving clarification to final product expectations. This includes answering technical questions and, when appropriate, giving the employee public praise for a job well done. Remember, when discussing recognition, it is said that "babies cry for it and men die for it." Recognition is a very strong behavior-controlling strategy used very successfully in supervising employees.

Your appearance at the work site, resulting in praise for your employees, will pay big dividends. Then, follow through as the employee gets closer to the deadline for delivery of his or her part of the project. Never delegate more than you can expect your employee to produce in the time allotted. If need be, give assistance to the project worker by providing additional employees when necessary to accomplish task to completion. Never delegate a task to an employee who does not have the skill set to be successful in the task. Be sure that you give your employees all the tools and assistance necessary to assure the employee's success. Grease the skids for the employee's positive outcome and brace yourself. You will be surprised just how much your employee can accomplish by the supervisor showing strong support for his or her work.

Warning about Praising

All employee praise, especially public praise, must be subject-oriented and specific to the performance of the employee receiving the praise. Thank the employee for a job well done when he or she has accomplished a task, stating the specific positive accomplishment. Empty-ended praise is seen as phony and something to fear; it will actually hurt your image and reduce the morale of the people you are supervising. Walk around to find your employee doing something right and then praise that behavior publically. This will produce repetition of the same kind of positive behavior—from that employee and any other employee who observed the praise. From that perspective, the praising process is a great tool for supervisors. However, giving made-up praise, or general praise that points to no specific accomplishment, reduces the professionalism of the praising process and is seen as suspect. It does more damage to employee morale than good.

Conclusion

It is obvious that stress and time management are definitely interconnected. The stress we experience, both at work and outside of work, may combine and trip us up on the job. This is important because, for the purpose of this chapter, we are concerned with how the clash of internal and external stressors affects our work performance. Of all the stressors we experience at work as a supervisor, stress emitting from the mismanagement of time must be considered critical. External stressors can only exasperate that work-stress experience.

We have only scratched the surface of the topic of time management. The reader is encouraged to continue this study from the many sources available. However, if nothing else, you should begin implementing some of the ideas expressed in this chapter.

The following concepts will help you to remember the most salient points of this chapter:

1. Remember that poor time management may be caused by stress; stress may be caused by poor time management.
2. Have something to write on and write with at all times.
3. All meetings are a drain on time management, regardless of how necessary. Minimize meeting time.
4. When you promise to deliver something, promise long and deliver short.
5. Be honest with yourself and others. Admit it when you do not have what it takes to accomplish a task. Consider partnering with another supervisor when these issues come up. Also, you may hire out tasks to trusted contract companies when you lack time or knowledge to complete them in a timely fashion.
6. Prioritizing will provide a clear view of which tasks to refuse to deviate from when someone asks for your time. Fight off the time thieves that reduce your productivity to focus on the tasks that count.
7. Stay off the phone unless the call is an emergency, strictly business, politically charged, or career-enhancing. In addition, do not text, Facebook, Tweet, or post on any social media. If a phone call is necessary, assign someone else to make it whenever possible. You can follow up on phone calls when you find the time. The phone is not your friend when you are trying to work on time management.
8. Task oversight is an essential component of time management. You must control the outcome of each project or work task you have delegated to others.
9. If you find you are doing more work yourself than you are delegating, you are probably not using the tool of delegation properly. Spend your time in follow-up and follow-through rather than working directly on the project tasks yourself.

10. Never leave a work task or project unsupervised for any reason. That is, be in control of the outcome of every work task that you delegate to an employee in your charge. Ultimately, no matter who does the work, you are responsible for the positive or negative outcome of every task you supervise.

11. Minimize external stressors. Problems in a supervisor's life outside of work have a definite negative impact on work performance by adding to the day-to-day internal stressors in the workplace. If you are trucking around external personal pressures, you are not going to be an effective supervisor at work. At the same time, the workplace can be a great stress reliever if you just work hard and bury yourself in work for 8 h a day. Remember each day to park your home-grown stress at the door before entering the workplace.

12. Recognition is a very strong behavior-controlling strategy that can be used very successfully in supervising employees.

Refer website http://www.ifpo.org for further information

End Note

1. Table 17.1; a simple time management form.

18

Employee Motivation Theory and Application

Eric Webb, Marianna Perry, Lawrence J. Fennelly

Part 1: Theory

Introduction

A motivated and emotionally engaged workforce is critical in any employment environment—even more so in the areas of public safety and asset protection. Creating an environment where staff feels appreciated, valued, and challenged develops a sense of pride and belonging in employees. Employees who appreciate and value their employer and associated job responsibilities are less likely to leave the organization, miss work, or expose the employer to liability and risk.

While the benefits of a motivated workforce are obvious to the novice manager, creating an atmosphere that fosters employee participation and motivation is difficult for even the most experienced supervisor or leader.

Unfortunately, there is no formula for fostering a positive, engaging work environment. Each individual employee is unique and presents different characteristics, history, and personality traits that may or may not respond to motivational techniques. The key to creating an environment that develops loyalty, creativity, and appreciation in employees lies within understanding the basic psychology of motivation and administering techniques diverse enough to meet the needs of heterogeneous employees.

As each organization is different, so are the keys to fostering motivation in those organizations. In this chapter, we will review the basic concepts of motivational theory. These theories, coupled with creative thinking, can provide management with the tools to create unique, effective, and responsive programs and policies that keep employees interested and engaged.

Theories of Behavioral Motivation

Maslow's Hierarchy of Needs

Through extensive research and analysis, social psychologist Thomas Maslow developed his well-respected theory of human motivation and responsive behavior.[1] Maslow's hierarchy of needs attempts to explain human psychological and social development through a series of progressive needs and desires that, once fulfilled, motivate the individual to develop the desire to pursue, then satisfy, the next subsequent and escalating need. To understand Maslow, one must meet the first need in its entirety before engaging in the next need.

Security Supervision and Management. http://dx.doi.org/10.1016/B978-0-12-800113-4.00018-3
Copyright © 2015 Elsevier Inc. All rights reserved.

Maslow's theory entails five fundamental human needs:

Level 1: Physiological needs: food, shelter, clothing
Level 2: Safety needs: self-preservation
Level 3: Social needs: a sense of belonging and acceptance
Level 4: Esteem needs: self-esteem and recognition from external sources
Level 5: Self-actualization: fully realizing one's full potential

There are three fundamental concepts Maslow promulgated in understanding his hierarchy: (1) behavior is affected by unmet needs; (2) individuals meet their most basic needs first and then escalate; and (3) fundamental needs take precedence over advanced needs.[2]

Maslow's levels of motivation translate well into the work environment. Each level can be related to an employee, from their initial hiring through promotion, training, and leadership. Understanding where an employee is within the organization, with reference to Maslow, may help management and supervisors determine the appropriate motivation and rewards for that individual.

For example, according to Maslow, the most basic fundamental needs of an individual (physiological and self-preservation) will motivate the applicant to seek employment. Employment offers the ability to provide food and shelter (Maslow's Level 1) and a means to maintain those achievements (Maslow's Level 2). A new hire can be classified within these paradigms. The new employee has been motivated to seek employment with your organization in order to meet fundamental needs, and is initially focused on learning the job in order to maintain employment that fulfills his or her need for self-preservation.

Remember, Maslow argues that individuals accelerate through the hierarchy of needs.[3] As one need is met, the next level of desire becomes essential. After an employee has met their basic needs and learned the skill set required to maintain employment (Levels 1 and 2), Maslow's hierarchy would suggest the employee begin to seek acceptance from coworkers and staff. Basically, once an employee understands how to do the job, they will seek to create social bonds with others that they are sharing the workplace environment. An employee at this stage may be receptive to programs or training that fosters a sense of teamwork or allows them to work with individuals they normally would not have an opportunity to meet. An employee at this stage may be receptive to shift work or overtime simply to expand opportunities to meet and relate to other members of the organization. Clearly, a new employee would not be an appropriate candidate for extensive rotation, overtime, or additional responsibilities as they are still engaged in a lower level of motivation. The new employee is focused on how to do the job in order to retain the job.

Once an employee has internalized the skill set required to be successful and has exercised opportunities provided by management to network within the organization, the next step in Maslow's theory is likely to develop. Level 4 of the hierarchy of needs seeks to meet self-esteem needs. At this point, the employee will be comfortable enough within the context of the organization to desire to contribute to the overall welfare or betterment of the operation. This may be the most difficult stage of effective management, but it also offers the most opportunity to motivate, develop, and retain effective employees. An employee desiring to fulfill esteem needs, will want to feel appreciated and needed within the corporation. This likely will manifest itself in employee suggestions to management, recommendations for improvements or changes in operating procedures, or even in the employee volunteering time or experience to contribute toward new ideas or procedures. A manager who listens to employee suggestions and takes them into consideration is more likely to foster a sense of loyalty than one who immediately rebukes such ideas. Even employee input that cannot be implemented offers management an opportunity to foster motivation. By communicating the reasons why a process cannot be adopted, coupled with appreciation for the employee's effort and input, management can instill the feeling of participation among the staff, thereby fulfilling the esteem needs of employees.

The final component of Maslow's need-based hierarchy entails self-actualization—in other words, a need to fully meet one's personal potential. Not every individual or every employee reaches this final step. Employees who do not feel valued by the organization or are constantly changing jobs (and therefore have not met their self-esteem or fundamental needs) will not seek to fully address their potential as an employee. However, individuals within an organization who do feel valued and secure in their employment, will look for ways to make their experience even more fulfilling. At this point, management should have in place programs for tenured staff that allow opportunities to achieve higher professional and personal goals. These individuals will seek to continue their education, obtain professional certification, or even cross-train within the organization to learn new skill sets. While this is the ideal scenario, an employee seeking to become as well rounded and valuable as possible will only do so after he has been properly trained, socialized, and recognized within the company.

While Maslow's theory certainly does not address every problem associated with employee motivation, it can be used as a guide to assist managers in determining where an employee is within their work experience. Subsequent appropriate motivators should be used to foster employee development and motivation.

Herzberg's Two-Factor Theory

In contrast to Maslow, Frederick Herzberg theorized that motivation (specifically in the workplace) is influenced by nonexclusive factors of job satisfaction and dissatisfaction.[4] Herzberg surveyed workers to determine what they appreciated about their jobs, as well as what frustrated them about their employment, which resulted in his two-factor theory.

Herzberg suggests that when certain factors are present they can provide motivation for employees. Herzberg simply and directly calls these motivating factors "motivators." Conversely, when other factors are absent, workers become frustrated and unsatisfied. Herzberg refers to these factors as his hygiene theory.[5]

The two-factor theory argues that successful managers must reduce job dissatisfaction by providing employees with hygiene factors.[6] These factors tend to relate to the environment in which one works and the context of that work. By providing safe working conditions, a reasonable salary, and benefits, employers meet the hygiene needs of their employees.

However, to truly engage and motivate employees requires that motivators must be implemented to encourage employee loyalty and growth.[7] Motivators include factors related to employee self-esteem and actualization. Common motivators may include responsibility, advancement, and recognition.[8]

In effect, Herzberg's theory may be readily combined with the ideas presented by Maslow. Where Maslow would argue fundamental needs must at first be met, Herzberg would see hygiene factors that require satisfaction. Maslow's subsequent pursuit of self-esteem and self-actualization is then reflected in Herzberg's motivation factors.

Many theorists actually combine the theories of Herzberg and Maslow into a single hierarchy of needs. However, for the purpose of this text, it is important to understand the unique concepts Herzberg presents to add to our understanding of employee motivation.

Reinforcement Theory

On a more fundamental level, the reinforcement theory seeks to explain motivation by examining consequences.[9] Knowing the result of certain behavior can affect the motivation of an individual to repeat the same behavior. Realizing positive benefits through exceptional performance, motivates employees to continue to strive to excel. Reinforcing positive behavior with rewards, motivates employees to continue that behavior. Subsequently, reinforcing negative behavior with sanctions deters employees from repeating certain actions.

In the security environment, it is all too easy to reinforce negative behavior through reprimands and sanctions. While it is certainly an occasional necessity, it often becomes the focus of supervisors in a paramilitary organization. Successful managers are those that take the time and initiative to communicate positive reinforcement to their staff. While rewards, benefits, and time off are excellent positive motivators, they may not always be practical or financially possible. Simply recognizing performance and expressing gratitude for that performance may be enough to foster a proactive environment where employees feel valued.

It is important to think creatively when implementing positive reinforcement. Employee-of-the-year (or month) programs can provide a cost-effective and easy opportunity to recognize performance. Progressive security employers do this in many cases. As an added incentive, the employee award is coupled with a premium parking space or company token of appreciation, and you now have a cost-effective positive employee motivation program in place that requires minimal administration.

Equity Theory

The equity theory, which was introduced by J.S. Adams in 1965, postulates that individuals make generalized calculations about their relative contributions and rewards extrapolated from their employment.[10] An employee will evaluate the time, effort, and skill they contribute to an organization and compare that with the benefits of the aforementioned employment: pay, health care, hours, etc. What this theory basically states is that employees will determine for themselves if their effort is being justly compensated. Adams' equity theory proves invaluable when it is used as a tool to analyze the effort and rewards given employees.

The equity theory argues that when employees put in relatively similar input but receive dissimilar benefits, work place stress and anxiety will occur.[11] The employee receiving less benefit is more likely to be absent and disinterested in his work. If the employee perceives that his or her effort is being less appreciated than similar efforts from other employees, the disappointed employee will not be motivated to contribute to the organization (beyond the minimal requirement to maintain employment).

Using the equity theory does not mean all employees must receive the same pay or benefits package. The theory recognizes that employees are making calculations based on perceived efforts and input in the work environment. An employee can recognize and appreciate another individual in the organization earning a higher wage if that person's experience, skill, and knowledge are readily apparent. The problem in this theory develops when employees of similar abilities begin to perceive unequal benefits derived from congruent employment.

While there are additional parts to the equity theory, it is imperative that security management professionals recognize that employees make these "work effort" calculations constantly. It is impossible to properly motivate an organization if members of the team do not feel they can get a fair shot at participating and earning benefits from the employer.

Practical Tools in Fostering Motivation

While theory is helpful in explaining employee needs and behaviors, managers need to perform and supervise staff in the real world. Effectively managing and serving the organization is infinitely easier with a highly motivated and responsive staff. The following tools can be easily exercised to foster such cooperation.

Leadership
Possibly the single most important factor in motivating employees is in the behavior and professional demeanor of senior staff and executives. Effective leadership is not necessarily the result of a magnetic personality; many quiet unassuming individuals have proven to be exceptional leaders.[12] The diminutive James Madison and boisterous Theodore Roosevelt prove that diverse personalities can be successful in motivating and managing people and organizations. To provide effective leadership for an organization, one must present clear goals, clarify responsibilities, and nurture increased authority in subordinates as their skills develop and grow.[13]

Participation
Providing employees input into the decisions that affect their environment is one of the most effective tools in fostering motivation. The more people feel they were involved in a decision, the more personal ownership they will have in their work.[14]

Training
Normally, a discussion of training needs for security staff focuses on new hire orientations, use of force, sexual harassment, and legal issues; however, training can be a

powerful motivator for employees. Beyond the rudimentary training provided to all employees, managers can reward employee interest and efforts through formalized training programs. When management recognizes an innate skill or trait an employee possesses, offering a formalized training program serves not only as positive reinforcement for the employee but also as a possible financial benefit for the organization. For example, having an employee who helps around the office with computer problems may provide an excellent opportunity for management to encourage formal computer network training at a local trade school. The employee obtains valuable experience, and possible certification, and management now has a multiskilled team member capable of saving the organization's time and money.

Rewards

Possibly the most difficult thing a manager can do is implement a good employee reward program. Very few security budgets have line items earmarked for employee rewards, nor is there ample petty cash available to meet this need. Fortunately, rewards can be implemented fairly cheaply if done with a little bit of creativity. Rather than large cash awards, simply providing monthly recognition in the form of an employee of the month reward can foster a sense of pride in an organization. Rewards can range from something as small as a certificate of appreciation or a desirable parking spot, to additional time off or restaurant gift cards. Regardless of what type of reward management chooses to provide, it must be done by leaders who are sincere and can effectively communicate with employees. Even the smallest reward when coupled with sincere appreciation can provide the valuable, positive reinforcement that addresses an employee's desire to feel valued within an organization.

Part 2: Application

How to Motivate

When the question of how to motivate was asked of a senior corporate security manager, he said that if he could figure out the answer to that question, he would be considered a genius. Many times, the answer to this question is not as difficult as it may seem.

The following are some ideas that are currently being implemented by security companies who are putting forth the effort to motivate their employees and create a workplace where security officers *want* to work, instead of a place where they *have* to work. If you as a manager or supervisor can discover the key to motivating your employees, you will have a healthy, thriving workplace.

Step 1. Establish a Set of Objectives for the Entire Department and Break It Down into Categories:
- Physical security
- Training and education
- Services

Step 2. Market the Security Program

- Reassign officers for greater visibility.
- Once a month, do the following:
  - Check every light inside and outside to assure properly functioning—even emergency lights.
  - Check and test *all* alarms.
  - Check and test *all* intercoms and public address systems.
  - If something is broken, have it repaired.
  - Check *all* fire extinguishers.
  - Make sure that your employees have what they need to perform the duties of their job effectively.
  - Write a report on each identified issue and send the list to management the first of every month.

Step 3. Diagnose Motivation Issues Accurately

- Determine what it is that management wants individual security officers and teams of security officers at a particular location to do, and ensure that the officers have been made aware of each task and function of each particular job.
- Are post orders up-to-date and accurate? In other words, look for a "disconnect" in the way things are really done and the way management perceives they are being done.
- As individual job tasks are completed, document them on a spreadsheet monthly to give the security team a sense of accomplishment.
- Check if the security officers are aware of how their job tasks fit into and affect the overall operation of site or organization.

Gather and check the intelligence data as it pertains to a specific site. If you disagree with the data, develop your own effective set goals and strategic objectives that are applicable. Consider exceeding the original set of goals.

Step 4. Manage Your Program, by Utilizing the Following:

- Monthly quality improvements.
- Problems are prevented by proactive inspections.
- Reports that are well-written and accurate should be rewarded and poor reports should be rewritten—with training.

Step 5. Work As a Cohesive Team and Unit

- For scheduling flexibility, cross-train all security officers assigned to a particular site in every position at the site so that any one of them can work any position on any shift or any day and effectively perform the required job functions of the site.
- Ensure site coverage by using a "living" schedule to accommodate security officers' personal/family obligations and allow them to swap to cover shifts/assignments. However, this must be done with the supervisor's involvement, to avoid confusion over scheduling that results in a lapse in coverage.

- Have procedures in place for last-minute emergency situations, such as illness, a sick child, car trouble, etc.
- Holidays and vacation are important, so accommodate security officer requests for time off, if at all possible. Use a rotating vacation schedule and be fair with granting time off for vacations and holidays.
- Reward good performance through perks such as gift certificates, uniform pins, certificates of award, etc.
- When there is going to be a change at a particular site, if at all possible, get your staff involved in the process. Converse with your team and tell them why there are going to be changes, and why the changes are necessary. This will allow them to "buy in" to your objectives and goals and work with you in the process, instead of working against you, which may result in morale issues.
- Tailor individual job assignments to achieve success and results, instead of having to deal with missed opportunities and failure.

Step 6. Measuring the Progress of Your Team
- Let your staff know that their work is measured by the quality of their reports and the accuracy of their observations while performing job functions.
- Find a way to recognize achievements and emphasize positive, rather than negative, reinforcement.
- Develop a rewards program as stated above, and ensure you follow through.
- Capitalize on successes and achievements with recognition and incentives.

Step 7. Use Communication to Motivate Your Team of Security Officers
- Come in early and stay late to meet and greet the officers on each of the shifts.
- Create a pass-on log for communication so the security officers can communicate to each other on every shift. This way, everyone will be aware of what is going on at the site.
- Communication is not a one-way street. It has to freely move from the top to the bottom, the bottom to the top, from right to left, and from left to right. It must be open and encouraged.
- Manage your security officers by walking around the site and interacting with them as they perform their job duties. Take note of any issues and concerns that they have with their job responsibilities.

Step 8. How to Deal with Security Officers Who Perform Poorly and Cannot Be Motivated
- Many of us have had to deal with the following situation: The reports look sloppy—illegible writing, incomplete or missing pertinent information, misspelled words, poor or no punctuation, etc. The security officer reports to work not bathed and unshaven, in a dirty uniform—a generally unacceptable and unprofessional appearance. This security officer may appear bored with his or her job, is frequently late or calls off,

comes to work out of uniform, etc. and does not have the skill set to do the job properly. It is evident that this security officer clearly has no pride in himself or herself or the job they have been hired to do.

- If any of the problems stated above are detected while the security officer is on probation, deal with it effectively—counsel and retain, and extend (in writing) the probation period.
- Document *everything* and terminate, if necessary, if you do not detect immediate improvement or effort made by the employee to change.

Step 9. Determine the Worst Job in Your Company

- Is the worst job performed by the employee who has not received any praise or recognition lately?
- Praise goes a long way to motivate individuals and is appreciated by the receiver. It makes employees *feel* appreciated, even if the job is low-status in the organization and not highly compensated.
- Praise employees for exceptional performance or when they go beyond what is expected to achieve a goal. Recognize their effort on a project so they can see their worth to the company.
- If you give everyone a raise—10% for example—and nothing else, this will not encourage employee motivation. Would 8% be better, with an additional 2% as an incentive? Here is an example: A baseball player is offered a $5 million a year contract and an additional $8 million in incentives and goals. This contract has a performance and reward incentive that can be achieved. Is the player motivated? We think so. It is the same concept.

Summary

Various theories of human behavior and motivation seek to explain why individuals react to specific situations. In the workplace, it is critical to understand the behaviors and needs that motivate employees. The new hire and the old veteran may come to work in the same environment and perform essentially the same duties, but they probably have dramatically different psychological motivations in performing that work.

Monetary compensation is only one of the motivating factors for an individual. Feeling a sense of pride and contribution to the organization is important, as well as a sense of appreciation by supervisory and management staff. An effective manager should understand the various theories of human motivation, then use those concepts to address the needs of individuals throughout the organization appropriately. Understanding what is needed to reinforce or motivate positive behavior is critical in fostering high-achieving, motivated employees.

While understanding such concepts is important, implementing appropriate solutions in the real world can be challenging. Managers can use a combination of rewards, training, employee input, and leadership to motivate staff. Assessing the various programs in use by both security and nonsecurity organizations is a good place to start.

Refer website http://www.ifpo.org for further information

End Notes

1. Huffmire D. and Holmes J., *Handbook of Effective Management: How to Manage or Supervise Strategically* (Westport, CT: Praeger Publishers, 2006), 117.
2. Muchinsky, 376.
3. See note 1 above.
4. Riggio R., *Introduction to Industrial/Organizational Psychology* (Upper Saddle River, NJ: Prentice Hall, 2000), 195.
5. Ibid.
6. See note 4 above.
7. See note 4 above.
8. See note 4 above.
9. Ibid, p. 189.
10. See note 2 above, p. 378.
11. Ibid.
12. See note 1 above, p. 24.
13. Ibid.
14. Allen, 176.

19

Supervising Across Generations

Gerald D. Curry

The Changing Landscape of Work

What type of people will occupy the workplace in the future? The demographics of the workplace have changed. Mitchell (2005) demonstrates that the workforce of today is tremendously different from previous periods in history, and supervisors will require new skills as they continually evolve into more accommodating and understanding leaders.[1] Supervisors will need to know how to effectively work together with people from multiple generations. In many instances, an older employee may have a younger and potentially more educated supervisor than has been experienced in previous generations. Wide swings of cultural challenges will become the new normal, according to Ball.[2] Many organizations are not equipped to deal with generational conflicts that may arise from varying degrees of workplace diversity. Current supervisors may not have the necessary skillsets to be successful in this new environment. This chapter presents tools and strategies to help supervisors effectively manage and bridge the potential generational gaps. The chapter concludes by highlighting six emerging trends that are shaping the global workplace.

Each generation has its own set of idiosyncrasies and unique norms. The current workforce is comprised of four general groups: veterans (the World War II generation), baby boomers, Generation X, and millenials (also known as Generation Y and Z).[3] Many myths are associated with each group, and this chapter is designed to help you gain a better understanding of their uniqueness and similarities. When people are born between two groups, they are commonly called *cuspers,* or the sandwiched generation. Regardless of when a person is born, everyone has a right to earn a decent wage and to do so without embarrassment or perceived harassment in the workplace.[4]

Supervising members of all four groups may be difficult at times, but it can be accomplished when equipped with the right information as well as sensitivity to employee needs. The successful security supervisor, after completing this chapter, should be able to:

- Identify members of the various generations and know the associated traits of each group.
- Clearly articulate workplace characteristics impacting the future workplace.
- Define the Titanium Rule and know how to apply it when communicating with members of different generations.
- Understand the importance of diversity and how prioritizing it improves effectiveness in the workplace.
- Identify emerging trends shaping the future workplace and its impact on society.

Security Supervision and Management. http://dx.doi.org/10.1016/B978-0-12-800113-4.00019-5

Examining the generational traits of each group provides additional insights into why these groups perform, interpret, and communicate in the manner they do. Smith (2012) recommends that supervisors pay close attention to every member of their team to ensure they create a safe, healthy, and productive environment.[5] Societal expectations are different for each group, and employees come to the workplace with their own unique perceptions about their employer and what they would like to achieve. Mitchell suggests that supervisors learn to balance their communications and create a wholesome environment for all.[6] However, blending the various generations into a wholesome unit is often easier said than achieved.[7]

Addressing Intergenerational Dynamics

Understanding the similarities and distinctions of each group offers a useful framework for fostering better relations, increased productivity, and even in improving revenue.[8] Understanding these generational traits will create a new awareness and provide a competitive advantage for supervisors. By embracing these distinctions, the supervisor will be able to communicate effectively with all groups on matters of importance. Fries (2013) recommends reaching people right where they are by communicating using relevant examples that they can understand. This will foster stronger relationships and deeper respect for the individual and broader groups.[9]

People communicate differently. To reach people where they are, it is important for supervisors to listen with attentive ears, not only to understand what is being said, but to identify the broader context and meaning behind what is being communicated—the *why*.[10] Each generational group has different values and ways to emphasize what is important to them. While one segment of the workforce may demonstrate a strong loyalty to the employer, another group may not. This disparity between groups can easily be misunderstood by supervisors, which may create animosity, cause isolation, or prematurely push some members aside if the communication or response is not measured.[11] Figures 19.1 and 19.2 provide some insights into the various generational groups.

Managing a multigenerational workforce requires a better understanding of each group. For each generation, there are particular experiences that highlight specific preferences, expectations, beliefs, and working styles. With this understanding, the supervisor can gain leverage in moving the individual and organization forward. Understanding basic interpersonal dynamics will improve workforce training programs, task assignments, and overall productivity. The more generational understanding a supervisor has and, most importantly, exhibits, the more likely the entire workforce will respond positively.

Veterans

Members of the veteran group have a deep respect for authority and do not mind hard work, but they are less tolerant to change and have a low threshold for risk.[12] They rely on their steep experience and readiness to mentor anyone willing to listen. When their

Overview of Generations

Generation	Year	Population
Veteran (WWII)	1925 – 1945	45 million
Baby Boomers	1946 – 1964	80 million
Generation Xers	1965 – 1980	49.1 million
Generation Yers (Millennials)	1980 – 1999	73.5 million
Generation Zers (Millennials)	2000 – Forward	96 million

* Statistics source is from U.S Department of Labor 2012

FIGURE 19.1 Generational populations.

Veterans (1925-1945)	Baby Boomers (1946-1964)	Generation X (1965-1980)	Generation Y (1980-1999)	Generation Z (2000-Forward)
• Watched parents struggle to make ends meet during Great Depression of 1930s • Very Careful with money, conservative, have great respect for authority • Fought in World War II or Korean War • Very loyal to their employers • Grew up without television • Job security very important, switching jobs not easily embraced • Team Players • Indirect in communicating • Loyal to the organization • Respect the authority • Dedication and sacrifice • Duty before pleasure • Obedience • Respond well to directive leadership • Seniority and age correlated • Adherence to rules	• Represent largest group in workforce • Will inflict largest "brain drain" when they retire • Often involved in both child care and elder care • Fought in wars abroad such as the Vietnam War • Used typewriters rather than computers • Important changes such as "the Pill", the civil rights movement and "Motown" era • Highly educated, desiring of better lifestyle than their parents • Big Picture/Systems in Place • Bring Fresh Perspective • Do Not Respect the Titles • Disapprove Absolutes and Structure • Optimism • Team Orientation • Uncomfortable with Conflict • Personal Growth • Sensitive to Feedback • Health and Wellness • Personal Gratification	• Witnessed many dramatic changes in economy and technology • First generation to be entertained by video games like Atari • High number of divorced parents, dual-income families and "latch key" kids • Accustomed to recurring economic recessions; familiar with oil shortages, terrorist attacks, soaring inflation • Skeptical, independent and entrepreneurial • Most well educated generation so far; great candidates for leadership positions • Positive Attitude • Impatience • Goal Orientated • Multi-Tasking • Thinking Globally • Self-Reliance • Flexible Hours, Informal Work Environment • Just A Job • Techno-Lateral • Informal – Balance • Give Them a Lot to Do and Freedom to Do Their Way • Questions Authority	• Grew up with technology such as the internet, computers, voice mail, video games • More globally minded than previous generations • Population three times bigger than Gen Xer population • Dual-income parents, divorces, daycare • Very protective parents (often termed 'helicopter parents') • Inquisitive, socially and environmentally conscious, concerned about the future, highly entrepreneurial • Have lived through one of the biggest economic booms in North American history • Often described as the generation with a sense of 'entitlement' • Confidence • Sociability • Morality • Street Smarts • Diversity • Collective Action	• Youngest group in the workforce now • Extremely techno-savvy; instant messaging preferred mode of communication (i.e., email is for old folks) • Protective parents; monitoring by adults is often seen as positive means of protection • Confident, happy and secure • Team players, like to engage in community service activities • More activities available to them than previous generations, team activities often co-ed • Heroic Spirit • Tenacity • Technological Savvy • Lack of Skills for Dealing with Difficult People • Multitasking • Need Flexibility

Data sourced by Dr. Jill Novak, University of Phoenix, Consumer Behavior, 2014.

FIGURE 19.2 Generational traits and characteristics.

reputation and wisdom is not respected or sought out, they tend not to complain, but instead carry on with little interference or notice from the broader group.[13] This generation was taught to obey rules and respect organizational structure.

Baby Boomers

The baby boomer group was raised in the era after World War II and the Korean War, where they saw the world playing out and evolving on black-and-white television.[14] This group's lifestyle centers on working; for them, finding a work–life balance is a nice idea but not a reality. This group of workers is living longer than previous generations, and they plan on remaining in the workplace well beyond traditional retirement age.[15]

Generation X

Generation X has a different mentality than baby boomers in that they work to live, instead of living to work. This group grew up with a higher rate of blended families than previous generations. Consequently, they developed behaviors (not values) of independence and are more willing to adapt than any other generation.[16] This group's behavior is more distrustful and cynical of authority.

Generation Y

The Generation Y group—commonly called millenials—is considered to be the "empowerment" generation. As children, they received medals for participating, not for actually beating the competition.[17] This group was encouraged to make their own choices and to question authority. Gen Y'ers expect employers to accommodate their expectations by giving more and creating a user-friendly workplace that is attractive and inviting.

Generation Z

Generation Z grew up with computers and the Internet, which plays a significant part in their understanding of the world. They are constantly connected and networked, and they expect the same from their company.[18] Remaining connected with interactive media, such as text and instant messaging, blogs, and multimedia players, is the norm. This "always-connected" mindset dominates one of the major frustrations and disconnects in the modern workplace.[19]

Workplace Characteristics

After carefully reviewing the uniqueness and differences of each individual group, one can better understand their motivations, thinking patterns, behaviors, and specific expectations required in managing such a diverse workforce. As previously mentioned, technology advancements have played a tremendous part in designing the future workplace Computers, cell phones, and virtual conferencing have made it possible to connect remotely to the office while physically being elsewhere. Several companies have made drastic economic decisions to close brick-and-mortar facilities and allow large numbers of their workforce to work from home or other remote areas.[20] Most employees view remote working or tele-working as a benefit because it offers the individual more flexibility, while also saving the organization the cost of paying utilities and lease payments for office space.[21]

The demand for supervisors to introduce more work–life balance initiatives is increasing, and business owners, chief executive officers (CEOs), and senior leaders are paying attention.[22] Work–life balance is more than having the opportunity for teleworking; it includes maternity leave for new mothers and fathers, time away to care for an elderly parent, tuition reimbursement, on-site daycare facilities, and flexible vacation rules.[23] Collectively, these benefits are playing just as much of an important decision as negotiating one's salary. Having the ability to work flexible hours is becoming a significant priority in accommodating a more transient and demanding lifestyle.[24]

Training and development is also becoming more of a priority. While older generations are more committed to their employers, the younger generations are more prone to career-hopping from company to company throughout their careers.[25] As a result, obtaining specialized skills and certification will become vitally important and supervisors and managers need to pay close attention to this desire. On one hand, some supervisors may be reluctant to make costly investments in a younger employee's training, understanding the employee may terminate his or her tenure at any moment. There is a more expansive view when examining training. The predominant thought is, "If we do not invest heavily in our employee training and professional development, then our competition will, and potentially will reap more market share in our industry." This opinion is more realistic for supervisors who work for companies that are well-vested in their industries and who support employee development. The senior leaders realize there is an economic risk in investing in employee training, but the consequence of not investing is far more detrimental. Carlson (2011) suggests that any company that dominates the competition with increased profits, is likely to have a robust training program.[26]

The older generations (veterans and baby boomers) are not as susceptible to change, while the younger generations expect mandatory training to be delivered in an online format, therefore affording more flexibility on when and how training should be completed.[27] Regardless of the training delivery method, program consistency yields better results. Supervisors who build consensus amongst the various groups and actively seek opportunities to collaborate when designing training programs tend to fare better than when training programs are created in isolation.[28]

Health care benefits are vitally important to all groups, but they receive more emphasis from older generations. As employees become older and are more likely to experience sickness and aliments, health care program protocols and requirements become increasingly important.[29] As younger generations start new families, health care becomes a priority. Health care is the top company benefit behind salary for all employees.[30]

C-Suite Priorities

Three important aspects occupy a senior leader's attention: people, process, and profit.[31] Of these three elements, people are the most important. Understanding how to properly manage and maintain an environment of value and respect is critically important to those who occupy the C-suite (top senior executives whose titles start with "chief" or the letter "c"). Creating an effective and productive workplace is a priority for leaders managing across generations.[32] Company policies are increasingly becoming transparent, with opportunities for collaboration and input from all employee stakeholders.

Ball emphasized that the person in the C-suite wants supervisors and managers to be culturally astute and equipped with the skills that enforce company standards and policies.[33] Internal company policies are designed to build positive work cultures and effective teams. To reach optimal organizational performance, attracting top talent has to be on the top of every CEO's list.[34] Learning how to transform the workforce through positive influences and expanding and enhancing the employee's experience is important every day. Supervisors must learn to lead by reducing and resolving conflicts in the workplace. Managing and eliminating conflict occurs when supervisors know their people, understand company policies, and collectively work toward increasing revenue.[35]

Conflict resolution occurs when ample attention is paid to understanding your workforce and cultivating cultural competence.[36] If individual members of groups do not invest the time to understand one another, it is very likely that they will experience more conflict. Learning cultural competencies from each group becomes increasingly important. Cultural competencies are a set of congruent behaviors, attitudes, and policies that come together in a system, agency, or among professionals and enable that system, agency, or those professionals to work effectively in cross-cultural situations.[37] Workplace demographics are changing and becoming diverse within genders, generationally, and racially.

Having the skills and ability to effectively communicate with your employees requires a special art. In this email-dominated society, far too many supervisors rely on keeping their workforce updated via email. A challenge that occurs when communicating across generations in this way is how emails are interpreted. Many times, employees do not have the time to read and truly digest the essence of what is being communicated. An email sent cannot be assumed as an email received. The generations have different email tolerance and interpretation levels and online habits that must be guided and disciplined.[38]

Claire Raines and Lara Ewing coined the phrase "Titanium Rule" in their book *The Art of Connecting*. The Titanium Rule provides the essential tools supervisors and managers need to connect across generations by asking appropriate questions, observing mannerisms, reading idiosyncrasies, noticing preferences, and understanding the way people dress. When equipped with this knowledge, supervisors and managers become better prepared to meet them where they are, and then gently engage them to find a common understanding. The Titanium Rule engages people according to their druthers, or as they would like a supervisor to treat them.[39]

In communicating across generations, the Titanium Rule is highly recommended because it yields the highest benefits in today's workplace when supervisors talk to veteran employees about their experiences.[40] The conversation will be better received if it is clear, concise, and direct. When assigning a task to a baby boomer, the supervisor should ask for input and allow the employee to contribute to the solution. Generation X'ers and Y'ers would prefer receiving the task by email or in text form, with the option to provide feedback via instant messaging or some other online platform.[41] The bottom line is that each generation is unique and prefers to process information and tasks differently. Supervisors and managers need to be keenly aware of how to proceed when communicating with their workforce.

Regardless of the generation, everyone wants to be valued.[42] Valuing each individual is critically important because it conveys respect and admiration.[43] When supervisors engage employees with respect, they respond with trust and loyalty. When trust and loyalty exist in the workplace, effectiveness and productivity is right around the corner. It is just a matter of time before the working environment is thriving with positive potential and tremendous possibilities. When working conditions are ideal, everyone is connected, and people feel valued and respected, conflict is reduced, and cynicism eliminated.[44]

Having a strong and disciplined employee recognition program is important. Vogel (2001) confirms that all generations enjoy being recognized for their contributions to the company, and supervisors are charged with the responsibility of submitting their best and brightest.[45] If a company does not have an employee recognition program, then leaders should consider creating one. Many companies start with an employee-of-the-month, employee-of-the-quarter, and annual recognition, and move toward using this program to rally the entire workforce. Each of these programs continually enhances the organization's quest for success.

Valuing Diversity

People are the primary concern to those who occupy the C-suite. Future recruiting efforts should cast a wider net than today, and consequently they will reach a more diverse candidate pool. Diversity in the workplace is necessary to create a competitive economy in a globalized society.[46] As corporate leaders and boardrooms continue to search for ways to increase market share, creating a more diverse workforce is one of the easiest ways to achieve this objective. Recruiting from a wider diverse candidate pool means possibly sampling a more qualified workforce.[47]

Diversity is more than just creating a workforce from various ethnicities and genders. Diversity fosters a more creative and innovative workforce that introduces new ideas, perspectives, and insights into the workplace. Bringing together workers with different qualifications and experiences potentially resolves internal conflicts quicker, by breeding innovation and creativity.

When the workforce is empowered to make decisions and execute meaningful programs at a lower level, it creates a higher degree of responsibility and trust within the workforce, according to Haugen (2013).[48] When leaders engage their employees in the environment where they reside and work, the employees respond with a renewed level of trust and respect for that leader.[49] Employees desire a leader who cares about, understands, and connects with them and their culture. When managing a diverse workforce, understanding cultural behaviour and ways of communication is critically important.

Leaders must understand the diverse culture they supervise if they are going to be successful. It is not enough to simply see the external skin color of people; leaders must take time getting to know the entire workforce. When time is invested in getting to know a person's motivation, thoughts, and behavior, everyone wins. For too long, affirmative action programs were confused with quota systems. Diversity is more than simply counting heads, but making heads count, according to Betances (2013).[50] Established diversity programs reach further than merely focusing on recruiting quota systems; they empower the entire workforce by leveraging the best talents, skills, and insight. Diversity programs should create transparent opportunities for the entire workforce to offer suggestions and present ideas without being embarrassed, hassled, or coerced.

To embrace diversity in its fullest, leaders must learn to appreciate people right where they are and realize the societal contributions each ethnicity has made in history. Being equipped with this knowledge will enhance supervisor-subordinate relationships through connectivity, which will separate good leaders from those that are mediocre. Leaders contribute value daily, and the workforce seeks those that care. Leaders of diverse groups know how to communicate and engage people in their natural habitat, and they do so with clear communication and directions.

Women as Leaders

The workforce is changing, particularly among women. Women are entering into careers once dominated by men and thriving in those industries in record numbers. The glass ceiling is crumbling and new opportunities are being presented to those who choose to lead. It has been reported that women bring empathy and intuition to leadership.[51] Women are living longer, appear to be more in tune with their feelings, and have an understanding of the workforce. Women leaders have been able to leverage these qualities to benefit the entire workforce.

In 1995, only 9.6 percent of corporate board seats of Fortune 500 companies were occupied by women; by 2013, that number had increased to 16.9 percent. Women comprise 47.3 percent of the labor force—and that number continues to increase—yet make up 50.8 percent of the US population.[52] These women earn approximately 60 percent of the undergraduate and master degrees granted, but only 12.4 percent of women are executive officers. The future is extremely promising and progressive for women increasing on all spectrums.

Astute leaders and supervisors are keenly aware of the growing demographics and harness female aspirations and talents by helping them develop into productive leaders. Women are the fasting-growing group of professionals in the workforce. More women attend and graduate from college than men, and they are entering the workforce at higher levels. The US Department of Labor predicts that women will continue to edge men out of senior management positions over the coming decades.[53]

Women from around the world a uniting and rallying around a common theme of making their voices heard, by demanding equal treatment in society and especially the workplace. Some cultures still hold arcane views of women that tend to intentionally hold them back, by not affording the same equal treatment as men. As social media continues to enlarge our global community, people are learning of tremendous achievements women are making in all stations of life, and these accomplishments are both inspiring and encouraging.

In the growing decades it should be expected to see women replacing men as world leaders and assuming the role of Presidents, CEOs, and global thinkers. The respect given to women will have a significant impact creating more of a societal focus on family, integrity, values, and productivity. Many of the prejudices and discrimination practices that continue to exist today, will be addressed and not tolerated by these women leaders because of shifting female priorities[54].

Managing Generations Successfully

Each generation has a distinctive culture and therefore different of their managers and supervisors. Being able to connect and communicate effectively with the workforce means being able to eliminate cultural barriers in the work environment. An organization's culture transmits the behavior of the workforce and how people feel in this environment. Katanga (2013) states that "culture is how organizations 'do things.'" What a company does, and how it does it, can be summarized by the culture it has adopted.[55]

Organizational culture is the behavior of humans within an organization and the meaning that people attach to those behaviors. Culture includes the organization's vision, values, norms, systems, symbols, language, assumptions, beliefs, and habits.[56] Leaders are responsible for establishing the culture within an organization. The workforce will conform to the boundaries and expectations senior leaders create. In an effort to eliminate cultural barriers, leaders should focus on establishing as much transparency as possible. Every generation exudes more confidence when their voices are heard by senior management.

As the workplace becomes more globally connected and geographically separated, teams become more commonplace; management methods are challenged by time zones and cultural demands. Senior management must prioritize the needs of its workforce in how it executes daily operations. The most miniscule undertaking should examine the second and third order of consequences that cultural effects have on every decision. Paying close attention to detail on how corporate decisions are interpreted will lead to a more inclusive workforce and eliminate cultural barriers.

Diversity is more than race, gender, or class distinction; it includes multiple generations, and the strengths and weaknesses everyone brings to the workplace by creating effectiveness and increased productivity. Understanding the complexities of what it takes to supervise large numbers of people is critically important to bridging gaps across generations.

Emerging Trends

The world will continue to evolve as new technologies are developed, people become more connected, and living patterns become more condensed. Some emerging trends are worth noting regarding what is to come over the coming decades: extreme longevity, new media ecology, the rise of smart machines and systems, a computational world, and a globally connected world.[57] Each of these concepts are further explained below.

Extreme Longevity

If one examines both the US federal and private workplaces, one sees an older demographic in which the workforce is older, healthier, and desiring to remain in the workplace longer. By 2025, Americans over 60 years old will increase by 70 percent, and people will be working long past 65 years old. The traditional career path of remaining with a company for 20 or 30 years is becoming obsolete, and the older generation is sticking around and occupying positions that were traditionally held by someone much younger.

As baby boomers become older, they are making more demands on the government and the broader society. Cries for extensions in health care benefits, social security, and more investment options for their pensions are becoming routine. This generation is placing more emphasis on healthy living, so they can live longer and take more advantage of their longevity.

Several reasons exist and positively impact this extension of longevity, such as medical technology in stem cell research, optimal new insights into DNA coding, and nutrition protocols. Additionally, people are visiting the doctor more than ever, so preventive medicine is having a huge impact on identifying early treatment opportunities. Society as a whole has started listening to physicians. Another factor contributing to sustaining life is advancement in technology connectivity. Media technology is having a tremendous effect on medical and nutrition awareness. With the use of smart technology, websites and blogs have been developed to educate society on medical trends. Even those living in isolated communities can now access industry thought leaders in specific domains. Collectively, all these activities contribute to living a more healthy and prolonged life.

New Media Ecology

To survive in this new environment, supervisors will have to learn a new language. New communication tools require new media literacies beyond text. Multimedia technologies are transforming communications and a new vernacular is required to keep pace. Once upon a time, a "hotspot" was the local diner, bar, or rendezvous where someone would go to on a date. A "cell" was a microorganism living inside of a person, and a "tweet" was the sound of a small little bird that flew. These terms have taken on new meanings, and media technology continues to push the limits by introducing new terms onto which society can latch.[58]

Today's multimedia platforms have changed the way people communicate, live, and exist. Media technology is making a significant impact on both recreation and behavior. Most places are under some kind of digital surveillance. Each intersection that one drives through captures an image, each swipe of a credit card tracks spending habits, and a cell phone tracks movement. This recorded data has the potential of becoming the new boundary for deciding one's moral compass and introduces a new concept—always on video.

Rise of Smart Machines and Systems

Smart technology is revolutionizing human interactions, productivity, and collaboration. As workplace automation increases, it will surely nudge human workers out of performing rote and repetitive tasks. Automation is critical to every domain in our lives, including teaching, medicine, security, combat, and virtually all forms of production. Machines are replacing or augmenting humans in several industries. Smart machines will establish new expectations and standards of performance.

Agencies will outfit these workplaces with a host of platforms and operating systems to compete with industry leaders. Most manual labor jobs will be automated, and those without the necessary skills, education, and training will enter into unemployment abyss. Becoming technology savvy by earning technical certifications will be essential in acquiring career-leading jobs, even more so than having an academic degree.

Industry giants are considering new concepts, such as bring-your-own-device, in communicating with their workforce. This concept allows employees the option of using the device with which they are most comfortable. This also creates the unusual demand of companies having multiple operating systems to be compatible with various devices and platforms. Smart technology will create unlimited access and communication opportunities for the broader society by reducing intermediate levels or gates that traditionally allowed permission.

Computational World

Data, data, data! Every object, interaction, and item will be converted into data—everything will become programmable. We have entered into a data-driven society where everything we do, see, and desire will be based on programmable data. Data will enable modeling of social systems, and micro- and macro-scale models will create unprecedented levels of complexity and completeness far beyond anything mankind has ever experienced before.

Today, patterns are tracked, monitored, and analyzed to make translatable sense, and then portioned out for decisions and action. To offer an example of the magnitude of how data is being harvested and used by everyday people, the Fitbit is a small device worn on a person's wrist that captures exercise activities, monitors sleep habits, records calorie intake, and various other daily performance data, and provides instantaneous updates on demand. This device can provide historical trend data to be used in making nutrition and fitness decisions. People now have complete autonomy to capture, monitor, analyze, and make informed health decisions about how they are going to live their lives. This level of control and insight never existed before, and with technology it is only going to increase.

From an industry perspective, the horrific events of the 9/11 attacks and the chaotic response during Hurricane Katrina taught the federal government huge lessons on the importance of data fusion and collaboration. Databases are now linked and networked globally to instantaneously translate input on facial recognition, credit card transactions, and global positioning systems. Several protocols are being fused together by computers to provide a deeper view into complex matters by offering complete analysis to make better decisions. It is reported that each day we produce as much data as society has effectively created throughout the entire history of mankind.

A Globally Connected World

An increased global interconnectivity puts diversity and adaptability at the center of organizational operations. It is important to first understand a few terms as we discuss this emerging concept. *Globalization* is the trend toward creating greater exchanges and integration across geographic borders. Europe and the United States no longer hold a monopoly on job creation, innovation, and political power. The rise in technology is allowing smaller countries to play politics, economics, and innovation on the world stage.

Multinational organizations from resourced and infrastructure-constrained developing countries are producing usable materials and products at a faster rate. These countries are no longer waiting on the larger countries' input, permission, or markets to drive prices and provide validation of their services. Advancements in technology have increased globalization and international trading at monumental levels in all industry domains.

Projections from the US Labor Department show that by the year 2030, the American workforce will need to fill 83 million replacement and new jobs. It is predicted by 2030, approximately 54 percent of new workers will be people of color. Today, a majority of the babies born in the United States are children of color. Within three decades, America will have no clear racial or ethnic majority, and more than half of the population will be people of color. These changing demographics demonstrate the need for an agenda that prepares the workforce for this reality.

Living patterns also are changing worldwide. People are moving from more rural communities to the cities where there are jobs. This changing demographic is causing overcrowding in cities around the world and creating a more transient society. People are moving from their native countries to live in areas where more opportunities exist. This shift in living and working patterns is making the world more globally connected and creating a mobile and agile workforce. Jobs that were once traditionally considered American are now being advertised and potentially occupied by a foreigner.

Conclusion

No longer will supervisors be able to be monofocused. Supervisors will need exposure to better understand concepts from multiple disciplines, which means they must become lifelong learners. Professional development is not only encouraged but expected. New media programs will change the way we communicate. Most events are being recorded in various forums, whether it be on Twitter, YouTube, Facebook, or the next-generation venue. New media forms are being developed to better leverage these communication platforms and more.

The changing demographics in society are overwhelming the existing infrastructure. The amount of information being generated is too large to be processed in a cogent and intelligent manner using today's standards of data processing. New thoughts must be developed with broader and deeper insights to successfully cater to societal demands. New philosophies, policies, and concepts will be required to help streamline a supervisor's thinking to get at those matters that create value for all mankind. The future is bright for those who prepare, yet limiting and unforgiving for those who do not.

Learning to supervise across generational borders will require talent, skill, patience, and most importantly, insight—insight into a world and industry that is evolving, with no limits or borders. Leaders and managers will have to adapt to make adjustments on the fly to accommodate rising pressures from their workforce. Creating an environment where new ideas can anonymously surface from the workforce will become important, and providing public forums to recognize the best and brightest will remain important. Supervising across generations will require dedication and attention to every minute detail, and leveraging technology to assist in this effort will also become important.

Friedman (2005) recorded that the world is flat, and with the technological advancements it is becoming smaller.[59] As technology continues to pull people together, it will become critical to ensure that all generations know how to leverage it in their favor. In this new environment, connecting with people right where they are, will become increasingly important. The human connection, especially from leaders and supervisors, will remain vital in order to exhibit employee valuation. The trait of expressing appreciation and pride in employee performance by leadership will not diminish or alter. Because of technology, leaders and supervisors will be required to be more understanding of human conditions than ever before.[60] Technology is faceless and emotionless, but this is where leaders will have to play an active role by inspiring their workforce to greatness.

Refer website http://www.ifpo.org for further information

End Notes

1. Mitchell B., *Understanding and M.D. Generations, Putting People First* (Orlando, FL: Achieve Solutions, 2005).

2. Ball J. and Legagneur A., *Of a Certain Age: Supervising the Next Generation* (Atlanta, GA: Reflective Practice: Formation and Supervision in Ministry, 2011).

3. See note 1 above.

4. Carlson C. et al., *Traditionalists, Baby Boomers, Generation X, Generation Y (and Generation Z) Working Together, What Matters and How They Learn? How Different Are They? Fact and Fiction* (New York, NY: United Nations Joint Staff Pension Fund, Talent Management Team, 2011).

5. Smith A. and Koltz R., *Counseling Supervision: Where is the Manual for Working With the Millennial Generation?* (Bozeman, MT: Montana State University, 2012).

6. See note 1 above.

7. Fries V., *One Size Does Not Fit All: Motivating a Multi-Generational Workforce* (Washington, DC: Right of Way, 2013).

8. Erbes K., *Managing Multiple Generations in the Workplace* (San Diego, CA: San Diego State University, Southern Area Consortium of Human Services, 2007).

9. See note 7 above.

10. See note 8 above.

11. See note 1 above.

12. See note 7 above.

13. See notes 1, 4 and 5 above.

14. See note 4 above.

15. See note 7 above.

16. See note 1 above.

17. See note 2 above.

18. See note 7 above.

19. See note 4 above.

20. Green, K. et al., *Diversity in the Workplace: Benefits, Challenges, and the Required Managerial Tools* (Orlando, FL: University of Florida, IFAS Extension, 2013).

21. See note 8 above.

22. See note 1 above.

23. Kosset E. E., Lobel S. and Brown J., *Human Resource Strategies to Manage Workforce Diversity, Examining the Business Case* (Radford, VA: Center for Promoting Ideas, 2013): vol. 4, pt. 16, accessed January 9, 2015. Available: http://www.ijbssnet.com.

24. See note 1 above.

25. See note 5 above.

26. See note 4 above.

27. Hatton-Yeo A. and Telfer S., *A Guide to Mentoring Across Generations, Generations Working Together* (Glasgow, Scotland: The Scottish Center for Intergenerational Practice, 2008): accessed January 9, 2015. Available: http://www.scotcip.org.uk/.

28. See note 1 above.

29. White G., *Diversity in Workplace Causes Rise in Unique Employee Benefits and Changes in Cafeteria Plans* (Little Rock, AR: Southern Arkansas University, Journal of Management and Marketing Research, 2013).

30. See note 1 above.

31. See note 8 above.

32. See note 1 above.

33. See note 2 above.

34. See note 8 above.

35. See note 5 above.

36. See note 8 above.

37. See note 27 above.

38. Egan M. E., *Global Diversity and Inclusion, Fostering Innovation Through a Diverse Workforce* (New York, NY: Forbes Insights, 2006).

39. Raines C. and Ewing L., *The Art of Connecting* (Location Unknown: AMACOM, 2006).

40. Ibid.

41. See note 7 above.

42. See note 1 above.

43. Vogel R., *Generation X Supervising the New Firefighters* (Ann Arbor, MI: School of Fire Staff and Command Program, Dept. of Interdisciplinary Technology, 2001).

44. See note 39 above.

45. See note 43 above.

46. Herman R. E., "A Leadership Evolution," appearing in *Employment Relations Today* (Boston, MA: John Wiley & Sons, Winter 2000).

47. Hansen T., *The Future of Knowledge Work, an Outlook on the Changing Nature of the Work Environment* (Location Unknown: Intel Corporation, 2012).

48. Haugen T., *Workplaces of the Future: Creating an Elastic Workplace, Resetting Horizons* (Location Unknown: Human Capital Trends, 2013).

49. Bennis W., *Still Surprised: A Memoir of a Life in Leadership* (San Francisco, CA: Jossey-Bass, 2010).

50. Betances S., *Winning the Future Through Education: One Step at a Time* (Chicago, IL: New Century Forum Inc., 2013).

51. Ouye J., *Five Trends That are Dramatically Changing Work and the Workplace* (New York, NY: Knoll Workplace Research, 2013): accessed January 9, 2015. Available: http://www.knoll.com/media/18/144/WP_FiveTrends.pdf.

52. Bureau of Labor Statistics, *Table 3: Employment Status of the Civilian Noninstitutional Population by Age, Sex, and Race* (Washington, DC: Bureau of Labor Statistics, 2013): accessed January 9, 2015. Available: http://www.bls.gov/cps/cpsaat03.htm.

53. See note 38 above.

54. Betances S., *Winning the Future Through Education: One Step at a Time* (Chicago, IL: New Century Forum Inc., 2013).

55. Watkins M., *What is Organizational Culture? And Why Should We Care?* (Cambridge, MA: Harvard Business Review, May 15, 2013): accessed January 9, 2015. Available: https://hbr.org/2013/05/what-is-organizational-culture/.

56. Tharp B. M., *Defining 'Culture' and 'Organizational Culture': From Anthropology to the Office* (Location Unknown: Haworth, 2009): accessed January 9, 2015. Available: http://www.haworth.com/docs/default-source/white-papers/defining-culture-and-organizationa-culture_51-pdf-28527.pdf?sfvrsn=6.

57. Author Unknown, *Workplace Forecast* (Alexandria, VA: Society for Human Resource Management, 2013): accessed January 9, 2015. Available: http://www.shrm.org/Research/FutureWorkplaceTrends/Documents/13-0146%20Workplace_Forecast_FULL_FNL.pdf.

58. Busch E. and Nash J., *Remote Work: An Examination of Current Trends and Emerging Issues* (New York, NY: Cornell University, ILR Center for Advanced Human Resource Studies, 2011): accessed January 9, 2015. Available: http://www.distantjob.com/Spring2011_CAHRSRemoteWorkReport.pdf.

59. Friedman T., *The World is Flat: A Brief History of the Twenty-First Century* (New York, NY: Farrar, Straus & Giroux, 2005).

60. See note 51 above.

20

The Supervisor's Role in Employee Relations

Inge Sebyan Black, Christopher A. Hertig

A great deal of the supervisors's time is spent *managing* employee relations. Employee relations primarily deal with complaints. Complaints are concerns, problems, or complaints that employees raise with their employers. In some situations, complaints are referred to as grievances, and they are quite similar. Handling complaints can be difficult and must always be done with the greatest attention to the applicable rules, policies, regulations, and laws. Properly addressing complaints will help to preserve morale, loyalty, and confidence in the supervisor by the employee. Improperly handling complaints, however, can be a major source of workplace discontent and could result in liability issues for the employer, as well as for the supervisor individually. Personal and company reputations may rest on the attention given to a complaint.

To address complaints, many organizations have specific procedures. These procedures can be varied, as private employers have different requirements from state to state or province to province; public employers have constraints based on civil service law; and both private and public may also be subject to collective bargaining agreements with employee unions. Regardless, any complaint procedure must be followed. Failing to do so may cause difficulties down the road should the complaint lead to administrative proceedings, a criminal trial, or a civil trial. Some jurisdictions have specific regulations for how long a complainant can wait before filing a complaint; for the US Equal Employment Opportunity Commission, the limit is 45 days. There are also quasi-governmental bodies, such as human rights commissions in some US states and Canadian provinces, which investigate complaints and have their own guidelines.

Regardless of the procedure in place, the supervisor must always strive to do the following:

- Resolve disputes in a timely manner.
- Provide a resolution satisfactory to all parties involved.
- Involve all necessary staff, including representatives from the employee union or human resources.
- Treat every complaint as a serious one. Some matters may not appear to be serious, but to the person making the complaint, they are.

- Be perceived as fair. Although some people will always complain of bias, employers and employees must be assured to every extent possible that the supervisor has acted fairly in response to a complaint. This is especially important from a liability standpoint as the perception of fairness (or lack thereof) may make the supervisor impeachable as a witness in a hearing or a trial.
- Be externally defensible if the decision made by the supervisor is challenged. Similar to the fairness issue, the supervisor must be able to articulate the reasons why the complaint was resolved the way that it was and point to any aggravating or mitigating factors. Failure to articulate this may open up liability issues for the employer or supervisor during a hearing or a trial.

When hearing complaints, deal with them immediately rather than letting them become a bigger issue that could lead to resignations. Issues left unresolved tend to fester, with the potential for results whose negative impact will far outweigh the effort not taken to resolve it. A matter that could have been resolved with verbal counseling instead becomes a termination followed by a civil suit for wrongful termination. Therefore, procedures for handling complaints should be respectful both of the rights of the employer as well as the rights of the employee. Should a complaint be decided by an arbitrator, examiner, judge, or jury, the failure to address a complaint when first made aware of it may be treated as the supervisor condoning that particular behavior; in an adversarial proceeding, the complainant will certainly present it in that manner.

Processing the Complaint

The supervisor should be familiar with his or her employer's procedures regarding complaints and follow them correctly. The supervisor should always meet with the complainant regarding the substance of the complaint. Such meetings should be held privately. During the meeting with the complainant, remember the following points:

- Allow the employee to talk without interruption and listen carefully.
- During the conversation, follow-up questions may be necessary to probe for specific facts. This is important in cases where a policy, regulation, or law has multiple elements that must be satisfied. Each of the elements must be addressed in the complaint.
- Discuss the supervisor's responsibilities regarding the complaint and the impact of any limitations placed on the supervisor.
- Discuss the employer's commitment to confidentiality as well as the restraints placed on the supervisor and the employer as a result of such confidentiality. This includes any legal or regulatory requirements, if applicable.
- Identify what kind of resolution the employee is seeking. If there are prescribed penalties for violations identified in the complaint, the employee should be made aware of them.
- If the complainant asks that no action be taken, that may also be taken into consideration. The complainant's reluctance to take action should also be addressed; the reluctance could be indicative of fear on the complainant's part, or it could be something else entirely. If possible, the complainant should be on record if there are

whistleblowing or retaliation concerns. Ultimately, the complaint may be pursued without the complainant's participation if enough evidence exists.

- If the complaint relates to the complainant's manager, the employee must be able to go to an impartial person of higher rank or position than the manager who is the subject of the complaint. This person may not necessarily be in the same organizational or command chain as the complainant.

After the interview with the complainant, the next steps are dependent upon the type of complaint. Other witnesses or persons involved may need to be interviewed to corroborate the complaint. Some of these interviews may be adversarial. It is also possible that information uncovered through witness interviews may lead the supervisor to reinterview the complainant.

The Importance of Documenting

The results of every meeting should be documented. There are several ways to accomplish this. The supervisor may take notes during the interview; this will depend on the comfort level of the interviewee. If permissible by law, the interview may also be recorded. Also consider having the employee write down his or her statement. For more formal proceedings, the supervisor may write down or transcribe the employee's statement and have the employee initial each page and sign. This provides a record of the individual attesting to the accuracy of their statement. Should there be an administrative proceeding or trial, this will preserve the substance of the statement at the time it was actually made.

In addition to documenting any interview conducted, documenting all evidence-gathering or other activity is imperative. In doing so, there are some things the supervisor must keep in mind. First and foremost, the supervisor must be objective at all times. It is not the supervisor's place to assign guilt or innocence. It is the supervisor's job to report the facts of the case. The supervisor should avoid speculating or rendering an opinion unless asked to do so; if that must occur, then it should be only conclusions that are supported by the available evidence.

Precision is also important. Dates, times, and locations must be exact whenever possible; if not exact, they must be estimated as closely as the evidence permits. Quotes must also be precise; however, this can be complicated at times because the human mind sometimes translates what it hears. Instead of the supervisor writing what the complainant said, the supervisor might be writing what the supervisor *thinks* the complainant said. Here, also, objectivity is essential. Any agreements or decisions that are made must also be recorded exactly. This includes identities of the parties involved as well as the officials empowered to authorize or make such agreements or decisions.

Precedents and Privacy

As part of the case documentation, the supervisor should identify any precedents related to the complaint and should include how prior complaints were addressed. This might be accomplished by reviewing security department records or by coordinating with human resources personnel. These precedents can help justify the actions ultimately taken or not taken. Once a decision is made or a course of action is decided upon, the supervisor should keep the complainant advised of the status of the complaint to every extent possible.

Privacy concerns will affect the investigation of every complaint. The complainant—particularly if "whistleblowing" is involved—has certain legal protection depending on the state/province or federal jurisdiction. Persons who are the subjects of complaints have certain due process rights. The supervisor must be aware of the liabilities incurred if information is unintentionally released or deliberately leaked. Corporate counsel should be consulted if the supervisor is uncertain about what can or cannot be released to a third party. Ultimately, information should not be released to any individual who does not have a "need to know." Parties that have a need to know might include human resources staff assigned to the complaint, the management officials that will decide what action the company will or will not take, or the legal counsel retained by the company. Parties that do not have a need to know might include department managers that are not involved in the complaint or security officers not involved in the investigation.

Dealing with Unions

Special care must be taken when dealing with employee unions. The steps described above must still be taken by the supervisor, but dealing with a union (bargaining unit) adds additional caveats to an investigation. For example, complaint resolution procedures are often spelled out within the bargaining agreement. The supervisor might have to follow different protocols for union members than for non union personnel, based on the bargaining agreement. Union members might be entitled to union representation for any hearing or interview. This can add additional stress to the interviewer because the union representative may attempt to deflect questions, obfuscate, or otherwise interfere with the investigative process. Some agreements may require that an outside arbitrator be used instead of handling a complaint internally within the company. If the security supervisor works for a government contractor at a government-run facility, there may even be additional civil service protections that must be respected. The supervisor must be aware of all of these considerations.

The End of the Investigation

As the investigation reaches its end and the supervisor has documented the interview, collected the necessary evidence, and drafted a report on the investigation, the final step is to submit the report to the proper authority. Different entities handle complaints in different ways. Some companies have boards or commissions that handle complaints. Others have specific managers designated for that purpose. Still others have the human resources department determine final resolution. The supervisor may be bound by a collective bargaining agreement to submit copies of the report to union representatives or an independent arbitrator.

As discussed earlier, some entities require complaints to be handled within a specific timeframe or in a particular manner. The supervisor must ensure, from the beginning of the investigation to the final report, that requirements for specialized incidents are met. Whistleblower protection, which is intended for company employees who complain that the company's internal operations violate policy, regulation, or statute, has different requirements from state to state or province to province. Anti-bullying and anti-harassment complaints also may have different requirements depending on the investigative entity.

Prevention

An additional—and often overlooked role—of the security supervisor is not only to receive and investigate complaints but to prevent or mitigate, where possible, the situations by which complaints can originate. In the absence of a complaint prevention or resolution process, supervisors must advocate for establishing one. A few simple prevention steps that companies can take are as follows:

- Have clear policies and procedures in place for complaints.
- Know the policies. As a supervisor, one should be able to articulate the policy and to understand how it is implemented and enforced. Supervisors must also know who is authorized to handle and investigate specific complaints.
- Know the laws—local, state/provincial, and federal. Understand the legal definition of such topics as harassment. The employer's legal counsel may be able to assist with this.
- Train all management staff who may reasonably be expected to deal with complaints.
- Be prepared to take steps to remedy the employee complaint. Any offensive conduct must be eliminated at any cost, up to and including termination of the employee perpetrating the harassment.
- Prevent any retaliation against those who complain or those who support a complainant.

Potential Legal Issues

It is imperative that supervisors be trained on harassment prevention. We can look to California as an example. In 2005, California enacted a law, Government Code Section 12950.1, which requires all employers with 50 or more employees to train all supervisors on harassment prevention, with 2 h of training every 2 years. It states that the training must be interactive and cover all state and federal laws prohibiting harassment. Although their guidelines on the subject of training are somewhat vague, this can be seen as an example of possible future state or provincial requirements. The California code further suggests that supervisors can be held accountable and *personally liable* if they ignore illegal conduct when they have the authority to stop it.

Consider having a policy specifically dealing with whistleblowing so that workers are encouraged to come forward with complaints. Various laws protect whistleblowers, such as the Sarbanes-Oxley law in the United States, public health regulations, safety regulations, etc. A generic policy for handling whistleblowers is a necessity, even if the particular situation is not covered statutorily at present. Organizations should always be prepared to uncover evidence of wrongdoing. The security function, by definition, plays a leading role in this.

Conclusion

Handling complaints is an important part of a supervisor's job. Supervisors who are adept at resolving the issues that concern their subordinates will form lasting bonds and earn the respect of those subordinates. Those who cannot master the skills to handle complaints will become isolated from the people they supervise and often witness an increased amount of dissatisfaction, absenteeism, and turnover. No one wins in that situation.

Refer website http://www.ifpo.org for further information

Security-Related Business Functions

21

Evaluation of Uniformed Protection Officers

Ronald R. Minion

Introduction

The line security officer plays a vital role in the success of any security organization. The level of motivation also creates an immediate impression regarding the organization that the officer is responsible for protecting. First impressions are lasting! A high performer does not necessarily make the best officer. A long-term solid performer—a protection officer who has been properly screened, trained, uniformed, and prepared for the job of protecting life and organizational assets—will get the job done best.

Once the officer is on the job, far too often security managers take a hands-off approach. However, this is the time when all officers need guidance and support to get the job done effectively. Good supervision and coaching leads to positive performance—performance that builds profits (whether contract or proprietary).

There is no magic to motivate the uniformed security officer. However, for too long, guard force managers have not paid enough attention to the officer's individual professional employment needs. The job cannot get done without expending human and financial company resources for the officer's support, leadership, and professional development. These two resources are indeed precious; hence, there must be a program—a plan that will work. Once organizational resources are committed to employee motivation, managers must know what they are doing and be aware of how the resources will be managed.

Many contract security companies are managed on the premise that the bottom-line profit results directly from the level of motivation of the line security officers. Therefore, the program presented in this chapter may seem like a departure from the traditional way that protection officers are managed. How company resources are expended to enhance motivation and productivity within the security force is a very important exercise in human resource management.

Officer Evaluation

Before discussing rewards, perks, or bonuses, there must be an accurate record of how well the officers are doing. This cannot be a "hit-or-miss" opinion expressed by a supervisor. Each officer must be scored/graded, and a report card must be generated. Managers should grade the officers and then grade the site/account in a holistic manner. This is the beginning of the team approach to guard management. The following questions must be addressed:

- How will the officers be evaluated?
- What criteria will be used?
- Who is responsible for conducting inspections/evaluations?
- How will results be verified and/or validated?
- How will officer performance be linked to team performance?
- How will feedback and results be provided to officer(s)/team(s)?
- What are the rewards for good performers?
- What are the sanctions for bad performers?

Step 1

Determine what job-related accomplishments and/or performance measures are most important to the evaluation process. The 10 most important factors to be assessed are as follows.

Dress/deportment: How well the officer presents and conducts himself or herself on the job will be a determining factor in the level of performance. Anecdotally, it is unusual for a sloppy officer to perform well, just as it is unusual to see a crisp and sharply turned-out officer perform below security management's expectations. The officers must have the tools to work with—a good uniform management program is essential.

Qualifications: There are numerous training and education opportunities available for protection officers. There are official certifications that accredit the officer's achievements/skills. The most important training programs directly linked to officer performance are first aid, cardiopulmonary resuscitation, nonviolent crisis intervention, occupational health and safety, Certified Protection Officer, protective security courses at private/government institutes, and professional college security programs leading to an associate or bachelor's degree.

Reports/notes: The officer who is capable of effectively taking notes during his or her tour of duty and able to translate the information to a useful report is vital to a successful security department. Electronic incident tracking often replaces the manual process; hence, officers must be familiar with how to use computers. Good security depends on every officer's contribution to record keeping and statistics.

Site operating procedures: All levels of the security unit should participate in the development and maintenance of effective standard operating procedures (SOP). Once these indispensable orders are complete, they must be continually updated. Good officers work hard at keeping security procedures current. An officer's knowledge and understanding of the application of site/post orders significantly enhances security.

Knowledge of site and facility orientation: Prior to permanent assignment to any post/site, the officer must be familiar with the physical layout of the property/facility to be protected. Site plans, supervised tours, duty checklist, SOP, and a written quiz at the completion of on-the-job orientation are all helpful in gaining a clear understanding of the physical plant.

Attitude: An officer with a positive attitude toward his or her employer, duties, responsibilities, and the site which must be protected, is essential for good security. Bad attitudes equate to bad security. An officer who has assumed a position in security as a "stop-gap" measure will seldom possess the right attitude. Good attitudes are developed through joint goal setting. Officers who have a say in how site security is managed, generally have the best attitudes.

Public relations: The protection officer is a public relations envoy for the organization he or she protects. The officer who has paid attention to the need for appropriate dress and deportment has taken the first step in the creation of a positive first impression with visitors, employees, customers, and corporate executives. The officer must understand how to be portrayed as the person in charge. An individual who exhibits a pleasant/upbeat image is vital to a successful public relations program.

Reliability: The ideal officer will come to work early to make sure he or she is fully conversant with the events of the previous shift. Once management recognizes an officer as reliable, he or she will be given more responsibility, which will ultimately advance the officer's security career. This officer knows his or her work, understands SOP, and works harmoniously with other officers on the security team.

Housekeeping and image enhancement: A sloppy officer, a sloppy security office, sloppy records, sloppy notes, and sloppy reports all lead to poor performance and poor security. In the overall pursuit of image enhancement, protection officers must work at looking sharp at all times. They must keep the security area tidy and maintain orderly records and reports. Good housekeeping equates to good security.

Permanency: Turnover is an ugly word in the private security community. However, it is also a fact of life for some security providers. New faces create disruptions in the life safety/asset protection program—not deliberately, but in the process of becoming acclimated to the security program. The experienced and qualified officer who dresses immaculately, produces quality reports, understands SOP, has the right attitude, exhibits public relations, is reliable, and keeps a tidy work station will stay longer, feel good about the job, and will be a credit to his or her employer and the security profession.

Step 2

Evaluation Format

All employees, regardless of their occupation, need feedback: "How am I doing?" "How does my work compare with my coworkers?" "How can I improve?" Protection officers are no exception. If they are left in the dark and can only guess as to how well they are getting their work done, they will soon become demoralized, negatively impacting performance.

The officer appraisal form in Figure 21.1 has been developed to accurately assess performance. This report is based on the 10 most important factors necessary for the attainment of an officer's success in the security workplace.

<u>**INSPECTION REPORT – OFFICER EVALUATION**</u>

Date: _____ Time: _____ Site: _____
Inspector: _____ Officer: _____

Evaluation Results
Ten success factors each graded 1 to 10. (1—unsatisfactory 10—outstanding)
Please circle appropriate grade.

Dress/Uniform...1 2 3 4 5 6 7 8 9 10
Qualifications..1 2 3 4 5 6 7 8 9 10
Quality of reports/notes.....................................1 2 3 4 5 6 7 8 9 10
Knowledge of orders 1 2 3 4 5 6 7 8 9 10
Knowledge of site 1 2 3 4 5 6 7 8 9 10
Attitude..1 2 3 4 5 6 7 8 9 10
Public relations...1 2 3 4 5 6 7 8 9 10
Reliability..1 2 3 4 5 6 7 8 9 10
Housekeeping..1 2 3 4 5 6 7 8 9 10
Permanency at site..1 2 3 4 5 6 7 8 9 10

Add up all values circled and enter the total: (Maximum possible: 100 points)
Total: _____

Comments: _____
_____
_____

Officer Signature & Date: _____

FIGURE 21.1 Officer appraisal form.

Step 3

Evaluation Process

The completed evaluations are invaluable documents that can be used extensively as a protection officer management tool. To effectively evaluate all officers on a particular site, a senior member of the force must be appointed to coordinate the project (inspection coordinator).

The inspection coordinator must work closely with the site supervisor, communicating proactively. The exercise must not be deemed as a "witch hunt," but rather a positive program designed to recognize good work by all officers. For this reason, presentation is everything. The officers must understand exactly how they are being rated, on what categories, and how they can meet or exceed expectations. These issues should be discussed prior to the evaluation and once again individually with the officers during the evaluation period. If the security staff is unionized, the collective bargaining agreement (CBA) will play a significant part in how evaluations are conducted. Any negotiations on a new CBA should include the employee evaluation process.

Once all of the evaluations have been completed, they must remain confidential and be delivered to a senior member of security management.

Step 4

Officer/Team Assessments
Based on the previously described collection of data, security management will be in possession of very valuable information that should not be left to gather dust. This data should be assessed by the inspection coordinator and discussed with the site supervisor.

Each officer must be given the opportunity to discuss his or her appraisals. It must be an exercise designed to enhance motivation and performance. It is a time to set goals rather than chastise. Each officer must be told of any shortcomings brought to light in the performance audit. Each officer must be told of the timing of the next evaluation and be instructed on how to improve performance as required.

By calculating each officer's rating, it is easy to determine a team score. Simply take the average of each officer's score, including the supervisor(s). At this point, managers should compile and determine officer/team grades. The results should then be discussed with the individual officers. The next logical step is to discuss the grade for the team with the whole team.

The client (i.e., not only the commercial customer but corporate management) will be impressed with company security professionals who have worked hard to develop a productive security organization. They will be impressed that the security staff they have contracted are put through a rigorous performance-measurement process that provides guidelines designed to eliminate bad performance among the protection service group.

This same process creates a level playing field for the security staff; each officer knows the rules. All team members must be informed as to when and what to expect from the next scheduled inspection, which should be conducted within 6 months.

Step 5

Goal Setting and Motivation
For this program to work, there must be realistic goals. If the overall average score was 70%, set a new target of 75%. This gives everyone on the team something positive to strive for. It will be amazing to see how (without any help from management) the team will establish a norm for good performance. Now, team members will discreetly sanction poor performers (and sometimes not so discreetly). Everyone wants to play on a winning team. The rising tide will lift all boats.

Ideally, there should be more than one team. If the team consists of a small proprietary security force, make each shift a separate team. If it is a large in-house group, identify each site as a team. If it is a contract company, the number of teams will potentially be unlimited.

Team standing will become very important to team members, but only with management impetus. The entire evaluation program has to be managed. Communicating information is vital to the overall success of the program. By placing a lot of emphasis on the results of the evaluations, management can significantly improve overall officer performance.

Validation of the process is essential. If management, supervisor(s), officers, and/or teams think the results are skewed, biased, or inaccurate, that is a problem. The source of the problem must then be identified: is the problem with communication, the design of the evaluation, the weighting applied (or not) to the scores? If the accuracy of the grades is in doubt, a private security consultant, a member of the human resources department, or another department within the organization can be recruited to do spot audits to confirm the correctness of the data.

After being certain that the evaluations and scoring were fair and reasonable, the next step is determining what to do with those who did not meet acceptable standards—the poor performers. Certainly, a confidential corrective interview is in order. If the deficiencies are serious, a written warning or counseling might be more appropriate. Most important, management must allow the employee an opportunity to improve. Security managers can turn a negative to a positive by skillfully communicating with the low-scoring officer. Individual coaching and encouragement will go a long way to improve future evaluations.

On the flip-side, the evaluation process will not be effective unless security managers have some ways to reward high performers. A letter of recognition, a certificate, a plaque, a bonus, gift certificate, a promotion, a lapel pin, medal of merit, a dinner with the boss, or a promotion might be effective. Different people respond to different incentives, so it will involve some thoughtfulness on the part of management.

In the same token, if management is going to score and rank the teams, they must somehow acknowledge or reward the high-performing team(s). Publish the rankings, tell other departments/divisions in the organization, have a write-up in the company newsletter, or give out rewards (e.g., a monetary reward to be divided by team members, team jackets, crests, individual/group certificates/plaques, pizza party).

Having described the need to address the different levels of performance that will be identified through an evaluation system, there is one caveat to taking actions based on the results of the evaluations. The first iteration of the evaluation system (whether they are done quarterly, biannually, or annually) should not involve taking actions to reward high performers or to address poor performers. The first iteration should be used to establish a baseline. Employees cannot show an increase or decrease in their scores without an initial score to begin with.

Ultimately, the goal is to improve performance through heightened motivation within the security organization. The perks/rewards are secondary to improved on-the-job officer performance. How to measure officer performance has always been a puzzle. With a solid evaluation system for the security staff, it now becomes possible to measure performance and increase efficiencies or address little problems before they become crises.

Refer website http://www.ifpo.org for further information

22

Statistical Analysis for Security and Supervision

Whitney DeCamp, Patricia A. O'Donoghue, Robert A. Metscher

The Collection of Data

Why does a security supervisor need to learn about the collection of data or research methods? The reasons are quite simple: the ability of managers and supervisors to sense, spot, and address problems before they become serious creates a tremendous advantage for the companies that employ them. Knowing about research and problem-solving processes assists supervisors in identifying problems and finding out more about the situation. By collecting and analyzing data, then displaying it as useful information, the security professional can answer fundamental operational and strategic planning questions.

Statistical analysis ultimately boils down to numerical results. With computer programs available to do the mathematical computations, most people using statistics can focus more on simply how to get the computer to do what they want and how to interpret the results. You do not have to be a mathematical wizard to do this—the average person can calculate and interpret meaningful statistics. There are three steps involved in statistical analysis:

1. The collection of data
2. The organization of data
3. The analysis of data

A raw dataset—that is, a spreadsheet or table with lots of numbers—cannot usually be understood by simply looking at it. To grasp the meaning of a vast amount of numerical data, its bulk must be reduced; that is, it must be made manageable. The process of abstracting the significant facts contained in the data and making clear and concise statements about the derived results, constitutes a statistical analysis. Common sense and experience are key elements in the analysis phase of information gathering. The purpose is to give a summarized and comprehensible numerical description of large amounts of information.

Operational considerations include the following:

- What do we do?
  - What programs, tasks, or actions consume our efforts?
- How does it support our objectives and those of the organization?

Security Supervision and Management. http://dx.doi.org/10.1016/B978-0-12-800113-4.00022-5

- Why are we engaged in these activities?
- How do we know?
  - How can we show our activities are efficient and effective?

Strategic considerations include the following:

- Where is the organization heading?
  - What goals represent the next horizon?
- What must we do to support that direction?
- Do our activities currently support that direction?
  - If not, how must we change?

Metrics and Data Collection

Today, more than ever before, security professionals are expected to be business savvy. Organizational leaders expect demonstrable efficient and effective returns for their protection investments and security leaders who are capable of providing that information. Throughout our industry, talk of "metrics" and their uses abound. Without complicating the topic, metrics may be grouped into the following broad categories:

- *Input/effort*: What raw materials or actions are committed to a program, task, or activity?
- *Output*: What is the immediate product of those actions?
- *Outcome*: What benefits are derived from the effort and results?

Historically, much emphasis has been placed on effort and output data. Unfortunately, this information is typically of little use in an organizational performance context. They often fail to demonstrate where or how the organization benefits.

Consider, for example, the deployment of some remote system, such as access control, alarms, or closed-circuit video systems. The goal of deploying this remote system is likely to improve the capability to govern a facility or investigate suspicious activity. To quantify this, the fictitious department might track the number of access permissions granted and revoked, the number of false alarm fines avoided, or the investigations completed remotely. These are all good data points to collect. They may even be comparable to other basic data to show change in costs based on a reduction in re-keying costs, or the management of alarm user accounts, and so on.

Once this information is collected, the next step in demonstrating a value to the organization is to consider what has been eliminated, what has been made more efficient, and how that can be presented. If the remote systems were meant to eliminate unnecessary travel to specific locations, how can that data be formatted into useful information? The distance and travel time to each location is a known quantity. Each unnecessary trip could be calculated to show the miles that were not driven and the time not spent traveling. These are real costs that translate into demonstrable efficiencies. The next step after that would be to show the increase in other activities that the untraveled time has made available to personnel. With just a little effort, data that are likely already being collected are then turned into a clear business case.

Ensuring the effectiveness of any data analysis program requires consistency. Data must be consistently collected, and accuracy is an implied requirement. The data must also be consistently formatted to facilitate convenient analysis. A specific value for a specific data point must be consistent. For instance, if a facility name is part of the data being collected, then everyone entering the data must use the same name. Failing to do so does not derail the whole process, but it does create unnecessary administrative overhead to clean the data later in the process. To avoid this annoyance, simply *collect consistent data consistently*.

Collecting data today is easier than ever before. There are now many free services online that eliminate the need for more than a few minutes to set it up. Smartphones offer a range of applications, including spreadsheets, which may be used for collecting near real-time data if an online service, such as Google Docs, is an unacceptable option for an organization. To be successful, it is essential to begin; it is not necessary to begin big or to wait while striving for perfection. Collecting some data will lead to a greater understanding of what data are desired and how they may be used. This, in turn, allows for revising and improving the collection and reporting process, which can become the start of an ever-improving process on its own.

Staffing Exercise

For an example, consider a problem that all managers face at one time or another: the staffing of the workforce. As a manager faced with this problem, you will need to collect some data. Here are some things to consider, statistically speaking. First and foremost, what is the total number of individuals that you will need to effectively run your day-to-day operation? Now, let us say that 70% are considered "old" employees—that is, they have worked in your security department for more than a year. The other 30% are "new" employees with the following attrition record:

- Within the first 4 months of their employment, 50% leave.
- Within the second 4 months, 20% leave.
- Within the next 4 months, 10% leave.

The conclusion: only 20% make it through the first year. After that, they become "old" employees. Among the old employees, the attrition rate is 30% a year (or 10% every 4 months. With these rates in mind, how should the company approach the problem of determining a hiring rate that will maintain a stable work force and resize the work force by any given percentage rate annually (depending on needs)?

Once organized and analyzed, this research and these data can be useful decision-making tools rather than a mass of incomprehensible statistical information. In addition, being knowledgeable about research and research methods helps professional managers to: (1) identify and solve small problems in the work setting; (2) know how to discriminate good research from bad; (3) appreciate and constantly remember the multiple influences of factors impinging on a situation; and (4) take calculated risks in decision-making, knowing full well the probabilities attached to the different outcomes.

Hurry Up and Wait Exercise

Consider a real-life example of how to organize data. As the manager of a security force charged with maintaining access control into a facility, the waiting lines and waiting-line behavior of customers is a never-ending concern. Waiting in line (generally referred to as queue) occurs when some employee or customer must wait for service or access into a facility. On average, it is possible to be a member of at least three queues on any given day.

From a manager's point of view, here are some of the considerations in solving this problem of waiting in queue. The manager must try to find the optimal point where the queues are short enough to minimize customer complaints. The same manager must keep in mind that it is not practical to provide such a service that no queue can develop. In effect, managers balance the increased cost against the customer complaints (which increase as the average length of wait increases). Data on time spent in queues can be broken into two categories: (1) the number of arrivals during a certain period of time, and (2) the time lost by personnel waiting for services (see Figure 22.1). More categories can be constructed to include the sheer number of persons waiting in line. This

Period (Hours)	Number of Arrivals	Service Time (Minutes)
1	0	7, 7
2	2	
3	0	
4	2	10, 10
5	1	5
6	0	
7	4	6, 7, 9, 12
8	7	3, 4, 6, 7, 9, 10, 15
9	5	4, 5, 5, 7, 10
10	0	
11	0	
12	2	4, 4
13	0	
14	0	
15	0	
16	1	10
17	0	
18	4	5, 5, 7, 10
19	1	8
20	1	10
21	0	
22	0	
23	0	
24	1	10
Total	31	231

Time analysis: 231 min total, for an average waiting time per arrival (231/31) of 7.45 min.

FIGURE 22.1 A chart documenting hypothetical arrivals and service minutes for each hour.

information may be used to determine if another service person should be assigned to the desk during a specific time of day, say between 7:00 am and 9:00 am in the morning when the line is the longest.

As Figure 22.1 illustrates, it is not only good customer service to provide two access control individuals at the desk but, more importantly, it is also cost-effective. The chief financial officer would love to hear how you saved the company money and used your personnel effectively with this one example.

Analysis of Data

Decision Making

If it was possible to predict the future with complete certainty, the structure of managerial decision would be radically different from what it is. There would be no excess production, no clearance sales, and no speculation in the stock market. However, because people do not live in a world of complete certainty, they usually try to make decisions by using the probability theory. Usually, managers will have some knowledge about the possible outcomes in a decision situation; by collecting and organizing information and then considering it systematically, managers often will reach a sounder decision than if they guess.

The concept of probability is a part of everyday life. When rain is predicted, people change their plans from outdoor activities to indoor ones. Managers who manage inventories go through a series of decision-making situations similar to changing plans from outside to inside. Both of these decision-makers benefit from their own assessment of the chances that certain things will happen. Determining the chance that something will happen is called *probability*. In probability theory, an event is one or more of the possible outcomes of doing something. For example, examine the classic coin-toss event. If someone tosses a coin, getting a tail would be an event; getting a head would be another event. This activity of tossing the coin in probability theory is called an experiment.

When conducting experiments in probability, two critical terms must be remembered: *mutually exclusive* and *collectively exhaustive* events. Events are mutually exclusive if one and only one of them takes place at a time. Consider again the example of the coin toss. There are two possible outcomes, heads or tails. On any single toss, either heads or tails may turn up, but not both. Accordingly, the event of *heads* or *tails* on a single toss is said to be mutually exclusive. The question to consider in determining whether the events are mutually exclusive is: can two or more of these events occur at one time? If the answer is yes, the events are not mutually exclusive. When a list is made of possible events resulting from this experiment and the list includes every possible outcome, this is a collectively exhaustive list. In the coin-toss example, the list "heads and tails" is collectively exhaustive, unless the coin lands on its edge. In analyzing data and decision-making, most managers should consider and use probabilities. If using probabilities, the concern should be with two situations: (1) where one event or the other will occur, and (2) the case where two or more events will occur.

Forecasting

Another very important element of analyzing data (in addition to probabilities) is forecasting. Every manager considers some kind of forecast in every decision that he or she makes. Some of these forecasts are quite simple. Take the case of the operations manager who forecasts Friday's workload on Thursday in order to grant a security officer time off. Other forecasts are more complex and usually involve long periods of time, cost, and government regulation for some future issue. No one forecasts with absolute accuracy. Nevertheless, decisions must still be made every day and they are made with the best information that is available.

Regardless of the forecasting technique used, the forecasting process stays the same:

1. Determine the objective of the forecast. (What is its use?)
2. Select the period over which the forecast will be made. (What are your information needs over what time period?)
3. Select the forecasting approach you will use. (Which forecasting technique is most likely to produce the information you need?)
4. Gather the information to be used in the forecast.
5. Make the forecast.

Forecasting Types

There are three basic types of forecasts: judgmental forecasts, extensions of past history, and casual forecasting models.

1. Judgmental forecasts

People tend to use these kinds of forecasts when "good" data is not readily available. A judgmental forecast is used to change subjective opinion into a quantitative forecast that can be used. The process brings together, in an organized way, personal judgments about the process being analyzed. Essentially, it relies primarily on human judgment to interpret past data and make projections about the future.

2. Extensions of past history (also called time-series methods)

Taking history as the beginning point for forecasting does not mean that October will be just like August and September; it simply means that over the short run, future patterns tend to be extensions of past ones and that some useful forecasts can be made by studying past behavior.

3. Casual forecasting modes

If considerable historical data are available and if there is a known relationship between the variables being forecast and other retrievable variables, it is possible to construct a casual forecast. This model is an example of forecasts, which relate several variables.

Consider the usage of decision-making skills and analysis of data in the inventory exercise below.

Inventory Exercise

For many security organizations, the inventory figure is an extremely large asset. Inventory difficulties can and do contribute to a business' poor image, lack of authority and control, and sometimes to the ultimate—failure. In this exercise, observe that skillful inventory management can make a significant contribution to the security operation.

There are two basic inventory decisions that managers must make as they attempt to accomplish the functions of inventory:

1. How many items to order when the inventory of that item is to be replenished.
2. When to replenish the inventory of that item.

The following aspects should be considered when deciding when to order:

1. Lead time

   If calling for home delivery of a pizza and it takes 30 min or less for it to arrive, then 30 min is the lead time for ordering.
2. Lead time demand

   Consider how many pairs of gloves, seasonal items, winter coats, or short-sleeve shirts are needed to keep in stock, then when the stock reaches a certain point, place the order.
3. Stockouts

   Have a contingency plan. Demand of items will continue, even in terrible weather (flood, snow, hurricane), strikes, or even transportation disasters. Consider them all and plan accordingly.
4. Safety stock

   Hold out some extra items, just in case. The term *safety stock* refers to extra inventory held as a hedge, or protection, against the possibility of a stockout. It is, however, always part of the total inventory.

Graphic Presentations

Columns of numbers have been known to evoke fear, boredom, apathy, and misunderstanding. While some people seem to "tune out" statistical information presented in tabular form, they may pay close attention to the same data presented in graphic or picture form. As a result, consider using graphs as opposed to tables. Here are two very basic examples of how to illustrate your results:

1. *Pie chart*: Pie charts are one of the simplest graphic methods, representing a circular graph with pieces that add up to 100%. Pie charts are particularly useful for visualizing differences in frequencies among a few normal-level categories. Pie charts provide a quick and easy illustration of data that can be divided into a few categories.
2. *Bar graphs*: The bar graph (or histogram) can accommodate any number of categories at any level of measurement and, therefore, is more widely used.

Determining Correlations and Causality

The statistics so far discussed have focused primarily on managing a business and monitoring staff. For any organization, these forms of statistics can reduce costs, as well as increase productivity and efficiency. However, when security enters into the equation, one can also turn to social statistics to provide additional information. For example, a retail loss prevention specialist might be interested in which demographic characteristics are most related to shoplifting. Alternatively, perhaps statistics could provide the specialist with clues to the optimum balance of accessibility for customers to reach an item, or for added security to prevent shoplifting. An item locked behind glass is less likely to be stolen, but it is also less likely to be purchased. How much security is too much security? Statistics from prior experimentation could provide answers.

Before getting too involved into these statistics, the purpose of this discussion should be made clear. This introduction to correlations and causality is intended to provide the reader with enough information to understand the importance and the underlying principles of statistics, as well as a meaningful way to interpret these statistics. Those interested in collecting and analyzing data should consult additional sources relating to research methods, correlation, and regression. The Statistical Package for the Social Sciences (SPSS) is a commonly used software package for this kind of analysis, although many other programs also are available. PSPP, for example, is a free software program designed to simulate the experience of more expensive packages, but at no cost (available at gnu.org).

There are several terms used in statistics that must be defined before delving deeper into the topic. A *variable* is something that can change or otherwise varies from person to person. An *attribute* is one of the possible characteristics within a variable. For example, sex is a variable, while male is an attribute. Similarly, height is a variable, while 5'11" is an attribute. In other words, a variable is a category and an attribute is some characteristic or measurement in a category. An *independent variable* is the cause in a relationship (or more precisely, the variable believed to be the cause) and a *dependent variable* is the outcome or effect in the relationship. A *correlation* is a relationship between two variables. It can be positive, in which having a high attribute with one variable is usually associated with a high attribute with another variable. For example, among children, a higher age is usually associated with a higher level of intelligence. This is a positive correlation. On the other hand, a correlation can be negative. Education and shoplifting could be an example of this. Hypothetically, a high number of years of education could be associated with a lower likelihood of shoplifting and vice versa. Simply put, a correlation indicates that there is some sort of a relationship between two things. If you know only one attribute of a person or thing, you might be able to make a reasonable guess as to a second attribute if a correlation exists.

A correlation, however, does not necessarily denote causality. To prove something caused something else, there are three requirements that must be met:

1. There must be a correlation between the cause and the effect.
2. The cause must occur before the effect.
3. The relationship must be not the result of a third variable.

It is the final requirement that is often most difficult to establish. In statistics, a relationship caused by a third variable is called a *spurious* relationship. An example of this could be found with shoe size and criminality. If we only looked at these two variables and claimed to have found causality, we would likely come to the conclusion that as shoe size increases, involvement in crime also increases. There are other variables that might account for most or all of this correlation. First, age is a factor because young children have a smaller shoe size and are less involved in crime. Second, gender has an effect on the relationship because men are more likely to be involved in crime and have a larger shoe size. Overall, a researcher would not be wrong to conclude that shoe size is related to crime, but that does not establish causality and hardly gives us the whole story. Additionally, knowing correlations can lead to useful security implications. Just because causality is not established does not mean the information is worthless.

The *experimental design* is the best way to establish causality. It is also the most effective way to test a change to procedure. In an experimental design, there must be at least two groups. The first group is the control group, which is not exposed to the experimental stimulus (or the change being tested). The second group is the experimental group, which is exposed to the experimental stimulus. The results can then be compared to see if the experimental group experienced changes the control group did not. As long as the participants (people, buildings, organization, etc.) were randomly assigned to one of the two groups, any changes observed only in the experimental group can be reasonably attributed only to the experimental stimulus. The stimulus can then be said to be the cause of the change.

The experimental design can be difficult to understand without an illustration, so here is an example. Let us say that a director of security for a chain of storage facilities with over 250 locations is interested in adding fake security cameras to deter would-be vandals. However, the organization will not authorize the expense without proof the concept will work. Determined to get the funding, the security director randomly chooses 25 of the locations to install the cameras (the experimental group) and does nothing to the other locations (the control group). After 1 year the security director notices a decrease in vandalism by 20% at the locations with the cameras, with a drop of only 10% at the other locations. What these statistics imply is that some part of the 20%, approximately one-half, is likely caused by other changes in policy or society. However, the majority of the decrease was unique to the locations with cameras and therefore is the evidence needed to acquire the additional funding. Likewise, testing the medicinal purposes of new drugs is a similar process. A random selection of participants (the experimental group) is given the drug and the remaining participants (the control group) are given a placebo. This is an extremely effective design, as care is taken to make sure people involved in both groups believe they are in the experimental group. In the storage facility example, it is possible even with an experimental design for a third variable to be involved. Security officers, for example, might have increased their patrols believing they were being watched if they were not informed that the cameras were fake. On the other hand, had the vandalism rates increased, the officers might have decreased patrols relying on the fake cameras to deter.

Using statistical *controls* is sometimes the best option for establishing causality if an experimental design is not feasible. These controls are simply additional variables added to the equation. As more controls are added, the impact of the independent (cause) variable on the dependent (effect) variable will decrease, but any conclusions will become more valid and accurate. A study by the US Census Bureau in 1987 illustrates the usefulness of this approach. It is a well-established fact that women make less money than men overall in the United States. When one reads this, one almost instinctively assumes there is a causality involving discrimination behind this relationship. However, once other variables are added (years on the job, marital status, type of occupation, education level, and many others), 60% of the difference between the income of men and women can be explained through other nondiscriminatory factors. This does not negate the fact that women make less than men, but it does partially explain it and increase our understanding of the problem.

When a researcher believes more than one cause exists, as is virtually always the case in social statistics, *multiple regression* can be used. Rather than testing each relationship separately, regression allows each possible cause to be tested simultaneously. For example, delinquent peers and the frequent witnessing crimes, both correlate with delinquency. However, because the two concepts are not unrelated (having delinquent friends will likely increase the amount of crimes witnessed), the two relationships should be tested together. This allows for the overlap in the concepts to be controlled and generates more accurate statistics.

There are other more advanced forms of statistics that have only recently become possible due to advances in computer technology. Path analysis, for example, allows tracking causality through mediating variables. Although in previous years a test would only have considered whether regular exposure to juvenile delinquents increases delinquency, today that test considers whether it also increases pro-delinquency beliefs and abilities and whether those have an impact on delinquency. This essentially allows us to use the statistical test in a flow chart. See Figures 22.2 and 22.3 for an illustration.

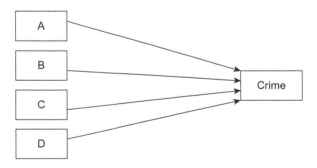

FIGURE 22.2 A graphical representation of a regression model.

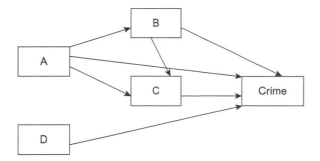

FIGURE 22.3 A graphical representation of a path analysis model.

Conclusion

Whether trying to influence people or justify your operating budget, use the information available to you to make predictions about future events and use statistics as an aid in testing your predictions. There is uncertainty with many managerial tasks, and the use of statistical analysis is no exception. However, using the probability theory and forecasting methods, along with simple mathematical formulas and percentages, will add authenticity to your decisions, and confidence in your conclusions. Statistics can be easily combined with virtually any other area of interest as well. For example, quantifying turnover rates and costs can help illustrate a potential problem. The financial impact of turnover (and various other problems) can be communicated more clearly when statistics are used to define and summarize problems. You can also turn to other people for experience and research to provide additional information. From industry-specific research to theory testing by criminologists, useful and informative statistics are plentiful.

Refer website http://www.ifpo.org for further information

23

Security Officer Scheduling

Gary Lyons, Brion P. Gilbride

Nearly all security supervisors, at some point in their careers, will be responsible for putting together a work schedule for their subordinate officers. Although technology has simplified the scheduling process in many ways, the supervisor must still understand not just where to place their officers, but *when* to place them. In determining a schedule, there are a number of factors involved, which include (but are not limited to) the following: how many officers are available; how many positions, locations, or posts must be staffed; the opening and closing hours of the locations; or whether overtime is authorized and how much. One factor that is itself complicating is identifying what skills are required at a particular post or location. Does an officer need to be bilingual, certified in cardiopulmonary resuscitation or automated external defibrillator use, or accredited to operate mobile X-ray equipment? Does the officer require other specialized training, such as vehicle searches, crowd control, or firearms?

For the supervisor who has not dealt with scheduling of personnel—and even for those who have—the correct and efficient use of the work force can be extremely challenging. There are an infinite number of ways to construct a working schedule, and wise use of employees' time has a profound effect on the bottom line. Immediate benefits of a good working schedule include increased effectiveness, better relationships, and longer retention of staff, along with greater client satisfaction. Effective scheduling is often the result of the scheduler's experience and individual creativity. To begin, it is essential to develop a baseline. Remember the old adage: "A failure to plan is a plan to fail."

Some key things to remember when developing a schedule are outlined in this chapter.

Define the Mission

What needs to be accomplished? In many instances, it is simply staffing a post for a defined period of time. In any case, the more specifically the assignment is defined, the better the chances of a successful final outcome.

Gather Information

This is where the majority of time and effort will be spent. Just as important as gathering information will be keeping that information organized, up-to-date, and accessible. Having to sort through disorganized or unreliable information will add additional time and

Security Supervision and Management. http://dx.doi.org/10.1016/B978-0-12-800113-4.00023-7

frustration to the scheduling process. Begin by identifying the basic requirements of the post. Note that some factors will be outside the scheduler's control. Some questions to ask include the following:

- How many hours will this post need to be staffed? Is it a 24-h post, or is it only open for a specified timeframe or on certain days?
- How many personnel are needed to safely staff this post at any one time?
- Is this a fixed post or is it a patrol area?
  - Are there designated times and locations that need to be patrolled or is it up to the assigned officer(s)?

Account for Controlled and Uncontrolled Factors

Controlled factors are issues that can be anticipated and planned for. These include the mix of full- and part-time staff available, anticipated overtime budget availability, planned vacation or military/medical leave days, holidays, facility operating hours, or specific training requirements for a post. Uncontrolled factors are issues that cannot be anticipated or planned for. These might include employees calling in sick, inclement weather, criminal activity, or mechanical failures such as water main breaks or power outages.

Account for Fatigue

Taking into account the role fatigue plays in security duties is often forgotten when scheduling staff for their various duties. Certain duties, such as monitoring closed-circuit television/digital video systems or patrolling on foot or bicycle, take their toll on the employee. According to the UK Center for Protection of National Infrastructure (CPNI), 12-h shifts are a greater risk to health and performance than 8-h shifts due to fatigue and stress. CPNI recommends balancing operational needs with the impact shift-work has on health and family considerations.[1]

Communication

Most personnel prefer to have a stable and predictable schedule so they can plan their personal lives. *Stability is a key to retaining staff.* If a post is operational over irregular time periods (e.g., from 4 to 8 am and again from 2 to 6 pm), staff should be made aware of the possibility that they will be needed to work irregular hours. Supervisors should address the impact of this in advance with the staff and note any concerns. These concerns can be used to identify potential "win–win" scheduling scenarios that fulfill the mission while accounting for employee scheduling preferences. For example, a single college student may prefer the evening and weekend hours that an employee with family responsibilities would find difficult.

Time-Off Requests

It is imperative that the employer have a clear and precise standard operating procedure (SOP) for employees to request time off. It is equally imperative that the supervisor understands this SOP and adheres to it. An effective SOP will lay out the responsibilities of employees when they request leave as well as the responsibilities of supervisors/managers when they grant leave, deny leave, or propose an alternative. The SOP must be kept up to date as far as any contractual obligations or even changes to the law. Several US states have recently passed laws mandating a certain amount of paid sick leave for businesses, subject to certain restrictions.

For employees, the SOP should have procedures for requesting leave in advance, such as requiring vacation time requests a minimum of 2 weeks in advance. This allows the supervisor to maintain control of the scheduling process and allows time to make needed adjustments. If sick leave or emergency leave is allowed, procedures for that should be developed as well. For example, consider requiring that employees seeking short-notice sick or emergency leave make their request specifically to a supervisor or manager. This eliminates the "telephone" game that is sometimes played where an employee claims to have called in but to a nonsupervisory employee, who might have forgotten to relay the message.

Contractual Requirements

If the security team contains members of a bargaining unit, there may be contract stipulations regarding when and how employees are scheduled. For example, seniority may impact post assignments, or the contract might require a certain minimum number of staff on shift, or leave requests may be managed via a process negotiated into the contract. Overtime assignments and shift differential may be in the contract as well, forcing the supervisor to consider available funding as a determinant in when and how to fill particular shifts.

It can be seen here that there are numerous factors to consider when developing a schedule for security staff. Some of these factors conflict with one another, and it will be incumbent upon the supervisor to determine how best to accommodate these factors. In doing so, the supervisor will develop a schedule for a predetermined time period. Where possible, the supervisor should develop more than one schedule for the time period; this allows alternatives to be considered, and gives the staff input on multiple versions that may help smooth over disagreements or otherwise reduce friction when one employee gets the schedule they prefer while another does not.

Keep in mind that there is no one way to create a schedule. As mentioned, developing multiple schedules creates more options for the supervisor to work with. It also allows switching to an alternative if the initial schedule is problematic or does not adequately support the organization's needs. Sometimes a schedule that looks great on paper is a nightmare in practice.

Figures 23.1 and 23.2 provide two schedule templates. Note that the schedule provided in Figure 23.2 has the potential to conserve resources in the following areas:

- Workers' compensation
- Vacation benefits

Name	Monday	Tuesday	Wednesday	Thursday	Friday	Saturday	Sunday
Officer A	0800–1600	0800–1600	0800–1600	0800–1600	0800–1600	Off	Off
Officer B	1600–2400	1600–2400	1600–2400	1600–2400	1600–2400	Off	Off
Officer C	0001–0800	0001–0800	0001–0800	0001–0800	0001–0800	Off	Off
Officer D	Off	Off	Off	Off	Off	0800–1600	0800–1600
Officer E	Off	Off	Off	Off	Off	1600–2400	1600–2400
Officer F	Off	Off	Off	Off	Off	0001–0800	0001–0800

FIGURE 23.1 Schedule I: 168h total, 24h a Day, 7 Days a Week, with three full-time and three part-time staff members.

Name	Monday	Tuesday	Wednesday	Thursday	Friday	Saturday	Sunday
Officer A	0800–1600	0800–1600	0800–1600	0800–1600	0800–1600	Off	Off
Officer B	1600–2400	1600–2400	1600–2400	1600–2400	Off	Off	1600–2400
Officer C	Off	0001–0800	0001–0800	Off	0001–0800	0001–0800	0001–0800
Officer D	0001–0800	Off	Off	0001–0800	1600–2400	0800–1600	0800–1600

FIGURE 23.2 Schedule II: 168h total, 24h a Day, 7 Days a Week, with four full-time employees required.

- Health insurance
- Uniforms
- Other "per employee" expenses

The reason these savings may be realized is that two fewer personnel are required for Schedule II. The use of full-time personnel means that any dissatisfaction with the scheduling is likely mitigated by the full-time position and fringe benefits that might accompany it. This helps create an environment conducive to viewing security work as a long-term career. Although Schedule II is less expensive, Schedule I could be used as a backup schedule in the event that Schedule II was unable to be implemented.

Challenges

A common challenge with scheduling is the lack of follow-up on the part of the scheduler (the supervisor, usually). Follow-up is important. A schedule can influence morale, for example. A schedule that accommodates most employees will make them happy, and happy workers are usually productive ones. A schedule that accommodates no one, sometimes can work as the employees do not feel that one employee is advantaged over another as far as the schedule is concerned. That said, a schedule that favors one person over another is a morale-killer. Supervisors who write schedules are human, and sometimes the temptation to "do somebody a favor" can be difficult to overcome. The same can be said if a perception exists that some individuals are always granted their time-off requests while others are routinely denied or alternatives proposed.

Another challenge with scheduling, particularly at sites used by the public, such as shopping malls or universities, is accounting for special events that sometimes occur at those sites. A special event might be a concert, a speaker, a sporting event, seasonal sales, or some other planned situation. Regardless of the event, in many cases the regular day-to-day duties must also be addressed and scheduled for. Flexibility is essential. When the schedule cannot flex, the employees must be communicated with—quickly and honestly—about what has to happen to accomplish the mission.

Conclusion

Effective scheduling is a continuous improvement process. Employee issues, weather, and clients' needs can change without notice and affect the most solid of schedules. There will be many instances when the planned schedule and the final outcome are inconsistent. The supervisor must be flexible. He or she must have a planned back-up schedule(s) for each post and a plan for implementing these back-up procedures. There must be regular communication with the staff about expectations when it comes to scheduling and shift work. The staff's comments and concerns should be taken into consideration where possible. Consultation with corporate counsel regarding any legal or contractual obligations is recommended, particularly if supervisors are unsure of how scheduling is affected by those issues.

Refer website http://www.ifpo.org for further information

End Note

1. *Human Factors in CCTV Control Rooms: A Best Practice Guide* (London, UK: Centre for the Protection of National Infrastructure, Date Unknown.) Accessed November 5, 2014. Available: http://www.cpni.gov.uk/documents/publications/2014/2014001-human_factors_cctv_control_rooms.pdf.

24

Improving Organizational Performance by Employing Total Quality Management

Tom M. Conley

The primary objective of any security program is to protect life, property, and information. Both proprietary and contract security programs have internal as well as external customers. While there are usually a wide variety of tactics, techniques, procedures and tools used in combination to accomplish this task, the core strength of all security programs boils down to people. With well-trained, professional people, things just seem to go well, from the day-to-day routine tasks to emergencies. Contrarily, things do not usually go all that well when people fail to possess the training and competencies they need to be successful.

Anyone who has spent even the slightest amount of time in a security supervisory or management position has almost certainly heard complaints from customers such as, "I like security officer X, but security officer Y does not seem to know what he is doing. I just do not have confidence in security officer Y." Or, the complaints may sound like, "I do not understand why your team of security officers cannot seem to do the job correctly and consistently. They always miss things that we have talked about being important, and they repeatedly cannot do them." Other customers may voice concerns over security officers telling inappropriate jokes or exhibiting inappropriate behavior while on post. These complaints may cost security companies accounts and give them a bad reputation with other organizations as well as with potential employees. The best way to avoid (or at least minimize) these adverse issues to a manageable level is for security companies to embed total quality management (TQM) principles and processes within their organizations. The good news is TQM is not overly complex to the point where its principles and methods cannot be grasped, nor is it too difficult for a security company or security department to integrate into its organization.

TQM has been defined in different ways. One definition that encapsulates the tenets of TQM is as follows:

> *A people-focused management system that aims at a continual increase in customer satisfaction at continually lower real cost. TQM is a total system approach (not a separate area or program), and an integral part of high-level strategy. It works horizontally across functions and departments, involving all employees, top to bottom, and extends backwards and forwards to include the supply chain and the customer chain.*

Security Supervision and Management. http://dx.doi.org/10.1016/B978-0-12-800113-4.00024-9

Not all people will agree with this definition. Some people refuse to acknowledge the existence of TQM, while others are doing all they can to embrace the concept. Still others are experimenting with TQM and trying to figure out what it means for their business. Whichever position an individual or organization might take, TQM is here to stay, as a way of doing business in a different way. The choice is to embrace TQM or be left behind by those who do.

So practically speaking, what is TQM and how is it used? It is imperative to understand that the concept of implementing TQM requires a fundamental change in the way an organization does business. TQM *cannot* be implemented simply as a program approach. To be successful and bring the organization and its people profound results, TQM *must* be implemented as a change in the way the organization does business. In a TQM environment, the key stakeholder shifts from the organization's officers and directors to the customer. The organization exists for one primary reason, which is to service the customer by providing the absolute best quality product or service for the lowest possible cost. The customer must be the primary concern and focus. If an organization takes care of its customers by meeting their needs, there will be ample profits for all people within the organization.

One key factor to implementing TQM in an organization is that senior management must be fully committed to the change. This commitment means that leadership must be provided for TQM efforts in and outside the organization, and TQM efforts must be adequately funded. Without the firm, long-term commitment of senior management, TQM will not be effective and the needed changes will not occur in an organization. The result will be that the organization will not gain a competitive edge and, over the long term, they may not be at all competitive with other organizations that do implement TQM as a way of doing business. Organizations must be effective and efficient in everything they do. The people in every organization should be asking, "Are we doing the right things?" and "Are we doing things right?" High organizational efficiency and effectiveness are at the core of TQM.

In addition to leadership and a total commitment to organizational change, the concept of TQM involves two disciplines, which combine and work in conjunction with each other: qualitative methods and quantitative analysis. Understanding qualitative methods and quantitative analysis is important because everything an organization does, involves a process. Some processes are simple, whereas others may be complicated. Typically, the more complicated the process, the more chance or probability there is for the occurrence of errors and inconsistencies. It is these errors and inconsistencies that cause organizations grief and lost profits. They affect the quality of a product or service, which, in turn, affects an organization's growth and possibly its very existence.

To understand the present and the future, one needs to understand the history of TQM. After World War II, the country of Japan was crippled, its economy was in ruins, and its spirit nearly broken. The United States decided to help Japan rebuild its economy. A United States government statistician, Dr. W. Edwards Deming, was asked to assist on the project of helping Japan. Deming had previously tried to help companies in the United States, but they had turned him away because the US economy was in good shape. There were plenty of workers, and because American companies were leading the world's industrial base, they thought that what Deming offered would be of no use to them. However, when Deming went to Japan, the Japanese listened. Deming taught them the quantitative and qualitative concepts of TQM. They learned ways to do things better and at a lower cost, while still maintaining high quality. The result of the ongoing work with Deming was remarkable. The Japanese went from having little or no impact on the global economy in the 1940s to having a significant impact by the 1970s. The major difference was the implementation of TQM.

During the 1970s, the US economy was not doing very well. Inflation and unemployment hit double digits and American workers continued to want more money and benefits. American companies had lost their competitive edge and were losing in the global economy. Meanwhile, Deming's work with the Japanese had become widely known and respected by American companies. By the early 1980s, American companies were definitely hurting. They called on Deming to help them in the same way that he had helped the Japanese. However, unlike the Japanese, most American companies were not really serious about making changes. They wanted a quick fix for their problems. Deming was selective in terms of what organizations he would work with, and he would only deal with the top people in an organization. If those top people were not committed, he was not at all interested in working with them.

Finally, companies such as Ford, Chrysler, Westinghouse, Harley-Davidson, and Motorola came around, as they were forced to commit to TQM for their survival. Deming helped them. The results of organizations implementing TQM as part of a new way of doing business were profound but predictable. The profits of companies increased because the quality of their products increased. By the late 1980s, American automobiles were known for their high quality and were priced competitively. People, once again, were proud to buy American. In addition to Deming, other people, such as Joseph Juran and Peter Senge, have worked tirelessly to help organizations become competitive and shift to the new way of doing business.

Deming used a system known as the *14 Points for the Transformation of Management* ("Deming's 14 Points").[1] He used these as a set of guidelines or operating principles for organizational leaders to focus on the changes they needed to make and to keep the focus on continual improvement. Deming's 14 Points are as follows:

1. Create constancy of purpose toward the improvement of products and services, with the aim to become competitive, stay in business, and provide jobs.
2. Adopt the new philosophy. We are all in a new economic age. Western management must awaken to the challenges, learn their responsibilities, and take on leadership for change.
3. Cease dependence on inspection to achieve quality. Eliminate the need for inspection on a mass basis by building quality into the product in the first place.
4. End the practice of awarding business based on the price tag. Instead, minimize total cost. Move toward a single supplier for any one item, in a long-term relationship of loyalty and trust.

5. Improve, consistently and forever, the system of production and service, to improve quality and productivity, and thus constantly decrease cost.
6. Institute training on the job.
7. Institute leadership. The aim of supervision should be to help people, machines, and gadgets to do a better job. Supervision of management is in need of an overhaul, as well as supervision of workers.
8. Drive out fear, so that everyone may work effectively for the company.
9. Break down barriers between departments. People in research, design, sales, and production must work as a team, to foresee problems of production and use that may be encountered with the product or service.
10. Eliminate slogans, exhortations, and targets for the workforce that ask for zero defects and new levels of productivity. Such exhortations only create adversarial relationships, as the bulk of the causes of low quality and low productivity belong to the system and thus lie beyond the power of the workforce.
11. Eliminate quotas. Eliminate management by numbers and numerical goals. Substitute leadership.
12. Remove barriers that rob the hourly worker of his or her right to pride of workmanship. The responsibility of supervisors must be changed from sheer numbers to quality.
13. Institute a vigorous program of education and self-improvement.
14. Put everybody in the company to work to accomplish the transformation. The transformation is everybody's job.

The purpose of Deming's 14 Points is to create a management system that focuses on ceasing to do some things and beginning to do others. It is to create an environment or climate in which employees can work with dignity and one with which they can take pride in their work. Deming's 14 Points exemplify a profound new way of thinking for the security manager and supervisor. Under the system of TQM, no longer is it the responsibility of the manager or supervisor to simply make certain that people are doing their job; rather, their responsibility is to focus on helping and enabling people to do their jobs better, through education and support. Ultimately, the objective should be to support the security officer so that the officer can support the organization's customer. This applies to both proprietary and outsourced security programs.

As was stated previously, proprietary and contract security programs have internal as well as external customers. This recognition is a critical part of the TQM process. An example of an internal customer in a proprietary security program is where the employees depend on the security program to provide them with adequate protection. An example of an internal customer in a contract security program is where the other employees within the organization depend on the security officers to provide employees in other departments with the information they need to do their jobs; for example, the payroll department needs accurate time records to pay the security officers. Provided an organization uses a contract security program, an example of an external customer in a proprietary security program is for the organization to ensure that the contract security provider is fully supported and paid in a timely manner. An example of an external customer in a contract security program is the protection of the client's people, property, and information. It is noteworthy to state that there can—and should—be many external customers, which includes public safety partners (e.g., police, fire, emergency medical technicians, emergency management).

So what is the link between TQM, Deming's 14 Points, and leading a security organization or function? TQM and Deming's 14 Points directly affect a security organization or function because the integration of TQM can and does directly affect the success of a security organization or function, or the lack thereof. People generally want to do the right thing and in the correct way for their employers. While there are exceptions, employees want to do a good job for their employers because doing a good job is not only the ethical thing to do, but it also provides employees with a positive level of job satisfaction. Conversely, even the best-intentioned employees do not feel good about their jobs or their organizations if they are not able to be successful. The simple truth is when a failure occurs in the workplace, it is most often attributable to a faulty process as opposed to a bad or ill-intentioned employee. Put another way, employees will succeed most of the time if they work within a process that enables them to be successful. What Deming understood with great clarity is that too often a faulty process is the direct cause of an employee not being successful. In the absence of an organization using TQM, the employee is almost always blamed for what is in reality a faulty process. In short, organizations that use TQM work hand-in-hand with their employees, their suppliers, and with their customers to solve process problems at all levels. This ultimately results in good employees being successful because they are working within a process that enables them to be successful.

The basics of any and all processes can be broken down into three separate but dependent areas of measurement: *inputs, actions, and outputs.* Using these three areas in the analogy of baking a cake, the inputs would be the ingredients for the cake as well as all the utensils, oven, measuring cups, and anything else that would be needed to make the cake. The actions would be the act of mixing the cake, greasing the pan, baking the cake, and frosting the cake. The output would be the actual cake. Seems straightforward and simple enough. Right? Not so fast. There are a few problems. First, what type of cake will be made? A chocolate cake with vanilla icing, or a traditional German chocolate cake? Or another kind altogether? This brings to light the first problem with the processes that many organizations use—there is no real process or, if one does exist, it is loose and ineffective.

Returning to the cake analogy, if the type of cake is not known or the attributes of the cake are not known, how can the necessary ingredients and instructions be identified? The short answer is that they cannot be identified. The lesson learned here is the first thing to do in any process is to clearly define the output. If the output is not clearly defined, there is no way to know what inputs are required and what actions are necessary in order to have the correct output. For the purpose of the cake analogy, once the output has been defined (a finished two-layer German chocolate cake ready to eat), what comes next? Some may cite a list of ingredients such as flour, sugar, baking soda, butter and so forth. However, they would be wrong. After defining the output, the second thing needed, which is also the first input, is a recipe for the two-layer German chocolate cake. The recipe is critical because it provides the guidance on the remaining inputs and contains what actions to take in order to obtain the output. In theory, if instructions are available and are followed precisely, the same type of cake can be baked over and over again and it will look and taste the same way every time.

Sadly, organizational leaders and managers too often run their organizations or departments in a manner analogous to directing their employees to bake a cake but not within the framework of a successful recipe (process). The employees do their absolute best to bake a great cake in the absence of having a successful process to follow. Then, when the cake does not turn out well, the manager tells the employees, "If you cannot bake me a cake that looks and tastes good, then I'll find others who will!" The employees have done their best, but they have failed to bake a good cake. The manager then fires those employees and hires replacements, in the hopes that the new employees will be able to "get the cake right." The new employees try their best, but fail again because of a faulty process. The manager blames the employees again. The ex-employees are frustrated because they did their best but could not get the cake right. This frustration by manager and employees alike repeats itself thousands of times per day all over the world—and this is the exact problem that is solved when organizations use the TQM approach.

Consider how the cake analogy would turn out differently in an organization using the TQM approach. First, for an organization that knows it needs to make cakes, it would likely hire employees with related experience. Secondly, managers would meet with the employees to discuss what type of cakes the company baked, what recipes are used, and what the outputs are as a result of those proven inputs and actions. The employees would be provided with training covering the processes used by the company. Then, when the employees start mixing and baking the cakes, the outputs would be predictable. These predictable outputs would enable the employees to be satisfied and have a sense of accomplishment in their jobs, and they would maximize the organization's profits. If the outputs were not as good as they should be, then everyone would examine the process and see what went wrong.

One of the key tools and benefits used in TQM is being able to measure outputs. The two general methods used to accomplish this are *quantitative data* and *qualitative data*. In short, quantitative data refers to the process of doing measurements on anything that can actually be scientifically measured, such as a person's weight, height, age, etc. Qualitative data, or "opinion" data, is information that cannot itself be scientifically measured but that is relevant. An example of qualitative data is the result of the data collected as a part of a survey. Quantitative data and qualitative data are both important and relevant in the TQM framework. Once again returning to the analogy of the cake, the quantitative data would be the ingredients, how the cake is mixed, and the time and temperature at which the cake is baked. The qualitative data of the cake would be how it looks, smells, and tastes. In the absence of using the TQM process, the cake would look, smell, and taste differently every time a cake was baked. These errors and inconsistencies in a process that cause each cake to look, smell, and taste differently are known as *variance*. One of the keys of TQM is reducing variance and thus keeping the errors and inconsistencies in a process within manageable limits.

Qualitative methods are an important part of TQM because they deal with human skills and conceptual thinking. While measurement is important, leadership and the ability to support people ultimately determine an organization's success or failure. This is especially true in the security profession because security professionals are in the people business. While security officers are required to know how to implement the tools they have to work with (alarms, access control, closed-circuit television, etc.), people skills make security professionals valuable to their employers and customers. Qualitative methods help to set the structure for organizational processes. Deming developed a very effective model known as the *Plan, Do, Study, and Act* (PDSA) cycle. The concept of the PDSA cycle, as depicted in Figure 24.1, is to plan the work and process, do the work within the process, study the outputs of the process, and then take action upon what needs to be changed, or take no action, depending on the results. The PDSA cycle then repeats with the improvements. This model provides managers and supervisors with a scientific method of learning how to make continuous improvements.

The quantitative analysis tools in TQM involve the actual measurement of outputs and are used to calculate variances. Measuring outputs, calculating and tracking variance, and integrating these into a process are critical to an organization's success in a TQM environment. There is no way to control outputs, only inputs and processes. In quantitative analysis, the variance is tracked and measured in a variety of ways. The idea of tracking and measuring variance is to keep the processes "in control." When a process is in control, it means that the variance of a product or service is within the specifications. When the variance of a product or service is out of control, it means that the process has a problem and the output is no longer within the specifications. It does not matter if the output is a cake

FIGURE 24.1 The PDSA cycle.

or a hubcap for a car wheel. If the hubcap fits properly on the wheel and it matches the color and strength of the specifications, the production process that made the hubcap was in control. However, if the hubcap has a defect in the coloring or strength, or if it will not fit on the tire because it is too small or too large, then the production process that produced the hubcap was not in control—rather, it was "out of control."

The key to consistent quality is keeping the process of a product or service in control. Ascertaining if a process is in control or out of control is determined by statistical variance. Every process has an upper control limit (UCL) of the variance and a lower control limit (LCL) of a variance. Back to our hubcap example, if the hubcap is too large, it would be above the UCL. However, if it was too small, it would be below the LCL. In both cases, the hubcap would be out of control. The only way for it to be in control, and not defective, would be for the circumference to measure less than the UCL but more than the LCL.

While determining the UCL and LCL of a process is important, it is necessary to always be working on ways that will bring the UCL and LCL closer together; thus, one should always be looking for ways to reduce variance even more than it has been reduced in the current process. It is essential that a process be brought in control before attempting to reduce variance within the process. Traditional methods of controlling variance are defined as an "acceptable" range of variance.

In a manufacturing-based setting, which deals with primary quantitative data, a good example of defining "conformity" in terms of upper and lower control specification limits usually deals with specific measurements. For example, a company that makes steel rods that are supposed to be 6 inches in length may have an allowable variance of ±0.01 inch. This means if the steel rod is more than 6.01 inches, then it is too large to be used. Conversely, if the steel rod is less than 5.99 inches, it is too small to be used. This approach tends to allow complacency concerning variation within that range (±0.01 inch). It assumes that a product just barely meeting specifications, just within the limit, is just as "good" as one right in the middle; however, a product that is just outside 6 inches (above or below ±0.01 inch) is "bad." Managers, supervisors, and line personnel must constantly be looking for ways to improve their systems and reduce variation in an acceptable level so that things stay "within control"—or, said another way, within the allowable variance. As was the case with our German chocolate cake, staying "in control" of the process will ensure that every cake baked will taste the same as the one before it. Whenever anything is out of control, the item is wasted, which costs the company money.

One example is pursuing the elimination of waste. In the 1980s, the Motorola Corporation committed to a campaign called Six Sigma, which aims to reduce variation so much that the chance of producing a defect is down to 3.4 defects per million—or, in other words, the product is 99.99966 percent perfect. The difference between the steel rod manufacturer example and Motorola is that the steel rod manufacturer settled for average variation, whereas Motorola reduced their variance until they had an almost-perfect process. By keeping the process in control, constant quality is maintained and defects are minimized. Therefore, production costs can be kept to a minimum and customer satisfaction can be kept high. This is a fundamental objective of TQM.

There is also a need to control variance in security. While security is a service and therefore far more qualitative than it is quantitative, there are key events in security that can and should be measured. Just one example is mobile patrol alarm response. Mobile patrol alarm response is a type of security service wherein a patrol officer in a car receives a call for service to respond to a customer location where an alarm signal has activated. For the purpose of this example, the alarm response time is defined as the period of time it takes a mobile patrol officer from the time of notification to when the patrol officer arrives on-site at the location of an alarm (Figure 24.2).

This response time is measured in rounded minutes. Again, for the purpose of this example, let us say the average time it takes all patrol officers to respond from the time of notification to the time of arrival is 9 min. Nine minutes is then the statistical "mean" or the average. However, that does not provide enough information to identify the variance. This is important because not every alarm call will be an exact 9 min response time. In fact, very few response times will be exactly 9 min. Therefore, it is necessary to determine the variance of time in order to know what time range it takes for alarm response. In other words, consider that an average alarm response call takes a minimum of 7 min and a maximum of 11 min. This means any time above 7 min but below 11 min is within the control range. Seven minutes would be the LCL and 11 min would be the UCL. In statistical (quantitative) terms, this means that the range between 7 min and 11 min will be the average response parameter 68% of the time. Why 68%? As depicted in Figure 24.2, these times are expressed in statistical terms of *normal distribution* via *standard deviation*. In this case, normal distribution is portrayed via standard deviation in the form of a bell curve. Because statistics is nothing more than variance squared, the bell curve paints a visual picture of what is occurring with the alarm response time data. Those who do not have an understanding of statistics need to acquire one in order to be effective managers.

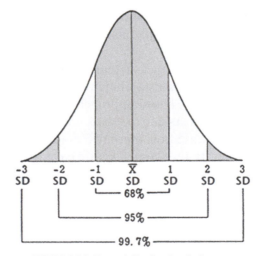

FIGURE 24.2 Normal distribution bell curve.

Applying this example to standard deviation and the bell curve means that the 9 min time is the average or mean. Everything above 9 min represents a plus standard deviation time, whereas anything below 9 min represents a minus standard deviation time. In this example, a response time falling within 7 min to 9 min is a −1 standard deviation and a response time falling within 9 min to 11 min is a +1 standard deviation. Any response time below 7 min or above 11 min is out of control, or outside of the UCL and LCL timeframe. This is the output of the inputs and actions. Being in control or out of control is how managers know if the alarm response time is or is not within the usual parameters. If it is not, it is time to find out why.

While determining the UCL and LCL of a process is important, it is important to always be working on ways that will bring the UCL and LCL closer together; thus, one should always be looking for ways to reduce variance even more. This is called "tightening the bell curve." Using the alarm response time example, perhaps a 9 min average response time is too long and/or the variance of 2 min each way from the 9 min mark is too much of a variance. What if a maximum of a 6 min response time is required? The *only way* to change the output—in this case, a 6 min average response time—is to change the inputs and actions. As changes to the inputs and actions are made, the data needs to be measured to see what impact the inputs and actions have on the process. Simply telling patrol officers they need to have a quicker alarm response time without adjusting the process is an exercise in futility—pointing out, with great clarity, why implementing a TQM system organization wide is so critical.

Some of the most common methods and tools used to measure and track processes and variation are process control charts, histograms, run charts, Pareto charts, cause-and-effect diagrams, deployment charts, fishbone diagrams, and scatter grams. These tools have individual purposes and can be used in conjunction with each other. Of course, to be able to employ quantitative analysis tools successfully, the user must have an understanding and competency of general math and basic statistics. An average person normally has the math abilities to add, subtract, multiply and divide. However, it is less common for the average person to have an understanding of statistics. Understanding statistics is fundamental to being able to implement and understand the tools that are used in the TQM environment.

By managers and employees working as a team and in one common direction for a common goal, the problem of low quality and high variance is corrected. Thus, the cake company that does not use a TQM-based approach would have high employee turnover, low employee morale, high costs due to waste, and a poor product that is inconsistent. It is not difficult to understand how these two diametrically opposed examples of cake-baking apply to the security business. Like the cake business, when things fail in security, they are overwhelmingly a process problem versus a people problem. If the processes are sound, security officers will likely be highly successful, which means the service to the customers will be consistently good.

There are several areas in which security managers and supervisors can contribute to their customers. One major area of contribution can be the act of formulating a value strategy for a customer. Every quality security department or outsourcing organization must have a value strategy to be successful and maximize the money invested in the security program. The value strategy is a comprehensive and well-defined plan that explains exactly how the security personnel from the security department or outsourcing organization will add value to the customer's organization. If a security department or outsourcing organization cannot explain why they should be there and what value they add to an organization, then they are open to budget cuts and being treated with a low level of corporate esteem. A well-detailed value strategy will prevent any "mutual mystification" about the mission of security personnel and will establish a measurement system to track variance and chart progress. With a clearly defined mission, a process can then be developed, which will facilitate the implementation of the mission and identify opportunities for continual improvement through variance reduction. It is essential that the value strategy be communicated to everyone in the organization. This will allow security officers to understand the broader mission of why they are on post and what their job *really* is.

The other major area in which security managers and supervisors can contribute to their customers is establishing and maintaining a comprehensive initial and ongoing training program. It is essential that all levels of security personnel receive adequate training. Not only do security skills and human relations training provide security personnel with much needed skill sets that enable them to function successfully, but training also fosters a sense of belonging to a team. Training additionally provides security officers with a belief that the organization truly cares about them as individuals and what happens to them when they are in the field. Of particular value is the effectiveness of training workers with little or no formal education, many of whom may earn low wages. Such employees have much to gain from general workplace and security-specific training because many lack the necessary skills to compete in an increasingly knowledge-dependent economy that is filled with challenges and stress.

In closing, let us consider a definition of TQM that personnel in security organizations can use effectively. TQM is a management system and philosophy that:

- Institutes a never-ending process of improvement and innovation.
- Is aimed at satisfying and exceeding the customer's needs and expectations.
- Institutes and embeds Deming's 14 Points into every phase of the organization's operation.
- Reduces costs through the elimination of waste and bottlenecks in the organization.
- Involves all people in the organization.
- Is supported by the culture.

The focus in all we do needs to be on the customer. The customer needs to be the key stakeholder and understand the value that officers owe, and can add, to their organization for the money invested in their security program. Anything short of this is unacceptable and will lead to a less than positive outcome.

The leadership challenge for today's security supervisor is both daunting and exciting. While the challenges have never been greater than they are now, the opportunity for growth has also never been as good. The choice of quality is up to each security manager and supervisor. Will you choose quality or mediocrity? One of those two choices will provide the security professional with a satisfying and rewarding career in security that will be a tremendous growth experience. The other will not. The golden rule is that only the customer is qualified to truly define the quality of the products and services others provide to them.

Refer website http://www.ifpo.org for further information

End Note

1. Deming, W. Edward., "The Fourteen Points for Management," appearing in *Out of the Crisis* (Cambridge, MA: The MIT Press): accessed January 15, 2015. Available: http://www.deming.org/theman/theories/fourteenpoints.

25

Project Management for the Security Professional: A Position in Transition

Franklin R. Timmons

Project Management: An Overview

Project management is the art of communicating, understanding business, developing processes, and moving them forward. In a world where businesses are ever changing and companies are being merged, purged, and submerged, project management is a key to the fundamental success of the organization.

An organization exists largely in support of projects. In the contract security business, the entire business model is based on projects and project management. These can be short term (30 days to 6 months) or long term (1–5 years) in nature. Because of this, the project manager must be one who can see the future, understand the needs of the business, and motivate and continuously improve productivity of the team that he or she serves. Knowing the internal and external customer is paramount to success.

Because society has become so dependent on computers and systems, the project manager has to be computer literate and system compliant. Today, reports can be generated and communication can be accomplished in what seems to be the speed of light. Email and documents can be electronically zapped across the world in seconds. In this advanced digital age, teleconferencing can allow for instantaneous review and feedback.

Based on the demands and criticality of the project/task that is to be undertaken, staffing for projects can become the single largest piece of the project manager's time and budget. Much of what the project manager does centers around the ability to improve productivity and reduce the bottom line. Maximizing the productivity of people, systems, and processes becomes paramount to the survival of the project manager and the business he or she represents.

History

In the mid to late twentieth century, the emphasis of the project manager was maximizing worker productivity, no matter what the method or the cost. This was done, in some cases, by brute force, a dogmatic management style, and overuse of unclear and nondescript disciplinary policies.

Security Supervision and Management. http://dx.doi.org/10.1016/B978-0-12-800113-4.00025-0

Even though financial rewards were sometimes plentiful, the major thrust or concern of the employee was job stability or the "job for life" syndrome. The employee knew (or felt like) they would be retained by the employer, if the employee maintained a suitable job performance record. In some cases, employees felt as though they needed an added layer of workplace assurance; in those cases, they voted for and were covered by collective bargaining agreements. The agreements were often viewed in a negative light by managers but seen as the way to preserve a working way of life by the employees. In actuality, managing a work force covered by a collective bargaining agreement is easier sometimes, because all the rules are spelled out in black and white. Many decisions were determined by seniority, and those most affected by the decisions or cutbacks were employees of lesser seniority. There are exceptions to this rule, but they are few and far between, even in right-to-work states.

In the past, many job functions were not automated. Because processes were stable or unchanging, often times the project managers became less dynamic in their thinking and their actions. When an occasional project arose, be it construction or process change, the person in charge of the task would usually be named from within the organization. They would cease working on their normal day-to-day duties and assume their new role, totally consumed by the parts and pieces of their project. Generally, the project managers interacted with local employees such as themselves, and relationships were already established and in place. The need for outside involvement was limited because the general knowledge base came from within the organization.

These early project managers had firm understandings of the business and developed true values of wisdom and commitment. They were relentless in their pursuit of excellence, but they were limited by the few business and personnel tools that they were given.

Transition to Today's World

Into the 1980s and 1990s, American business continued to evolve. Businesses realized that they could streamline operations and reduce costs by instituting a new policy that would come to be known as *outsourcing*. Instead of maintaining their own employees for whom they had lucrative benefit and retirement packages, companies began opting to outsource these positions to contract organizations. In many cases, the contract companies had little or no benefits; those positions that did have benefits were substantially reduced from that of the company seeking to outsource.

Sometimes, outsourcing resulted from facility closings and companies physically moving production to other locations and countries. It may have meant moving certain functions of the work force into a contractor role. Often, when the latter occurred, many of the employees who worked for the business migrated across to the contract company or contract function. These contract companies continued to evolve, across the board and in many disciplines. Engineering, maintenance, security, and even entire contract operating companies were examples of this massive paradigm change in the American work culture.

With the advent of this contractor growth, so came the growth of the project manager to manage and lead the work activity.

Project Management: A Security-Specific Challenge

In the "old days," the senior security person on a job was generally given a paramilitary designation, such as lieutenant, captain, or major. Then, often times, below them were several more layers of command, usually with military or law enforcement designations. There was very little flexibility in command structure, and normally situations at the site did not change. Life went on, as a day-to-day activity and tasks were very manual, at best.

In the early 1990s, automated access control and closed-circuit television (CCTV) systems made their way onto the security playing field. Owners of facilities and businesses decided that they could now have a machine fulfill the function of the human being and operate at a substantial cost savings.

As we turned the corner into the twenty-first century, it became apparent that electronic systems were only getting bigger and better. Globalization was causing businesses to improve their local area networks (LANs) and wide area networks (WANs). Security monitoring stations, command centers, control rooms, etc., began monitoring systems from various parts of the United States and beyond. Access and CCTV systems that were once hardwired to the central computer server were now being placed in more remote locations and being controlled over the companies' LAN and WAN. Officers were now able to complete functions remotely, such as opening doors and gates, and communicating with employees in the field.

The People Piece

The number-one asset for any project manager must be his or her people. The people must know how to go out on a daily basis and make the entire program work.

Selecting the right people for the job is very important for success. Thorough job descriptions, including detailed activities and core competencies, are critical. Degrees of higher learning may be important on paper, but certificates from technical schools attesting to the technical competence and skill set of the worker could be paramount. Officers standing post or working control rooms or infusion centers must be able to communicate orally and use electronic devices. They must understand and be able to use the tools that are provided. Advanced degrees may be an effective indication of program management skills, but they may not be indicative of the ability to effectively use the necessary tools at a work station.

An organization may be plagued with high turnover rates that erode stability and rob the organization of experience and wisdom. Additionally, the added costs for continuous processing, training, and equipping of new personnel are an important consideration.

Today's project manager is faced with motivating people from a very diverse cultural and education global perspective. In the past, workforces were generally regionalized and the educational background of the prospective employee was well established and limited to the geographic area for the local job site. Because our world has become so diverse and mobile, the project manager will need to understand a multitude of cultures and, in some cases, languages, as well as definitely manage different academic levels. Often, these considerations will be directly related to the ability to find a suitable workforce based on hiring requirements and stipulations for the job. Many jobs are slightly more than minimum wage, and they often require background checks and drug screenings. Many times, even though unemployment rates are high in some regions, the employable work force for that area or for that specific job category has already been capped.

Project managers must communicate, motivate, and lead. They must also identify accountabilities for individuals and then hold them accountable. This must all be done in a way that will ensure that the organization and the employees are successful and will continue to grow. Many organizations will use semiannual or annual performance reviews. The project manager must decide if this process is viable and adds value or if they should implement a less formal system for providing frequent feedback.

Communication

Communication is essential for the success of the organization. The various forms of communication are covered in other parts of this book. However, it is still necessary to highlight and reinforce several key elements.

In today's electronic world, where thoughts and statements are streaming at the speed of light, it is critical that face-to-face communication is accomplished. The use of mechanical devices makes it impossible to observe body language or read nonverbal responses to statements that could be critical to the success of the project. Email and texting have a place in our society, but in many cases direct face-to-face communication cannot be replaced.

By completing face-to-face communication, whether it occurs one-to-one or in a group setting (staff meeting), we set the stage for effective and continued communication should the electronic pathways suffer from disruption. Projects can suffer substantial setbacks if communications are disrupted. System outages that occur from construction activities, acts of god, or extended planned preventative maintenance programs can cause major disruption to a project.

When speaking with employees, another critical piece of communication is not only in sending the message, but also in receiving the a message. Active listening skills are essential. Employees must be heard and understood. To be heard, they must be allowed to speak. Listening often includes repeating back or using three-way communication. This is accomplished by verbally repeating back to the employee what you thought they said, followed by the employee confirming the communication as correct. This helps ensure a complete understanding.

Effective Communications Exercise

To better illustrate effective communication, a quick and simple exercise can be completed. The exercise involves a minimum of three people: a facilitator, a speaker, and a listener. The group will need a Tinkertoy set.

Methodology

With both the speaker and the listener out of the room, the facilitator will take the Tinkertoy set and divide the pieces equally among the speaker and the listener. The facilitator will build an object with the pieces designated for the speaker. The listener will only be assigned necessary parts. Any unused parts should be cleaned from the table and placed back into the box.

The model or object that was built will be placed on one side of a small table, with the parts of the object still to be assembled on the other side. A solid divider will be placed in the middle of the table so that the listener cannot see the object that has already been made. Then, with instructions from the speaker, and with a set time of 3 min, the listener will assemble the object using the parts in front of them based on the instructions from the speaker. The listener is encouraged to ask questions for clarification, but cannot show parts for verification or look at the already assembled model.

Desired Outcome

This exercise will help the parties understand the value of clear, concise communication; the value of asking questions for clarification; and the importance of standard nomenclature and definitions. One person may call a round object a wheel, whereas another person may call it a disc.

Motivation

Motivating employees can be one of the hardest concepts for the project manager to grasp and then maintain. Often, project managers are struggling with their own identities and ways to motivate themselves, but now they are called upon to motivate others. The project manager may sometimes feel overcome with a sense of futility and helplessness.

It is essential for the project manager to have a clear understanding of the expectation of the job and the mission. The project manager has got to continuously check and adjust those expectations, as roles and responsibilities continue to grow or be modified. Motivation may mean changing the course and adjusting the way you do business. An applicable saying is "If you always do what you have always done, you will always get what you have always gotten." The bottom line is, nothing will change unless you change the methods used, by the way you do it or with the people involved.

Leadership

Leadership is often confused with supervision. A leader is not always a supervisor, but a supervisor or project manager must always be a leader. Leadership includes inherent qualities, such as honesty, trustworthiness, dependability, reliability, perseverance, and being able to ask what is next. A leader is never satisfied with the status quo and is always trying to improve the lot of others, himself or herself, and the organization.

Identify Accountabilities

The project manager is the pivotal person to ensure goals and objectives are aligned and synchronized. The goals and objectives of the company must be understood and accepted by the project manager. The project manager then must establish priorities and accountabilities that best match those of the company and will lead to successfully attaining those goals and objectives.

The project manager must assist the employees in establishing their accountabilities and duties to ensure the company's goals and objectives are being met. If these are not aligned, the project will not achieve successful resolve of required activities.

Holding Employees Accountable

The project manager is directly responsible for ensuring that employees get the job done. This is generally accomplished through periodic progress checks and observations. One saying that has particular merit in this situation is "inspect what you expect."

The Program Piece

Managing the program is an essential piece of the pie. Without the program, there is no work. However, you cannot manage a program that you do not understand. So, we have to start by understanding the program.

A project manager must always make certain that he or she has a clear understanding of the commitments. These commitments are spelled out in the contract, or various letters or memorandums of understanding. These commitments should be identified on a master list, shared with employees, and the status checked periodically with the client. Commitments can also be actions or promises made to improve work processes or the general lot of the employees themselves. They will want to know the status, and here is where a tie back into the communication can be made.

Once the commitments are identified, then resources can be allocated to complete the tasks. When we talk about resources, it may mean adding additional staff or providing training to existing personnel so that they can be cross-trained. Often, we view cross-training as a negative aspect of employment; however, if done correctly, cross-training for many employees is seen as improving their worth to the company and ensuring more job opportunities and pathways for promotion. Cross-training can be a motivational tool; although it is often poorly communicated and forms employee perceptions that become their realities.

The System Piece

The project manager does not have to be a systems expert, but he or she must have a fundamental understanding of how the systems operate and work for the fulfillment of the mission. Systems implementation requires a level of person–machine interface. In today's working environment, understanding the systems is a crucial function. Understanding how the system interfaces with the mission, and the limitations of the system, are also critical.

Many systems are affected directly by the way they are set up and are only as good as the information that is inputted, and the knowledge of what information, or reports, can be retrieved. One critical element that today's project manager must have the answer for is the question, "What is the operational contingency plan or business continuity plan for the failure of a system or many systems?"

For example, several years ago there was a major spring storm that disrupted the activities of a security command center. Two-way radios and mobile phones, which were routinely relied upon for communication, were rendered ineffective when towers were damaged. When phone and two-way radio communication proved to be less than effective, the young supervisor turned to a senior manager and said, "What do we do now?" The senior manager identified the fact that when the National Weather Service issued an all clear, runners would be methodically dispatched to open lines of communication and provide sheltered personnel with updates. The young supervisor looked in a puzzled way and asked, "What are runners?" Runners are designated personnel, not necessarily members of the protection force, who have specific routes to travel, specific messages to relay and, if possible, specific alternate means of communications to allow for updates and status.

No matter what system is in place, project managers have to ensure that they know what the contingency plan will be—and that all of their personnel also know.

The Business Piece

The project manager must be an effective business person. He or she can never lose sight of the fact that the company they serve and all the employees exist to do one thing—to make money.

Schedules must be realistic, understood, and communicated to all employees. This may be accomplished different ways for different-sized organizations. A smaller organization might best be served with regular staff meetings where schedules are discussed and input is received. Larger organizations may be better served by having a scheduling group; the information is then transmitted through published schedules and "all-hands" meetings.

The clients must be regularly briefed and their alignment and consensus received. There is nothing worse than the clients being surprised by their observation of the project or when reviewing schedules and finding mistakes.

Teams should be challenged to think ahead and look for schedule drift, especially if the drift is to the right. Schedules drifting to the right generally mean negative budget impacts, extended schedules, and a strained impact on morale.

The Wrap

Looking at all the facets of project management, one can truly see that this is a very dynamic and diverse role. The project manager can never overlook the value of the individual employee, the individual contributors, and the team. He or she will be called upon to motivate, align, provide guidance, oversee, and drive the organization. The project manager can never lose sight of the needs of the organization and what it will take to make all the members of the team successful. Above all, the project manager and his or her team can never stop communicating.

Refer website http://www.ifpo.org for further information

Technology in Security

26

Security Technology: A Management Perspective

James J. Leflar Jr.

Chapter Learning Objectives

- Gain an understanding of the primary purpose of security within an organization.
- Discuss the importance of organizational culture and the relationship with security technology.
- Identify the basic security technology most security officers are likely to encounter.
- Review the deployment of security technology in an office environment.
- Discuss the ethical behavior expected of a security officer in connection with technology.

Introduction

Security in the twenty-first century is a dynamic and critical component to an organization. The fundamental purpose of the security function within an organization is to maintain the safety and security of personnel and property assets (intangible and tangible) of an organization. The aforementioned purpose includes all personnel at a facility—employees, contractors, and visitors. Also, it includes all property, such as proprietary knowledge, electronic data, and reputational assets. This chapter discusses the relationship between security technology and risk management, the importance of aligning departmental goals with organizational goals, and the critical nature of organizational culture on the ethical performance of security duties. This chapter focuses on the importance of understanding how security fits into the business scheme of an organization and the basics of integrating security technology into that organizational perspective.

Security, Risk, and Organizational Management Dependencies

Efficient organizations are more interdependent and running on leaner budgets than in previous generations. To appreciate the management perspective of a modern organization, it is necessary to understand the holistic, risk management-oriented approach that a modern security professional takes to address the interdependencies between security and integrated business strategies. Modern security is no longer your grandfather's approach to security. The security function of an organization exists to support the business operation. Every organization, even nonprofit and governmental, has business functions associated with the management of the organization. Organizations with a culture that fosters the open exchange of information between business functions are more likely to develop positive, dynamic relationships between managers. Many organizations use a risk management program to maintain and ensure the survivability of the organization. The security function is a key stakeholder in the risk management process.

An effective, efficient, and modern security function aligns departmental goals with the strategic goals of the business. This alignment ensures that the security program is performing activities that are valuable and necessary to the organization. Because the security function seeks to align departmental goals with strategic goals, the security program uses information from the risk management process to determine the risks that should be addressed. According to Norman (2012),[1] security programs are developed to manage organizational risk in an organized and methodical way. The risk assessment is an evaluation of the organization in accordance with approved criteria. The assessment should be comprehensive throughout the organization to include each facility/office. The site-specific assessments provide excellent information necessary to determine the risks from a security perspective. Organizational management determines how to treat the risks. The treatment of risks falls into the basic categories: accept the risk and do nothing, address the risk with actions to ameliorate or eliminate the risk, or transfer the risk to another party, such as an insurance company. Therefore, security measures that address risk issues for a facility are based on the risk evaluations for the organization or the facility. Engaging in the risk management process is an example of the security function aligning itself and its practices with the strategic level of the organization. The selection and use of security technology is a deliberate decision-based process that relies on the foundation of risk management; the technology is justified as a risk treatment.

A dynamic security environment requires a security professional who embraces technology changes. This results in greater opportunities and capabilities for the security officer to perform his or her job. To benefit from the technological advances, the user must remain proficient in the use of the relevant technology. Modern-day security presents great opportunities for personal and professional development, but that growth is dependent upon a well-grounded education for the security practitioner. Embracing ongoing, lifelong education is the most important quality of a security professional. Maintaining a current educational level is the only way to keep abreast of risk management, and in particular, security technology. The foundation of understanding technology is an understanding of how and why technology fits into a business function. Simply knowing how to operate a computer or maneuver around an access control program is not the only important aspect of technology. Understanding the business perspective and the perceived value of the technology-security interdependency is crucial.

While security-related technology has changed on a regular basis, the fundamental principle of security has remained the same for many years: to maintain the safety and security of personnel and property assets of an organization. Security technology is a valuable tool in accomplishing that principle.

Security Measures

The security measures at a facility or office suite are determined and installed to achieve particular risk treatment goals. The existing level of security measures are evaluated or compared against the desired level of security protection. The determination to achieve a certain level of security protection is based on the respective organizational security appetite. This appetite, or acceptable approach to security, may be based on industry best practices or government requirements. For example, federal contractors often must comply with the National Industrial Security Program Operating Manual, and banks must comply with appropriate banking regulations. However, most corporate organizations do not have mandatory security requirements—they have business requirements.

The organization's security department creates a security program based on the business goals of the organization. This program details what security is going to accomplish, when the activities will occur or be completed, how the organization will accomplish those goals, and why it is important to accomplish the goals. Security should clearly indicate how they will help achieve the business goals for a fiscal year. For instance, a business goal could be to achieve a 99% customer satisfaction rating. While security is not responsible for this entire goal, they can contribute by ensuring the customer areas are safe and secure, customer information is securely maintained within the organizational systems (hard copy or electronic), and security officers provide exceptional customer service. As noted above, the primary goal of the security function is to protect the safety and security of personnel and property assets of an organization. To achieve that goal, the security professional selects the necessary tools to create an overlapping series of security measures resulting in a security-in-depth approach.

Organizational Culture and Types of Security Technology Measures

The culture of an organization establishes the underpinnings of the organization. This is extremely important to understand because the culture determines the essence of the organization. The culture of a company tells the employee how to behave, dress, and communicate, and also determines the acceptable level of security. The culture will dictate whether the security measures are "in your face" or very low key. A considerable amount of effort and thought are expended in planning the security measures of a new facility. As discussed earlier, the guiding security principle is the protection of the people and the property of the organization. While this may be a guiding principle, it does not control or limit how the security measures are selected and implemented.

The approach that is normally taken to develop the approved security measures for a facility is often described as a layering effect or security-in-depth. This means that each security measure (layer) augments all of the other countermeasures so that the result is a more difficult target to reach. If one measure fails to stop an intruder, the others are in place to prevent access. Common external countermeasures are security fences, adequate lighting, maintenance of grounds (trees and shrubbery), bollards, security officers performing tours, and access points for personnel and vehicles. The key issues are to provide security personnel with clear visibility of the grounds and to prevent people from gaining unauthorized access. Many of these traditional security measures are fairly low-tech and may not even stand out as security technology measures.

The development of a facility security plan is often a combination of obtrusive and unobtrusive security measures that balance the need for security and the cultural need to remain inviting. For instance, adequate exterior lighting, allowing clear sight of both sides of a walkway and low-cut shrubbery, are examples of unobtrusive security measures. A security officer at the front door inspecting every photo identification card is much more intrusive. Some organizations have a culture that embraces overt security and are not concerned with reducing the visibility of the security technology. For instance, a government research center does not try to hide the security measures. Naturally, not all of the security measures are obvious or communicated to the staff. The security technology types we will focus on in this chapter are the most common types a security officer is likely to encounter: closed circuit video, access control, and intrusion detection.

Closed Circuit Video

Organizations embrace closed circuit video (CCV) because it serves several important functions directed at achieving annual organizational goals. CCV systems provide a reliable means of monitoring and recording activity in and around the facility. CCV equipment has dramatically improved over the years and continues to do so. The video is used to prevent, respond to, and recover from incidents. Prevention is achieved through security officers actively monitoring the video screens, and looking for potential problems at the earliest stage of the incident. When something suspicious is identified, the officer alerts patrol officers or the local police to respond and investigate. The recorded data allows the organization to assist the police in a criminal investigation or the organizational lawyers with a civil action. The protection of CCV data is extremely important to preserve it as potential evidence in a criminal trial or a civil lawsuit. Liability usage is sometimes forgotten by security practitioners, but it is often the critical component to defend against fraud, thereby successfully recovering from the incident. For instance, someone may falsely claim to slip and fall on organizational property, and the CCV coverage is the only record to document the fraud. The professionalism and dedication of the security officer assigned to use the CCV equipment is often the difference between success and failure. Demonstrating the documented security program intent of the CCV system is facilitated by the security officer performing his or her respective duties as expected. A CCV system may be intended as proactive, reactive, or both. Proactive use of the system requires the security officer to actively be engaged in the use of the technology; that is, monitoring the cameras and acknowledging the alerts. Reactive use is based on the recording of activity for future review in accordance with reported incidents. It is more common that both approaches are used to provide a more robust and valuable security measure to the organization.

Strategically placing cameras throughout the exterior and interior of a facility increases the ability of the security officer to see and record activity in the facility and the adjoining grounds. The placement of cameras is a carefully considered practice, utilizing a security plan intended to achieve the primary goal of protecting personnel and property assets of the organization. A camera is selected according to the role it will play and its capabilities. Cameras are designed as either analog or digital/IP (Internet protocol). Figure 26.1 provides a basic explanation of the camera types and benefits. Any selection and deployment of a camera must be in conjunction with site-specific considerations. Selecting the appropriate camera for the location and purpose will determine the probability of success. For instance, the selection of an infrared (thermal imaging) camera to record individuals entering the front doors of a facility would be a poor choice. A better selection would be a 5-megapixel IP camera with both normal and low-light capabilities.

Camera Type	Purpose of Camera	Advantages	Disadvantages
Fixed	• Fixed-position camera • Typically used to monitor doors and fixed areas of interest	• Inexpensive; more cameras can be placed for less money • Provides excellent facial images • Provides excellent coverage of a specific area	• Locked in a fixed position • Manual realignment necessary to move position
Pan-tilt-zoom (PTZ)	• Camera has the ability to pan, tilt, and zoom • Allows for movement of camera to monitor incident or follow a person as they move	• Has the ability to pan left/right, tilt up/down, and zoom in on activity • Tour programming allows for a planned series of movements • Camera can be set to detect and follow the movement of a person walking	• Expensive • Best used as a real-time investigative tool for security • Camera covers additional areas other than where the event is taking place
Panoramic	• Provides a continuous 180° or 360° picture	• Provides more of a full vision approach to understanding what is happening, similar to a bird's-eye view	• Each sensor takes one camera slot on the recorder. If there are five sensors to create the panoramic view, the recorder must allot five cameras slots.
Low light	• Provides low-light camera imaging	• Provides a picture in low light	• Picture may be grainy
Thermal imaging (infrared)	• Detects the heat signature of a person in complete darkness	• Can locate a person by their body heat in complete darkness	• Expensive • Best to augment infrared camera with low-light camera

FIGURE 26.1 Basic camera types.

Security industry practices are moving toward IP cameras because they use newer, more robust technology. IP and network-based technology allows for the transmission of data through the network to remote viewers. For example, a security director located in one facility would be able to view cameras located in another facility through the company network. Kruegle (2007)[2] correctly indicates the improved capabilities of the security officer through the use of CCV, but also the ability to network the CCV system to other locations, providing an added layer of security. As technology changes and equipment capabilities improve, the user has more choices, but the fundamental concept of why to use the equipment remains the same. To benefit from those changes, the security plan must rest on a solid foundation of business/organizational principles and goals.

Electronic Access Control

Electronic access control is a powerful management and security tool to assign and track access into secured areas. The commercially available systems are fairly consistent across manufacturers and provide the ability to manage permissions into secured areas via an access smart card, key fob, or other access device. There are many advantages to using an electronic access control system instead of a metal key system. With the right access card, it can double as a key and a source of identity verification. Photo identification (ID) cards are very common and allow a security officer to verify that the photo on the card matches the person using the card. Also, some card readers have the capability to require a personal identity number (PIN) or biometrics to accompany the use of the access device to verify the user is the assigned card holder. This is referred to as two-factor verification and is very common in higher security areas, such as data centers or document vaults.

The components of a typical system consist of a server/computer to operate the program software; a control panel that interfaces the door equipment with the software; power for the equipment; a lock device (door strike, magnet lock, optical turn-stile, electric door handle, etc.); the card reader; door contacts; the passive infrared (PIR) request-to-exit (REX) detector; and the manual request-to-exit button. The manual request-to-exit button is always included with a magnet lock, but not normally with other locks. An exception to that rule is when it is necessary to include a door release button or paddle to comply with ADA regulations. All of these devices work together to limit access into a space and also track those who have access rights. Many systems have the capability to flash the ID card photo on the monitor at the security desk of the user as the card is presented at a card reader. This is another use of technology to assist the security officer in performing his or her duties.

Fail Safe and Fail Secure

Fail safe and fail secure, both describe slight variations in the equipment that reflect the way the equipment functions. For instance, the door strike locking device is either fail safe or fail secure. This is a commonly misunderstood description by nonsecurity personnel. Both types are safe and reliable. Fail safe means that when the power fails, the lock powers down and the door is open. Fail-safe locks require a consistent flow of electricity to power the lock and often feel warm to the touch. Fail secure, on the other hand, means that when the power fails, the door remains locked; fail-secure locks only need power to release the lock. Fail-secure functionality is often more desirable because the door remains locked in a power failure. Consider this example: if someone wants to enter a secure room, they need only pull the fire alarm to unlock fail-safe doors. Fail-secure functionality keeps the doors locked.

Electric Strike Locks

Door strikes are very safe and reliable locks if used correctly. From the unsecure side of a room, the door handle must always be locked; from the secure side, the handle must be unlocked. This functionality allows people to leave the secured space at all times. Often referred to as a storeroom function handle, this prevents people from becoming trapped during an emergency. There are exceptions to this rule with the secure side being open to free egress. For instance, many data centers require card access to enter and leave the space. This allows for more accurate tracking of personnel in the space. If there is a card reader on the secure side, there will also be an emergency request-to-exit button to override the door lock for use during an emergency. The use of electronic access control is intended to augment the security program and protect people and property; trapping people during an emergency is never acceptable.

Magnet Locks

Magnet locks normally appear at the top of a door and are very common on double doors (a magnet lock per door) and glass doors. The electricity powering the locks keep the doors secure as long as the power is active. If the power fails, the locks release and the doors are unlocked. Relying on only the magnet lock to secure the doors may be a serious security concern and often prompts other means to secure the doors. As with the electric strike locks noted above, the equipment associated with securing a door with a magnet lock is augmented with an emergency request-to-exit button. This emergency release (request-to-exit) button cuts the power to the door lock during an emergency when the power is not cut to the door locks. An example of an emergency where the power does not cease is a bomb threat evacuation. An access control system is always connected to the building fire alarm system. This connection allows the power to cease powering the locks, resulting in unlocked fail-safe locks.

Intrusion Detection Systems

Often referred to as a burglar alarm, an intrusion detection system (IDS) is used to detect unauthorized access into a space or call for assistance. This security measure is another opportunity to provide a layer or an added depth to the security protection for a facility. The IDS countermeasure can be used to protect a single room or the entire external perimeter. The IDS uses a combination of sensing devices, such as motion detectors and glass breaks, to determine if someone has entered the space. The system is armed (active) when the space is empty and disarmed when the building is open. An added feature to the IDS approach is the duress alarm (panic button) that allows a user to call for assistance. An example of a popular use of the wireless duress alarm button is when someone falls and requires medical assistance. In an office setting, the button can be portable (wireless) or affixed in a single location and connected to the panel via wires. A duress button is an important security tool and is often factored into protection plans for a facility. Providing personnel with a constant means of calling for help is critical to actual security and to reducing the fear of an incident. A duress button is simply an input point on the IDS control panel that operates in the same way as a door contact. When the system is activated,

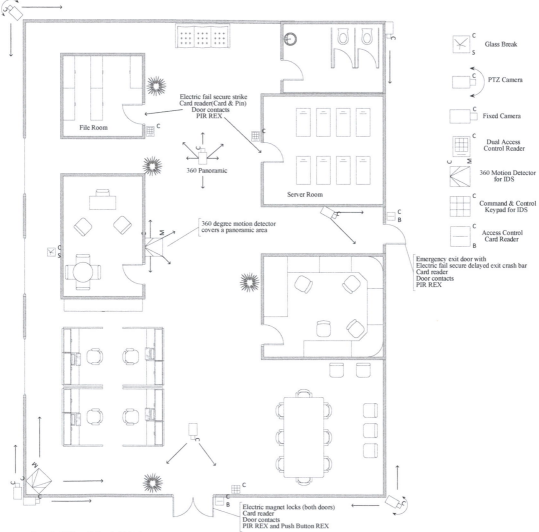

FIGURE 26.2 Security technology in use.

either by the depression of the duress button or the opening of an armed door, the signal is sent to the central monitoring station (CMS). The personnel at the CMS follow the instructions for the facility, such as calling the local police department.

Figure 26.2 provides a simple illustration of the deployment of security technology in a typical office. This example assumes the security officers are either at another facility or there are no officers assigned to the office. If the officers are at another facility, it is reasonable to assume the CCV system and access control systems are networked to the other site. If there are no officers at another facility, the systems are running on automatic and there is no active monitoring. The cameras provide a complete picture of the exterior of the site. The use of pan-tilt-zoom (PTZ) cameras is only justified if there is active monitoring. The interior use of CCV is necessary to provide coverage of the entry/exit doors and the sensitive areas within the office. The access control system database has records of each user and these users have certain permissions associated with a respective ID access card. Those with permission are granted access through a door, but there is a threat to this security measure. People without clearance may follow those with clearance through a door. The cameras will capture this activity, but this is a reactive security posture. When the office is closed, the IDS is activated and the motion detectors provide primary real-time security coverage of the perimeter. If someone forces a door open, the system will notify the central monitoring center for a response. If a window is broken, the glass break will also notify the monitoring center. This is an example of how the various pieces of security technology work together to provide security-in-depth. The security measures provide a certain protection that augments the other protective measures. Each works in harmony with the others to provide a complete security posture for the site.

Ethical Issues and the Use of Technology

Ethical behavior is expected from security personnel at all times. To facilitate our discussion, it is necessary to establish a common definition of ethical behavior. According to BusinessDictionary.com (2014),[3] ethical behavior is consistent with values commonly recognized as good within society. This definition provides a general understanding of ethical behavior without fully exploring the topic of ethics. That exploration is outside the scope of this discussion. The key element in the definition is the identification of the values viewed as "good." Those values include, but are not limited to, telling the truth, not stealing from others (this includes not stealing from organizations), not harming others, and keeping one's word. When security officers are hired, there is some sort of vetting process to remove those applicants with a criminal history or a history of unacceptable behavior, but the system is never perfect and applicants who engage in unethical behavior sometimes get through the process. Behavior that falls into a criminal category (theft, fraud, etc.) normally results in not being hired or involuntary separation of employment. Behavior that is not criminal but still unacceptable is really the target of our discussion.

Security officers are entrusted with technology that allows them to use their own discretionary powers to perform their jobs. When discretionary decision-making is permitted by the security officer, which is common, there are opportunities for questionable actions. Because security officers may be contract employees working at a client site, they may not be totally

systems, a single, well-trained officer is capable of watching an entire facility and calling for assistance from a remote location. However, the capabilities of the technology are only as good as the deployment and planned use of the security measures. The officers must understand how and why to use the security technology. An understanding of the organizational culture will make the difference between success and failure in the security field—security is very much an activity surrounding and involving people.

The ethical use of security technology is of critical concern. The use of advanced technology allows an officer to have access to highly sensitive information. The people associated with the organization rely on the security officers to act in an ethical manner and perform the duties assigned to those officers in a professional and diligent fashion. Trust is the most important relationship expectation between the organization and the security officer.

Refer website http://www.ifpo.org for further information

End Notes

1. Thomas L. Norman, *Electronic Access Control* (Waltham, MA: Elsevier Butterworth-Heinemann, 2012), 23.

2. Herman Kruegle, *CCTV Surveillance: Analog and Digital Video Practices and Technology* Second Edition (Burlington, MA: Elsevier Butterworth-Heinemann, 2007), 3.

3. BusinessDictionary.com, (2010): accessed October 1, 2014 http://www.businessdictionary.com/definition/ethical-behavior.html.

27

Fire Protection Systems and Special Hazards

Matthew J. Millsaps

Overview

A common type of emergency that requires the response of security personnel is an activation of a site's fire detection or suppression system, often in the form of a fire alarm. These responses must be approached with the utmost urgency, as the risk of fire within a facility can have a catastrophic impact on operations from both a **life safety** *and* **asset protection** standpoint. The report of fire must be planned for, as it often requires a coordinated and systematic response with outside agencies, such as the local fire department, emergency management system, and utilities contractors.

The security supervisor plays a vital role in these incidents because they must have an understanding of the capabilities of the fire protection systems that are in place, know how to locate and isolate the point of alarm based off of detection system data, and be knowledgeable of any special hazards that may exist. Beyond this, the security manager must also be able to: ensure adequate manpower and resources are available to facilitate the safe evacuation of occupants; size up and assess the magnitude of the event; and attempt to contain and control it. Thus, these incidents can quickly become the most taxing and resource-intensive calls for service that security teams will face.

Principles of Fire Science

At the most basic level, fire is a process of rapidly occurring, self-sustaining oxidation accompanied by heat and light. It is composed of four equally important elements:

- Heat
- Fuel
- Oxygen
- The chemical chain reaction of the previous three elements

This is generically referred to as the *fire square* (or in some texts, the *fire tetrahedron*).[1] For fire to occur, all four of these elements must be present; if you remove any one of these, the fire will be extinguished. Otherwise, with no attempts at mitigation, a compartmentalized fire will progress through the combustion process until it ultimately exhausts

Security Supervision and Management. http://dx.doi.org/10.1016/B978-0-12-800113-4.00027-4

its supply of fuel or oxygen, eventually dying naturally. Thus, within a compartment, the phases of fire are as follows:

1. Incipient stage
2. Growth stage (the endpoint of this stage is flashover)
3. Free-burning stage
4. Decay stage

Although the names of these phases (often called stages) vary from text to text,[2] it is during the incipient stage that extinguishment will be most easily and successfully attained, and will yield the greatest benefit of reduced fire loss and survivability of occupants.

Because of this, most fire suppression systems target the incipient stage for both detection and suppression interventions. As fire develops and spreads throughout the fuel load, a process called *pyrolysis* occurs. This is what accounts for the chemical chain reaction needed for fire to continue, and it is also what creates the byproducts of the combustion process (heat, light, and smoke/toxic gases).

Fire extends or spreads as heat is transferred from hotter objects to cooler objects. This occurs through three different means:

- Conduction
- Convection
- Radiation

The use of water or other wet extinguishing agents inhibit the heat transfer process by cooling the fuel, thus absorbing or taking away the heat.

If unimpeded, the process of heat transfer to the various fuels located in a building will create a self-sustaining fire that will progress rapidly through the previously discussed stages, often reaching flashover (an Immediately Dangerous to Life and Health or IDLH condition) in a matter of minutes.[3] Attempts at controlling a fire after the incipient stage often create a flow path for fire advancement and increased oxygenation, which will ultimately lead to a true *hostile fire event* driven by the type of fire and available fuels.

Fire is divided into five different classes based on the type of fuel that is burning, and extinguishment is dictated by disruption of the fire square specific to these classes[4]:

- *Class A*: Ordinary combustibles (wood, paper, fabric)
- *Class B*: Flammable liquids (fuel oil, gasoline)
- *Class C*: Electrical fires
- *Class D*: Combustible metals (often found in industrial settings)
- *Class K*: Kitchen or cooking oils (restaurants, cafeterias, etc.)

It is important that the security supervisor understand this, as the primary fuel load at a particular location generally dictates the extinguishing agent(s) present within the structures fire protection or sprinkler systems. It is also important for all officers to understand and be trained in these classes, for even initial attempts at containing small fires must be made with a fire extinguisher rated for the type of fuel that is burning.

The most common fire extinguishers found in the business, industry and residential settings are made of a dry chemical agent and rated for Class A, B, and C fires (ABC or "dry chem" extinguishers); however, there are also extinguishers that specifically combat these classes individually. Likewise, Class D and K fires each have extinguishers specifically designed to handle these fuels, consisting of dry powders and wet chemicals respectively. Important to note is the Class A extinguisher. This extinguisher consists of 2.5 gallons of pressurized water and may be found in older facilities or installations that maintain a fire brigade. Although these "water cans" are highly effective on ordinary combustibles, they can promote fire spread if used on Class B or K fires, pose a shock hazard if used on Class C fires, and can create an explosive reaction if used on Class D fires. Again, all officers and supervisors should seek training in basic fire safety skills.

Building Construction Classification

As each type of fire is classified, so is each type of construction. There are certain similarities in the design or engineering of a building that present unique circumstances when exposed to fire. These construction types are[5]:

- *Type I*: Fire resistive (those with spray on fire proofing or fire resistive material)
- *Type II*: Noncombustible (concrete block or masonry construction)
- *Type III*: Ordinary (a combination of masonry load bearing walls and wood framing)
- *Type IV*: Heavy timber or mill (framing with robust lumber)
- *Type V*: Light wood frame or stick built (most modern homes)

For the most part, all of the buildings and facilities that the security officer will encounter fit into one of these categories. The type of construction, coupled with factors such as occupancy type and anticipated fire load, determine the necessary types of fire protection systems.

The construction qualities of a structure also support its *gravity resistance system*.[6] The ultimate catastrophic event that can happen to a building during a fire is a full or partial structural collapse. When engineered properly, the forces and loads that the building will be exposed to on daily basis will be factored into its structural elements and connections. Often, however, the potential of available fuel for combustion, referred to as the *fire load* and measured in terms of *heat release rate*, is not weighed heavily into the design or engineering process.[7] As lightweight and composite construction materials have become the norm in design standards, primarily for cost savings purposes, the need for rapid and early fire control measures must be recognized by the security manager.

Requirements and Consensus Standards

Fortunately, in most commercial or industrial occupancy structures, nationally recognized codes or consensus standards are adhered to in the design and construction process. Just as there are mandated codes and regulations regarding such things as electrical service

(National Electric Code), water and sewage systems, and building construction (Uniform Facilities Criteria), there are codes that specifically focus on fire threat and life safety. Responsibility for compliance to the codes is within the purview of a fire protection engineer. The fire protection engineer should be involved in all aspects of a building or expansion project, from the initial planning phases through to the final inspection process.

In the United States, there are two agencies that primarily concern themselves with the creation of standards for fire safety: the US Occupational Safety and Health Administration (OSHA) and the National Fire Protection Association (NFPA).

OSHA, which is a division of the US Department of Labor, deals with fire safety in general industry as well as specialized domains such as shipyards, marine terminals, and the construction industry. OSHA also has responsibility for recordkeeping regarding safety incidents, workplace accidents, serious injuries and fatalities, and enforcement actions. OSHA, as a US government regulatory agency, conducts investigations and inspections; OSHA also can levy fines and penalties for violations of the Occupational Safety and Health Act or OSHA regulations.

NFPA is a committee that releases consensus standards every 3 years. This means that their recommendations are based on the guidance of industry experts; although not law, they are considered to be the industry "norms". The NFPA publishes the NFPA the 101: Life Safety Code, which has generally been adopted as law nationally. NFPA 101 covers numerous topics, and should be available to all security managers, especially those involved in physical security planning or regulation compliance and enforcement. Specifically, NFPA 101 deals with numerous things, including (but in no way limited to) the following:

- Occupancy classification
- Means of egress
- Detection and extinguishment systems
- Interior finishes
- Fire resistance ratings of building characteristics such as firewalls, doors, fire stops, and draft curtains

NFPA is what drives the needed fire protection signaling and suppression appliances to be incorporated into a site's infrastructure. If the Security Manager has an understanding of the type of facility they will be tasked to protect, they can use the appropriate NFPA code to better determine the type of fire protection system that is necessary. There are also several standards that relate to fire protective measures that lie outside of the actual engineering of the building. The need for certain types of fire extinguishers, respiratory protection standards, fire watch crews, closed-circuit video, and investigation procedures are just a few examples of the guidance that can be obtained through NFPA. This will be particularly useful information to those security personnel who have the responsibility of conducting codes compliance and safety inspection duties. Some of the NFPA standards with which a supervisor should be familiar are as follows:

- NFPA 1: Fire Code
- NFPA 72: National Fire Alarm and Signaling Code

- NFPA 10: Standard for Portable Fire Extinguishers
- NFPA 13: Standard for the Installation of Sprinkler Systems
- NFPA 14: Standard for the Installation of Standpipe and Hose Systems
- NFPA 51B: Standard for Fire Prevention During Welding, Cutting, and Other Hot Work
- NFPA 704: Standard System for the Identification of the Hazards of Materials for Emergency Response
- NFPA 730: Guide for Premises Security
- NFPA 731: Standard for the Installation of Electronic Premises Security Systems
- NFPA 921: Guide for Fire and Explosion Investigations
- NFPA 1001: Standard for Fire Fighter Professional Qualifications
- NFPA 1072: Standard for Hazardous Materials/Weapons of Mass Destruction Emergency Response Personnel Professional Qualifications[8]

In total, the NFPA releases in excess of 300 consensus standard documents that address almost every type of occupancy or industry, as well as every imaginable hazardous condition or event that may occur. It is outside of the scope of this chapter to list all of them, but security managers should be familiar with the extent of their scope as well as how to access them. A general index of the NFPA standards, as well as the opportunity to access them using a subscription service, can be found at www.nfpa.org.

Fundamentals of Fire Protection Systems

For the purpose of this chapter, a facility's fire protection system can be considered to consist of two separate components that may or may not be interconnected:

- The fire detection system
- The fire suppression system

A *fire detection system* is the mechanism that recognizes smoke, fire, or hazardous conditions and, in turn, alerts occupants and emergency responders to the emergency. This system can be as simple as a fire alarm pull station, or more complex in the form of a heat, flame, or smoke detector system. In most commercial or industrial facilities, the fire detection system can be activated either manually by occupants or automatically by detectors, which in turn activates a system of audible and visual warnings (usually as a combination of a horn or bell, and strobe or flashing lights). These alarms may be locally reported (notification only to those occupying the structure); however, they are often transmitted to emergency personnel. The detection activation may be part of any of the following types of systems:

- A *local protective system*, where only the facility is notified
- An *auxiliary protective system*, which ties into a municipal alarm box system
- A *remote station*, which notifies the fire communications center
- A *central station*, which notifies a private monitoring center who in turn notifies 911
- A *proprietary protective system*, which covers multiple different occupants within the same facility but notifies locally, such as to a security watch desk

For the security manager, it is paramount to determine what type of notification system the facility's detection system uses, especially in the case of local or propriety monitoring. The duty of receiving and interpreting the initial alarm point will often be a responsibility of the security team.

The *fire suppression system*, on the other hand, is the actual plumbed system that is in place to suppress fires in their early stages (sprinkler systems) or assist firefighters in firefighting activities (standpipe systems). In some cases, this is in response to the detection system activation (preaction and deluge systems); however, in most cases, it is in direct response to the fire threat. In fact, it is often the suppression system activation that causes the detection system to alert, as most alarm systems have water flow alarm sensors that trip when water moves into, or is discharged from, the system. Standpipe systems are used by fire crews to make fire attack easier; they provide access points in a facility to attach fire hoses, known as "attack lines." Although the security manager should be aware of fire department connection points, the sprinkler system is what will be addressed here.

Sprinkler systems use a system of piping to provide discharge points of water (sprinkler heads) in the event of a fire for the protection of life and property. A basic system would consist of a water supply (often from the public water grid) that is drawn into a building with assistance from an auxiliary fire pump. As the water enters the building (usually at ground level), it passes through a valve assembly and travels up a wall through a large pipe called a riser to the ceiling level. It then goes laterally across the ceiling through a feeder line, and is distributed across the ceiling through branch lines that project perpendicularly off of the feeder. The actual sprinkler heads are spaced at regular intervals along these branch lines to assure uniform distribution of water over a certain area.

Sprinkler heads come in various shapes and sizes, and have different heat ratings. A sprinkler is essentially a water spray nozzle with a round-shaped deflector that propels water out over a distance. In normal conditions, there is either a piece of soft metal or plastic covering the nozzle outlet. When a specified temperature is reached (such as through flame impingement or radiant heat), the metal or plastic fusible element melts, allowing water to be discharged.

Sprinkler systems generally fall into one of six different types:

- *Wet pipe system* (always has water ready in the piping)
- *Dry pipe system* (water is brought into the system when a head opens; often used in buildings with no heat to prevent frozen pipes)
- *Deluge systems* (often used in industrial settings where fire could rapidly spread; they deliver massive amounts of water over a large area)
- *Preaction systems* (a two-stage system that is generally dry; however, when a detector activates, the system charges and stands by until a head opens)
- *Residential systems* (these are designed *only* for life safety, with no regard for property protection)
- *Specialty systems* (unique systems that do not fall within standards)

The type of sprinkler system as well as its engineering relates directly to the NFPA occupancy classification[9] that the facility falls into: light-hazard class, ordinary-hazard class, or extra-hazard class.

There are also a variety of special occupancy conditions recognized by the NFPA. These include occupancies that possess special characteristics that accelerate the development and advancement of flame spread, such as:

• High-piled combustible material
• Flammable liquids
• Combustible dust
• Chemicals and Explosives

NFPA 13, *Standard on Installation of Sprinkler Systems,* is what drives the types of systems needed for a particular occupancy. Again, this can be very complicated, and it correlates with other factors, such as building construction type and available water supply. These very technical aspects of fire protection are a function of fire protection engineers. Security leaders who are tasked with the inspection of systems must receive recognized fire prevention training and work closely with fire protection specialists.

Other Fire Protection Systems (AFFF, FM220)

Aside from fire extinguisher and sprinkler systems, there are other fire protection systems that are used in certain specialized environments. One system, aqueous film-forming foam (AFFF), was developed by the US. Navy during the 1960s and is currently in use both militarily and commercially, particularly in aviation safety and oil refineries. AFFF is a type of foam that performs two functions: It smothers a fire, robbing it of oxygen. It also leaves a layer of film on the fuel supply that prevents the fire from reigniting once the foam has cleared away.[10]

FM220 systems were developed to replace clean-agent fire suppression systems that used halon. These systems were common in data centers, computer mainframes, and server rooms because halon systems do not use water to suppress a fire, meaning that expensive IT infrastructure would not be damaged. Halon systems suppress a fire whether used as a liquid or a gas. In either form, no residue is left behind. Due to halon's nature as an ozone-depletion agent, since 1994 the production or import of halon has been banned in the United States, including halon 1301 which was commonly used in fire suppression systems, via the Clean Air Act.[11]

Although halon systems remain legal, other systems such as the FM220 fire suppression system were developed to replace them. Developed by DuPont, the FM220 uses liquefied gas (a type of heptafluoropropane) to suppress a fire without leaving a residue behind.[12]

Hazardous Materials, Explosives, and CBRNE

The presence of hazardous materials (Hazmat) has become the norm at almost any job site. Traditionally associated with the industrial or manufacturing setting, almost all commercial facilities store or use hazardous substances to some degree. For example, a hotel or resort may maintain substances such as chlorine or bromine for swimming pool maintenance, while educational facilities often have chemistry laboratories and industrial cleaning solvents. Churches and religious organizations store fertilizers and oxidizers for cemetery lawn care, and bulk fuel storage to power heating and boiler systems. Even in residential settings, personal hobbies such as model rocketry, military history, spelunking, and firearms ammunition reloading can result in the storage of hazardous materials. On a more illicit side, the clandestine manufacture and preparation of illegal drugs such as methamphetamine, gamma hydroxybutyrate, and methylenedioxymethamphetamine (MDMA or Ecstasy) can turn virtually any environment into a hazardous materials threat.

Along the same line, the threat of domestic terrorism and criminal activity pose a constant risk to business, industry, and critical infrastructure in the form of explosive materials and weapons of mass destruction. Post 9-11 trends that continue to plague security personnel and emergency responders are suspicious packages, suspected improvised explosive devices, and "white powder" investigations with concern of exposure to weaponized Anthrax. These types of "black swan" events can disrupt facility operations for prolonged periods of time until the threat is proven or ruled out, and they are often managed in the initial stages by security or protection officers.

Hazardous materials are classified by the United Nations/Department of Transportation (UN/DOT) into nine separate hazard classifications based on characteristics of the substance or element. For the most part, any commercial vehicle transporting in excess of 1000 pounds of a substance(s) is required to display a placard indicating which of these classifications the substance(s) on board falls into[13]:

- Class 1: Explosives
- Class 2: Compressed gases
- Class 3: Flammable liquids
- Class 4: Combustible solids
- Class 5: Oxidizers
- Class 6: Poisons
- Class 7: Radiation
- Class 8: Corrosives
- Class 9: Other regulated material (ORM-D)

Many of these hazard classes are broken down further into subclasses; however, that is outside the scope of this chapter. Also, most Class 1, Class 7, and certain Class 5 and 6 materials are required to be placarded despite the amount. Every security officer should be aware of these classifications, especially those functioning at shipping terminals or logistics hubs and other sites with heavy vehicle traffic; a good idea of hazards present can be obtained simply by recognizing what materials are being transported into and out of the complex.

For fixed facilities or buildings, the NFPA requires a sign to be attached to the structure to provide emergency responders with an instant snapshot of the hazardous material threat inside. The NFPA 704 marker system, often called a "fire diamond," is a four-sided color-coded placard that indicates the risk materials on site present relating to the following:

- Fire (red panel)
- Health (blue panel)
- Instability (yellow panel)
- Special characteristics (white panel), such as asphyxiant gasses, water reactivity, and oxidizers

The risk these hazards create to each of these categories are graded with a numbering system, from 0 (no risk) through 4 (severe risk). Specifics relating to this hazard marking system can be obtained from *NFPA 704: Standard System for the Identification of the Hazards of Materials for Emergency Response.*[14]

Again, any security manager or supervisor working at a site in which hazardous materials may be stored, or utilized in the course of operations, should be knowledgeable in the specifics of these hazards. Security staff should also be reminded that, in many cases, exposure to hazardous materials in certain conditions can pose an immediate threat to life and health. Therefore, any incident involving an uncontrolled release of hazardous substances should be evaluated by a specialized Hazardous Materials Response Team. Security managers should ensure that an emergency plan is established and in place that identifies who would respond to contain and mitigate such an emergency, as well as any clean up contractors that the client may wish to use for post-emergency disposal or removal.

CBRNE

Because of recent world events, the threat of the use of unconventional weapons and weapons of mass destruction must be understood and prepared for. The acronym CBRNE stands for Chemical, Biological, Radiological, Nuclear, and high Explosives and generally includes agents and weapons that can be employed in an act of terrorism.

A **chemical attack** is the deliberate release of a toxic gas, liquid, or solid that can poison people and the environment. Chemical weapons are often aerosolized when deployed to kill or seriously injure or incapacitate victims and their signs and symptoms of exposure appear very quickly. Many of these chemicals serve their purpose as toxic industrial materials, and are often relatively easy to obtain compared to other types of weapons of mass destruction.

As a whole, there are four classes of chemical agents used for terrorism purposes:

- *Nerve agents:* These include sarin, tabun, V agents, and soman and are designed to disrupt the pathways in which the nerves transmit messages.
- *Blister agents:* They include mustard gas and lewisite compound; they are caustic agents that cause large and painful blisters to the skin and internal membranes.
- *Blood agents:* They include hydrogen cyanide and any cyanide-containing gas; these agents disrupt respiration on a cellular level, causing hypoperfusion and cell death.

- *Choking agents*: These poisonous gases, such as chlorine and phosgene, attack the lungs and result in respiratory failure.[17]

A fifth category—which, unlike the others, typically does not cause permanent injury—is *irritating agents* (often called "riot control agents"); this group includes mace, capsicum, and tear gas. These agents are often employed by law enforcement to temporarily incapacitate people through irritation to the skin and mucosa, eyes, mouth, and throat. There are also agents, such as adamsite, that cause transient nausea and vomiting.

Treatments for these agents vary, and many of these chemicals can cause death in a relatively short time frame with only slight exposure. Security personnel working in environments in which these agents may be used, should be properly trained in the use of personal protective equipment, such as powered air purifying respirators and antidote kits, including the Military Mark-I Auto Injector and the Convulsion Antidote for Nerve Agent kit for nerve agent exposure.

According to the US Centers for Disease Control and Prevention (CDC), **biological weapons** release viruses and bacteria, or their toxins, for the purpose of harming or killing citizens. Biologic agents can be delivered covertly, and the onset of signs and symptoms may begin several hours or even days after the attack has occurred. Often, emergency responders are unaware of an attack until numerous casualties begin arriving at health facilities presented with similar complaints. Biological weapons can be deployed with simple tactics, and they are extremely effective at low dosages (up to 14 billion times more so than chemical weapons by weight). Fortunately, they are hard to obtain, and a tremendous knowledge of science and technical laboratory etiquette is required to successfully grow or manufacture these agents. By and large, there are four types of biologic agents that could be employed for a terrorist attack[18]:

- *Viral agents*: Viruses such as smallpox and Ebola virus, which are microorganisms that grow in living cells and do not respond to antibiotics
- *Bacterial agents*: Single-celled organisms such as anthrax, Q-Fever, and the plague, which can invade human tissue or produce toxins in the body
- *Rickettsia*: Bacteria pathogens transmitted by fleas, lice, mites & ticks through ingestion, contamination or inhalation causing Spotted or Typhoid Fever (Infection)
- *Biological toxins*: Toxic substances that yield from generally nontoxic biologic organisms; for example, ricin, which comes from the castor bean, and abrin, which comes from rosary peas
- *Fungi*: Certain fungi can cause infections in immunocompromised persons and to some degree healthy adults; this causes concern for agro-terror, in that crops and food supplies can be devastated if contaminated.

Biological agents are considered to be Class 6 under the UN/DOT hazard classification system discussed earlier. The CDC further breaks down biologic agents into three categories (A, B, and C) based on factors such as availability, ease of dissemination, and public health effect, with Category A being the highest priority and C being the least.[19]

Radioactive and **Nuclear** terrorist threats, although listed separately in the acronym, can be addressed together for the purpose of this discussion. **Nuclear** generally is associated with the fissionable reaction (detonation) of uranium and plutonium, while **radioactivity** regards all other isotopes, such as Cobalt-60 and Cesium-137, which would be associated (in terms of a threat) with a dirty bomb or aerosolized dispersal. Despite the means of deployment, the mass contamination of a populous with radioactive material could cause widespread devastation. Although the use of ionizing energy as an engineered weapon is considered to be a relatively low threat compared to other weapons of mass destruction, a dirty bomb or nuclear detonation is still possible. Security personnel should be familiar with some common terminology and fundamentals of radioactive material.

There are four types of radiation:

- *Alpha*: These energetic positively charged particles are a product of radioactive decay. They lose energy rapidly when passing through matter and can be completely shielded by a sheet of paper. They are generally not considered a threat outside of the human body, but they can be lethal if inhaled or ingested.
- *Beta*: These fast-moving positive or negative charged electrons can penetrate farther than alpha; however, they are less harmful. Some beta particles may penetrate the skin; nevertheless, they are stopped by clothing or thin metals such as aluminum, which is >0.10 inches thick.
- *Gamma*: These high-energy waves travel great distances at the speed of light. Although they have the ability to penetrate many types of materials, several feet of concrete (or other dense material) can stop them.
- *Neutron*: These high-speed particles can penetrate many materials. Unlike *alpha*, *beta*, or *gamma*, these particles can make something radioactive through a process called *neutron activation*.[20]

The security manager must understand that most myths and urban legends surrounding nuclear energy and radioactive materials are false. When exposed to radioactive energy, people do not "glow green," nor are they "vaporized." The reality is that being exposed to radiation is essentially unnoticeable. You do not feel it immediately, and you cannot see it. Thus, it must be detected using meters or instruments such as dosimeters, which should be available to staff.

The risk of contact with **explosive** material or the suspicion of its presence (i.e., a suspicious package) has become a very real threat for the modern security professional. The ease of which *improvised explosive devices* (IEDs) can be manufactured, as well as the mainstream use of blasting agents and military-grade munitions in commercial industry, creates a true hazard for security professionals. A detonation or explosion, whether as a result of terrorist activity or industrial accident, is a devastating event that can result in substantial impact on life and property.

Modern security supervisors should be familiar with explosives and be able to recognize their components and precursors. IEDs and bombing events are covered in great detail elsewhere in this text; however, it should be kept in mind that, due to their incendiary nature, the initial notification of a detonation or explosion may come in the form of fire alarm activation.

Fire Alarm Response

The response to an alarm for fire, or the protocols followed at the discovery of such conditions at a facility, will hinge primarily on the response plan or operating guidelines. Focus should be placed on aiding and ensuring evacuation, locating and isolating the hazardous condition, and directing the local emergency responders into the scene. Working as a part of a *unified incident command system* should be a goal of the security manager, who will be able to provide outside agencies with key information regarding site access, fire department connections, and sprinkler system components, as well as information relating to occupant accountability and potential hazards that exist within the facility.

The US Fire Service has long adopted the acronym RECEO-VS as the tactical priorities for fire officers at fire scenes. This acrostic stands for the following[15]:

- *Rescue*: Freeing trapped occupants or evacuating the premises
- *Exposure*: Determining the areas adjacent to the fire and susceptible to flame spread
- *Confinement*: Containing the fire to prevent it spreading
- *Extinguishment*: Using water or extinguishing agents to put the fire out
- *Overhaul*: Ensuring that the fire is completely out and not continuing to burn
- *Ventilation*: Removal of toxic gas and smoke from the atmosphere
- *Salvage*: Preservation of property to protect from water and fire damage

This information is provided not to try to teach firefighting tactics to security personnel, but to familiarize protection officers with the fire departments on-scene operational objectives.

Studies have demonstrated the significance that *flow path* (air movement) plays in the acceleration of fire growth, flashover, and conflagration. This data emphasizes the importance of early isolation of the fire and combustion process. Thus, during day-to-day patrols and rounds, simple measures, such as ensuring that fire doors are unblocked and that man doors and exit points remain closed, can dramatically reduce the risk of a small fire becoming a catastrophic event.[16]

The protection officer's role during a fire or hazardous condition should be identified and preplanned prior to an actual incident. Other than the use of fire extinguishers or facility suppression appliances, officers should not actively partake in fire suppression activities without proper training and equipment.

The best thing security staff can do operationally is assist in the safe evacuation of occupants and in confining the fire. This can be accomplished by basic measures, such as the following:

- Using crowd control techniques and public address to encourage a calm, orderly exit.
- Ensuring occupants use the stairs as opposed to elevators. Most commercial structures have pressurized stairwells that lead to the exterior. This creates a safe and smoke-free route for egress with adequate oxygen.

- Being familiar with and directing people to the closest exits.
- Ensuring doors are shut and exterior doors and windows are not unnecessarily propped or left open.
- Activating fire doors or draft curtains, if trained.
- Knowing how to interpret fire alarm panel information to determine alarm point or location.

As a security supervisor, the response to an alarm of fire should be rehearsed and planned for. Security operations staff should know their roles and expectations. The supervisor then will need to focus primarily upon: maintaining accountability of their personnel as well as building occupants; and interfacing with the emergency responders to assume a role in the incident command structure as an "expert" in the facility's operations, hazard areas, and fixed fire suppression apparatus. The supervisor must also assess other issues that may require security mitigation, such as crowd control and escort duties, which may be required in the case of event/recreational venues or secure/limited access sites.

Fire Investigation and Documentation

The investigation of fire events and the determination of their origin and cause will be driven by policy and the capabilities of your staff. Depending on circumstance, these investigations may be handled internally; turned over to local, state, or federal law enforcement or fire officials; or be conducted as a joint venture between your security administration and outside agencies. No matter what, the determination of cause and origin must be made by a trained fire/arson investigator as defined by NFPA 1033: *Standard for Professional Qualifications for Fire Investigators*, and NFPA 921: *Guide for Fire & Explosion Investigations*.

The investigation of fires has become technically and scientifically advanced. In the past several years, advancements in technology such as computer-generated fire modeling, arc mapping, new data collection, and accelerant detection methods, as well as a better understanding of fire behavior and growth, have forced the investigator to rely upon science for determination of cause. Thus, NFPA 921 calls for the use of the scientific method when attempting to identify the specific cause of the fire.

For every case, the investigator must:

1. Identify the problem
2. Define the problem
3. Collect data
4. Analyze the data
5. Develop a hypothesis
6. Test the hypothesis
7. Draw a conclusion

336 SECURITY SUPERVISION AND MANAGEMENT

In doing this, Chapter 17 of NFPA 921 requires the investigator to examine four critical elements before a determination of origin can be made:

- Witness information
- Fire patterns (burn marks, demarcation lines, etc. that indicate movement and intensity)
- Arc mapping (evaluating the electrical circuit system)
- Fire dynamics (fire behavior and modeling)

Ultimately, the fire investigator must make a conclusion on the cause of a fire. There are only four acceptable causes of fire recognized by NFPA 921:

- Natural
- Accidental
- Incendiary/arson
- Undetermined

Assuming the security supervisor will not be the one conducting the fire investigation, the best way to assist investigators is to document the incident and encourage officers to act as the "eyes and ears" of the scene, providing detailed and accurate descriptions of what they witnessed during the event.

The security supervisor must also ensure containment and isolation of the scene to prevent scene contamination or the spoliation of evidence. **Spoliation** can be defined as the loss, destruction, or material alteration of an object that has, or potentially has, evidentiary value by someone who is responsible for its preservation. Generally, this responsibility would fall to the person charged with the security or integrity of the scene. Although the process of fighting and overhauling fire lends to an amount of destruction, spoliation would be excessive or unnecessary destruction, even if accidental. Therefore, maintaining the integrity of the scene is a particularly important role.

The investigation of fire is a highly technical and unique discipline that has specific legal authorities and evidentiary rules (such as *negative corpus* evidence) that do not apply to other types of criminal investigation. With that in mind, the security manager should strive to have a well-defined policy dictating who is responsible for investigating these types of events.

Because fires often lead to significant destruction of evidence of ignition sources, detailed documentation of the scene and factors observed during the fire can provide valuable assistance to investigators. Aside from normal reporting of who, what, where, when, and why information relative to a standard incident report, other forms of documentation may be necessary and helpful for the security officer to employ, such as the following:

- Diagrams/sketches
- Photographs
- Note taking
- Video

- Maps
- Tape recordings
- Witness logs
- Scene logs

It is also important for witnesses to be identified and initial statements be taken early after the incident. In the case of a small office building, the identification of potential witnesses may be easily discovered using access control records or employee work schedules. In a shopping mall or mass gathering (concert, sports event, etc.), witness identification may be more complex and additional officers may need to be called to help rapidly identify and obtain their contact info and preliminary statements. Other means of witness ID include closed-circuit video footage, ticket or sales slip information, or vehicle registration (parking lot) numbers.

As has been emphasized throughout this chapter, your agency's handling of these low-frequency, high-impact events should be planned for and driven by policy. Fire investigation is a specialized science that needs to be conducted by experts. The supervisor should refrain, at all costs, from making any speculation or statement regarding determination of cause without consulting with persons specifically trained in this unique aspect of investigation. These investigations may require input assessment by law enforcement investigators, insurance company representatives, corporate management, and fire officials. Thus, the best role that security staff can provide is scene security and accurate reporting of initial scene findings.

Conclusion

The security manager cannot merely respond to an alarm. They must understand what an alarm means, how it is activated, how to respond safely, among many other things. If a fire can be extinguished, the security manager must understand how to extinguish the different types of fires that might be encountered in a residential, commercial, or an industrial setting. With the increase in terrorist activity worldwide in the twenty-first century, the security manager must also be aware of the unique difficulties posed by CBRNE attacks, however rare or unlikely they might seem to be.

Refer website http://www.ifpo.org for further information

End Notes

1. NFPA, *The Fire Triangle and Fire Tetrahedron* (Quincy, MA: National Fire Protection Association, Date Unknown): accessed January 15, 2015. Available: http://www.nfpa.org/press-room/reporters-guide-to-fire-and-nfpa/all-about-fire.
2. Ibid.
3. Ibid.
4. Ibid.

5. Frassetto R., *Understanding Building Construction Types* (Tulsa, OK: FirefigherNation, February 1, 2012): accessed January 15, 2015. Available: http://www.firefighternation.com/article/truck-co-operations/understanding-building-construction-types.

6. Michael J. D., *Building Construction: Understanding Loads and Loading* (Fair Lawn, NJ: Fire Engineering, June 1, 2010): accessed January 15, 2015. Available: http://www.fireengineering.com/articles/2010/06/building-construction-understanding-loads-and-loading.html.

7. Babrauskas V. and Peacock R. D., "Heat Release Rate: The Single Most Important Variable in Fire Hazard," appearing in *Fire Safety Journal* (Burlington, MA: Elsevier, 1992): vol. 18, accessed January 15, 2015. Available: http://fire.nist.gov/bfrlpubs/fire92/PDF/f92019.pdf?origin=publication_detail.

8. *Document Information Pages (List of NFPA Codes & Standards)* (Quincy, MA: National Fire Protection Association, Date Unknown): accessed January 16, 2015. Available: http://www.nfpa.org/codes-and-standards/document-information-pages.

9. *Hazard Classification for NFPA 13 Sprinkler Design* (Boston, MA: Massachusetts Department of Fire Services, Division of Fire Safety, May 2010): accessed January 17, 2015. Available: http://www.mass.gov/eopss/docs/dfs/mfa/training/hazard-classification-6-28-10.pdf.

10. *Aqueous Film-Forming Foam* (Washington, DC: Naval Research Laboratory, Date Unknown): accessed January 17, 2015. Available: http://www.nrl.navy.mil/accomplishments/materials/aqueous-film-foam/.

11. *Questions and Answers on Halon and Their Substitutes* (Washington, DC: Environmental Protection Agency, Date Unknown): accessed January 17, 2015. Available: http://www.epa.gov/ozone/snap/fire/qa.html.

12. *DuPont FM-200 Waterless Fire Suppression Systems* (Wilmington, DE: E. I. DuPont de Nemours and Company, 2014): accessed January 17, 2015. Available: http://www2.dupont.com/FE/en_US/products/FM200.html.

13. *Nine Classes of Hazardous Materials* (Washington, DC: Federal Motor Carrier Safety Administration, Date Unknown): accessed January 17, 2015. Available: http://www.fmcsa.dot.gov/sites/fmcsa.dot.gov/files/docs/Nine_Classes_of_Hazardous_Materials-4-2013.pdf.

14. *704 Marking System* (Jefferson City, MO: State Emergency Management Agency, Date Unknown): accessed January 17, 2015. Available: http://sema.dps.mo.gov/docs/programs/Executive/merc/LEPC%20Manual/704%20MARKING%20SYSTEM.pdf.

15. *Module 3: Developing an Action Plan* (Indianapolis, IN: Department of Homeland Security, Date Unknown): accessed January 17, 2015. Available: http://www.in.gov/dhs/files/Decision_Module3_SM.pdf.

16. *Live Fire Test with FDNY Will Guide Improvements in Fire Department Tactics* (Washington, DC: National Institute of Standards and Technology, July 11, 2012): accessed January 17, 2015. Available: http://www.nist.gov/el/fire_research/fire-071112.cfm.

17. Masden J., *Chemical Warfare Agents* (Whitehouse Station, NJ: The Merck Manuals, September 2013): accessed January 17, 2015. Available: http://www.merckmanuals.com/professional/injuries_poisoning/mass_casualty_weapons/chemical_warfare_agents.html.

18. *Biological Weapon* (Chicago, IL: Encyclopedia Brittanica, 2015): accessed January 17, 2015. Available: http://www.britannica.com/EBchecked/topic/938340/biological-weapon.

19. *49 CFR 173.134 – Class 6, Division 6.2* (Ithaca, NY: Cornell Law School, Legal Information Institute, Date Unknown): accessed January 17, 2015. Available: http://www.law.cornell.edu/cfr/text/49/173.134.

20. *Radiation Basics* (Washington, DC: U.S. Nuclear Regulatory Commission, Date Unknown): accessed January 17, 2015. Available: http://www.nrc.gov/about-nrc/radiation/health-effects/radiation-basics.html.

28

Identity Documentation and Verification

Charles T. Thibodeau

The world is awash with false, altered, or otherwise illegally used documents that allow individuals to gain access to a facility, location, or even a country in which they have no right to be, or to disappear by creating a new identity. These new identities are often forged from existing public records. Identity documents are central to the average person's existence, and the ability of another person to utilize one's identity is no laughing matter. Some of the 9/11 hijackers, for example, used fake identity documents to enter the United States prior to the attacks. Those fake identity documents ultimately made it possible for terrorists to board commercial airliners, hijack those aircraft, and crash them into densely populated office towers to kill as many people as possible. In the security profession, terrorists and criminals are not the only users of false, fraudulent, or altered identity documents. Young adults between the ages of 18 and 20 years use them to gain access to bars, nightclubs, and other establishments, using many of the same techniques that criminals, terrorists, or intelligence professionals use.

Thus, this chapter is essentially a paper chase. It introduces how identity documents are prepared, purchased/obtained, and used. The methods used by security professionals and law enforcement to help verify a person's identity are discussed. Immigration-related documents, such as permanent resident cards and visas, are explained in an American context as their system is the most complex. This chapter also examines what the private sector has contributed in developing better screening verification capabilities so the criminal element in this world can be impeded and stopped.

Some of the identity documents to be examined include the following:

1. *Birth certificate*s: A document that verifies a person's date of birth, name, and place of birth. Place of birth is an essential element of citizenship. Typically issued by the town, county, or state/province in which the birth occurred.
2. *Social security cards*: In the United States, this document contains a national identity number connected to a Social Security Administration account. In Canada, the Social Insurance Number serves the same purpose. The social security numbering system itself is based on the geographical area in which the card was issued, as well as the citizenship/status of the recipient.

3. *Driver's licenses*: A document that verifies a person's date of birth, and current address, biometrics such as a current picture of the person's face, height, weight, color of hair, color of eyes. Typically issued by the state/province after minimum age, driver training, and documentary requirements are met. Accepted the in United States and Canada as the most common identification document among adults. Variations exist for persons unable or unauthorized to drive.

4. *Passport*: A document that verifies a person's citizenship, date of birth, and place of birth. Extensive vetting and multiple identity documents are usually required in order to obtain one. Once obtained, good for multiple years.

5. *Refugee/aslyee travel document*: In the United States, this document is used by noncitizens to travel outside of the United States for extended periods without jeopardizing their refugee or asylee status. Requires an application and the timing of the application is specified by US law.

6. *Residency permits ("Green Cards" or I-551)*: A document that verifies US lawful permanent residency status; must be renewed every 10 years. Holders can enter/exit the United States with this card, together with a valid passport from their country of citizenship. Subject to time restrictions.

7. *Work authorization permits*: A document that verifies that a noncitizen worker is who they say they are, and they have a legal status that authorizes them to work in the United States.

8. *Visa*: A document issued by a sovereign nation through their embassy and/or consulate. In the United States, can be for immigrant or nonimmigrant. The visa is a document with security features like those of a passport and is placed inside the bearer's passport. In the United States, Mexican and Canadian citizens can obtain a Border Crossing Card, which is identical to the I-551 and functions as a visitor's visa.

9. *Transportation Worker Identification Credential (TWIC)*: A smart card issued by the Transportation Security Administration (TSA) in the US. Used by dockworkers, merchant mariners, airline employees, and others.

If the people coming to the United States are holders of any of the identity documents listed above, and either the document is fraudulent or the person is an impostor to a legitimate document, it is imperative that they be intercepted, regardless of their reasons for coming. Once such persons have entered the country, it then becomes possible for them to blend into large cities or areas with significant ethnic populations. The ultimate fear is that such persons are members of a group hostile to the country.

The manufacturers of these fraudulent documents are quite proficient, and it has become increasingly difficult to discern alterations in a document even with a thorough visual/tactile inspection. However, there is still a risk in manufacturing a fake document, meaning that the safest thing to use is a legitimate document. To obtain a legitimate document under false pretenses, however, requires some ingenuity. To create a fraudulent identity using a legitimate identity document, means that there must be an initial document or piece of evidence on which the subsequent identity documents are based. This is referred to as a "breeder document."

The Breeder Document

The birth certificate is often referred to as a "breeder document." If an individual can successfully obtain a birth certificate, they can assume that identity as their own because birth certificates have no photograph or biometrics by which to identify the true and rightful holder of the document. The individual may now, with this breeder document, obtain additional and more secure forms of identification issued legitimately based on the birth certificate. The birth certificate is the easiest document to obtain and duplicate for of the purpose of assuming someone else's identity; birth certificates are mainly ink on paper with a raised seal. Few other security features are incorporated into birth certificates.

Birth certificates are issued by the town, county, or state/province in which the birth occurred. They are legal, public documents and as such are accessible to others. There may be a fee, or perhaps the inquirer must provide a justification, but fees can be paid and justifications can be fabricated—if a justification is even requested by the clerk or registrar that issues the document. Because there is no picture identification or biometric identifier on a birth certificate, it is easy for an individual seeking it to contend they are, in fact, the person listed on the birth certificate. If an individual can obtain a legitimate copy of a birth certificate of someone with similar age or birth date, that is an added bonus. Birth certificates are not reconciled with death certificates—in the United States, only the Social Security Administration is concerned with that, and as a government bureaucracy it does not move quickly. Thus, it is possible to impersonate a recently deceased person because there is no link to their death certificate.

Once the birth certificate is obtained, the "breeding" can begin. The birth certificate can be used to apply for a driver's license in a state or province. This is a rite of passage for teens in many Western countries, where it may otherwise be unusual for a minor child to have photo identification (ID) unless he or she has a passport. The driver's license, which might have some proof-of-address or testing requirements, will further establish the identity of the individual; licenses are issued by the state/province after at least minimal vetting and driver's licenses generally have seen improved security features in the last 10 to 15 years. With the driver's license, the individual now has a stronger and *legitimate* form of identification that will allow them access to government offices, airplanes, and various other facilities. With a driver's license, the individual now has enough identification to rent an apartment, set up utilities, rent a car, drive a car, etc. Most importantly, the driver's license can now be used to procure additional identification.

Alternatively, the individual might apply to the Social Security Administration for a Social Security card based on the birth certificate. To be issued a social security number, the main parameter that must be met is legal presence in the United States. A birth certificate from a US municipality or county establishes that fact. As social security numbers are often issued shortly after birth, a photo ID is not required to obtain a social security card. This document is important as a corroborating piece of identification. Social security numbers are used, rightly or wrongly, as a national identification number. The social security number is used on driver license applications, rental applications, by K-12 and postsecondary schools, and employers as a unique identification number; the Internal Revenue Service uses it for tax filing purposes; and it is used for other purposes.

Thus, no matter how much security a local, state, or federal government entity incorporates into identity documents, possession of a breeder document enables access to highly secure documents, as well as making it possible to evade counterfeit and fraud-detection measures by virtue of its unquestionable authenticity. Consider how criminal elements might have become aware of the breeder document concept. The clerk at the local county clerk's office or Department of Motor Vehicles tells people what documents they will and will not accept, and usually why. Trial and error will eventually lead to success as different documents successfully pass muster with the clerk. The internet has made this process even simpler as most government entities put instructions on their websites telling exactly which documents are acceptable.

The Social Security Card

Once a criminal has obtained a legitimate birth certificate document, he or she can now use that legitimate document (to which he or she has no right to as an impostor) to obtain other documents. One such document contains a number that is used in many facets of everyday American life, and that is the social security number. In Canada, a similar system exists with the social insurance number. This number is commonly used as an identifier by schools, hospitals, employers, the Internal Revenue Service, and others because each number issued to a person is unique. One does not even have to be a citizen to obtain a social security number; persons present legally in the United States get a social security number because they need one to secure employment. The only document needed for a citizen is a "certified copy of a document showing a birth, marriage, or divorce that took place in the United States."[1]

At this point, the terrorist or criminal has two vital pieces of identity: a birth certificate and a social security card. While there are security features on the social security card, the card is typeface on paper and can be easily duplicated. In addition, a social security number can be "decoded" via the Internet using sites such as SSN Validator.[2] If checking a social security card using this method, the state of issuance, date of issuance, issuance status, SSA Death Master File, and current status of the social security number can be obtained.

The Driver's License

The driver's license, particularly in North America, is one of the most versatile identity documents there is. Issued by the state/province, it has a photograph, security features, and is accepted by banks, rental car companies, airlines, government entities, and most everyone else as a valid, legitimate form of identification. Using a driver's license to hide one's identity can be accomplished in three ways, as there is a photograph involved:

- A borrowed or stolen ID of a close look-alike
- A purchased fake/altered ID from a criminal ID maker
- An authorized ID obtained by use of a breeder document

The upside to the photographic driver's license is that it is possible for a security professional to catch an impostor to a legitimate document or a fake/altered document. It will not be possible for that professional to catch the holder of a legitimate driver's license obtained unlawfully through breeder documents.

Security professionals assigned to access control, particularly at a pub, bar, or nightclub, should be aware of the following:

1. *Borrowed driver's license ID*: Identifying an impostor to a driver's license requires very close observation of the details on the license. Often, an underage person seeking access to a bar will use another live individual's identification, such as a friend or relative close in age and appearance.

The best way to intercept someone that is an impostor to a legitimate identification that belongs to another person is to be prepared. Working conditions are rarely optimal for security professionals, but it is best if there is a table/counter to work on, adequate overhead lighting, a magnifying glass, and three lights (these can be separate or can be obtained all in one device): a strong flashlight, a handheld fluorescent light, and a handheld ultraviolet light.

If an Internet-connected device, such as a tablet or laptop is available, this can be used to research legitimate driver's license designs for comparison. In addition to the Internet, there are publicly available books that contain every driver's license and state/provincial-issued ID, since many jurisdictions have multiple versions of identification cards that look superficially similar. One such book is the *Law Enforcement Guide to Identification and Illegal ID Use*.[3]

Other signs to look for include expiration dates. People who borrow another person's driver's license do not want it to be confiscated by security at the bar (which some states/provinces permit), so the safest thing for them to do is use an expired document. This way, it is of no value to the true holder of that driver's license and thus confiscation is not a concern. Some jurisdictions will "clip" the corner of a driver's license that is about to expire, indicating that a new license has been requested but has not yet been issued; the clip technically invalidates the document because it is considered a mutilation. There will typically be a supplemental document or letter from the issuing agency to go with the clipped document. Oftentimes, when the new license arrives, the old one is not surrendered.

2. *Fake or altered driver's license*: These might be easier to detect because it is almost impossible to make a fake or altered driver's license that cannot be detected. The most effective tools for detecting a fake or altered driver's license are the human eye and the human finger.
   a. The security professional should feel the card. A digital photo will not feel like it is raised off of the card. A photograph substituted, no matter how thin the paper and adhesive, will feel different. The edges of the photograph are where this will become most apparent. Feel the edges of the card itself. They should feel smooth, as if cut with a die. If the card feels rough, chances are the card itself is fraudulent. In recent years, most jurisdictions have moved away from laminated driver's license cards and into cards printed on plastic.

b. Is the card printed vertically or horizontal? Most drivers' licenses are printed horizontally, but some states do print the licenses of people under the age of 21 vertically to make it easy for bouncers, security, or law enforcement to recognize almost instantly. Cards printed vertically for a person older than 21 are more likely to be fraudulent.

c. The security professional should visually examine the card. Is the card multicolored and embossed with holographs or other forms of security built into the card? Is there color-shifting ink—ink which color appears to change when the card is tilted?

d. Is there a magnetic strip and additional information on the back of the card? Many fraudulent cards are only half-complete. If one side is blank, chances are that card is bogus. If there is a magnetic strip present, it should be able to be read; there are publicly available card readers that can read the strip on the back of a driver's license. If the card cannot be read, it might be fraudulent.

e. The security professional should match the photograph on the driver's license to the person presenting it. Close attention should be paid to the nose, eyes, ears, ear lobes, chin, and Adam's apple. These will be the easiest features to quickly scan between photograph and person, and they are the most difficult to alter without surgical assistance.

f. In addition to the facial features already mentioned, any piercings, tattoos, scars, or other blemishes or deformities should be checked. Although these can be covered up or removed, the presence or absence of a scar may be questioned, such as for a scar that might have been obtained after the driver's license photo was taken.

g. In addition to physically and visually examining a document, one should also question the person presenting the driver's license about the information on the card. While questioning, observe the person's facial expressions and body language when they respond. Do they act nervous, develop a tick near the eyes, or do their eyes turn up toward the ceiling while thinking about their answer? These kinds of body language are outward signs of their anxiety and nervousness, or that they may need time to recall what they memorized from a borrowed or fake ID.

3. *Breeder document–obtained ID*: If the driver's license is obtained via a breeder document process, the individual tasked with examining identification will not find anything because they are looking at a legitimate card issued by a government bureaucracy. A security professional will probably get a feeling that something is "off" about the individual, but as the identity document is clearly legitimate, it will be more difficult to deny access. At this time, questioning the individual might be the only way to develop a way to deny them.

While a trained intelligence operative might have backup forms of identification, others will not plan that far ahead—leaving the additional option of asking for supporting documentation. A person who claims to be "Giacomo Rossini" will likely not just have a driver's license, they'll also have credit cards, a library card, a pistol permit, an identification for their workplace, or other documentation that will tend to support their insistence that they are in fact "Giacomo Rossini." If the person can produce additional proof of being who they say they are, like a picture ID from work, a medical ID card without the picture but the correct name and address, or a credit card in their name and address, then it increases the likelihood that they will gain access to the facility.

In this case, it will do no good to question because the person will know everything about the person in the driver's license picture ID—it is legal and the picture is most likely them. In extreme cases, a home phone number could be requested and called for verification. If using this technique, the person's reactions should be carefully observed. If there is subterfuge, such as the person giving their own cell phone number instead, the suddenly ringing phone will be an indicator that the person seeking access has been untruthful. Within reason, particularly when dealing with customers or clients, give the benefit of the doubt and seek alternative ways to confirm their identity.

For bars, clubs, and other establishments, controlling access is always difficult. Inevitably, there will be young-looking 21- to 23-year-olds who are really hard to judge. On the other side, there will also be 20-year-olds who look 25. The job of checking IDs must cover all the bases and will sometimes be defeated. The important thing for the person manning the entry door is that they can articulate the different ways that they determined a person's identity. As long as the security professional takes reasonable steps, liability for an incident or accident may at least be mitigated.

Some fake driver's licenses can be easily identified because they are printed vertically on one side of the card while the other side is blank. Typically, a state driver's license is printed horizontally with a magnetic strip and printed information on the back. Also, many documents use color-shifting inks, holograms, watermarks, or microprinting—features that usually cannot be duplicated without specialized equipment or software. This means that many fake identity documents are poorly constructed and therefore easy to detect. For more information on security features, visit http://www.gpo.gov/pdfs/customers/security_glossary.pdf.

The Seriousness of the Threat

The importance of verifying a person's identity is not just an issue for bouncers, bars, or nightclubs. The seriousness of the breeder document, as well as identity theft, document fraud, or similar issues, have been underscored by the events of recent history. As for how serious the threat is, back in the 1990s, Osama bin Laden was one of the leaders of a terrorist group called al Qaeda that was operating in Iraq, Afghanistan, Pakistan, Syria, and other places. He was one of the main designers of the infamous 9/11 attacks on the Twin Towers in New York City, and the attack on the Pentagon in Washington, DC, USA. These locations were attacked by three hijacked commercial airliners when terrorists flew planes with nearly full loads of jet fuel into the iconic Twin Towers, killing nearly 3,000 people. Simultaneously, the same group of terrorists flew a third plane into the Pentagon, in Washington, DC, where they killed 125 people.

The importance of the breeder document is underscored further by the "Millennium Bomber", a terrorist name Ahmed Ressam who was caught at the US./Canadian border in

1999. Ressam told investigators that Osama bin Laden, through al Qaeda, set up a school to teach terrorists how to make false documents. Ressam was an excellent student and became an expert in producing passports. During interrogation, Ressam told how he was able to fly all over the world with doctored and illegal identification papers, including passports. In addition to professional manufacturing by the likes of Ressam, there are other experts making fraudulent driver's licenses and other types of identity documents.[4] Those who produce these fraudulent documents have no interest in what happens to the purchaser afterward; it is a business transaction to them. Knowing that a purchaser is highly unlikely to report problems with a document forger or vendor to the local authorities, opens up the door to a variety of unpleasant situations, making trying to purchase a fraudulent identity document quite risky.

The Passport

The passport is the ultimate in identification documents. If there were a hierarchy of identification documents, the passport would be at the very top. The passport is proof of a person's citizenship—proof of the bearer's entitlement to rights guaranteed to them by the country in which they are a citizen, which includes the ability to enter and leave the country's territory. Given the importance of the passport, the security features used in them are both numerous and increasingly complex. The vetting process for obtaining these documents is typically extensive, requiring several forms of identity documents that are often independently verified. For example, if a person presents a birth certificate issued by the Canadian province of Ontario, the government office issuing the passport may contact the hospital listed on the birth certificate to confirm that there is, in fact, a record of the person having been born at that hospital. The importance and value of having a document that permits international travel means that passports are a sought-after target for identity thieves, criminal organizations, and terrorist entities. Given the security features and vetting involved in obtaining a valid, legitimate passport, they are often stolen and used by impostors; it is simpler to alter a person's appearance to resemble a legitimate document than to alter the document to resemble the person.

Border authorities in most Western countries have extensive training in recognizing fraudulent documents as well as impostors, meaning that an altered document has to be near-perfect to avoid detection. Coupled with biometric systems in place at many entry points means that even with a legitimate document, an impostor might be foiled by an iris scan or a fingerprint mismatch. What does all this mean? It means that the most effective way to obtain a passport that will withstand both human and technological scrutiny is to obtain a genuine document that has only been used by the impostor that carries it. The impostor's biometrics become associated with the travel document. If the impostor uses a breeder document to transition from birth certificate or baptismal certificate to driver's license to passport, the impostor can use the same details over and over, making the cover story easier to maintain; the impostor supplies the details as he or she obtains the other documents rather than having to memorize stolen passport data that belongs to someone else.

Consider that what really killed almost 3,000 people in the 9/11 attacks was not the aircraft crashing into the buildings, but that the perpetrators were able to enter the United States. Also remember that an individual only has to enter the country successfully once; after they are in, they can hide, assimilate, or remain mobile. The documents used by the 9/11 terrorists allowed them to take seats on those ill-fated aircraft. Some of the 9/11 terrorists did not even have fraudulent documents; they entered the country with legitimate documents and visas obtained by false pretenses. At that time, there was little auditing of the individuals and what they claimed to be doing once they entered the United States. For further information on how identity documents are used, see *Crossing Borders: How Terrorists Use Fake Passports, Visas, and other Identity Documents*, which contains a comprehensive description of how passports and visas are illegally used to gain access to any country by thousands of terrorists.[5]

Refugee/Asylee Travel Documents

The reader should note that only US agencies and laws are used for reference in this section. Different countries have different laws and regulations regarding the entry/exit policies and/or documentary requirements for persons granted refugee status, asylum, or other noncitizen status.

United States Citizenship and Immigration Services (USCIS) is the US government agency that deals with the needs of refugees and asylees. From time to time, these refugees or asylees need to travel outside of the United States, and to do so they file a Form I-131 to inform USCIS of their need to travel outside of the country. There are stipulations for both refugees and asylees that they will not depart the United States while their application is being processed. If they depart, their application is considered abandoned. They apply for the I-131 to travel outside the United States without jeopardizing their refugee or asylee status. Even with the I-131, their travel is subject to certain restrictions concerning how long they can remain outside the United States.

By law, a refugee or asylee with a travel document has to notify USCIS no less than 60 days prior to their departure. Once they leave, however, no one knows what they do or where they go once outside the United States. They could be honest and be looking in on a sick parent or attending a relative's funeral. They may have escaped with their life and little else. They may be gathering the rest of their family to bring them to safety. Or, they could be taking classes on how to recruit Americans to go to training in Afghanistan and return as terrorists.

The I-131 application permits the request of one of three kinds of documents. They are:

1. *The Advance Parole Document:* This document is best understood as a pass that permits the bearer to re-enter the United States without jeopardizing the bearer's pending applications with USCIS. This document does not replace a passport but is accepted by an air carrier in place of a passport and/or visa. The Advance Parole Document serves as the person's authorization to travel into and out of the

United States without granting them a legal status. This is used most often by refugees who are in the process of applying for, or adjusting their existing status to, legal permanent resident. Persons who have an application or an adjustment-of-status in process are generally not permitted to depart the United States as their application is dependent on their presence inside the United States.

2. *The Refugee Travel Document:* This document, which looks similar to a passport, is for persons granted refugee or asylee status who have a need to travel outside the United States for an extended period.
3. *The Re-Entry Permit Document:* This document is for lawful permanent residents who need to remain outside the United States for extended periods without jeopardizing their resident status. In spending significant time outside the United States, legal permanent residents place themselves in jeopardy of being ordered removed from the United States upon their return. If US Customs and Border Protection believes a permanent resident is not actually residing in the United States, they can take action based on that belief.[6]

Green Card Residency Permits

A United States Permanent Resident Card (Form I-551) is an identity document that verifies the permanent residency status of the holder. The I-551, referred to as a "green card," is so named because from 1947 to 1967 the background color of the card that people carried to prove their status while living in the US was green. This is the identity document issued to the lawful permanent residents mentioned above.

People with the status of permanent residents are known as lawful permanent residents (LPRs). As such, these individuals are allowed to live and work in the United States. It is important to realize that these people are not citizens but are otherwise afforded all the rights and legal protection that the Constitution extends to citizens.

Permanent residents of the United States must carry their I-551 at all times. Failing to do so is a violation of the Immigration and Nationality Act, incurring the possibility of a fine up to $100 and/or imprisonment for up to 30 days for each offense. Only the federal government can impose these penalties. It is also illegal to carry an expired, inaccurate, or damaged alien registration card.

There are many reasons why the United States requires a green card for permanent residents. In the United States, a green card is proof for noncitizens of their right to live and work permanently in the United States. Green card holders can travel freely within the United States, can enter and leave the country more easily, and can hold down jobs with virtually any employer within the United States. This permanent residency card is also the first step to becoming a naturalized US citizen. The green card makes it easy to distinguish legal residency and work authorization between those who have been granted lawful permanent resident status in the United States versus those who are present on immigrant visas, nonimmigrant visas, or those not legally present.

Immigrant and Nonimmigrant Visas

A visa is a document obtained at a US Embassy or Consulate granting a foreign traveler permission to apply for admission into the United States at a port of entry. It is not a guarantee of entry into the United States. US Customs and Border Protection Officers determine if, and for how long, an alien is admitted. Visas contain many of the same security features that are found in passports and on driver's licenses.

There are two types of visas: immigrant visas, for people who intend to live permanently in the United States, and nonimmigrant visas, for people who wish to visit the United States temporarily (for tourism, medical treatment, business, temporary work, or study). In addition, there are several countries who meet the criteria for a waiver of the visa requirement for short-term visits; these are referred to as "visa-waiver countries."

Typical Types of Visa Fraud and Consequences

A visa is subject to the same abuses as other documents discussed in this chapter. The most common types of visa fraud are as follows:

1. Use of a "breeder document", where a false identity with supporting documentation are submitted as application materials for a visa.
2. The person being interviewed by a consular officer provides the necessary information to justify the issuance of a visa, but information that would refute that justification is withheld. Such information might include criminal history and association with people known to be criminals or participants in groups designated as terrorist organizations by the government granting the visa.
3. The person being interviewed by a consular officer misrepresents their reasons for requiring a visa. For example, a person seeks to obtain a visa to study in the United States, they set up corroborating evidence to support that contention, but then simply fail to attend school or pay tuition after they arrive. The school merely confirms to the government the status of the student (enrolled, unenrolled) when requested. As mentioned earlier, once the individual has gained entry, they are virtually undetectable. This type of fraud is often used by people who want to immigrate to the United States but cannot obtain an immigrant visa.
4. The person has procured a legitimately issued visa with another's identity by illegal means. The person presenting the visa will be the impostor. If the superficial features are similar enough, the visa may escape notice by a border official; again, coupled with biometrics, this is a risky proposition as the legitimate visa holder's biometrics will not match those of the impostor.

A huge issue with nonimmigrant visa holders in the United States is that some of those who enter on a legitimate nonimmigrant visa either fail to comply with the terms of the visa or fail to depart in a timely fashion. Failing to comply with the terms of the visa occurs when, for example, a person enters the United States as an F-1 student, after a semester drops out of school, then finds a job and stays. The person is considered "out of status" as they entered on a student visa and are no longer a student. That person can be subject to removal from the United States. Failing to depart in a timely fashion is commonly referred to as an "overstay." For example, a B-2 visitor for pleasure can be admitted to the United States for up to six months, at the discretion of the US Customs and Border Protection Officer that admits them. If that B-2 visitor stays for nine months, they have overstayed their status and are subject to removal from the United States. Note that three of the 9/11 attackers were people with valid visas who went missing before the attack. In 2013, Tamerlane Tsarnaev and his younger brother, Dzhokhar Tsarnaev, killed three people and injured an estimated 264 people using a homemade explosive device placed at the finish line of the Boston Marathon. The Tsarnaev brothers entered the United States on valid student visas but rarely attended class.

Transportation Worker Identification Credential

The Transportation Worker Identification Credential (TWIC) was established by an act of Congress in 2007. The TWIC rules set forth regulatory requirements to implement enhanced security in the maritime transportation environment. Administered jointly by the Transportation Security Administration (TSA) and US Coast Guard, the TWIC ensures that individuals who might pose a threat cannot gain unescorted access to secure areas of the nation's maritime transportation system.[7]

What Is a TWIC Card?

The TWIC cards are tamper-resistant biometric credentials for workers who require unescorted access to secure areas of ports, vessels, outer continental shelf facilities, as well as all credentialed merchant mariners. The TWIC is a "smart card" containing a digital photo and fingerprint linking the card and the card holder. It is a card that looks like an access control card but it is embedded with three access card technologies. First of all, it is a picture ID card. It has a chip, known as an integrated circuit chip (ICC), which stores the holder's information and biometric data. The chip can be read by inserting it into the reader or holding it near a proximity contactless reader. The chip can also be read by swiping with a magnetic strip and barcode reading method.[8]

What Companies Do to Address Identification Problems

Many companies in the United States are serious about facility security, and demand to know with certainty who is inside their facilities at any given time. This is accomplished through an access control system that relies on verifiable identification. These systems are only effective when the inspection and evaluation of identity documents are an integral part of the system, and when employees are subject to such verification through the issuance of tamper-resistant photo identification badges. Consider that some employees come to work and are verified five times a week by the same security personnel for years on end—this element of familiarity adds to the protection level of the badge.

Doors built into the access control point will prevent unauthorized access to the main parts of the building. To access the doors at an access control point, a card-swipe, proximity reader, biometric system, or other access control arrangement would be used by the employee to automatically verify their identity and allow access into the facility. Or, a security professional may need to see the identification and admit the employee. Visitors, vendors, or contractors would be subject to different procedures, which might include specialized badges to wear, mandatory escorts from authorized company employees, or other measures as appropriate.

The determination to allow access through any checkpoint should be made based on measures such as evaluation of the picture on the identity document, the biographical information (date of birth, home address, physical characteristics of the person), and review of other information voluntarily surrendered by the person being evaluated. The security professional should feel free to ask questions based on the information on the identity document and the information provided by the person themselves. The person seeking access must answer these questions accurately or their access will be denied.

In addition to the identity validation at the access point, companies should also make it a policy for any employee to challenge someone who does not display a valid badge or otherwise appears to be out of place. If the person who was identified by an employee in the interior of the building states that they do not have a badge, the front desk is to be called and informed of the situation immediately and security should initiate some kind of protocol. No other action is to be taken by the whistle blower. The level of badge-wearing compliance in any secured facility is a measure of just how much security exists.

When challenging someone for their identification, whether at the initial access point or somewhere within the facility, the following modes of observation will be the only way to ascertain whether the individual being challenged might be a threat to persons or property:

1. *Verbal communications*: Information gathered by general conversation or formal questioning.
2. *Nonverbal communications*: The appearance of the individual being questioned regarding body language, and numerous points of unalterable characteristics of the face of the person, comparing those characteristics to the person's face on the photograph of the picture ID. The positioning of the hands, and places the eyes keep focusing, are indicators of whether a person will fight, run, strike a particular location, etc.
3. *Written documentation*: This includes the information contained on the identity document(s) presented, any information written in a visitor's log, and supporting documentation—anything provided by the individual or found on their person or in their belongings.

Conclusion

Security professionals have a need to know who is in their facility or on their property at all times. To ensure that knowledge is effective, security professionals must first be aware of the types of documents they will encounter. Once that is understood, the security professional must then learn how to tell if each of those documents is genuine or fraudulent. Different documents have different levels of security, and the security supervisor must make sure that the officers or staff have the tools at their disposal to help them determine genuine from fraudulent. As security professionals learn to distinguish genuine from fraudulent documents, they must also learn to identify fraudulent people (impostors) comparing them to their legitimate documents. Therefore, observation skills *and* elicitation skills are essential to success. The security professional does not need to memorize everything about a document, but it is imperative to know where to find the correct information. A vague "this doesn't look right" is not enough—to articulate this to a regulatory agency, law enforcement official, or an administrative hearing, the security professional must have facts at their command (Figure 28.1–28.8).

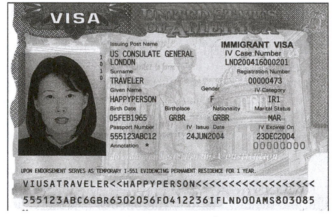

FIGURE 28.1 US visa.[9]

FIGURE 28.2 US legal permanent resident card (I-551), 2007–present.[10]

FIGURE 28.3 US passport.[11]

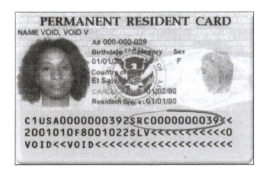

FIGURE 28.4 US legal permanent resident card (I-551), pre-2007.[12] (Note: These are valid until their expiration date passes.)

FIGURE 28.5 Canadian permanent resident card.[13]

FIGURE 28.6 US social security card.[14]

FIGURE 28.7 Canadian social insurance card.[15]

FIGURE 28.8 TWIC card.[16]

Refer website http://www.ifpo.org for further information

End Notes

1. *Social Security Number and Card* (Washington, DC: Social Security Administration) accessed October 3, 2014. Available: http://www.ssa.gov/ssnumber/.

2. *SSN Validator.* Crime Time Publishing Co., accessed October 3, 2014. Available: http://www.ssnvalidator.com.

3. Office of Juvenile Justice and Deliquency Prevention, *Law Enforcement Guide to Identification and Illegal ID Use* (Washington, DC: U.S. Department of Justice, Office of Justice Programs, February 2001) accessed October 3, 2014. Available: http://www.udetc.org/documents/FalseIdentification.pdf.

4. *A Terrorist's Testimony* (Boston, MA: WGBH, 2010) accessed October 4, 2014. Available: http://www.pbs.org/wgbh/pages/frontline/shows/trail/inside/testimony.html#3.

5. Oriana Zill, *Crossing Borders: How Terrorists Use Fake Passports* (Boston, MA: WGBH, 2010) accessed October 4, 2014. Available: http://www.pbs.org/wgbh/pages/frontline/shows/trail/etc/fake.html.

6. *How Do I Get a Refugee Travel Document?* (Washington, DC: U.S. Citizenship and Immigration Services, October 2013) accessed October 4, 2014. Available: http://www.uscis.gov/sites/default/files/USCIS/Resources/D4en.pdf.

7. *Program Information* (Washington, DC: Transportation Security Administration) accessed October 4, 2014. Available: http://www.tsa.gov/stakeholders/transportation-worker-identification-credential-twic%C2%AE.

8. *TWIC – Transportation Worker Identification Credential* (Woods Hole, MA: Woods Hole Oceanographic Institute) accessed October 4, 2014. Available: http://www.whoi.edu/sbl/liteSite.do?litesiteid=23632.

9. U.S. Citizenship & Immigration Services, accessed October 14, 2014. Available: http://www.uscis.gov/i-9-central/acceptable-documents/list-documents.

10. Ibid.

11. See note 9 above.

12. See note 9 above.

13. Canada Border Services Agency, accessed October 15, 2014. Available: http://www.cbsa-asfc.gc.ca/publications/pub/bsf5023-eng.html.

14. Social Security Administration, accessed October 15, 2014. Available: http://www.ssa.gov/history/reports/ssnreportex.html.

15. Government of Canada, Services for Youth, accessed October 15, 2014. Available: http://www.youth.gc.ca/eng/blog/2011/21.shtml.

16. Transportation Security Administration, accessed October 15, 2014. Available: http://blog.tsa.gov/2010/08/talk-to-tsa-response-recognizing-twic.html.

Emergency Management

29

Integrated Physical Security Systems

Jeffrey A. Slotnick

As the security industry has advanced, so has technology. To understand the importance of physical security to the security operation, one must understand the different concepts and technologies that are involved. Securing the facility is just as important as securing the people who work there, their visitors, and their clients.

Physical security technologies can be divided into several areas:

- Barrier systems
- Intrusion detection
- Visitor management
- Video technology
- Integrated operations centers

The physical security industry is in a period of dynamic change. This change has been facilitated by significant advances in technology and the application of technology to the physical security industry. Physical security can no longer be defined as "guards, gates, and guns." ASIS International defines physical security as "that part of security concerned with physical measures designed to safeguard people; to prevent unauthorized access to equipment, facilities, material, and documents; and to safeguard them against a security incident."[1]

The basic concepts that apply to the physical security practitioner are to deter, detect, delay, and respond to the adversary. This has not changed. What has changed over time is the technology used to facilitate these functions. For example, the first patent for contact cards was submitted in 1970. In 1984, the first commercial cellular telephone networks came into existence. In the 1990s, security camera systems used video cassette recorders for image and data storage.

By contrast, today there are networked physical security systems using physical security information management (PSIM) systems. PSIM systems provides a platform and applications that collect and correlate events from existing disparate security devices and information systems into a high-speed usable format. Before discussing advancements such as PSIM systems, the fundamentals of physical security must first be understood.

An *integrated physical protection system* is the combination of people, procedures, and equipment designed to protect assets or facilities against theft, sabotage, or other malevolent human attacks. Integration connects several different types of hardware devices and developing software interfaces so that devices can exchange information and be monitored and/or controlled by trained personnel from one or more locations. This integrated

Security Supervision and Management. http://dx.doi.org/10.1016/B978-0-12-800113-4.00029-8

approach to physical protection provides better security coverage with fewer human resources. This is not to say that technology will displace manpower; human interface is essential to monitoring and response. When combined with technology, humans work much more efficiently. In this manner, technology augments human capabilities and provides checks and balances to counteract wrongdoing. Successful security systems emphasize a growing awareness of technological developments and their integration with human resources, so that all can communicate more efficiently. Technology is a double-edged sword; it allows humans to be more efficient and responsive; however, if poorly managed, technology can also reduce the level of security.

Detection, Delay, and Response

With any physical security system, there are three criteria against which performance should be validated: detection, delay, and response. Management of these three criteria is essential to managing an effective integrated security system.

Detection

Detection concerns the ability of the system to recognize and/or identify a threat or adverse action. Detection of a threat or adverse action does not exist in a vacuum; the probability of detecting a particular threat is dependent on the type of system(s) in use. Detections must be identified as to location and type of detection; once identification is made by the system, it should be evaluated by a human. The time between sensor activation (detection and notification) and assessment (human evaluation) is an important metric. An efficient and effective system will provide rapid and accurate detection and assessment. If detection or assessment is delayed, it allows an adversary time to complete its task and depart the area. The longer the time between sensor activation and assessment, the greater the opportunity is for the adversary to be successful. A key principle in an effective integrated physical protection system is: *detection is not complete until the alarm is assessed.*

Delay

A delay provides obstacles to slow the adversary and increase adversary task time. Delay is commonly accomplished via barriers such as fencing, cages, bollards, access control points, turnstiles, and hardened rooms in a layered design. The intent is to cause an adversary to require many different kinds of skills and tools to be successful in breaching the series of delays.

Response

The response function begins at first detection. A response force, even if it is one person, must be prepared to position itself to engage with a threat. First detection tells the force "get ready to move." The function entails two components: interruption of the adversary and nullification. These two components entail the following considerations:

- How fast can detections be identified, assessed, and passed to the response force?
- Can the response force reach the right place, with the right number of people carrying the right equipment?
- Will the response force reach the right place at the right time? If it takes longer to arrive at the scene and deploy than it takes for the adversary to complete their task, then the adversary is successful.
- Will the response force possess the capabilities needed to engage the threat? For example, if the adversary is three trained terrorists with military experience, small arms, and explosives, a single county sheriff will likely be inadequate to defeat this adversary.

Layered Security or Security-In-Depth

Layered security relates to concentric circles of protection (Figure 29.1) and is often referred to as "security-in-depth." In this concept, there are multiple rings or layers of security, where each layer is more complex and requires a different skill set and tools to breach.

The first layer is located at the boundary of the site, and additional layers are encountered as one moves inward through the building toward the high-value assets. The first boundary also provides the first opportunity to detect that an adverse action is taking place, requiring technology that is capable of sensing and detecting the start of an event be both present and operational.

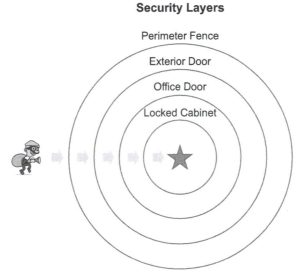

Security Layers

Perimeter Fence

Exterior Door

Office Door

Locked Cabinet

FIGURE 29.1 Layered security.

Basic Principles of Security Layers

Access to a facility can be divided into use areas. For example, the most exterior layer is for guests, contractors, and deliveries. The next layer is mixed use, perhaps for meetings between employees and guests. The most interior layer is the most protected and is only accessible by qualified employees. Depending on the facility and/or the nature of its business, there might be more than three layers. Having multiple layers ensures that an intruder will not be able to gain access to sensitive and controlled areas. Security professionals can decrease an adversary's odds of successfully breaching a location by adding layers, increasing the effectiveness of existing layers, or both. To rely on a single physical security layer means that the adversary only has to win one time.

Employee security awareness can create an invisible, yet very effective, security layer. Most employees, however, lack security awareness. In that situation, it must be taught to them. A training program regarding security awareness might be a solution. It does not have to be complicated. It can merely be reminding people of simple things: locking doors, being aware of their surroundings, locking their computers, etc. A trained employee is an advocate—an extra set of eyes and ears.

Current Thinking in Physical Security Technology

Enterprise security risk management (ESRM) is a "process for identifying, analyzing, and communicating risk and accepting, avoiding, transferring, or controlling it to an acceptable level considering associated costs and benefits of any actions taken."[2] To achieve a highly developed state of integrated security risk management, it is imperative to build security, safety, and resilience across domains by connecting efforts to prevent crime and terrorism, enhance security, safeguard information assets and technology, and ensure resilience to disasters. This is critical in assuring enterprise health and security, and ensuring enterprise longevity. ESRM is not an end in and of itself, but rather part of sound organizational resilience practices that include planning, preparedness, program evaluation, process improvement, and budget priority development. ESRM should enhance an organization's overall decision-making processes and maximize its ability to achieve its objectives in the face of adversity.

The function of physical security has traditionally been to secure people and buildings. The industry historically has been slow to absorb new technology, relying more on security officers and physical barriers. As enterprise risk management (ERM) and organizational resilience management (ORM) evolve to address all aspects of security and risks across all stakeholders, physical security has come under increased scrutiny. Numerous examples of physical security breaches leading to major organizational losses, both in terms of assets and brand damage, have led to the security function and physical security reporting to board level. Globally, new roles have been created within large organizations, where chief security officers (CSO) and chief information security officers (CISO) have responsibility for ESRM, including physical security. Subsequently, management reporting, policy compliance, and key performance indicators have entered the physical security function, requiring more efficient working practices and monitoring tools. Integrated security systems with high levels of integration address these organizational requirements.

Integrated security information management systems provide a platform designed to integrate multiple unconnected security applications and devices and control them through a comprehensive user interface. The system collects and correlates events from existing disparate security devices and information systems (video, access control, sensors, analytics, visitor management, networks, building systems, etc.), which allow security personnel to identify and proactively resolve threat situations. Physical security systems integration presents numerous organizational benefits. These include increased control, improved situational awareness, management reporting, and data analytics. Ultimately, these solutions allow organizations to reduce costs through improved efficiency and to improve security through increased intelligence and refinement of analytical information, allowing for trend analysis.

An integrated physical security system has six key capabilities:

1. *Collection*: Device management collects data from any number of disparate security devices or systems including video technology, intrusion detection, access control, visitor management, and barrier systems.
2. *Analysis*: The system analyzes and correlates the data, events, and alarms to identify real situations and their priority levels.
3. *Verification*: The relevant situation information is presented in a quick and easily digestible format for an operator to verify and communicate the situation.
4. *Resolution*: The system provides standard operating procedures (SOPs), step-by-step instructions based on best practices and an organization's policies, and tools to resolve the situation.
5. *Reporting*: All the information and steps are tracked for compliance reporting, training, and potentially, in-depth investigative analysis.
6. *Audit trail*: The system also monitors how each operator interacts with the system, tracks any manual changes to security systems, and calculates reaction times for each event.

Business rules and requirements that govern integration should be used for physical security integration and in building an information architecture for governing and managing enterprise risk. Integration combined with real-time data analytics helps make the business case for the security function. This combination supports metrics and key performance indicators that can show continual improvement and added value.

Physical Security Technologies

Various technologies can be integrated into a comprehensive system. A key concept is that the various sensors, cameras, barriers systems, visitor management systems, and access control devices communicate data to a network where data is converted into meaningful information, which is interpreted by an operator for appropriate action.

Barrier Systems

Barrier systems are comprised of a number of components, such as fencing, vehicle entry portals, and personnel entry portals. Barrier system elements include single and double fences, lighting, personnel gates, vehicle gates, clear zones, and restricted areas. These systems can be coupled with a number of associated technologies, including access control systems, analog/digital video, video analytics, electronic locks, door position switches, intercoms, and others. Some or all of these systems can be integrated. For example, an employee approaches an entry portal, uses their access control card, and the video system compares a photograph on file to the credential and video image being captured at the moment. Once all proofs are certified, the access is granted.

Fencing

Figure 29.2 shows a security-rated fence. Fencing is designed and rated according to what it is designed to stop. For example, one grade of fencing only stops people, while another can stop a 20,000-pound truck traveling 50 miles per hour.

There are a number of fence-associated technologies, including monostatic and bistatic microwave, ported coaxial cable, taut wire, strain gages, and fiber optic—all of which can be integrated.

Personnel Entrance

Figure 29.3 shows a secure personnel entrance. A number of technologies are incorporated here, including card access, lighting, magnetic locking mechanisms, video, and of course turnstiles. One item to consider on any portal is the concept of throughput. Throughput is the amount of people, vehicles, or materials that can pass through a portal within a given time frame. This is important because security must observe a fine balance between effectiveness and efficiency. It would be impractical to have an employee wait in a long line to be screened for entry, as this takes time away from work and equates to significant loss of work hours over time.

FIGURE 29.2 Security-rated fence. *Image courtesy of Ameristar Fence Products.*

FIGURE 29.3 Personnel entrance.

FIGURE 29.4 Vehicle entrance. *Image courtesy of Ameristar Fence Products.*

Vehicle Entrance

Figure 29.4 shows two examples of barrier systems at a vehicular entry control point. These devices can be automatically actuated in an integrated system based upon a pre-configured set of circumstances.

Intrusion Detection

Intrusion detection systems consist of both interior and exterior technologies. They include active and passive infrared, sound and glass break detection, vibration detection, and capacitance detectors. Many facilities are now using video analytics for intrusion and motion detection.

Access Control

The term *access control* refers to the practice of restricting entrance to a property, a building, or a room to authorized persons. Physical access control can be achieved by a human (e.g., a guard or receptionist) through mechanical means such as locks and keys, or through technological means, such as access control systems like a turnstile. Lock-and-key management systems may also be employed as a means of further managing and monitoring access to mechanically keyed areas or access to certain small assets.

An access control system determines who is allowed to enter or exit, where they are allowed to exit or enter, and when they are allowed to enter or exit. Historically, this was partially accomplished through keys and locks. Due to the issues with keys and locks relating to accountability, record keeping, and the costs of rekeying, many organizations have chosen to use electronic access control. There are also bridging technologies, which use intelligent key systems to account for each key in an electronic system. By electronically issuing keys, one can restrict access, audit all usage, and safeguard. By using these systems, physical keys are accounted for and available at all times. Intelligent key systems can be integrated into a larger physical security system.

Electronic access control uses computers to solve the limitations of mechanical locks and keys. A wide range of credentials can be used to replace mechanical keys. The electronic access control system grants access based on the credential presented. When access is granted, the door is unlocked for a predetermined time and the transaction is recorded. When access is refused, the door remains locked and the attempted access is recorded. The system will also monitor the door and alarm if the door is forced open or held open too long after being unlocked.

Access control has three principal components, with each being more complex and providing a higher level of security. First is an item that is physically possessed, such as an access control card or door key. Second is a piece of information such as a personal identification code or password. Third is a biometric feature such as a photograph, fingerprint, or iris scan. These features can also be used in combination with the each other, which is referred to as multifactor authentication.

A typical credential is an access control card or key-fob. There are many card technologies available, including magnetic stripe, bar code, Wiegand, capacitance, proximity 125-kHz proximity, 26-bit card-swipe, contact smart cards, and contactless smart cards. Also available are key-fobs, which are more compact than identification (ID) cards and attach to a key ring. Biometric technologies include fingerprint, facial recognition, iris recognition, retinal scan, voice, and hand geometry. Built-in biometric technologies found on newer smartphones and iPads can also be used as credentials in conjunction with access software running on mobile devices. Some of the system components include the access reading unit, intelligent field panel, computer, system, software, archive storage devices, communications network, and integrated subsystems. Proximity readers can be active or passive.

Standards for Access Control Systems

The US government established standards for access control cards, which incorporates the standardization of technologies. These standards were established per the Homeland Security Presidential Directive (HSPD) 12, *Policy for a Common Identification Standard for Federal Employees and Contractors*. HSPD 12 was meant to eliminate the wide variations in the quality and security of identification used to gain access to secure facilities with the potential for terrorist attacks. The initiative was intended to enhance security, increase government efficiency, reduce identity fraud, and protect personal privacy by establishing a mandatory standard for secure and reliable forms of identification.[3]

The National Institute for Standards and Technology proceeded to develop the Federal Information Processing Standard (FIPS) 201, *Personal Identity Verification (PIV) of Federal Employees and Contractors*, released in March 2006. The FIPS 201 standard specifies the architecture and technical requirements for the common ID card issued to federal employees and contractors. It describes the requirements for the system to verify personal identities, including personal identity proofing, registration, and issuance, as well as the detailed specifications that will ensure interoperability among PIV systems of federal departments and agencies.[4]

Visitor Management

Most facilities have visitors, contractors, and clients coming to their facilities. Accordingly, most security departments monitor who enters a facility, where they have permission to be, who they will be visiting (or who invited them), and for how long. This is accomplished by entering and managing visitor information into a log. Front desk staff and security officers in most organizations today use paper-based systems, which can be inaccurate and inefficient, thus wasting valuable time and money.

This process can be made more efficient—and to a great extent, automated—by using an integrated visitor management system. There are a number of visitor management systems available on the physical security market. They typically take an existing credential, such as a driver's license, and scan it to populate information fields and generate/issue a temporary access card. A visitor management system allows organizations to streamline the check-in process for visitors and contractors, thereby creating efficiency. They can collect and recall accurate data of current (and even pending) authorized visitors in real time. This helps monitor employee, visitor, and facility safety and security. Additional support and efficiency can be gained via electronic signatures or preregistration through a web-based portal.

Visitor management solutions can be integrated with other incident reporting platforms to take advantage of access to existing personnel, banned/watched subjects, and location interaction. For example, if an enterprise has multiple locations, a single registration process can reduce the need to create duplicate visitor information for each location or multiple redundant information entry. When integrated with other physical security systems, visitor management becomes a critical service to any security environment by providing accurate information during an emergency or building evacuation. Additionally, when integrated with the access control system's database, employees who have forgotten their badges can swipe their driver's license at a kiosk or visitor management station. If the database confirms that the person is a current employee, it prints a paper badge valid for that day. Another benefit of integration is the ability to check a visitor's identification against national and local databases, as well as in-house databases for potential security problems.

Video Technology

There are few subjects that dominate publications, education sessions, negotiations, and actual deployments as much as video surveillance does. Video surveillance has made a

FIGURE 29.5 Video surveillance system.

huge impact in many other industries as well. It is frequently a compliance requirement, such as with gaming establishments, data centers, traffic light systems, license plate recognition, credit card and ATM transactions, to name a few.

Video surveillance systems (Figure 29.5) are often more precisely called analog video surveillance or IP video surveillance, to indicate their use of conventional or network-based connectivity. In terms of integration, network-based video surveillance is most easily integrated. Integrated video is used in many situations, including transit, loss prevention, educational campuses, banking, sports venues, residences, gaming, and public safety.

The three primary uses of video surveillance systems are observation, forensic review, and recognition. Integrated video can be used in conjunction with varying physical security systems to increase security. For example, consider when a vehicle approaches an entry portal and a license plate reader scans the license plate. The scanned license plate is matched or correlated to the access control identification card; if authorized, the system lowers a barrier to permit entry.

Cameras come in many types, such as fixed, fixed zoom, pan-tilt-zoom, dome, and miniature cameras (Figure 29.6). A recent addition is 180 and 360° cameras, which have multiple cameras in the same dome, allowing for a wide range of viewing options.

Intelligent Video and Video Analytics

Basically, intelligent video reduces the vast amount of information contained in video, making it more manageable for systems and the persons responsible for operating them. Using intelligent video, the video surveillance system automatically performs an analysis and/or tagging of a captured video. Applications range from analytics, such as video

FIGURE 29.6 Exterior video camera.

motion detection and audio detection, to more advanced systems including camera tampering detection, people counting, virtual fences, and vehicle license plate recognition. The applications performing these analyses are also referred to as video content analysis (VCA) or video analytics (VA). Network video cameras with video analytics applications are never idle; they are constantly analyzing video streams, ready to send alarms or perform actions regardless of human involvement.

Intelligent video systems support the operator in detecting suspicious activities, such as people moving in the wrong direction or people trying to manipulate cameras, and can automatically start the recording of video and alert appropriate staff. It accomplishes this by detecting, classifying, and tracking multiple objects simultaneously. It can also detect events such as motion, movement in the wrong direction, entering/exiting, running, loitering, and people interaction; and can also detect and classify traffic rules, such as illegal U-turns, vehicles pulled off road, and objects left unattended or removed.

Integrated Operations Centers

There are many technologies that can be integrated to provide a common operating picture. The *common operating picture* is the collection of data provided by integrated systems and is typically observed in what is best described as an operations center. Operations centers can range in size from small, with a single operator and single bank of screens, to large operations centers with multiple stations, operators, and supervisors (Figure 29.7). In an operations center construct, many technologies can be integrated, including access control cards, door contacts and strikes, video cameras/video analytics, guard forces, alarm monitoring, buried sensors, above-ground sensors, entry systems, lighting, barrier systems, and biometrics.

When the operations center concept is combined with well-written policies/procedures and effective training, it creates a formidable capability that can protect an enterprise, provide early warning of impending incidents, and add significant value. Integrations and data analytics in real-time helps build the case for the business case to include the security functions by supporting metrics, key performance indicators, and improvement.

FIGURE 29.7 Operations center.

Conclusion

The security industry has really only scratched the surface of integrated systems and their capabilities. All organizations—and especially large enterprise organizations—are subject to the same manmade (crime and terrorism), natural (earthquake and flood), and technical (chemical release) disasters. In the twenty-first century alone, many organizations have suffered great losses as a result of terrorism, military, natural disasters, or technological disasters. Global organizations that do not prepare for catastrophic events will suffer significant loss of life, property, and resources—or may cease to exist altogether. Integrated systems and the timely information they provide, facilitate and expedite preparedness and help to ensure success of the enterprise.

Refer website http://www.ifpo.org for further information

End Notes

1. ASIS International, *Security Management Standard: Physical Asset Protection ANSI/ASIS PAP.1-2012* (Alexandria, VA: ASIS International, February 24, 2012), 57, c.47.

2. Office of Risk Management and Analysis, *DHS Risk Lexicon, 2010 Edition* (Washington, DC: U.S. Department of Homeland Security, National Protection and Programs Directorate, Date Unknown), 12.

3. *Homeland Security Presidential Directive 12: Policy for a Common Identification Standard for Federal Employees and Contractors* (Washington, DC: U.S. Department of Homeland Security, July 22, 2012): accessed January 7, 2015. Available: http://www.dhs.gov/homeland-security-presidential-directive-12.

4. Computer Security Division, *Personal Identity Verification (PIV) of Federal Employees and Contractors* (Washington, DC: U.S. Department of Commerce, Information Technology Laboratory, August 2013): accessed January 7, 2015. Available: http://dx.doi.org/10.6028/NIST.FIPS.201-2.

30

Managing Critical Incidents and Large-Scale Special Events

Eloy L. Nunez, Ernest G. Vendrell, Scott A. Watson

Introduction

In the post-9/11 era, it has become increasingly fashionable for security professionals to discuss how the disciplines of physical security and information technology are converging and thus changing the very nature of protective services. While these discussions are both important and positive, they fail to fully address the rapidly shifting nature of today's security threats. The central reality of security in the post-9/11 world is that the complex nature of critical incidents necessitates an interdisciplinary response.

Security professionals must be prepared to deal with a wide variety of critical incidents including crime, weather-related emergencies, cyber-attacks, terrorism, product tampering, and a whole host of other issues. To adequately respond to today's critical incidents, security professionals must have an understanding of not only traditional security disciplines and information technology but also general business practices, risk management, crisis management, business continuity, disaster recovery, and public safety to name just a few. Convergence is indeed coming, but it is much grander than what is encompassed in the current discourse (www.csoonline.com/fundamentals/abc_convergence.html).[1] The words of Benjamin Franklin at the signing of the Declaration of Independence ring as true for security professionals today as they did for the founding fathers in 1776: "We must all hang together, or assuredly we shall all hang separately."

Most experts today are predicting that corporations, businesses, law enforcement agencies, and various other governmental entities in the United States and around the world will be confronted with critical incidents that are likely to increase in number and level of severity.[2–5] As a result, planning for critical incidents has taken on greater importance as well as a renewed sense of urgency. In particular, the terrorist threat is increasingly decentralized and more difficult to detect, cyber-attacks continue to grow in number and pose a significant threat to our nation's public and private infrastructure, and the short and long-term costs of addressing natural hazards continue to rise.[6]

Critical incidents are unanticipated incidents of high consequence, such as natural disasters, hazardous materials spills, transportation disasters, terrorism, workplace violence situations, and other similar life-threatening situations. The extraordinary dimensions of these situations require special organizational skills and abilities on the part of emergency response personnel in order to attain a successful outcome. Although the exact time and place of a critical incident cannot always be anticipated, that does not mean that it cannot be planned for. Contingency planning for a wide array of critical incident scenarios is a long-established practice for organizations in the military, as well as the public and private sectors. We may not know where and when a tornado or terrorist attack is going to occur, but we would be remiss in not planning ahead of time for such eventualities.

Closely related to critical incident planning is the planning for special events. The fundamental principles of planning are the same for the unanticipated incident as they are for the anticipated event. The only difference is that with the event, the time and place are known ahead of time to the planners which is a great advantage, but does not relieve the planners of the responsibility of planning for contingencies within the scope of their special event plan. It does not take a lot for a preplanned event to turn into an unanticipated critical incident in a hurry. Consequently, emergency response plans that provide the necessary structure for managing critical incidents and preplanned large-scale special events are of vital importance to any organization. Besides helping to save lives and reduce property loss, a well-thought-out emergency response plan can serve to lessen an organization's potential liability. Developing a comprehensive emergency response plan is, therefore, one of the most essential functions that a security supervisor or manager can perform.

Scope of the Problem

Unfortunately, many organizations lack a good emergency response plan. This can ultimately lead to a variety of negative consequences, ranging from adverse publicity to significant operating losses as well as loss of life. On the other hand, when organizations realize that emergency response planning is vital, they create and circulate elaborate policies and procedures designed to deal with a variety of emergency and disaster situations. Moreover, these organizations usually feel confident that they are prepared to deal with any contingency. Their emergency response plans detail specific actions to take in the event of a catastrophic event and outline specific steps that should be employed during the ensuing recovery effort. However, far too often, this is where the planning process ends. Typically, the planning document is filed away and forgotten until a critical incident occurs.[7,8] This is quite problematic because it is unlikely that the emergency operations plan will be effective without the active participation of those who are likely to implement the plan in times of crisis.[9]

Emergency Planning Considerations

Clearly, an emergency response plan cannot be applied to every potential crisis situation. However, a comprehensive plan that takes into account potential natural, technological, and man-made threats and involves key personnel in the planning process can help an organization to systematically manage emergencies in an effective and efficient manner. Therefore, the planning process is a key element that forces security managers and supervisors to explore viable options that can be employed in the event of a critical incident. For this reason, oftentimes there is considerable discussion regarding which is more important—the plan or the planning process.

The Components of an Effective Emergency Response Plan

Being prepared for critical incidents involves four important components: planning, reviewing, training, and testing. These are the cornerstones of any emergency response plan, and it should be noted that it is a circular rather than linear process. Perhaps Nudell and Antokol (1988) explain this concept best when they describe the above components, when implemented, as an umbrella of preparation against the thunderstorms of a potential crisis.[10] According to the American Society for Industrial Security, effective emergency planning begins with the following[11]:

* Defining an emergency in terms relevant to the organization doing the planning
* Establishing an organization with specific tasks to function immediately before, during, and after an emergency
* Establishing a method for utilizing resources and for obtaining additional resources during the emergency
* Providing a recognizable means of moving from normal operations into and out of the emergency mode of operation

Incident Command System

With regard to establishing an organization with specific tasks and a method for utilizing resources, it should be noted that there exists a recognized system with a predetermined chain of command as well as a proven structure for an organized response to a critical incident. Referred to as the incident command system (ICS), it uses common terminology that is descriptive and decisive, yet not difficult to understand, in order to control personnel, resources, and communications at the scene of a critical incident.[12–14]

ICS was developed in the early 1970s after a series of major wildland fires in southern California resulted in a number of recurring problems among emergency responders. Some of these included nonstandard terminology, nonstandard and nonintegrated communications, unmanageable span of control, and lack of the capability to expand and contract as required by the situation.

Although originally a fire service control system, ICS has since been adopted by a wide variety of local, state, and national emergency management and law enforcement organizations due to its many documented successes. Today, it serves as a model all-risk, all-agency emergency management system. ICS principles have been proven over time in government, business, and industry. In fact, ICS has been endorsed by the International Association of Chiefs of Police (IACP) and the American Public Works Association (APWA).[12,15]

There is also a legal requirement for using ICS because there are federal laws that mandate its use by individuals responding to hazardous materials incidents. Specifically, the Occupational Safety and Health Administration (OSHA) rule 1910.120, which became effective from March 6, 1990, requires that all organizations that handle hazardous materials use ICS. Non-OSHA states are also required by the Environmental Protection Agency to use ICS when responding to hazardous materials incidents.[12,15]

In essence, ICS is a well-organized team approach for managing critical incidents, as well as preplanned special events. It uses common terminology, has a modular organization (which means that it can expand/shrink according to the needs of the situation), has a manageable span of control (the number of subordinates one supervisor can manage effectively; usually 3–7, the optimum is 5), and uses clear reporting and documentation procedures. In effect, emergency response personnel can view ICS as an incident management toolbox. Not every tool in the toolbox will be used for every situation, but the tools are available should they become necessary. Additionally, it is important to note that ICS can be used for all types of incidents regardless of size. However, it is essential that all emergency responders understand their specific roles when using ICS.[12,13,15,16]

The ICS structure is built around five major management activities or functional areas[12,15]:

- Command: sets priorities and objectives and is responsible for overall command of the incident
- Operations: has responsibility for all tactical operations necessary to carry out the plan
- Planning: responsible for the collection, evaluation, and dissemination of information concerning incident development as well as the status of all available resources
- Logistics: responsible for providing the necessary support (facilities, services, and materials) to meet incident needs
- Finance: responsible for monitoring and documenting all costs; provides the necessary financial support related to the incident

These five management activities or functional areas form the foundation of the ICS organizational structure. The activities can be managed by one individual in the event of a small incident, or a fully staffed ICS structure that addresses all five functional areas may be needed to manage larger or more complex events. In both cases, it is important to note that the incident commander is the individual in charge at the scene of a critical incident until properly relieved. The incident commander is also responsible for assigning personnel to the other functional areas (operations, planning, logistics, and finance) as needed.

ICS organizational structure (Figure 30.1) and procedures enable emergency response personnel to work safely together to take control of a critical incident. They can also assist organizations to effectively and efficiently manage the aftermath of a critical incident.

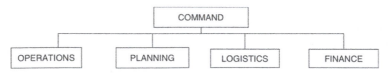

FIGURE 30.1 Basic incident command system organizational structure.

Common Requirements for Effective Critical Incident Management

Regardless of the type of crisis, a series of common requirements must be taken into account for an organization to be successful when a critical incident occurs, including the following[10]:

- Deciding policy
- Assessing threat
- Identifying resources
- Selecting crisis team personnel
- Locating the crisis management center
- Equipping the crisis center
- Training crisis team personnel
- Testing contingency plans and emergency procedures
- Dealing with the media
- Dealing with victims and their families
- Dealing with other affected persons (e.g., employees)
- Getting the organization's normal work done during the crisis
- Returning to normal after the crisis (both operationally and in human terms)

Vulnerability Analysis

With regard to the threat assessment above, many times this procedure can be accomplished by using a simple numerical rating system on a chart (using a scale of 1–5, with 1 as the lowest and 5 being highest) listing: potential emergencies (e.g., fire, flood, and terrorist attack); estimating the probability of each emergency occurring, assessing the potential human impact (death and injury); property impact (losses and damages); potential business impact (loss of market share); and finally, the strength of the internal and external resources that may be available (5 being weak resources and 1 indicating strong resources). Next, is to total the score for each emergency, taking into consideration that the lower the score, the better. Although somewhat subjective, the comparisons will be of significant assistance in determining planning priorities. In the example shown in Figure 30.2, we would be most

Type of Emergency	Probability +	Human Impact +	Property Impact +	Business Impact +	Internal Resources +	External Resources =	Total
	L 1-5 H	L 1-5 H	L 1-5 H	L 1-5 H	W 5-1 S	W 5-1 S	
Fire	3	5	5	5	2	4	24
Earthquake	2	4	4	4	2	3	19
Hurricane	4	4	4	4	3	4	23

FIGURE 30.2 Vulnerability analysis chart.

vulnerable to the fire scenario closely followed by the hurricane threat. We would be less vulnerable to the threat of an earthquake.[17]

The Emergency Operations Center

An emergency operations center (EOC) serves as a centralized area for the management of emergency operations. The EOC is where decisions are made by the emergency management team based on information provided by emergency responders and other personnel.[17]

The EOC can range from a dedicated, well-equipped center (comprehensive emergency communications capability including radio, telephone, fax, computer, and television; self-sustaining power sources; bathroom, eating, and sleeping facilities for staff; etc.) to an ad hoc room that is used as circumstances dictate. Of particular importance is that an organization identify its requirements ahead of time and establish the type of arrangement that best suits its needs.[10,11]

Although the EOC should be near senior management, it should not interfere with everyday operations. In addition, an alternate site should always be selected ahead of time. Hawkes and Neal (1998) states that "an effective command center ready to respond to any emergency is a critical component of any headquarters security plan" (p. 54).[18] They further contend that "a successful command center is the result of careful planning, clearly defined structure and job descriptions, and comprehensive training" (p. 54).

Media Relations

Lukaszewski (2013) contends that prudent organizations identify threats, assess vulnerability, and determine risks to effectively prepare for crisis events.[19] Preplanning leadership actions assist organizations in meeting pre-established objectives during the critical initial stages of a crisis. In particular, Lukaszewski emphasizes the importance of creating policies and establishing responsibilities based on likely scenarios.[19] This enables leadership to identify what actions should be taken, and by whom, in times of crisis.

Procedures for dealing with the media also cannot be overlooked. When a critical incident occurs, the security manager will undoubtedly be pulled in many different directions. Faced with a considerable number of important tasks, the security manager may not view media relations as a primary concern. However, being prepared ahead of time to deal with the media can help an organization get through the incident without the additional damage that can be caused by misinformation and speculation. In addition, the negative publicity that an organization receives as a result of a critical incident can have far-reaching effects. The organization's image and business can be adversely impacted. Litigation is bound to result as victims, the families of victims, employees, customers, and perhaps various interested outside parties will seek to lay blame and recover damages. Attorneys are compelled to examine every newspaper account and television report of the incident. They will, of course, be looking for statements from representatives of the organization for any admission or confirmation that the organization was in some way negligent.[20]

Nuss (1997) defines a crisis as "an event requiring rapid decisions involving the media, that, if handled incorrectly, could damage the organization's credibility and reputation" (p. 1).[21] He further provided a number of effective crisis communication steps that organizations should consider:

- Have a media plan.
- Build a relationship with the media before a crisis strikes.
- Train employees in crisis communications.
- Maintain a good relationship with the media after a crisis.

Lukaszewski states that "the principal ingredient of a crisis is the creation of victims. It is the presence of victims and how they are managed that creates a crisis" (p. 16).[19] Furthermore, according to Lukaszewski, avoiding responsibility and shifting blame can lead to negative consequences for an organization and its leadership.[19]

Cooperating with the media provides an organization with a number of important benefits that far outweigh the benefits of denying them access. In particular, it provides the organization with an opportunity to provide its side of the story. This is important because, oftentimes, the spokesman for the organization can make available background information that may provide a different perspective on the situation. Furthermore, working with the media may prevent reporters from seeking out secondary sources that are typically less informed and more likely to misrepresent the organization. Consequently, it is far better to have the organization give an accurate statement of the situation as opposed to leaving it up to the reporter to locate an "informed" source, which can lead to speculation and misinformation. Saying nothing also has its own risks. Ignoring bad news will not make the incident go away, and usually this tactic raises additional questions.[20]

The Federal Emergency Management Agency (FEMA) provides a number of important considerations for dealing with the media in an emergency[17]:

- Designate a trained spokesperson and an alternate spokesperson.
- Set up a media briefing area.
- Establish security procedures.
- Establish procedures for ensuring that information is complete, accurate, and approved for public release.
- Determine an appropriate and useful way of communicating technical information.
- Prepare background information about the facility.

FEMA also provides the following guidelines when providing information to the media during an emergency[17]:

- Give all media equal access to the information.
- When appropriate, conduct press briefings and interviews. Give local and national media equal time.
- Try to observe media deadlines.
- Escort media representatives to ensure safety.
- Keep records of information released.

- Provide press releases when possible.
- Do not speculate about the incident.
- Do not permit unauthorized personnel to release information.
- Do not cover up facts or mislead the media.
- Do not place blame anywhere for the incident.

It is also important to note that in many organizations, crisis communication is assigned to security, rather than it being a corporate communication or legal department responsibility. For this reason, Lukaszewski contends that constructive relationships among all staff functions relative to preparedness need to be established in advance.[19]

It is quite evident that although safety issues are always the top consideration, a security manager or supervisor cannot overlook the importance of an effective crisis media relations plan. This plan must be implemented quickly during a critical incident to provide accurate and timely information while safeguarding the reputation and interests of the organization.

Developing the Emergency Response Plan

Obviously, the development of a comprehensive emergency management plan requires considerable time and effort, and sufficient time should be provided for its completion. Representatives from key organizational units must be involved from its inception, and upper management support is essential throughout the entire process. Many times, this can be readily accomplished by having the chief executive officer or facility manager issue a mission statement that introduces the emergency management plan, its purpose, and importance to the organization, as well as defines the structure and authority of the planning team. Additionally, it is important in the initial planning stages to select an individual within the organization to assume responsibility for the plan and act as the planning team leader or coordinator.

Ultimately, capabilities and hazards should be analyzed, specific roles and responsibilities carefully outlined, and critical company products and services identified in order to ensure a coordinated and effective response when a critical incident does occur. This will typically involve meeting with outside groups and establishing mutual aid agreements where appropriate. Gillepsi emphasizes that mutual aid agreements enhance preparedness and that emergency response is more effective when public and private organizations cooperate.[22]

According to the Federal Emergency Management Agency (2006), some outside groups or agencies to work with could include the following[17]:

- Local police department
- Local fire department
- Emergency medical services
- City or county office of emergency management
- Local emergency planning committee
- City or county government officials

- Public works department
- Electric utilities
- Telephone companies
- Volunteer agencies such as the American Red Cross, Salvation Army, etc.
- Essential contractors
- Suppliers of emergency equipment
- Company insurance carriers
- Neighboring businesses
- Trade associations
- National Weather Service

In crisis situations, organizations respond differently based on variations in tasks, level of preparedness, as well as political considerations. Conferring with outside groups or agencies ahead of time will undoubtedly avoid confusion and delays during the response phase of an emergency, improve coordination and communication during the management phase of the incident, and help organizations transition to the recovery phase much faster. However, it is important to note that these agreements should clearly define the type of assistance as well as the procedures for activating the agreement in order to avoid unnecessary conflict.

Integrated Systems Approach to Special Event Planning

Coordination between agencies, organizations, and other stakeholders during a critical incident is paramount for the successful outcome of the incident. Nowhere is the scope of interagency, multistakeholder cooperation more evident than during the planning of a large-scale special event such as a political convention, global economic summit, or a sporting event such as the Super Bowl or the Olympics. These large-scale special events typically take at least a year of planning and encompass a broad array of participants from many fields and disciplines. The problems associated with integrating so many stakeholders in such a complex planning environment are self-evident, but what is often ignored are the learning opportunities that these large-scale special events provide—an ideal setting for planning participants to share ideas and learn from each other. These large-scale events act as *focusing events* where interdisciplinary knowledge is shared, ideas are exchanged, and innovations are hatched.

As stated earlier, the incident command system provides a modular organizational structure that is ideal for planning large-scale special events. Equally important is the use of a universal language that allows for the effective communication and exchange of ideas between disciplines of various agencies and organizations. ICS terminology is universally known and avoids industry-specific jargon or geographical colloquialisms that hinder communications between elements in crucial incidents and in preplanned special events. ICS provides both the structure and the process that are ideal for planning and managing complex incidents and events. However, ICS alone is not sufficient for understanding

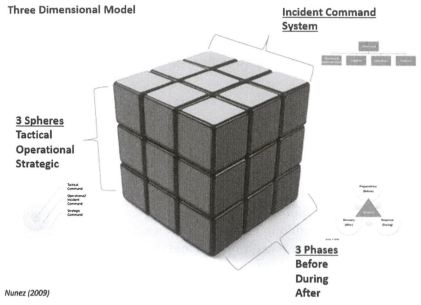

FIGURE 30.3 Three-dimensional model for planning special events.

and managing such complex systems. To fully grasp the complexity of large-scale special event planning, it is important that we conceive it as a three-dimensional model, in which ICS is only one of the three dimensions.

Figure 30.3 illustrates the components of the three dimensional model for planning special events. The first, and most important, is the ICS structure and the processes associated with it. While many critical incidents result in the activation of only some of the modular components of ICS, the planning of a large-scale special event will require the full scope of an ICS organizational structure.

The second component of the model can be simply stated as *before, during,* and *after.* FEMA uses a four-phase emergency management model that includes preparedness, response, recovery, and mitigation[23]. Nuñez (2009) argues that mitigation is a process which occurs before, during, and after a critical incident, and should not be considered a phase in itself.[24] According to the Nuñez model (Figure 30.4), mitigation is an overarching process that encompasses the preparedness, response, and recovery phases. This is important because the planning of a large-scale special event incorporates all three different elements: the *before,* the *during,* and the *after.*

The third component of the three-dimensional model consists of three concentric circles denoting the *strategic, operational,* and *tactical* spheres of command (Figure 30.5). The middle ring of the circle pertains to the operational planning for the main event. Within this ring is the command structure (ICS) for the localized event itself (e.g., the Super Bowl, the G-8 Summit). The bulk of the planning normally focuses on this sphere. Typically, command and control for the operational sphere during the event is located at a predetermined incident command post (ICP).

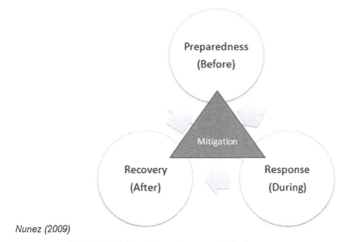

Nunez (2009)

FIGURE 30.4 The three-phase model of emergency management.

Nunez (2009)

FIGURE 30.5 Three spheres of command.

The inner ring of the circle pertains to the tactical sphere. The tactical sphere comes into play when an unanticipated localized critical incident occurs during the special event. Such localized critical incidents include, but are not limited to, situations such as active shooters, chemical spills, bombings, and localized weather disasters. Tactical response is basically a contingency within the broader operational plan. Command and control of the localized incident is typically located at an ad hoc tactical operations command (TOC).

The strategic sphere pertains to the broader stakeholder environment surrounding the event area of operations. The strategic sphere is also a part of the overall plan and serves as a contingency in the event that an unanticipated incident cannot be locally contained, and in which the assistance of elements, not assigned to the main operational sphere, are needed. For example, a mass casualty incident during a Super Bowl would likely result in the activation of a multijurisdictional mass casualty plan involving the hospitals and resources of surrounding counties, states, and the federal government. The strategic command sphere is typically located at a predetermined Emergency Operations Center (EOC), at a distance from the main area of operations. During large-scale special events, the EOC typically deploys at a Level 2 activation, and is ready to mobilize to a Level 1 activation if necessary.[25]

As the three-dimensional model illustrates, the planning for a large-scale special event is really several plans in one. It involves a full-fledged ICS structure—planning for the before, during, and after. It also involves strategic, operational, and tactical planning. The complexity of the planning process can be better managed by understanding the three major dimensions of this model.

Reviewing and Integrating the Emergency Response Plan

Once the initial plan is completed, it is essential that its various components be reviewed in depth by planning team personnel and revised as necessary. The draft plan could then be presented to key management personnel as well as any individual who may be required to perform or provide support services. Many times, a tabletop exercise provides an excellent opportunity to review potential critical incidents with key personnel because problem areas can be readily identified and discussed. The plan can then be modified accordingly and later presented to the chief executive officer for final approval. On approval, the plan can be distributed to all affected personnel who should be required to sign that they have received the document. It is then important that the plan be quickly and clearly communicated to all affected personnel.[5]

It is imperative at this point that the plan be fully integrated into the organization's standard operating procedures (SOPs). According to FEMA, "SOPs and checklists provide the detailed instructions that an organization or individual needs to fulfill responsibilities and perform tasks, assigned in the EOP [emergency operations plan]" (p. 3).[26] Clearly, a comprehensive checklist that includes major planning, implementation, training/ testing, response, and recovery components would be an invaluable asset to any organization's emergency response plan.

Training and Testing

After the plan has been finalized, communicated to all affected personnel, and integrated into the organization's standard operating procedures, it must be thoroughly tested. An emergency response plan will not work properly unless realistic training is provided and it is thoroughly tested prior to implementation in an actual emergency. Testing the plan helps to identify problem areas, as well as inherent weaknesses, that must be corrected in order to ensure that the plan will work as designed. Training and testing, thus serves to identify areas in need of improvement, thereby enhancing coordination and communication among emergency response personnel.

The first step in the training process is to assign a staff member responsible for developing an overall training plan and the requisite goals and objectives for each component. Additionally, a determination must be made as to the following:

- Who will actually perform the training?
- Who will be trained?
- What type of training activities will be employed?
- What materials and equipment will be needed?
- When will the training take place?
- Where will the training take place?
- How long will the training last?
- How will the training be evaluated and by whom?
- How will the training activities be documented?
- How will special circumstances be handled?
- How will training costs and expenses be budgeted?

It should be noted that critiques, or evaluations, are an important component of the training process and must be conducted after each training activity. Sufficient time should be allotted for the critique, and any resulting recommendations should be forwarded to the emergency planning team for further review and action. Additionally, organizations should consider how to involve outside groups and agencies in the training and evaluation process. As previously mentioned, this could certainly help to avoid conflict and increase coordination and communication when a critical incident does occur. Emergency response training can take a variety of forms. FEMA's Emergency Management Guide for Business and Industry describes six types of training activities that can be considered[17]:

- Orientation and education sessions: Sessions designed to provide information, answer questions, and identify needs and concerns.
- Tabletop exercise: This is a cost-efficient and cost-effective way to have members of the emergency planning team, as well as key management personnel, meet in a conference room setting to discuss roles and responsibilities and identify areas of concern.
- Walk-through drill: The emergency planning team and response teams actually perform their emergency response functions.
- Functional drills: Designed to test specific functions such as medical response, emergency notifications, and communications procedures, although not necessarily at the same time. The drill is then evaluated by the various participants and problem areas are identified.
- Evacuation drill: Participants walk the evacuation route to a predesignated area where procedures accounting for all personnel are tested. Participants are asked to make note of potential hazards along the way and the emergency response plan is modified accordingly.
- Full-scale exercise: An emergency is simulated as close to real as possible. Involves management, emergency response personnel, employees, as well as outside groups and agencies that would also be involved in the response.

Practical "hands-on" training always provides personnel with excellent opportunities to use skills that are taught and to learn new techniques and procedures. For emergency response training, simulations such as tabletop exercises, drills, and full-scale exercises are particularly valuable for practicing decision-making skills, tactical techniques, and communications. Moreover, simulations serve to determine deficiencies in planning and procedures that can lead to modifications to the emergency response plan.[10,11,17]

"Model City" Simulator

Perhaps one of the most successful and creative ways of teaching critical incident management to emergency response personnel is through the use of a "model city" simulator board. As the name implies, a "model city" simulator represents a small community with a residential area, business district, and industrial park. The simulator provides a realistic environment needed to give participants the feeling of actually having managed a critical incident and to immediately see the results of their actions. In essence, students get to practice decision-making skills in a realistic environment where there are no repercussions for making a mistake.[27,28]

The goal of this training is to provide participants with a "game plan" that can make the difference in taking control of an incident or allowing it to mushroom out of control. The primary focus is on training operational personnel to manage the initial 30 minutes of a critical incident by employing a series of critical tasks or decisions. These include the following:

- Establish communications: Advise dispatch to hold the air and allow only emergency radio traffic or request that a separate frequency be assigned for the incident.
- Identify the "hot zone": It is very important to identify the hot zone immediately in order to limit additional exposure to danger.
- Establish an inner perimeter: An inner perimeter should be set up quickly. It is used to control and contain the area and prevent the initial situation from getting worse.
- Establish an outer perimeter: The outer perimeter is used to control access to the affected area. It is not an offensive position and should be located well outside of the hot zone.
- Establish a command post: The command post should be established outside of the hot zone, between the inner and outer perimeters. It does not need to be located with a view of the scene. Initially, the command post can be your vehicle or any other suitable temporary location with communications capability.
- Select a staging area: The staging area should be large enough to accommodate the arriving emergency resources for transfer to the scene as needed. It must be located outside of the inner perimeter at a safe and secure location.
- Identify and request additional resources: Quickly assess the need for additional resources at the scene and direct resources to the staging area. Examples of additional resources are local police, fire, emergency medical services, HazMat (hazardous materials), public works, utility companies, the National Guard, federal and state agencies, the American Red Cross, etc.[27,28]

The advantage of a critical incident management program using a "model city" simulator is that training shifts from discussing emergency response issues at the "tabletop" level to actually practicing handling an incident in a realistic, simulated environment. Learning to implement a standard set of tasks or procedures under these conditions will undoubtedly assist emergency response personnel to quickly take control and limit the growth of a critical incident, thereby affording a much greater opportunity for bringing the situation to a successful outcome.[27,28]

Evaluating the Emergency Response Plan

Regardless of the training schedule selected, a formal audit of the entire emergency response plan should be conducted at least once a year. Furthermore, in addition to the yearly audit, the emergency response plan should be evaluated, and modified if necessary, as follows[17]:

- After each drill or exercise
- After each critical incident
- When there is a change in personnel or responsibilities
- When the layout or design of a facility changes
- When there is a change in policies or procedures

Of course, any modifications or changes to an emergency response plan should be communicated to affected personnel as soon as possible. Similarly, changes to the planning document should be incorporated and distributed in a timely manner.

Terrorism's Impact on Crisis Management

The events of September 11, 2001, had a profound impact on the way the nation perceived the threat posed by terrorist groups. Despite a series of highly publicized and well-coordinated attacks on the United States' interests abroad during the 1990s, the public was largely unprepared for the potentially catastrophic violence posed by small groups of committed individuals.

As security professionals, it is easy to deride this lack of preparedness; however, it must be remembered that prior to September 11, 2001, the public's exposure to terrorism, while significantly troubling, did not come close to approaching the impact of the World Trade Center, Pentagon, and United Airlines' Flight 93 attacks.

In the 1980s, terrorist tactics generally included the hijacking of airliners and seizing of hostages to create uncertainty, promote fear, and engineer an environment of international drama on which to publicize their cause. By the 1990s, terrorist tactics changed. While kidnappings still occurred, bombings and other high casualty-producing attacks became more commonplace. The attacks on the US Embassies in Tanzania and Kenya, as well as the bombing of the Khobar Towers in Saudi Arabia, the seaborne assault on the USS Cole in Yemen, the domestic acts of terrorism on the Alfred P. Murrah building in Oklahoma City, and the first World Trade Center bombing in 1993 are but a few examples.

Over time, terrorist attacks shifted from the deadly, yet limited, actions choreographed to obtain worldwide attention to catastrophic, casualty-dense attacks designed to shock the populace with high body counts while simultaneously destroying or damaging critical infrastructures.[29-32]

Today, we are seeing yet another shift in terrorism strategy, especially among Jihadist groups. As the global war on terror has progressed, Western governments have shared information, frozen assets, and captured or eliminated numerous terrorist leaders. This coordinated campaign has degraded the capability of Jihadist terror organizations to conduct catastrophic attacks outside of their main spheres of influence. Jihadist organizations have adapted to this situation by making extensive use of social media to encourage individual Western sympathizers to conduct small scale attacks in their own countries.[33]

By encouraging "lone wolf" terrorists, the Jihadists are seeking to reduce the risk of failed operations in the United States and other Western countries. After all, a lone terrorist does not have to worry that co-conspirators will compromise his operation. This "leaderless resistance" comes with a cost as the terrorist forgoes attempts at spectacular operations in favor of smaller attacks that are more likely to succeed.

Some recent examples of lone wolf attacks include the following:

- October 20, 2014: A Canadian man with Jihadist sympathies uses his vehicle to run over two Canadian soldiers in Montreal. The man is eventually shot and killed by authorities.
- October 22, 2014: A Canadian man with Jihadist sympathies shoots a Canadian solider at a war memorial in Ottawa and then proceeds to enter the Parliament building before being killed by authorities.
- October 23, 2014: An American man with Jihadist sympathies in New York City attacks police officers with a hatchet.

If done well, this leaderless resistance/lone wolf strategy provides little or no warning of a pending operation. As a result, the importance of awareness on the part of individual citizens has become even more important to the prevention of terrorism.[34]

This change in terrorist strategy will require those engaged in crisis management to be prepared to deal with the implications of both large-scale attacks and smaller, but more frequent, acts of aggression.

Post-9/11 Era: The Public Sector

In the days following the attacks on New York City and Washington DC, the US government, in direct response to the terrorist actions of 9/11, enacted significant changes to its security programs.

- President George W. Bush issued an Executive Order to establish the Office of Homeland Security as part of the White House Staff.
- In March of 2002, the President issued Homeland Security Presidential Directive 3, authorizing the establishment of the color-coded Homeland Security Advisory System designed to alert government agencies, the private sector, and the citizenry to the changing risks of terrorist attacks.

- On November 25, 2002, President Bush signed the Homeland Security Act of 2002, which reorganized the reporting structure of 22 government agencies under the auspices of the newly created Department of Homeland Security.[35]

The purpose of these initiatives was to

- Streamline the efforts of government agencies involved in security-related activities so as to increase cooperation and enhance efficiency
- Reach out to the private sector in order to promote cooperation.[35]

The challenges in implementation, however, were enormous. Each agency had its own culture, management style, procedures, priorities, and sometimes even rivalries. Only time and experience would tell how effective these efforts to reorganize the government's protective services might be.

This test came rather soon. On August 25, 2005, Hurricane Katrina made landfall in Louisiana. This powerful storm impacted a wide geographic area and displaced a large number of people. In the final analysis, the death toll was estimated at more than 1,800, thereby serving to illustrate the magnitude and scope of the disaster. In particular, Hurricane Katrina exposed a number of weaknesses in our nation's emergency management system, to include its capacity to respond to large-scale, catastrophic events. Seventeen FEMA failures in the aftermath of Hurricane Katrina can be attributed to a number of factors:[36]

- After 9/11, FEMA lost its status as an independent agency, and the FEMA Director was no longer in a cabinet level position with direct access to the president,
- FEMA lost preparedness and mitigation personnel and funding to other priorities within DHS.
- The change from an all-hazards approach, to a focus on terrorism prevention, weakened overall national response capabilities.

However, in response to the noted problems, a number of changes occurred that granted more authority to the president and clarified the mission of FEMA and DHS. Collectively, the legislation passed is known as the Post-Katrina Emergency Management Reform Act of 2006 (PKEMRA). PKEMRA requires that all emergency management functions be consolidated and placed back into FEMA, which would be given elevated status within DHS. The goal was to prevent another Katrina debacle from occurring again.[36]

Post-9/11 Era: The Private Sector

As is typical with high-profile events, the initial reaction to the September 11 attacks was a flurry of activity to examine organizational security and business continuity issues. Budgets temporarily increased, as did the overall interest in security products and services. As time passed and attacks on the homeland were prevented in the short term, a separation process began to take hold. As one may expect, companies that deemed their risks to be lower reduced their budgets to pre-9/11 levels and went back to business as usual.

Firms deemed to be at higher risk, such as utility companies, financial institutions, public venues, and organizations designated as critical infrastructure by the Department of Homeland Security, changed their security programs more significantly. Not surprisingly, the level of commitment to security, business continuity, crisis management, and disaster recovery expressed by the private sector is a result of perceived risk, vulnerability, potential impacts to operations, and a changing regulatory environment.

Since the war on terrorism has become a long-term feature of US foreign and domestic policy, security, crisis management, business continuity, disaster recovery, and related disciplines are seeing, and will continue to see, the following changes:

1. While some terrorist organizations may still try to conduct spectacular operations, far more attempts will focus on low level, conventional terrorist attacks by lone wolf operatives.
2. Weapons of mass destruction will eventually be used against the United States.
3. Out of necessity, increased cooperation will occur between the public and private sector.
4. As critical infrastructure becomes more protected, soft targets such as shopping malls, schools, and movie theaters will become terrorist targets.
5. The demands for high quality security personnel will increase.
6. Government regulation regarding the selection and training of security personnel will increase.
7. Government regulation of recovery-related activities in the private sector will increase.
8. Demand for people with professional certification, training and formal education in security management, business continuity, crisis management, and disaster recovery will increase.
9. The need for general education of the populace on terrorism and related issues will significantly increase.
10. Community Emergency Response Teams (CERT) will become a more prominent part of public safety.

Professional Development

An emergency response plan is a dynamic process that must be kept up-to-date and consistent with an organization's operations and identified vulnerabilities. Therefore, security managers and supervisors must continually scan their internal and external environments in order to anticipate and plan for problems that could have an adverse impact on their organizations. One way of accomplishing this is for security managers and supervisors to read extensively, become familiar with the numerous emergency/disaster organizations and services available, and maintain an active network with other professionals in their field, as well as in allied disciplines. Two excellent emergency/disaster-related resources to consider are the annual Disaster Resource Guide,[37] as well as the many resources available from various federal, state, and local emergency management agencies.

It should be noted that FEMA, through the Emergency Management Institute (EMI), offers an Independent Study Program consisting of a series of self-paced courses. Each set of course materials includes practice exercises as well as a final examination. The average time of completion is 2–14 h, and individuals who score 75% or better are issued a certificate of completion by EMI. The courses are offered free of charge to those who qualify for enrollment. In addition, college credit may be obtained after successful completion of the courses.[38]

Summary

Both public and private sector organizations are becoming increasingly aware of the need to plan for the effective management of critical incidents. Security managers and supervisors are expected not only to prepare well-written plans for these events but also to have a plan in place that works and is understood by all. This requires that the plan be tested through training, thereby ensuring that responding personnel can immediately initiate emergency management operations. Besides helping to define the technical, interpersonal, and organizational dynamics of critical incident management, these activities assist emergency responders to become familiar with the roles and responsibilities of all personnel, including outside groups and agencies, at the scene of a critical incident.

Refer website http://www.ifpo.org for further information

End Notes

1. CSO Magazine Online, *CSO fundamentals: The ABC's of physical and IT convergence.* Retrieved March 2, 2007 from http://www.csoonline.com/fundamentals/abc_convergence.html.

2. Federal Emergency Management Agency, *A whole community approach to emergency management: Principles, themes, and pathways to success* (2011). Retrieved from: http://www.fema.gov/media-library-data/20130726-1813-25045-0649/whole_community_dec2011_2.pdf.

3. Sylves R. & Waugh W. Jr., *Disaster management in the U.S. and Canada* (Springfield, IL: Charles C. Thomas, 1996).

4. Paschall R., *Critical incident management* (Chicago, IL: The Office of International Criminal Justice, 1992).

5. Gigliotti R. & Jason R., *Emergency planning for maximum protection* (Boston, MA: Butterworth-Heinemann, (1991).

6. Department of Homeland Security, *The 2014 quadrennial homeland security review* (2014). Retrieved from: http://www.dhs.gov/sites/default/files/publications/2014-qhsr-final-508.pdf.

7. Joyce E. & Hurth L., "Booking your next disaster," *Security Management* 41(11) (1997): 47–50.

8. Reid K., "Testing murphy's law," *Security Management* 40(11) (1996): 77–78, 80–83.

9. Perry R. & Lindell M., *Emergency planning* (Hoboken, NJ: John Wiley & Sons, Inc., 2007).

10. Nudell M. & Antokol N., *The handbook for effective emergency management* (Lexington, MA: Lexington Books, 1988).

11. American Society for Industrial Security, Standing Committee on Disaster Management, *Emergency planning handbook*. (Dubuque, IA: Kendall/Hunt Publishing Company, 1994).

12. Federal Emergency Management Agency, *Incident command system training* (2008). Retrieved from: http://training.fema.gov/EMIWeb/IS/ICSResource/index.htm.

13. Woodworth B., *The incident command system: A tool for business recovery. Disaster Resource Guide* (Santa Ana, CA: Emergency Lifeline Corporation, 1998).

14. Dezelan L., "Incident management system," *Law and Order* 44(8), (Wilmette, IL: Hendon Inc., 1996).

15. Federal Emergency Management Agency, *Incident command system instructor guide* (Washington, D.C.: US Government Printing Office, 1995).

16. Arata M. Jr., "Finding order amidst the chaos," *Security Management* 39(9) (1995): 48–53.

17. Federal Emergency Management Agency, *Emergency management guide for business and industry.* (Washington, D.C.: US Government Printing Office, 2006).

18. Hawkes K. & Neal J., "Command performance," *Security Management* 42(11) (1998): 77–83.

19. Lukaszewski J., *Lukaszewski on crisis communications: What your CEO needs to know about reputation and crisis management* (Brookfield, CT: Rothstein Associates, Inc., (2013).

20. Gardner R., "Getting ahead of the headlines," *Security Management* 41(7) (1997): 115–19.

21. Nuss R., *Effective media crisis communication during a critical incident* (Winter Springs, FL: Nuss and Associates, Inc., 1997).

22. Gillepsi D., "Coordinating community resources," in *Emergency management: Principles and practice for local government* eds. T. Drabek & G. Hoetmer (Washington, D.C.: International City Management Association, 1991), 55–78.

23. Lindsay B.R., *Federal emergency management: A brief Introduction. CRS Report for Congress* (Washington, DC: Congressional Research Service, 2012).

24. Nuñez E., *Intervention strategies. Lecture presented for the Saint Leo University Criminal Justice Program Command School* (Tavares, FL: Lake County Sheriff's Office, 2009).

25. Miami-Dade Government, *EOC Activation Levels. Miami-Dade Fire Rescue* (October 12, 2012). Retrieved September 10, 2014, from http://www.miamidade.gov/fire/about-activation-levels.asp.

26. Federal Emergency Management Agency, *Guide for all-hazard emergency operations planning* (Washington, DC: US Government Printing Office, 1996).

27. Faggiano V., McNall J., & Gillespie T., *Critical incident management: A complete response guide* (Boca Raton, FL: CRC Press, 2011).

28. BowMac Educational Services, Inc., *Critical incident management instructor notebook* (Rochester, NY: Author, 1992).

29. Jenkins B., "The new age of terrorism," in *The McGraw-Hill homeland security handbook*, ed. D.G. Kamien (New York, NY: McGraw-Hill Companies, Inc., 2006), 117–130.

30. MIPT Terrorism Knowledge Base, (2007). Retrieved March 2, 2007 from http://www.tkb.org/.

31. Kean T.H., et al. *The 911 Commission report: Final report of the National Commission on Terrorist Attacks Upon the United States* (Authorized Edition) (New York, NY: W. W. Norton, 2004).

32. Stern J., *The ultimate terrorists* (Cambridge, MA: Harvard University Press, 1999).

33. MSA, *Worldview No. 25: U.S. intelligence concerned over al Qaeda threats* (2014). Retrieved May 21, 2014 from http://www.msasecurity.net/Portals/91068/docs/U.S.%20Intelligence%20Concerned%20Over%20al%20Qaeda%20Threats%2005.21.14.pdf.

34. Stewart S., *Stratfor Security weekly article: The recent lone wolf attacks: Trend or anomaly?* (2014). Retrieved October 30, 2014 from http://www.stratfor.com/weekly/recent-lone-wolf-attacks-trend-or-anomaly?topics=296.

35. Haddow G. & Bullock J., *Introduction to emergency management*, Second Edition (Burlington, MA: Butterworth-Heinemann, 2006).

36. Haddow G., Bullock J., & Coppola D., *Introduction to emergency management*, Fifth Edition (Burlington, MA: Butterworth-Heinemann, 2014).

37. Rainey K., *Disaster resource guide* (Santa Ana, CA: Emergency Lifeline Corporation, 2014).

38. Federal Emergency Management Agency, *Emergency Management Institute, independent study program* (2014). Retrieved from http://www.training.fema.gov/IS/.

Investigations

31

Managing Investigations

Robert A. Metscher

Introduction

Security professionals throughout the industry are responsible for managing investigations. Whether it is a complex loss investigation, interviewing unwanted visitors, or simply taking a report for a customer accident, there will be investigations that require monitoring to ensure completeness. After all, a poorly completed accident report could cost a company a significant amount should it lead to litigation. It is because of this often-concealed responsibility that security supervisors and managers should be capable of adequately managing investigations.

Key Management Points

Organizational Function and Role

Within every organization, an investigation function exists. This function may have developed out of need due to a response to an incident. This incident could have been an accident, employee complaint about a manager, significant theft, or network intrusion. In the smallest organizations, the function may be nothing more than an extension of the duties for one or more employees. As organizations grow, they may allocate resources for a dedicated investigative role. Over time, additional investigative functions may develop into dedicated roles.

Each organization employs their investigative capabilities somewhat differently. For instance, the organization may divide loss, accident, employee relations, and information system investigations across different departments or investigative units. The organization may also designate one investigative unit that conducts all investigations for other internal departments. Managers and supervisors should be aware what role their investigative teams fill within the organization. If the investigative function is divided between multiple entities, then coordinating with other investigators will prove valuable. First, it may reduce "turf" problems if investigations are conducted or extended into another group's normal domain. Second, and more important, this coordination will expand the range of skills and tools available within investigations.

Organizational Investigative Process

Just as each organization inherently has some sort of investigative function, it also has a process for investigations. In many instances, the process exists as little more than a

Security Supervision and Management. http://dx.doi.org/10.1016/B978-0-12-800113-4.00031-6

semi-agreed-upon series of actions. In more established investigative programs, the process may be rather formal. Any manager charged with overseeing investigations should develop a documented investigative process if one does not exist.

Investigations have several similarities to projects within an organization. Unlike regular operations, projects consist of a specific start and end point. They further have a defined scope or boundaries describing what is desired, what resources will be consumed, how long it should take, and what the deliverable should look like. Investigations also have clear start and end points, boundaries, and an expected deliverable at the end. The value of recognizing these similarities may be found in the management of the process, the measurement of activities involved, and a periodic review of investigative efforts to improve efficiency and effectiveness.

Just a little analysis of any prior investigations or discussions with stakeholders can yield at the very least a rudimentary series of investigative steps. This initial draft may be tested with hypothetical investigations or compared with previous investigations and refined as necessary. The documented process should be capable of showing each stage of the organization's investigative process from the time the initial lead is developed until it is formally disposed of or delivered to the final customer Figure 31.1. The construction of an organizational investigation process should include the communication and reporting that occur throughout the process, and at what point another department is notified of the investigation, or at what threshold a senior executive is informed.

Such a clear and documented process serves a few purposes. First, it provides investigators with guidance on conducting an investigation within the organization. Whether the investigator is new or seasoned, a documented process ensures some consistency with all investigations. If one investigator must pass an investigation to another investigator, having a documented process offers a frame of reference for the progress of the investigation. Second, the documented process provides senior management insight and reassurance that there is a process. Senior managers rarely have a strong understanding of any investigative methodologies, except those presented in the media or popular culture. Given the level of inaccuracy found in these sources, it makes sense to educate and reassure organizational decision makers. Lastly, a documented process demonstrates to external examiners the existence of a formal process. The existence of these reporting methods, such as anonymous telephone hotlines, may be required by regulation. Demonstration that each lead or report is documented, along with the process it follows, may reduce any additional inquiries concerning the validation of such a reporting program.

Key Management Skills

Communication

The skill of communication is somewhat vague, particularly in the context of being a manager or a supervisor. Security departments essentially have several different customers, including organizational management, employees, vendors, customers, and any member

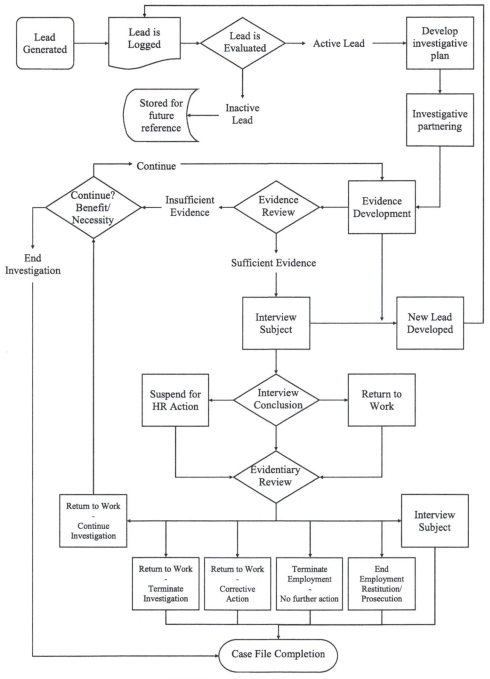

FIGURE 31.1 Investigation process.

of the public who may have a legitimate reason to be on the premises. Concise communication is necessary in three separate contexts to lay the foundation for successful information transfer within an organization. First, communication with the security staff or other personnel responsible for submitting documentation cannot be underrated, as it is these individuals that you must count on to accomplish the mission you are supervising. Second, communication with organizational management can be a tricky endeavor, often because security must distribute information to more than one department. Finally, communication with organization members—and in this case, through committees or when responding to a complaint—can make or break the overall security program. A quick look at these aspects may provide insight as to how they are approached and handled with respect to investigations. Whenever disseminating information to persons or groups outside the security department, it can be helpful to use an information dissemination checklist (given at the end of the chapter) to aid in organizing data, clarifying issues involved, and preventing the release of information or sources that could hinder future security operations.

Departmental

Within the security department, information should be shared fairly readily. Even so, there is a certain level of formality that must be maintained. Where that level exists is truly a departmental or organizational matter. If operations management software is not available, moving information from one shift to another can become a monumental task, which can be overcome with a pass-on book, a simple desk log (see Conclusion), or a formal email process. Oncoming members can verify that a note has been read by initialing the information. Simple desk logs can be useful in reviewing activity levels, and officers can also use them as a reference; these logs may be handwritten, or a hardcopy printout of the activity may be stored in an operations database. Memoranda should be reserved for formal communication pertaining mainly to personnel action issues and office policies, while incident information should be contained in the departmental report format or database. Open communication within the department is a key factor in bringing all available investigative resources into use, but security professionals must respect the need to compartmentalize some information. A clear example of this occurs when a complaint is made concerning the conduct of a member of the security department and the manager or supervisor must investigate the allegation. This information should be kept confidential and compartmentalized from other members of the security department.

Organizational Management

Investigations in general, and internal investigations specifically, can be extremely sensitive. Managers often want to know "everything" and they want to know it "now." If no policy exists, then the security supervisor must come to an agreement with those to whom he or she reports. It is not always prudent to share all current information; should a leak develop within management, then a relationship of continuous conflict will evolve. Also, members of management who are not versed in protocols used by a security department can hamper or significantly damage an investigation by demanding specific activities. However, it is also important to coordinate with operations management to compensate for any changes in staffing due interviews disrupting workflow, or suspensions/terminations. It is irresponsible and counter to being a responsible organizational manager to unnecessarily disrupt operations for the sake of the investigations. When possible, communicating with operational managers could avoid the problem. In addition, it is important to act impartially toward management decisions based on investigative conclusions. Investigators seek answers and explanations, not convictions or terminations. If an opinion or suggestion is solicited, then be forthright and logical; however, at all times, your statements should be from a professional standpoint.

Organizational Staff

If there are no current employee committees on security topics, then it may be worthwhile to organize one. It is through this type of involvement and communication with line employees that you, as the supervisor, can get a feel for how security services are perceived by the organization or customer. Acting on information gained in such meetings will greatly increase the security department's credibility. In providing quality service, this credibility will ultimately dictate the level of involvement in security matters by line employees. Put the minutes from these meetings in a monthly bulletin to further increase communication. If you, the supervisor, lack the time or informational content for a security bulletin, then consider sharing your information with a related department, such as safety or human resources. Whether delivered on paper, through email, or as a link to an internal web page, newsletters are a powerful tool, but technology is creating more robust options. Blogs (weblogs) may be used internally as a timely medium for communication. Instead of waiting for a monthly newsletter, a blog post can be made available each day or multiple times per week. It is also important to remember that the same technology can easily link to information on the web, such as articles, white papers, photographs, and video clips, to add some more interactive content to the traditional black-and-white paper newsletter. The more line employees that mention the security department's capabilities or consider it a resource, the more likely management will take notice and provide more resources.

Records Systems

The finest investigation in the world is all for naught if the information is not stored in an easily retrievable and logical manner. Consequently, it is the responsibility of the supervisor and manager to maintain or develop a strong filing system. Such a system must make accommodation for documents dealing with a wide variety of subject matter as well as various access levels. Even for computer-based filing of any kind—formal databases, spreadsheets, or reports in specific computer directories or folders—there are a few considerations to keep in mind.

Among the computer-based systems are quality investigation management software programs. These products and services specialize in offering one place to store all investigative records. This may include written documentation, scanned images of documents, video or specific images, as well notes associated with the investigation. As with many automation tools, it is essential to configure this program properly before deploying it into the operational environment. Poorly configured software may result in considerable unnecessary effort after the fact. However, a well-configured product or service can streamline the investigative documentation and reporting process, thereby driving a high level of efficiency.

Incident/Activity Numbering Practices

Numbering systems associated with cases, incidents, or activity reports can be a deciding factor in the quality of a filing system. Creativity is the key that allows a numbering system to provide quick reference information while remaining uncomplicated. Although the most simplistic system would be to just number incidents from 1 to 9999, little information about the activity involved can be ascertained without physically searching the file. On the other hand, using just the names of those involved as a means for sorting can raise issues of privacy and may cause complications for multiple incidents or similar names. A numbering system that contains some portion of the activity's date, location, type of incident/investigation, and a counting sequence can provide easy reference. With the increase in the use of computer reporting and storage systems, such numbers can allow for the sorting of databases to measure the levels of various types of occurrences.

For example, the case number 2007-0102-4-2-0123 could represent an event occurring on January 2, 2007 (2007-0102) at a specific location or zone (4), which was a customer accident (2); by a simple count, it was the 123rd event that year (0123). Such numbering systems provide a great deal of flexibility that can be directly translated into a tracking tool for activity monitoring, focusing audit efforts and lead development within investigations. Moreover, for larger case files, it is perfectly feasible to have a master incident number, such as the one above, and to further assign an additional number as a suffix (-1, -2, etc.) for each document within the case or file. This extra effort can be of great use should any information within the case file need to be specifically referenced in a later report. Furthermore, categories need not be limited to numerals, with just 10 options per digit; letters may be used as well, giving each digit a total of 36 potential categories of data. Also, by separating each segment of the incident number into individual spreadsheet cells or database fields, it becomes considerably easier to develop management reports by whatever data may be recorded.

Location of Files

Files should be carefully separated as much as space will allow. This aids in preventing information being accidentally "shared" or shared unnecessarily. Divisions of files can be based on the type of investigation involved, with internal investigations being the most sensitive and important to protect from unnecessary perusal. Realistically, members of the security staff who are not directly involved with the investigation do not need full access to internal files. However, they do need to know the type of activity an individual was conducting if they are to prevent it in the future. Security managers and supervisors should also carefully restrict access to internal training or personnel files maintained within the department. These are, in essence, partial mirrors of documents maintained in the human resource department and should be provided the same level of confidentiality.

Specific types of files that should be separated as much as possible include the following:

- Internal training files
- Security department activity tracking forms
- Customer accident reports
- Employee accident reports
- Internal investigation files
- External investigation files
- Equipment maintenance records
- Exception reports—new and old

Keep in mind that as a manager you are responsible for tracking people, their activity, and activity within the organization in general. It is important to share all the appropriate information with your staff, but to provide the same level of individual privacy as does a human resource department in dealing with security staff personnel records. It can be hard to keep some files locked away from your staff and it can cause some questions to be raised about trust, but these can be addressed from a standpoint of the nature of the information and an employee's expectation of privacy. Remember that your employees' curiosity is an important ingredient in preventing or investigating losses, but as their supervisor you must keep this in check with regards to personnel information.

Personnel Concerns

Assigning Investigators

Investigators are often assigned to investigations merely by being the first to answer the phone or arrive at a scene. Needless to say, this is certainly not the optimal method for matching skills to problems, but it may be the most reasonable under the circumstances. Ideally, in an environment with limited manpower, investigators should be equally capable to handle any investigation. This may very well be the case, but keep in mind that there can be factors within an investigation that warrant the attention of a person with a specific interest. When an individual is an investigator or dons the investigation "cap," it is his or her imagination, creativity, and most of all curiosity that ensures a successful outcome. Consequently, officers who are only concerned with the "what" and not the "why" may not be strong investigators and should be encouraged to be more inquisitive.

In a perfect world, a supervisor would have all the resources and could serve as a specialized investigator for any situation, but as a general rule this is not the case. Supervisors must be able to remove or add investigators to an investigation without overlooking the impact on those individuals involved. To avoid conflicts that result from reassigning investigators, supervisors should consider possibilities, such as using partnering or specializing/centralizing some activities.

It may be very difficult to maintain partner teams in an environment with normally limited resources, but it is possible for a supervisor to assign a secondary or investigative partner on a case-by-case basis. This allows the flexibility to place skills where they are best suited while avoiding problems caused by removing individuals from an investigation. This can also create an even distribution of extra work should an investigator leave the organization. With a fixed partner team, the termination of one partner will leave that individual's entire caseload on the other partner, which could become quite burdensome if these should require court appearances or liaisons with outside organizations. For those organizations not equipped with case management software, investigators should maintain an individual case log. In this situation, it is rather easy to redistribute a departing investigator's cases. Case logs should be designed to reflect the aspect of investigations that are choke points within your investigative process.

Another option available to supervisors is the designation of longer-term activities to one individual. For instance, if your organization has a problem with vandalism or more specifically "tagging," it may be more efficient to assign one officer to handle all these investigations. This does not mean that other officers cannot conduct the initial inquiry and photograph the evidence, but it does imply that the designated individual should track this activity and liaison with the appropriate outside agencies. This is a useful method for lateral promotions that give senior officers more responsibility and experience. This also assists in developing a complete and standardized reporting system for a particular type of activity.

Motivating, Tracking, and Evaluating Investigators

Ensuring that all programs are improved continuously is a clear role of management. Whether that improvement is found intentionally or through accidental experimentation, an improvement in overall efficiency or effectiveness cannot be ignored. Programs that continue to exist without improvement may very well be eliminated or absorbed by a more efficient program. When striving to improve a program continuously, it is essential to collect data about the activities involved. Investigations are no different, although many might argue that every investigation is unique. A number of activities that occur may be tracked. Some activities may not be tracked too accurately, and "pretty accurate" may be sufficient for establishing working metrics.

A short list of activities to track might include the following:

- Investigation start/end dates
- Investigation type and/or loss type (cash, property, etc.)
- Task times (research, video review, interviews, travel, reporting, etc.)
- Start date of employees causing losses
- First loss date of employees causing losses

From the list above, a number of metrics may be derived with limited effort:

- Total leads unresolved
- Total active investigations
- Total investigations by type
- Average work hours per investigation (this may be broken into smaller categories)

- Total losses identified or resolved
- Average travel time required per investigation
- Average tenure of employee causing losses
- Average loss per day for employees causing losses
- Any of the above by investigator compared to team

There are three primary goals for developing and utilizing data from the operations. One is to measure the performance of individuals and the team, and ultimately to improve the overall process. Knowing which investigator is more efficient, while still being thorough, may help develop improved practices. Identify time-consuming administrative tasks that may be automated or eliminated to provide investigators with more time for other tasks. Time is often the most precious resource, and it may be difficult to measure well. Eliminating mundane or perfunctory tasks also serves to improve morale. Another reason for data collection is to tell the story of the operation to those outside of the investigative role, like senior managers. Many outside have trouble visualizing what investigators do with their time. If their only other reference is popular culture, the life of an investigator looks pretty cool—and very inefficient. Giving organizational decision makers a clear image of the resources required by investigations is essential to demonstrating the value of the investigative function. Lastly, and maybe of greatest value, is to use the collected data to find solutions that eliminate investigations. Remember that investigations are typically directed at unexplained problems. If the data may predict what conditions drive these problems, then finding solutions to alter or eliminate these conditions is of real value. Consider being able to show senior management that a particular source of loss, such as a common injury or pilfered property, has been eliminated, thus creating a recurring savings for the organization.

When collecting, collating, and presenting data, be diligent in recognizing that it represents the effort of people. Much of it will represent the effort of the investigative role being managed. These individuals need to be recognized and reassured that their efforts are noticed. Many times, motivating individuals has less to do with showing them their shortcomings and more to do with recognizing their efforts and encouraging improvement. Treating investigators as professionals and expecting professional performance will assist with driving improvement. The backbone of a good investigation is not generally exciting, high-profile work—rather, it is laborious surveillance and endless document review. This can cause an investigator to cut corners or to become more cursory in their work. An ironhanded supervisor can impede investigations by stifling the necessary initiative within investigators, yet a passive supervisor would indirectly cause investigations to falter or become weaker. Motivational methods can be directly tied to supervisory tracking and evaluation efforts of investigators; however, the supervisor must know each member of the team and what motivates them as individuals. Efforts to motivate the individual separate from the team must be made as is necessary and to strengthen the investigator's tie to the team. There are a virtually limitless number of ways to motivate, and a supervisor must use some creativity and sound judgment when developing these efforts. Here are some useful tools to encourage, track, and evaluate an investigative team:

1. Develop a monthly or quarterly review/counseling program. These need not be long counseling sessions, but merely a 15- to 20-min session for each agent at the beginning or end of each month. The supervisor can write a few objectives and points of improvement for the investigator to reach within the month and identify topics that the agent will receive training on in that month. In turn, the agent can write concerns or suggestions about the points listed and any comments about the department's operations. This not only provides useful documentation to support an annual review, but it also gives the individual a feel for his or her overall performance. For the supervisor, this can offer valuable insight into the attitudes of the department and likely avenues for future motivation and improvement. It should also be noted that supervisors must be prepared to receive some fairly harsh criticism from their staff and that such criticism must be acted on but not retaliated against. If the staff is willing to write their criticisms, then they are concerned about their workplace and are not simply "punching the clock." This is positive and can be harnessed.

2. Hold well-defined meetings regularly. Keep these as short as possible by using a standard naming system that helps to identify the purpose. Names such as solution meetings, planning meetings, and organizational affairs meetings can create the right mindset prior to attendance. Limit the agenda to one or two topics per meeting and strive to keep these under 30 min in length. Never forget that meetings should ultimately increase productivity and not become a barrier. If necessary, designate an individual to act as a facilitator to prevent the meeting from being sidetracked.

3. Allow the staff some say in general operations. Foster an open environment that encourages suggestions that can streamline operations. Do not be afraid of using some of these ideas. By incorporating everyone's ideas, the staff gains a feeling of ownership of the department, and consequently their interest and concern will increase further. Improving investigative efficiency permits more investigations to be undertaken.

4. Develop a "lessons learned" journal. This can consist of a list of all cases with short entries describing the circumstances. Also include actions that should not be repeated (hence, lessons learned) as well as compliments for activities that are handled exceptionally well, and the agent's name. This provides a lasting acknowledgment of an investigator's achievements.

5. Various charts can be used to show progress and organize activity. Considering that investigations are similar to projects, many tools available within project management may be helpful for tracking and evaluating investigations. There are many free resources describing these tools; in addition, many free add-ons to software, such as for Microsoft Excel, are available. The investigation process discussed previously, as well as other processes, may be graphically represented in flowcharts. The wide variety of ways to graphically represent data, provides a means of gaining insight

into the overall investigation effort, as well as to specific aspects that may need improvement or refinement.

Investigation Issues

Initiating and Prioritizing Investigations

Investigations are initiated for many reasons and in diverse circumstances; however, the security supervisor is often directly responsible for those generated by exception reports, audits, or unique incidents. These investigations must be prioritized and worked into the department schedule. The security supervisor should seek to have a staff investigator handle much of the so-called "legwork" so as not to cause a slighting of supervisory duties. This in no way implies that the supervisor can simply pass off the work he or she just does not feel like doing, but instead offers training and experience opportunities for other investigators. Supervisors can use all investigations in which they are directly involved as an opportunity to mentor another experienced investigator.

Once an investigation has been initiated, lead sheets (which for practical purposes can be index cards) should be created for each lead that is discovered. These can then be systematically researched or divided up among agents for follow-up. These lead sheets should contain basic information about the investigation (incident number, type of incident, date, etc.) as well as the lead itself. Similar leads can be grouped onto the same sheet, as they will most likely be researched at the same time. Any information that is discovered from the lead should be briefly noted on the lead sheet; any evidence (receipts, photographs, vouchers, etc.) will most likely be kept separate from the lead sheet itself. Completely researched leads that provide no further leads can then be returned to the primary investigator or the case file, while any further leads can be noted on the original sheet before a new sheet is created and researched. Lead sheets are of unquestionable value when an investigation is paused or stopped, especially if the primary investigator leaves the organization during this time. In addition, this type of documentation allows the supervisor to quickly review investigations to determine the level of effort and effectiveness of an investigator.

Prioritizing investigations should not occupy more than a few minutes of a supervisor's time, but these decisions can have a great effect on the security department, the parent organization, and the public's opinion of the organization. Careful consideration must be given to high-profile incidents or when senior executives are implicated in wrongdoing. Failing to properly judge the amount of emotion behind an investigation or the opinions of organizational staff, management, and the public could cause serious embarrassment to the parent organization. Factors for prioritizing investigations include, but are not limited, to the following:

- Emotionally charged issues (i.e., workplace violence, hate crimes, stalking)
- High-profile incidents (media or prominent figure involved)
- Organizational management interest
- Total investigative resources available

- Total protection obligations
- Likeliness that activity investigated will cease quickly
- Number and quality of leads
- Solvability factors considered and reviewed
- Whether there is a witness.
- Whether the suspect can be named, located, described, or otherwise identified.
- Whether the suspect vehicle can be identified.
- Whether the stolen property is traceable.
- Whether there is clear motive present.
- Whether there is significant physical evidence present.
- Whether there is a positive report concerning physical evidence by a trained technician.
- Whether it is reasonable to conclude that the case may be solved by normal effort.
- Whether there are limited opportunities for anyone but the suspect to have clearly committed the crime.

Investigative priority is a frequently changing situation, with investigations being set aside for periods of time when necessary. A word of caution goes with this: avoid unnecessary shuffling of investigations. If an investigation is nearly complete, there is little reason to drop it simply because of an artificial priority system.

Investigative Follow-Up

The security supervisor is directly responsible for ensuring the completeness of case files and all documentation included within, and therefore must take several actions during and after an investigation. The supervisor must monitor progress, coach investigators, and be prepared to summarize the investigation to management on its completion. This is a tall order, but it is essential to building departmental credibility with organizational management and outside agencies.

As discussed previously, progress reporting can occur in several different ways, as well as being an inherent part of the coaching process. It is important to identify an investigator's improper actions as quickly as possible to prevent them from occurring again and to recognize proper actions in an equally timely fashion. One coaching method includes three steps on identifying the incorrect action. First, a positive activity is recognized and encouraged, followed by the incorrect actions being verbalized to the individual and the correct way explained or demonstrated. The positive reinforcement can be placed at the end, but it illustrates one way to correct behavior while avoiding an unconcerned presentation of the supervisor's interest. As the investigator is coached through the investigation, the progress can be easily monitored. It is with the more experienced investigators, who may not seek assistance often, that progress must be monitored through other techniques.

Another extremely important tool for coaching investigators is to play "devil's advocate." As long as the investigator knows that you are not attacking them personally or questioning their character in a real sense, this can be very useful and often quite fun.

Simply question all aspects of the investigator's report and try to put yourself in the shoes of a defense attorney. By attempting to find holes in the report or case and picking at them, it becomes possible to search for other information and aid the investigator in remembering the important aspects of the investigation. At the right time, this can be very enjoyable for all involved, and it is also useful for giving newer investigators a feel for questions they may be confronted with in the future. The operating terms here are informal and impersonal. In all ways, prevent the investigators from feeling that their peers are personally attacking them.

In addition to ensuring that parts of a case file are complete, take the time to make sure that the case file contains all of the appropriate parts. Develop checklists that aid in keeping files complete from start to finish. Checklists should seek to eliminate relevant problems through prevention rather than merely identifying the existence of a problem after the fact. For example, begin with the completeness of the prepared case file to ensure that all necessary forms are present at the start, which also serves as a reminder of the requirements of the various parts of the case file. Again, try to keep paperwork to a minimum, as it should contribute to the overall productivity rather than creating extraneous work. When using an electronic database, the reporting of many of these actions and requirements may be automated.

Once the investigator has completed the case file, the supervisor can write a summary of the case in the lessons learned journal. Later, this can be used as an executive summary in memos forwarded to organizational management. The summary should be extremely brief, identifying unique aspects of the case, actions taken, and the current disposition. The following is an example of such a summary:

> *Review of alarm access reports identified access activity at the satellite location outside of normal business hours. Subsequent surveillance and investigation identified a total of approximately $5,000 in potential loss through property theft, and identified newly hired manager John Smith's code as the one used for access. During the interview, Smith admitted to the theft of property totaling $5,000 from the satellite location as well as $2,300 in fraudulent invoices for undelivered services. Smith agreed to pay restitution in full and criminal charges have been filed. Total loss in this case is approximately $7,300. A new exception report has been developed to aid in a more timely identification of similar loss opportunities.*

After the case file is completed, the supervisor must review further aspects of the case, such as evidence preservation, and conduct one last review of all the paperwork. Proper preservation of evidence can prevent uncomfortable courtroom situations. The local prosecutor's office should be contacted and preservation practices reviewed. Any time that evidence may be maintained outside of a police evidence operation, it is likely that some questions will be raised about chain of custody and access. A little extra time spent on this matter may lend considerable credibility to one's department in the future. Moreover, it is important for the supervisor to review all cases with investigators prior to their court appearances. The investigators should do the same for the supervisor on the days of his or her appearances. The fact that court appearances can occur months or even years after an investigation is completed, makes this review and drilling of great importance. This is just another application of the old adage "a gallon of sweat in training is better than a pint of blood in battle." Keep this in mind when an investigator grumbles about the extra effort.

Information and Intelligence

Investigative supervisors are expected to have volumes of current information literally at their fingertips at any given time. They need to have a firm understanding of local and regional trends that could affect their organization. Collecting and maintaining information can be a very useful tool with little extra effort in the long run. Using a card filing system like the one mentioned earlier, it is possible to track activity in the vicinity of the organization, which quite possibly becomes the source of a lead in a later incident. When using an electronic database, trend reporting capabilities are considerably easier than with paper-based intelligence. Intelligence analysis software programs, such as the Analysts' Notebook by I2 (www.I2.com), are powerful tools for correlating data quickly.

Information can be located from a variety of open sources, such as newspapers, phone books, crisscross directories, and the web. Newspapers often have a section on police-reported incidents in the area. This can be of tremendous value in recognizing activity trends in the immediate area. When one is at a court appearance, it only makes sense to listen to the other cases being heard—if any activities relate to your organization, then make a note of this. It is possible that a robbery could occur in a mall parking lot while the tenant stores remain unaware of this activity. If your organization is located in or around the area, this information might be useful in determining staffing needs and informing employees. As with any information collection and storage function, it is important to regularly purge the records to maintain just those that will be useful.

Any information provided by an individual, whether solicited or not, must be carefully reviewed to determine credibility. The following questions represent the minimum scrutiny that such provided information should receive.

- Why did this event happen? At this particular time? At this location?
- Why is this information being provided to us? In this fashion? With this slant?
- Does this information stand up when compared to all other data available? Why or why not?
- Will another person or group benefit by others believing this information? How?

Always keep in mind that information may be false or incorrectly organized. This may be intentional or not; however, the result is the same. Investigators must seek to corroborate any information to ensure its accuracy.

Conclusion

Nearly all security supervisors are responsible for managing investigations of one type or another. An accident investigation in one organization may be as important as a theft investigation in another organization. It is the supervisor's responsibility to ensure that investigations are complete, accurate, timely, and meet the needs of the organization. Minutes spent preparing can save hours in unnecessary effort. Supervisors need to create strong investigation support measures such as filing, mentoring, and information storage to gain the greatest long-term value from the investigative process.

Information Dissemination Checklist

1. Check existing notes.
2. Update facts and data.
   - Identify information that, if leaked, would be detrimental to the intended security department activity and remove it being mentioned as much as possible.
3. Consult with other staff (other departments as appropriate).
4. Identify target audience.
   - Primary audience (e.g., president of operations)
   - Secondary audience (e.g., CEO or president and all other vice presidents)
5. Prepare key messages.
   - Does this activity directly affect operational efficiency?
   - Does this activity affect profitability?
   - Does this activity affect morale?
   - Could this activity have been largely prevented?
   - Are suggestions necessary to effectively prevent negative impacts of this activity?
6. Develop positioning statement.
7. Develop theme.
8. List examples or an analogy.
9. Provide quotes.
   - Sound or video bites
   - Excerpts from reports and written statements
10. Role-play potential questions and answers.

Refer website http://www.ifpo.org for further information

32

Interviewing

Brian D. Baker, Brion P. Gilbride

A foundation of the professional protection officer's duty rests on the ability to communicate with others on both an interpersonal and investigative level. The ability to communicate in an inquisitive and detail-oriented manner is a skill acquired through training and experience; it should not be viewed as procedural questioning and manual recording of responses. The ability to ask a question and to receive an answer is relatively simple form of communication with which everyone has experience. What distinguishes routine questioning from actual interviewing rests in the skill of the interviewer—the security professional. The skill of interviewing requires practice, and with practice comes experience. As with other skills, when interviewing is not practiced, the ability to verbally interact with others in an inquisitive fashion is weakened.

This chapter provides an overview and foundation regarding interviewing techniques that the security or protective services professional can use in a variety of situations. For supervisory personnel, this chapter will help identify ways to train and develop interviewing skills in their subordinates. Two groups of individuals that will also benefit are students and public service professionals who are seeking to transition into the professional security organization career. The material presented here will be useful to the student who may not have exposure to interviewing, as well as to the public service professional transitioning from a military or law enforcement role who seeks to understand the nuances of interviewing in the security or protective services context.

Interviewing Defined

Interviewing means different things to different people. The security or protective services professional is most often called upon to conduct a few primary types of interviews. The purpose of an interview is to obtain information that will resolve a problem or prevent a new problem. Most interviews conducted by security professionals fall into one of these three categories:

- Accidents and incidents, including crimes
- Risk assessment (prevention)
- Internal policy or compliance

Even though most security and protective services professionals do not possess arrest powers, police and private security have competing interests. Security overlaps the order maintenance function of policing, but the goals of security are the actual protection of people and assets on the property for or on behalf of the employer or client.[1] Some interviewing techniques used by law enforcement do not translate well into the private sector, but given the number of former law enforcement professionals working in the security or protective service professions, it is important for supervisors to understand which interviews their subordinates routinely conduct, as well as the techniques appropriate to each kind of interview.

What Interviewing Means to the Supervisor

Supervisors within a security organization should consider positive encouragement to all officers in order to evaluate their role as an investigator. Regardless of the actual title of the position, or type of uniform worn while on post, all officers should be encouraged to develop investigative skills, of which interviewing and communication should be a priority. Depending on the situation or the post orders and duties, the officer's duty, to have *verbal contact* with clients, visitors, or others, requires the need to develop professional rapport and a goal-oriented conversation to gain necessary information. As the officer gains experience and develops the skill of interviewing, promotion or recognition may follow both formally and informally within the organization, and the officer will be respected for his or her investigative ability.

Why the Skill Is Important

Everyone needs to have interviewing skills. Shyness, a spirit of intimidation, introversion, fear of public speaking—all of these supposed barriers can be overcome through encouragement and development of skill through experience. Likewise, the bold, extroverted, very serious, or "type A" personalities also need positive direction and practice to enhance their interviewing skills. The idea that an officer is a weak communicator or, alternatively, has too strong of a personality, are just a few of the obstacles to overcome for a good interview. Consider the importance of reaching a balance as an individual officer, and recognize that contact with other employees or the general public may already be tarnished by negative perceptions toward uniformed personnel in authority or in enforcement duty. Likewise, the supervisor should consider the importance of leadership in reaching a consistent balance of interviewing skills among the entire security team, thus helping overcome stereotypes, and images of abuse of authority and lack of trust.[2]

Officer/Supervisory Participation

It is important to note that a security officer or supervisor may not be involved in all aspects of an investigation and may only perform specific tasks, such as interviewing a specific individual about a specific matter. Nevertheless, that interviewer must be adequately briefed on the investigation to the extent that he or she may follow up on responses made by the individual during the interview. The interviewer, time permitting, should consider reviewing statements already taken.

Shyness

An area of academia that has considerable influence on the impact of interviewing (on the interviewer, interviewee, or both) is the study of shyness. Indiana State University's Shyness Research Institute offers several practical suggestions for overcoming shyness that translate ideally to the role of a security supervisor and security officer as an investigative interviewer. As a starting point, a supervisor should encourage officers to examine themselves and try to self-identify their level of introversion or extroversion, their shyness levels, and their learning styles. Beyond this, some of the Shyness Research Institute's recommendations to overcome shyness include the importance of limiting emotions and fears, developing conversation skills, treating others with courtesy and respect, and practicing talking to others in various settings.[3]

Demeanor

Two of the most important assets that the security officer has are appearance and attitude. After setting a physical and psychological presence for the interview, the communication of *who, what, when, where,* etc., is a process of conversation. Appearance may seem like an odd topic for a chapter about interviewing, but a security professional's dress, grooming, and physique all play a role in conveying authority and commanding presence.[4] What is said via a professional appearance is that the security professional takes his or her job seriously. If the security professional is perceived as sloppy in appearance, that perception may carry over into the interview and ultimately affect the quality or amount of information obtained.

Attitude is the companion of appearance. A security professional should present a posture of confidence and sincerity at all times. A security professional who is sometimes casual or engages in horseplay or unprofessional conversation will have a difficult time being taken seriously when duty requires it. Smiling and looking happy when appropriate is part of depicting a positive attitude. Eye contact and an erect stance, with a nonthreatening positioning of the hands, is also good practice in order to extend that confident appearance. Whereas, standing cross-legged or placing hands in one's pockets is perceived as inappropriate if one is trying to convey a professional demeanor. Likewise, the security officer who is overly stern, with fixed frown and deep stare, may be intimidating or make others uncomfortable.

It takes practice to gain control of appearance and attitude. Some organizations provide a limited number of uniforms, and this may require some part by the officer to launder and alter the uniform to fit properly. Physical fitness is also an integral part of this category, and the officer should try to exercise to improve health and ability; however, unless the security professional is required to exercise as part of an employment agreement, some will not. Physical fitness will help portray the perception of being capable and confident to others. The uniform should be appropriate to the physique of the officer and tailored to fit comfortably and modestly for both genders and all body types. Shoes and belt should be in good condition and polished. Again, this may take additional and even uncompensated practice by the officer.

Practicing a positive attitude begins with simple steps. A commitment to make eye contact with others is a great start, as is giving a smile, nod, or greeting when encountering the general public. Acknowledging others, according to the culture of your organization and including your geographic regional culture, whether addressing a person by his or her first name or "Mister," "Miss," or even "Sir," or "Ma'am." In the United States, there are regional variances on the approval of using the term "Ma'am"; for addressing females, it seems that use of "Miss" is more universally polite.[5]

When interviewing or interacting with others, practice giving a slight nod of the head to confirm that you are both hearing and understanding/comprehending what is being communicated. Tilt your head at a very slight angle left or right and change the frame of your lips and mouth if appropriate. Do not tilt your head to a significant angle that makes you appear overly sensitive or as though you are communicating with an emotional child. Simple and slight expressions and movements confirm to the subject that you are listening, paying attention, and understanding.[6]

Rapport

No discussion of interviewing is complete without mentioning rapport. Rapport, essentially, is the development of a relationship between the interviewer and the interviewee. When rapport is established, the interviewee is at ease with the interviewer and is readily answering questions in what is perceived as a truthful manner. People are generally pleasant to someone who is pleasant toward them. It is this simple idea that, when understood properly, makes a security professional an asset to the organization based on the ability to obtain reliable, accurate information in a timely fashion while simultaneously keeping most clients or customers pleased with the experience (or at least not angry about it).

How an interviewer establishes rapport with an interviewee and how long it takes to establish rapport are subject to a number of variables. The personality types of both the interviewer and interviewee play a role. It is easier for an interviewer to establish rapport when he or she comes across as truthful, sincere, and noticeably takes an interest in what the interviewee has to say. It is easier to establish rapport with an interviewee who is not in fear of being accused of something or being detained pending the arrival of law enforcement. If that interviewee has had positive experiences with the security professionals or law enforcement in the past, he or she is more likely to be at ease. If the interviewee just witnessed something and wants to be helpful, it should not be difficult to establish the rapport necessary to find out what happened.

Demeanor and shyness, which were discussed earlier, can impact the development or rapport with an interviewee. If the security professional conducting the interview assumes a "bladed" stance (e.g., does not signal openness to the interviewee) and if the interviewee has had military, law enforcement, or personal defense training, he or she may react according to their training and cease being cooperative. If the interviewer crosses their arms or rolls their eyes when the interviewee is answering a question, that may be interpreted as the security professional not believing the interviewee's answer, and the "eye roll" is generally considered disrespectful. No security professional, regardless of experience or training, will elicit information from someone who feels they are not respected. If the demeanor is not professional, the rapport will be minimal or nonexistent.

Shyness, which during an interview might be expressed by the security professional as an inability to make or maintain eye contact, can also affect rapport, as can using a lot of long ("pregnant") pauses between questions or a lot of "um," "uh," and other conversational fillers. As discussed earlier, security professionals are expected to project a certain amount of authority when dealing with clients or the public in general. If any of the behaviors described above are occurring during an interview, the subject being interviewed may conclude that the interviewer is either unsure of his or her authority, or that he or she lacks authority entirely. This can take rapport from the "excellent" range to "none at all" very quickly. Habits and demeanor generally must be controlled in order to create an environment where rapport will flourish.

A final element of rapport, which is related to demeanor in a way, is the use of language. Different people have differing commands of their native languages. A solid interviewer does not have to be eloquent or flowery, but that interviewer must be easily understood. In fact, many times the interviewer must gauge the language to use based on their perception of the language capabilities of the interviewee. In terms of maintaining a professional demeanor, the security professional should not use slang, profanity, jargon, or grammatically incorrect language when interacting with the public. When interviewing a subject, it is sometimes necessary to use slang, profanity, jargon, or grammatically incorrect language if that is what is necessary to be understood. Sometimes this is a cultural issue as well; if the interviewer and interviewee are of different cultures, their expectations may be different.

To give an example of how cultural differences affect rapport, consider the scenario of a security professional searching the baggage of people entering a facility accessed by the public, such as an office building with multiple tenants. If an individual from certain cultures is asked about whether there is any money in their baggage prior to the search—which is not an unusual question to ask because it gives the security professional the option to give the person their money to hold while the baggage search is completed—they may lie and tell the security professional that there is no money. The reason for this sometimes is that in the country this individual is from, the local police or customs authorities will take their money during a search and keep it. Therefore, the individual lies to the security professional searching the bag because they fear the security professional is asking so that they might take the money.

Why Language Is Important

Suppose that a review of closed-circuit television footage depicted an employee talking to a stranger outside the employee entrance of a facility and then later holding the door open for that stranger to enter. It would be immediately necessary to speak with that employee to determine why they allowed the stranger through the employee entrance and to understand for what circumstance or pretext. The security officer making contact with this employee should likewise be considerate and careful of the terminology used during the verbal communication. Although this investigative interview is inquisitive, the term "questioning" should not be used. In a polite and professional manner, the officer should merely ask to "speak with" the employee; the purpose is not to be accusatory as though this employee is a co-conspirator, but merely to portray this as a follow-up investigation.

In comparison to law enforcement, security organizations can successfully use soft language,[7] which has a better context to civilian, commercial, and industrial clients. Even in a hard security environment, such as a power plant or military installation, professional and considerate communications with others can translate into rapport and respect for the role of the security officer. In the jargon of the security organization, the officer interviews subjects, witnesses, victims, and employees. But in face-to-face contact with these individuals, the security officer "talks with" people who can "provide assistance" or who "may have information that is helpful" in explaining an incident. *There should be nothing in using the selection of softer terminology to infer that a security officer is vulnerable to deception, lacks authority within the organization, or is hindered from using assertive or challenging deportment when appropriate.* The level of the interview must rise to the skill of the officer and within the goal of the investigation, depending on the situation and the personality and rapport that is developed with the subject. Just as there are different models for handling employee discipline and conflict,[8] it is up to the supervisor to help empower officers to be willing to confront contradictions and to dig deeper for details that need investigation. Likewise, the interviewing officer is not the final judge. When, or if, an interview reaches conflict, the officer should have the skills to de-escalate or involve the supervisor as mediator.

Depending on the function of the security organization, officers and supervisors may have varying levels of interaction with law enforcement officials (liaison). Law enforcement officers are busy and in some areas may have limited experience and understanding of professional security. When reporting information to law enforcement, it is important that all communication be concise and directed to the immediate need. Do not use terminology that is in the jargon and lingo of the police field. Avoid talking the way you hear police officers on television or the movies. When it comes to the police officer's understanding of the security organization, the security officer is typically viewed as a responsible agent representing the property owner or client company; a police officer may be indifferent to the extent of interviewing skill or training that the security officer possesses. To effectively liaison with law enforcement, the security officer must present a verbally organized synopsis of the incident and explain plainly to the police officer why the police have been summoned.

Interviewing versus Interrogation

In popular culture, interrogation is a consequential activity that not only is associated with confessions of guilt, but it can also take on unpopular images of abuse and torture.

Interrogation can conjure movie depictions of bright lights in smoke-filled windowless rooms or urban legends of strong-arm tactics, torture, threats, and physical abuse. In some countries, abusive tactics used by law enforcement and government officials are quite real. They have no place in a professional security, law enforcement, or government organization.

Regardless of the purpose of the communication—whether with a witness, a victim, or a suspect—the interaction between this person and the security professional is an *interview*. There are different types of interviewing that fit different situations. For example, a security officer on patrol who encounters a stranger inside a perimeter fence may challenge that individual and conduct a brief investigative interview to determine the person's identity and their purpose for being on the property. Another security officer may respond to a motor vehicle accident that occurs in the parking lot of a shopping mall, thus also requiring an investigative interview with the drivers to complete an accident or incident report. In each of these examples, the purpose of the interview is to gather information that may be required for follow-up or future action by the security organization or by the client. In these general examples, the contact is *professional* (unemotional), *inquisitive* (questioning and conversational), and *limited* (concise) to the activity or incident immediately present.

During the investigative interview, if the investigating officer determines that there may be a violation or criminal offense occurring, this finding would still require the officer to act within the scope of his or her training, authority, and procedures of the security organization. In many cases, the officer would not have authority to physically detain the person and begin a course of accusatorial and confrontational questioning. Such questioning is referred to as a *custodial interrogation*[9]; by authority under the law, it is limited to law enforcement officers only. This is because whatever the subject states may be used in a criminal trial. Criminal procedure would dictate the rights and protections of the person being questioned, and information such as a confession of guilt would be formally used against the person in court. Security officers and protection agents not only typically lack the legal authority to conduct questioning in a detention setting, but often lack criminal procedure training and could find themselves in significant civil or criminal jeopardy if they violate another person's rights.

To avoid the risk of personal and organizational liability for violating the rights of others, the security organization should have clear procedures for investigative interviews and should train officers in the scope and limits of their jurisdiction and duties. In non–law enforcement scenarios, the right to detain a person for a criminal offense may be limited to the recovery of property (e.g., a retail theft detention) or a protective detention (e.g., use of a defensive force incident). The duration of the detention should be brief and limited to the time that a criminal suspect transitions over to a law enforcement officer for formal arrest and prosecution. In the security officer's incident report narrative, terminology should characterize the conversation and verbal communications as an *interview*, not as an interrogation.

Whether speaking or writing, the individuals who are interviewed by security officers should be referred to either formally or neutrally, but not in hostile or inferential terms.

Perhaps the most neutral term for an individual that could be relayed to a written report is the word: *subject*, or for unidentified individuals: *unknown subject* or *the individual*. When the identity of a person is known, the person's name should be used in all verbal and written reports. It is important to avoid police and law enforcement terminology when conducting or reporting on an interview; their terminology is specific to their unique situation. The security officer's information could appear in a number of places—the chief executive officer's desk, corporate counsel, a regulatory agency, a civil court, a criminal court, an administrative hearing, or some other venue. Knowing this, a stranger or a known trespasser, or a person positively identified or encountered in the commission of a crime or violation, should be neutrally referred to as a *subject*. Respect and simplicity should be common goals in the security organization.

The Administrative Interview

As in the examples above, there are different types of interviews. In many organizations, the security team conducts or participates in internal investigations, regulatory compliance, ethics compliance, or administrative investigations. These investigations also require interviews, but the nature of the interview may have a more limited scope and a more definitive purpose, as opposed to a witness interview or a field interview. The administrative interview is a fact-finding interview to report on a specific individual or course of conduct—the results of which are usually provided to a specific decision maker within the organization. One distinction between an investigative interview and an administrative interview is that the administrative interview may be used for either the employee's benefit (e.g., due diligence for job promotion) or detriment (e.g., termination for sexual harassment of another employee).

The security professional's role as a subject matter expert, and corporate resource for investigations, makes them a primary agent to support human resources departments, compliance officers, industrial safety professionals, corporate counsel, and operations executives with specific inquiries. Due to the civil, regulatory, or organizational nature of such investigations, it is imperative that any associated proceedings be void of inference or reference to criminal law or law enforcement-type terminology that might portray the employee as being involved in criminal wrongdoing. Most often, these interviews are introduced as "an administrative matter" or "an internal review."

Other types of administrative investigations may include sexual harassment, contract violations, bribery or improper influence, financial irregularities, environmental law violations, or other potential legal minefields. Such interviews may begin in an "administrative" and non-confrontational style, but depending on the findings and responses, the need for the investigator to expand on questioning and follow-up questions upon every statement becomes critical.

Some organizations require that an employee cooperate honestly with any administrative investigation. This means that it may be possible to discipline or even terminate an employee if they refuse to cooperate or if their response is found to be deceptive.

Regardless, in situations where termination is a possibility, the investigator may consider using a *voluntary release* or *consent to interview* form for the subject to sign. This release form may also contain language stating the company's policy on cooperating with administrative matters.

The administrative interview typically seeks to determine what someone knows and how they know it to be true or false. Because of potential legal issues involved with certain violations, particularly those that may lead to administrative or civil actions against the employee, the interviewer may request a written statement from the subject. This can serve as both verification and summary of the information. A subject who consents to an interview but refuses to provide a written statement may also be in violation of company policy regarding administrative investigations.

Due Diligence Investigations

Due diligence investigations are interesting because the information obtained through them can be used toward different outcomes—a person is promoted to a position of trust within the organization, or perhaps is declined a promotion based on potentially derogatory information. The objectives for risk management and suitability are clear. The company is within its rights to decide in the interests of the company to select a specific individual. Even so, some risk remains that an adversely impacted individual may challenge the company's decision through legal or regulatory action. The result of a professional internal investigation used to support an administrative decision may be called into court as part of the company's defense.

In due diligence investigations where the interviewers are checking references and verifying past experience, some interview questions are standard for each interview, lending consistency to the process. A proficient interviewer will identify appropriate follow-up questions and discussion throughout the interview. Often, the subject leads the investigator to other questions—some of which have similar observations and information, and others that might have distinctly different observations. Therefore, although a due diligence interview begins with asking specific questions of a specific individual for a specific purpose, the proficient interviewer can adjust the scope of their questioning and, by extension, the investigation itself.

Challenges for the Interviewer

There are a number of potential legal pitfalls that come into play when interviewing a witness, victim, or suspect. Security professionals should avoid having unobserved and closed-door contact with members of the opposite gender. If this situation is unavoidable, an audio/video recording should be made of the entire encounter and stored with the case file. In situations without witnesses or a recording that corroborates/verifies the interview, the security professional could make themselves vulnerable to accusations of inappropriate contact or even sexual harassment. By including security staff, a supervisor or manager, human resources representative, or any other individual unconnected to the interview or case in question, will help mitigate this vulnerability. Security managers should work to develop training and implement procedures to minimize this vulnerability to the greatest extent possible, while still enabling the security professional to perform effectively; however, this can be a difficult line to walk. In addition, documentation of the interview itself and any statements made or transcribed must be kept with the case file, along with the identity of any witnesses to the interview. These witnesses and documentation establish accountability should the company need to mount a defense against accusations of impropriety. Some organizations have begun using body-mounted cameras to record and help mitigate false claims against officers. Security managers should always consult corporate counsel before purchasing or utilizing these technologies.

Another potential impediment to a free and forthcoming interview can be peer pressure. Although it is natural for people to be curious about an incident and some may provide information or perspective, others will want to avoid any involvement or even the appearance of involvement. This may be due to cultural factors where it is shameful or distasteful to come into contact with authority figures. Should anyone attempt to involve themselves or otherwise interfere with an interview, the security supervisor should briefly interrupt the interview and politely request privacy and cooperation. It may be the case that the supervisor will have to halt the interview and identify a more secure location in which to finish, or the supervisor might even have to obtain contact information and conduct the interview at a later date and time. It is for these reasons that interviewing inside a vehicle or outside of a residence is often more conducive to interviewing. The priority should be on obtaining the best information possible as soon after the incident as possible, but sometimes reality interferes; when it does, the security supervisor must adapt.

Rudeness and indifference are another common challenge interviewers are faced with. Eye contact, staring, and blink rate are some of the easiest and noticeable signs that someone is disinterested and not paying attention. Sunglasses can often be a barrier to view eyes in a conversation; therefore, in an environment where there is any type of obstruction (sunglasses, shields, safety glasses, etc.) the other movements of the head and facial expressions can help to determine a positive attitude and active listening. Verbal responses—even if limited to "okay," "right," or "I'm following you"—are positive phrases that can encourage communication. Distractions such as text messaging or telephones should be avoided; with practice, these devices can be managed during interview settings. Consider past experiences when others were rude or conveyed disinterest—these can become some of the best lessons for how a security officer should not act if a good attitude is to be developed.

Things to Remember When Conducting an Interview

Interview in a discreet manner, privately and individually. Being discreet does not imply that interviews must always be done in closed rooms or inside a patrol vehicle.

Discreet refers more to a tone of voice and an air of privacy, where the communication is out of range of the ears of others, but not necessarily out of view.

There may be circumstances where an effective interview may involve asking a group of witnesses, "Can someone tell me what happened?" This leading question is useful for evoking a response and beginning the investigation. From there, the security professional can control the situation by obtaining names and contact information from some of the lead witnesses and quickly separating them. This is done so that the interviewees are not influenced by one another's responses to the security professional's questions. Inevitably, there are exceptions, for example, when the witnesses report similar observations, a group interview may be useful for getting immediate and urgent information.

The Impact of Note-Taking on the Interview Process

No matter how excellent one's interviewing skills are, it is not possible to remember everything that one or more people have said regarding an incident. The longer that the interview process takes, or the more people being interviewed, the more likely it becomes that the security professional might inadvertently confuse names, dates, details, or even one interviewee's story with another. Therefore, it is essential that the security professional develop note-taking skills in addition to the interviewing skills. The notes may become evidence in an administrative matter, civil suit, or criminal case via a subpoena, and this must be kept in mind at all times.

Notes are especially important at the beginning of an incident, as soon as the officer safety concerns have been addressed. The small details that might be jotted down for the inevitable report later are: the time a call was received; the condition of a victim; the time the security professional notified the local police; the time the security professional functioned as incident commander while waiting for the hazardous material team to arrive; or the time a suspect was physically restrained and handcuffed. (See Chapter 35: "The Importance of Report Writing to the Security Operation" for more information)

A unique dynamic occurs during an interview when the subject observes note-taking. An open writing pad or a pen in the investigator's hand can become a point of focus by some nervous subjects. Sometimes inexperienced investigators conducting an interview in a dictation form, ask questions and then write word for word the response given. Although there are certain interview formats, such as taking a sworn statement, where this approach might be appropriate, it is generally inflexible and does not readily support eliciting information from an interviewee.

If a complex administrative interview is conducted by one person who simultaneously asks questions and notes the answers, then that interviewer will be concentrating on writing words instead of listening. Conversely, the interviewee will be concentrating on what is being written instead of providing information. The interviewee may even gauge his or her answers based on what the security professional is perceived to be writing down—the idea being that either the interviewee will want to be helpful and therefore try to talk about things the interviewer appears interested in, based on the note-taking, or the interviewee wants to mislead the interviewer by steering the conversation elsewhere.

An experienced investigator may begin an interview by first writing down the subject's name and contact information, and then closing the notebook and proceeding with an open dialogue. The goal of interview questions should be consistent with the fundamentals of any investigation—the questions of *who, what, where, when, how,* and *why.* This is where having some familiarity with the case that involves the interviewee is essential. The investigator can quickly and concisely introduce his or her role and the purpose of the interview. Asking a very open question such as, "Tell me what happened here," is often enough to start a subject's dialogue. More skill and communication may be needed if the subject is hesitant or uncooperative. Without the notebook and pen in hand, the subject will more openly having a conversation than when they are "getting involved" or "making a statement." As the interview progresses, the subject may provide details such as the name of another witness, a date, or a description of some person or thing. At this point, the investigator can allow the subject to finish a sentence, stop him or her, and tell him that it is necessary to write this information down. When done properly, the interruption appears natural and does not disrupt any rapport that has developed. The investigator, upon gaining the interviewee's understanding of the reason for the interruption, may then finish taking the note(s), close the notebook, and continue. In this particular style, the investigator is focused on having the subject fully complete his or her statement.

After the initial round of interview questions has ended, the next step is for the investigator to retell the story he or she has just taken notes on and ask the interviewee to confirm or reiterate certain points. Also, at each point noted, the investigator can ask follow-up questions regarding the particular subject. This style allows the investigator to develop rapport by listening, and then gains the partnership of the subject as he or she "helps" with notes.

In more complex interview situations, such as an administrative interview, it may require a second person to serve as a note taker. The use of this second investigator to serve as note taker is to help to record details without distracting the flow and narrative of the subject. By positioning a note taker out of the direct line of sight of the subject, the interviewer and subject can maintain a conversation allowing the key facts to be quickly written down.

In some cases, the use of a recording device may take the place of the note taker; however, subjects may have an equally uncomfortable and inhibited reaction when a recording device is being used. Recorders may be useful for obtaining a formal statement, as in the case of an admission to a violation or a formal claim, but otherwise these devices may cause anxiety with both the subject and investigator, thus impeding a free-flowing narrative.

Conclusion

The importance of the interviewing role to the security professional generally cannot be understated. For those who supervise security professionals, it is imperative not only that the supervisor understand the different aspects of conducting an interview, but also that the supervisor be able to develop this ability in subordinates. Some interviews can be time-consuming, such as when the officer has to reinterview people because the security professional missed key information, failed to ask follow-up questions, or generally could not establish rapport. These situations will have a negative impact on an investigation—and consequently, the reputation of the security professional or even the organization for which he or she works.

Refer website http://www.ifpo.org for further information

End Notes

1. Rick Ruddell, Matthew O. Thomas, Ryan Patten. *Examining the Roles of the Police and Private Security Officers in Urban Social Control.* (International Journal of Police Science & Management, 10 October 2010) 13(1), Accessed April 9, 2015. Available: http://www.academia.edu/1115424/Examining_The_Roles_Of_The_Police_And_Private_Security_Officers_In_Urban_Social_Control.

2. David Weisburd, et al. *Police Attitudes Toward Abuse of Authority: Findings From a National Study* (Washington, DC: U.S. Department of Justice, National Institute of Justice, May 2000) Accessed April 9, 2015. Available: https://www.ncjrs.gov/pdffiles1/nij/181312.pdf.

3. *How Do I Overcome Shyness?* New Albany, IN: Indiana University – Southeast, Accessed April 9, 2015. Available: http://www.ius.edu/shyness/faq/how-do-i-overcome-shyness.html.

4. Lt. Chris J. Cole. *Improving Your Command Presence.* (San Diego, CA: Law Officer Magazine, 31 March, 2011) Accessed April 9, 2015. Available: http://www.lawofficer.com/article/tactics-and-weapons/improving-your-command-presenc.

5. Angier N. *The Politics of Polite.* (New York, NY: New York Times, 28 August, 2010) Accessed April 9, 2015. Available: http://www.nytimes.com/2010/08/29/weekinreview/29angier.html.

6. Straker D. *Head Body Language.* (Changing Minds.org, 11 November, 2007) Accessed April 9, 2015. Available: http://changingminds.org/techniques/body/parts_body_language/head_body_language.htm.

7. *Soft,* MacMillan Dictionary, Accessed April 9, 2015. Available: http://www.macmillandictionary.com/dictionary/american/soft#soft__6.

8. Chirasha V. *Management of Discipline for Good Performance: A Theoretical Perspective.* (Online: Online Journal of Social Sciences Research, 17 July, 2013) Accessed April 9, 2015. Available: http://onlineresearchjournals.org/JSS/pdf/2013/jul/Chirasha.pdf.

9. *Miranda Rights,* Miranda Rights.org. Accessed April 9, 2015. Available: http://www.mirandarights.org/custodialinterrogation.htm.

33

Introduction to Vehicle Searches

Brion P. Gilbride, Lawrence J. Fennelly, Marianna Perry

In the security profession, there is a need to maintain awareness of what is coming onto or what is leaving the premises. The vast majority of people who enter or depart the property will do so in a vehicle, whether a passenger vehicle or a commercial truck. Therefore, security officers should have an understanding of the staggering number of locations in which contraband might be hidden in a vehicle generally. Contraband can be items legal to have in possession, such as documents, equipment, or intellectual property; it can also be items that may not be legal, such as weapons or narcotics.

Security officers will be called upon to observe vehicles as they enter or depart, and in certain situations may be called upon to search all or part of a vehicle. Before security officers can be involved in a vehicle search, there are a number of considerations that must be addressed. First, and foremost, is whether or not the security officer has the legal authority to conduct a search. In most jurisdictions, *only* duly sworn law enforcement officers may conduct a search incident to arrest or seize any evidence of a crime that is found as a result of such a search. Although there are some jurisdictions that grant limited police powers to security officers in certain instances, this is highly unusual.

What a security officer may be authorized by law to do is to observe and record items in plain view. The term "plain view" means that an item must be visible from *outside* the vehicle, such as through an open door or a window. The officer cannot enter the vehicle; he or she should not even touch it. Any items in "plain view" should be recorded by camera if possible. If any illegal items are observed, security officers should immediately notify law enforcement, secure the area around the vehicle, and await further instruction from law enforcement officials. Bear in mind that security officers may be called upon to testify in a court of law about everything that occurred, especially prior to any law enforcement arriving on scene. Security officers should document the timeline of events from the initial contact through the notification to, and arrival of, law enforcement officials.

The few security officers who might possess the legal authority to enter a vehicle will be subject to the same prohibitions that sworn law enforcement officers are subject to—particularly with regard to probable cause. In a nutshell, *probable cause* for an arrest is defined as a reasonable basis for believing that a crime may have been committed; for a search, it is defined as the reasonable basis for believing that evidence of a crime is present in the specific location to be searched.[1] Any individual with police powers that include authority to search and/or arrest must receive intensive and ongoing training in these matters throughout their careers.

Security Supervision and Management. http://dx.doi.org/10.1016/B978-0-12-800113-4.00033-X

If a security officer is legally authorized to conduct a search of a vehicle at all, it will likely be in the form of a consent search. A consent search simply means that the person in control of the vehicle agrees to allow the security officer to search the vehicle. If the law and company policy permit these kinds of searches, security officers should obtain the consent in writing—and any consent form must be reviewed by legal counsel to ensure it is legally sound. If consent is refused, the only recourse security officers will likely have is to refuse the vehicle entry into the premises. If consent is revoked after initially being given, the security officers must cease any search immediately; again, their only recourse is to refuse the vehicle entry into the premises.

Even if security officers have consent to search a vehicle, or are authorized by law to do so, there are a number of other issues that must be addressed first. These issues include the following:

- What are the legal restrictions, if any, to conducting a consent search of a vehicle on private property?
- What are corporate policies and/or procedures regarding the search of vehicles on company property?
- Are employees, contractors, and/or visitors told that their vehicles are subject to searches if they enter the property? Is there signage posted at entry points and other conspicuous locations?
- If security officers are legally allowed to search a vehicle:
  - Will the vehicle need to be moved?
  - Where are the occupants while the search is conducted?
  - Are searches documented? If so, how, and by whom?
  - Do security officers understand that if they encounter a suspected illegal item, they must not touch or tamper with it in any way and immediately discontinue the search to notify law enforcement?
  - Are searches recorded on video?
  - If a vehicle is damaged during a search, is the company or the individual security officer liable for the damage?

The above list is by no means exhaustive. Depending on the nature of the facility or the nature of the search, other questions may also present themselves. Corporate counsel should be involved in any and all legal research and should review all policies and procedures relating to the searching of vehicles or property on company premises. Security officers and their supervisors must be fully cognizant of what their legal authorities are, as well as what authorities are granted them by the company. If the security managers do not work directly for the company but instead are contract employees, the contract must also incorporate these stipulations. If possible, the authority of the contract security officers should be spelled out in the contract as well as any policy or procedure documents.

The information provided in this chapter is intended to familiarize security staff with the different types of vehicles that may be encountered. Although not all-inclusive, it provides security officers with an awareness of some easy-to-use indicators for when they are examining a vehicle in plain view or conducting a consent search. Because all jurisdictions are not the same, when in doubt security officers should consult with law enforcement authorities if they suspect something untoward may be occurring. The information in this chapter is provided on the assumption that all legal requirements have been addressed and that security officers can conduct a search of the vehicle(s) in question.

An additional complication to any search situation will be the occupant(s) of the vehicle. If the security officer is merely going to examine the vehicle by walking around the exterior, looking through the windows or using a flashlight for illumination, the safest course would be to keep the occupants in the vehicle. This way, if an occupant intends something untoward, they will have to open a window or a door and that will allow precious seconds for the officer to react or seek cover. If, however, the search is more intensive, officer safety must determine the action taken. Occupants should wait near the area where the search is being conducted, but not so close that they can interfere with the search or distract the officer(s) conducting it. Additional officers should be stationed near the occupants to maintain control of them during the search. As the vast majority of searches involving security officers will include the consent of the occupants, this will often be a matter of asking the occupants to stand and wait. Not everyone will always be cooperative, however, and that must be taken into consideration as well. Every situation is different, and every facility allows for different measures to be taken. Some locations will be conducive to a vehicle search, and others will not.

Commercial Vehicles

The most common search situation security officers will encounter will be part of perimeter security. Specifically, it is the search of vehicles seeking to enter or depart the property. Simply put, there are two main types of vehicles that security staff will encounter at an entry point. One is passenger vehicles, such as cars, light trucks, and sport-utility vehicles, and the other is commercial trucks, which include box trucks, tractor/trailers, tankers, and flatbeds.

Before discussing how to search a commercial truck, the biggest question that must be asked is: "What is the purpose of the search"? Security officers cannot search a truck if they do not know what they are searching for or why they are searching for it. The "what" and the "why" will oftentimes dictate "how" the search will be conducted as well as "where" the search will be conducted and "who" will do the searching. Part of the answer to this big question lies in identifying the specific (and sometimes unique) threats to the facility.

If, for example, the primary concern is to detect explosives or a vehicle-borne improvised explosive device (IED), the search may not need to be intrusive and time-consuming. At some facilities, searching the outside of the commercial truck and into the trailer from the rear doors, or with nonintrusive equipment such as a truck X-ray or sniffing canine, will be sufficient and can be done relatively quickly. If the main concern is narcotics or weapons, the search may be more intrusive, which will cause the search to take longer and probably also present an officer safety concern depending on the response of the occupant(s). Truck drivers are accustomed to being stopped and searched, whether by the Department of Transportation officials for motor carrier safety, weigh stations, or customs inspections when crossing international borders, so they are less likely to protest. This does not mean that they will not protest an intrusive search.

Once the purpose of the search is determined, the "how" can be addressed. If the vehicle searches are being conducted at entry points, they need to be conducted in such a way as to not impede the movement of traffic on the roadway outside the facility. Either the search needs to be quick enough to maintain traffic flow, meaning that the search be will not-at-all thorough in the absence of nonintrusive inspection equipment, or the searches must be moved away from the entry point to another location. This would present a host of additional safety and logistical considerations, but it would allow for a more thorough search.

Security officers must always be cognizant of their physical safety. To search a commercial vehicle, whether cab/tractor or trailer, it will be necessary to climb up onto the truck and to climb back down afterward. The vast majority of truck searches will be conducted outside, regardless of the weather conditions. Falls are not unusual, particularly during inclement weather. For safety, security officers should use the "three-point contact" method. This method concerns maintaining two hands and one foot, or two feet and one hand, in contact with either the ground or the vehicle at all times. Compensation claims for falls are common, and the back and neck injuries that sometimes result are expensive both in terms of treatment and lost time.

Figure 33.1 features the tractor, or cab, of a truck. There are different configurations of these, but generally there will be seats for the driver and a passenger, and a sleeper cabin may be included in a space behind the driver and passenger seats. There will be an engine compartment in the front, fuel tanks, compartments to store tie-down chains and similar items, cables behind the sleeper that attach to the trailer, and other features. There are a number of natural voids in and around the tractor/cab that are large enough to permit concealing items of various sizes, particularly those with shapes that are malleable.

FIGURE 33.1 The tractor (cab).[2]

The exterior gas tank(s) are large enough to be a potential explosive threat, and items can be smuggled there as well if sufficiently protected from the fuel inside.

For a cursory search, a tractor/cab can be checked fairly quickly. Most cabs have hoods that lift toward the front of the truck, unlike the hood of a car that lifts up toward the rear. The hood itself usually includes the cowlings that cover the front wheels, and the entire front cover often moves as a single piece. This means that the entire engine compartment can be checked quickly. Note that items *can* be deep-concealed within the engine; however, accessing them would involve dismantling at least part of the engine—this would probably not be an immediate threat to a facility in most instances.

Behind the tractor/cab will typically be a trailer. Trailers come in a variety of types. Some are open while others are enclosed. Some are designed to hold liquids, whereas others designed to hold gases. Some are designed to hold dry solid goods. Consider the diagrams of trailers shown in Figures 33.2–33.4.

The flatbed trailer pictured in Figure 33.2 shows that searching one is fairly straightforward. A crossbar runs lengthwise underneath the flatbed itself, but this crossbar is actually two crossbars running parallel to each other. The spare tire is often stored in the significant void between the two crossbars, along with ladders, tie-down chains, and other equipment. This is an easy area to physically check and it is important because that void is not visible unless one ducks underneath the trailer. A substantial amount of contraband could fit in that void and be concealed by a tarpaulin or similar cover. Most truckers carry some kind of tarpaulin to use as a cover for loads or as padding, so it is an easy thing to overlook.

FIGURE 33.2 Flatbed trailer.[3]

FIGURE 33.3 Tanker.[4]

FIGURE 33.4 52-foot box trailer.[6]

The tanker pictured in Figure 33.3 is typical and can haul a variety of liquid and semiliquid products, ranging from pasteurized milk to unleaded gasoline. The tank itself may be single-walled or double-walled. It may have one continuous chamber or it may have several chambers. The chambers may all hold the same commodity or they may hold different commodities; this is typical of gasoline tankers, which might carry regular unleaded, mid-grade unleaded, and super unleaded in separate chambers on the same truck. Tankers generally can carry 11,000 US gallons or 42,000 liters of liquid.[5]

Tankers are much more difficult to search. In the absence of nonintrusive inspection equipment, there is really no way to physically see or examine inside the tank itself. On balance, it is also unsafe for anyone to open, enter, or hide items inside a loaded tanker. More likely a concealed item will be on the tanker chassis itself. Some tankers have tubes on the side of the trailer bed in the void between the curve of the tank and the bed itself. These tubes often hold the hoses and connectors necessary to pump out the contents of the tanker. These tubes, for example, are also a void large enough to contain a significant amount of contraband or a device capable of detonating a tanker full of fuel.

There are numerous and significant safety issues involved; even if the cargo is nontoxic, there are confined-space issues. To safely search a tanker could potentially involve breathing apparatus, specialized suits, or other equipment that is most likely expensive to obtain and maintain and has significant training obligations associated to it. If the cargo is hazardous, there are additional considerations. The threat in these situations is not merely the ability to conceal items on the trailer or the exterior of the tanker; the threat sometimes comes from the contents of the tanker itself. These contents cannot necessarily be concealed, as any hazardous material must be placarded in a way that identifies that the contents are hazardous, and in what way. An additional and not often considered threat, is that a tanker containing a food product could have something introduced *into* it rather than something being concealed on or inside the tanker.

Although the flatbed and tanker trailers are common around the world, the trailer that security personnel will see most often is the 52-foot box trailer, hereafter referred to as the 52-ft, and shown in Figure 33.4). Typically, this trailer can hold 60,000 lbs. or 27,000 kg of goods.[7] The primary challenge concerning the 52-ft is that threats can be concealed within the trailer just as easily as on the chassis it sits upon. These trailers can hold nearly anything, from bulk product to palletized goods to boxes. Some of these products can be physically searched without much difficulty beyond climbing into the trailer. Others can be "tunneled," where the searcher can remove items from in front and push them out behind themselves to reach a particular location in the trailer.

A concealment method not unique to the 52-ft but difficult to spot is the false wall. A false wall is placed at the end of the trailer closest to the tractor/cab. The false wall is set in a few feet from the actual trailer wall and mimics the style (often plywood) and the braces. If done properly, where the screws in the braces and the condition of the plywood match the other parts of the trailer, it is difficult to spot without a laser range-finder. A 2-foot gap created by a false wall in a 6-foot high trailer leaves space for a significant amount of weapons, narcotics, or any other contraband.

Seals

Although applicable to various types of trucks, most often seals are found on 52-ft trailers and shipping containers being transported on a trailer chassis. Seals are typically plastic or metal, and their purpose is to demonstrate for anyone checking that a trailer door has not been opened since the seal was put on. Seals are often numbered, and the number is used as a check that one seal has not been substituted for another. Figures 33.5–33.7 show three examples of commonly used seals. In simple terms, the bolt seat is the most difficult to remove and requires bolt cutters. The plastic and cable seals can be cut with wire cutters or other smaller cutting implements.

FIGURE 33.5 Bolt seal.[8]

FIGURE 33.6 Plastic seal.[9]

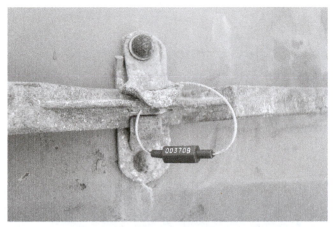

FIGURE 33.7 Cable seal.[10]

It is not unusual for security officers to verify that seals are intact or that the seal number on the seal matches the number on the paperwork. Certain government programs, such as the US Customs–Trade Partnership Against Terrorism (C-TPAT), encourage seal verification and motor carriers agree to consent searches as part of their participation in the program. It is these searches that are typically conducted by security officers.

Passenger Vehicles

Passenger vehicles are ubiquitous in modern society. Security officers will encounter them each and every day. The threat presented by a passenger vehicle varies depending on the environment. The officer safety issues presented also vary for the simple reason that passenger cars typically can hold more people and offer more entry/exit points for them. Nevertheless, security officers will be called upon to deal with passenger vehicles every day.

Passenger vehicles, regardless of size, are made up of an engine compartment and hood in the front, with the passenger cabin directly behind. The passenger cabin will have a minimum of one seat but may have several. There may be two entry doors or four, with storage space beneath the floors or under the seats. The vehicle may have a separate, inaccessible trunk or perhaps the rear seat(s) fold down to provide access. The vehicle may be a sport-utility vehicle (SUV) with no separate trunk/cargo space. The spare tire may be on the inside or on the outside. There are natural voids depending on the design of the passenger vehicle, and there are thousands of designs—remember that there are 20 years' worth of vehicle makes and models that are still being driven regularly, as well as older or more obscure makes and models.

Figures 33.8 and 33.9 show cutaway images of two passenger vehicles: a Volkswagen Scirocco and a Honda Ridgeline. In these cutaway images, it is possible to infer where some voids exist in these two vehicles. Inside the fenders above the tires, for example, are

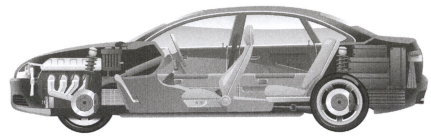

FIGURE 33.8 Car-Cutaway.[11]

FIGURE 33.9 Car-Cutaway.[13]

places where items can be hidden that would not be too difficult to access. Although difficult to see in Figure 33.8, the different shapes, sizes, and locations of natural voids are readily apparent in Figure 33.9. Fenders, panels, carpets, or other obstructions may have to be removed to get to them, but they are there.

The removal of fenders, panels, carpets, or other obstructions is where the security officer's attention should be focused, even during a cursory search. Places where carpets appear to have been removed and put back are something to watch for as the carpet can never quite be put back in place the same way. Therefore, places where the carpet appears to be pulled up may indicate that removal was done to access a void beneath it. In many newer-model vehicles, the panels are put in with plastic pegs, not screws. Pegs are easily lost and/or damaged. If marks around the pegs suggest that they have been pried off, it may have been to access a void on the other side. If screws or bolts holding a fender in place look unusually clean, it may be that tools used to remove them knocked residual dirt/grime off or scratched them. Remember that it is entirely possible that screws and

FIGURE 33.10 Interior view of the front driver and passenger seats in a passenger car.[14]

pegs are moved for legitimate repair-related reasons. Treat these as indicators—one indicator may be nothing, but two indicators might be a sign of someone deliberately manipulating the interior of the vehicle.

The discussion about voids and obstructions has not differentiated between the exterior of the vehicle and the interior. Consider Figure 33.10, which shows the area in and around the front driver's and passenger's seats. The security officer can sometimes search these areas without disassembling the vehicle:

1. *The seats.* The seats provide a decently sized area in which to hide contraband, firearms, etc. Items can be fitted around the padding or the padding moved and replaced to accommodate these items. Add-on seat-covers can further camouflage any openings made in the seat to hide items. The best way to search these is to push on them or even sit on them. Does the seat feel like a car seat should?
2. *The doors.* The only thing between the interior door panel and the exterior of the door is the hardware that operates the window and the void that holds the window when it is lowered. This is also a sizable space in which to hide contraband. Flat items such as currency bundles are ideal for the door-panel spaces. Two easy ways to check the door without disassembling it is to first lower the window. If the window cannot be lowered or lowered completely, something might be interfering with the window or the arm that lowers/raises it. If the window does lower, shining a flashlight into the void at the top of the door that the window moves up and down through, should make most of the void visible.
3. *The dashboard center console.* The center console is more common now than it used to be. This is the area that houses the environmental controls and car radio, and often has spaces to hold sunglasses and other accoutrements. There is generally space behind the console to hide items, but it is difficult to reach. The spaces on the sides of the console,

where it touches the carpets in front of the driver's and passenger's seats, should be examined to see if any of the fasteners holding the console in place have been tampered with or if the carpet that touches the sides of the console has been moved.

4. *The vents.* The vents include not only the vents in the center of the console but the vents on the far sides of the dashboard (next to the doors) as well. The significance of the vents is derived from the ability to sniff the air after turning on the cold or warm air regulator. If marijuana is hidden behind the vents, for example, the smell will be detectable.

5. *The dashboard.* Much of the dashboard, particularly on the passenger side once the airbag is removed, is a void. Although it is possible to see into parts of the dashboard from the vents or the glove compartment, to thoroughly search it the dashboard must be disassembled. As with the center console, the security officer might look for areas where the dashboard has previously been disassembled, such as the fasteners or scratch marks.

Examples of Concealment

There are many places to hide contraband inside any vehicle. Locations and indicators have been discussed. This section presents some images of concealed items. Figure 33.11 shows packages concealed in the backing of a fold-down rear vehicle seat. Figure 33.12 shows a firearm concealed in the center console/armrest. Figure 33.13 shows packages hidden in the rear fender of a Jeep Liberty. Figure 33.14 shows cigarettes concealed inside a tire.

Tires

Be cognizant of the tires. Figure 33.14 gives a sense of just how much can be stuffed into a vehicle tire. SUV and light truck tires can hold more, and commercial truck tires are bigger

FIGURE 33.11 Packages behind rear seat.[15]

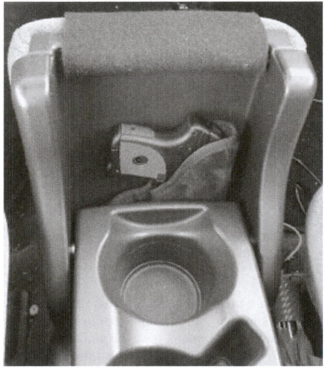

FIGURE 33.12 Firearm in center console.[16]

FIGURE 33.13 Packages in rear fender.[17]

FIGURE 33.14 Cigarettes inside tire.[18]

still—tires are a common place to hide items. A potential advantage for the security officer is that it is sometimes obvious that a tire has been tampered with. However, if a smuggler has access to tire mounting equipment, it will be much harder to tell; the equipment makes it possible to remove the tire from the rim, load the tire, and return it to the rim. Also, it is not always easy to find or access some tires. For passenger cars, trucks, and SUVs, there will be four tires. The size of the tire varies considerably between a smart car and a Chevrolet Tahoe.

If searching a commercial truck, notice that there are typically four tires on each axle at the rear of the trailer instead of two. The outer two tires are visible just by walking around the trailer. The inner two tires, however, are only visible when they touch the ground, and can only be seen from certain angles. Figure 33.15 gives an idea of how this looks.

Certain kinds of commercial trucks, such as dump trucks or trucks that haul heavy loads of rock or gravel, have an extra axle where the tires do not always touch the ground. It is typically near the center of the trailer.

Spare tires, for both commercial trucks and passenger vehicles, are important for security officers to examine. Spare tires are also not always easy to find. On commercial trucks, they are typically found beneath the trailer, either in a side compartment or hanging from a bracket. There may be more than one spare tire as well. On passenger cars, they are either inside a natural void in the trunk, or they are on the exterior of certain cars such as Jeeps, Humvees, or Toyota's FJ Cruiser.

Spare tires are easier to examine because, in most cases, the security officer can easily remove the spare tire and replace it. There are two simple methods one can use to get a sense of whether a tire might have contraband concealed within it. One way is to take the spare tire and drop it from a height of 4–5 feet in the same position it would be if it was on the axle. It should bounce consistently, like a ball. If it does not, or if the bounce is weak or

FIGURE 33.15 Tractor/trailer with rear axles visible.[19]

lopsided, there *may* be items in the tire. Another option is to "tap" the tire by placing one hand on the sidewall of the tire and using a small hammer or flashlight to tap the opposite sidewall. If the vibrations are felt by the hand touching the tire, then that area of the tire has nothing but air. If the vibrations are extremely weak or not felt at all, it may be that something is inside the tire at that location.

A Note on Gas Tanks

Gas tanks can have items concealed in them that will not interfere with the operation of the vehicle. It is very dangerous to search or remove a gas tank without proper training and safety precautions. It is possible, with the right equipment, to be able to remotely look into the filler cap and see into the gas tank safely, using a particular kind of scope.

A Real-Life Case of an Improvised Explosive Device in a Vehicle

Figure 33.16 is an image the US Federal Bureau of Investigation made for the case of Faisal Shahzad, the man who parked a car bomb in New York City's Times Square in 2010. The car bomb, fortunately, failed to detonate and Shahzad was arrested. The vehicle in question was a 1993 Nissan Pathfinder. In the rear seats and cargo area of the Pathfinder, there were two 5-gallon gasoline cans, a metal container holding 250 pounds of a urea-based

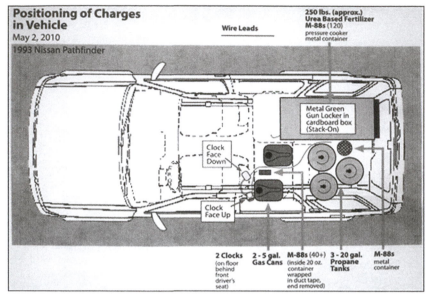

Positioning of Charges in Vehicle
May 2, 2010
1993 Nissan Pathfinder

Wire Leads

250 lbs. (approx.)
Urea Based Fertilizer
M-88s (120)
pressure cooker
metal container

Metal Green
Gun Locker in
cardboard box
(Stack-On)

Clock
Face
Down

Clock
Face Up

2 Clocks
(on floor
behind
front
driver's
seat)

2 - 5 gal.
Gas Cans

M-88s (40+)
(inside 20 oz.
container
wrapped
in duct tape,
end removed)

3 - 20 gal.
Propane
Tanks

M-88s
metal
container

FIGURE 33.16 Faisal Shahzad's Nissan Pathfinder.[20]

fertilizer, three 20-gallon propane tanks, a small container holding M-80 fireworks (equal to one-quarter-stick of dynamite), and wires running from the fertilizer and propane tanks to two clocks in the rear seat area. None of these items were concealed; if the windows were not heavily tinted, the items would have been visible to anyone who looked in the window. The weight of all this was under 500 pounds, well below the maximum load for a Nissan Pathfinder.[21]

Documentation

Any searches or inventory of property that are conducted on vehicles should be logged. For routine or cursory searches, it may not be necessary to write an incident report, but managers should maintain a log indicating the date and time the search occurred, who performed the search, the license plate(s) of the vehicle, and the driver of the vehicle. For commercial vehicles, the information should also include a summary of what cargo (if any) is aboard, any seal numbers, and whether the seals were broken to inspect the cargo.

For situations where more intensive searches are being conducted, such as campus security officers conducting a consent search of a vehicle parked on university property, a full incident report should be written. This report should include the reason(s) for the search, what was searched, who participated, the date and time that the search occurred, the identity of the occupant (or occupants), who consented to the search, how they consented to the search (verbal, written) and at what time this consent was granted. This is all in addition to identifying what, if anything, was found during the search. As previously mentioned, it is possible that the security officer(s) who conducted the search will have to testify in a legal proceeding regarding the events surrounding a search, and any report should be written with this in mind.

Conclusion

Vehicle searches are a legally complex activity that, in some security disciplines, are something security officers are periodically called upon to do. In those situations, it is imperative that security officers and their supervisors know exactly what they can and cannot do, legally or by company policy, with regards to searching vehicles on their property. If security officers are authorized to conduct vehicle searches, it is important to understand how to conduct them safely. The materials discussed in this chapter will help in that understanding, but the most effective thing a security officer can do is to request training on the legal ramifications involved. If vehicle searches are part of the security officer's duties, he or she must maintain proficiency. Even something as simple as using a company car for practice would be beneficial.

Remember: When in doubt, reach out to local law enforcement and seek guidance. Failure to perform due diligence in these matters could impede a criminal case and possibly subject the company or the security officers to legal liability. Reaching out to local law enforcement contacts for tips on concealment methods is also a prudent idea as vehicles and concealment methods are always changing.

Refer website http://www.ifpo.org for further information

End Notes

1. *Probable Cause* (Ithaca, NY: Cornell University, Legal Information Institute, Date Unknown), accessed January 25, 2015. Available: http://www.law.cornell.edu/wex/probable_cause.

2. *191-376-5141 – Search a Commercial Vehicle for Explosive Devices or Prohibited Items at an Installation Access Control Point* (Location Unknown: QuinStreet Inc., Date Unknown), accessed December 13, 2014. Available: http://www.armystudyguide.com/content/SMCT_CTT_Tasks/Skill_Level_1/1913765141-search-a-comme.shtml.

3. *191-376-5141-1 – Search a Commercial Vehicle for Explosive Devices or Prohibited Items at an Installation Access Control Point.*

4. *191-376-5141 – Search a Commercial Vehicle for Explosive Devices or Prohibited Items at an Installation Access Control Point.*

5. Gilbride B. and MacDougall A., *Links in the Chain: Vulnerabilities Between The Points* (Alexandria, VA: ASIS International, Supply Chain & Transportation Security Council, 2013), 3.

6. See note 4 above.

7. See note 5 above.

8. *Bolt Seal – Model QUEENSEAL High Security* (Pembroke Pines, FL: American Seals, Date Unknown), accessed January 23, 2015. Available: http://www.americanseals.com/bolt-seals/bolt-seal-model-queen-seal-high-security.

9. *Pull Tight Cable Seal – Model JoeGuard Series 10* (Pembroke Pines, FL: American Seals, Date Unknown), accessed January 23, 2015. Available: http://www.americanseals.com/cable-seals/pull-tight-cable-seal-model-joeguard-series-10-inch.

10. *Steel Cable Seals* (Punta Gorda, FL: Secure Cargo Alliance, 2013), accessed January 23, 2015. Available: https://www.securecargo.org/content/steel-cable-seals.

11. *Volkswagen Scirocco Mk1 Cutaway Diagram* (Location Unknown: The Car Hobbby, October 30, 2012), accessed: January 23, 2015. Available: http://thecarhobby.blogspot.com/2012/10/scirocco-mk1-cutaway-diagram.html.

12. *Archives for the 'Vehicles Engine Diagram' Category* (Location Unknown: Information2Share, August 26, 2011), accessed January 23, 2015. Available: https://information2share.wordpress.com/category/vehicles/vehicles-engine-diagram/.

13. *Show History* (Chicago, IL: Chicago Auto Show, 2005), accessed January 24, 2015. Available: http://www.chicagoautoshow.com/history/2005/.

14. Koerner B. I., *Alfred Anaya Put Secret Compartments in Cars So the DEA Put Him in Prison* (New York, NY: Wired, March 19, 2013), accessed December 13, 2014. Available: http://www.wired.com/2013/03/alfred-anaya/all/.

15. *Proactive Drug Interdiction and Vehicle Concealment* (Easthampton, MA: SRR Training, 2005), accessed December 13, 2014. Available: http://www.srrtraining.com/ProactiveDrugInterdictionandVehicleConcealment.html.

16. *Concealed Carry in the Car – Ruger LCP in My Chevy Impala* (Location Unknown: GunDetails.com, November 16, 2012), accessed December 13, 2014. Available: http://gundetails.com/concealed-carry-in-the-car-my-set-up/.

17. *CBP Officers Arrest Mother of Four With Marijuana Load at El Paso Port* (Washington, DC: U.S. Customs & Border Protection, July 18, 2011), accessed December 13, 2014. Available: http://www.cbp.gov/newsroom/local-media-release/2011-07-18-040000/cbp-officers-arrest-mother-four-marijuana-load-el.

18. McDermott K., *Smugglers' Secret Tricks to Send Cigarettes Into Europe: Pictures Reveal Belarusian Gangs Fit Cars With 'Smoke Holes' Where Dozens of Fakes Can Be Stashed* (London, UK: The Daily Mail, April 10, 2013), accessed January 24, 2015. Available: http://www.dailymail.co.uk/news/article-2306779/Smugglers-secret-tricks-send-cigarettes-Europe-Pictures-reveal-Belarusian-gangs-fit-cars-smoke-holes-dozens-fakes-stashed.html.

19. *How to Succeed in the J. B. Hunt Lease Purchase Program* (Location Unknown: The Keystruckers, September 5, 2010), accessed January 24, 2015. Available: http://thekeystruckers.com/2010/09/05/how-to-succeed-in-the-j-b-hunt-lease-purchase-program/.

20. *The Times Square Case: Terror Suspect Arrested; Case Continues* (Washington, DC: Federal Bureau of Investigation, May 4, 2010), accessed January 24, 2015. Available: http://www.fbi.gov/news/stories/2010/may/timessquare_050410/times-square-case.

21. The Times Square Case: Terror Suspect Arrested; Case Continues.

34

Crime Scene Response and Evidence Collection

Andrew R. Reitnauer

"Every contact leaves a trace."—Edmond Locard (1934)[1]

"Wherever he steps, whatever he touches, whatever he leaves, even unconsciously, will serve as a silent witness against him. Not only his fingerprints or his footprints, but his hair, the fibers from his clothes, the glass he breaks, the tool mark he leaves, the paint he scratches, the blood or semen he deposits or collects. All of these and more, bear mute witness against him. This is evidence that does not forget. It is not confused by the excitement of the moment. It is not absent because human witnesses are. It is factual evidence. Physical evidence cannot be wrong, it cannot perjure itself, and it cannot be wholly absent. Only human failure to find it, study and understand it, can diminish its value." (Kirk, 1953)[2]

Editor's Note:

Crime scene response and evidence collection is an integral part of the investigative process that requires specialized training and knowledge. Security personnel must at all times be cognizant of the laws governing their jurisdiction with regard to crime scene and evidence preservation/collection guidelines. Security departments should have a written procedure detailing the responsibilities and legal limitations applicable to their staff for all evidence-related matters, and any questions should be directed to local law enforcement or a local government attorney's office.

Introduction

The two quotes at the opening of this chapter are primary examples of why we conduct a crime scene investigation within the criminal justice field. The first quote was given by Edmond Locard, a French forensic investigator spanning the 19th and 20th centuries. All of forensic science is based upon the premise that when a person enters a scene, no matter the timeframe, they will leave something behind and remove something from the scene. In other words, there will be a transfer of substance, allowing for a connection to be made. As stated by Paul Kirk in the second quote, the common inference is that fingerprints, tire and foot impressions, firearm evidence, and biological material get transferred. The analysis of this evidence will be performed by a trained forensic scientist in a controlled laboratory

Security Supervision and Management. http://dx.doi.org/10.1016/B978-0-12-800113-4.00034-1

environment. However, the actions of the first responders will dictate the recovery and integrity of the evidence throughout the investigation process.

The role of the crime scene responder in an investigation is to collect and analyze evidence at a forensic level. This participation in the process may only be performed after the security of the crime scene has been established, logs maintained, and observations passed onto the crime scene investigator. The sensory observations made by personnel upon arrival at a scene cannot only lead investigators toward a specific pathway of evidence collection, but they may also dictate the level of safety precautions needed to establish crime scene protocols. Responding officers must be aware of these aspects of the investigation, and supervisors must assume responsibility for the security of the incident.

Upon Arrival

In addition to following protocols for officer safety, upon arrival, you should stop, look, and listen! What do you see? Is there a smell in the air? What is the current weather condition? What vehicles are present? Are the doors and windows secure?

The first responder to any scene of a crime will change the conditions of the scene permanently—it is inevitable. However, thorough notes of the observations made upon arrival will assist investigators in determining what evidence is probative. When possible, responders should attempt to document the scene through photography to add a visual record of the scene as present on arrival.

The security supervisor must designate the secured boundaries of the scene by using clear markers and posting personnel at entry points to establish the perimeter. Supervisors must also designate someone to begin maintaining an access log, which includes name, title, enter and exit time, and reason for entry (Figure 34.1). This access log will become part of the crime scene examination record, and under the laws governing discovery (e.g., Rosario material, Brady Rule, derived from "People of NY vs. Rosario" and "Brady vs. Maryland") may be turned over to all parties during the litigation process. All parties

Incident Access Log

Date: _____
Location: _____
Incident number: _____
Supervisor: _____

Name	Title	Time in	Time Out	Purpose	Officer

FIGURE 34.1 Example of an incident access log.

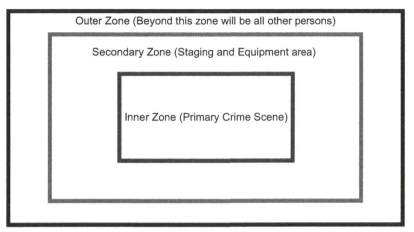

FIGURE 34.2 Crime scene security zones.

documented on the access log should enter the crime scene with the knowledge that the action of entering the secured perimeter may require them to be called as a witness at trial.

Crime scene security must be divided into three distinct areas or zones (Figure 34.2). The outer perimeter must secure the area from bystanders, onlookers, and the media. The secondary zone should act as a staging area for safety concerns, equipment storage, communications, and the incident command center. People who have a role in the crime scene but are not active investigators may be permitted access into the outer zone. The inner zone shall encompass the active crime scene. This perimeter must be monitored at all times, and only those persons who have an active role at the scene may be granted access. Persons entering the inner zone must be cognizant of physical evidence and their own safety. Personal protective equipment (PPE) must be worn at all times within this area.

Personal Protective Equipment

First responders to a crime scene must be aware of their surroundings and identify the type of PPE that must be used at a scene. In addition to safeguarding against the transfer of evidence from the responder to the scene, PPE will protect against any harmful elements of the crime scene, both seen and unseen. The most common types of PPE that will be employed at crime scene are the following[3]:

- *Protective gloves:* Nitrile is preferred over latex due to common allergic reactions and protection in the event of contact with some organic solvents.
- *Protective face mask with eye shield (or protective glasses):* Often at a crime scene, there is the potential for bloodborne pathogens, toxins, and particulates that could be inhaled. The use of a protective mask will assist the user in preventing contamination. In addition, the use of a mask will also prevent the deposit of saliva from the responder into the scene.

- *Steel-toed shoes:* These types of shoes are especially useful in outdoor scenes and construction settings.
- *Shoe covers:* In the event of a biological contaminant, such as blood or other bodily fluids, shoe covers will protect the surface areas of the shoes from collecting these contaminants.
- In the event of a high-risk biological scene, the responders may need to wear a Tyvek suit or a protective coat.
- First responders must also be cognizant of the potential use of a respirator. In certain types of crime scenes, there could be a chemical odor, toxic fumes, or lack of breathable air.

Photographic Documentation

One of the first concerns for a security supervisor should be the immediate documentation of a crime scene. This is dependent on the size of the crime scene and the ability of the supervisor to document the scene due to lack of equipment, weather, inability to simultaneously protect the scene and document it, or other relevant factors. Once the safety of all people has been established, one must be mindful of the transient nature of evidence. The environment can move evidence, certain parts of evidence can change state, and overall conditions may change. After a fire, debris may fall, smoke will clear, and damage areas can change. The initial documentation of damage may assist crime scene responders and arson investigators in determining the cause of the fire or fuel source. Metal objects may burn to ash, and the temperature that they were exposed to can determine the fuel that was burning. Likewise, the presence of a discernable burned object can tell the investigators the temperature of the fire. An example is the discovery of an aluminum can that has been burned to ash. Aluminum will typically burn around 1900° F; thus, one can infer that the fire at the scene was burning at a high temperature. Often, an incendiary fuel source, such as gasoline, can lead to higher temperatures in a fire. All of these items should be photographed as soon as possible. Later, we will discuss the elements of overall and evidentiary photographs.

All photographs must contain three elements: the subject, a scale, and a reference object. Crime scene photographs should always be in focus, with the subject of the photograph as the main object of the scene. There should always be a scale or ruler present. This will allow the investigators the ability to resize the image to accurately reconstruct the scene. Also, investigators can implement photogrammetry, or a discernment of measurements, throughout the scene, based upon the scale present and projecting it throughout the remainder of the photograph. A reference object should always be included in crime scene documentation to allow an overlap of the subject matter. By including a fixed point or object, such as a door, light switch, furniture or other object, investigators can splice together the scene to gain a full understanding of the layout and contents. The overall photographs must be a fair and accurate representation of what is seen. Any change in color may misidentify an object for investigators and possibly

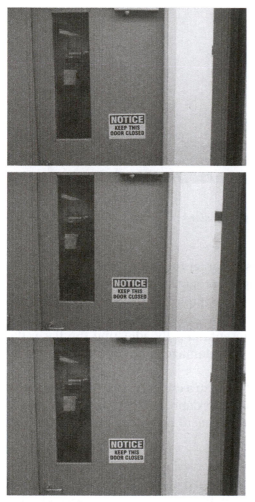

In this photograph, the white balance, or color of lighting, is incorrect. The overall composition of the photograph has a yellow tone. This photograph is not an accurate representation of the scene.

Although it is a closer depiction of the scene than the photograph directly above, this image is also incorrect. The color balance of this photograph depicts the overall scene as having a blue hue.

This photograph shows the door in the correct composition and depicts the colors correctly. The tones of the walls and the "Notice" sign are white, as seen at the scene.

FIGURE 34.3 Comparison of image color balance.

jurors (Figure 34.3). Preliminary overall photographs should attempt to capture the locations of evidence and identifying features of the scene, such as addresses, vehicle identification numbers and serial numbers, footwear/tire mark impressions, and the conditions of the scene.

Any evidence that is marked for future collection or examination must be documented thoroughly and as early in the crime scene investigation as possible. The introduction of additional persons or influences may alter the appearance, location, or existence of this evidence. In addition to an overall photograph, medium-range photographs should be taken to document the evidence in greater detail. While the purpose of the overall photograph is to document the conditions of the scene and the relationship of objects, the medium range photograph serves to document the appearance of an object. In all

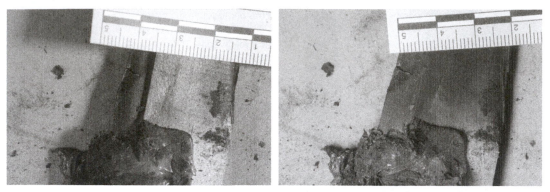

Photograh 1   Photograh 2

FIGURE 34.4 Which is the correct representation? *(Photo courtesy of Andrew Reitnauer.)*

photographs, a scale must be included, as well as a marker to indicate the identity of the object in question. Again, objects of medium-range photographs must be a fair and accurate representation of what is seen. Adjusting the photographic principles or lighting may allow the photographer to achieve this goal.

In Figure 34.4, photograph 2 is a correct representation. By adjusting the flash, the reflection from the charring was omitted, allowing the damage to be captured as seen by the investigator.

If any evidentiary photographs are to be taken for use in a critical comparison examination at a later time, guidelines must be followed in accordance with the best practices of digital evidence. In general, the basic components of macro or evidentiary photography are as follows:

- The digital image must be captured in a lossless compression format. The two widely accepted lossless compression formats are tagged image file format (TIFF) and RAW. TIFF is a universal file type, whereas RAW files are proprietary based upon the manufacturer of the camera. Specialized software may be required to open and enhance a RAW image.
- The camera must be on a grounded platform, such as a copy stand or tripod. In general, the human body cannot stop natural vibrations with a camera shutter speed slower than 1/60 of a second. Using a grounded platform will allow the subject matter to be in complete focus.
- The camera shutter must be controlled by a remote cord or by using the timer mode. The simple action of depressing the shutter control will cause the camera to vibrate, losing focus of the subject matter.

Most criminal justice agencies have made the transition to digital photography. Digital photographs have been accepted as evidence since the mid-1990s, culminating in Resolution 97-9 by the International Association for Identification.[4] As reported by Steven Staggs,[5] two landmark cases led to Kelly-Frye hearings (Kelly-Frye refers to preliminary hearings whereby the judge determines whether or not to permit particular scientific evidence) allowing the admissibility of digital evidence:

> ***State of Washington versus Eric Hayden, 1995:*** *A homicide case was taken through a Kelly-Frye hearing in which the defense specifically objected on the grounds that the digital images were manipulated. The court authorized the use of digital imaging and the defendant was found guilty. In 1998, the Appellate Court upheld the case on appeal.*

> ***State of California versus Phillip Lee Jackson, 1995:*** *The San Diego (CA) Police Department used digital image processing on a fingerprint in a double-homicide case. The defense asked for a Kelly-Frye hearing, but the court ruled this unnecessary on the argument that digital processing is a readily accepted practice in forensics and that new information was not added to the image.*

The responding officer must also maintain a photo log if any photographic documentation is taken. The log should contain the date and time of the photograph, the subject matter, and any additional notes. All photos must be logged whether or not they are of sufficient quality for future usage. Misfires may occur, however, they must still be logged. An example of a photo log is shown in Figure 34.5. These logs must be maintained within a case file or incident report, as they are a part of the examination record and discoverable material at trial.

Principles of Digital Photography

Photographers must be cognizant of the principles of photography that will guide the composition of the image itself. In discussing the operational parts of the digital camera, one must consider the sensor array. This part of the camera is analogous to the traditional film negative and is comprised of a number of individual sensors. The more sensors that

<u>**Photograph Log**</u>

Date: _____
Location: _____
Incident number: _____
Supervisor: _____

Date	Time	Initials	Subject	Comments

FIGURE 34.5 An example of a photo log.

are present on the array, the higher the resolution potential of the camera. These sensors are red, green, or blue, which are the three primary colors of a digital image. In the natural world, green is twice as prevalent as the other colors; therefore, the sensor array has twice the amount of green sensors than red and blue.

When taking the photograph itself, there are three controls to the camera: ISO, shutter speed, and aperture. The ISO setting (International Organization of Standards) controls the "speed" of the film. In a digital camera, this setting controls the coordination of the individual sensors to capture motion or low-light settings. The shutter speed controls the amount or duration of light that passes through the lens and is captured by the sensor array. By controlling the time factor so that the iris controlling the lens is allowed to remain open, the photographer can control the exposure of the photograph. Finally, the aperture is the feature of the camera that controls the depth of field, or the depth of focus of the image. By controlling the diameter of the lens opening, the aperture can control the depth of the subject matter that will be in focus. Figures 34.6–34.8 outline the ISO, shutter speed, and aperture settings.

In Figure 34.9, the evidence markers are arranged in increasing distance from the camera. The change in the aperture settings allows the markers in the distance to be in focus as compared to the markers closest to the camera. By altering the aperture settings, the

FIGURE 34.6 High ISO on left, where the image appears "grainy." Correct ISO on right. Photo taken at a distance of approximately 150 yards. *(Photo courtesy of Andrew Reitnauer.)*

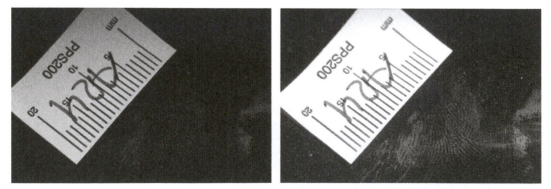

FIGURE 34.7 Photograph on the left was underexposed due to the shutter speed being set too fast, when compensated for, and allowed to remain open longer, the shutter speed corrected the exposure of the photograph in the image on the right. *(Photo courtesy of Andrew Reitnauer.)*

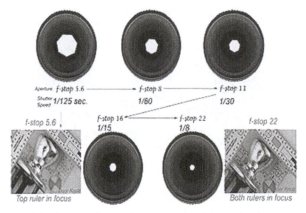

FIGURE 34.8 The change of the lens iris due to the aperture settings. *(Photo courtesy of Nicholas Petraco.)*

FIGURE 34.9 Photos depicting the various aperture settings. *(Photo courtesy of Andrew Reitnauer.)*

FIGURE 34.10 To avoid flash reflections, the flash must either be removed from the camera body, creating an angle, or bounced off of the ceiling. *(Photo courtesy of Nicholas Petraco.)*

photographer can choose the depth of the photograph that will be in focus. If the main subject of the photograph is to be in focus but the background subject matter is to remain out of focus, the aperture setting should be set low. Alternatively, choosing a high aperture setting will allow the background behind the main subject matter to remain in focus within the photograph.

Use of Flash

External flash units are helpful tools when responding to a crime scene and for the proper documentation of evidence. The white balance of a photo flash unit is set to mimic daylight to ensure the proper color balance of the subject matter. Today's digital cameras are designed to communicate electronically with the flash unit, ensuring that the exposure of the photograph will be appropriate for the selected photographic mode (programmed auto, aperture priority, shutter priority, and manual).

The photographer must be mindful of the reflections that can occur due to the directionality of the flash and the position of the subject matter. To avoid flash reflections, as demonstrated in Figure 34.10, the flash must either be removed from the camera body, creating an angle, or bounced off of the ceiling. Manufacturers of ceiling paint use a very consistent tone of white, which reflects the light from a camera flash, dispersing the light evenly over the space. If equipped with remote flash units, the photographer may also create multiple angles of light, or light a transparent surface (i.e., glass) from behind as well. Figure 34.11 is an example of a window that was lit from behind using transmitted lighting from an external flash unit.

Collection of Evidence

At a crime scene, the paramount concern must always be officer safety. This is also true for the collection and packaging of evidence. The security supervisor must ensure that all personnel maintain their safety throughout the evidentiary collection, packaging, and

FIGURE 34.11 An example of a window that was lit from behind using transmitted lighting from an external flash unit. *(Photo courtesy of Andrew Reitnauer.)*

transportation process. Once it is determined that the scene is safe for responders and that all conditions and evidence have been documented properly, officers must rely on their PPE throughout the collection process.

All personnel who will be handling evidence must wear proper gloves. This will ensure the integrity of the evidence by minimizing the risk of the transfer of epithelial DNA and latent fingerprints. Also, proper gloves reduce the risk of exposure to any possible contaminants while handling the evidence. Biological evidence, such as blood, saliva, semen, or other bodily fluids, may be present. Taking the proper steps, such as when responding to a medical biohazard condition, will help to ensure your health and safety.

Biological contaminants are not the only hazard that supervisors must consider. In the event of an explosion, fire, or chemical release, those collecting evidence must consider a chemical exposure as well. Many commonly encountered chemicals can be toxic to the skin if handled improperly. As can be encountered in an industrial setting, the reaction levels to a known chemical must be considered when handling. In addition, items may have sharp edges that must be protected against. Knives and cutting tools, broken glass, and metal shards can all become a hazard during the evidence collection process.

When packaging evidence for transport and further examination, one must not only consider the safety of those handling the item itself, but the integrity of the evidence. The basic types of evidence packaging are paper bags, cardboard boxes, envelopes, plastic bags, paint cans, and plastic sheet protectors. All of these types of packaging can be used; however, they all have a specific purpose and use. The use of the wrong type of packaging can damage or destroy the evidence, rendering any forensic examination useless. All sharp objects and firearms must be secured within the package, in the form of zip ties, string, or other nondestructive material, to ensure the safety of everyone involved. Staples and tape should not be used to secure an item of evidence within the package, and under no circumstances should staples be used to secure forms or other paperwork to the evidence packaging. The use of staples will not only compromise the integrity of the package but could damage the evidence packaged within. Figure 34.12 is an example of the damage that can be done to evidence while using staples.

Most items collected from a crime scene should be packaged in a clean paper bag or cardboard box. The use of these types of materials will allow any excess moisture to evaporate while maintaining the integrity of the evidence. If allowed to remain in the evidence packaging, excessive moisture can cause mildew or mold to grow, especially if packaged in sealed plastic. All sharp objects must be packaged in a sealed cardboard box and secured properly. Figures 34.13 and 34.14 demonstrate the proper way to secure firearm evidence and sharp objects within a cardboard box. Note the placement of the

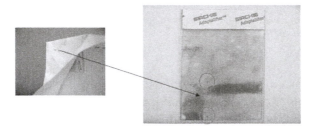

FIGURE 34.12 An example of the damage that can be done to evidence while using staples. *(Photo courtesy of Ioan Truta, Boston Police Department.)*

FIGURE 34.13 The proper way to secure sharp objects within a cardboard box. *(Photo courtesy of Ioan Truta, Boston Police Department.)*

FIGURE 34.14 The proper way to secure firearm evidence within a cardboard box. *(Photo courtesy of Ioan Truta, Boston Police Department.)*

zip ties, securing the evidence within the package while minimizing the friction, of the package and the tie, to the evidence itself. As noted in Figure 34.14, all firearms must be rendered safe prior to packaging, and any magazines must be removed from the firearm prior to packaging. The supervisor must be prepared to assist with firearms in the event of any questions regarding safety. **All firearms must be treated as if they are loaded!** In the event that assistance is needed in handling a firearm, err on the side of caution and request assistance.

All evidence collected from a fire scene or suspected arson must be placed in a clean paint can and sealed. The potential presence of hydrocarbon accelerants can evaporate; if packaged in a paper bag or cardboard box, their concentrations or even presence may evaporate. These items, or their representative samples, should be placed in individual cans and sealed completely. The fire debris chemist may perform tests on the vapors present in the can while still sealed, ensuring the proper measurement of accelerant type and amount.

Tape and adhesive items must be packaged in a plastic sleeve. Placing these items in a paper bag or cardboard box will allow the adhesive side to stick to the packaging itself. This will cause the transfer of fibers to the tape, potentially damaging evidence and destroying the integrity of the packaging itself. By packaging the tape in a plastic sleeve, the tape will remain flat and any adherence to the sleeve itself will not destroy any potential evidence or cause the transfer of any trace evidence to the adhesive. Figure 34.15 is an example of the proper packaging of tape evidence within a plastic sleeve.

Any questioned document evidence or paper evidence collected can be packaged in a plastic bag, which includes paper currency. If any items are wet, they must be allowed to air dry before placing in the plastic bag; alternatively, these items could be packaged in a paper bag or box. If there is any suspected biological evidence on the

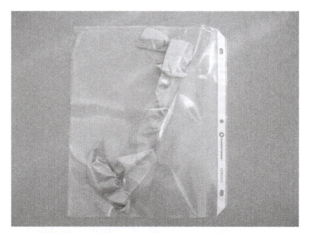

FIGURE 34.15 An example of the proper packaging of tape evidence within a plastic sleeve. *(Photo courtesy of Ioan Truta, Boston Police Department.)*

paper, it must be packaged inside a proper container to maintain the integrity of the biological evidence.

After placing the items in a container, the packaging must be completely sealed. There must be no holes or breaches within the outer package that could lead to a compromise of the evidence. If the container is a cardboard box, all sides of the box seams must be covered by tamperproof tape, to include any holes caused by the placement of zip ties or string. Paper bags must be folded over twice and sealed with tamperproof tape. Plastic bags and envelopes must be folded and secured, prior to the placement of tamperproof tape. All paint cans must have the lid fully secured, and the rim must be covered with tamperproof tape. In all instances, a second layer of clear packing tape may be applied over the tamperproof tape to ensure the security of the seal. A basic rule of thumb regarding the seal is that if you can fit a pencil into an opening, there is not a proper seal present. Figures 34.16–34.19 show some examples of proper packaging and seals.

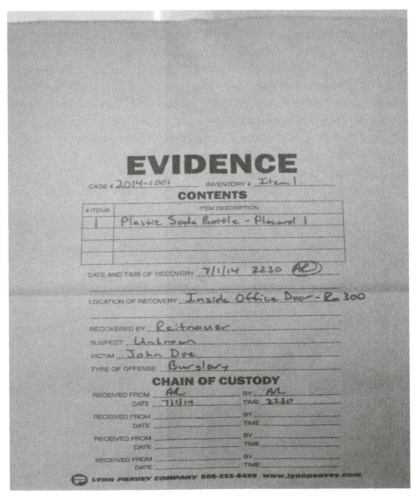

FIGURE 34.16 Example of paper evidence bag. *(Photo courtesy of Andrew Reitnauer.)*

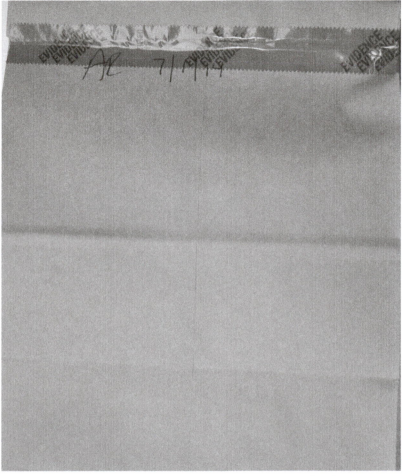

FIGURE 34.17 Example of a Proper evidence seal. *(Photo courtesy of Andrew Reitnauer.)*

All seals must bear the following:

- Initials of the person sealing the evidence
- Date of seal
- Agencies may require the incident number be placed on the seal; when not a requirement for the seal, the incident number must be present on the package

All packages must indicate the following:

- Incident number, address, or location
- The item number(s) contained within the package. While each package must contain only one item, multiple packages may be packaged together in a larger container.
- The date and time of collection
- The name of the collecting officer
- If applicable, a voucher or invoice number

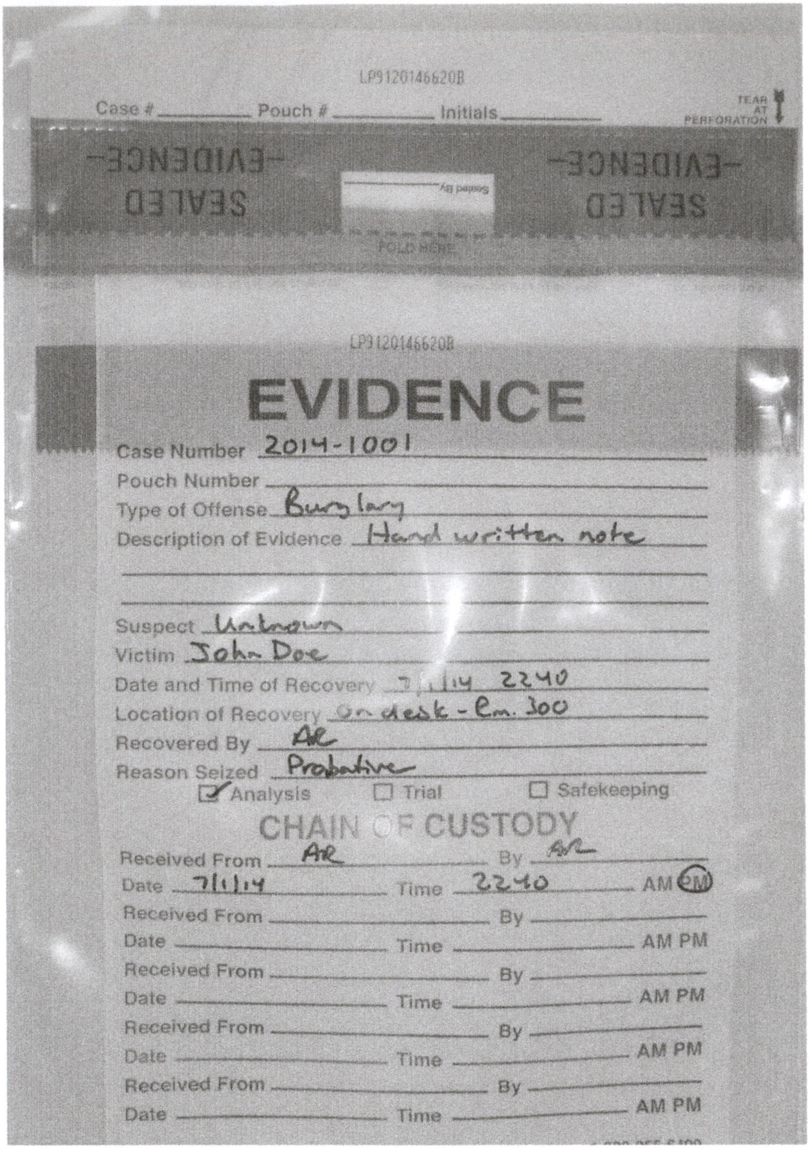

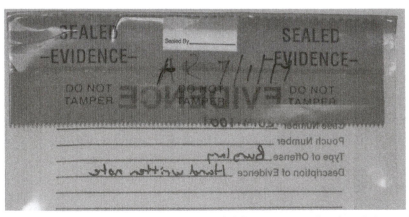

FIGURE 34.18 Example of a plastic evidence bag. *(Photo courtesy of Andrew Reitnauer.)*

FIGURE 34.19 Example of a proper evidence seal. *(Photo courtesy of Andrew Reitnauer.)*

Summary

The security supervisor is responsible for the initial response of personnel, maintaining officer safety, setting up a secure perimeter, and possibly for the documentation and collection of evidence at a crime scene. Thorough documentation must be maintained from the initial response through to the final stages of involvement. Security personnel may be directed to document the access to the crime scene, in addition to documenting the conditions of the scene. It is a requirement to maintain access logs and complete notes to document any sensory observations and conditions upon arrival. If responsible for photographic documentation, the supervisor must serve as a technical leader, ensuring the proper documentation of the overall scene, location of evidence, and potentially any critical comparison evidence to be used in a forensic analysis at a later time. By knowing the type of evidence being collected and the potential forensic use during analysis, the supervisor can recognize the proper evidence collection and packaging procedures to ensure the integrity of the evidence. By following these guidelines, the initial response, security protocols, and evidentiary concerns may all be obtained in a safe and proper manner.

Refer website http://www.ifpo.org for further information

End Notes

1. Edmond Locard (1934), Locard's Exchange Principle. Accessed 4/13/15 www.forensichandbook.com/locards-exchange-principle.

2. Paul L. Kirk, *Crime investigation: Physical Evidence and the Police Laboratory* (Interscience Publishers, Inc.: New York, 1953).

3. Barry A. J. Fisher and David R. Fisher, *Techniques of Crime Scene Investigation*, Eighth Edition (CRC Press, 2012).

4. I.A.I. Resolution 97-9. http://www.theiai.org/member/resolutions/August 1,1997/RES97_9.PDF.

5. Steven Staggs, *The Admissibility of Digital Photographs in Cour*. Crime Scene Investigator Network. Date Accessed 3/12/14. http://www.crime-scene-investigator.net/admissibilityofdigital.html.

35

The Importance of Report Writing to the Security Operation

Christopher A. Hertig, Lawrence J. Fennelly,
Brion P. Gilbride, Tucker Beecher

Reports are used by management to analyze critical problems
Philip P. Purpura, CPP

If one were to query most security supervisors about the most pressing problem they have with their subordinates, there is an excellent chance that the reply would be: "Poorly written reports." The main reason that this reply is heard is that report writing is a skill. As with any skill, some people have natural talent, some can develop talent, and some cannot. Report writing is not just an activity—it is a process. The process begins with obtaining information (often through interviewing), documenting that information, and presenting that information in a format that will be useful to a variety of audiences, from company managers to police to judges and attorneys. A well-written report should be constructed so that an individual not involved with the situation could take the written report into a legal proceeding and testify to the facts of the case with confidence.

Why Report Writing Is Crucial

The process of report writing cannot be discussed without first understanding why report writing is a critical skill for security professionals and why the supervisor must be proficient at both writing reports as well as reading and editing them. First, the written report provides a *permanent record* of something that occurred in a particular place over a particular time frame. This permanent record aspect is important for several reasons. The written report will often be accompanied by some kind of evidence—photographs, diagrams, voice recordings, video recordings, call logs, Internet provider (IP) address information, or other material. When a report is well written, the accompanying evidence will tend to support it. When a report is poorly written—whether by inability, inattentiveness, or compromised integrity—the evidence will tend to highlight the flaws, errors, or omissions. This permanent record provides context to the other information or evidence.

Second, the written report preserves the integrity of a case. Perceptions change over time, regardless whether that occurs intentionally or unintentionally. For example, if a crime is committed and a case is initiated in the criminal justice system, that case could

Security Supervision and Management. http://dx.doi.org/10.1016/B978-0-12-800113-4.00035-3

take years to resolve. The written report preserves the perceptions of the author(s) or other parties involved *at the time the incident occurred.* This is important because memories become fuzzy and people move to distant locations, retire, or even die. Once the testimony of an individual becomes unavailable, the written report is all that remains to convey what that individual saw or heard. If the report writer omits information or puts incorrect or even false information in a report, that carelessness or integrity failure is also preserved.

Third, the written report provides information about an event in a particular place during a particular timeframe that can then be analyzed for its intelligence value. One way the intelligence value of the written report has increased exponentially is with the availability of commercially aggregated data and public record databases. For example, with a license plate number, public records make it possible to trace the plate to the make, model, and year of vehicle as well as the registered owner, his or her address, and other information. Other public records make it possible to trace address history, website registrations, criminal histories, social media activity, and hundreds of other types of information.

The written report also allows the aggregation of other report information in order to conduct trend analyses on a particular location (or group of locations), a certain type of activity, a definitive date and time range, on specific perpetrators, or some other combination of factors. Trend analyses have just as much intelligence value as the information itself because they allow security managers to focus existing resources and can provide leverage in requesting additional resources or funding. The emergence of "big data" and analytics in recent years has enabled pattern recognition in a universe of data so large that humans cannot possibly analyze all of it. Yet, as computers grow more and more powerful, they also become more capable of identifying patterns in seemingly disparate data. This becomes especially important as security departments and information technology (IT) departments become partners in investigating criminal activity and other threats to the organization—both virtual and physical.

Situations That May Require Written Reporting

To determine if a report must be written, there must be an understanding of what situations might warrant a written report. A situation that warrants a written report is usually referred to as an *incident.* An incident can be many things: a criminal activity, a vehicle accident, a fire alarm, a water main break, a power outage due to weather, and a medical emergency are some common incidents. Incidents can be simple, such as a fire alarm tripped by kitchen activity, to complex, such as a multivehicle accident with fatalities. Some incidents can be handled by one security officer, whereas others may require not just security officers but law enforcement, fire, emergency medical, or hazardous material personnel. Some incidents will require obtaining information from the individuals or groups involved, whereas others will require reporting on visible evidence such as tire marks, broken glass, or a fire. Once it is apparent that an incident has occurred, the next step is to gather information about the incident that might be relevant to a written report.

How Information Is Collected

To write a report, there must be something *to* report. Gathering information for a report can involve one or more techniques, from personal observation to interviewing to downloading or reviewing data. For the security professional, the bulk of the reporting will be based on interviews, thus making interviewing a critical investigative skill. Without conducting an effective interview, there will be no useful information on which to make notes. This is true at the various junctures of the investigative process, from initial questioning of witnesses to focused interviews with suspected wrongdoers. The interview can provide corroborating information from witnesses, exonerating or alibi information from potential suspects, or even confessions from detained individuals. Security managers must ensure that subordinates are able to conduct an adequate interview. Some individuals are naturally skilled at eliciting information, while others need to develop that ability—but develop it they must.

Managers must also make subordinates aware of the difference between interviewing a witness, which is generally not adversarial because most people want to be helpful, versus interviewing a suspect. In the interviews that can be adversarial, a person skilled in countermeasures can divert an interviewer away from questions that implicate that person. Interviewing is a key component of an investigation. The astute security manager makes sure that his or her subordinates are proficient at it. Interviewing is like note taking, managing of incident scenes, conducting surveillance, and conducting searches, in that information gleaned from these activities is placed into a report. An officer or investigator who can improve his or her interviewing ability has a better chance of becoming more proficient at report writing. So too does one who gets better at surveillance or searching. The effective supervisor or manager knows this and does everything possible to enhance their subordinates' report-writing subskills.

The Importance of Notes

Once information is collected, it must be recorded. Taking notes while investigating or responding to an incident is important for officers. Using those notes to assist in report writing will help one to recall facts that were documented when dealing with the situation as it occurred. Note-taking is especially useful while interviewing because it enables the officer to directly quote an individual and ensures the most accurate representation of the interview short of recording it, which should be done when possible and if it is legally permissible. Note-taking enables the officer to keep information organized which becomes crucial when the actual writing of the report takes place. A copy of the notes should be kept with the report for clarification purposes. It is also possible that an officer's notes might be subpoenaed for a criminal or civil case; depending on jurisdiction, there may be regulations regarding which notes have to be maintained and for how long.

Six Important Points of Report Writing

Every written report should be clear and concise. If a report is clear and concise, it will answer or address six basic questions:

1. *What?* What happened? Describe the incident or situation.
2. *Where?* The exact location of the occurrence. The more specific, the better.
3. *Who?* The security officer must address as many *who*s as possible. "Who" includes the following:
    a. Victims
    b. Witnesses
    c. Responding personnel: security, law enforcement, fire department, emergency medical services (EMS), others
    d. Callers and contacts: who reported the incident, who was notified and by whom
4. *When?* The security officer must address as many *when*s as possible. "When" includes the following:
    a. When was the report received?
    b. When did responding personnel (security, police, fire, EMS) arrive or depart?
    c. When did the incident occur?
    d. When were notifications made?
5. *Why?* This involves judgment and opinion and may not be easily proven, but it may be very important in judgment of guilt or liability. Officers must be careful here not to speculate. Any judgment or opinion rendered must be based on the information available and nothing else. Speculation will detract from the credibility of the author and the report itself.
6. *How?* How did it happen? Detail the chain of events to the greatest extent possible, and acknowledge gaps in information where they occur.

It is imperative that security personnel realize that the audience for a report may be as small as the security shift supervisor or as large as a court of law. The report may become part of a local file, part of a civil/criminal case, an administrative or quasi-judicial proceeding, or an internal investigative activity.

Consider the following scenarios to gain an understanding of where a written report might be seen—both inside and outside of an organization.

- *An employee slips and falls:* This report might go to the safety manager, human resources, the corporate insurance provider, corporate counsel, or a government regulatory body, such as the U.S. Occupational Safety and Health Administration. The report could be used to address insurance claims, liability lawsuits, or administrative proceedings.
- *Property is stolen and an arrest is made:* This report will be provided to local law enforcement. When the arrest is made, the report is given to the district attorney and ultimately the arrestee's defense attorney. The report may also go to the corporate

insurance provider and corporate counsel. The report could be used to prepare a prosecution, defend against a prosecution, address insurance claims, or address liability lawsuits.

* *A water main breaks and a networking equipment room is flooded*: This report might be given to the corporate IT department, the corporate insurance provider, or the local utility company that maintains the damaged pipe(s). The report could be used to justify damage awards, address liability lawsuits, or to obtain replacement equipment under warranty.

Other Report Writing Tips

The timing of writing a report is sometimes as important as the report itself. In a nonemergency situation, the security officer should write a report on an incident as soon afterward as possible.

Such an incident report should be completed prior to the end of the shift. It is incumbent upon the security manager to ensure this is taking place. Woe unto the manager who has to explain to the executives or the insurance company that a report is unavailable and also lacks a legitimate reason for the delay. Legitimate reasons for not writing a report immediately after an incident might include the following:

* A high-stress situation, such as where a security officer is fired upon by a criminal and has to return fire or otherwise defend himself or herself or others. The officer must be given time to de-stress and dissipate the adrenaline released during the incident. The officer might therefore write a report on the incident the following day.
* A mass-casualty incident, such as an explosion in a manufacturing plant, where emergency medical response, damage assessment, or other business continuity operations take precedence. The responding officers might write separate reports, or they might write parts of an "umbrella" document that covers the incident as a whole, or both.
* Extreme fatigue, which often occurs in combination with a high-stress situation or a mass-casualty incident. Officers who have been on duty for abnormally long hours or have engaged in unusually strenuous activity may require rest before they can competently report on an incident. This is not merely, "I'm tired. Can I write this up tomorrow?"

The language used in a written report is important. Statements must be as precise and as accurate as possible. Writers must ensure that the words they use are appropriate—slang terms should be avoided unless the writer is directly quoting someone. Jargon or industry terms should be avoided unless they are necessary; if used, then the writer should explain clearly what they mean. For example, writing that "Officer Smith searched the suspect's person, clothing, and belongings for concealed weapons or other dangerous items" is clearer than "Officer Smith conducted a pat-down." Although most security professionals will understand what a "pat-down" is, an administrative inquiry, insurance company, or an attorney might question it or simply not know what that is.

The references included in a report are also significant. Many reports written by security officers serve, in a sense, as an accusation against an individual or a group. To lend credibility to the report as well as to the accusation itself, the security professional must cite what law, rule, regulation, or policy was violated. In doing so, the security professional must be aware not only of what elements constitute the violation, but how their interviews and evidence support those elements.

If theft involves the taking of the property belonging to another person or entity, the report should establish to the extent possible what property was taken, who it belonged to, where and when it was taken, who was found in possession of it, and whether the individual who was found with it had a right to possess it.

The Supervisor's Responsibilities

The role of the supervisor in the report-writing process is nearly as important as the writer's role. The supervisor is the first line of defense before a written report is distributed. The supervisor must protect both the author and the employer, and he or she provides this protection by reviewing the report before anyone else sees it. The supervisor must proofread the report for grammar and structure, monitor the writing quality itself, and review the report to ensure all relevant information is present and in sufficient detail. The supervisor might verify details or ask the report writer about the specifics of the incident. The supervisor must protect the employer by ensuring that the reports are approved and grammatically correct, coherent, and contain the necessary information to help executives, insurance companies, corporate counsel, and others understand what occurred during the incident being reported. The supervisor must protect the security officer by ensuring that the officer's written report reflects well on the organization by being grammatically correct and coherent and that it contains the necessary information.

Proofreading is important for the security supervisor. The supervisor must have enough of a command of language and understanding of the various incidents that occur to be able to effectively evaluate a security officer's report. If an officer writes an incomplete report, the supervisor should return the report to the officer for resubmission and explain, if necessary, what is lacking in the report. If an officer writes a sloppy report with misspelled words and run-on sentences, the supervisor should return the report to the officer for resubmission and identify the misspelled words and run-on sentences that need to be fixed. Many security providers now use computers to write reports, and if so, the grammar-check and spell-check should be completed prior to the report being submitted to the supervisor.

There are techniques for proofreading that can be used by both the security officer and the security supervisor. Reading the report out loud can identify errors; the ear will hear what the mind chooses not to see. Editing one's own report requires a level of objectivity most people do not possess, and reading aloud can overcome that. Having a third party, such as another security officer or another security supervisor, review the report can identify errors, gaps, or omissions that the author and supervisor might have missed, particularly if the third party is unaware of the incident being reported.

In addition to proofreading, the supervisor must also evaluate the report to ensure that the six points (who, what, when, where, why, and how) were adequately addressed. If that is not the case, the supervisor must ensure that an explanation is contained in the report to explain why such information is missing. A supervisory review may identify additional information that the report writer can obtain to improve the report, or may identify information that the officer failed to include because of the possible negative impact on the author. This is a particular danger in "use of force" complaints. Saying that the "subject was directed to the ground" does not specify what techniques were used, which can leave the incident open to various interpretations. The following gives a more detailed impression of what occurred: "While attempting to control the subject's movements by clamping subject's bicep above the elbow to direct him to an adjoining room, subject actively resisted and tried to strike Officer Smith. Writer utilized a straight-arm bar to safely bring the subject to the ground so that Officer Smith could apply handcuffs…"

The supervisor must also become an expert on differentiating the writing styles of his or her subordinate security professionals. No two people think or write exactly the same way. If two people received a similar education, or have similar experiences, their writing style may show similarities, but they will still not be exactly alike. Variations in writing style can take many forms. Some are taught to put two spaces after a period in a sentence, while others only put one. People from different regions or countries spell certain words differently. For example, the word *colour* is used in the United Kingdom, whereas the word is *color* in the United States. People from different regions use different expressions to describe the same thing. Once a supervisor becomes accustomed to a subordinate's writing style, any deviations to that style becomes apparent. This might be indicative of fatigue or of being interrupted repeatedly while trying to write the report. Deviations also might mean that someone uncomfortable with report writing is using a template written by another and unconsciously has adopted the other's writing style. Unfortunately, deviations in writing style could also relate to omitting information or creating a story rather than reporting a factual event. It is incumbent upon the supervisor to be alert to these changes in style, whether such changes are overt or subtle in nature.

Testifying

Testifying in legal (criminal or civil court) or quasi-legal (disciplinary hearings, administrative agency hearings, labor arbitration hearings) proceedings is the final step. Presenting testimony in a proceeding is the epitome of an investigation. There are some who believe that testimony starts with the taking of notes for the report. One could probably argue that it starts earlier, with the interview or initial approach to the incident under review. Whatever the case, testimony is the presentation of an investigation. It is where the officer shows his or her work on the case. It is also, like report writing, an exercise in communication: answering questions based on the report.

When teaching someone how to testify, the relationship between testimony and the written report becomes clear. If a security professional testifies on behalf of a plaintiff, the defendant's attorney has only one job: to cause the judge or jury to doubt that testimony by challenging or attacking the report written by that security professional. Challenges to the descriptions of persons and objects drive home the importance of attention to detail. Questions about the officer's source of information illustrates the criticality of attributing everything learned to its proper source. Queries regarding the definitions of words in the report emphasize the need to use simple terms, avoiding technical jargon or "legalese." Ultimately, what did not appear in the written report but *should* have, becomes the ammunition needed to cause the judge or the jury to doubt the reliability of anything contributed to the case by that security professional.

Reports that are detailed, accurate, and organized will lead to testimony that is equally detailed, accurate, and organized. This aids not only the security professional who wrote the report and testified to its contents, but also the security supervisor who supported the professional during the investigation and reviewed the work product before releasing it. The benefits of proper report writing that leads to proper testimony are legion. The security professional can improve his or her presentation and public speaking skills with a friendly audience, such as corporate counsel or the prosecuting attorney. Presentation and public speaking skills are further improved by the adversarial audience of the defendant's attorney or defense counsel and by the neutral audience of the judge, jury, arbitrator, or fact-finder. Security managers can improve relations with prosecutors' offices, investigators, or local law enforcement when subordinates provide detailed, accurate, and organized reporting and testimony.

The security professional who omits information from a report or falsifies information within a report may also be identified through testimony, and may be forced to further omit or falsify during sworn testimony. If that occurs and opposing counsel has access to information such as visitor logs, access card swipes, camera footage, or other contradicting evidence, the lack of integrity or the ethical failure will be uncovered for all to see. Such an unmasking will be public record in a legal or quasi-legal proceeding, with all of the negative public relations impact that follows. The security supervisor can defend against this by ensuring the validity of the report at the time it is written or filed. Otherwise, the security supervisor becomes complicit in the loss of credibility.

Conclusion

In discussing the importance of report writing to the security enterprise as a whole, it is important to remember that the best-written reports are those supported by thorough preparatory work, which will lead to effective testimony. The more effective that an officer's interviewing and note-taking skills are, the more detailed the report will be. The more detailed the report, the more thorough the testimony will be. A detailed report mitigates the ability of opposing counsel to attack it.

The security supervisor plays a key role in this arena. It is the supervisor who supports subordinates by ensuring reports are as detailed as possible and as professional looking as possible. It is this same supervisor who supports the employer by ensuring that quality in report writing is maintained. It is this same supervisor who protects both employer and employee by ensuring the integrity of the information provided, as well as the security professional who investigates the incident and writes the report.

Refer website http://www.ifpo.org for further information

36

Apprehension and Detention Procedures

Matt Stiehm

Scenario 1

Jim works as a loss prevention manager for a major retailer in an urban location. The store has had several thefts from the jewelry department over the past two weeks. The stolen items are valued around $500. The suspect(s) are described as a male and female team who approach the counter and request to see a series of mid-priced rings, bracelets, or earrings. The couple gets the clerk to bring out five to seven pieces to look at, and then the team has a third suspect who approaches the counter and distracts the clerk for a moment. The male then reaches, grabs, and palms one of the items and places the item in his pocket. The male walks off, while the female talks with the clerk for a few more minutes and asks for help with another item or two. She thanks the clerk for showing her the items and walks off to meet up with the male and exit the store. Jim has reached out to nearby retailers and they are experiencing similar thefts. Through this outreach, Jim obtains descriptions of the three suspects.

Using a digital camera system, Jim observes the jewelry counter. He sees a male and female approach the clerk that matches the description of the suspects. He watches the described pattern of behavior as above, and sees the man "palm" and place the item in his front pocket. Jim maintains constant observation of the male suspect and observes the male suspect leave the store. At the same time as he is maintaining observation of the suspect, he calls the clerk to get the value of the "stolen" item. The item is valued at $150.

Jim notifies the store manager that he will make an apprehension of the male outside the store, and requests the assistance of a clerk to "standby" while he approaches the male. Jim approaches the male when he is outside of the store vestibule. Jim identifies himself as the loss prevention employee for the store and gives the reason for the stop. What authority does Jim have in making the stop, (detention), and what authority or ability does he have to use force?

Scenario 2

A security professional is standing post at the front of a bar to screen patrons prior to entrance. The purpose of screening is to ensure the safety of all patrons and that they have a good time. The security professional sees an obviously intoxicated individual who is cutting in line and

Security Supervision and Management. http://dx.doi.org/10.1016/B978-0-12-800113-4.00036-5

attempting to get to the front. The bar is a stand-alone building with a private parking lot. The line is clearly established, and all of the other patrons have been following directions. The intoxicated individual is getting louder, and as the person passes one set of patrons, someone speaks up and tells the individual to go to the back of the line. A verbal altercation occurs, and the intoxicated individual takes it one step further and makes threats of violence to the group that has objected to the line cutting. The security officer calls for backup and waits to approach the intoxicated individual. The security officer is clearly identifiable in a blaze yellow uniform, with the word "Security" on the back and front. The security officer provides clear direction to the individual to stop, otherwise the person will be asked to leave. The individual continues, and the security officer orders the individual to leave the property. The individual refuses, and what follows is a common security interaction: the individual is taken to the ground and handcuffed. The individual is then escorted to a "quiet" area, where police can be called to deal with him.

Introduction

Protection officers in today's society are tasked with a variety of roles from uniformed security, executive protection, loss prevention, corporate security, and everything in-between. In these roles, they sometimes have the authority to make an arrest, or to apprehend and detain a suspect. Simultaneously, today's society has become more violent and individuals are not willing to follow authority. Accordingly, the question needs to be asked: what does the law permit a private security professional regarding arrests or apprehensions and the use of force that sometimes is necessary in those situations? Understand that the role of security and its connotations are different than the role of law enforcement. Security can be more proactive and has more authority than law enforcement under specific circumstances.

Generally, the apprehension of a subject causes tension. This tension is derived from the approach, response, transportation, detention and ultimately the individual's release. Examining this process is not complex, but is essential. There are many considerations involved in the actual approach and detention. These considerations will vary depending on the laws of a particular jurisdiction, on the corporate policies, safety concerns, and liability concerns.

Nothing in this chapter should be construed as legal advice. Protection professionals should consult with corporate counsel to ensure compliance with laws, policy, and procedure. All material presented here is done so in good faith and intended to be informative and to serve as a reference. That said, to conduct an exhaustive review of all state laws would be time-consuming and not appropriate to this forum.

Protection officers should be aware of the differences between types of crimes. The least serious is usually referred to as a summary offense, which is the equivalent of receiving a ticket—a fine, possible probation, but nothing more. This category might include trespassing, littering, jaywalking, or many motor vehicle-related violations. Misdemeanor offenses are more serious but do not include what most would categorize as major crimes.

Misdemeanor offenses are typically punished by less than a year in prison, fines, and/or probation. Misdemeanors include such things as driving while intoxicated, simple assault, harassment, reckless driving, or theft/shoplifting. Felonies are the most serious, and are punished by prison sentences in excess of 1 year. Felonies include murder, manslaughter, rape, aggravated theft, aggravated assault (or assault with a weapon), and many others. In most states both felonies and misdemeanors are classified as criminal offenses.

Authority

Laws and the Private Person

Security professionals exercise a wide variety of authority. Consider the first scenario at the start of this chapter. What authority does Jim have? First and foremost, he is an agent of the store, and many US states allow for shopkeepers to make "stops" to prevent shoplifting. Jim also has the authority to execute trespass warnings to individuals on the property. Finally, and most importantly, many states allow for Jim to "arrest" individuals under what is commonly known as a "citizen's arrest." Each of these authorities would be provided for within statutory law for a particular state. (Please check local laws to ensure correct interpretation and understanding—if there are any questions, consult an attorney.)

Citizen's arrest (or private person's arrest) generally allows for a private person to make an arrest of an individual who has committed a misdemeanor in the citizen's presence, committed a felony in the citizen's presence, or with whom the citizen reasonably believes has committed a felony.

Here are some relevant state laws for reference. It is incumbent upon each reader to review their specific laws, as there are some variations.

Minnesota: 629.37 When Private Person May Make Arrest. *A private person may arrest another:(1) for a public offense committed or attempted in the arresting person's presence; (2) when the person arrested has committed a felony, although not in the arresting person's presence; or (3) when a felony has in fact been committed, and the arresting person has reasonable cause for believing the person arrested to have committed it.*[1]

Louisiana: Code of Criminal Procedure, Art. 214. Arrest by private person; when lawful. *A private person may make an arrest when the person arrested has committed a felony, whether in or out of his presence.*[2]

Oregon: 133.225 Arrest by private person: *(1) A private person may arrest another person for any crime committed in the presence of the private person if the private person has probable cause to believe the arrested person committed the crime. A private person making such an arrest shall, without unnecessary delay, take the arrested person before a magistrate or deliver the arrested person to a peace officer. (2) In order to make the arrest a private person may use physical force as is justifiable under ORS 161.255.*[3]

Oregon: 161.255 Use of force in defense of premises: *(1) A person in lawful possession or control of premises is justified in using physical force upon another person when and to the extent that the person reasonably believes it necessary to prevent or terminate what the person reasonably believes to be the commission or attempted commission of a criminal trespass by the other person in or upon the premises. (2) A person may use deadly physical force under the circumstances set forth in subsection (1) of this section only: (b) When the person reasonably believes it necessary to prevent the commission of arson or a felony by force and violence by the trespasser.*[4]

Understanding the citizen's arrest laws provides for a foundation of what a private protection officer can lawfully do when acting either as an agent of the organization, company, or even as an individual. The employer or company does not have the authority to discourage or prevent an employee from (1) reporting a crime, or (2) protecting themselves from being attacked or becoming a victim of a crime. There are also some additional laws that govern actions of the private person should they arrest someone. For example, many states require that law enforcement be contacted as soon as possible to continue control of the arrest. Many states also mandate that the person being detained must be told the reason for the stop (detention or apprehension). There is also some implied ability to use force or, in some cases, actual statutory provision for some modicum of force to control the individual being detained. Please consult corporate counsel regarding the use of force as a protection professional.

Laws and Shoplifting

Coupled with this authority of a private person's arrest, most states allow for agents of a business to conduct stops related to shoplifting to prevent loss to the store. A sample of state laws regarding shoplifting is provided below. It is incumbent upon each protection officer to check their state or provincial laws, and with corporate counsel for any clarification. Arizona, for example, specifically references the authority granted to a merchant or a merchant's agent.

Arizona: 13-1805 Shoplifting; detaining suspect; defense to wrongful detention; civil action by merchant; public services; classification.

(A) *A person commits shoplifting if, while in an establishment in which merchandise is displayed for sale, the person knowingly obtains such goods of another with the intent to deprive that person of such goods by:*
   (1) *Removing any of the goods from the immediate display or from any other place within the establishment without paying the purchase price; or*
   (2) *Charging the purchase price of the goods to a fictitious person or any person without that person's authority; or*
   (3) *Paying less than the purchase price of the goods by some trick or artifice such as altering, removing, substituting or otherwise disfiguring any label, price tag or marking; or*
   (4) *Transferring the goods from one container to another; or*
   (5) *Concealment.*

(B) *A person is presumed to have the necessary culpable mental state pursuant to sub-section A of this section if the person does either of the following:*

    (1) *Knowingly conceals on himself or another person unpurchased merchandise of any mercantile establishment while within the mercantile establishment.*

    (2) *Uses an artifice, instrument, container, device or other article to facilitate the shoplifting.*

(C) *A merchant, or merchant's agent or employee, with reasonable cause, may detain on the premises in a reasonable manner and for a reasonable time any person who is suspected of shoplifting as prescribed in subsection A of this section for questioning or summoning a law enforcement officer.*[5]

At first glance, section C seems pretty straightforward. However, it is not and this is where advice of corporate counsel is essential. To understand why, section C must be broken into individual pieces. Consider the following list:

- "A merchant, or merchant's agent or employee"
- "with reasonable cause"
- "may detain on the premises"
- "in a reasonable manner"
- "for a reasonable time"
- "suspected of shoplifting as prescribed in subsection A of this section"
- "for questioning"

The importance of consulting counsel prior to drafting policies or procedures on when and how to detain someone or affect an arrest cannot be overstated. In the breakdown of section C, the common denominator is definitions. The security professional must be educated regarding who constitutes a merchant or their agent/employee. He or she must understand what constitutes reasonable cause and how to articulate that cause to counsel, to law enforcement, or other interested parties. A security professional may detain someone on the premises only if they understand what area constitutes the "premises." Is it inside the store? Outside the store? In the parking lot? If the store is in a shopping center, does a neighboring store constitute "premises"? How does one know how long a reasonable time is, or what is considered a reasonable manner? Counsel will be able to research the legal answers to these questions.

In Georgia, there is a specific part of the criminal code that establishes a defense for merchant's that detain someone suspected of shoplifting. This is often referred to as "Merchant's Privilege" or "Shopkeeper's Privilege."

Georgia: 51-7-60 Preclusion of Recovery for Detention or Arrest of Person Suspected of Shoplifting Under Certain Circumstances.

Whenever the owner or operator of a mercantile establishment or any agent or employee of the owner or operator detains, arrests, or causes to be detained or arrested any person reasonably thought to be engaged in shoplifting and, as a result of the detention or arrest, the person so detained or arrested brings an action for false arrest or false imprisonment against the owner, operator, agent, or employee, no recovery shall be had by the plaintiff in such action where it is established by competent evidence: (1) That the plaintiff had so conducted himself or behaved in such manner as to cause a man of reasonable prudence to believe that the plaintiff, at or immediately prior to the time of the detention or arrest, was committing the offense of shoplifting, as defined by Code Section 16-8-14; or (2) That the manner of the detention or arrest and the length of time during which such plaintiff was detained was under all the circumstances reasonable.[6]

Miscellaneous Laws

Aside from shoplifting, what other crimes occur within the realm of professional security? The answer is anything and everything. Remember, there are far more security professionals than law enforcement officers working in the world. That means far more opportunity to encounter criminal activity. Security professionals are unlikely to encounter a homicide, but it happens. They will encounter the following much more often:

- Theft: Taking something from another with the intent to permanently deprive, there is both felony and misdemeanor theft. The threshold between misdemeanor and felony is usually based on value. Think of someone at a ball game or state/county fair who takes someone's purse or wallet.
- Theft by deception: Using deceit, trickery, or a rouse to perpetuate a crime and obtain an object of value, ownership, or property through deception. One of the scenarios at the beginning of this chapter was an example of theft by deception.
- Receiving stolen property: The acquisition of goods with the knowledge that they have been stolen, extorted, embezzled, or unlawfully taken and having the intent to deprive the owner of the goods knowing they were ill-gotten.
- Robbery: Taking something from another with the intent to deprive by the use of force or fear. Most people think of strong arm robbery or the traditional gun/knife robbery where money is taken from a gas station clerk.
- Assault: Verbally threatening someone with bodily injury. Typically involves profanity. "I'll kick your ass" would suffice in most jurisdictions.
- Battery: Nonconsensual physical contact with another individual that results in bodily injury. A bar fight is a common example. An assault is typically the follow-up to a bar fight.
- Domestic abuse/battery: Nonconsensual physical contact with another individual with which the person is in an intimate (married) relationship. There are specific classifications of relationship that make it a domestic assault.
- Rape: Nonconsensual sexual intercourse between one individual (actor) and victim for the purpose of sexual gratification.

Use of Force

Most state laws allow for some modicum of defense or others when it comes to the application of force. In the private persons arrest statutes, most states allow for some modicum of force. Pennsylvania law states that the agent of a business may use as much force as reasonably necessary for the detention of the subject to be detained, while Nevada developed guidance on how much force is appropriate. Nevada developed guidance for "lethal" force, and did so in the case of *State of Nevada v. Rolland P. Weddell*. An examination of state laws regarding the use of force by a "private person" during an arrest highlights both similarities and differences in the laws.

Kansas: Private person's use of force in making arrest.

(a) *A private person who makes, or assists another private person in making a lawful arrest is justified in the use of any force which such person would be justified in using if such person were summoned or directed by a law enforcement officer to make such arrest, except that such person is justified in the use of deadly force only when such person reasonably believes that such force is necessary to prevent death or great bodily harm to such person or another.*[7]

Missouri: Private person's use of force in making arrest.

(2) *A private person acting on his own account may, subject to the limitations of subsection 3, use physical force to effect arrest or prevent escape only when and to the extent such is immediately necessary to effect the arrest, or to prevent escape from custody, of a person whom he reasonably believes to have committed a crime and who in fact has committed such crime.*

(3) *A private person in effecting an arrest or in preventing escape from custody is justified in using deadly force only*

    (3) *When he reasonably believes such use of deadly force is immediately necessary to effect the arrest of a person who at that time and in his presence*

        (a) *Committed or attempted to commit a class A felony or murder; or*

        (b) *Is attempting to escape by use of a deadly weapon.*[8]

It is hard to determine the veracity of each state's use of force statutes as most lawsuits against security professionals do not reach the supreme judicial court at the state or federal level. These cases are typically settled. The federal case law that provides for some foundation is that of *Graham v. Connor*, which involves law enforcement. Even so, it provides for a foundation of what is considered reasonable. As noted in the March/April 2013 edition of the Campus Law Enforcement Journal:

> *In the first case, Graham, a diabetic was in a car with his daughter. Graham and his daughter were attempting to get some orange juice for Graham who was having a diabetic reaction. Graham entered a store, but due to long lines, left without purchasing anything. Graham told his daughter to hurry to another store. An officer observed Graham's quick entry and exit from the store, and stopped them to conduct an investigation. During the course of the investigation, Graham became upset and was handcuffed. While handcuffed, Graham sustained injuries. In turn, Graham filed suit against the department and the officer for excessive force. The Supreme Court found that officers are liable when any level of force is deemed excessive. However, the definition for what is excessive is determined after each situation, and is lacking an*

objective guideline. "The reasonableness of the situation and force used is determined on the spot, considering all the circumstances" (Champion, 1997, pp. 196–197). So what does this mean for officers? It sets up a standard that officers cannot be judged for their use of force, without looking at the context of the situation in which the force was used. This standard is based and argued under the 4th Amendment to the Constitution, (i.e., specifically search and seizure), since the application of force is a seizure.[9]

What does this mean for professional protection officers? Cases that address the use of force are few and far between. This means that security professionals in many instances are working in a space that is not clearly defined. It is clear that state law allows for a private person to make an arrest. With that arrest authority, however, is a vague, undefined, and untested ability to use force. In the real world in which the security professional works, he or she will at some point encounter a situation that requires the use of force. It is only a matter of time before case law at the federal level is on point and provides for a foundation. Until such time, security professionals must follow the guidance at hand—guidance that consists primarily of organizational policy and/or legal advice from corporate counsel.

Store Policy

Turning again to the scenarios, along with relevant state law, Jim would have the authority to act within the scope of his store's policies and procedures. Policies and procedures might limit the behavior of loss prevention employees or protection officers, but this does not negate any lawful authority provided by state statutes. The policy can say whatever the company wants it to, but it cannot supersede the law. The reality is that even staying within the boundaries of the law, company policy may still be violated and that has consequences of its own, such as formal punishment or termination.

Policies and procedures should clearly provide a foundation upon which a protection officer can do any job. This should apply to anyone working within the security field. These policies and procedures have their place within the security/protection fields. The reason is that there needs to be some sort of organizational restrictions and guidance regarding certain activities, especially those that could subject the company to liability if done improperly. The organization sets the course for what is allowed on duty, and company policies or procedures are restricted only by applicable law.

Policies regarding detentions and arrests should include a number of elements. These include but are not limited to:

- Identification of employee: How does the security professional identify himself to the person being stopped? This should be both verbal and nonverbal. Company-issued identification or credentials must be shown to the individual being detained in addition to a verbal identification, such as: "I am a loss prevention agent with Target."
- Purpose for the stop (apprehension, detention).
- Guidance on the application of force, which could take many forms. Within legal boundaries, what does the company explicitly permit or forbid the security

professional to do? Are distinctions made between passively resisting persons and actively resisting ones?

- In making an apprehension or detention, can restraints (handcuffs, shackles, flex-cuffs) be utilized?
- Notifications: At what point does law enforcement need to be notified? Store management? If the apprehension or detention involves a juvenile, when are parents/guardians notified? How are these notifications documented?
- Reporting: What incident report forms must be completed? Are there separate forms for use-of-force incidents? What information must be captured in the report to satisfy law enforcement, the corporate insurance carrier, and corporate counsel?
- Release: What procedures are followed when releasing an individual to law enforcement? What procedures are followed when releasing an individual because law enforcement declines to respond? Or if exculpatory evidence is identified? How is the release documented? Are any notifications required?

Some companies have comprehensive policies on apprehension and detention and use-of-force that incorporate federal, state, and local statutes, while some small stores do not have polices at all. In many cases, including retailers such as Target, Kmart, Sears, Best Buy, Herbergers, JC Penny, Gander Mountain, and Saks Fifth Avenue, a store large enough and profitable enough to have an internal loss prevention component or security division will likely also have a legal division that can craft these policies.

Loss prevention positions are somewhat different than uniformed security positions. When the employee is clearly and distinctly in a uniform, the purpose is to provide for an overt security presence. Regardless of position, whether uniformed or undercover, the authority for a private person making arrests remains the same. If a security provider does not have policies and procedures regarding arrests and detention, they must be developed and subject to legal review as soon as possible. A memorandum of understanding (MOU) or a set of post orders will not be sufficient. Policies must provide clear direction on the "when" and "why" of apprehension or detention but should not include the "how". For example, company policy might be that a security professional will not approach, detain, or otherwise interfere with an individual who has shoplifted or stolen anything with a retail value of less than $5. The reasoning behind such a policy is that there is set standard or "floor" beneath which the expense and/or potential liability from engaging in an apprehension or a detention outweighs the value of any possible recovery.

Tactics

Professional Protection Officer

Once the "when" and the "why" of apprehending or detaining an individual are understood, equal attention must be paid to "how". When a security professional determines that a person meets the necessary legal/procedural criteria and decides to approach a person, they must act. First and foremost, a professional should understand that sometimes the right, appropriate, and reasonable thing to do is nothing but contact law enforcement and allow properly equipped individuals to respond. Sometimes the odds are against individual protection officers, and discretion and individual safety is paramount. There are a host of theories and tactics that can be applied to making contact with a "bad" individual. The reality is that as a security professional one does it on a daily basis with all individuals and does so with limited respect, weapons, training, and/or backup.

Contact

In looking at how to contact the "actor" or "bad guy" one must understand the context first, and determine the level of crime or criminal transgression that has been committed. For example, a loss prevention agent observes a 14-year old girl shoplifting $20 of makeup products versus another girl who is on-site during an armed robbery. While these are examples at opposite ends of the danger spectrum, they provide for a clear understanding that not everything is black and white. Approaching an individual can be dangerous; a 14-year-old girl can hurt or kill just as readily as a full-grown adult. There is, however, the "scalable" likelihood of anything bad happening. Once the decision to make contact has been made, take into account who is being approached, where, when, for what reason, who will make the approach, and how the approach will be made. Consider these elements individually:

- *Who is being approached*: The security professional must assess the person they intend to approach. Is it one individual or is it more than one? What are the physical characteristics of the individual? Do they move as if they might have something concealed under their clothing? Do they appear to be scanning approaches, exits, looking for an advantage should an encounter occur? Are they physically larger or smaller than the security professional(s) making the approach? Is the individual male or female? These questions and more will impact how the approach occurs, or if it occurs at all.
- *Where will the approach take place*: Where is the safest place to stop, approach, or deal with the individual that is committing the crime/violation? Is it better to stop someone outside of the store, in an isolated area, or out in view of where plenty of witnesses will be present? For a security professional, this is an individual decision, guided by organizational policy. For a loss prevention professional, stopping someone outside of the store provides for a better foundation regarding the elements of the crime of shoplifting. Working as an executive protection specialist and providing protection for the principal is key, so the terms of an approach may not be perfect.
- *When will the approach take place*: There are sometimes situations when an individual needs to be contacted immediately, such as with a fight, assault, or other violent crime. The "when" is "right now." However, with some of the other crimes and transgressions, sometimes the "when" can be in a few minutes. There are no laws that state that action must be taken immediately (absent of imminent harm to the individual or those the security professional has a duty to protect). Not needing to approach right away allows for backup to arrive, for video cameras to be trained on the area, for law enforcement to be notified, or for any other reason.

- *Why is the approach being made*: This refers more to articulable facts, legal necessities, or other information that will be requested by law enforcement, or needs to be shared with the person being apprehended/detained. Security professionals must articulate their reason(s) for making the stop. They do not necessarily have to be the actual reasons, but they must say something. Persons are more likely to cooperate if they feel the security professional is being upfront about what is happening. Also, if the reason(s) cannot be articulated, it may be that taking action itself may not be necessary.
- *Who will make the approach*: Who should approach the individual? Should a manager or supervisor be present? Should there always be one officer to contact and another to cover or observe? The "who" is often a tactical decision as most people tend to calm down when they are outnumbered or see no other option besides de-escalating.
- *How will the approach be made*: "How" is an important tactical question. Does the nature of approach call for someone with extensive training versus an untrained or inexperienced officer? Force is inevitable even with compliant individuals as a patdown search for weapons, taken for officer safety purposes, will involve making physical contact with an individual in locations most people do not want to be touched. If an altercation is expected because the person is known to be belligerent when approached, how will the approach be conducted to minimize or mitigate that belligerent behavior?

Distance

Generally, one wants to stay 1.5 to 3.0 arm lengths away. This is close enough to move in and close the gap for initiating "arrest and control techniques," yet far enough away that one can have an advantage to leave or flee. Think about staying off to the side, and not directly in front, and "bladed" with what is referred to as a weapons or dominant hand back (Figure 36.1).

When there are multiple individuals to contact, the security professional must maintain control and vision of the entire group. When possible, separate the primary offender from the group and isolate that individual. If that is not possible, strong verbal commands will be necessary to obtain and/or maintain control of the situation. If there is more than one security officer, the second and subsequent officers can take a variety of positions. The purpose of additional officers is to provide "visual" deterrence for both the person(s) being apprehended as well as any bystanders. Back-up officers should take control of a situation if, and only if, the primary officer is clearly not in control or has created a "safety/security"

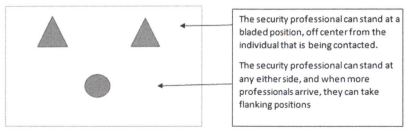

FIGURE 36.1 Arrest and control techniques.

threat to himself or herself, or others. These are both significant judgment calls and can only be made at the scene. Most professional security officers have been involved at one time or another in an incident during which they were faced with a potential officer safety issue caused by mishandling of an incident.

When approaching, be aware of the distances involved, particularly if there are any barriers that could be used as cover/concealment. Distance determines the ability to initiate force, defend against force, or flee from it if necessary. Watch the individual's hands and body position. The hands are one of the few things that can hurt you. Hands themselves are weapons; a few minutes of watching mixed martial arts (MMA) will demonstrate how true that is. Hands are more dangerous when holding knives, guns, pepper spray, or improvised weapons, such as a beer bottle or a baseball bat.

Movement

The security professionals must be in control of the entire situation, and part of controlling a situation is directing the movement of the individual(s) involved. Individuals should be told specifically and clearly where to move, what to move, how far to move it, and sometimes why they are being told to do so. Generally, asking for assistance or for individuals to cooperate will work, as people usually want to be helpful. Asking people to move is a regular part of the security professional's duties; the purpose of movement in apprehension/detention is primarily about safety and privacy. Most security professionals operate under the authority of the property owner, meaning that at minimum security professionals possess the authority to ask people to leave the property and/or provide for a criminal trespass warning.

In a situation where apprehension is a possibility or a certainty, moving the individual to a more secure or less visible location is important for a number of reasons. Some individuals will be less compliant/more combative if they have an audience. Isolating them from individuals that can exacerbate the situation is wise from a safety perspective. Verbal commands and officer presence alone may be sufficient to get an individual to move. Sometimes force must be used, such as an escort hold or "come-along." Isolating them also allows them to calm down or de-escalate without "losing face." Someone who feels humiliated will not be cooperative. There are tactical advantages as well; the security professional can move a person into an environment where it is easier to control them—to a more-confined area, an area with fewer or more easily controlled exits, or an area easily accessible by backup officers or law enforcement.

Weapons

Usage

There are a variety of defensive tactics available with which to physically control an individual. They include the "empty-hand" control or "escort" hold, and weapons such as collapsible baton, pepper spray, Taser, and firearms. Knowing not just when but how to use these defensive tactics is imperative—force is always a game-changer. Yet sometimes the presence of those implements can have a calming effect on the situation. That said, liability stakes increase when force is involved—and usually exponentially if weapons come into play.

Some security professional are permitted to carry weapons. Such professionals must be fully trained, regularly qualified, and protected by comprehensive organization policies that specifically address use-of-force. Each weapon has different positive and negative aspects. Each weapon system is designed for specific "target" areas. Weapons carry different liability and training requirements as well.

Electronic Incapacitation Devices

An electronic incapacitation devices (ECD) is commonly referred to as a Taser. However, Taser is a brand name; there are other manufacturers as well. ECDs, when used correctly, create neuromuscular incapacity. There are a variety of limited effects, as well as limited potential for personal injury. ECDs must make contact with an individual to be effective. They can be fired from a handheld device at a distance using "darts" or "probes," or can be physically touched to the individual by the security professional. These weapons are most effective at close quarters (i.e., less than 21 feet). The target's area should be in line with manufacturer requirements.

Batons

Batons come in two basic designs: straight or side-handled. As with the Taser, the straight baton is typically referred to as an "ASP," with ASP being the actual name of the baton manufacturer. Side-handled batons are known by the name "PR-24." Both types of batons come in collapsible varieties as well. Regardless of the name, each type of baton has a different system for training, use, and deployment. As with ECDs, security officers can only use this weapon in close quarters. Large muscle groups are the primary target area for a baton strike; however, other target areas can be utilized with proper training, such as nerve centers and pressure points. The visibility of the baton, particularly the deployment of a collapsible baton, can have a deterrent effect. This weapon can seriously injure or even kill an individual, although this is not a common occurrence. There is also moderate risk that in using this weapon the security professional could lose control of it during an altercation.

Chemical or Pepper Spray

Chemical spray, or what is commonly referred to as pepper spray, is carried on the belt in a canister. The canister or chemical is limited and is disbursed typically as a stream, a spray, or a type of foam. The general location or target area is the face. However, different mixtures and manufacturers have different requirements, and target areas must be aligned as appropriate. Chemical agents or spray generally impact the ability to see and cause temporary but intense burning sensation in and around the mouth/face/eyes.

Defensive Tactics

Anytime security professionals are provided with training, the inclusion of use of force training is imperative. Ideally, there should be regular updates on the application of force as well as human interaction dynamics. There are a variety of systems of defensive tactics that can be used, but all are based on the same general principles of how people move and react. A good system provides for understanding on how to control a human during the context of contact or apprehension. Handcuffing and searches should be taught in conjunction with defensive tactics, as they are integral parts of the apprehension process.

With any weapons or empty-hand defensive tactics, the training should include significant amounts of practice, and that practice should be as realistic as is safely possible. Using real-life scenarios is recommended; security professionals should practice scenarios that they are likely to encounter while on the job. The training needs to incorporate communication, such as body language, proxemics or nonverbal communication, and verbal skills. Training scenarios should teach and reinforce all stages of a potential encounter.

Handcuffing and Searching

The ability to control someone with handcuffs is a decision not to be taken lightly. To handcuff someone is to deny them freedom of movement. The security professional must be certain that the law permits them to apply handcuffs or restraints to another person, and if so, the security professional must understand how to do it safely, what to do after restraints have been applied, and how to safely release someone. At times, handcuffing someone is essential for safety purposes and is a prudent thing to do.

Security professionals must be trained in the proper use of handcuffs. They must understand how the locking mechanisms work, how to apply them correctly using only one available hand, how to determine tightness, how to position a person prior to handcuffing, and how to approach them. Also, after someone is handcuffed, the individual should be searched at least for concealed weapons or handcuff keys. The area accessible to the hands of the handcuffed person should be searched immediately. This includes the waistline of the pants, pockets, or any other area the person might be able to move their cuffed hands to. Remember, also there are people nimble enough to move their rear-cuffed hands to the front of their body. There are numerous ways to conceal a small handcuff key on the body, and it is even possible for a cuffed individual to break open the handcuffs (unlikely, but possible). Persons being handcuffed and searched should be moved out of public view when possible and safe to do so.

Emerging Trends

As protection officers become more widespread throughout society and their roles change, there will be a greater expectation that they can approach, interview, calm, restrain, and/or detain individuals in a professional manner. Protection officers are the first or second line of defense in most environments and we depend upon them. They will require more and more training, similar to that which law enforcement receives, as the responsibilities grow more complex. In addition, security professionals will have to maintain relations with the public and the organizations they serve. They must be ever vigilant against inappropriate or inadequate tactics that can readily spoil those relations.

Refer website http://www.ifpo.org for further information

End Notes

1. 2014 Minnesota Statutes, *When Private Person May Make Arrest* Chapter 629, Section 629.37. Accessed December 21, 2014. Available: https://www.revisor.mn.gov/statutes/?id=629.37.

2. 2014 Louisiana Code of Criminal Procedure, *Arrest by Private Person, When Lawful* CCRP 2014. Accessed December 21, 2014. Available: http://www.legis.state.la.us/lss/lss.asp?doc=112362.

3. 2013 Oregon Revised Statutes, *Arrest by Private Person* Chapter 133, Section 133.225. Accessed December 21, 2014. Available: https://www.oregonlegislature.gov/bills_laws/ors/ors133.html.

4. 2013 Oregon Revised Statutes, *Use of Physical Force in Defense of Premises* Chapter 161, Section 161.225. Accessed December 21, 2014. Available: https://www.oregonlegislature.gov/bills_laws/ors/ors161.html.

5. Arizona Criminal Code, *Shoplifting; Detaining Suspect; Defense to Wrongful Detention; Civil Action by Merchant; Public Services; Classification* Title 13, Section 1805. Accessed December 21, 2014. Available: http://www.azleg.gov/FormatDocument.asp?inDoc=/ars/13/01805.htm&Title=13&DocType=ARS.

6. Georgia Criminal Code, *Preclusion of Recovery for Detention or Arrest of Person Suspected of Shoplifting Under Certain Circumstances* Title 51, Chapter 7, Section 60. Accessed December 21, 2014. Available: http://law.justia.com/codes/georgia/2010/title-51/chapter-7/article-4/51-7-60.

7. Kansas Code, *Private Person's Use of Force in Making Arrest* Chapter 21, Article 32, Section 21–3216. Accessed December 23, 2014. Available: http://law.justia.com/codes/kansas/2011/Chapter21/Article32/21-3216.html.

8. Missouri Revised Statutes, *Private Person's Use of Force in Making an Arrest* Chapter 563, Section 563.051. Accessed December 23, 2014. Available: http://www.moga.mo.gov/mostatutes/stathtml/56300000512.html.

9. Stiehm M., *Campus Security/Public Safety Use of Force* (West Hartford, CT: International Association of Campus Law Enforcement Administrators, March/April 2013): vol. 43, pt 2, Accessed December 23, 2014. Available: http://community.iaclea.org/resources/viewdocument/?DocumentKey=605375f1-e221-4809-9be1-b2af124b2250.

Current Issues in Security

37

Espionage: A Primer

Brion P. Gilbride

Gentlemen do not read each other's mail.
Henry L. Stimson, US Secretary of State, 1929

When you think of espionage, what is the first thing that comes to mind? Perhaps you imagine shadowy government agents trading briefcases full of secrets in a dark alley, the CIA and KGB, or James Bond/007. This is what most people, regardless of where they are in the world, understand about the business of espionage. The reality is that governments do collect all manner of information on the operations and activities of other countries, both friend and foe. Also, part of this reality is that businesses and individuals collect information on each other—whether for business advantage, revenge, protection, or any other reason.

Espionage, in essence, is stealing secrets. Secrets can be in nearly any form—a document, an email, computer files, recorded conversations, text messages, etc. Who keeps secrets? Governments do, as do companies and people. The original recipe for Kentucky Fried Chicken is a secret. The schematics for a new machine may be a secret. Negotiations for a merger between two companies, plans for a brand-new aircraft carrier, and a list of spies with official cover working in Turkmenistan, are all secrets. There are thousands of examples. If another entity—either a corporation or even a government—got its hands on one of these secrets, consider what the impact would be. A competitor's product may beat your employer's product to market, costing millions in revenue. A government may begin feeding misinformation to your government's spies because it now knows who they are. Two companies may not merge; instead, your company fails while the other survives. The outcomes are legion, and most of them are bad.

Espionage in History

If the previous examples seem vague, there are plenty of real-life examples. In November 1778, General George Washington ordered that a spy ring be established to operate in New York City and supply information on British troops. The ring, called the Culver Spy Ring, operated until 1783. None of the members were ever caught. Methods used by the spy ring included pseudonyms, writing messages in invisible ink, and designing a numerical substitution system to identify people and places. During the ring's 5 years, its successes included thwarting a British attack on Rhode Island in 1780, as well as the capture of British Major John Andre—the spy who had led the Americans to Benedict Arnold.[1]

Security Supervision and Management. http://dx.doi.org/10.1016/B978-0-12-800113-4.00037-7

In the period after World War II, the Soviet Union was able to produce an atomic bomb years before anyone thought they could. They had help from several people; one was noted scientist Klaus Fuchs, who worked on the Manhattan Project. The scientists involved in the Manhattan Project developed the atomic bombs that were ultimately dropped on Nagasaki and Hiroshima, Japan at the end of the war. Fuchs passed along information on bomb design and assembly when he worked in the United States; when he moved to London, he passed along information on plans for a hydrogen bomb. To whom did he pass this information? The Soviet Union.[2] Fuchs was arrested in February 1950 and sentenced to 14 years in prison.

During the 1980s, an Iraqi scientist working on Saddam Hussein's nuclear program used his memory to identify foreign recipients of a restricted report so that he could obtain copies of it for Iraqi use. In his book *The Bomb in My Garden*, Dr. Mahdi Obeidi described his search for a particular report on the design of an atomic weapon. He tracked down this report to a library at the University of Virginia. When Dr. Obeidi went to see it, he learned that he would need to complete paperwork and provide identification for security purposes. To avoid leaving anything incriminating behind, Dr. Obeidi protested that the paperwork would take time and asked if he could briefly peruse the report to confirm it was the particular report he was looking for. The university agreed, and Dr. Obeidi was given the report. In doing this, Dr. Obeidi had the paper in his possession long enough to review the list of people to whom copies were provided to at the time it was published. This list contained the name of an Italian professor of Dr. Obeidi's acquaintance who may not have been subject to restrictions such as those placed by the University of Virginia. In this way, Dr. Obeidi was able to obtain a copy of the report without anyone in the United States knowing that he did so. In the United States, his attempt to access the report at the University of Virginia likely would have been reported to the authorities.[3]

Espionage in the Twenty-First Century

As demonstrated, different varieties of espionage have been used over the years. As the amount of information amassed by people and the methods of storing or transporting all of that data have exploded, the threats generated by espionage have changed. Espionage cases from the twenty-first century demonstrate some of the differences. In June 2013, an Indian national living and working in the United States was arrested and charged with theft of trade secrets. This person allegedly downloaded 8000 files from Becton Dickinson's computer servers for a disposable pen injector that the company was developing. The files were stored on external hard drives, thumb drives, and other storage devices.[4] This case is currently pending.

On February 28, 2007 Hanjuan Jin, a naturalized US citizen of Chinese descent from Aurora, Illinois, was intercepted at Chicago O'Hare International Airport attempting to board a flight to China. In her possession were more than 1000 electronic and paper documents that were property of Motorola. During her trial in 2011, a number of facts came to light. Jin joined Motorola in 1998 and worked until taking a leave of absence in 2006. During this leave, Jin obtained a job with Sun Kaisens, a Chinese communications company with connections to the Chinese military. On February 15, 2007 Jin returned to the United States and resumed employment with Motorola on February 26. Jin made multiple visits to Motorola between February 26 and 27; during those visits, Jin downloaded hundreds of technical documents from Motorola's servers and transported numerous hard-copy documents out of the facility. Among the materials seized from Jin on February 28 at O'Hare Airport were descriptions of specific Motorola product features, classified Chinese military documents, and $30,000 in cash. Jin was convicted on three counts of theft of trade secrets but was acquitted on three counts of economic espionage on behalf of China.[5]

On May 20, 2013, a man named Edward Snowden boarded a flight from Hawaii to Hong Kong. In his possession, or under his control at that time, were numerous files and documents containing classified information on US intelligence and diplomatic activities throughout the world. Snowden is believed to have obtained these items via his work with the US National Security Agency (NSA) as a contract employee. Prior to this work, Snowden had worked for the US Central Intelligence Agency from 2007 to 2009 as an information technology (IT) specialist, and before that for the NSA as a security guard.[6] It was primarily his IT background that enabled him to find and then copy the materials he ultimately fled with. Among those materials were documents relating to NSA capabilities concerning the collection, recording, and analysis of international and domestic phone calls involving the United States.[7]

Sabotage

Espionage cannot be adequately covered without discussing its evil twin, sabotage. Sabotage occurs when an individual takes an action that interferes with normal business or government operations. Keep in mind that the action does not have to be physical, such as pouring sugar into the gasoline tank of a car to prevent the engine from working properly. It can be something simple, such as renaming an important computer file so that others cannot find it. Being able to commit sabotage requires many of the same elements that committing espionage requires—particularly, opportunity or access to items or systems that can be sabotaged.

In 2013, a train carrying nuclear waste derailed in Bessines-sur-Gartempe, France. On the same day, a passenger train derailed south of Paris, in Bretigny-sur-Orge. Subsequent investigation of both rail accidents revealed that a part called a "fishplate," used to link to pieces of rail together, became loose. The loosening of the fishplate caused the two rails to which it was fastened to come apart, causing the derailments.[8]

In 2010, two Russian nationals and one Kazakhstan national were arrested near an Effingham, Georgia power plant after being spotted by a park ranger. A search of their nearby vehicle found a machete, shovel, wire cutters, and ski masks.[9] The intentions of these three men are not clear, but the presence of equipment that would be useful for breaching a fence or cutting electric wires suggests that their intentions were not good.

In 2011, a man was arrested after placing a homemade bomb at a natural gas pipeline substation in Okemah, Oklahoma. The bomb was found by an employee and fortunately did not detonate.[10] Had it done so, it would have caused significant damage to the natural gas company's infrastructure—the pipeline and substation—and possibly killed people who worked or lived in proximity to the line.

How Can Espionage Be Conducted?

The practices involved in committing espionage, referred to as tradecraft, have varied over the years. In many ways, tradecraft was and is dependent on what forms of information are available. In the days before computers, information had to be memorized and transmitted verbally, written down, or transmitted via a communication device (i.e., radio, telegraph). Capturing or stealing information had a certain element of risk in those days because one could be caught in the act of using the communication device or intercepted while actually carrying the evidence of espionage. To protect information, governments devised codes to deter others from intercepting it. The discipline that evolved from this practice is referred to as *cryptography*.

Tradecraft, especially before computers became widespread, relied partly on equipment being simple to use, reliable, and most importantly, concealable. One of the simplest ways, and riskiest, is to pass information from person-to-person via a handoff. This can be done out in the open but is subject to detection if there is any surveillance. This method is easily applicable to twenty-first century espionage activities; however, instead of paper or microfilm, the items passed are encrypted thumb drives or small DVD disks. The risk here is that if the person is intercepted by security officials, then the evidence is right there on their person. Another method to pass information is by using a "dead-drop." A dead-drop occurs when one party leaves an item or package in a prearranged place, which is later retrieved by another party. This is less risky in that the parties are not seen together; however, just like the person-to-person handoff (also known as a "brush-pass"), if the party with the item is intercepted by security officials the evidence is right there.

Information being transported may also be concealed via encryption. Before computers, information was often disguised using codes generated by a cipher machine. A code and a cipher are not the same thing. A Khan Academy lesson on codes and ciphers defines a code as "mapping from some meaningful unit into something else." In other words, in a code, one typically smaller or lesser complex component is substituted for a larger component. A cipher is defined as "mechanical operations (known as algorithms) which are performed on the individual or small chunks of letters."[11] A cipher, therefore, is the exercise used to create the code. If a cipher is used to create a code, the same cipher can be used to break it. When transporting information, an additional level of safety can be provided by encryption, such as a one-time pad (OTP), in which a cipher is: "a series of numbers randomly keyed to letters that can be put into clear text only by someone having an identical OTP."[12]

Communications technology in the pre-computer age also made espionage risky. Telephones were not wireless, so unless someone was using a radio, there was no way to capture transmissions out of the air—the transmission line itself had to be accessible in order to eavesdrop. Such devices were called *taps*. In some instances, the cable carrying conversations could be tapped but not individual phone lines. The United States did this with a cable running beneath the Sea of Okhotsk to intercept Soviet communications at the naval base in Petropavlovsk. The operation, called Ivy Bells, required a submarine and divers to install a tap and later to retrieve and replace the recording tapes.[13] A conversation between two people in a room could also be recorded via a transmitting device called a *bug*. Bugs could be concealed inside the room but were detectable via scanning equipment or by someone physically finding it.

Other tradecraft concerned the creation or use of identity documents. One of the ways to protect an organization that is committing espionage is to have the perpetrators of such acts disguise their identity. In the twentieth century, this might have involved photo-substituting within a legitimate passport, applying for a driver's license using a fake birth certificate so as to have a real document on a phony person, or altering one's appearance to match a legitimate person or identity document (i.e., as an impostor). The widespread use of biometrics in the twenty-first century, from fingerprints to palm prints to retinas, has made these methods far more complicated to use, but not impossible.

In the digital age, a number of things have changed. Most telephone calls, including cellular phones and satellite phones, are broadcast through the air to towers or satellites. This means unencrypted conversation can be intercepted without having to physically enter a site or install a tap on a phone line. Encryption technology has become far more powerful and accessible to the public than it used to be; however, computing power has multiplied exponentially, to such an extent that encryption can potentially be defeated. Bugs have become smaller and more powerful—there is no longer a need to hide a bug in a room when they can be concealed on a person. A bug could be concealed in nearly anything, and most cellular phones that people use come with recording and photographic capability that is near professional quality. All this technology is accessible to the general public. Like telephone calls, the data transmitted by wireless networks, smartphones, and other devices can be intercepted without having to physically install a recording device or enter a restricted space.

In the digital age, most of the world's information or data is stored on computers, servers, or devices that can communicate with computers or servers. If someone accesses information on a company's computers or servers to which they are not authorized or entitled, that falls pretty clearly under espionage. Espionage might also include someone denying a company access to proprietary information or data. If a person hacks into a company's computer and wipes (erases) the hard drives, they have accessed information to which they are not authorize or entitled *and* also gone a step further by altering or destroying such information.

To give an idea of the scale of the changes between papers and tape recordings versus digital storage, consider the following comparison. Instead of passing documents or microfilm, an espionage agent might pass a DVD disc or a USB thumb drive. Consider how much more information a USB thumb drive can hold versus actual paper or microfilm: 32-gigabyte (GB) thumb drives are inexpensive; if 1 GB is analogous to 900,000 pages, multiply that by 32—that is just shy of 29 million pages. If the book *Atlas Shrugged* is 1000 pages long, then 28,800 copies of it can be stored on a single thumb drive.

Social Engineering

Social engineering is a recent phenomenon. It encompasses both the use of technology and person-to-person techniques to elicit information. If a person can be convinced to unintentionally or inadvertently give up information, a level of plausible deniability is created for those seeking unauthorized access to that information. This activity is referred to as *social engineering*—"the art of gaining access to buildings, systems, or data by exploiting human psychology, rather than by breaking in or using technical hacking techniques."[14] In simpler terms, social engineering is a confidence game. The social engineer tries to bluff his or her way into the information being sought.

CSO magazine published an article in 2008 that described some of the tactics used by social engineers. For social engineering to work, the "engineer" must convince the target that he or she is someone who is entitled to the information they are seeking. The engineer might use company-specific jargon to convince the target that he or she is an employee of the company, in particular one of higher rank than the target. The rank confers the additional advantage of making the target less likely to question something from a higher-up in the corporate hierarchy. Other tactics include using a recording of the company's "on hold" music to simulate a call from an internal phone—the idea being that the target hears the familiar music and assumes the person is calling from elsewhere within the company. Combine this with "spoofing" the caller identification (i.e., the target's phone displays a different caller ID number than the actual incoming call) and the tactic can be quite effective. Social networking sites such as LinkedIn and Facebook have made the lives of social engineers easier, as many people share too much about their personal and professional lives via those sites. In addition, the frequent changes to the security settings of those sites, makes it difficult for even prudent persons to keep their information secure.[15]

Motivations

It is not enough to understand how data might be captured or transmitted to effectively defend against it. It must also be understood why a person or an organization might want to intercept a company's secrets. According to the Defense Human Resources Activity,[16] some reasons why a person might engage in espionage include the following:

Increasing prevalence of personal financial problems and/or compulsive gambling
Diminishing organizational loyalty
Ethnic diversification and/or allegiance to a global community

The first reason, and the most common, is money. The data held by a company can be quite valuable in some instances. Design specifications, blueprints, customer data, and financial data could be turned over to another company or even another government for remuneration or other consideration. An employee who lives beyond his or her means could be susceptible to this, as might one who gambles compulsively or is overwhelmed by serious medical bills for a spouse or other relative.

Diminishing organizational loyalty is an interesting and more recent phenomenon. During much of the twentieth century, it was possible to start working for a company and stay with them for an entire 20- or 30-year career. This meant there was considerable loyalty between the company and its employees, who knew if they worked hard that the company (via their pension) would take care of them in their old age. In the twenty-first century, this outlook has fallen by the wayside for a variety of reasons. It is no longer uncommon for someone to hold the same position with different companies, or to change jobs entirely. The downside to feeling less loyalty to one's employer is that it removes a significant mental barrier to violating one's integrity—or enabling the rationalization of taking something from the company.

Ethnic diversification and/or allegiance to a global community is also a recent phenomenon. Populations in many countries are much more diversified than they were 50 years ago. Back then, people emigrated to the United States to become American or to Canada to become Canadian. In the twenty-first century, however, a hyphenated description has become common. *Chinese-American* denotes someone who emigrated from China to the United States, while *Indo-Canadian* describes someone from India who moved to Canada. The distinction described here is between a person who emigrates to become a citizen of their destination country and one who temporarily emigrates to take advantage of opportunities or benefits accessible in the destination country with the goal of returning "home". This change has occurred with the prevalence of organizations such as the United Nations or the European Union in favor of the traditional nation-state. The ability of the average person to easily and quickly move from one place to another anywhere on the globe and the general interconnectedness of the world via the Internet (as we know it) has also contributed to this change. However, if the emigrant must choose between the country they have immigrated to and the country they have emigrated from, with whom will they place their loyalty?

Security Clearances and Classifications

Governments have come up with systems to identify information that they want to keep secret. Governments also have procedures to identify and vet persons who can be permitted to access such secret information. Security classifications generally are used to restrict government-held or government-related information. These classifications are applied to any information that, if exposed, would adversely affect national security. This kind of information is commonly referred to as *classified information*. To obtain access to classified information, a security clearance is required. There are different levels of security clearance, depending on the nature and sensitivity of the information classified at that particular level.

A person does not need to be a government employee to be granted a security clearance. Many private companies working on government contracts, particularly those of a military nature, employ persons with security clearances. Regardless of their employer, if a person requests a security clearance, a background investigation will be conducted. The intensity of the investigation varies, but background investigators ultimately have to learn enough about the person so that an adjudicator can determine that person is not a potential security risk:

> *It must be determined that the individual's personal and professional history indicates loyalty to the United States, strength of character, trustworthiness, honesty, reliability, discretion, and sound judgment, as well as freedom from conflicting allegiances and potential for coercion, and a willingness and ability to abide by regulations governing the use, handling, and protection of classified information.[17]*
>
> U.S. State Department, "All About Security Clearances"

The procedures vary by the nature of the entity granting the clearance, but essentially the grantor of the clearance must be satisfied that the person requesting it will not steal, leak, or lose the information to which they have been granted access.

Trade Secrets

In the private sector, trade secrets are analogous to classified information. Trade secrets are information that, if exposed, would impact the health (and sometimes the very existence) of the company that possesses them. The Legal Information Institute at Cornell University described six factors under US law that will typically determine whether or not information can be referred to as a trade secret:

- The extent to which information is known outside the company
- The extent to which information is known by employees and/or others involved with the company
- The extent of measures taken by the company to safeguard the information
- The value of the information to the company and its competitors
- The amount of effort or finances expended in the development of the information
- The ease at which the information could be duplicated by others

These factors are straightforward. Something that is not secret cannot be a trade secret. Information that is not protected (e.g., published on the company's Internet site) cannot be a trade secret. Information that is valuable because of the resources used to develop it can be a trade secret as long as it is known to a minimum necessary number of people and is protected via encryption, a safe, armed guards, or some other method. Note that this is different than a patent; a patent requires disclosure of information in order to receive protection, and for a limited amount of time. A trade secret is a secret until it is exposed.[18]

An article submitted to the European Parliament on November 28, 2013, states that in order for information to be considered a trade secret, it must meet all of the following:

- It is not generally known among or readily accessible to persons within the circles that normally deal with the kind of information in question.
- Has commercial value because it is secret.
- Has been subject to reasonable steps by those in control of the information to keep it secret.[19]

As you can see, the definitions of a trade secret are quite similar. Simply, the information cannot be already known or accessible, it must be protected as a secret, and it must have some value by virtue of being kept secret.

What Can Security Do About Espionage in the Twenty-First Century?

Companies and governments are more vulnerable to espionage now than ever before. The sheer volume of information stored in a nonphysical format and the multitude of methods by which to intercept such information makes security, and especially cybersecurity, more relevant to company operations and to maintaining the bottom line. Some of the espionage methods described above can only be detected by IT professionals, such as the introduction of an unauthorized thumb drive onto the company network or the attempted accessing of restricted files. Methods such as the dead-drop or the person-to-person handoff can only be detected by observation via video or by someone witnessing the event. Persons attempting to access company data via wireless transmission can now stay far enough away from the facility that law enforcement may be the only ones to detect such activity. Background investigations conducted by the human resources (HR) division take on additional importance with the increasing number of emigrants living and working in a particular location.

The importance of cultivating relationships with the corporate IT department, the corporate HR department, as well as the appropriate law enforcement entities cannot be understated if the fight against espionage is to be successful. Tactics such as "red teaming"—where security professionals deliberately try to penetrate an organization in order to identify weaknesses—are becoming more and more common in both government and the private sector. Security awareness is also important. The "general population" company employees will supplement good security practices if they understand why they need to do something. Security professionals can support that by making periodic presentations to the employees. If presentations can include the corporate IT department or law enforcement, that will have additional impact.

Refer website http://www.ifpo.org for further information

End Notes

1. Williams V., *Culper Spy Ring* (Mount Vernon, VA: George Washington's Mount Vernon, Date Unknown): accessed December 29, 2013. Available: http://www.mountvernon.org/educational-resources/encyclopedia/culper-spy-ring.

2. Weinstein A. and Vassiliev, *The Haunted Wood: Soviet Espionage in America – The Stalin Era* (New York, NY: Random House, 1999), 319–20.

3. Obeidi M. and Pitzer K., *The Bomb in My Garden* (Hoboken, NJ: John Wiley & Sons, 2004), 77–9.

4. Sampson P. J., *Former Engineer at Bergen County Based Becton Dickinson Charged with Stealing Trade Secrets* (Woodland Park, NJ: North Jersey Media Group, June 8, 2013): accessed June 8, 2013. Available: http://www.northjersey.com/mahwah/former_Becton_Dickinson_engineer_charged_with_stealing_trade_secrets.html.

5. Dollear S. and Samborn R., *Suburban Chicago Woman Convicted of Stealing Trade Secrets from Motorola Before Attempting to Travel to China* (Chicago, IL: United States Attorney, Northern District of Illinois, February 8, 2012): accessed January 5, 2014. Available: http://www.fbi.gov/chicago/press-releases/2012/suburban-chicago-woman-convicted-of-stealing-trade-secrets-from-motorola-before-attempting-to-travel-to-china.

6. Greenwald G., MacAskill E. and Poitras L., *Edward Snowden: The Whistleblower Behind the NSA Surveillance Revelations* (London, UK: The Guardian, June 8, 2013): accessed June 10, 2013. Available: http://www.guardian.co.uk/world/2013/jun/09/edward-snowden-nsa-whistleblower-surveill/print.

7. McCullagh D., *NSA Spying Flap Extends to Contents of U.S. Phone Calls* (San Francisco, CA: CNET News, subsidiary of CBS Interactive, June 15, 2013): accessed June 16, 2013. Available: http://news.cnet.com/8301-15378_3-57589495-38/nsa-spying-flap-extends-to-contents-of-u.s-phone-calls/.

8. Author Unknown, *French Police Investigate Sabotage in Nuclear Train Crash* (Paris, France: RFI, July 19, 2013): accessed January 24, 2014. Available: http://www.english.rfi.fr/europe/20130719-french-police-investigate-sabotage-nuclear-train-crash.

9. Komanecky, De A. *Effingham Deputies Call Feds after Arresting Russians with Shovel, Wire Cutters Outside Georgia Power Plant* (Savannah, GA: Savannah Morning News, September 9, 2010): accessed September 11, 2010. Available: http://savannahnow.com/effingham-now/2010-09-09/effingham-deputies-call-feds-after-arresting-russians-shovel-wire-cutters.

10. Author Unknown, *Okla Man Sentenced for Trying to Bomb Gas Line* (San Francisco, CA: San Francisco Chronicle, December 5, 2012): accessed December 8, 2012. Available: http://www.sfgate.com/news/crime/article/Okla-Man-sentenced-for-trying-to-bomb-gas-line-4094321.php.

11. Author Unknown, *Codes and Ciphers* (Mountain View, CA: Khan Academy, Date Unknown): accessed January 24, 2014. Available: https://www.khanacademy.org/math/applied-math/cryptography/ciphers/a/ciphers-vs-codes.

12. Royden B. G., "Tolkachev, a Worthy Successor to Penkovsky," *Studies in Intelligence* 47, no. 3, Unclassified Edition (2003): accessed January 18, 2014. Available: https://www.cia.gov/library/center-for-the-study-of-intelligence/csi-publications/csi-studies/studies/vol47no3/article02.html.

13. Yenne B., *Secret Weapons of the Cold War: From the H-Bomb to SDI* (New York, NY: Berkley Books, 2005), 242–43.

14. Goodchild J., *Social Engineering: The Basics* (Framingham, MA: CSO Magazine, December 20, 2012): accessed January 25, 2014. Available: http://www.csoonline.com/article/514063/social-engineering-the-basics.

15. Goodchild J., *Social Engineering: Eight Common Tactics* (Framingham, MA: CSO Magazine, November 6, 2008): accessed January 25, 2014. Available: http://www.csoonline.com/article/460135/social-engineering-eight-common-tactics.

16. Author Unknown, *Insider Espionage is a Growing Threat* (Arlington, VA: U.S. Department of Defense, Defense Personnel Research Activity, Date Unknown): accessed January 19, 2014. Available: http://www.dhra.mil/perserec/adr/counterintelligence/insiderespionage.htm.

17. Author Unknown, *All About Security Clearances* (Washington, DC: U.S. Department of State, Date Unknown): accessed January 24, 2014. Available: http://www.state.gov/m/ds/clearances/c10978.htm.

18. Author Unknown, *Trade Secret* (Cornell, NY: Legal Information Institute, Cornell University, Date Unknown): accessed January 24, 2014. Available: http://www.law.cornell.edu/wex/trade_secret.

19. European Commission, *Proposal for a Directive of the European Parliament and of the Council on The Protection of Undisclosed Know-How and Business Information (Trade Secrets) Against Their Unlawful Acquisition, Use and Disclosure* (Brussels, Belgium, The European Parliament, November 28, 2013): accessed January 24, 2014. Available: http://eur-lex.europa.eu/LexUriServ/LexUriServ.do?uri=CELEX: 52013PC0813:EN: NOT.

Cyber Security

Jeffrey L. Colorossi

Information security has traditionally been about protection of electronic data, services, and systems. For many people, this equates to the Internet, their work computer systems, or the online retail services they use. Cyber security, while often used interchangeably with information security, extends far beyond the protection of computer systems. Critical infrastructure systems such as water, power, heating and air conditioning, and communications, including mobile devices, all rely upon computers systems and make up the larger focus of cyber security. Our context, while inclusive, will show how information security has become a facet of the broader scope: cyber security. It is important to note that, in many ways, cyber security is a natural and logical progression of traditional security methodologies, modified to address the unique nuances of digital technologies. Making one an expert in cyber security is beyond the scope of this text; rather, this chapter will provide an introduction into many aspects of cyber security to establish a foundation for future research and study. Relevant resources provided in the text and at the end of the chapter will aid and encourage security professionals at all levels in furthering the knowledge and skill sets they bring to their teams.

Internet Security Primer

Protection of personnel, facilities, services, and durable goods was once an entirely hands-on, physical endeavor. Introduction of technology systems such as closed-circuit television, audio recording equipment, and, to a lesser extent, communications devices were instrumental in evolving professional security services. The development of computers by educational institutions, medical research facilities, and the military introduced a new means for sharing knowledge, automation, communication, and ultimately a new vector for crime and malicious activity. ARPANET, the first interconnected network, was created by the US Defense Advanced Research Projects Agency in 1966 to enable computers in remote locations to communicate directly with each other.[1] ARPANET was the very beginning of the Internet that we know today. While that first network was limited to four remotely connected computers, it demonstrated the feasibility of rapid and direct communications using computers by sharing information pertaining to military and educational research.

Over the next 20 years, ARPANET expanded exponentially until in 1988 there were more than 100,000 computers interconnected around the world. Robert Tappan Morris (son of a chief scientist with the National Security Agency [NSA]) was a graduate student attending

Security Supervision and Management. http://dx.doi.org/10.1016/B978-0-12-800113-4.00038-9

Cornell University when he created a worm (a program that automatically replicates from one computer to another) that he claimed was to "gauge the size of the Internet." Morris launched his worm from Massachusetts Institute of Technology to hide its source. The worm took advantage of several weaknesses in the computer systems it touched, causing an estimated 6,000 computers to crash. For his efforts, Morris became the first person prosecuted under the Computer Fraud and Abuse Act (Title 18).

Initially, universities and research facilities sold Internet access by the minute to users. Cliff Stoll was an astronomer at the Lawrence Berkley Laboratory assigned to their computer laboratory to track user billing. His book, *The Cuckoo's Egg: Tracking a Spy through the Maze of Computer Espionage,*[2] details his efforts in tracking and ultimately leading authorities to an unauthorized user stealing access time from across the globe. A relatively short book, it provides a unique and very accurate insight into the early challenges of tracking computer activity and showcases one of the first international computer break-ins. Little did Stoll know his experiences would become commonplace in the twenty-first century.

The early 1980s ushered personal computers into mainstream use. Businesses and individuals alike began to take advantage of this new technological marvel, quickly becoming dependent on electronic bulletin board services (BBS), electronic mail (email), and ultimately web browsing. The ARPANET was unable to support the ever-increasing volume of users and, out of necessity, the Internet was born. By 1992, there were more than a million computers connected to the Internet; as it expanded, the amount of information available to anyone with access to retrieve it also expanded, further extending the potential avenues for abuse and misuse. Over the next 20 years, access to the Internet quickly migrated from limited per-minute charges to the often free and unlimited access for nearly everyone. During this same timeframe, computer crime and the ever-increasing need for security flourished. An early example of the increase in malicious activity was SQL Slammer. SQL refers to *structured query language* and is a method of extracting information from database systems. SQL Slammer was a worm that infected Microsoft SQL database servers globally, demonstrating in less than 10 min the broad reach and ever-increasing risk of Internet use. View the global spread of SQL Slammer here: http://www.pbs.org/wgbh/pages/frontline/shows/cyberwar/warnings/slammermap.html.

Figure 38.1 presents a short timeline of notable computer security events extracted from public news feeds and security breach reports. A security breach is any incident that bypasses security controls, resulting in the unauthorized access to systems, data, or services. Several state and federal laws require organizations experiencing a breach to provide notifications to affected customers, partners, and government agencies.

Confidentiality, Integrity, and Availability: The CIA Triad

Confidentiality, integrity, and availability (CIA), as the basis for information security, are equally important to the broader realm of cyber security (Figure 38.2). **Confidentiality** refers to ensuring that information (known as data) is only accessible to someone with a need to know. Access controls and data encryption protect confidentiality for most cyber

Year	Event
1991	The number of computer virus records exceeds 1000
1992	The number of connected computers exceeds 1,000,000
1994	Kevin Mitnik arrested for computer fraud ($80+ million in damages)
1994	250,000 attacks on Department of Defense computers
1996	China requires computer users to register with the police
	New York Stock Exchange shutdown by computer attacks
1997	First firewall developed to protect computers
1998	Solar Sunrise: Intruders infiltrate >500 military, government, and private computer systems
1999	CyberWar: first-time computer attacks used in war (Serbia and Kosovo)
2000	I Love You virus causes $1 billion in damages
2001	Code Red and Nimda viruses cause >$28 billion in damages globally
2002	Dedicated denial of service attack knocks out critical Internet services
2003	Recording industry sues 261 individuals for computer piracy
	SQL Slammer spreads globally in under 10 min (see text)
2004	Windows finally ships with a built-in firewall
2005	Web application attacks begin to emerge as primary method of compromise
2007	TJ Maxx data breach loses 45.7 million credit and debit cards: cost, $257 million
2008	Pay Card Industry Digital Security Standards (PCI-DSS) released to protect credit card transactions
2009	Commission on Cybersecurity for the 44th Presidency was created
	Heartland Payment Systems breached, losing 130 million debit and credit cards
	Department of Veterans Affairs loses records of 76 million veterans
2010	Botnets send >40 million spam email messages per day
2011	Sony: 100 million records lost, Epsilon: 60 million records lost; security giant RSA all breached
2012	Hacking collective "Anonymous" attacks for a cause
2013	White House issues executive order on improving critical infrastructure cybersecurity
	Target breach exposes 40 million credit and debit cards
2014	Edward Snowden releases NSA-classified records

FIGURE 38.1 Twenty years of notable security events, assimilated from public news feeds.

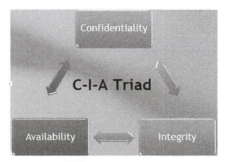

FIGURE 38.2 CIA triad.

systems. Access controls are a system of permissions that ensure data or data systems are appropriately protected and accessible by only those with proper authority. For example, a human resources (HR) database might be restricted to allow managers to view (read) information pertaining to their staff while allowing HR personnel to manage and modify the same records. This is an example of role-based access controls, where personnel were assigned the roles of manager or HR based upon their organizational responsibilities. Assigning permissions based on roles often simplifies the administration of data access.

Information is stored on computers digitally (simply put, as 1s and 0s), which the computer interprets as either data or program code. The human readable form of this data is plain text. To protect data, it is often necessary to render it unreadable to both user and computer without the use of specific tools, permissions, or processes. One of the preferred methods of protecting data is through encryption. Data encryption uses mathematical algorithms or calculations (remember to the computer data is just 1s and 0s) to hide the contents from those not authorized to view it. Although it is possible to "break" the encryption using specialized software and extremely powerful computers, this could easily take thousands of years when an appropriately strong algorithm is used. On the other hand, users and computers with proper access to the algorithm can easily decipher (unencrypt) the data and use it. Occasionally, one might hear the term *obfuscation* used in conjunction with encryptions; these are completely different processes, with obfuscation merely jumbling of or masking over the data. Obfuscation in most cases is a trivial protection to bypass.

Data for many sensitive purposes, including financial transactions, legal documents, and medical records, require a high level of assurance that the information has not been altered. **Integrity** refers to keeping data inviolate or unaltered by unauthorized personnel. Like confidentiality, encryption plays a role in protecting data integrity; however, hashing plays an equally important role. Hashing (also known as a *message digest*) is also performed using a mathematical algorithm; however, rather than altering the presentation of the data, a hash value is created that is unique to a given set or subset of data. Think of it as a compact digital file signature. The calculated hash is then safely stored and used only to verify that data was not changed while either in storage or in transit. For example, the mere addition of a space or punctuation mark to a document would completely change the calculated hash value, proving alteration of the data. MD5 and SHA1 are examples of hashing algorithms. MD5hash and Winmd5 are examples of file hashing tools. The forensics section discusses further uses for hashing.

Figure 38.3 shows how adding a period to the sample sentence (left) completely changes the resultant hash (right).

Clear Text	MD5 Hash
Cyber security requires diligence	43aee90f7e43087eeebb5acd4074f18a
Cyber security requires diligence	5adb51faf57985eb36fa00a0dd61d77e

FIGURE 38.3 MD5 hash examples.

Availability focuses on ensuring that authorized users have access to data, services, and systems whenever needed. Availability can often be likened to system uptime, which would lead one to ask what security has to do with the role of infrastructure and support systems. Denial of service has become a major, organizationally-impacting event that cyber security professionals deal with. A denial of service (DoS) is an attack that prevents access to data, systems, or services. A dedicated denial of service (DDoS) attack uses large compromised networks of many computers in a concerted attack. Defense of availability is often a concerted effort between network and security teams. System load balancers, web application and network firewalls, and active monitoring are key measures taken to protect against denial of service attacks. Firewalls are specialized network systems that control, monitor, and restrict network traffic flow as a defensive measure. In the expanded arena of cyber security, protection of critical infrastructure systems becomes imperative when a denial of service attack could endanger large portions of the populace.

Authorization and Authentication

Cyber security relies on some key controls to ensure accountability. **Authentication** is the process of ensuring that one is who they claim to be. The process of authentication uses one or more of the following factors:

1. Something a person knows: This is commonly a username, password, or passphrase.
2. Something a person is: Use of a unique physical characteristic such as fingerprints, retina scan, or voice recognition. Biometrics is the use of physical attributes in computer authentication.
3. Something a person has: Use of a unique physical device that can be associated with a specific individual, such as a government identification card, security token, or key.

Traditionally, individuals authenticate by use of a username and password. Both elements are something the individual knows; therefore, this is single-factor authentication. While the use of complex passwords has been shown to be effective at reducing account compromise, modern computers are powerful enough to break short and weak passwords in a matter of minutes, hours, or days. Complex passwords consist of a combination of upper-case letters, lower-case letters, numbers, and special characters. Passphrases are often much easier to remember, providing a mechanism for users to easily remember long and relatively unbreakable passwords. Passphrases are created by stringing many words together without spaces and by changing some of the letters to numbers or special characters. Figure 38.4 shows an example of converting a phrase into a passphrase. Note the use

Original Phrase	Passphrase
Mickey Mouse has two big floppy ears	M!ck3yM0us3H@s2BigFl0ppyE@rs

FIGURE 38.4 Example of passphrase creation.

of capital letters for the first letter of each original word and the replacement of other letters with numbers or special characters. Randomness greatly increases the strength of the resultant passphrase. Additionally, on Windows-based systems, passwords greater than 14 characters are significantly more difficult to crack than passwords of lesser length.

Two-factor authentication requires the use of two factors, such as username/password with a security token or a biometric reader with a personal identification number (PIN). A security token provides a unique and regularly changing code that is synchronized with the system the user is accessing. While the "something a person has" (password) might be easily guessed, an attacker would still require the security token (something a person has) in order to compromise the authentication process. Two-factor authentication is becoming commonplace; however, diligence in protecting each factor is critical to preventing compromise. It is also important to remember that even if two-factor authentication is used, it must be done in a secure manner. The debit card (something a person has) and personal identification number (PIN) (something a person is) is a simple example of two-factor authentication; however, most PIN numbers are four characters, thus limiting the number of possible combinations to 9999 and making it easy to use "brute force." The European Union (EU) has enacted requirements for the use of EMV (Europay, Mastercard, and Visa) "chip and PIN" credit cards. The chip and PIN card contains a small memory chip that helps authenticate the card. This mechanism also requires the user to have a PIN. More secure than the magnetic stripe credit cards with signature in use in America today, the chip and PIN cards are becoming mandatory in the United States in 2016. Retailers electing not to use the new cards will be held responsible for any fraudulent transactions that might occur.

Authorization refers to the level of access granted an individual to data, systems, or services. Access controls regulate authorization and work hand-in-hand to protect cyber systems. Once authenticated, a user must then be authorized to access the desired resource(s). File, folder, and share permissions are common methods of controlling access. Data owners can restrict access on a need-to-know basis by granting read, modify, and execute permissions on files, folders, and shares. Nonrepudiation extends the concept of authorization and applies it to assurance, particularly in reference to electronic communications. It is often a simple practice to spoof (falsify) where an electronic communication comes from. Through use of authentication and digital signatures, nonrepudiation ensures that the sender actually sent the communication and the recipient actually received it; neither can deny their part in the communication.

Risks, Threats, and Vulnerabilities

Viewed holistically, cyber security encompasses a broad spectrum, touching nearly every aspect of our lives. In the most simplistic terms, the primary role of cyber security is to manage risk. Before we define risk, it is important to understand the key contributors to risk—specifically threats, vulnerabilities, and asset value. When calculating the asset value, one must look beyond mere acquisition cost and consider sundry costs associated with all aspects of the cyber asset. Take, for example, a critical computer server that contains customer information. While the price of the hardware and software might be relatively low, the cost of the customer data carries a much higher price. For this reason, the Ponemon Research Center *2014 Data Breach Report*[3] estimated the average corporate cost of a data breach at nearly $3.5 million US dollars, with a per-record cost of $194.

Many definitions exist in the information security community regarding risk, threats, and vulnerabilities. Even the major standards bodies, such as the National Institute of Standards and Technology (NIST), International Standards Organization, and European Network and Information Security Agency, all define threats and risk differently. They all agree, however, that vulnerability is a flaw, weakness, or lack of security control in hardware, software, or a system process that exposes the system to compromise; simply stated, vulnerability is an exposure to compromise, and most system compromises are the direct result of exploitation of identified vulnerabilities. For example, an error in the code of an operating system or associated program might result in a system or application failure during routine operation. This error condition introduces a vulnerability that is ripe for compromise by an attacker. Vulnerabilities are not limited to coding errors; rather, system configuration settings pose an equal risk and carry a real likelihood of exploitation. Standardized configuration guidelines, such as those provided by NIST and the Center for Internet Security (CIS), help reduce vulnerabilities due to configuration settings.

Knowledge of both the vulnerability and the existence of a tool or method for exploiting that same vulnerability is a **threat**. Security researchers often dedicate much of their time to identifying vulnerabilities in systems and developing tools with which to exploit the vulnerability. Vendors and manufacturers frequently provide updates for vulnerabilities identified in their systems. Furthermore, vulnerabilities are called "zero day" vulnerabilities until the manufacturer or vendor identifies a fix or releases a patch. Major security conferences such as Blackhat, Defcon, and CanSecWest all offer competitions and rewards to security researchers who identify new ways to compromise systems and demonstrate them at their conference. In many cases, such release of information regarding vulnerabilities follows a responsible disclosure; however, this is not always the case.

Responsible disclosure is the private notification to a vendor or manufacturer regarding a vulnerability in the system or piece of software with the intent of allowing them a reasonable time to patch before public disclosure. Many manufacturers have created a "bounty program" for researchers who identify vulnerabilities in their systems in exchange for a commitment that the researcher will not reveal the vulnerability to the public. It is important to note that there are researchers who identify vulnerabilities and immediately post them to public hacker forums, such as Full Disclosure (http://seclists.org/fulldisclosure/). It is also common practice to post the actual exploit code to assist others in reproducing the exploitation scenario. Security practitioners regularly monitor such sites as a proactive approach to defending against zero-day vulnerabilities—or in the case of hackers, as a method of identifying new ways to compromise target systems.

Many cyber security companies employ security researchers specifically to seek out zero-day vulnerabilities to protect customer systems. When vulnerabilities in systems are identified, the manufacturer is notified as part of the service. Vupen Security (http://www.vupen.com/english/) takes a different approach, employing security researchers to identify vulnerabilities; however, rather than informing the manufacturer, Vupen sells details of the vulnerabilities to the highest bidder. This controversial approach has been very lucrative for researchers, who can earn from $5000 to $100,000 for identified vulnerability details.

Cyber security controls and decisions are determined by risk. In its simplest form, we define **risk** as the likelihood that a threat will exploit a vulnerability. To calculate risk, we use the equation: Risk = Vulnerability × Threat × Asset value. Organizations must carefully prioritize risk based upon the risk equation and how it impacts the overall business operation. One must also consider probability (likelihood) when assessing threats and risk. If tools are readily available, exploitation relatively easy, and value gain for the attacker high, then there is a high probability that the threat will be realized. The risk officer and/or the chief information security officer (CISO) for cyber systems must carefully weigh these factors when assessing risk and allocate resources or direct actions accordingly.

Risk can be addressed by one of four approaches: acceptance; mitigation; transfer; or a combination of the three. **Risk acceptance** means that an organization has evaluated the risk and made the determination that taking action to mitigate or remove the risk is not worth the cost or effort. For example, a computer system that is normally disconnected from the Internet is vulnerable to a remote access attack due to running an operating system that is no longer supported. The system will be replaced in 2 years and changes to the existing system are cost prohibitive due to old technology. The organization agrees the risk is sufficiently low that operation will be allowed to continue until the new system comes online in 2 years. Another common example of risk acceptance focuses on organizations that elect to delay patching critical system vulnerabilities based on the systems location in the network. This is a common approach for servers located behind a network firewall.

Risk mitigation is a process for applying alternative controls to limit possible damage or loss should the threat be realized. In this scenario, removing a network interface card to guarantee the system is not connected to the Internet is an example of mitigation. **Risk transfer** is a form of mitigation that is becoming very popular as both the attack vectors and capabilities of malicious actors increase. Organizations may hire third parties to defend their systems from attack or purchase "breach insurance" to protect the company from the monetary impact of a breach. Breach insurance, which is very similar to malpractice insurance, offsets the cost of breach notifications and credit protection services required by state and federal law. Some breach insurance also protects organizations against the cost of lawsuits in the event of a breach.

Defense in Depth

In medieval times, rings of defense protected a castle: a mote, high walls, archers, and boiling oil. Each was a solid defense by itself but not enough to defend against a large attack; however, together they provided a well-rounded defensive front. The concept, known as defense-in-depth, carries directly over into cyber security and is the hallmark of a mature cyber security program. A familiar mantra in cyber security is that a defender must protect against a nearly limitless number of possible cyber-attacks, whereas an attacker need find only one hole to penetrate a system. Defense-in-depth bolsters defenses by providing a broad, redundant, and protective barrier against attack and subsequent compromise. Elements of defense-in-depth exceed mere technical controls, however. While cyber security policy and program are the principle elements, a well-rounded defense-in-depth program considers many more factors. It is important to recognize that cyber security is not a one-size-fits-all solution, and it is imperative that the CISO holistically views the systems and data under his or her purview to ensure adequate and appropriate controls are in place.

Policy and Program

The cyber security policy is the first step to protecting cyber assets in any organization and is the foundation of an overall cyber security program. While one might consider the cyber security policy part of the organizational security policy, the scope and complexity for a given organization may be such that having a separate policy might be the most effective approach. The CISO is responsible for developing, implementing, and maturing the cyber security program. Historically, the CISO would report to the chief information officer (CIO); however, organizations are realizing the importance of security and beginning to assign the CISO to higher level reporting, often to the chief financial officer (CFO), risk officer (RO), and in many cases the chief executive officer (CEO). Furthermore, by moving security out from under the CIO, it relieves the burden of conflict when the CIO is responsible for services and security controls that may impede those services.

This text previously introduced the concept of policies; however, there are elements of cyber security that dictate additional considerations on top of the standard security policy. Larger organizations will often create separate policies to address key focal points. Additionally, many topics covered by separate policies are also covered in an organization's acceptable use policy to simplify the policy review process for employees.

Acceptable Use

General users are possibly, albeit unintentionally, one of the biggest risks to an organization's cyber security program. User education is critical in protecting any cyber system, and the acceptable use policy is a big tool in educating users. Acceptable use defines how users interact with cyber systems, what constitutes appropriate use, and what activities are unacceptable. It establishes organizational controls and places responsibility for security on all users. Key aspects of an acceptable use policy should include Internet use, social media use, password requirements, remote access restrictions, data protection requirements, and actions for cyber incidents. Acceptable use is organizationally specific and therefore, the examples listed above are suggested guidelines rather than required aspects of an acceptable use policy. Policy effectiveness is a direct function of organizational support. It is critical to have senior leadership support and organizational buy in for the security program success. It is also recommended that all members of the organization review the acceptable use policy annually.

Access Controls

Cyber system access closely resembles physical access controls. Individuals are granted access proportionate to their assigned tasks and nothing more. This ensures proper segregation of responsibility and establishes a security hierarchy that can be managed on a need-to-know basis. In the cyber realm, this concept is known as "least privilege." Adherence to least privilege requires organizations to ensure proper system configuration, and optimally, access is assigned based upon requirements necessary for one to perform their defined role. Separation of duties (SOD) is another access control approach ensuring that system-level access is also restricted based upon work responsibilities. A common weakness in access controls exist when shared user accounts are allowed. A shared account is one where multiple users know the credentials, thereby reducing access control effectiveness and removing the accountability afforded by individual accounts.

Security Configuration

Modern cyber systems are often complex, highly interconnected, and open to public access. The complexity stems from a number of factors, including operating system, hardware, applications, and support systems. As complexity increases, so too does the need for standardization. As indicated previously, an attacker only needs one point of entry to compromise a system, and the misconfiguration of a lone network device could be that entry point. System hardening is the first step in establishing a cyber-defensive position. Hardening is a process for configuring and patching systems to minimize the potential vectors of attack. CIS (http://www.cisecurity.org) has developed a set of security templates based upon identified industry best practices for hardening common cyber systems based upon manufacturer, operating system, and purpose. NIST also offers standard hardening guidance for cyber systems.

Identified vulnerabilities have been exploited in many systems. When vulnerabilities are identified, it becomes incumbent upon the manufacturer to develop patches to mitigate the vulnerability. Until a patch is released, system administrators and managers must find alternative methods to protect the system. Organizations should establish patch management processes to ensure manufacturer patches are promptly and expeditiously applied. Windows-based systems can use a system management server (SMS), whereas Linux-based systems might use a system called "puppet" to manage deployment of system patches. The vendor/manufacturer patch service does introduce a risk that organizations must take into consideration when making decisions on whether or not to patch their systems. Security researchers and hackers obtain new patches the same time everyone else does; while administrators should be applying the patches, the researchers and hackers are analyzing them to see how they change the system. This knowledge allows them to reverse-engineer the patch and quickly develop exploits for those systems not patched.

Incident Response

During the early years of the Internet, individuals and organizations were under the misconception that their systems were secure and impenetrable; even today, this is a common belief in many organizations. Events in recent years described at the beginning of this chapter, highlight the idea that it is *not* a matter of *if* an organization will experience a cyber-breach, *but rather when* a breach will occur. Proactive security processes are designed to protect cyber systems; however, it is imperative that organizations have a defined process for responding to an eventual attack. The incident response policy defines how an organization will respond to intrusion. The Federal Emergency Management Agency (FEMA) has established standard response processes for casualty and disaster scenarios. The principles defined by FEMA, and discussed in Emergency Management Unit - #5, are easily extended to respond to cyber casualties, adjusting responder actions to the nuances of the digital systems involved.

Key aspects to cyber incident response include the following:

- Define an incident response (IR) team. Comprise the IR team of personnel knowledgeable in cyber systems, communications, HR, and legal. Specify a core team and augment as necessary.
- Establish a communications plan. Communication is key to every successful response plan. Trying to figure who to call in an emergency can significantly hamper response and recovery efforts.
- Train the IR team. Administrators often assume they know how to respond to an incident because they work on the system daily. However, it is easy to wipe out all traces of the issue and prevent future mitigation of an existing problem if IR processes are not followed.
- Define a specific tool set. Incident response tools must be relied upon to support investigations and restore system operation. Use of tools that are new or untested, places the system under undue risk during a critical situation. Additionally, such tools might exhibit unintentional responses that further complicate the situation.
- Establish cyber scenarios and develop action plans to respond to them. Over time, this library of scenarios will increase along with the IR team experience and skills.

Cyber incident responders perform two unique roles in an investigation: forensics analysts and incident handlers. While the skill sets overlap to a certain extent, each requires a different primary focus. Responding to a system compromise requires advanced knowledge of the systems being examined, including an understanding of the "normal" indications. It is impossible to recognize when something is abnormal if one does not know what it looks like when it is normal. The **incident handler** is responsible for detecting, responding, and resolving cyber incidents. The handler is responsible for execution of the incident handling steps, assessment of attack vectors (including malicious software [malware] and network threats), attack tools and techniques, system activity assessment, and maturation of the IR process. The incident handler will leverage system logs, firewall logs, intrusion detection system alerts, and access records as part of the investigation into the incident. Suspected malicious files may be analyzed in an isolated "sandbox" to determine exactly what the file does without further propagation. Live connection (attacker still active in the system) scenarios provide the incident handler with the ability to view the attackers' activity in real time. Several educational organizations offer specialized incident handler training and certification. Check out the educational resources at the end of this section for more information.

The **forensic analyst** is responsible for evaluating digital evidence left behind at the scene of the crime. Dr. Edward Locard (1877–1966) was a forensic scientist, known as the French Sherlock Holmes, who formulated the basic principle of forensics: "Every contact leaves a trace." While the concept of cyber did not exist during his time, Locard's principle applies equally to all cyber security investigations. When a perpetrator passes through a crime scene, footprints, fingerprints, personal objects, and other key traces are left behind. A forensic analyst seeks similar traces, primarily in digital form, to determine the who, what, when, where, and how of the incident.

The forensics analyst relies heavily on software tools that enables him or her to recover data from electronic storage media and devices. One of the common misconceptions regarding computer technology is that once a computer hard disk drive has been formatted, all prior information is lost. In order to fully remove data from magnetic media, it is necessary to overwrite the entire device, often multiple times, to prevent data recovery. Using forensic recovery software, an analyst can examine the device at a very low level and recover most (if not all) of the information stored on the device, provided it has not been overwritten. An examination of a computer hard drive during an investigation might include recovery of email messages that were sent or received, photographs or images viewed on the computer, and data files. The broad adoption of cell phones and smart devices presents an interesting challenge for forensic analysts because most of the newer devices are manufacturer unique, requiring use of special hardware and software specifically made for the given device or series of devices.

Another significant and emerging challenge to forensic investigation is the increasing prevalence of "anti-forensic" tools. Many software programs exist to circumvent or compromise forensic investigations. For example, TimeStomp is a tool in the popular penetration testing suite Metasploit (http://www.metasploit.com), which gives a malicious user the ability to modify system time stamps. Time stamps are assigned to files and folders automatically by the system and are used to determine when the file was created, last accessed, and last modified. By changing the time stamps, a person with malicious intentions might modify evidence to hide involvement in a crime. Steganography is the science of hiding information and is another popular anti-forensics approach that involves embedding data into images. This renders the data completely hidden; unless known to exist and the proper tools are used, it is nearly impossible to retrieve the data from the image. One way to determine if information is hidden in an image is to compare a suspect image to the original of the same image; if the file size is different, there may be data hidden within it. Several educational organizations offer specialized forensics analysis training and certification. Check out the educational resources at the end of this section for more information.

Ethics and Cyber Security

No discussion of cyber security would be complete without considering the role of ethics. Cyber security practitioners are in a position of trust and their reputation hinges on maintaining that trust. They are frequently exposed to sensitive information during the course of their work, often as a result of their involvement in a cyber-related investigation. Regardless of content, the practitioner should never share or disclose such information, except where failure to disclose would constitute a crime or place someone at significant risk. There are cases where information gained must be disclosed by law, such as evidence of child pornography or threats on government officials. Protection of sensitive information is critical; while not under a proper nondisclosure agreement (NDA), there is an expectation of trust placed upon cyber security professionals. The "need to know" concept, discussed previously, directly applies to the cyber security professional, and failure to follow those guidelines is a breach of ethics and denotes a loss of trust. Corporate reputation, or personal reputation for that matter, is critical for success in the business world. An ethical issue can as easily taint an individual or corporation's "brand" as a data breach. Therefore, it is imperative to approach all cyber operations with the highest regard.

Hand in hand with ethics is the concept of the "legal right to investigate." Cyber system administrators, users, or managers respond to cyber incidents, often under unique circumstances. It is important to recognize when to investigate and when to seek assistance. Administrators, for example, are very familiar with their system operation and the locations of critical information; when unusual events (such as a security breach) occur, they are quick to start "looking" to determine what happened. This ambition, while well intentioned, can result in a loss of evidence and invalidation of the investigation if the person is not properly trained. Investigations follow specific procedures designed to protect evidence and ensure adherence to due process and due diligence. It is important to understand when to conduct an investigation and more importantly, what the scope and potential impact of that investigation should be. Numerous examples have been seen in the media where a computer support person identified inappropriate use and took actions that later resulted in their being fired—or worse. In one case, a repair technician with a chain-computer retailer was attempting to repair a customer's computer when he came upon child pornography. The technician proceeded to make a DVD copy that he turned over to the police as evidence, only to find himself arrested for the production of child pornography. As an investigator or incident responder, if you suspect child pornography exists on the system, the investigation should stop and law enforcement immediately notified. Further viewing or copying is a federal crime and might result in prosecution.

The investigator must keep the scope of the investigation appropriate. It is a violation of the Computer Fraud and Abuse Act (Title 18, United States Code) to hack into another computer system without proper authorization. In 2014, a White House Commission on the Theft of American Intellectual Property expressed that "without damaging the intruder's network, companies that experience cyber-theft ought to be able to retrieve their electronic files or prevent exploitation of their stolen information." The entire report is available at http://www.ipcommission.org/report/IP_Commission_Report_052213.pdf. While the law clearly defines hacking as illegal, there have been instances where the line has been tested. In 2005, an employee of Sandia National Laboratories was investigating several computer breaches. In an effort to determine the attackers' identity, he began to track them backwards using hacker tools to bypass firewalls and other devices. When he reported his efforts to the company, he was instructed to cease his investigation. Recognizing the attacks were coming from outside the country, he reported his findings to the Federal Bureau of Investigation (FBI; under the whistleblower statute) and was subsequently fired. The employee later settled with his former employer; however, this is an example where the lines between hacking for malicious intent and hacking in defense begin to blur. Hacking back is an issue that will merit close attention as more and more organizations experience cyber-attacks.

The Many Faces of Cybercrime

The US Justice Department (DOJ) defined computer crime as "any violations of criminal law that involve a knowledge of computer technology for their perpetration, investigation, or prosecution."[4] Applied in 1989, this definition is still applicable and logically encompasses cybercrime. The DOJ later clarified the definition by specifying the following:

1. Events where computers are the target of the crime, such as theft of software or hardware
2. Events where computers are used as an instrument of the crime, such as sending spam or threats
3. Events where computers are the subject or victim of the crime, such as directly hacking into a computer system

It is important that security professionals understand the evolving mechanisms of cybercrime and what response or actions are appropriate. We will begin with a discussion on hackers and the role they play in cybercrime. Then, we will examine targets of cyber inopportunity from four threat perspectives: personal, organizational, critical infrastructure, and organized crime. While each carries aspects of the others, we will delve into the particular nuances of each section.

The Role of Open-Source Intelligence

Open-source intelligence (OSINT) is at the heart of all cyber security activity and commonly associated with the intelligence community. OSINT refers to the tremendous amount of individual or organizational information freely available on the Internet. Previously available via newspapers, library resource centers, government offices, and universities, Internet interconnectivity has made such information far more accessible for nearly anyone. OSINT data mining over the Internet enables businesses to perform competitive advantage analysis, allows researchers to expand their available sources, and gives attackers a simple avenue for footprinting their targets. Government records are commonly stored online; business records related to publicly traded companies are public records stored online; social networks gather everything anyone is willing to post online to share with others; educational research documents shared with other educational institutes are available via public Internet shares. Although expensive commercial software is available for performing such data collection, many free open-source specialized tools can perform complex scans of the Internet, seeking any available information related to nearly anything. OSINT is highly valuable to organizations to research the competition; however, it is equally useful to cyber attackers. Imagine how knowing exactly what computer systems are used, office locations, or even sensitive employee information could further enable an attacker to compromise an organization.

Maltego is one such OSINT tool extensively used for information gathering. Maltego excels at both data collection and correlation. It has the ability to identify websites an individual has used, multiple email address, memberships to online services, and a plethora of other personal and valuable pieces of information. Maltego provides a method of visualizing information gathered, further simplifying the correlation of data collected. Another tool frequently used for performing OSINT is Shodan-HQ, an online search tool used to target specific systems (rather than user information) to identify vulnerable characteristics such as operating systems, default access credentials, and unprotected devices.

Threat Actors: Hackers, Crackers, and Script Kiddies

Hackers, crackers, and script kiddies—oh my! The news and movies have glorified hackers as nearly superhuman in the things they can do with computers for several years; however, there is far more than chivalry and glamour in the art of computer exploitation. The term *hacker* has traditionally described a skilled programmer who attacks systems for knowledge and the educational value, whereas the term *cracker* relates to one who breaks into systems for malicious purposes. On the other hand, script kiddies are unskilled hackers who attempt to hack into systems using automated tools rather than knowledge to manipulate the systems. The term *hacker* has now morphed to mean anyone who breaks into cyber systems, regardless of intent. The DOJ categorizes hackers and crackers all as hackers. There are three categories of hacker to facilitate identification of the good guys and the bad guys; however, regardless of classification, if a hacker breaks the law, they can face fines and jail time.

White-hat hackers are security professionals who try to find the weaknesses and vulnerabilities before the black-hat hackers do. White hats are hired to protect systems through a regimen of security testing in an effort to identify weaknesses before the attackers do. The black-hat hackers attack systems with bad intent, often for monetary gain in one form or another. The primary difference between white hat and black hat is permission. Although they usually have similar skills, the white hat only performs hacking after obtaining permission (referred to as a "get out of jail free card"). Black hats, on the other hand, attack whenever they want. Gray hats are hackers who try to walk the fine line between legal and illegal. Often, they are legitimate security practitioners by day and hackers by night. As previously stated, regardless of the hat worn, hacking without permission is illegal and is punishable under the Computer Fraud and Abuse Act.

The next obvious question is why anyone would give permission for someone to hack into their systems. Penetration testing is a form of system validation where white-hat hackers conduct system attacks using the black-hat hacker methodology. These hackers are often certified by an authoritative body and bonded to show that they have the proper skills and capabilities to perform this sort of testing. Certified Ethical Hacker (CEH) and Certified Professional Penetration Tester (CPPT) are two such certification paths. An in-depth system knowledge is crucial for success in performing security testing.

Not all hackers use knowledge or monetary gain as their motivation. Rather, some hackers attack to make a statement or express a viewpoint. Attacking cyber systems for a cause or political purpose is known as *hacktivism*. Hacktivists have made the news due to several high-profile system attacks. The most notorious group of hacktivists is the collective known as Anonymous. The group claimed responsibility for several high-profile attacks, including Sony Media, HBGary Federal, and various US law enforcement organizations, largely due to their ability to avoid detection. The US government developed a system named The Onion Router (TOR) that allows relatively anonymous access and untraceable use of the Internet. Also known as the "DarkNet," this system is heavily used by individuals attempting to hide their actions, including hackers, criminals, and pedophiles.

TOR consists of access nodes and a special client that connects users to the access nodes. The client automatically selects an available access node and, once connected, moves from node to node until reaching the desired exit node. All further connections within TOR are anonymized to prevent the user from being tracked backwards over the Internet. This system relies on being able to trust the servers running TOR nodes. An operator of a TOR node has the ability to track a user back to the immediately prior node. As such, a group of operators could potentially track a user over TOR. Several government agencies, including the CIA, NSA, and FBI have been suspected of running TOR access nodes. The hacking group Anonymous used TOR extensively to hide their identity and source locations. It was not until the FBI identified and turned one of the primary Anonymous members into an informant that the rest of the Anonymous was identified and apprehended.

Another hacktivist with very different intentions became highly visible during this same period of time. A hacker going by the name of **th3j35t3r** is a self-professed anti-jihadist. The name **th3j35t3r** (the Jester's cyber handle) is written in "leetspeak," a form of computer slang where numbers and special characters are substituted for normal letters of similar construction. Described as a "lone wolf cyber patriot" for his efforts toward attacking and taking down Jihadist websites, The Jester uses various cyber-attack tools, including a DDoS tool he created called XerXes. The cyber equivalent of Robin Hood from literature of old, he would identify malicious cyber groups and attack them rather than the usual targets of hacker attacks. The Jester has been credited for helping to identify members of

Anonymous. His most notable attack was against the Westboro Baptist Church for staging protests at US veterans' funerals. The Jester's escapades are nicely detailed in a report on the SANS Reading Room (http://www.sans.org/reading-room/whitepapers/attacking/jester-dynamic-lesson-asymmetric- unmanaged-cyber-warfare-33889).

Targets of Cyber Inopportunity

The cyber target landscape is rapidly expanding. Originally, Internet access was extremely limited, being only available through government departments, military entities, and universities on a pay-by-the-minute basis using extremely slow computer modems. System exposure was, as a result, relatively low due to the small number of systems connected, immaturity of the systems, and limited technical capabilities of their users. It was during this period when critical systems were beginning to be interconnected and computer security was of very little concern.

Fast forward 30 years and more than three-fourths of the US population has a personal computer and Internet access. The capabilities of even the most basic systems far exceed the capabilities of the "high-end" computers of the 1970s. For example, the guidance computer (GC) used to get the Apollo 11 rocket to the moon was a 1.024 MHz system with 2 kb of memory; this would equate to storing about 24,000 words. When compared to a modern system, the GC is about 1/1,000,000th the power of a modern laptop computer running a quad-core 2.40 GHz processor with 64 GB of memory. The NASA Office of Logic Design offers an excellent series on the Apollo mission computers, with an interesting look into the computers used on early space flights (http://klabs.org/history/build_agc/).

Personal Risk

Not only do modern computers have considerably higher capabilities than those of previous decades, but there are significantly more computers connected to the Internet. The US Census Bureau reported that in 2012, 78% of households had Internet access, compared to only 8% in 1984 (http://www.census.gov/hhes/computer/files/2012/Computer_Use_Infographic_FINAL.pdf). Personal computers (including work-related user systems) are used for nearly every aspect of our daily lives. For example, retail stores provide online and direct-to-home purchasing, utility companies support automated billing, and financial institutes provide mechanisms for managing all aspects of our financials, from bill paying to investments. Such activities make personal computers a very valuable target for thieves and other attackers. By their very nature, personal computers store sensitive information such as bank and credit card account numbers, medical records, purchase records, and other vital information. Such personally identifiable information (PII) is a common target for attackers, and particularly identity thieves. Identity theft has been steadily on the rise for several years. At the time of writing, 47 states have laws requiring breach notification, specifically for protecting consumers from identity theft and other forms of crime. Identify theft captures sensitive information that allows the attacker to impersonate the victim to directly either access their accounts or create new accounts; either method gives them access to funds and services at the victims' expense. Javelin Strategy and Research's 2012 Identity Theft Report[5] states that more than 12.6 million people in the United States were victims of identity theft in 2012, for a net loss of more than $21 billion.

Cyber Stalking and Cyber Bullying

The reach of the Internet—and in particular, social media—has made access to anyone's personal information a relatively trivial task. Cyber stalking is the act of using computer systems for tracking the activities of another individual. Cyber bullying, on the other hand, is the act of using computer systems to threaten and harass another individual. Each is extremely intrusive and violates both civil and criminal laws in many states. Cyber stalking and cyber bullying are serious issues, particularly within public schools. According to reports by the US Department of Education, US Department of Justice, and US Department of Health and Human Services, nearly 25% of high school children have been the victim of cyberbullying. Whereas bullying is normally thought of as an in-person occurrence, cyberbullying can happen anywhere, at any time, and be completely anonymous. Social media practices, such as posting selfies (self-taken portraits), geotagging (geographic coordinates of longitude/latitude embedded in photos taken with many mobile devices), and a desire to share everything one does on social media sites, makes tracking of individual activities likes, and dislikes very easy for stalkers and bullies.

In 2013, the suicide deaths of two young girls aged 12 and 13 brought the danger of cyberbullying to the national media and public eye. Both girls were the victims of bullying online via social media. As security professionals, one of the most important services we can provide is education in how to recognize and defend against cyberbullying. These tragic events could have possibly been avoided through education and awareness of the signs of cyberbullying.

The US Department of Health and Human Services has established a website specifically to educate parents, students, and educators on the dangers of bullying (which includes cyberbullying). The following indicators might provide early identification of a victim of cyberbullying:

- Unexplainable injuries
- Lost or destroyed clothing, books, electronics, or jewelry
- Frequent headaches or stomach aches, feeling sick or faking illness
- Changes in eating habits, like suddenly skipping meals or binge eating. Kids may come home from school hungry because they did not eat lunch.
- Difficulty sleeping or frequent nightmares
- Declining grades, loss of interest in schoolwork, or not wanting to go to school
- Sudden loss of friends or avoidance of social situations
- Feelings of helplessness or decreased self esteem
- Self-destructive behaviors such as running away from home, harming themselves, or talking about suicide

Cybercrime

Organized Crime Groups

Organized crime existed long before the emergence of the personal computer; however, the breadth and reach of the Internet has been like a shot of adrenalin for cybercrime. Cyber criminals are able to gather virtually unlimited information on targets from government sources, social media, and data aggregation services that buy and sell personal information. Where victims of organized crime used to be local to the criminal, the Internet provides a means for attacking nearly anyone from anywhere in the world.

The business of cybercrime is flourishing with attack tools including malware, encryption tools, and data mining services offered for sale or lease based upon a defined price scale. A search on the Internet, and particularly the DarkNet, will quickly reveal a wide array of developers offering services to create, and vendors offering to sell, toolkits and exploit kits. Toolkits contain software that allows cybercriminals to spread their malware, infecting targets and gathering information. Exploit kits are software packages that automate the job of compromising the targets systems, often including their own delivery mechanism such as an email server. Like regular commercial software, these crimeware packages come complete with a service and support contract that ensures regular exploit and tool updates.

CryptoLocker is a popular malware kit that allows the purchaser to create custom phishing messages containing links to malicious software. When a recipient clicks a link, malware is loaded onto their computer, encrypting the entire contents of the computer hard drive in the process. Victims are required to pay large sums of money to have their information unencrypted. Another popular Crimeware kit, ZEUS, originally focused on banking fraud by capturing user credentials to move and steal money. ZEUS has evolved and advanced to the point where it is now a command-and-control (C&C) system for a broad range of attacks including spam, currency mining, and DDoS. Command-and-control systems remotely manage thousands of compromised computers. Cloud services have enabled ZEUS vendors to offer it as a paid service where attackers rent time on the ZEUS botnet rather than having to setup and maintain their own attack infrastructure. This software or service as a platform significantly lowers the attackers' risk.

Research by anti-malware analysts show that the crimeware packages are becoming as advanced from a software development standpoint as any other commercial software package. Reverse engineering and analysis show code development characteristics that rival anything available from a commercial software developer. Reverse engineering is a process of analyzing a software program to determine what it does and how it does it without having access to the source code. Advanced encryption and packing (method of hiding program code from casual review) methods make reverse engineering of these packages very difficult. Reverse engineering a software package will often aid in determining the source of the application due to the languages used within the software code.

Critical Infrastructure Threats

In March 2000, the residents of Maroochydore in Queensland, Australia, found millions of liters of raw sewage flowing into public parks, rivers, and even the grounds of the Hyatt Regency hotel. Now one might ask what this event is doing in a discussion of cyber security. Vitek Boden worked for a company that implemented remote supervisory control and data acquisition (SCADA) control systems. After being turned down for employment by one of his customers, Boden used stolen SCADA control equipment to perform more than 46 attacks on the city's waste management system; he became the very first person prosecuted for conducting a cyber-attack against **critical infrastructure** systems.

We define critical infrastructure as those systems and assets either physical or virtual that are so vital to a country that destruction or incapacitation would have debilitating effect on the safe and stable operation of that country. One of the primary methods for maintaining critical infrastructure involves **industrial control systems** (ICS). As a type of *industrial control system*, SCADA devices make up the centralized management, monitoring, and control systems for industrial processing, power and communication infrastructure, manufacturing, and facility management systems. While actively used since the early 1970s, SCADA systems were often proprietary systems built without industry standardization. Unlike the technology devices in use today, often replaced every few years, the life expectancy of SCADA systems was often 40 to 50 years. Unfortunately, the early computer systems evolved and the newer systems became incompatible with these "legacy" SCADA devices necessitating the continued use of the older computer and control systems. In an effort to automate and simplify management, organizations began finding ways to connect these older system to the wide-open Internet; connecting systems that were developed without security and access controls made them a juicy target for attack.

In 2013, the White House issued an executive order, Improving Critical Infrastructure Cybersecurity, directing a mutually cooperative framework for protecting the nation's critical infrastructure. The National Institute of Standards and Technology (NIST) is the guiding body for establishing policies and procedures for technical government operations. NIST developed the *Framework for Improving Critical Infrastructure Cybersecurity* in support of this presidential order (http://www.nist.gov/cyberframework/). The executive order further directed the Department of Homeland Security (DHS) to update the National Infrastructure Protection Plan. DHS released *NIPP 2013 Partnering for Critical Infrastructure Security and Resilience* in response (http://www.dhs.gov/national-infrastructure-protection-plan).

Each document compliments the other, each with the primary goal of protecting the national critical infrastructure. NIPP 2013 calls for a concentrated effort to minimize risk through partnerships amongst government, academia, owners/operators, tribal leadership, and nonprofit organizations. NIPP focuses on the aspects common to basic protection skills:

- Identify, deter, detect, disrupt, and prepare for threats and hazards to the nation's critical infrastructure
- Reduce vulnerabilities of critical assets, systems, and networks
- Mitigate the potential consequences to critical infrastructure of incidents or adverse events that do occur

NIST has long concentrated on technical controls in addition to policy, procedures, and standards. The cyber-security framework focused previous efforts on protecting our critical infrastructure along with educating organizations that have rarely considered security from an information technology perspective. However, infrastructure advances are not limited to industrial systems. Utility companies have been working to develop a smart-grid using "smart meters" to facilitate remote monitoring of gas, water, and electric use. Researcher, Mike Davis[5], demonstrated a proof-of-concept attack against smart meters creating a simulated worm that propagated across 22,000 smart meters in a 24-hour period.[6]

Attention on the threat to critical infrastructure became headline news when coordinated zero-day attacks, against Siemens' ICS systems used in the nuclear facilities in Iran, caused the physical destruction of high-speed centrifuge devices used for creating nuclear weapons fuel. While not specifically targeting "critical infrastructure", the *Stuxnet worm* successfully caused these devices to self-destruct; this demonstrated that such an attack, not unlike an attack against SCADA systems, was not only possible but also highly effective. Extensive research by Symantec into the mechanisms used by Stuxnet suggested a joint venture between Israel and the United States and revealed six key factors in the attack's success:

- The code was complex and highly advanced, beyond what is normally seen in malware, and written in multiple languages.
- The attack vector was by USB portable drive rather than over the Internet.
- The digital certificates (electronic file signatures) that were used were legitimate, possibly stolen rather than forged, ensuring that the worm would be "trusted" by any system it was installed on.
- An unprecedented four zero-day vulnerabilities were used in the attack software.
- The attacks suggested inside knowledge of the Siemens PLC operation.
- The worm attempted to communicate with remote control servers in other countries.

Home electrical supply line management is now moving to *smart meters* that allow the power company to remotely read, enable/disable, and maintain electrical distribution to homes and businesses from a central management center.

Advanced Persistent Threats

Advanced persistent threats (APT) are garnering significant attention within the media and the cyber-security community. APT is a stealthy and highly complex continuous attack process. APT are commonly associated with government and nation-state organizations targeting industry, military, and other high-value targets. Critical infrastructure is a prime target for APT and recommendations of the critical infrastructure protection plan specifically address many of the risks attributed to APT. The 2009 attacks against dozens of major US organizations, including Google, DOW, Northrop Grumman, and Morgan Stanley, are an example of an APT. Named Operation Aurora, the attacks were directly attributed to hackers from China. APT attacks commonly take advantage of multiple system vulnerabilities, including vulnerabilities that have existing patches provided by the manufacturer. While this might appear counterproductive, the relative success of APTs is evidence that many organizations still neglect the patch management responsibilities, leaving critical systems vulnerable to compromise. The Mandiant Intelligence Center produced a public report, *APT1: Exposing One of China's Cyber Espionage Units*, detailing their investigation of advance persistent attacks originating from China. Their efforts identified a specialized group suspected to be state-sponsored that demonstrated exceptional hacking and exploitation skills. Several of their attack methods involved use of previously unknown zero-day vulnerabilities, further highlighting the importance of proper system security management. The entire report is available on the Mandiant website: https://www.mandiant.com/resources/resource/apt1-exposing-one-of-chinas-cyber-espionage-units.

Attack Mechanisms

The number of attack methods of bad actors, whether they are hacktivists, corporate spies, or nation-state hackers, is nearly limitless. The following is an overview of some of the more prevalent categories of attacks. Further information on each is available at the links provided at the end of the section.

Social Engineering

Social engineering has long been the preferred method of obtaining sensitive and high-value information. The art of persuasion is invaluable to children asking for new toys, teenagers convincing the teacher that the dog ate their homework, employees convincing the boss to give them a raise, and police interrogating suspects—each is an example of a form of social engineering. Social engineering really entered the cyber arena with the emergence of spam/phishing attacks, as described earlier, and custom tools for conducting such attacks. The goal of social engineering is to convince someone to do something they normally would not do, such as installing malware, giving up personal information, or revealing login credentials.

The Social Engineering Toolkit (SET) is an exceptional tool for conducting cyber-based social engineering attacks. This tool has the capability to mirror popular web pages and then embed malicious software into the custom web page. SET also has a built-in email server that will send email to the designated victims containing links to the newly created malicious website. SET integrates with security testing tools such as Metasploit to build exploit packages that can be deployed by SET.

BotNets

Wide-scale attacks frequently leverage robot networks (BotNets) to maximize the strength of the attack while maximizing the attackers distance from the attack. BotNets consist of primary servers known as command-and-control servers that act as centralized coordination servers. C&C servers are managed by a core group of attackers known as "bot herders." Participant computers, "bots," compromised by various attacks that install the client software, are managed by C&C servers to perform various attack functions.

Malware Category	Malware Purpose
Virus	Self-replicating software that performs malicious actions on infected computer systems.
Trojan horse	Non-self-replicating software that performs malicious actions on a system while impersonating a legitimate program. (Remember the Trojan horse from Troy.)
Spyware	Software commonly embedded in computer systems via browsers that track a computer's activity and reports back to a central collection server.
Ransomware	Software that restricts access to a system and demands money to restore access.
Keylogger	Hardware device or software that captures every keystroke on a computer and saves it or forwards it to an attacker.
Botnet client	Remote control program that joins a computer to a botnet for performing remote coordinated attacks against other systems.
Rootkit	Malicious software installed and normally hidden from the operating system. Rootkits often have more access to the system than the system administrator has.
Shellcode	Custom code injected into a system as part of an exploit that creates a user shell (similar to the old DOS windows) into the operating system.

FIGURE 38.5 Common malware.

Spam, Phishing, and Spear Phishing

Spam is the practice of sending unsolicited massive bulk email deliveries to a large number of recipients. The email content is often product advertising, goods and services, political propaganda, or malicious software. Phishing is a common method of luring victims into giving up personal information such as user credentials, credit card information, or to launch an attack. Phishing involves sending emails (often as part of a spam attack) to potential victims in an effort to gain their trust and ultimately their bank account. More advanced phishing attacks involve the attacker researching the victim to identify information that can be used to further gain the victim's trust. For example, knowledge of an employee role would allow an attacker to tailor a phishing email specifically to that individual or individual's position in an effort to increase the victim's trust.

Malware

Malware is an overarching term referring to software that has a malicious function or component. This includes bot clients, viruses, Trojan horses, and various utilities. Figure 38.5 explains some of the more common malware.

Advancing Your Cyber Security Career Options

Cyber security, as we have learned, is a relatively new area of expertise. The continual evolution of technology and cyber solutions necessitates developing skill sets that evolve with these changes to protect and defend cyber systems, regardless of purpose. There is a significant shortage of trained cyber security professionals. Protection officers and service providers are in a unique position to develop the skills internally to better support their customers and fill the current gaps. Additionally, many cyber jobs very closely parallel their noncomputer counterparts. Forensics, for example, is an area of continuous change and skilled forensic analysts are in high demand. Forensic services are used by law enforcement, corporate investigations, private investigators, and financial systems auditors. Forensics also plays a large part in the incident response process when attempting to determine the source and, more importantly, the extent of a breach.

Incident handlers are skilled in coordinating response efforts, prioritizing actions, and assessing incidents holistically. Handlers are expected to have a broader understanding of systems involved in incidents, and personnel with prior information systems experience are especially suited to tackle this area of training.

Security testers/penetration testers (pentesters) are the most advanced cyber security roles, uniquely positioned to conduct security assessments for clients. A penetration test (pentest) is the process of attacking a system from the perspective of and using the same tools as a hacker or attacker would use. Many organizations have outside requirements to conduct annual penetration tests. Qualified testers are in high demand and earn a premium salary.

Cyber Security Resources

There are many resources available by which to increase your knowledge and skills in cyber security. The following resources are just a small sampling and are not endorsements; rather, these are industry leaders in cyber security education and training. Some of the offerings are free, whereas others charge for the training.

General cyber security:

1. National Institute of Standards and Technology (NIST; http://www.nist.gov): NIST has established standards for all aspects of cyber security for government agencies. NIST is recognized as an industry standards and best practices organization.
2. Department of Homeland Security (DHS; http://www.dhs.gov/topic/cybersecurity): DHS offers resources and training classes across the country in general cyber security, incident response, and security testing. In many cases, this training is completely free.
3. SANS Institute (http://www.sans.org/): The SANS Institute provides training and resources globally in all areas of cyber security. One of the more useful resources is the SANS Reading Room, where research papers are published for public access.

Forensics and incident response:

1. US Computer Emergency Readiness Team (US-CERT; http://www.us-cert.gov): Established in 2003 for protection of the US infrastructure, US-CERT defends and coordinates actions against cyber-attacks across the country. It also provides training and educational resources to aid organizations in improving their incident response processes.
2. Software Engineering Institute (SEI) of Carnegie Mellon University (http://www.sei.cmu.edu/training/p28.cfm): SEI offers advanced management training in incident response practices and operations.

3. SANS Digital Forensics and Incident Response (DFIR; http://digital-forensics.sans.org/): SANS has developed an entire group around developing DFIR training and resources. The SANS Incident Response and Forensic Toolkit (SIFT) is one of the more valuable resources available from SANS. SIFT is a LiveCD that you can boot from a computer that contains all of the tools needed for a forensic or incident response investigation. A LiveCD is an operating system on CD or DVD that the computer can be started from effectively bypassing the installed operating system. SIFT is available here: http://digital-forensics.sans.org/community/downloads.

Refer website http://www.ifpo.org for further information

End Notes

1. Abbate, J. E., *From ARPANET to Internet: A History of ARPA-Sponsored Computer Networks, 1966-1988.* (Philadelphia, PA: University of Pennsylvania, 1994) Available: http://search.proquest.com.login.capitol-college.edu:2048/docview/304104775/fulltextPDF/1AB08590A99D49F2PQ/9?accountid=44888.

2. Clifford Stoll., *The Cuckoo's Egg: Tracking a Spy Through the Maze of Computer Espionage* (New York, NY: Doubleday, 1989).

3. *2013 Cost of a Data Breach Study: Global Analysis* (Traverse City, MI: Ponemon Institute LLC, 2013) Available: https://www4.symantec.com/mktginfo/whitepaper/053013_GL_NA_WP_Ponemon-2013-Cost-of-a-Data-Breach-Report_daiNA_cta72382.pdf.

4. National institute of Justice US Dept of Justice, Computer Crime: Criminal Justice Resource Manual 2 (1989) [hereinafter DOJ CComputer Crime Manual]. A derivative definition of computer crimes is "those crimes where knowledge of a computer system is essential to commit the crime." Jo-Ann M. Adams, Comment, Controlling Cyberspace: Applying the Computer Fraud and Abuse Act to the Internet, 12 Santa Clara Computer & High Tech L.J. 403, 408 (1996).

5. Davis, M., *SmartGrid Device Security, Adventures in a New Medium* (Seattle, WA: IOActive, 2009) Available: http://www.blackhat.com/presentations/bh-usa-09/MDAVIS/BHUSA09-Davis-AMI-SLIDES.pdf.

6. Pascual, A. and Miller, S., *2013 Identity Fraud Report: Data Breaches Becoming a Treasure Trove for Fraudsters* (Pleasanton, CA: Javelin Strategy, 2013) Available: https://www.javelinstrategy.com/uploads/web_brochure/1303.R_2013IdentityFraudBrochure.pdf.

39

Workplace Violence: Prevention, Mitigation, Response, and Recovery

Inge Sebyan Black

Introduction

Security professionals throughout the world have taken on the task of educating and training businesses and their business counterparts on how to address and prevent violence in their workplace. Although it has been repeatedly said that companies need to have a workplace violence program, it should be said more firmly that companies **must have a** *well-defined* program in place—one that the chief executive officer endorses, is approved by legal, and lets their employees know that employee safety is the top priority. Leaders must be taught how to prevent a workplace violence incident, identifying potential problems, and steps in communicating a problem in order to minimize losses and mitigate the event when it occurs, because it will. **There is no magic solution to stopping the violence** because the perpetrator will not be as obvious as one might think. They may not give the warning signals companies have trained employees to spot, or they might give several indications but to different people. Companies must mitigate the risk and mitigate losses through training, planning, and being prepared. Companies must not use the same-old security approach of reacting to a problem, but instead they must be proactive.

The Risk

Workplace violence needs to be seen as a *risk* that requires implementing risk-based programs, such as risk assessment. The assessment, which should be a specific workplace violence assessment, will provide an understanding of the likelihood of a possible workplace violence threat and recommended solutions. If companies do not accept and acknowledge the possibility of a violent incident occurring at worksites, signs of potential problems will be missed—as will the chance to develop solutions to avoid it.

So what would cause companies to make workplace violence a serious component of their strategic management initiative? To be successful in delivering a solid workplace violence prevention program, senior management must be totally committed to it.

Security Supervision and Management. http://dx.doi.org/10.1016/B978-0-12-800113-4.00039-0

OSHA

The problem of workplace violence is extremely serious. It is serious enough that the US Occupational Safety and Health Administration (OSHA) issued a Directive on Workplace Violence on September 8, 2011.[1] This directive outlines enforcement procedures for OSHA field officers to help them investigate employers for alleged workplace violence. OSHA's general duty clause requires employers to maintain a workplace that is free from recognized hazards that cause or are likely to cause death or serious physical harm. OSHA can cite and fine employers for failing to provide workers with adequate safeguards against workplace violence after an investigation. This Directive does not require OSHA to respond to each complaint or incident related to workplace violence, but it does help to provide guidance for field officers to determine whether an investigation should be pursued and if a citation is appropriate. This directive is an initiative on OSHA's part to examine the issues surrounding workplace violence. Although OSHA issued guidelines for preventing workplace violence for health care and social service workers in 1996 and also late-night retailers and tax drivers in 1998, few citations were ever publicized after these guidelines were put in place. In recent years, there has been a heightened interest in the subject of workplace violence and OSHA has fined and cited employers on the basis that death or physical harm was likely to result from hazards which the employer knew or should have known about.

Violence in the workplace has had devastating effects on businesses, both financially and in lost lives. Employers have a legal and moral obligation, along with the responsibility, to provide a safe and secure work environment. Every day, thousands of employees are subjected to workplace violence in one form or another. Workplace violence includes any use of physical force against or by a worker that causes or could cause physical injury, threatening behavior, harassment, veiled threats, and intimidation. It also includes anger-related incidents, rape, arson, property damage, vandalism, and theft. Incidences can occur at off-site business-related functions like conferences, trade shows, social events, or meetings, but we refer to it as workplace violence because it takes place at work. The US Bureau of Labor Statistics reported that assaults and violent acts, including homicides, accounted for 18% of the overall fatal work injuries in 2010.[2]

When talking about the legal responsibility or duty of employers to safeguard employees, customers, and others from preventable harm, the employer's obligation to respect employee rights and appropriately manage these investigations must be remembered. Having recognized the possibility of workplace violence is the first step in planning and mitigating such an event when it occurs.

Identify the Risks

When considering the critical components of what every business should consider to effectively address the issue of workplace violence, one must begin by identifying the internal risks, which need to be examined just as external variables such as domestic violence, stalking, and other forms of unknown, aggressive behavior that enters the workplace must also be examined. It is impossible to understand all the psychological and physical factors that might push an individual into committing a violent or aggressive act. For this reason, workplace violence is a very complex issue. We must look at all aspects of the risk/threat spectrum and be prepared to respond to any type of violence, whether it is an active shooter, suicidal employee, or domestic partner. Everyone reacts differently to stress, which makes it nearly impossible to determine which stressors might lead a particular person to commit a violent act.

To review all of the risks, it is critical that a violence risk assessment, specifically identifying the risks associated to workplace violence, is performed. Having a security risk assessment is an extremely important process in identifying security concerns and risks. During the security assessment, our process is often to identify assets, identify specific events that would cause loss of assets, estimate the frequency of such losses, estimate the potential impact of such loss, and finally identify ways to mitigate such losses. When evaluating various options of mitigating loss, consider how feasible the option is and the cost versus benefit. A workplace violence needs assessment will go beyond review of general vulnerability to assess the possibility of violence from internal and external sources. Companies must attempt to identify threats that might pertain to a particular industry type or organization, relationships that exist between a perpetrator and an organization, or relationships that may exist between a perpetrator and a current or former employee. Consider factors such as the following:

- Are employees working alone, at a remote location, or at night?
- Do employees handle cash or other valuable assets?
- Do employees work with the general public?
- Is the workplace in a high-crime area?
- Is the business targeted for terrorism, animal rights, or human rights?
- Is this workplace known for high-stress, threatening behavior?
- What physical security is currently in place (e.g., identification badges, access control, closed-circuit video, lighting)?

These are just a few of the factors to consider in a violence needs assessment. Each workplace site will have unique factors to consider.

Threat Assessment Team

Having a workplace violence policy is not enough without the full commitment from senior management. With senior management involved, a team of leaders from various units of the business will be needed to devise a plan of what will be delivered, how it will be delivered, and to whom. This team of leaders can be referred to as the "threat assessment team" and should include representatives from a variety of disciplines, including legal, human resources, security management, and the employee assistance program. If employee unions are present, a union representative should be included. The key is to have a multidisciplinary approach, drawing on the different parts of the management structure, with different perspectives and areas of knowledge. It would also be helpful to include a member of local law enforcement.

Remember to identify the personnel who will carry the primary responsibility for preventing and responding to incidents of violence. Companies must provide them with the necessary resources, policies, procedures, or guidelines that will assist them with a coordinated response. Training a threat assessment team helps to maintain lines of communication and authority, and guide the incident management process before a threat or violent incident occurs.

Some ways to start planning include the following:

- Contract for an impartial, complete risk assessment and specific violence assessment. This should be designed to evaluate risks from within and outside the company.
- Institute a written workplace violence policy developed by management and employee representatives. Incorporate multiple disciplines to research and write this policy. Use clear examples of acceptable behavior. Use firm, clear, and concise language.
- Institute a firm harassment and zero tolerance policy.
- Communicate the company's view on workplace violence and harassment.
- Involve every employee.
- Implement an incident reporting system.
- Prioritize training and frequency of training for new hires and existing employees.
- Give the receptionist extra training in the areas of detection and facial recognition.
- Train front-line supervisors and management.
- Train management on nonviolent conflict resolution.
- Mandate annual training to re-enforce policies.
- Develop partnerships with local police and emergency departments, as well as a mutual aid agreement with another business.
- Conduct tabletop exercises, including partners.
- Monitor and adjust training as needed based on statistics of success and intervention.
- Outline and communicate the investigation process and investigate every incident.
- Offer a confidential employee assistance program (EAP), allowing employees to seek help and provide support services for victims of violence.
- Have plans for sheltering in place, along with a safe zone off-site.
- Maintain copies of company diagrams and property off-site.

Supervisors and managers should have specialized training on their roles in identifying and reporting ways of diffusing aggressive behavior, conflict resolution, employee relations, personal security measures, and communication skills. These are by no means inclusive as there are other aspects on which managers should be trained.

Workplace Violence Prevention Policy

The workplace policy must be written using firm, clear, and concise language. It should be clearly communicated, both at the new hire orientation as well as ongoing, that there is zero tolerance with regards to threats and violence. The policy should emphasize the employer's commitment in providing a safe and secure workplace environment, along with a clear definition of unacceptable behavior. The policy should state the code of conduct, prohibiting all threats, violent behavior, and other behavior that might be interpreted as intent to cause physical harm.

After the policy is written and communicated, it will be important to require prompt reporting of suspected violations along with enforcement of the policy. The policy should also include the following:

- All reports to management to be confidential and treated with discretion.
- All reports to be promptly investigated.
- Every witness and complainant to be treated fairly and impartially while investigated.
- Include guidelines for investigative staff and training/qualifications.
- Identify how information about potential risks of violence will be communicated to all employees, if necessary.
- Investigations should be free from conflicts of interest (i.e., employees are not investigated by their supervisors).
- Human resources should communicate problematic employees with security.
- Offer an EAP program to all employees.
- Make a commitment for non-retaliation to an employee that makes a report in good faith.
- State any applicable regulatory requirements.
- Indicate discipline for any policy violation.

Train to Identify Warning Signs

Security professionals know that some employees may have a higher risk of behavior issues or tendencies. Training and experience are the keys to understanding what behaviors might lead to violence. Every attacker has different psychological characteristics, so it is helpful to be aware of behavioral clues that cause someone to act out. In many cases, attacks are perpetrated by individuals who display some of the following characteristics:

- Prior history of violence: Involvement in previous incidents of violence, verbal abuse, antisocial activities, disruptive behavior.
- Domestic situations: An employee caught in a domestic dispute or family turmoil may impact the workplace.
- Suspicious behavior and indicators
- Mental disorders: Mood swings, depression, bizarre statements, paranoid behavior, overly aggressive, unstable behavior
- Life-changing events: Sudden loss of a family member or pet, extreme medical changes, divorce, or other major life changes
- Financial stresses: Bankruptcies, mortgage arrears, or heavy debt load
- Obsession with another employee: May be romantic or not
- Chemical dependence: Drug or alcohol abuse
- Increased interest in weapons: Ownership of guns or gun collection, other offensive weapons, talking a lot about guns
- Disgruntled employee: An employee feels the company no longer cares about him or her, other employees create a sense of mistrust, recently laid off or terminated

Education and Training

Companies need to consider what training to provide and to whom. Training also needs to be repeated periodically and updated based on changes in policies, physical elements, or risk factors. Training for employees should include understanding what workplace violence is, identification of early warning signs of workplace violence, and to whom and how to report it.

It is important to communicate to all employees that every employee needs to be responsible for a safe and secure work environment. Each employee can help ensure a safe environment by following established access control procedures and preventing piggybacking, which allows others to enter while the employee is entering. Employees should also be instructed on the companies reporting procedures, including behaviors that are red flags or indications of a potential employee matter such as a domestic issue. This is important because statistics show that a perpetrator kills, on average, three to five innocent bystanders, besides their intended victim.

Training for supervisors and managers should include all of the training employees receive, along with training in the following:

- The issues of workplace violence
- Supervisor/manager's role in identification of violence
- Ways to de-escalate or diffuse violent behavior
- Recognition of behavioral clues
- Conflict resolution
- Communication skills
- Personal security options
- EAP if available
- Various cycles of anger and managing anger
- Crisis management
- High-risk terminations
- Security procedures
- Emergency procedures relative to a violent incident

A Violence-Free Workplace

A recap to safeguarding the workplace from violence requires incorporation of a variety of procedures, such as the following:

- Use hiring practices that incorporate comprehensive background checks on new hires but also random or annual background checks on the current workforce.
- Incorporate a zero-tolerance policy.
- Establish a procedure for employees to report problem behavior through anonymous ways (e.g., employee tip line) and ensure an immediate and useful response.
- Foster a work environment that supports the reporting of misconduct and also prohibits retaliation to those who report the conduct.

- Investigate all incidents, and properly document.
- Implement procedures for investigation of misconduct, ensuring they are viewed as fair.
- Implement specific workplace violence training for new hires, annual training for current employees, and specialized training for management.
- Conduct a risk assessment with a workplace violence assessment.
- Utilize a threat team and any threat plans.
- Incorporate a fully integrated facility security program, utilizing structural barriers, identification badges, access control and lighting, key control, locks, documentation, communications, closed-circuit video, and environmental design.
- Use the security system to it's most benefit.
- Review termination practices, with an eye toward having a plan for high-risk terminations.
- Liaise with local law enforcement, medical staff, hospitals and fire department.
- Develop an emergency plan, including evacuation procedures and disaster recovery plans, and update both frequently.
- Develop partnerships with other similar businesses.
- Evaluate and update workplace violence policies and plans as necessary.

This list is noninclusive, and each individual business will have specific needs beyond what is presented here.

Everyone plays a role in preventing violence through observation, communication, and reporting. No organization can afford to ignore the issue of workplace violence as lives are lost daily due to such tragedies. Make the commitment and be proactive through initiatives, planning, exercising, and mitigating. Commitment will make the difference in how many lives are lost.

Refer website http://www.ifpo.org for further information

End Notes

1. OSHA Guidelines for Preventing Workplace Violence.
2. U.S. Bureau of Labor Statistics, U.S. Department of Labor, 2012, General Duty Clause, Section 5(a)(1).

40

An Overview of Security Risk Management Concepts

Kevin E. Palacios, Kevin E. Peterson

Modern life is full of all types of risk—no individual, community, organization, or place is immune from them. For this reason, a meaningful strategy to identify and manage risks is essential. It is something we all do, whether locking our car, keeping our passwords private, or looking both ways before crossing the street. Why? Because unaddressed risks can result in loss events, and these events cause consequences that may range from minor inconvenience to complete devastation.

Organizations such as businesses, government agencies, associations, and nonprofits benefit from a well-defined process for identifying and managing risk. This chapter outlines some considerations in such a process from a security and assets protection perspective and summarizes some models that can support such a process. To form a foundation for this discussion, a general overview of *risk management* is appropriate, and that is where we begin.

The concept of risk management has developed over time and originated in the financial investments arena. The various types of risk that exist in twenty-first century society include the following:

- Personal
- Financial
- Business
- Technology
- Operational
- Reputational
- Legal
- Security

Because many of these risk types either overlap or are interrelated, a comprehensive view of risk management is well advised. The emerging field of enterprise security risk management (ESRM), which will be discussed later in the chapter, is an intelligent framework for implementing such a comprehensive view. Another indicator of interaction among various risk types and the means to address them lies in international and national standards. Many such standards are written to recognize the multiple facets of risk, and some even address risks in a consolidated fashion. One example is the soon to be released (as of this writing) American National Standards Institute (ANSI)[1] Standard on Risk Assessment, which is being developed under the joint auspices of ASIS International and the Risk and Insurance Management Society (RIMS). Other examples include the following:

- ISO Standards
    - ISO 31000—Risk Management
    - ISO 27000—Information Security
    - ISO/PAS 22300—Corporate Protection and Business Continuity
- ANSI Standards
    - Auditing and Management Systems: Risk, Resilience, Security, and Continuity
    - Business Continuity Management
    - Chief Security Officer—An Organizational Model
    - Management System for Quality of Private Security Company Operations
    - Organizational Resilience: Security, Preparedness, and Continuity Management
    - Security Management Standard: Physical Asset Protection
    - Supply Chain Risk Management
    - Workplace Violence Prevention and Intervention
- ASIS Guidelines
    - Business Continuity
    - Facilities Physical Security Measures
    - Information Assets Protection
    - Pre-employment Background Screening
    - Private Security Officer Selection and Training
    - Workplace Violence Prevention and Response

Such standards and guidelines help security professionals and others think more globally and avoid the common trap of addressing risks in a vacuum or within a disciplinary "silo." The mindset of risk management helps avoid phrases like "that's not within our area of responsibility," "let them worry about that," or "not my job!" As security consultant Kevin Palacios, CPP, put it:

> *Historically, within both public and private organizations, risk management has been segmented and compartmentalized into "silos". Clearly, there is a tendency to classify risks in different categories which are mutually exclusive. This seems to be the result of the way in which our mind tries to solve problems: differentiating and sorting to better handle them. Existing organizational structures assume that the consequences of an unexpected event will be more or less limited to a particular area or section of an organization.*

(Palacios, 2014)[2]

Most ISO and ANSI standards follow a "plan–do–check–act" (PDCA) approach. Also known as the Deming cycle, PDCA is a management method whereby a step-by-step

---

[1] American National Standards Institute.

approach is employed to control a business process and ensure continuous improvement. It begins with a deliberate planning process, followed by a pilot or trial implementation under close scrutiny. The *check* step involves determining if the desired results were achieved in the trial or pilot, and if necessary a return to the *plan* step. Finally, once the process has been proven, the *act* step incorporates the new process into the existing infrastructure or business practices of the entity.[3] This concept fits seamlessly into a security risk management program because both are designed as a continuous and ongoing function to ultimately support an organization's strategic goals.

The value of standards in risk management was summarized nicely by Kevin Palacios when he said: "Standards-based management systems are the only way to gather 10 years of cumulative experience rather than acquire one year's experience 10 times."[4] Security professionals need to skillfully employ management systems and analytical tools in order to understand the overall context in which the organization operates. This effort should recognize the following:

- Critical organizational objectives
- The need to identify and measure hazards and the financial cost associated with them
- The ability to evaluate different types of risks, residual risk and risk tolerance
- A process to control and monitor results of risk mitigation strategies

Security Risk Management Models

To help meet the objectives discussed above, a number or organizations have taken a proactive stance over the past 30 years or so. As a result, a wide variety of models or methodologies now exist for implementing risk management programs. Some of them are the CARVER method (US Army), analytical risk management (US government), risk assessment methodology[2,5] (Sandia National Laboratories/US Department of Energy), RAMCAP (US Department of Homeland Security), and others. A number of models have been developed in the European Union, Australia and Canada as well, with many of them focused on critical infrastructure protection and/or cyber security.

Each of these models has advantages and disadvantages, and each works better in some applications than others. Security professionals must be careful when selecting a risk management/assessment model to guard against the tendency to misapply a given model or over-rely on one model over another without recognizing the distinctions among them.

All credible models have two things in common. The first is how they describe the functions of the security risk management process. An effective model will always recognize the following *functions* in one form or another:

- Assessment (defining and measuring the specific situation at hand)
- Controls (risk mitigation measures)

---

[2] Risk assessment methodology (RAM) is actually a series of models, each tailored to a particular sector of critical infrastructure such as water systems, dams, chemical facilities, electrical transmission, etc.

- Evaluation (determining how well the mitigation strategy is working)
- Monitoring (continuously checking for changes in risk factors and their implications)

Credible models will also consider some form of each of the following *risk factors*, which comprise the management process:

- Assets (all forms of organizational assets and, when possible, a determination of value)
- Threats (including threat actors and threat methods)
- Vulnerabilities
- Impact (also known as consequences)
- Mitigation (measures taken to address the risk–sometimes called "controls)

Like the PDCA approach, the security risk management process is meant to be cyclical or ongoing rather than static. This is absolutely essential because the risk factors are constantly changing, and those changes may have a drastic effect on extent and nature of the actual risk.

It should also be noted that the term *criticality* is often used as part of the lexicon in security risk management models. Criticality is actually used in two different ways depending upon the specific model in use—and practitioners should ensure they understand how the term is being used in the particular model being employed. It may be applied to the *assets* risk factor to describe the relative criticality of each asset. In this regard, it is a measure of the *value* of an asset. However, criticality may also refer to the *impact* risk factor and connote the *severity* of a loss event and its consequences. Both uses of the term are common and proper, but security professionals should be mindful of its use.

Finally, such models—and how they are applied—should consider that many risks are difficult to measure or even perceive before a loss event occurs. Therefore, practitioners should avoid the temptation to use the risk management process as an excuse to play "Monday morning quarterback" or engage in the "hindsight bias." In addition, risk management must always work toward achieving the organization's strategic or business goals. The process does not operate in a vacuum. This recognition provides strategic direction to a business, so that both protection and nonprotection managers understand what creates value and what destroys that value. The pursuit of opportunities requires an in-depth understanding of the risks to take as well as the pitfalls to be avoided.

A Generic Security Risk Management Model[3,6]

A general model for risk management follows the basic assets/threats/vulnerabilities/impact/mitigation paradigm, as shown in Figure 40.1. The first step in such a process is to clearly identify and articulate the organization's assets. Remember, you cannot have a successful security program if you do not know what you are protecting.

[3]This section is largely extracted from "Primer on Security Risk Management," a white paper by Innovative Protection Solutions, LLC. Used by permission.

Risk Management Process

FIGURE 40.1 A general security risk management process. *Source: Innovative Protection Solutions, LLC.*

Assets

Identifying assets, however, may not be as straightforward as it may seem. As mentioned, no effective security program can be implemented without a thorough understanding (on the part of both the asset owner *and* the security professional) of what it is that is being protected—or *should* be protected. When looking at an organization's assets, three types should be considered:

- Tangible
- Intangible
- Mixed

Too often, asset owners and security professionals focus exclusively on tangible assets or on those which appear on the accountant's balance sheet.

Assets must also be "valuated" somehow in order to set priorities and determine relative worth to the organization or mission. The value of assets is frequently expressed in dollar amounts, but assigning such a number is not always possible, particularly in the case of intangible and mixed assets. Even when dollar values are assigned, a credible number that can reasonably be defended may be elusive, and often times it simply cannot be determined. Security professionals should be careful to ensure that a realistic valuation of assets is in place before continuing with the development of a risk management program.

Threats

Any individual, organization, or agency faces a wide variety of threats. These fall into the three categories: *intentional, natural,* and *inadvertent.* Intentional threats are those perpetrated by an adversary against a specific target. Examples include criminal acts, terrorist attacks, arson, theft, white collar crime, intellectual property theft, and others. Natural threats include storms, natural disasters, power or utility outages, pandemics, and the like. The most difficult to quantify are inadvertent threats. These consist of accidents, errors, and unintentional acts that may be caused by an individual, but in a nonmalicious manner. A comprehensive threat assessment will consider all three categories of threats.

What is needed is a balanced approach to threat assessment. Of course, some types of threats will be more prevalent at certain times and in certain places. Effective security risk management strategies, however, must be based on a realistic, full-scope, and balanced threat assessment.

Vulnerabilities

The most common view of *vulnerability* is a security weakness or problem. Although this can be the case, we must also recognize that some vulnerabilities are simply existing conditions or business practices that support mission accomplishment. For example, engaging in sales by e-commerce can be viewed as a vulnerability, but it may also be an essential way of conducting business for a particular company. One perspective on vulnerability is that it is anything which facilitates or allows a threat to be implemented or increases the magnitude of a loss event.

Vulnerabilities should be evaluated in any assessment or risk management program by the degree to which they would allow a threat action (sometimes called a *threat vector*) to successfully result in a loss event or elevate the impact of that event. Inadvertent threats and associated vulnerabilities are generally the most difficult in any organization to identify and measure. This should not, however, be used as an excuse for neglecting this aspect of the overall risk posture.

Impact

Bringing together all the information that has been collected on assets, threats, and vulnerabilities allows the practitioner to perform a risk analysis. A risk analysis also considers the potential *impact* or *consequences* of a loss event. This step looks at the level of severity of a loss event if it does occur. In other words, if a particular incident happens, it should be determined how seriously it will affect the organization in terms of the following:

- Its ability to perform its mission
- Death, injury, loss, or decreased productivity of its people
- Financial losses (both direct and indirect costs)
- Effects on market share or competitive advantage
- Reputational or brand degradation
- Sustainability of operations and organizational potential

In some cases, it is difficult to collect the data needed to conduct a thorough analysis. As noted security consultant and author James Broder states:

When experience (history) has provided an adequate database, loss expectancy can be projected with a satisfactory degree of confidence. In new situations, however, or in situations in which data have not been or cannot be collected, we have insufficient knowledge on which to base our projections.

(Broder, 2012, p 27)[7]

Our advice is to simply do the best job possible given the circumstances.

It should be noted that it is advisable to determine the risk factors in any given assessment (threat, vulnerability, and impact) by committee. In other words, assessments should be performed by a multidisciplinary team of subject matter experts in order to reach credible and justifiable numbers as input to the analysis. Justifying the numbers is the area where assessors are most often challenged by clients, executives, and decision makers in terms of reporting their risk analysis results.

Although there are many effective and time-tested approaches to calculating risk results (as discussed in the previous section on risk management models), a simple approach is often the most useful. One such approach uses the formula shown below to calculate the overall risk:

$$\text{Risk} = (\text{Threat} \times \text{Vulnerability} \times \text{Impact})^{1/3}$$

Using this formula, which multiplies the risk factors rather than adding them, recognizes that if any single factor is zero, the resulting risk is zero (at that time and place). In this approach, the evaluation factors (threat, vulnerability, and impact) are rated on a 0 to 100 scale. Such a scale is easy for people to understand because they are accustomed to thinking in terms of percentages. Using the cubed root also places the overall risk figure back on the 0 to 100 scale —again making it easy for people to understand and to visualize using charts and graphs.

Risk analysis results should be presented to the client or decision maker in a manner that assists them in understanding the data and making decisions. This includes placing the identified risks in a priority order or into priority categories to help show, from the assessor's perspective, which risks should be addressed first.

Mitigation

After a thorough risk analysis, the next step is to recommend a suite of protective measures that effectively addresses the relevant risks while considering available resources and minimizing any adverse impact on the enterprise's mission and operations. In other words, now that we know the problem, how do we fix it?

As indicated in the risk management process diagram (Figure 40.1), this step involves a number of subtasks. They generally include the following:

- Selecting appropriate tools and measures as part of the overall strategy
- Testing those tools/measures to ensure they operate as expected in the specific environment they will be used and that there are no unexpected conflicts among systems, policies, and procedures
- Implement the measures (may be done on a pilot or limited scope basis at first, and then fully implemented if appropriate)
- Train security staff, employees, facility users, maintenance staff and others as needed to maximize the effectiveness of the tool and reduce disruption

Although this model is very straightforward, it has wide appeal and is highly effective in a variety of settings, organization types, and security applications. Aspects of the process may be automated to leverage modern incident management systems and other analytic tools or implemented in a low-tech manner as desired (Peterson, 2011).[8]

Another Perspective: The ARES Model

Origin of the ARES Model

The model for the administration of revenue, environment and security (in Spanish *Administración de Rentabilidad, Entorno y Seguridad*), the ARES model, was developed in Ecuador to integrate protection management (logical and physical security and business continuity) into existing models (or even already implemented systems) of quality, safety, health, and environment. For the purposes of this discussion, the integrated management of environment, health, safety, security and quality (EHSSQ) will simply be referred to as ARES.

The model follows a strategic/operative approach and integrates concepts of strategic planning, theory of processes, quality management systems, and indicators of internal management and control, and it seeks to meet the information needs of all stakeholders. It helps understand the interdependencies between risks, how risk materializes, and how this can increase risk impact in another area of the organization. As such, it justifies actions to mitigate risk aimed to reach multiple sectors of business, generating savings and efficiency.

The vision behind the ARES model is twofold: first, to define a common language among the various parties concerned with organizational risks, and second, to generate strategic alignment. This is important because, if not properly managed, different types of risks can endanger all the objectives of the organization (including its primary objectives).

The ARES model represents a framework for considering the stages of identification, assessment, control, and monitoring of risks within an integrated, comprehensive, multidisciplinary, and participatory approach. Its key segments are prevention, mitigation, and response, as shown in Figure 40.2.

Integrated: ARES contributes to the achievement of objectives. The process of "thinking in risks" should not immobilize the action or the organizational dynamics (it may even help earn money). The prevention–mitigation–response cycle should not be considered as isolated actions, independent of the rest of the functions of the organization, but must become part of the overall management system. The administration of business risks is not a project, a product, or an action that is performed a single time (or even by external consultants to the organization); it must be assumed as a continual and ongoing process that is performed every day in the organization itself.

Comprehensive: ARES consists of organized efforts to protect people, information, assets, reputation, and the environment. It summarizes and welcomes all best practices, legal requirements, and applicable standards.

Multidisciplinary: Based on techniques from administrative sciences, statistics, psychology, physical security, safety and occupational health, and occupational medicine, ARES requires many specialists.

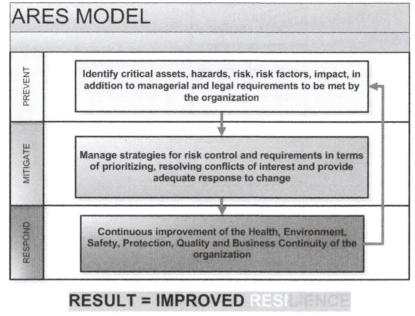

FIGURE 40.2 The ARES model.

Participatory: Risk management is a task for all. It calls for participation at all levels. ARES is based on a leadership model whereby all parts and levels of an organization are represented and actively participate in the process.

The creation of an "ARES culture" is not a matter of isolated events, but a comprehensive training, coaching, communication and information program to include the following:

- Visible and active leadership of the directorate to develop and maintain the support of an ARES culture
- Effective communication that motivate workers to develop their role with ARES
- Promotion of competence (knowledge, skills and attitudes) for a responsible contribution
- Participation and commitment at all levels

Phases of the ARES Model

Implementing a model of business risk management requires a thorough knowledge of the organization to establish a policy of prevention/mitigation/response, to define goals and objectives, to plan and integrate these activities, and to implement and measure compliance with the purpose of verifying that they have decreased losses and risks have been controlled.

The model has seven phases that create a virtual spiral designed to ensure a sustainable long-term system (see Figure 40.3). The phases are as follows:

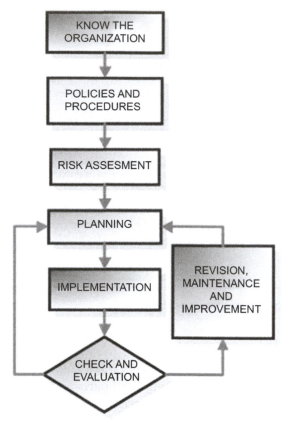

FIGURE 40.3 Layout of the ARES model.

1. Know the organization
2. Policies and procedures
3. Risk assessment
4. Planning
5. Implementation
6. Check and evaluation
7. Review, maintenance, and improvement

The establishment of integrated risk management in the company involves the introduction of a plan that includes organizational structure, the definition of functions, practices, procedures, processes, and resources necessary to carry out this action.

Know the Organization

To protect an organization, it is first necessary to understand it and have a clear mission, vision, and objectives. ARES requires a clear vision of the following:

- Hazards, risks, and consequences
- Legal requirements
- Existing programs
- Resources of tools available

The objective of this phase is to identify critical objectives of protection (people, information, assets, reputation, and environment) that are part of what is called the core business (heart of the business). This focuses attention on the hazards that are more relevant to the organization, which can really affect the survival, growth, and revenue of the company.

Policies and Procedures

The key word in developing an ARES model is *responsibility*. Each individual in the organization must assume responsibility for it, beginning with management who should support and promote this process. If an organization does not have policies and procedures for prevention, mitigation, and response correctly established and disseminated, it is because they are not aware that this is a tool that helps achieve business goals. An organization without this is at a competitive disadvantage. To this end, leaders must establish the commitment of the highest management through the alignment coaching of values and beliefs.

Integrated Risk Management Policy

A unified ARES business policy defines the strategic management and describes principles to which the organization aims, and simultaneously provides a standard against which achievements must be measured. This policy must be regularly reviewed and updated to align with operational requirements. ARES policy must be relevant to the activities, products, and services made (not only approved) by the management; this requires the organization to identify an organizational risk manager who has been given the authority to supervise and implement it. The policy affects all of the activities and decisions, including those related to the selection of resources, information, design, and operation of systems at work; design and supply of products and services, as well as the control and destruction of waste.

The unified risk management business policy contributes to the good business execution, caring for and development of the physical and human resources. It reduces costs and legal responsibilities by developing organizational structures and a *culture* that supports the control of the business risks, ensuring the full participation of the stakeholders.

Integrated Risk Management Procedures

The definition of procedures that are suitable and valid for the organization is one of the cornerstones to an effective implementation of the ARES policy. Its primary purpose is to translate the good intentions of the policy to daily practice, ensuring that activities and specific tasks are sufficiently coordinated.

RISK ASSESSMENT

Through the risk assessment process, the security professional balances consequences, countermeasures, and related costs until the residual risk decreases down to values close enough to the tolerable risk. The organizational definition of "tolerable risk level" must be explained in the form of a procedure to avoid conflict between areas with different "visions" of risk. The level of maximum acceptable risk must be defined as a range or rather than a specific number. Otherwise the possible solution sets or options would be unnecessarily limited. The intention is to optimize (not necessarily reduce or eliminate)—to balance risks and impacts created by the business, its products, and services before they even exist.[9]

PLANNING

Planning involves a process that helps to identify what action(s) need to be taken and how an entity can know when those actions have occurred. To measure the prevention–mitigation–response, a set of indicators must be defined so that the success can be measured. If it cannot be measured, it cannot be managed. Indicators should be developed based on the priorities of the company's strategic plan.

The indicators should be as follows:

- Measurable: accurate and complete data
- Time constrained: data that is necessary and accounts for a particular timeframe
- Relevant: does not measure things that are not important
- Specific: pointing toward what will be measured
- Achievable: easy to understand and evident when the management is "right" or "wrong"

Some recommended categories of indicators are financial, administrative, technical, operational, and human. For each of the indicators, the first thing to be defined is the value or level of goals to be accomplished.

IMPLEMENTATION

For implementation, the ARES model uses the guidelines of the Method of Operational Risk (MOR) developed by the US Navy in 1989. ARES is designed to enable individuals to identify and measure hazards, evaluate risks, and implement controls to reduce the risk associated with any action or operation. The ARES implementation operates at three levels according to four principles, and it follows five steps:

The ARES levels are as follows:

Operational: a continuous analysis and "something fast"
Tactical: implementation of the five-step process
Strategic: involving careful study of available data, diagrams and analytical tools as well as formal testing and monitoring of long-range hazards

The ARES principles are as follows:

1. Accept the risk when the benefits outweigh the cost of mitigation.
2. Do not take unnecessary risks.

3. Anticipate and manage risks (risks are more easily controlled when identified early in the planning process).
4. Risk decisions should be made at the appropriate level in the organization.

The ARES steps are as follows:

1. Identify hazards.
2. Assess risks.
3. Make decisions regarding how to address risks.
4. Deploy countermeasures.
5. Monitor compliance and effectiveness.

CHECK AND EVALUATION

This phase aims to evaluate the results by comparing them with a service-level agreement. This evaluation involves periodic reviews, tests, post-incident reports, lessons learned, performance appraisals, and exercises. Continuous assessment is implemented through three processes:

* Continuous monitoring of the management system
* Management of nonconformities and preventive or corrective actions
* Inspections and audits

To implement this phase, a set of indicators should be developed for each organization in which the ARES model is in place. These indicators serve as a benchmark and tool to measure the effectiveness and efficiency of the process in consideration of overall objectives. The role of the security department is essential to identifying, measuring, preventing, mitigating, and responding to a growing number of risks. Departments must be able to measure the probability and potential consequence of risks in order to fully support management. Without these measurements, management has no measurements to assess and prioritize what actions to take.

Indicators are any metric that is easy to measure. The purpose of an indicator is to obtain general information about the performance trends in order to systematically track the progress. ARES indicators are used to understand the adequacy of the quality controls, security, health, information, protection, and business continuity.

REVIEW, MAINTENANCE, AND IMPROVEMENT

An important element in the management of business risk is to learn from all the relevant experience and apply what has been learned. The application of these lessons must be accomplished systematically through an ongoing review based on the indicators and data collected via audits. The commitment to continuous improvement in the preventive action involves the continuing development of ARES policy and criteria for its implementation.

In summary, the application of an integrated, holistic, interdisciplinary, and participatory management system can offer significant advantages in terms of managing all-source risks to any organization.

Benefits of Integrated Risk Management

No management process can create an environment free of risks. However, the effective administration of risk management allows any organization to operate more efficiently in an environment in which risks are constantly changing or evolving. The three major benefits of the enterprise risk management are the strategic alignment of risk management to the strategic business goals, the increase in resource efficiency, and the improved risk reporting that results.

Refer website http://www.ifpo.org for further information

End Notes

1. American Society for Quality, *Plan-do-check-act cycle* (2015). www.asq.org, Accessed February 2015.
2. Palacios K., *Model for the integrated management of business risks* (Quito, Ecuador: IPC Foundation, 2014).
3. See note 1 above.
4. See note 2 above.
5. Broder J. and Tucker E., *Risk Analysis and the Security Survey*, Fourth Edition (Waltham, MA: Elsevier Butterworth-Heinemann, 2012).
6. See note 2 above.
7. See note 5 above.
8. Peterson K., *Primer on security risk management, white paper* (Herndon, VA: Innovative Protection Solutions, LLC, 2011).
9. Vellani K., *Strategic Security Management: A Risk Assessment Guide for Decision Makers* (Burlington, MA: Elsevier Butterworth-Heinemann, 2007).

41

Standards, Guidelines, and Regulation for the Security Industry

Ann Y. Trinca

All security businesses have an interest in ensuring their products and services not only meet customer or client expectations but also comply with applicable government regulations. Customers and clients, on the other hand, have an interest in ensuring their purchases of security products and services amount to money well spent. To accomplish this daunting task, businesses and consumers seeking guidance often turn to organizations that publish documents known as industry standards and guidelines. In general, adherence to these standards and guidelines is voluntary. However, any particular standard or guideline, or an aspect or portion thereof, has the potential of becoming mandatory if adopted into law by a government or legislature. Hence, security professionals seeking to stay ahead of their field make it a priority to keep up with relevant industry standards and guidelines.

The most respected and well known publisher of international standards is the International Organization for Standardization, more commonly known as ISO. In the United States, the American National Standards Institute (ANSI) is the official voice of American standards. Businesses, professionals, and consumers looking for security-specific guidance turn to the highly regarded standards and guidelines published by ASIS International, the preeminent worldwide organization for security professionals. The Security Industry Association (SIA) also has a significant influence in the sphere of electronic security and has published a number of well regarded standards enabling integration of security components. As the leading advocate for fire prevention and safety, the many standards and codes published by the National Fire Protection Association (NFPA) have also had a direct and significant impact on security technologies and operations. Standards have also been developed in the payment card industry (PCI) by the PCI SSC (Security Standards Council), an organization established in 2006 to mitigate data breaches and payment cardholder data fraud.

This chapter provides an introduction to these organizations, highlighting a few of the better-known published standards and/or guidelines of each. Also included in this chapter is a discussion of state regulation of the private security industry, with particular emphasis on security officers. By no means do the standards, guidelines, and regulations featured below represent an exhaustive list. In fact, it is important to understand that many new standards, guidelines, and regulations relevant to the security industry are in the works; of those already published, many are currently being updated or revised. This continuing evolution of standards, guidelines, and regulations indeed reflects the industry's dynamic nature. What can be said with certainty is that standards, guidelines, and regulations play a central role in how organizations conduct their operations, how consumers make choices, and how the industry as a whole evolves to meet changing security demands.

ISO—International Organization for Standardization

ISO is the largest publisher of voluntary international standards. ISO defines standards as "a document that provides requirements, specifications, guidelines or characteristics that can be used consistently to ensure that materials, products, processes and services are fit for their purpose."[1] Since its beginnings in 1946, when 65 delegates from 25 countries convened in London, ISO's influence and reach as grown significantly. ISO today includes national standards institute organizational members from 165 countries and a full-time staff of approximately 150 headquartered in Geneva, Switzerland.[2] Over the years, ISO has published more than 19,500 international standards, which address virtually every facet of technology and business. The use or adoption of these international standards has many benefits for businesses, consumers, and governments alike, as each has a vested interest in ensuring that materials, products, processes, and services meet acceptable levels of quality (Figure 41.1).

All ISO standards are the result of a highly rigorous development process that reflects the consensus of international subject matter experts. ISO management system standards are generic in the sense the standards can be adopted by any business, including service organizations and product manufacturers, as well as both small and large entities (Figure 41.2).[4]

There are a number of ISO Standards that directly impact the security industry, such as ISO 9000, Quality Management; ISO 31000, Risk Management; and ISO 27001, Information Security. An overview of each is provided in Figure 41.3.

As a way to demonstrate an organization's committee to quality systems, services, or products, many entities seek "ISO certification" by an external certification body.[11] Within competitive industries like security, ISO certification can be viewed as a positive discriminator. In its 2013 Survey of Certifications,[12] ISO reported data regarding certificates issued for compliance to ISO 9001:2008, Quality Management Systems, ISO 27001:2005, Information Security Management Systems, and others. As these numbers reveal, ISO certification is being sought in impressive numbers worldwide (Figure 41.4).

Benefits	
For business	Cost savings, reduced waste and errors, greater customer satisfaction, access to new markets, increased market share, environmental benefits
For society	Consumer confidence in product and service safety, reliability, and quality
For governments	Developed with the input of experts from around the world, standards provide an important resource for governments in developing laws and regulations and facilitating global world trade opportunities.

FIGURE 41.1 Benefits of ISO international standards.[3]

---

1. ISO standards are developed in response to a market need. ISO does not unilaterally decide to develop a new standard. Rather, ISO responds to market demand and industry requests, which may originate from industry stakeholders, including consumer groups.
2. ISO standards are based on global expert opinion. ISO standards are developed by groups of experts from around the globe. Through a systematic and lengthy process, these experts determine each standard's scope, key definitions, and content.
3. ISO standards are developed through a multistakeholder process. Technical committees include industry experts, consumer associations, academia, nongovernmental organizations, and government representatives.
4. Standards are based on a consensus. ISO standards are developed using a consensus-based approach that considers stakeholder input.

FIGURE 41.2 Key principles in the development of ISO standards.[5]

ISO 9000: Quality Management Systems[6]:
- Relevance: Service and product quality are important to many: to service providers, product manufacturers, consumers, and governments as well. Such quality is best enabled through a management system that emphasizes well established quality management principles.
- Details: The ISO 9000 series is among ISO's most popular and well known standards. The series address different aspects of quality management, providing guidance to ensure product and service quality meet customer expectations. The standards also provide a framework in which quality is continually improved. Included in the ISO 9000 series are:
  - ISO 9001:2008 provides the requirements for a quality management system and includes eight management principles: customer focus; leadership; involvement of people; process approach; system approach to management; continual improvement; factual approach to decision making; and mutually beneficial supplier relationships.[7] More than a million companies and organizations in over 170 countries have implemented this standard, and many have sought voluntary and optional certification as evidence of their conformity to the standard.[8]
  - ISO 9000:2005 discusses basic concept and language.
  - ISO 9004:2009 discusses ways to increase quality management system efficiency and effectiveness.
  - ISO 19011:2011 provides guidance for quality management system audits.

ISO 31000: Risk Management Standard[9]:
- Relevance: All organizations have an interest in safeguarding their assets, including their people, property, and professional reputation. The ability to manage risk effectively in an uncertain environment is essential to organizational stability and growth.
- Details: ISO 31000:2009, *Risk Management—Principles and Guidelines*, sets forth basic principles and a risk management framework and process. The standard helps ensure organizational resources are allocated wisely to address identified threats.

ISO 27001, Informational Security Standard[10]
- Relevance: Information represents the most valuable asset to many organizations. Organizations of all sizes are faced with the continuing challenge of protecting their vital information assets.
- Details: The ISO 27000 series of standards address information assets, including financial information, intellectual property, employee, and other information. Within the series, ISO/IEC 27001 is the best-known standard related to information security management system (ISMS), a comprehensive and systematic approach that incorporates a risk management process. Many organizations seek voluntary certification to the ISO/IEC 27001 standard.

FIGURE 41.3 ISO 9000, ISO 31000, and ISO 27001.

ISO Standard	Number of Certificates in 2013	Number of Countries/ Economies	Top 3 Countries: Number of Certificates	Top 3 Countries: Growth in Number of Certificates
ISO 9001:2008	1,129,446	187	China Italy Germany	Italy India United States
ISO 27001:2005	22,293	105	Japan India United Kingdom	Italy India United Kingdom

FIGURE 41.4 Number of ISO standard certificates.

ANSI—American National Standards Institute

In the United States, ANSI serves as "the voice of the US standards and conformity assessment system" and is the official US representative to ISO.[13] Founded in 1918, ANSI's mission is "to enhance both the global competitiveness of US business and the US quality of life by promoting and facilitating voluntary consensus standards and conformity assessment systems, and safeguarding their integrity."[14]

ANSI does not actually develop standards itself; rather, what are commonly thought of as "ANSI standards" are actually developed by more than 250 "standards developing organizations (SDOs)" accredited by ANSI.[15] To become an "American National Standard", not only must the document originate from an SDO, it must receive the ANSI review board's approval, signifying that the standard was developed through an open, balanced, and consensus-based process.[16] Thousands of security-related standards are available for purchase online from ANSI's eStandards Store.[17]

ASIS International

In the security industry, ASIS International has taken a leading role in the development and publication of standards and guidelines on a broad range of security topics. ASIS *standards* "set forth industry-recommended best practices, establish requirements, and provide tools and processes for implementation,"[18] whereas *guidelines* "offer a collection of suggested practices aimed at increasing information awareness."[19] Within the organization, the task of overseeing this responsibility falls upon the ASIS Commission on Standards and Guidelines. Committees are formed comprised of subject matter experts from the widest array of industry representation. This ensures all ASIS International standards and guidelines are developed in a balanced and impartial manner, consistent with ISO and ANSI standards.[20] The rigorous, comprehensive, and lengthy process involved in the development of each ASIS standard and guideline has resulted in an impressive resource collection relied upon by thousands of security professionals worldwide. Standards and guidelines continue to be developed by ASIS International to meet the needs of its growing global membership of more than 37,000 (Figure 41.5).

Published ANSI/ASIS International Standards[21]
- Auditing Management Systems for Risk, Resilience, Security, and Continuity—Guidance for Application (2014)
- Business Continuity Management (2010)
- Chief Security Officer (CSO)—An Organizational Model (2014, replaces 2008 edition)
- Conformity Assessment and Auditing Management Systems for Quality of Private Security Company Operations (2012)
- Management Systems for Quality of Private Security Company Operations—Requirements with Guidance (2012)
- Maturity Model for the Phased Implementation of a Quality Assurance Management System for Private Security Service Providers (2013)
- Maturity Model for the Phased Implementation of the Organizational Resilience Management System (2012)
- Organizational Resilience: Security Preparedness and Continuity Management Systems—Requirements with Guidance for Use (2009)
- Physical Asset Protection (2012)
- Quality Assurance and Security Management for Private Security Companies Operating at Sea—Guidance (2013)
- Supply Chair Risk Management: A Compilation of Best Practices (2014)
- Workplace Violence Prevention and Intervention (2011)

Published ASIS International Guidelines[22]
- Business Continuity (2005)
- Facilities Physical Security Measures (2009)
- General Security Risk Assessment (2003)
- Information Asset Protection (2007)
- Pre-employment Background Screening (2009)
- Private Security Officer Selection and Training (2010)
- Workplace Violence Prevention and Response (2005)

FIGURE 41.5 Published ANSI/ASIS international standards.

SIA—Security Industry Association

The SIA has developed and published standards aimed at enabling easy integration of diverse components, as well as predicable levels of performance.[23] Within the association, members of the SIA Standards Committee ensure that the standards they develop are coordinated and consistent with other existing standards (Figure 41.6).[24]

NFPA—National Fire Protection Association

The National Fire Protection Association (NFPA) is an international nonprofit organization with over 70,000 members worldwide.[25] Founded in 1896, its mission is "to reduce the worldwide burden of fire and other hazards on the quality of life by providing and advocating consensus codes and standards, research, training, and education." To date, the NFPA has developed and published over 300 codes and standards.[26] A few of these are listed in Figure 41.7 and illustrate the intersection between fire, life safety, and security.

- ANSI/SIA CP-01-2014- Control Panel Standard, Features for False Alarm Reduction
- ANSI/SIA DC-09-2007-SIA DCS-Internet Protocol Event Reporting
- ANSI/SIA MSD-01-2000-MSD Monitoring Practices Standard
- ANSI/SIA PIR-01-2000-PIR False Alarm Immunity Standard
- OSDP (open supervised Device Protocol)
- SIA AC-01-1996.10-Access Control-Wiegand
- SIA AC-03-2000.06-Access Control Badging Guideline
- SIA AV-01-1997.11-Audio Verification-2 Way Voice Standard
- SIA BIO-01-1993.02 (R2000.06)-Biometric Vocabulary Standard
- SIA DC-01-1988 (R2001.04)-DCS Computer Interface (CIS-1) Technical Report
- SIA DC-02-1992.02 (R2000.05)-DCS Generic Protocols Technical Report
- SIA DC-03-1991.01 (R2003.10)-DCS SIA Format Standard
- SIA DC-0402000.05-DCS SIA 2000 Standard
- SIA DC-05-1999.09-DCS Ademco contact ID Standard
- SIA DC-07-2001.04-DCS Computer Interface (CIS-2) Standard
- SIA GB-01-1994.12-Glassbreak False Alarm Reduction Standard
- SIA GB-02-1996.07-Glassbreak False Alarm Sounds Technical Report
- SIA PID-01-1995.12 (2006.06)-Point ID Sensor Multiplex Protocol Standard
- SIA RF-01-1997.04-Short Range RF Definitions Standard
- SIA TVAC-01-2001.04-TVAC-CCTV to Access Control Standard

FIGURE 41.6 Published SIA standards.

- NFPA 1: Fire code
- NFPA 10: Standard for Portable Fire Extinguisher
- NFPA 70: National Electrical Code
- NFPA 70E: Standard for Electrical Safety in the Workplace
- NFPA 72: National Fire Alarm and Signaling Code
- NFPA 75: Standard for the Fire Protection of Information Technology Equipment
- NFPA 101: Life Safety Code
- NFPA 220: Standard on Types of Building Construction
- NFPA 232: Standard for the Protection of Records
- NFPA 601: Standard for Security Services in Fire Loss Prevention
- NFPA 730: Guide for Premises Security
- NFPA 731: Standard for the Installation of Electronic Premises Security Systems
- NFPA 921: Guide for Fire and Explosion Investigations
- NFPA 1600: Standard on Disaster/Emergency Management and Business Continuity Programs

FIGURE 41.7 Published NFPA standards.

PCI SSC—Payment Card Industry Security Standards Council

The PCI SSC was established in 2006 to combat the exploding number of data breaches and fraud cases. The council has promulgated key payment card industry standards, including the Data Security Standard (PCI DSS), Payment Application Data Security Standard (PA-DSS), and PIN Transaction Security (PTS) requirements. The five founding organizations, including American Express, Discover Financial Services, JCB International, MasterCard, and Visa, have all incorporated the PCI DSS into their data security operations. The importance of standards is best underscored by the data breaches of several major corporations, resulting in shaken customer confidence, reputational damage, and enormous financial losses.[27]

Federal Regulation of Private Protective Security Officers

Private security officers play an important role in national security. The significance of their role is reflected in the Private Security Officer Employment Authorization Act of 2004, federal legislation signed into law by President George W. Bush, which authorizes fingerprint-based criminal history checks of state and national criminal history records to screen private security officers and applicants.[28] Access to Federal Bureau of Investigation (FBI) criminal history records is a significant tool to identify individuals who may lack the requisite qualifications for being a security officer, a position that demands a high level of confidence and trust.

Federal Government Contracts

Aside from federal legislation, the federal government exerts significant influence over private security through its government contracting process. Numerous federal agencies contract with private security providers to secure their facilities and occupants. Such contracts typically set forth detailed specifications relating to security officer age, experience, education, physical and medical standards, training, background, and licensing. Thus, contractors who wish to do business with the federal government must agree to employ only individuals who meet the security position's minimum qualifications.

Figure 41.8 contains some of the security officer qualifications included in a US Department of Homeland Security (DHS), Federal Protective Service (FPS) Protective Security Officer (PSO) contract.[29] DHS/FPS is responsible for the security of over 9000 federal facilities, overseeing over 15,000 private security officers involved in the contract guard program.[30] The broad scope of these DHS/FPS contract requirements is a compelling illustration of how the federal government can effectively direct the PSO industry, not through legislation, but through the government contracting process itself.

State Regulation of Private Protective Security Officers

In the United States, government regulation of the private security industry has traditionally been at the state and sometimes local (county or city) level. The vast majority of states have passed laws regulating the private security industry, including PSOs. While it is beyond the scope of this chapter to review each state's laws and regulations, this chapter will provide a brief overview of the state regulation of the private security industry, with particular focus on security officers located in the top five most populated states. According to the 2010 United States Census, these states include California, Texas, New York, Florida, and Illinois.

Department of Homeland Security/Federal Protective Services:

Security Officer Requirements

General Qualifications of PSOs:
- U.S. citizen or lawful permanent resident with approval
- Social security card issued by Social Security Administration
- High school diploma or GED from an accredited institution recognized by the US Department of Education
- At least one of the following experience/education levels (3 years of security experience within the past 5 years, or 3 years of military or national guard active duty or reserve service; or successful competition of a state certified law enforcement education and training or police officer's standard training course)
- Ability to fluently speak, read, comprehend, and compose coherent written reports in English
- Completion of a Lautenberg amendment statement/domestic violence certification annually.

Medical and Physical Qualifications:
- Pre-employment medical/physical examination and every 3 years thereafter by a licensed physician
- Must meet medical standards related to vision, hearing, speech, cardiovascular system, chest and respiratory system, gastrointestinal system, genitourinary system, endocrine and metabolic system, musculoskeletal system, hematology system, neurological system, psychiatric disorders, dermatology, medication, organ transplantation and prosthetic devices
- Must meet physical demands, including frequent and prolonged walking, standing, sitting, and stooping, up to 12 h per day, either indoors or outdoors, during daytime or nighttime
- Must be able to withstand extreme heat, humidity, cold, severe weather including snow, sleet, rain, hail, wind
- Must be able to remain calm in stressful situations, including confrontations with angry, distraught, disturbed, or violent persons
- Must be able to remain on post up to 4 consecutive hours without sitting, eating, or relieving bladder/bowels
- Must be able to remain alert for up to 12 h, with ability to mentally and physically react quickly to a variety of unexpected and dangerous situations
- Must be able to use senses, including sight, hearing, smell, and touch to discern unusual or dangerous situations
- Must be able to use post security equipment, including metal detectors, X-rays, closed-circuit video, handcuffs, baton, and firearm at any time while on duty
- Must be able to subdue violent or potentially violent or disturbed individuals, or intervene in a crisis by providing emergency first aid or resuscitation
- Occasional running, sprinting, lifting heavy weights, moving heavy objects, climbing stairs when responding to emergencies, facility evacuations, and giving pursuit

Screening for Illegal Drugs:
- Urine drug screening must be conducted during initial pre-employment screening and recurring medical examination, every 3 years
- Drug screenings must conform to U.S. Department of Health and Human Services Substance Abuse of Mental Health Service Administration's (SAMHSA) "Mandatory Guidelines for Federal Workplace Drug Testing Programs."
- Drug screenings must be conducted by laboratories listed on SAMHSA's "Current List of Laboratories Which Meet Standards to Engage in Urine Drug Testing for Federal Agencies."
- Contractor must perform random drug screenings of 10 percent of all PSOs over a 12-month period.

FIGURE 41.8 Common DHS/FPS Contract Requirements for Protective Security Officers (PSOs).

Department of Homeland Security/Federal Protective Services:

Security Officer Requirements

Government Suitability Determination:
- PSOs must receive a favorable suitability determination, conducted by the government.
- This requires the contractor to submit the following documentation on behalf of each PSO: contractor information worksheet; two forms FD-258, fingerprint chart; DHS form 11000-9, Disclosure and Authorization Pertaining to Consumer Reports Pursuant to the Fair Credit Reporting Act; foreign national relatives or associates statement; Lautenberg amendment statement; standard form (SF) 85P, questionnaire for public trust; standard form 85P-S, supplemental questionnaire for selected positions; signed e-verify confirmation notice; and OF 306, declaration for federal employment.

Security Clearances:
- In addition to suitability determinations, some contracts may require the contractor and/or PSOs to have security clearances if they will have access to sensitive or classified national security information.
- Background investigations must meet the investigation requirements set for the National Industrial Security Program Operating Manual (NISPOM).[31]

Training:
PSOs must successfully complete both initial and recurring/refresher training provided by either the contractor or government:
- Contractor-provided basic training (64h) covering: Overview of the Department of Homeland Security and the Federal Protective Service; ethics and professionalism; principles of communication; professional public relations; understanding human behavior; the law, legal authorities, jurisdiction and responsibilities; crimes and offenses; search and seizure; authority to detain; use of force, crime scene protection, rules of evidence; security guard administration; post duties; patrol methods and patrol hazards; general response procedures; access control; crime detection, assessment and response; safety and fire prevention; records, reports and forms; special situations; code adam; terrorism, anti-terrorism, and weapons of mass destruction (WMD); workplace violence; civil disturbances; bomb threats and incidents; hostage situations; sabotage and espionage; defensive tactics; use of handcuffs; review and examination (50 question multiple-choice test)
- Contractor-provided firearms training (32h)
- Contractor-provided less-than-lethal weapons training (8h: 4h baton, 4h OC spray)
- Contractor-provided refresher training: Within three years of basic training (or the previous refresher training conclusion date), 40h of refresher training[32]; annual refresher training up to 4h for baton, and up to 4h for OC spray
- Government-provided orientation training (8h) covering: rules and regulations; bomb threats and natural disaster responses; report writing, notes and required FPS forms; telephone and radio communications; and role of local, state and federal police agencies
- Government-provided training on weapons detection training program (WDTP) (16h initial training) covering: Point PSO; metal detector operator, walk-though metal detector; metal detector operator, hand-held metal detector; X-ray machine operator
- Government-provided annual refresher training (8h)
- The contract also specifies the qualification course of fire for both handguns and shotguns. Armed PSOs must qualify initially and semi-annually.
- PSOs must complete training and receive certification in first aid, CPR, and AED (automated external defibrillator). The frequency of this training is determined by the certifying body (e.g., American Heart Association or American Red Cross)
- PSOs must pass exams associated with training courses.

State and Local Requirements:
- In addition, the contractor and PSOs must abide by all state and/or local requirements.

FIGURE 41.8 Common DHS/FPS Contract Requirements for Protective Security Officers (PSOs). Cont'd.

It is important to note that state regulation of the private security industry and PSOs varies widely. A few states have no regulation, or regulation is accomplished at the local level, while other states have significant regulation. State regulation can vary on several dimensions, including whether regulation is focused at the company level (e.g., whether the organization provides contract security officers, or employs its own proprietary security officers for its own facilities) or at the individual level (e.g., whether the security officer is unarmed or armed), or both. Who does the regulating also varies. In some states, for example, regulation is accomplished by designated boards, while in others, the state police department may be charged with this responsibility. Thus, definitive generalizations cannot be easily made.

It can be said, however, there is a growing trend toward increased regulation at the state level, as well as growing interest among state regulators to promote the professionalism of the private industry as a whole. These trends are reflected in the growth of the National Association of Security and Investigative Regulators (NASIR), founded in 1993 by regulators representing seven states. Today, renamed the International Association of Security and Investigative Regulators (IASIR), membership now includes 35 regulatory agencies or boards in 24 states, seven Canadian provinces, and the United Arab Emirates.[33] Its objective is to promote "the professionalism of the private security, private investigative, alarm and related industries" through its goals of "enhancing applicant processing and records management; advocating for expedient background investigation and fingerprint processing; disseminating information on insurance/bonds; keeping abreast of and sharing information about new licensing technology; promoting effective state regulation and enforcement; assisting in education and training standards; eliminating unlicensed activity; developing harmony between law enforcement and the regulated industries; influencing federal legislation; formulating model laws and regulations; assisting states in developing and enforcing laws and regulations; encouraging reciprocity between states; and providing training and education opportunities for state regulators."[34] IASIR's website contains basic licensing information, including contact information and links to state regulators. This information provides a good starting point when researching state requirements.

State Regulators

A look at *who* regulates the private security industry in the top five most populated states immediately reveals the variation between states. Figure 41.9 lists the state administrative entities that oversee state security licensing and/or registration programs, as well as their website links.

Legal Regulatory Authority

State statutes establish the basis for regulation, while administrative rules and regulations provide details on the implementation of licensing programs. Figure 41.10 references the underlying legal regulatory authority of the top five states.

State	Administrative Agency
California	• California Department of Consumer Affairs (DCA), Bureau of Security and Investigative Services (BSIS) • http://www.dca.ca.gov/bsis
Texas	• Texas Department of Public Safety, Private Security Bureau • http://www.txdps.state.tx/RSD/pbs/
New York	• New York Department of State, Division of Licensing Services • http://www.dos.ny.gov/licensing/
Florida	• Florida Department of Agriculture and Consumer Services, Division of Licensing • http://www.freshfromflorida.com/Division-Offices/Licensing
Illinois	• Illinois Department of Financial and Professional Regulation • http://www.idfpr.com/dprdefault.asp

FIGURE 41.9 State administrative agencies.

State	Legal Regulatory Authority
California	• California Business and Professions code; Division 3, Professions and Vocations Generally; chapter 8.5, Locksmiths; Chapter 11, Repossessors; Chapter 11.3, Private Investigators; Chapter 11.4, Proprietary Security Services; 11.5, Private Security Services; Chapter 11.6, Alarm Companies • California Code of Regulations, Title 16, Professional and Vocational Regulations; Division 7, Bureau of Security and Investigative Services
Texas	• Occupational Code; Title 10, Occupations Related to Law Enforcement and Security; Chapter 1702, Private Security • Texas Administrative Code; Title 38, Public Safety and Corrections; Part 1, Texas Department of Public Safety; Chapter 35, Private Security
New York	• Private Investigators, Bail Enforcement Agents and Watch, Guard or Patrol Agencies License Law; Article 7, General Business Law; Article 7-A, Security Guard Act • Employees Rules and Regulations, Title 19 NYCRR, Part 170 (Security Guards), Part 174 (Security Guard Companies)
Florida	• Florida statute, Title XXXII. Regulation of Professions and Occupations, Chapter 493 (Private Investigative, Private Security, and Repossession Services); Title XLVI. Crimes, Chapter 790 (Weapons and Firearms) and Chapter 776 (Justifiable Use of Force) • Florida Administrative Code and Register, Chapters 5N-1 (Private Investigative, Security and Repossession Activities, Schools)
Illinois	• Illinois Compiled statute, 225 ILCS 447, Professions and Occupations, Private Detective, Private Alarm, Private Security, Fingerprint Vendor, and Locksmith Act of 2004 • Illinois Administrative Code, Title 68 Professions and Occupations; Part 1240 Private Detective, Private Alarm, Private Security, Fingerprint Vendor, and Locksmith Act of 2004

FIGURE 41.10 Legal regulatory authority.

Regulated Private Security Entities/Functions

Reflecting the trend toward increasing state regulations, the top five states reveal extensive regulation of private security and related functions at both the individual and organizational level. Figure 41.11 lists the categories subject to state regulation, whether though a licensing or registration process.

State	Regulated Private Security Entities/Functions
California	Private Patrol Operators and Security Guards; Proprietary Private Security Officer and Employer; Private Investigators; Alarm Company Operator and Alarm Company Employees; Locksmith Companies and Locksmith Company Employees; Repossessor agencies and Repossessor Agency Employees; Training Facilities and Training Instructors
Texas	*Agency Classifications*: Private Security Services Contractor Company (Class B license); Private Investigator Company (Class A license); Combination Private Investigator/Private Security Services Contractor Company License (Class C license) *Individual Classifications*: Security Officer (commissioned and non-commissioned); Private Investigator; Security Consultant; Security Salesperson; Employee of License Holder; Electronic Access Control Device Installer (includes Gate Operators); Alarm Salesperson; Alarm Systems Installer; Alarm Systems Monitor; Branch Office Manager; Guard Dog Trainer; Locksmith; Instructor; Personal Protection Officer; Owner, Officer, Partner, Shareholder, Manager, Supervisor
New York	Watch, Guard or Patrol Agency; Security Guard; Private Investigator; Armored Car Carrier; Armored Car Guard; Bail Enforcement Agent; Central Dispatch Facility; Security or Fire Alarm Installer
Florida	*Agency and School License Classifications*: "B" Security Agency (main office); "BB" Security Agency Branch Office; "AB" Security and Private Investigative Agency Branch Office; "DS" Security Officer School or Training Facility; "A" Private Investigative Agency (main office); "AA or AB" Private Investigative Agency Branch Office; "R" Recovery Agency (main office); "RR" Recovery Agency Branch Office; "RS" Recovery Agent School or Training Facility. *Individual Classifications*: "D" Security Officer; "M or MB" Manager of a Security Agency; "G" Statewide Firearm License; "K" Firearms Instructor; "DI" Security Officer Instructor; "C" Private Investigator; "CC" Private Investigator Intern; "M or MA" Manager of a Private Investigative Agency; "E" Recovery Agent; "EE" Recovery Agent Intern; "MR" Manager of a Recovery Agency"; "RI" Recovery Agent Instructor"
Illinois	*Security Professions*: Private Security Contractor; Private Security Contractor Agency; Private Security Contractor Agency Branch Office; Armed Proprietary Security Force *Private Detective Professions*: Private Detective; Private Detective Agency; Private Detective Agency Branch Office. *Alarm Professions*: Private Alarm Contractor, Private Alarm Contractor Agency; Private Alarm Contract Agency Branch Office. *Canine Professions*: Handlers, Trainers, Instructors. *Collection Professions*: Agency and Branch Office. *Detection of Deception Professions*: Examiners and Trainees. *Locksmith Professions*: Locksmiths; Locksmith Agency. *Also regulated*: Firearm Control Card (FAC); Permanent Employee Registration Card (PERC); Approved Training Course School; Approved 20-Hour Basic Training Program; Approved 40-Hour Firearm Training Course; Firearm Instructor.

FIGURE 41.11 Regulated private security entities/functions.

Security Officer Requirements

While the top five states vary in their licensing/registration categories, they share the following similarities with respect to security officers. All require security officers to meet minimum age requirements; to provide proof of identity and legal right to work; to submit fingerprints to accomplish state/federal criminal background checks; and to complete

State	Minimum Age	Criminal Background and Fingerprints	Proof of Identity and Right to Work	Proof of Training Completion
California	Yes	Yes	Yes	Yes
Texas	Yes	Yes	Yes	Yes
New York	Yes	Yes	Yes	Yes
Florida	Yes	Yes	Yes	Yes
Illinois	Yes	Yes	Yes	Yes

FIGURE 41.12 Minimum security officer requirements.

and/or submit proof of minimum training requirements from an authorized training school or training provider. In addition, all licenses/registrations are for a specified term (i.e., 2 years is typical), require fees, and must be renewed on a timely basis.

Figure 41.12 is *not* a comprehensive list of all requirements for security officer licensing or registration. Rather, it is intended to provide examples of different state requirements. Because of frequent changes in law and, in particular, administrative rules and regulations, readers are urged to review the latest statute, administrative rules and regulations, and the most current forms. Also, while a careful review of forms is a logical initial step to understanding state licensing/registration requirements, forms alone do not reflect the multitude of other legal requirements to which security officers are subject.

In California, for example, in order to work as a security guard for any Private Patrol Operator or in-house (proprietary) employer, the security guard must be registered with the California Bureau of Security and Investigative Services. A security guard registration is valid for a 2-year period. Registration requirements include the following: must be at 18 years old; must undergo a criminal history background check, both through the California Department of Justice (DOJ) and FBI; and must complete 40h of required training (i.e., 8h must be completed prior to being assigned to post; 16h must be completed within the first 30 days; and 16h must be completed within the first six months). Armed security guards must apply for a firearm permit, which requires 14 additional training hours (8h classroom and 6h range) on topics including moral and legal aspects, firearms nomenclature, weapon handling and shooting fundamentals, emergency procedures, and range training. Security guards carrying tear gas and batons must complete approved training courses for each.

In Texas, security officers must be registered with the Department of Public Safety to a licensed company. To accomplish this, applicants must submit fingerprints through the Fingerprint Applicant Services of Texas. The application must also include a copy of the applicant's training completion certificate: Level II for noncommissioned (unarmed) security officers; Level III for commissioned (armed) security officers; and Level IV for personal protection officers. Applicants without a Texas identification (ID) card or Texas driver license must submit a copy of an out-of-state ID card, out-of-state driver license, or military ID. Applicants who are not US citizens must include a copy of their Alien Registration Card, and nonresident aliens must also submit a copy of a current Work Authorization Card.

In New York, security guards must be registered with the New York State Division of Licensing Services. At time of application, the following must be submitted: the completed, signed application; copy of certificate showing completion of an 8 h pre-assignment course; signed DMV consent form; receipt that provides proof of fingerprint completion; additional supporting documentation; and course completion certificate for 47 h of firearms training, if applying for armed security guard registration. Training requirements for unarmed security guards include 8 h pre-assignment training, 16 h on-the-job training within 90 days of employment, and 8 h annual in-service training for each calendar year. Armed security guards must compete 8 h pre-assignment training, 16 h on-the-job training within 90 days of employment, 47 h firearms training (possession of a valid New York State pistol permit and security guard registration is a prerequisite to course enrollment), 8 h annual in-service training, and 8 h annual firearms training.

In Florida, an individual who performs the services of a security officer must have a Class "D" license. Applicant requirement includes: must be at least 18 years of age; must be a citizen or legal resident alien of the United States or have been granted authority to work in this country by the Department of Homeland Security, US. Citizenship and Immigration Services (USCIS); must provide current residence (not P.O. box) address; must submit fingerprints for background check, and must submit proof of successful completion of a minimum of 40 h of professional training provided by a school or training facility licensed by the Department of Agriculture and Consumer Services. In addition to the Class D license, armed officers must have a Class "G" statewide firearm license and complete an additional 28 h of firearms training.

In Illinois, security guards must obtain a Permanent Employee Registration Card (PERC), requiring a completed application, registration fee, and security clearance documents. Applicants must also complete the following training requirements, including: 20 h of classroom basic training within 30 days after commencing employment; 8 h additional training (may be site-specific and may be conducted on-the-job) within 6 months of employment; and 8 h annual refresher training. Upon completion of training, a certification must be signed by the instructor or employer. Armed security officers must complete an additional 20 h approved firearm training course.

Organizational or Company-Level Requirements

In addition to the licensing or registration of individual security officers, those states that regulate private security typically often place even greater requirements on licensing the entities that employ security officers. These more stringent regulations are arguably justifiable. Owners and other individuals representing management have the ultimate responsibility for ensuring compliance, thus higher expectations and standards imposed at the organization level are logical.

At the organizational or company-level, most states impose minimum age, experience, education, position of authority, insurance and/or bond, and other requirements on the owners, partners, officers, and/or managers. A growing number of states now require at least one individual, typically referred to as the "qualifying manager", "qualifying party", or "license holder" to successfully pass a written examination as a condition to being granted an agency license. The subject matter of the exams typically include a basic understanding of security officer operations, with a particular focus on the regulatory requirements applicable to both employers and security officers. State exams widely vary in scope and difficulty, with some examinations requiring diligent study of extensive and detailed rules. Significant fees are often associated with license applications. These fees, coupled by rigorous exam and prior experience requirements, can serve as an effective barrier to licensure and entry into the guard service business (Figure 41.13).

In California, an individual or organization that operates a business protecting people or property must be licensed as a Private Patrol Operator. Each individual, partner, and corporate officer meet the minimum age requirement (18 years or older) and undergo criminal history background checks. In addition, to be licensed as a Private Patrol Operator, a "Qualified Manager" who will manage the operations on a day-to-day basis must be designated. This individual may be an owner, partner, or corporate officer, or an individual hired to fill this role. Qualified Managers must be 18 years or older, undergo criminal history background checks, and pass a rigorous 2 h exam on the California Private Security Service Act and other business and security related topics.

In Texas, a guard company must be operated under the direction and control of one responsible manager. The designated manager must: be at least 21 years old; have passed the manager's exam; have at least three years' experience in the field, including at least one year of experience in a managerial or supervisory position; and must undergo background checks. Texas sets forth detailed background requirements including: must not have been convicted, in any jurisdiction, of a felony level offense; must not have been convicted, within the past 5 years, in any jurisdiction, of a Class B misdemeanor or equivalent offense; must not currently charged with, or under indictment for, a felony, or a Class A misdemeanor; must not currently charged with, a Class B misdemeanor; must not have been found by a court to be incompetent by reason of a mental defect or disease and not have been restored to competency; must not have been dishonorably discharged from the

State	Exam Requirement	Exam Name	Exam Format
California	Yes	Private patrol operator (PPO)	100 questions; multiple choice Closed book; 2 h
Texas	Yes	Qualified manager'	140 questions Multiple choice; open book; 2 h
New York	Yes	Watch, guard or Patrol agency	60 questions Multiple choice; closed book
Florida	No	N/A	N/A
Illinois	Yes	Private security contractor	75 questions; multiple choice; closed book; 90 min

FIGURE 41.13 Exam Requirements for Licensure as Security Guard Company/Agency.

United States armed services, discharged from the United States armed services under other conditions determined by the Board to be prohibitive, or dismissed by the United States armed services if a commissioned office in the United States armed services; and not be required to register in this or any other state as a sex offender.

In New York, to be licensed as a Watch, Guard or Patrol Agency, an applicant must: be at least 25 years old; be a "principal" in the business; have passed the exam within the last 2 years of the application; be free of disqualifying criminal convictions; and be able to demonstrate two years "experience" or "equivalent experience." New York defines "experience" as "two years of full-time security experience, such as sheriff, police officer, or security guard in a governmental agency of with a licensed private investigator or WGP agency" and "equivalent experience" as "two years in a position where the primary duties were the performance of security guard services or two years' experience reviewing and supervising the work of at least three persons performing security services."

In Florida, any individual, partnership, company or corporation that provides private security services must obtain a Class B (Security Agency) License and be under the charge of a designated manager who holds a Class M (Manager of a Security Agency) License. While Florida requires background checks and sets for a minimum age of 18 for managers, it currently does not has an examination requirement or minimum experience requirements. The manager requirements in Florida illustrates the wide range of regulation, even with the most populated states.

In Illinois, individuals and organizations in the business of providing private guard, watchman, security, or patrol services must be licensed as a Private Security Contractor or Private Security Agency. Applicants must be at least 21 years old, pass criminal background checks, and pass a rigorous exam. Illinois also has stringent experience requirements, including a minimum of three years' experience out of the 5 years immediately preceding application as a full-time manager for a licensed security contractor agency, a manager of a proprietary owned security force employing 30 or more registered personnel, or full-time supervisor in a law enforcement agency. Alternatively, applicants can meet this requirement through a combination of both experience and education, including a bachelor's degree in police science (or a related field) or business from an accredited college or university, plus 1 year of experience in the areas mentioned, or an associate's degree in police science (or a related field) or business, plus 2 years of experience (Figure 41.14).

State	Minimum Age	Experience	Insurance or Bond	Criminal Background and Fingerprints
California	18	1 year	Yes	Yes
Texas	21	3 years	Yes	Yes
New York	25	2 years	Yes	Yes
Florida	18	2 years	Yes	Yes
Illinois	21	3 years	Yes	Yes

FIGURE 41.14 Minimum Qualifying Manager/Party Requirements for Licensure as Security Guard Company/Agency.

Compliance Challenges

Security service providers face numerous challenges in attempting to remain in compliance with state and/or local laws. A few of these include: understanding the wide variation of requirements between jurisdictions; the difficulty tracking and coordinating training and license or registration applications and renewals; the lack of responsiveness of understaffed and underfunded agencies or boards who administer and enforce licensing and registration programs; and the high penalty costs and reputational damage associated with program violations. Because of these hurdles, security providers must be especially proactive in understanding the licensing and registration requirements for the jurisdictions in which they operated.

International Regulation

The trend toward increased regulation of the security industry is seen beyond the United States. The United Nations Office of Drugs and Crime (UNODC) notes the worldwide increase of civilian private security services and the corresponding need for industry oversight.[35] Its publication entitled, *State Regulation Concerning Civilian Private Security Services and Their Contribution to Crime Prevention and Community Safety* provides practical guidance for lawmakers and policymakers seeking to effectively regulate the civilian private security industry.[36] Topics address in this comprehensive reference include the role of civilian private security in crime prevention and community safety; the multitude of issues involved in the regulation, including the rationale, basis, and scope of regulation, licensing, codes of conduct, confidentiality, weapons, use of force, and working conditions; the issues relating to enforcement, inspection and complaints; training; and relevant international standards related to the safeguarding of human rights.[37] Those with an interest in gaining an international perspective will find this document to be an excellent launching point for further research.

Emerging Trends

Just as standards and guidelines are playing an ever more important role in the security industry, there is a trend toward increased government regulation, not only in the United States but worldwide. This arguably reflects the growing influence, maturity, and professionalism of the private security industry—a trend that is only likely to continue.

Refer website http://www.ifpo.org for further information

End Notes

1. *Standards* (Geneva, Switzerland: International Standards Organization, Date Unknown): accessed January 18, 2015. Available: http://www.iso.org/iso/home/standards.htm.

2. *The ISO Story* (Geneva, Switzerland: International Standards Organization, Date Unknown): accessed January 18, 2015. Available: http://www.iso.org/iso/home/about/the_iso_story.htm.

3. *Benefits of International Standards* (Geneva, Switzerland: International Standards Organization, Date Unknown): accessed January 18, 2015. Available: http://www.iso.org/iso/home/standards/benefitsof standards.htm.

4. *Management System Standards* (Geneva, Switzerland: International Standards Organization, Date Unknown): accessed January 18, 2015. Available: http://www.iso.org/iso/home/standards/managem ent-standards.htm.

5. *How Does ISO Develop Standards?* (Geneva, Switzerland: International Standards Organization, Date Unknown): accessed January 18, 2015. Available: http://www.iso.org/iso/home/standards_developm ent.htm.

6. *ISO9000 – Quality Management* (Geneva, Switzerland: International Standards Organization, Date Unknown): accessed January 18, 2015. Available: http://www.iso.org/iso/home/standards/managem ent-standards/iso_9000.htm.

7. *Quality Management Principles* (Geneva, Switzerland: International Standards Organization, Date Unknown): accessed January 18, 2015. Available: http://www.iso.org/iso/qmp_2012.pdf.

8. See note 6 above.

9. *ISO31000 – Risk Management* (Geneva, Switzerland: International Standards Organization, Date Unknown): accessed January 18, 2015. Available: http://www.iso.org/iso/home/standards/iso31000.htm.

10. *ISO/IEC 27001 – Information Security Standard* (Geneva, Switzerland: International Standards Organization, Date Unknown): accessed January 18, 2015. Available: http://www.iso.org/iso/home/standard s/management-standards/iso27001.htm.

11. *Certification...* (Geneva, Switzerland: International Standards Organization, Date Unknown): accessed January 18, 2015. Available: http://www.iso.org/iso/home/standards/certification.htm.

12. *The ISO Survey of Management System Standard Certifications 2013* (Geneva, Switzerland: International Standards Organization, Date Unknown): accessed January 18, 2015. Available: http://www. iso.org/iso/iso_survey_executive-summary.pdf?v2013.

13. *About ANSI* (Washington, DC: American National Standards Institute, Date Unknown): accessed January 18, 2015. Available: http://ansi.org/about_ansi/overview/overview.aspx?menuid=1.

14. Ibid.

15. *Frequently Asked Questions* (Washington, DC: American National Standards Institute, Date Unknown): accessed January 18, 2015. Available: http://webstore.ansi.org/faq.aspx.

16. Ibid.

17. Ibid.

18. *Standards* (Alexandria, VA: ASIS International, Date Unknown): accessed January 18, 2015. Available: https://www.asisonline.org/Standards-Guidelines/Standards/Pages/default.aspx.

19. *Guidelines* (Alexandria, VA: ASIS International, Date Unknown): accessed January 18, 2015. Available: https://www.asisonline.org/Standards-Guidelines/Guidelines/Pages/default.aspx.

20. *Standards & Guidelines, Quick Reference Guide* (Alexandria, VA: ASIS International, 2010).

21. *Published* (Alexandria, VA: ASIS International, Date Unknown): accessed January 18, 2015. Available: https://www.asisonline.org/Standards-Guidelines/Standards/published/Pages/default.aspx.

22. *Published* (Alexandria, VA: ASIS International, Date Unknown): accessed January 18, 2015. Available: https://www.asisonline.org/Standards-Guidelines/Guidelines/published/Pages/default.aspx.

23. *About SIA* (Silver Spring, MD: Security Industry Association, Date Unknown): accessed January 18, 2015. Available: http://www.siaonline.org/Pages/AboutSIA/Mission.aspx.

24. *SIA Standards Committee* (Silver Spring, MD: Security Industry Association, Date Unknown): accessed January 18, 2015. Available: http://www.siaonline.org/Pages/Standards/SIA-Standards-Committee.aspx.

25. *NFPA Overview* (Quincy, MA: National Fire Protection Association, 2014): accessed January 18, 2015. Available: http://www.nfpa.org/about-nfpa/nfpa-overview.

26. Ibid.

27. *About Us* (Wakefield, MA: PCI Security Standards Council, Date Unknown): accessed January 18, 2015. Available: https://www.pcisecuritystandards.org/organization_info/index.php.

28. The Private Security Officer Employment Authorization Act of 2004 became law as part of the Intelligence Reform and Terrorism Prevention Act of 2004, Public Law 108–458.

29. This information was derived from DHS/FPS Solicitation Number HSHQE5-14-R-0001, issue date 1/24/2014. Statement of Work (SOW), Section 5, Qualifications of Personnel, includes 12 pages of requirements; SOW, Section 6, Training, includes seven pages of requirements. The requirements provided herein are particular to this solicitation and may not be the same in other DHS/FPS or federal agency contracts.

30. Reese S., *Federal Building and Facility Security: Frequently Asked Questions* (Washington, DC: Congressional Research Service, June 17, 2014): accessed January 18, 2015. Available: https://www.fas.org/sgp/crs/homesec/R43570.pdf.

31. The National Industrial Security Program Operating Manual (NISPOM) is available from the U.S. Department of Defense, Defense Security Service, or mail in a request for the publication to Superintendent of Documents, U.S. Government Printing Office, Mail Stop SSOP, Washington, D.C. 20402–9238 (ISBN: 0-16-045560-X).

32. Refresher Training topics are similar to those provided in Basic Training.

33. International Association of Security and Investigative Regulators (IASIR), http://iasir.org.

34. International Association of Security and Investigative Regulators.

35. *State Regulation Concerning Civilian Private Security Services and Their Contribution to Crime Prevention and Community Safety* (New York, NY: United Nations Office on Drugs and Crime, April 2014): accessed January 18, 2015. Available: http://www.unodc.org/documents/justice-and-prison-reform/crimeprevention/Ebook0.pdf.

36. State Regulation Concerning Civilian Private Security Services and Their Contribution to Crime Prevention and Community Safety, 4.

37. Ibid, p. 5–6.

42

The Relationship Between Corporate Security and Information Technology Professionals

Kevin E. Peterson

One unmistakable trend in security management is the growing interconnectedness between security professionals and information technology (IT) professionals. Regardless of organizational structure, size, mission, or reporting chains, members of each field need to work together more and more. That is not to say however, that the nature of this relationship is not shaped to some degree by these organizational characteristics. This chapter will consider some of these organizational characteristics and also address the security/IT relationship in terms of particular security disciplines and functions.

There is no universal model for the security/IT relationship, and this has both positive and negative implications. On the positive side, a "one size fits all" approach would not effectively and efficiently serve every type and size of organization—or even every geographical location. Interactions among the key functions of *information technology, IT security, and traditional security* must be tailored to the specific mission, size, culture, and scope of the organization. At the same time, however, many organizations (especially small or entrepreneurial businesses) struggle with establishing a "best fit" relationship by trial and error—or even worse, they simply ignore the issue. An effective solution requires deliberate analysis and planning, which takes the following into account:

- How each of the three key functions contribute to the mission
- The size and scope of the organization in terms of people, facilities, and global reach
- The primary functions or services performed by the organization
- The organization's overall security/assets protection objectives and priorities
- The type of people who comprise the organization and its partners
- The regulatory and legal environment in which the organization operates

Why is this relationship relevant to contemporary organizations? Increasingly, people rely on information systems, the Internet, wireless devices, and cyber-infrastructure to accomplish tasks in their personal lives, the workplace, and other venues, such as associations, civic activities, houses of worship, and schools. Information systems and related devices are not only a nicety—they are a necessity in many situations. They are used for scheduling, communicating, documenting, planning, socializing, banking, shopping, reading, image sharing, and researching. This is just as true in business and government arenas, where just about any critical function involves some sort of information processing or system. Of course, the areas of security, asset protection, and loss prevention are no different. In fact, according to ASIS International President, Dave Tyson: "The greatest challenge facing security management professionals is the velocity of data and technology."[1]

The natural conclusion from these facts is that security professionals, IT professionals, and IT security professionals must all work together more closely and, as discussed in this chapter, rely on one another to satisfy the mission needs. In other words, effective collaboration among these domains becomes a mission-essential.

The Venn diagram in Figure 42.1 illustrates that the domains of information technology, IT security, and traditional security have both overlapping and non-overlapping interests. This is true of any organization whether in the private sector, public sector, international arena, or another venue. The intersection of the three domains represents that venue in which all three interact and must work together to meet organizational goals. However, one cannot neglect the areas where only two of the three domains overlap. A significant challenge, in many cases, is how to balance attention and focus on the three-way intersection, the two-domain overlap, and the segregated portions of each domain.

It is important to note that the position and size of each domain are constantly moving, and therefore the size and nature of the overlapping areas also change. (There will always be some overlap, however.) The changes can be driven by specific incidents, general events, global forces, markets, available technology, risk factors, or simply time. For example, a terrorist bombing may cause a significantly expanded focus on traditional security, while temporarily reducing the attention dedicated to IT security. A large-scale data breach, however, may have the opposite effect.

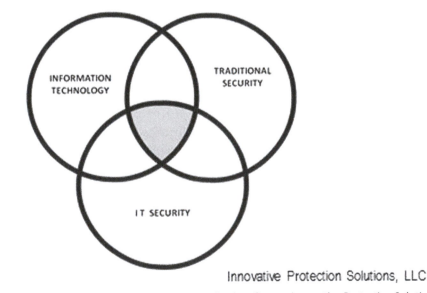

Innovative Protection Solutions, LLC

FIGURE 42.1 Interaction of three domains in any organization. *Source: Innovative Protection Solutions, LLC.*

It is imperative that security professionals (and their colleagues in IT) monitor these changes and react accordingly—in other words, remain agile.

The concept of *enterprise security risk management* (ESRM) recognizes the interaction among the three domains and incorporates the contributions of other organizational functions, such as legal, human resources, facilities, occupational health and safety, regulatory compliance, public/media relations, ethics, and business continuity. The idea is to take a holistic view toward protecting the organization's assets, involving all relevant parties and enabling the core mission.[2] The security department plays an integral role in any ESRM program. As stated in a 2009 *CSO Online* article on the role of a chief security officer (CSO): "The job of the enlightened security leader is to help those executives see their common challenges and address them in a way that facilitates cooperation between departments."[3] In short, ESRM is all about relationships and focusing them on a goal. In almost any organization, the proactive engagement of the security department, the IT department, and IT security are critical to the process.

The remainder of this chapter will discuss the influence of organizational characteristics and specific security functions on the nature of the relationship among the three domains.

Organizational Characteristics

Within any organization—whether public sector, private sector, or another type—two main characteristics influence the interrelationships among security, IT, and IT security: a) the mission and nature of the organization, and b) how those three domains are structured within the management hierarchy. These characteristics are in play regardless of the size of the organization—from an entrepreneurial high-tech startup with a few team members, to a small independent medical clinic, to a huge multinational corporation. Each entity has a mission and "personality" as well as an operating structure for management and operation of the enterprise. These will always play a role in functional interrelationships—how they work and how effective they are.

Mission and Nature of the Organization

Entities vary widely in their missions. Some examples include retail, manufacturing, high-tech, biotech/pharma, health care, entertainment/leisure, transportation, agriculture, food and beverage, telecommunications, government, and publishing. Each industry sector is unique, and organizations within each sector are distinct. For example, a large urban hospital may be very different from a rural/regional health center. Even in similar settings, one business may have a different personality and culture than a neighboring one. Cultural or environmental factors may include the management style, customer service emphasis, supply chain relationships, historical background, and the audience to which the organization caters. All of these aspects will influence the supporting functions of security, IT, and IT security, as well as how they interoperate.

Some organizations rely more heavily on IT infrastructure and capabilities than others. In fact, some rely almost entirely on IT and simply cannot perform their mission without a fully operational network running. According to an article posted by Gartner, a well-respected IT research and advisory firm, a typical figure cited for the cost of network downtime (on average) is $5600 per minute (or well over $300,000 per hour).[4] Other organizations operate in a relatively low-tech environment, but all experience some aspects of the interaction among the three domains.

In addition, respect and trust may play a key role in the nature of the relationship. Past President of ASIS International, Daniel Kropp, mentioned that in his current role as the security director of a large consulting firm, he has a strong working relationship with the IT staff. Although the IT staff is extremely engaged in meeting their day-to-day mission requirements, they recognize the need to support the traditional security function, and trust the security staff enough to allow them to integrate "their" systems with the corporate IT infrastructure. This requires a fairly robust level of technical expertise within the security department, but it also allows a high level of efficiency when adjustments need to be made to electronic security systems at the headquarters or any of the remote sites.[5]

The size and scope of the organization will also have a significant effect on how the domains relate. For example, a large multisite operation may organize any of the three domains on a regional basis or even centralize management of them from a headquarters location. Alternatively, there may be dedicated security, IT, and/or IT security staff at every single site. Some or all of the services may be outsourced enterprise-wide or at certain locations. No matter what the structure of these services is at any given time, it is advisable to periodically evaluate the structure and recommend any appropriate realignment actions for improved operational effectiveness or overall efficiency.

Organizational Structure

In terms of organizational structure, again, each organization is different. In fact, for a number of years there has been great controversy and debate over the issue of "who should report to who" in the security and IT arena in the typical organization. In a 2009 survey conducted among 100 large corporations, Strauchs reported: "One challenge to effective working relationships is a disparity in the reporting levels or position in the organizational structure of security versus IT." According to the survey, "about 73% of IT department heads report to top-level management, whereas only 40% of security department heads do."[6] Most security professionals believe that this situation is improving as more senior executives recognize the co-equal level of responsibilities of security and IT functions.

Still, actual practice varies widely in this regard. Here are the common arrangements that exist in typical organizations around the world:

- The CSO, chief information officer (CIO) and chief information security officer (CISO) report independently to the same executive (e.g., a vice president or senior vice president).
- The CSO, CIO, and CISO report independently to different executives.

- The CSO and CIO report independently to the same executive, but the CISO reports to the CIO.
- The CSO and CISO report to the CIO.
- The CISO reports to the CSO, separate from the CIO.
- The CIO and CISO report to executives and a security director reports to mid-level management.

There are pros and cons to each arrangement. From the traditional security professional's perspective, the second and last items on the above list represent adverse circumstances, but the nature of the organization and its mission may dictate such a structure. The first situation on the list is generally considered the preferable one in terms of the ability of the traditional security professional to influence the organizational decision making and resource allocation processes.

In any case, the three functions must work together collaboratively and cooperatively in order to ensure effective assets protection and mission achievement for the organization. Sadly, another finding from the Strauchs survey was as follows:

72% of the respondents claimed that their physical security department had a "cooperative" relationship with their IT department. Yet almost half indicated that the two departments "never" or "rarely" meet with each other.[7]

This may indicate a disparity between perception and reality when it comes to a "cooperative relationship" versus the kind of true collaborative and interactive environment that is necessary for effective mission achievement.

Leveraging IT for Security Disciplines and Functions

Almost every day around the globe, we see new evidence of security and related functions relying on information technology. Let us look at some of the ways this is occurring. The following paragraphs highlight some of the current applications for IT in each of the primary security disciplines that reside in a typical organization.

Physical Security

This is probably the most obvious arena where IT and traditional security are coming together. This is true in terms of the following:

- Electronic security systems
- Structural security
- The human element of physical security

In electronic security systems, the functions of surveillance, access control, and intrusion detection are becoming increasingly sophisticated. Many such systems now operate, communicate, and/or are managed via Internet protocol and wireless devices. More processing is being performed onboard cameras and other security "edge devices" while there is growing reliance on sophisticated database and knowledge management technologies to support such systems.

One security consultant was "enlightened" recently when meeting with the managers of a small commercial office building where some security upgrades were being considered. At the table were the building owner, building engineer, the property manager, and two IT staff members. This is just one indicator of the growing importance of the interaction among the three domains.

Video surveillance is a cornerstone of the revolution in blending IT infrastructure and physical security functions. In a survey conducted among 150 corporate IT professionals, Vince Ricco of Axis Communications reported for *SecurityInfoWatch*:

What was surprising was the extent to which IT was already supporting video on existing networks and providing video servers, storage and even backup storage [a significant commitment based on sheer volume].

Another surprise was the widespread usage of video analytics. …it was significant to find that 80 percent of the respondents currently leverage video surveillance footage for business intelligence purposes [and] 40 percent of the respondents…were using some form of cloud-based storage.[8]

Ricco went on to state, "IP video is beginning to blur the lines between IT and physical security."

"In 2010, when IP video was just beginning to overtake analog, the reaction of many IT departments was 'not on my backbone.'"[9] This, however, is obviously changing.

Access control and intrusion detection systems are also being managed increasingly by remote and wireless devices. Security officers are also using much more technology to support their functions, including visitor management, patrol, article screening, and emergency response. Just one of many examples is the Los Angeles International Airport, where many of the security control center functions are now managed in a distributed fashion using smartphones and tablet computers. This promotes faster and broader information sharing on threats, incidents, and conditions that affect the security and safety posture of the operation.

Although this trend renders tremendous advantages and efficiencies, it also calls to our attention the need to consider more fully the "security of our security systems." Increased reliance on IT introduces potential vulnerabilities—which also increases the importance of close collaboration with not only IT professionals, but also the IT security staff.

Personnel Security

Information technology is providing strong support in this discipline as well. One example is the fact that "smart" databases can now be accessed instantaneously on a 24/7 basis to support background investigations, threat assessments, and incident investigations. Personnel information, as legal and appropriate, may also be shared with security staff members to support investigations, access determinations, and other key functions.

In addition, computer-based training, running on the IT backbone, facilitates security awareness and education as well as reporting mechanisms for suspicious activity, fraud, waste and abuse, sexual harassment, misconduct, espionage, and other malicious activities. Such reports can be immediately distributed to appropriate departments or people and acted on in a simultaneous and coordinated manner. It also brings efficiencies to more routine functions, like documenting required training and managing the security/ safety aspects of employee travel.

Information Security

The relationship among the three domains with respect to information security is obvious. It should be noted that "information security" encompasses both IT security and traditional information security (and in some cases, other elements such as due diligence and market entry planning). Traditional information security covers a wide range of functions, including identifying and controlling proprietary information, protecting intellectual property, counter-competitive intelligence, and insider threat mitigation. All of these functions can be supported by the IT infrastructure, databases, and other automated processes.

Security Administration and Management

This is another area where information technology is having a tremendous impact. Probably the most obvious effect is that of automated incident management systems. These systems are commonly in place in organizations of all types. Today, they have become extremely user-friendly and have the capability of serving a wide variety of functions, including the following:

- Entry of incident reports by security officers
- Visitor management (one time and recurring)
- Safety and security advisory sharing (with image support)
- Access control system management
- Integration with building control systems and sensors
- Integration with and control of surveillance systems
- Investigation support and management
- Post-event analysis

As Brian McIlravey, Co-CEO of PPM, an incident management system provider, put it:

Since individual security devices and systems provide more information than ever before, integrated security systems collect astronomical amounts of data that needs to be extracted and analyzed meaning there's no question of Big Data's importance and its effect on security.[9]

Incident management systems provide an extremely valuable tool for generating, analyzing, and applying that data. They also support security program evaluation and management by incorporating metrics and enabling data-driven decision making at both the tactical and strategic levels.

In this respect, information technology facilitates a true enterprise security risk management program by moving the decision-making process from one that may be largely composed of guesswork or anecdotal evidence to one that is truly evidence-based. According to a white paper published by the ASIS International CSO Roundtable, in navigating the maze of technology available to establish and develop an efficient ESRM program:

The first priority…is to determine what types of data need to be aggregated and analyzed; this also means cultivating a good working relationship with the IT department.[10]

In a related survey conducted by the CSO Roundtable, "[n]early 60 percent of CSOs said IT was incorporated into their risk management strategy…"[11] This demonstrates the tremendous importance of these relationships in real-world business organizations around the world and in today's globally interconnected environment.

Security IT versus IT Security

A frequent source of confusion or misunderstanding is the tendency for professionals to fail to make a clear distinction between "IT security" and "security IT." Although many will dismiss this as mere semantics, noted security consultant John Strauchs wrote that "insights can be gained…by analyzing the professional lexicon of IT and security practitioners."[12] The distinction is increasingly important, and a clear understanding (and articulation to members of executive management) of these concepts is essential. Figure 42.2 lists some of the elements of each function and demonstrates that those elements are not the same.

IT Security	Security IT
▪ The protection of information systems, peripherals and the data that resides on them. ▪ Efforts to ensure confidentiality, integrity and availability of information with respect to information and communications systems. ▪ Managing hardware, software and firmware solutions to information systems risks. ▪ Conducting user training, monitoring compliance with related policies and procedures.	▪ Access control and security systems databases. ▪ Integrated access control, visitor management, surveillance and incident management systems. ▪ Connectivity with life safety, communications and building control systems. ▪ Interconnected security and Human Resources systems and databases. ▪ Security system and surveillance management over Internet Protocol. ▪

Innovative Protection Solutions, LLC

FIGURE 42.2 The distinction between " IT security" and "security IT". *Source: Innovative Protection Solutions, LLC.*

Obviously, both functions are critical to an effective security risk management program in any type of contemporary organization. However, they must be approached individually, with the clear understanding that they are mutually supportive but not the same thing. It is incumbent on traditional security and IT security professionals to educate one another on this issue.

Outsourcing

Within the realm of both traditional and IT security, there are many functions that can be, and often are, outsourced in many organizations. Although this can be a very efficient and effective approach, some caution is warranted in terms of developing a prudent outsourcing strategy. Organizations should identify what functions should be outsourced (and to what degree), and then practice due diligence in the source selection process.

Related functions that are commonly outsourced in whole or part include the following:

- Data center operations
- Cloud support
- Records management (hardcopy and electronic)
- Email services
- Mobile device services
- Imaging and transfer services
- Data/information/device destruction
- Computer forensics

Organizations such as the National Association for Information Destruction (NAID) and ARMA International (a professional association for records management) provide resources and can assist in developing policies, programs, and practices for managing both hardcopy and electronic information. Both organizations can also recommend vendors with the proper credentials, capabilities, and certifications to meet just about any information management needs. Liaison with or active participation in such organizations is highly recommended.

As indicated in a recent article:

More than half of U.S. states [and many countries around the world] today have enacted data protection laws and regulations, growing from just 15 states a year ago. Penalties for noncompliance can include fines, civil and criminal prosecution, even leading to jail time and business closure.[13]

Furthermore, according to the CSO Roundtable white paper:

What is not commonly realized is that a number of IT regulatory requirements call for some type of risk management program.[14]

Many such programs intimately involve traditional security department functions such as physical security, personnel security, investigations and information security—as well as the obvious role of both IT and IT security. This presents not only one more opportunity, but in fact a mandate to collaborate and coordinate.

Looking to the future, readers must acknowledge that these domains are constantly changing, and that the pace of change is increasing. This will have an impact on both operational and organizational aspects of every entity globally, although for some perhaps more subtly than others. In the conclusion to his chapter in the book *Security in 2020*, John Strauchs provides a rude awakening that every security professional should consider:

> *By 2020, many of the things we take for granted will be extinct, such as print newspapers, iPods, most desk-top computers, supermarket checkout lines, car keys, and a legion of other obsolete technologies. The security industry must do whatever it takes to ensure that its profession does not become aged and unfit.*[15]

How will this affect the relationships among traditional security, IT, and IT security as the future becomes the present? We should not only think about such eventualities, but also prepare for them by developing forward-thinking security and asset protection strategies—and by preparing ourselves and the next generation of security professionals for success.

Refer website http://www.ifpo.org for further information

End Notes

1. *Convergence Thought-Leader Aims to Expand Outreach to Information Security Stakeholders* (Alexandria, VA: ASIS International, January 19, 2015.) Accessed February 6, 2015. Available: https://www.asisonline.org/News/Press-Room/Press-Releases/2015/Pages/Dave-N.-Tyson,-CPP,-Assumes-Presidency-of-ASIS-International.aspx.

2. Kevin Peterson, *Physical and Traditional Security for IT Professionals* (Chambersburg, PA: Tapestry Technologies, 2010). Presentation/course materials.

3. Derek Slater, *How Security and the CSO Can Create Business Value and Competitive Advantage* (Framingham, MA: CSO Online, December 3, 2009.) Accessed February 6, 2015. Available: http://www.csoonline.com/article/2124612/it-careers/what-is-a-cso–part-2.html.

4. Andrew Lerner, *The Cost of Downtime* (Stamford, CT: The Gartner Blog, July 16, 2014.) Accessed: February 6, 2015. Available: http://blogs.gartner.com/andrew-lerner/2014/07/16/the-cost-of-downtime.

5. Daniel Kropp, *Interview with Santanya Mahoney, Michael Ott and author* (Arlington, VA: January 21, 2015).

6. Strauchs J., *Future of Corporate Security. Appearing in Beaudry, Mark; Tyska, Louis; and Fennelly, Lawrence. Security in 2020* (Alexandria, VA; ASIS International, 2010) p. 46.

7. Ibid.

8. Vince Ricco, *Survey Reveals IT's Changing Attitudes About IP Video* (Ft. Atkinson, WI: SecurityInfoWatch, January 21, 2015.) Accessed February 6, 2015. Available: http://www.securityinfowatch.com/article/12037275/esg-survey-reveals-its-changing-attitudes-about-supporting-ip-video-deployments.

9. Brian McIlravey, *Big data and incident management's role in the future of systems security, presentation at ISC West*, April 22, 2014.

10. C.S.O. Roundtable, *Enterprise Security Risk Management: How Great Risks Lead to Great Deeds, A Benchmarking Study* (Alexandria, VA: ASIS International, April 2010.) Accessed February 6, 2015. Available: https://www.rims.org/resources/ERM/Documents/Enterprise Security Risk Management.pdf.

11. Ibid.

12. See note 6, Strauchs, p. 48.

13. Federgreen, R., *"Mission Critical: Examination of New Data Protection Laws,"* (Tucson, AZ: National Association for Information Destruction (NAID), 15 January 2015.) Accessed February 6, 2015. Available: http://www.naidonline.org/nitl/en/blog/index.html.

14. See note 10.

15. See note 6, Strauchs, p. 51.

43

International Perspectives on Security in the Twenty-First Century

Paul A. Caron, K.C. Goswami, Ona Ekhomu, H.D.G.T. Oey,
Bruce W. Dobbins, Erik D. Erikson

Introduction—*Paul A. Caron*

A security professional working in today's dynamic operating environment has a daunting task. The supervisor will be ultimately responsible for advising and working in areas ranging from risk mitigation and personnel security to the identification of environmental considerations in international settings. The supervisor will be advising customers on matters such as active and passive threat solutions, all while serving in the capacity of the adaptive leader that the client is looking for them to be. This chapter aims to provide a comprehensive understanding on current international security concerns, ranging from civil considerations to terrorist activities and insurgencies, to security management concerns in the international stage.

The world is not flat; therefore, the preparation and mindset leading up to time working abroad should reflect a multidimensional approach to comprehending the intricacies of the sociocultural, economic, and general threat response upon which one would be required to provide accurate and timely insight. Despite the fact that emerging threats are growing much faster pace than seen in the last century, it is today's adaptive professionals that make a difference in the roles of security professionals, protecting both assets and lives simultaneously.

The Transformation of Threats in Today's Security Professional's Operating Environment—*Paul A. Caron*

The security professional's operating environment (SPOE) is changing drastically. The days of worrying about potential threats to managed assets and persons protected in the form of organized crime, insider threat to systems, abductions, etc. are not as clear as they once were. Today, we see a multitude of challenges presented not only daily but almost hourly to the community. Advances in technology and communication, such as social media outlets, and advances in personal communication devices (smart phones) have accelerated information sharing to yield actual real-time products that were once only attainable for corporations or media companies.

In today's SPOE, a teenager in a war-torn country can conduct live video surveillance through a smart phone, upload it to a website or file sharing program within seconds, and can share live tangible intelligence on movements, tactics, and other information potentially critical to security operations. Understanding where criminal elements and terrorist organizations are headed based on ideological, technological, and changes in their operating environment will ensure continued success as a security professional.

Threats are rapidly transforming based on individual and regional goals and aspirations. Until recently, most terror and criminal factions (including gangs) were content to operate with a linear command and control model (defined hierarchy and structure). Despite some organizations operating historically in a more cellular model (e.g., Al-Qaeda) due to its success in protecting operational knowledge and plans, the key in this model was always one thing: secrecy and speed do not mix.

Secrecy and speed do not mix well because nothing is real time. Whenever an attack or terrorist act is desired, every set of instructions or coordinating measures has to be passed down the line. Today, groups like the Islamic State (IS) have a command and control model that is more group-oriented and based on an immediate common goal. Unlike traditional hierarchical models, IS deploys its commanders regionally on a geographic basis. This ensures that lower-level leadership is grown locally within the organization, and in the absence of leadership (someone gets a drone strike), everyone else can still carry on successfully.

Couple this newly found *Terror 2.0* doctrine with their successes via social media, video propaganda, and greater international popular support in youth circles. That means a greater transformation than ever before. Threats to facilities and other critical areas are not just accomplished via kinetic attacks (bombings, physical damage, etc.) but are now executed remotely with "denial of service" (DoS) attacks, malware, sabotage facilities etc. No longer is it simply a protest that leads to damage in the SPOE but rather a multidimensional approach to security that has to be embraced more today than ever.

This transformation has to be constantly reviewed and studied in order for the SPOE to remain fluid and dynamic, ready to adapt to changes. Understanding what the SPOE encompasses—coupled with a plan on how to track, quantify changes, and identify indicators and warnings that can be tied to a net result, hopefully leading to positive change—will ensure the ability to rapidly identify threats and mitigate risk.

Anatomy of Terrorism—*K.C. Goswami*

Historically, insurgencies, insurrections, civil disobedience, and acts of terrorism have been tied to manifestations of long-standing grievances of members of the population acting against the local administration/government. If local administrators are unable to address the problem, or do not care about the inspirations and expectations of the populace, minor issues that could have been addressed at the inception stage take a monstrous form and threaten to break the fiber on which the societies exist. In these early stages, there has yet to be a movement that acquires the form of mass upsurge overnight. It is a low simmering discontentment of ideas, adoption, and formation of leaders and active participants that transform into manifestos and finally ideologies. The causes of this discontentment ultimately transform from passive into active movement and can be disparate in nature (i.e., social, ethnic, economic, cultural, or religious). Unfortunately, many people feel that governments remain ignorant or unconcerned during the initial stages, uncoordinated and unresponsive during the formative period, and helpless and reactive during the final stages of militant movements.

Causative Factors

At the outset, one must understand that there is not only a cause but a *popular cause* for any discontentment in a segment of society that would compel people to pick up arms against the bona-fide government. The popular causes most commonly seen are:

- Administrative
- Political
- Economical
- Social (religious, ethnic)

Public Reaction

Public reaction can be demonstrated in various ways. Reactions can range from roadside protests and graffiti on the walls to letters sent to the local media. Escalation in this form may graduate from a whisper campaign in closed rooms to agitation, clear civil disobedience, and ultimately to acts of terrorism and in extreme cases attempts to destabilize the government in the form of an insurgency.

Indicators

At each stage, these public responses graduate from minimal indications of civil unrest to legitimate threats. If the local administration or government intelligence agencies are unable to detect, analyze, and respond to them in time, the momentum behind the movement becomes too strong and places the government into a reactive posture.

Government Response

The government response to these indicators can range from unconcerned or indifferent to overreactive. Instead of a succinct and coordinated policy to redress the grievances of the masses, the government may instead adopt a policy of appeasement. Instead of being proactive, the government becomes reactionary, passing the initiative into the hands of hard liners. During this time, it is common for the masses to believe that the government has succumbed to the pressures being placed on it. This not only emboldens the group but ultimately serves as a catalyst that activates other such organizations that might otherwise have remained dormant, awaiting a weak or incoherent response from the government.

Popular Response

The populace essentially observes and monitors the government's response closely and reacts accordingly. Their reaction can be based on simply resigning to fate or by displaying resentment in some form, graduating slowly to defiance and thereafter to militancy and insurgency.

Recommended Government Response

It is said that "a stitch in time saves nine." A proverb more appropriate to tackling complex situations would be difficult to find. Timely discussions and addressing aggrieved masses can yield far more positive results both in the short and long term. Understanding these causative factors, coupled with appropriate responses, can enable a security professional to consistently remain proactive and ready for challenges within their operating environment.

Civil Considerations/Terrorist Activities—*Bruce W. Dobbins*

There is an apocryphal Chinese curse that states, "May you live in interesting times." Many security professionals believe that their times are the most "interesting" and, indeed, that new tools, theories, and methods must be developed to address these "new" realities. However, many security concerns are common concerns faced by security professionals for thousands of years. One must look to the fundamentals of the profession, applying those fundamentals with foresight, insight, expertise, and in a disciplined and structured approach, if one is to provide the service and duty of care that customers and clients expect and deserve.

Why They Do It

We see evidence of terrorist activities almost every day on the news. A neighborhood, school, village, or market has been attacked by a terrorist organization with a car bomb or suicide bomber. In some cases, like the multiphased attacks in Mumbai, India that occurred between November 26 and 29, 2008, killing 164 people, these attacks take place in a simultaneous and coordinated multilocation manner that can paralyze an entire metropolitan area. These attacks were preceded on March 12, 1993, by a coordinated 13-bomb terrorist attack in Mumbai that killed 257 people. Unfortunately, news reporting does not adequately provide sufficient detail regarding the quality and character of the civil defense response to these attacks, or the attempts by local authorities to plan ahead once the risk of an attack has turned into an actual incident that has become reality.

This type of threat falls under the category of civil disorder, also characterized as civil unrest or civil strife. This category is used to describe forms of unrest that are intentionally caused by one, or more than one, person(s). This situation is generally the result of major social problems that have resulted in a group/movement that is too weak to take on a government directly; but not so weak that it cannot marshal resources to complicate life for both the government and a nation's people. Mumbai in particular is also faced with terrorist attacks used as a form of national policy and persuasion (or punishment) that is coordinated, and supported, by a neighboring nation. The resort to terrorism is actually an expression of weakness; intended to emphasize the importance of the cause of those planning a terrorist event and also demonstrate to the population that the government cannot protect them or restore predictability to their normal lives.

Even those not directly involved with the terrorist event(s) have their lives influenced by the realization that they may become the victims of a terrorist act at any time while, concurrently, being unable to do anything about it. In this situation, realizing that their government is powerless to guarantee their safety undermines their respect for that government and, as a result, the power and influence of that government over their population. This is precisely the situation that the terrorist organization seeks. This situation is compounded when public utilities such as water or power supplies are interrupted, causing economic damage to a nation's economy by the threat of civil disorder and the unpredictability of public safety.

Preparing for the Worst

Preparation for the premeditated civil disorder resulting from a terrorist attack requires a coordinated and holistic series of proactive measures designed to detect and prevent terrorism. They must also minimize the damage that results from a successful terrorist act and maximize the impact of postattack recovery efforts. These plans and preparations include all levels of the security services including military, police, border and infrastructure security services, civil defense, medical services and private security services. Together, they must make efforts to psychologically prepare the population to deal with the aftermath of a successful terrorist attack. This preparation should include a coordinated effort to encourage participation by the population in surveillance and reporting activities that support their security services' efforts to disrupt terrorist attacks before they occur.

The most important component of this effort is an honest discussion with local leaders and communities regarding what to expect in the aftermath of a terrorist attack and how to help community leaders ensure the maintenance of calm and the dissemination of fact-based information to the communities as soon as possible. A successful communication effort during a crisis helps to encourage popular belief in the competence of local authorities as well as to discourage the promulgation of baseless rumors. Emphasis needs to be placed upon detailing precisely what the local citizens can do to help in practical terms. The senseless issuance of threat warnings by local security and governmental organizations does nothing but enhance the anxiety of the local population and increase the circulation of information via rumors and hysteria. Government organizations should maximize the effort to tie all information provided to the local community with actual, tangible actions that the population can take to aid in the response and recovery effort.

The engine that drives successful response and recovery efforts is the planning that ensures continuity of government during a coordinated and large-scale terrorist attack.

Governments must be able to continue performing essential functions that rest upon key pillars of competence that include the following:

- Effective leadership
- Staffing competence
- Multilevel coordinated communications
- Adequate command and control facilities

Continuity of government plans need to result from the coordination, development, and implementation of teamwork with all available security, emergency response, and medical facilities and services located within the community. The result needs to be a standardized continuity program management cycle that ensures continuity of response and command coordination across all services and organizations that will be tasked with assisting in a post-terrorism response.

It is critically important that this civil disorder planning be supported by an adequate legal foundation rooted in the legal tradition of each specific nation. It is no longer feasible to rely strictly on laws that provide for criminal sanctions for terrorist activities as if a terrorist act is simply another category of crime. There needs to be separate laws that provide the required legal framework with which to deal specifically with terrorism threats that include, at a minimum, the following:

- Adequate categories of crime in place, including violence, treachery, and other actions that are considered detrimental to civil safety and public order.
- Pre-emptive actions against suspected and/or imminent terrorism threats that can be taken without unnecessary delays.
- Adequate maintenance of a multicultural and multireligious community, where the preservation of peace is of paramount importance.
- Criminal laws that allow for robust terrorism-related investigations free of unnecessary legal bureaucracy while maintaining essential freedom for the citizens.
- A provision for expanded-scope investigation to support intrusive surveillance, enhanced monitoring, and prolonged detention that might otherwise be required to ensure effective counterterrorism operations.
- An adequate protection for officers of the law, security forces, and other officials who are considered essential to antiterrorism operations.

Planning and Practice: The Tie That Binds

Relatively small investments in preparation and practice can improve the effectiveness of the initial response to coordinated terrorist attacks and speed up the recovery process. This also increases the likelihood that there will be sufficient continuity of government to provide effective coordination of security and medical services while simultaneously keeping the population informed and engaged in the response and recovery process.

People must train to defend themselves against terrorist attacks; because the terrorist will most certainly be trained to attack *them*. Traditional recruits from organized terrorist groups will undergo significant levels of training that at a minimum would most likely include the following:

- Psychological indoctrination to the ideals of their group
- Basic combat and weapon training
- Advanced combat training that might include advanced weapons and explosives training
- Commando training in small groups specializing in small unit tactics and perhaps other more unusual terrorist training, such as maritime navigation

Security supervisors and managers should strive to train their security and emergency response team members to anticipate that terrorists will:

- Conduct advanced reconnaissance of their intended target sites in great detail—in order to be able to vanish, and then reappear after security forces believe they have cleared an area and moved on.
- Use a terrorist planning process that may take years to mature (and since the terrorist organizations have time, their reconnaissance will be much more difficult to identify as the pattern analysis becomes much more complex).
- Use cocaine and LSD, among other controlled substances, during attacks to sustain their energy and be able to stay awake and functional for 50 h or more. We may also see an increased use of steroids over time.

Security and emergency response organizations must be trained to support a 3–5 day response scenario, at a minimum, and not just tactics and procedures required to conduct simple "confront and overcome" types of engagement.

All organizations that have something/anything to contribute to community-based terrorism response must be included in planning, coordination, training, and exercise related to pre- and post-incident preparations. Any successful response to a single terrorist attack, much less the response required by a large-scale and coordinated multi-attack situation like those faced repeatedly in Mumbai, India, requires the ability for a community to maintain continuity of government while maximizing the ability to mitigate the impact of a successful attack. A successful surviving capability to cordon/contain a terrorist attack minimizes the number of casualties that result. Mutual assistance from surrounding communities and government entities needs to be incorporated into planning and training as well, if those communities and entities are to play a significant part in the response to a terrorist event.

Emerging Trends

The interconnection of this world continues to make information regarding terrorist practices, procedures, weapon procurement and manufacture, and communities/clients easier to both identify and target. Recent history teaches that one must assume that a terrorist organization knows as much about planning and the ability to respond to a terrorist event as any community or government organization does, and that communities and government organizations must plan accordingly.

Summary

A security professional is responsible for protecting the client's assets and, in an international environment, this role includes advising communities, and perhaps governments, as to best practices when preparing for terrorist surveillance and responding to foreseeable terrorist attacks. With this in mind, the classic tools of security assessment and management still form the foundation for developing the planning and response capability required to address and respond to terrorist-related activity worldwide. It is the employment and application of the fundamentals of the security profession with foresight, insight, and expertise that allows security to provide the service and duty of care that customers expect and deserve.

Religious Considerations and Local Governance Issues—*Ona Ekhomu*

Religion has historically been one of the primary drivers of terrorism. The Zealots, who in the first century launched terrorist attacks against the Roman rulers of Jerusalem, used Judaism to organize and promote their political agenda. The Islamic fundamentalists' belief in martyrdom and suicide terrorism has been traced to the Shiite imam Hussein bin Ali who, in October 680, was slain on the bank of the Euphrates River during a religious revolt. Religion may not be a cause of terrorism so much as it is used as a tool to organize politically motivated action based on violence. Terrorists use religion to reach a wide audience, gain sympathizers and recruit new fighters. It can be argued that political motive is the ultimate driving force.

Local governance issues, such as corruption, injustice, political and economic marginalization, poverty, political violence, or struggle for economic resources, have also tended to give rise to terrorism in Africa. Many African nations became independent in the 1960s and have had over 50 years' experience as nation states. Even so, prior to independence those same Africans countries suffered colonial exploitative governance from the British, French, Portuguese and Dutch. The model of leadership inherited by local elites was one of domination and brutality rather than participation, partnership and citizenship. New political elites have tended to behave like their colonial predecessors. This has created internal crises in some nation states, and where these crises were not properly handled the result was terrorism and insurgency.

Problem Analysis

The policy issue may be formulated as follows: Given that religious and local governance issues frequently lead to security breaches and cause preventable losses, what is the role of the security manager/supervisor in protecting his or her organization against terrorist attacks?

While government security agencies tend to focus on the task of protecting society at large from terrorist attacks and other violent crimes, corporate security managers and supervisors must carefully assess threats and vulnerabilities and develop threat mitigation measures that will protect people, property, information, and the mission of the organization, regardless of where they are located.

Terrorist threats abound in society and they arise from a variety of sources. However, regularly conducting risk assessments on religious issues and governance issues will give security managers an ability to forecast the occurrence of security breaches that may negatively impact the organization. For example, despite the fact that the suicide bomb attack on the United Nations (UN) building in Nigeria, on August 26, 2011 was predictable and foreseeable, the UN security managers did not emplace adequate countermeasures to prevent the attack. Only after the attack did the security managers declare that, despite intelligence reports, the UN did not believe the threats against the facility were credible.

Religious Considerations

Religious fundamentalism and extremism have given rise to a number of terrorist groups in Africa. Boko Haram, a terrorist group in Nigeria, has its aim at the imposition of strict Sharia rule over the northern part of this West African country. In other regions, Al Shabab fighters have radicalized young Muslims in Somalia and Kenya, and commenced with a campaign of terror in those East African nations. The largest country in Africa, Sudan, recently split into a Muslim North (Sudan) and Christian South (now known as South Sudan).

The armed conflict in Sudan raged between the Sudanese Army and the Sudan Revolutionary Front (SRF) for over three decades with an estimated 1.4 million casualties. This conflict was between the Muslim north that had ruled the country since independence and the Christian/animist south. A political solution based upon a plebiscite finally divided the country. In the Central Africa Republic (CAR), religious violence has led to immense political instability and a cycle of violence between Muslims and Christians. The CAR, with a population of 4.6 million inhabitants, broke into violent conflict when Muslim Seleka rebels, many from Chad and Sudan, deposed President Francois Bozize in March 2013. The Anti-Balaka militia, comprising mostly of Christians, fought back, targeting Muslims in their campaign. The Seleka rebels were forced to step down in January 2014. Atrocities, including murder, rape, and recruitment of child soldiers, were committed by both groups during the armed struggle.

The rise of terrorism in Nigeria can be directly linked to religious issues. The Maitatsine Islamic religious riots in 1980 were led by a fundamentalist Muslim cleric, Mohammed Marwa. Those religious riots claimed over 5000 lives in Kano City, northern Nigeria. The Maitatsine riots also claimed thousands of lives in other northern Nigerian cities, including Bauchi, Maiduguri and Yola. The city of Kano is frequently the theater of violent religious conflicts. In one case, an Ibo man by the name of Gideon Akaluka was accused of desecrating the Holy Quran. He was beheaded and Muslim youths mounted his head on a stake and paraded it around the city for public viewing.

Christian/Muslim armed conflicts have also occurred in the areas of Kaduna State and northern Nigeria, starting usually from the Zangon Kataf and Kafanchan local governments (or counties). Religious riots occurring in Christian areas result in Muslim casualties while conflicts in the predominantly Muslim Northern part of Kaduna State results in Christian casualties. In addition to killing innocent persons and whole families in the most bestial manner, properties are burnt, businesses looted and those that survive usually take refuge in military installations.

Nigeria

Since 2009, Nigeria has been combating religious terrorism waged by the Boko Haram sect. This fundamentalist Muslim group initially provided members with welfare and preaching. However, after the brutal killing of 17 members of the sect by the police during a funeral procession in July 2009, the leader Sheikh Mohammed Yusuf declared war on the Borno State government and the Nigerian Police Force. On July 26, 2009, Boko Haram fighters attacked the Dutsen Tashi police station in Bauchi but the attack was repulsed. They also attacked the Wudil police station in Kano and likewise in Yobe State. Boko Haram fanatics were later counterattacked by the military in an operation where Sheikh Yusuf was captured on July 30, 2009. He was extra-judicially murdered by the police at the state headquarters of Borno State Police Command in Maiduguri.

Since then, Boko Haram has mounted a terror campaign in Nigeria. The sect has raised the black-and-white Jihad flag in northeastern Nigeria and captured many local governments and towns in the areas of Borno and Adamawa. They bombed the Nigeria Police Force Headquarters in June 2011. Boko Haram has bombed military installations, local government buildings, district head (monarch) palaces, schools, markets and beer gardens. These Boko Haram attacks usually consist of AK-47 assaults against unsuspecting targets. In a second wave of attacks, improvised explosive devices (IEDs) were tossed against security patrols, buildings and other targets. The terror group subsequently migrated to suicide bombing, throat slitting, petrol bombing, and kidnapping girls to serve as sex slaves, cooks, for forced marriages, and human trafficking. In April 2014, Boko Haram kidnapped over 200 schoolgirls from the Government Girls Secondary School in Chibok, Borno State. This mass kidnap caught the attention of the world in a campaign tagged "Bring back our girls." Boko Haram remains the biggest security challenge faced by the government and people of Nigeria today.

Central African Republic

The religious conflict in Central Africa is also between Christians and Muslims. The Selleka rebel group overthrew the Christian-led administration and established itself as the government. Christian groups have resorted to violence in order to dislodge the Muslims. French troops and soldiers from other African countries are maintaining peace in CAR.

Uganda

The Lord's Resistance Army in Uganda led by Joseph Kony has waged a relentless terror campaign against the people of Uganda. His group claims that they want real Christianity to be practiced in Uganda. Joseph Kony's terrorism is sectarian in nature as it is with Christians at war with Christians. The Lord's Resistance Army has killed thousands of people in Uganda. The United States Special Forces are working with the Ugandan military in an effort to track down this terrorist.

Egypt

This North African country is predominantly Muslim in population. The Muslim brotherhood, the political party of deposed President Mohammed Morsi, is a fundamentalist group interested in foisting its beliefs on the secular Muslims in that country. Irked by the intolerance of the brotherhood, the military took over power from President Mohammed Morsi in July 2013 and installed a judge as president. Egypt has since elected a new President, General Abdulfatah Al Sisis (Rtd) but sectarian attacks have intensified.

Mali

This is a predominantly Muslim country that has been politically stable. However, Al Qaeda-linked fighters in 2012 tried to overrun the country. The Ansar Dine terrorists seized Timbuktu, Gao, Kidal and other northern Malian cities. The French government ordered in troops to prevent the fall of Bamako, the country's capital. Leading a coalition of nations that included Nigeria, the French chased out the Al Qaeda fighters. Elections were held in 2013 that produced a new president, Ibrahim Boubacar Keita. Ansar Dine terrorists continue to attack rural areas in Mali.

Other countries with sectarian issues include Somalia, Algeria, Tunisia, and Mauritania.

Role of the Security Manager

Often, the security manager of a bank, oil and gas, or telecommunications company will carry a weapon to defend his or her company. The role of the manager, however, is to carefully analyze the risks, compute the criticality, assess the vulnerability, determine the probability of a terrorist incident, and then design creative countermeasures that will protect organizational assets—people, property, information, and mission. Depending upon the national laws, the mitigation options available to security managers vary. In the Republic of South Africa, private security personnel may bear firearms; such is not the case in Nigeria. However, private security managers usually engage in partnership with the police or the military in Nigeria for protection of assets. In Nigeria's maritime domain, indigenous private security companies approved by the Nigerian Navy provide naval boats with which offshore platforms are patrolled and protected. This public–private partnership also provides escort to vessels in Nigerian waters to protect oil assets against piracy.

On land, private security managers work with the Nigeria Police Force and State Security Service to protect VIPs against violent crimes such as bombings, assassinations, kidnappings, armed robberies, assault, etc. Security Managers and Supervisors are required to be familiar with security practices and resources in their areas of responsibility in order to provide adequate asset protection.

Security Tips

1. Security managers must establish intelligence units in order to develop a constant flow of information from open sources. This information should be subjected to occasional rigorous analysis to determine if a threat pattern is evolving.
2. Security managers may purchase computerized criminal intelligence analysis tools (CIA tools) to assist them in connecting the dots that exist on the intelligence map.
3. Risk assessment and adversarial threat assessment will help the security officer identify imminent danger.
4. Vulnerability assessments are extremely important. The security manager should identify potential weaknesses before adversaries can exploit them.
5. *Emergency Planning:* The security manager must have a plan for all emergencies possible—fire outbreak, bomb explosion, active shooter, civil disturbance, chemical attack, biological attack, etc. The best time to prepare for an emergency is before it happens. Drills must be part of planning that anticipates business continuity imperatives.
6. *Emergency Preparedness:* Properly resource the organization for emergency and disaster resources including body bags if necessary. Other essential equipment includes face masks, torchlights, and call lists for government response agencies.
7. *Security Awareness:* Security awareness training should be part of the corporate culture in order to harden the corporate population against terrorist threats. Corporate security managers should develop and implement security consciousness and survival programs.

Security Management and Supervision General International Security Concerns—*H.D.G.T. Oey*

Not everything that counts can be counted, and not everything that can be counted counts.

Sign hanging in Einstein's office at Princeton

As the world changes more rapidly, the challenges of the modern corporate security professional increase exponentially. As the complexity of companies and of society as a whole increases, security issues have to be assessed in relation to "everything else that's important." Networked systems, information operations, cybercrime, (social) media, and ideological manipulation make it difficult to conclusively decide "what's important and what counts." This presents a challenge for management to develop an effective strategy that translates into hands-on operational decisions. Security professionals need to augment existing management and problem-solving skills with new methods as analog solutions tend to fail in a digital environment.

How This Century Differs From Centuries Past

During the past centuries the western world has been focused on expansion, growth, technological advancements and an increase in personal liberty. Most countries developed and evolved in similar but secular ways. They kept their borders closed and their monetary units independent. Societies and countries alike were separate entities with individual identities, preferences and habits. The pillars of which were firmly held in place by economic balance, religious values, political order and societal hierarchy. Beginning in the 1960s and 1970s, this began to change, propelled in a different direction by the sexual revolution and social expansion. Mental and physical freedom integrated societies and countries laterally, and combined with the unparalleled materialism of the 1980s, the walls of society were happily breached by pauper and politician alike. Countries integrated as the Berlin Wall fell and communism was defeated only to generate even more social integration and mental, vocal and physical freedom. Even with all of the newfound freedom, the beginning of the 1990s saw a new phenomenon was already virally spreading its footprint. The power of computer science and information technology made a giant leap forward feeding off the freedom and economic seeds that were sown decades earlier. With the Internet, freedom not only expanded yet further, it developed a whole new dimension of freedom and made possible the inception of a new paradigm: a holistically networked society that operates much like a biological organism. The cells are the people, the organs the systems, and the blood the information.

With the twenty-first century, society has moved into the information age. Society is becoming increasingly more difficult to grasp because of the rapid development of social, physical and digital environments that are characterized by the following elements:

The twenty-first century is:

- Networked, adaptive, creative, positive
- Proactive, holistic, engaged, social
- Sustainable, responsible, constructive
- Multidimensional
- Viral, digital, quantum

In the twenty-first century, new phenomena are being encountered such as social media influence, viral competitive behavior, cybercrime, networked corporate espionage, and artificial identities. This is in addition to, not in place of, existing problems. This has created increasingly more complex issues—issues that are more chaotic and interrelated than before. This new phenomena influence thoughts and habits and generate emerging behavior that in itself affects not only the phenomenon it originated from but also other phenomena on an unprecedented scale. The interconnectedness of individuals, families, groups, tribes, populations, and territories is increasing exponentially through recent technological advancements in the use of Internet, social media, smart phones and geospatial information technology. This affects the peoples' perception of the world and its problems, but more importantly it affects understanding why a company or organization is less efficient.

It is not difficult to see how seemingly unrelated phenomena such as Facebook and Twitter affect operations and how competitors have an increased effect on the market through competitive intelligence. Therefore, a modern company needs to transform problem solving skills to match the networked twenty-first century reality. It means looking at problems holistically (i.e., in relation to "everything else"). For example, the Russian involvement in Ukraine, the rise of the Islamic State, Ebola in West Africa, and the immigration crisis in the United States all have in common the fact that a singular linear solution, like a border, is declining in efficacy in the face of networked, interrelated, and viral phenomena.[1]

Corporations and governments have the perception that transformation costs money and time, and that during a recession there is not enough money but ample time available. The paradox of a recession in a networked world however is that the opposite is true: there is enough value but limited time! To understand this concept, look at Metcalfe's Law. Transformation and adaptation to the information age is different than change in the twentieth century because in a networked world Metcalfe's Law applies. The information age has two essential characteristics:

1. Networked connections
2. Knowledge dominance[2]

According to Metcalfe's Law, the value of the network increases exponentially (squared) proportional to the number of active users.[3] When the value of the network increases the value of shared knowledge will increase exponentially as well (Figure 43.1).

This will generate knowledge dominance where the network is most active. The importance of the implications of Metcalfe's Law is twofold. First, it means that linear development of governments and corporations is favorable in the early stages of a networked society (the end of the twentieth century); however, once the network grows and gains momentum, the linear improvement is not fast enough and these organizations will increasingly lag behind the networked ones. Secondly, in a short amount of time, networked users can assign a considerable value to a certain piece of information that will

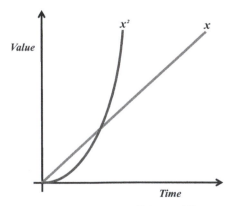

FIGURE 43.1 Exponential development according to Metcalfe's Law (x^2) compared to linear development (x).

not be recognized as valuable by someone outside the network. The result of which is that blind spots will start to develop that may only be discovered when it is too late.

In a sense, the perception of time is equivalent to a frog being slowly heated in a pan. By the time the water comes to a boil, it is too late. Corporations and governments alike do not adequately realize that they are developing slower than the world around them. If corporations, governments, and organizations do not start to develop themselves exponentially, they will find it increasingly difficult to adapt to reality and they will decrease the value they add to society.

Criminal organizations and subversive governments organically use the possibilities the information age offers. As a result, these networked groups evolve faster with time and no adequate protection can be offered by doing what used to work in the past. The hacking of the Belgian Ministry of Foreign Affairs in which confidential NATO files regarding Ukraine were stolen, exemplifies the vulnerability of linear organizational development.[4]

In order to transform problem solving capabilities to connect with twenty-first century reality and complexity, people will have to act progressively, assertively and proactively. While in the twentieth century, business models focused primarily on growth and outperforming the competition, while in the twenty-first century, business models seem to focus on information dominance and surviving the competition.

Survival of the Smartest

Research has shown that intelligent, well-motivated people, working together in a group, often collectively decide on the wrong conclusions.[5] They did not fail because they were ignorant—they failed because they followed a poor process to arrive at their conclusions. An interesting question that arises is why a corporate decision-making process usually is not part of a business continuity plan. Business continuity management is a part of security management and has been well established within the corporate governance system (Figure 43.2).

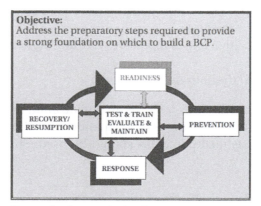

FIGURE 43.2 Readiness—the first step in developing a business continuity plan (ASIS).[6]

In order to maintain continuity and avoid bankruptcy, three elements are of vital importance in the twenty-first century:

1. A corporate decision-making process
2. Knowledge dominance
3. An agile organization

It is not a matter of whether one can afford to do this; it is a question of whether one can afford not to.

The Corporate Decision-Making Process

The corporate decision-making process uses a well structured approach and focuses on developing and managing knowledge instead of information. Knowledge is being defined as "analyzed information placed in context of the competitive environment" and contains the elements in Figure 43.3.

Decision makers (management) can lead their companies proactively by using the perks of a networked world. It starts by holistically analyzing oneself and the commercial operating environment of customer and competitor systems (competitor model). Developing a direction based on past experience and future probabilities is where knowledge management comes into play.

Knowledge Management

Knowledge management is the development, dissemination, integration, and retention of information and knowledge in a networked organization. Unlike a government agency, a corporation exists by the virtue of making money. Corporate knowledge management does not make money for the company in a primary fashion. It does not add to the EBIT (Earnings Before Interest and Tax), but does safeguard against being blindsided and out-maneuvered by the competition. Knowledge management creates the following:

- Reduction of uncertainty
- Reduction of losses
- Increase in situational awareness
- Increase in creative, positive, and competitive work atmosphere
- Higher effectiveness
- Higher contribution to "the bottom line"

Analysis plays an essential role as it allows an organization to define and decide "what is important in relation to everything else." Depending on the complexity of a specific problem, different analysis methodologies should be used. Simple linear problems are

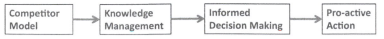

FIGURE 43.3 Corporate decision-making process.

solved using singular techniques. Complex phenomena require advanced modeling such as Multi-Disciplinary Analysis or System of Systems modeling.

An Agile Organization

An agile organization is flexible, resilient, and uses its networked corporate structure to use the power of Metcalfe's law (network value and knowledge dominance) in a positive manner. In order to achieve this situation, all parts of a company should work together much like the cells in a biological organism.[7] In an economic recession with a declining market, it is illogical to expect growth. The business model of an agile organization allows it to proactively adapt itself to a changing environment (survival). All corporate governance processes should be integrated and strive to collectively support an agile corporation with knowledge dominance.

Tools to Develop a Systemic Understanding of the Operating Environment in the Twenty-First Century

> *We cannot solve problems by using the same kind of thinking we used when we created them.*
>
> —*Albert Einstein (1879-1955)*

The twenty-first century has become the information age. The world is becoming more complex, chaotic, and interrelated. This affects the way problems are perceived, but more importantly, it affects the way problems are understood and resolved. As criminal innovative ideas and subversive creative technologies emerge, adequate protection cannot be provided using existing methodologies. Problem-solving skills need to be transformed to match the new reality. This paradigm shift is also referred to as changing from Newtonian thinking to quantum thinking. It refers to looking at problems holistically—in relation to "everything else."

The Paradigm Shift

Twenty-first century problems tend to be a multifaceted, complex aggregate of interacting systems that operate interactively like a biological organism. Consequently, the way to analyze and understand such a complex situation cannot be reached through a linear analysis (Newtonian) process. Newtonian models assume the world is continuous and single-valued. The real world however is disconnected complex, and multistate.

The mismatch of Newtonian models with real-world biological systems indicates that several Newtonian assumptions currently used to analyze systems are providing misleading and/or incomplete assessments. This process has been described as a paradigm shift. In a paradigm shift the same question asked twice gets two different answers. The difference depends on the underlying assumptions made about the world. New methodologies for warning intelligence can be developed based on quantum rather than Newtonian thinking. This means these methodologies view the problem as a whole (holistic) and from a different (nonlinear) perspective and generate higher order "solution spaces." This change in thought is the intrinsic meaning of the term *transformation*.

The way to allow for a change in thought and to analyze such complex problems is through the intelligence-led security approach that allows analysis of different problems from simple to complex.

The Three Gate Model

Contemporary security management methodologies call for an integrated approach to mitigate a company's vulnerabilities. In essence, an organization can be penetrated by breaching one or all of three gates. These gates are referred to as the logical, physical, and personnel gates.

Intelligence Analysis

Information is not knowledge

—*Albert Einstein (1879-1955)*

Many security issues are countered by passive and/or reactive measures, such as building a higher fence or creating a more heavily guarded facility. It is focused on deterring the threat, not on deterring the cause or origin. In order to deter the cause, the security domain will have to move from reactive to proactive measures. This means creating insight from the incidents and information that is already known. Knowledge grows where intelligence is abundant. The process of deriving intelligence from information is called intelligence analysis. Effective intelligence analysis is derived from a systematic process. Studies show that smart, well-motivated people often agree on the wrong solution. As stated earlier: they do not fail because they are stupid. They fail because they follow "a poor process in arriving at their decisions"[8] (Figure 43.4).

A Systematic Process Is the Most Effective Way to Facilitate Good Analysis[9]

Although this looks straightforward, many intelligence products do not match reality. This is due to the problem being more complex than the analytic method used on it. Human evidential reasoning is mainly adequate for frequently experienced events. Reasoning heuristics, evolved to be cognitively efficient and effective in our high-base rate world, often resulting in biased reasoning (grossly over- or underestimating probabilities) when faced with low-base rate events, such as deception.[10] Deception is relatively rare, so it is unsurprising that people are poor at counterdeception. Heuristics can result in the following analytic errors that hinder effective counterdeception.

- Poor anomaly detection: Analysts miss environmental cues of anomalies, or prematurely dismiss anomalies as irrelevant or inconsistent with other intelligence;
- Misattribution: inconsistent or anomalous events are often attributed to collection gaps or processing errors, rather than to deception;

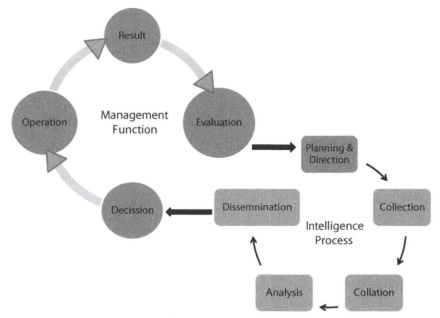

FIGURE 43.4 The intelligence cycle showing function and process.

- Failure to link deception tactics to deception hypotheses: When they do notice anomalies, analysts usually fail to recognize anomalous evidence as indicators of deception[11];
- Inadequate support for deception hypotheses: Analysts fail to link their assessment of an adversary's deception tactics and goals to the adversary's strategic goals; i.e., analysts fail to test denial or deception COAs (course of actions) against all the available evidence.

These analytic pitfalls can be avoided by proper analytical training and by using the intelligence led security analytic process (ILS). The ILS is analysis-driven and generates actionable intelligence for policymakers. Generally, one side (evidence) can be seen as the traditional security domain. The other side (assumptions) can be seen as the traditional intelligence domain. Integrating both in an "all sources context" generates knowledge and defines proactive measures. It allows for both linear and non-linear complex problems to be addressed.

Proactive Risk Management

Risk management strategies as described and standardized by ASIS International focus on the detect–delay–respond (DDR) cycle. Although effective, the methodology does not allow for detection of emerging technologies, nor does it advocate a proactive posture. Augmenting the existing DDR cycle with counterintelligence and knowledge management methodologies, to allow for the deterrence or disruption of threats, will move operations from the reactive to the proactive realm. It allows proactively sensing what dangers are moving to exploit unconscious vulnerabilities.

System of Systems Analysis

The most beautiful thing we can experience is the mysterious. It is the source of all true art and science.

—Albert Einstein (1879-1955)

To understand any phenomenon, ask the following question:

How do we create the necessary understanding of the operating environment, the competition as an adaptive entity within that environment, and ourselves, so we can determine how to most effectively and efficiently influence a potential adversary's perceptions, capabilities, and decision making?

The answer to the question begins with a deliberate and thorough analytical process before a crisis actually unfolds. That process is called a system of systems analysis (SoSA).

This approach advocates viewing the competition (or opposing group) as a complex adaptive system of interrelated systems on strategic level. SoSA attempts to identify, analyze, and relate the goals and objectives, organization, dependencies and interdependencies, external influences, and other aspects of the various systems and subsystems. The objective is to determine the systemic significance of each element relative to the overall system's goals and intentions. This helps assess the systemic dependent variables of the various elements and determine how decision makers/management can change corporate strategy and operational decisions.

Viewing a competitor as a complex system of systems increases the insight into the complex relationships, interdependencies, strengths, and vulnerabilities within and throughout a competitor's political structure, military (operational) capabilities, economic system, social structure, and information and infrastructure networks. Analysts capture the results of SoSA in "knowledge maps" and databases that support effects-based management. SoSA is primarily used by analysis units or think tanks but can be applied on a smaller scale using a methodology called "red teaming" or alternative analysis.

Conclusion

To understand and model a potential threat or vulnerability, decision makers should be encouraged to make timely and educated operational decisions by investing in the following:

- Transforming the protective (passive) function of security to include an early warning (proactive) function
- Integrating the intelligence domain with the security domain
- Creating (European) Standards and Definitions for the Security and Intelligence domain
- Creating and providing a curriculum of applied security and intelligence training courses to expand general knowledge
- Creating a platform information exchange—a networked database in which security professionals can develop, share, and retain knowledge

Protection of Assets Managed in Times of Conflict—*Bruce W. Dobbins*

The more things change, the more they stay the same. Consider the looting and destruction of museums and artifacts in Iraq after the US invasion, then remember the looting and destruction of museums throughout Europe during the Second World War. While the destruction of an international legacy is a tragedy for the world; it still pales before other security concerns faced when a region is at war—whether those security concerns originate as the result of the 2003 Iraq invasion or the current security problems caused by the emergence of ISIS today.

The security manager must focus specifically upon the assets that they are personally responsible for protecting on behalf of a client or firm. While that assessment process will no doubt be influenced by what is happening around them; the focus must be limited to the protection of the assets under their control—or that the company controls. Narrowing this discussion allows one to keep the scope of the discussion within reasonable limits while still addressing all of the key considerations.

The function of security is always focused on the protection of people, first, then property. Therefore, the concerns in asset protection include the staff within the threat area and the protection of the firm's reputation. In addition, security is, in the loss control function, also very concerned about the reduction of loss as a function of protecting or enhancing the profitability of the firm. Security managers must concurrently adopt a multifaceted approach that covers the entirety of the asset protection process in a mutually supportive holistic fashion.

Using the traditional WAECUP (Waste, Accident, Error, Crime, and Unethical Practices) model is certainly the best place to start; if vulnerabilities cannot be identified or quantified, the comprehensive approach to asset protection cannot be applied. Since these threats are interrelated, they must be understood and addressed as a package—and are more important when addressed within an international environment. Consider just a few of the big chunks that we would be responsible for as the security manager of a regional office for an international firm:

- Personnel security (in both work and residential locations), from the VIP to the lowest local-hire clerk, including methods of transport and routes taken between work and residence—bearing in mind that the company's response to a kidnapping, of even a local hire, may have devastating consequences for the reputation of that firm if not handled properly.
- Physical security at the sites of the work, the residential and common recreational locations, as well as the commonly used methods and routes of transport between these sites that include hardened physical methods as well as close coordination with local authorities.
- IT security in all of its forms—especially protection against cyber-attack and industrial espionage but also including the maintenance of both a reliable power supply and the physical integrity of the computer facilities. Infrastructure is a commonly overlooked, yet vital, component of IT security.

- Protecting cash and other small tangible assets that are both easy to transport and easy to lose track of in the midst of a crisis.
- Developing and implementing approved emergency response, contingency, and business continuity plans, to include the evacuation of staff and critical assets from a region in time of war or social disruption.

Where Is the Threat?

The question of "where is the threat?" cannot be addressed until it is understood what will be protected, the value and vulnerability of those assets, and the options regarding the levels of protection that can be practically provided. An armed attack can be deterred by providing armed guards (for instance); but there can never be absolute protection against a competently led and equipped armed attack—alternative contingency strategies must be prepared that include timely and safe evacuation of staff and preparation of essential assets that must also be evacuated. Many times, this means being close enough to the community (and what passes for a government in the local area) to be able to anticipate and assess the likelihood of an attack and evacuate staff and assets (if necessary) in advance of that attack. Reliance on government-provided warnings and information, while important, is not effective as such information usually is not actionable. Planning and implementation of security measures must stay ahead of an evolving security threat. Remember: complacency kills. The security professional must be out among and within the community where company/client assets are located. Security support must be proactive—not reactive—and flexible enough to adjust to evolving and changing threats before those threats become reality.

Know What Must Be Protected

The question of "where is the threat?" also cannot be addressed until it is understood what needs to be protected—the assessed value and vulnerability of those assets, and the ability to provide a predictable level of protection for those assets. This requires conducting some level of security risk assessment (SRA) for any site where the company does business (especially including all residential sites/areas), and then considering those sites as a functioning interconnected and interrelated system. For instance, assessing the communications connectivity between each site that not only includes the integrity and reliability of transportation links (lines of communication [LOCs] that include bridges, tunnels, route options, etc.) but also the communication methods to be used. As an example, consider using radios as opposed to cell phones if the cell phone tower is going to be jammed within minutes of a regional crisis unfolding.

When conducting an SRA, it is important to follow these key steps:

1. **Classify** the site in terms of function and importance—a site may be of limited functional value but have immense cultural or reputational value.
2. **Identify** the key components within a site that would do great damage if compromised (e.g., a computer database), stolen, or destroyed

3. **Rank** the components in priority order for each site and, if that site is a part of a greater system, then within that system as well.
4. **Review** that list against the actual assessed threat—both in the capability of a threat to do damage, and in their ability to identify in advance the value of the assets under protection.
5. **Assess** all vulnerabilities against those identified threats (everything from hacking and the malfeasance of an employee, to armed attack).
6. **Compare** the current security posture against those identified vulnerabilities.
7. **Re-rank** the resulting vulnerabilities and focus available security resources on mitigating those vulnerabilities. Prioritize your resources based upon what a potential perpetrator can know about the operations.

Using the CARVER(S) methodology is a simple yet important way to organize the analysis when going through the SRA process. It is also excellent for briefing senior leadership/management regarding the identified threats, vulnerabilities, and countermeasures. This methodology includes the cold-blooded questioning of the security posture and the firm's assets in the following key CARVER(S) areas:

1. **C**riticality: How important is that particular asset (or component)?
2. **A**ccessibility: How easy can a threat gain access to that asset?
3. **R**ecoverability: How long would it take your operations to recover from the loss of that asset?
4. **V**ulnerability: What is the level of threat-related exposure of that asset?
5. **E**ffect: What is the scope and magnitude of the consequences of that asset loss, including reputation and economic impact to the firm?
6. **R**ecognizability: How easy is it for a threat to identify your asset?
7. **S**hock: What would be the local, national, and international reaction to a successful attack against this asset and/or facility?

Planning and Practice: The Tie That Binds

Once the security manager knows what to protect, how vulnerable it is, and has implemented protection options to mitigate those vulnerabilities, the next step is to plan for and practice how to respond to those threats should they become real.

It is especially important, within an international context, to consider routes of ingress and egress from a location and how to get assistance into that area in times of turmoil as well as how best to evacuate staff and assets when necessary. This will require prioritizing which assets are expendable and which must be protected and saved. It is also vital to consider and plan for the possibility that one or more employees may be engaged in malfeasance and feeding confidential security information to a threat source. In this analysis, people always come first. Detailed planning must ensure the staff has sufficient resources to safely evacuate; resources including supplies, money, and documentation. The key is to keep planning and response ahead of an evolving crisis. The recent banking crisis in Egypt upon the demise of the Mubarak government, caused chaos in the streets and the inability to conduct Internet-based transactions, comes to mind. Regional banks, and their security personnel, should have foreseen this possibility and had plans in place to deal with it—years before it happened.

There will be times when a company will plan on destroying an asset rather than allowing it to be compromised. For instance, with adequate internationally based cloud backup, destroying a computer system and hard drives may secure the protection of valuable information contained within that asset-system. Planning for these eventualities must be multifaceted so that all planned actions support each other and the implementation of a unified coordinated response to a security crisis. In addition, key personnel must be specifically tasked, trained, and drilled as to how to carry out these responsibilities in times of crisis, well in advance of that crisis arriving.

Conclusion

A security professional is responsible for protecting a client's assets. In an international environment, this traditional role is further complicated by the presence of nontraditional and transnational threats. Yet, the classic tools of security assessment and management still form the foundation for developing a planning and response campaign to address any security situation.

ANSI/ASIS, PSC1, Aspects on Implementation—*Erik D. Erickson*

A company receives an invitation for bid (IFB), and considers responding. But the bid requirements specify that the security services need to comply with the ANSI/ASIS PSC.1:2012 standard. This standard is known as the "Management System for Quality of Private Security Company Operations—Requirements with Guidance." The job of the security manager is to make sure that this compliance is met. An order is given to the training manager in human resources to start this project and there is concern about how long will it take. An axiom of project management and linear programming: "Project management is essentially about time, quality, and money—pick two!" Most of the time it is not possible to have something ready on time, and maximizing quality, and keeping within the budget.

The training manager receives the PSC.1 standard and replies, "This is too vague, where are all the criteria?" These are not standards; they are just very general requirements with interpretable guidelines. How can guidelines be audited? How can those abstract concepts outlined in the proposed international standard be reduced into auditable steps?

An audit is a means of evaluating the effectiveness of a company's internal controls. It is a process of evaluating the way an organization presents its internal operations. Maintaining an effective system of internal controls is the key to achieving the company's business objectives, reporting on its operations, and preventing fraud or misappropriation of its assets. An audit answers the questions of "How effectively is the business run?", "Does the business meet the standards it set for itself, its stakeholders, and its clients?" Think of an audit as a medical checkup. A quality audit is to a regulated company what a medical examination is to a patient. It is a necessary procedure for evaluating a system's general "health" and for "diagnosing" problems in order to correct them.

At first glance, PSC.1 appears to provide some measurable standards for a security operation. However, what PSC.1 is suggesting seems to be some general guidelines, but no real specifics. After further review of the guidelines, it becomes apparent that these guidelines are mostly abstractions. Security managers must have specific standards to audit against, not abstractions.

The project manager, first-line manager, or security trainer must take those abstract guidelines and reduce them down into specific, concrete standards in which to measure. The saying comes to mind, "If it can measured, it's a fact; otherwise it's an opinion."

Security directors or company owners do not want opinions; they want specific answers that lead to results. They want information with which they can position their company to be more competitive. This applies to security auditors as well; companies do not want general opinions, they want specific recommendations on how to improve their operations. They want to know what the major nonconformities are and how to correct them in the shortest timeframe.

The task of trainers and educators is to make the complex simple. They simplify the complex by dividing and conquering. Abstract tools are needed to dissect and analyze the abstract. To understand the abstract, the following tools are needed:

1. Understanding of linguistic concepts; semiotics, and semantics (e.g., the "ladder of abstraction" by S.I. Hayakawa; and "semantic triangle" by I.A. Richard).
2. Understanding a few important ideas from set theory from mathematics.
3. Understanding basic concepts from object-oriented programming languages.

These simple theories are excellent analogies in which to better understand abstractions, and they help us simplify amorphous concepts.

Hayawaka's ladder of abstraction is an analogy (a linguistic comparison) between several elements of a set and another set of elements, and their relationship. The ladder of abstraction helps us visualize and conceptualize the relation between the abstract and the concrete (Figure 43.5).

FIGURE 43.5 S.I. Hayakawa's Ladder of Abstraction, as it applies to weapons.

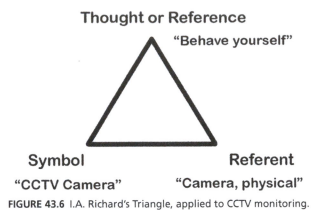

Thought or Reference
"Behave yourself"

Symbol
"CCTV Camera"

Referent
"Camera, physical"

FIGURE 43.6 I.A. Richard's Triangle, applied to CCTV monitoring.

Richard's semantic triangle helps to visualize the relation between objects and their respective meaning. The triangle is composed of three linguistic components: a symbol, a referent, and a reference. The "referent" is the object itself, such as a closed-circuit television (CCTV) camera. The "symbol" is a representation of the "referent", such as a sign with the words "Smile, you are on closed circuit television." The "reference" is that thought is generated in your mind when you think of the "symbol" or its "reference." In this case, the "reference" might be that "I am being observed on camera, I had better be well behaved" (Figure 43.6)

From set theory, understand that a set is a collection of elements. Another set, if equivalent, will have the same elements within the set. For example, if set "A" has the following elements (a, b, c, d) and set "B" has (a, b, c, d) then set "A" is equal to set "B" (A = B).

A security guard protocol for accepting and receiving a revolver will be different from a protocol for accepting and receiving a pistol. Why? Because the set of components that comprise a revolver are not the same as the set of components that comprise a pistol. For example, a revolver has the following simplified components: barrel, frame, handle/grip, trigger group, sites, hammer, and cylinder. The set of a revolver, set "A," contains elements (a, b, c, d, e, f, g). The set of components for a pistol are: barrel, frame, handle/grip, trigger group, sites, hammer, magazine. The set for a pistol, set "B," contains elements (a, b, c, d, e, f, m).

In Figure 43.7, there are two distinct sets of firearms: revolvers and pistols. They have elements in common (the intersection that includes elements: a, b, c, d, e, f, and the shaded area with diagonal strips). They also have elements that are not common too (elements that are mutually exclusive, 'g' and 'm'). A revolver has a cylinder (g), but does not have a magazine (m). However, a revolver and pistol both belong to a larger set of objects known as handguns. And handguns, along with another set of elements, rifles, are members of the larger set of firearms. In the writing and designing of rules of force, or use of force continuum, the ladder of abstraction and concepts from the set theory will be encountered.

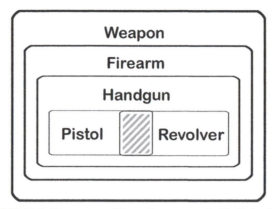

FIGURE 43.7 Using sets and Venn diagrams to clarify distinctions.

A class of weapons is abstract. The word weapon is an abstraction that includes many subclasses. These subclasses might be abstractions themselves: a handgun, a long gun. A subclass of weapons would be firearms. Typical firearms have subclasses of revolvers, pistols, carbines, rifles and shotguns. Why is this important? A security trainer writing a protocol for issuance of a handgun must be aware of these distinctions.

From a computer programming point of view, training is "programming." The generalized instruction set is a super class of instructions that contain methods transferred to other classes or objects. These instructions or methods are inherited to the subclasses. Think of instructions being giving from the president of a company that will apply to all employees of the company. It is a "top-down" communication; think of it as a river that flows downward. An example of a set of instructions that applies to everyone in the company is the "mission statement." Objects, classes, methods, inheritance, and polymorphism found in object-oriented programming are great tools to help security trainers be specific and think in a logical manner.

Moving up the ladder of abstraction, above the level of firearms is a larger class known as weapons. A Taser or Stinger is weapon that is not a firearm. It does not use ammunition that uses a primer, cartridge, powder charge (propellant), or a bullet, so these types of weapons are not classed as firearms. Training in weapons will include open and closed hand attacks and defenses. A human hand is a weapon. A human hand is an object that can be touched, it is concrete physical object. A weapon on the other hand (no pun intended) is a super class of objects, it is an abstraction.

In training as well as security auditing you need to be able to understand the ladder of abstraction and move up and down the ladder to apply this new standard PSC.1.

How are abstractions relevant to Section 9 of PSC.1 (Operation and Implementation)?

9.1 Operational Control:

a) Comply with legal and other regulatory requirements;

The operational word here is "comply," the first line manager or supervisor needs to understand what comply means. Does it mean to fill out this paperwork so that the security officer declares that "he or she will comply with all legal and other regulatory requirements"? Does a signature by the employee constitute compliance? Or, is it really a means to "lump and dump" the responsibility on to the employee?

What are the "legal" and "regulatory requirements" to operate in a particular country? Does everyone in the company understand what these are? Do these abstract concepts "map" into concrete concepts? (Mapping is a correspondence between two classes of objects.) How does comply or compliance "map" into the audit?

For example, one legal requirement for security officers might be to be at least 18 years of age. This can be audited by means of photo identification and verification. When identification is not readily available, such as a birth certificate, at least a high school diploma or equivalent should be provided for audit, as diplomas and transcripts can always be verified.

Another example is: what does "abide" actually mean to a security officer or a security auditor:

From PSC.1, Section 9.1.1:

c) Abide by local and applicable international laws, including international humanitarian, human rights and customary laws, as well as other obligations as described in this standard.

Security trainers should first tackle this by teaching security students about applicable local and international laws. Assume that the universal declaration of human rights for security officers is a two day course (16 h) to include a 50 question multiple choice exam. The students pass the exam with a 70% and that satisfies the 9.1.1 requirement, correct? No, that does not meet the requirement of "abide." "Abide" only applies directly to the security officers. They in the end will be judged by their actions as to whether they have "abided" by or conformed to human rights.

The trainer takes the abstract and makes it concrete. The trainer takes those abstract concepts such as human rights and nails them down to the concrete world of the security officer. The trainer must make things simple for the students. For example, the set of understanding of the student is = SKA1. The set of "desired" understanding of the student is = SKA2, this is arrived at by arrived at by the level of skills, knowledge, and abilities (SKAs) that the student needs to achieve.

$$SKA1 - SKAX = SKA2$$

Draw pictures, make Venn diagrams, or do something else. Create "references" for students to associate these ideas to the words they hear from you, the trainer, and to their thoughts. Use the three elements of Richard's semantic triangle. Basically, the trainer must create associations that have meaning and relevance to their students.

To understand what the student needs to understand (SKAX), one must understand all the elements of SKA1 (what it is that the student knows at that moment) and SKA2 (what it is that the student needs to understand to meet the requirements of the training necessary). Most instructors do not take the time to understand SKA1. There is no time to evaluate each and every specific security official's "SKA1," or to have the tools to diagnose this lack of understanding. Most instructors do not really understand all of the elements that comprise of set SKA2, and they not taken time to write these elements out. Instructors need to put these elements into what are known as "observables".

"Observables" are the elements in which one can "observe" with the five senses; touching/feeling, tasting, hearing, seeing, and smelling. The famous "sixth" sense is an amorphous abstraction of those five senses, which remains undefined. It is a "feeling" or a "suspicion.") The "sixth" sense is not auditable. During interviews, for example, most interviewers are not paying attention to all of their sensors. Interviewers that only rely on one or two of their sensory perceptions (two or three of their five senses), are therefore limited in their observations. How do they shake hands? How do they act or react under questions of stress? How do they smell?

In PSC.1, Section 9.2.5 Procurement and Management of Weapons, Hazardous Materials, and Munitions, there is the subsection "d" that deals with "Controls over their identification, issue, use, maintenance, return, and loss." If a security provider lacks specific procedures for this, the security managers will need to draft definitive procedures for each type of weapon. Consider what happens from the perspective of corporate responsibility. A corporation needs to continue for its stakeholders, but business continuity might be interrupted due to a lawsuit, because a procedure was not written down. In implementing policies and procedures there may be some resistance from those who cannot understand the reasoning behind it. To avoid misinterpretation of a procedure or protocol it is better to be as specific as possible. Always remember the KISS principle in teaching: Keep It Simple, Stupid!

Consider a firearms protocol with the following procedures:

1. Treat all firearms as if they are loaded.
2. Do not point the firearm (barrel) at anything you do not wish to destroy.
3. Do not put your finger on the trigger until you are ready to shoot.

Next is the protocol for the issuance and receipt of firearms (specifically handguns):

Handgun protocol: Observe all firearm safety procedures

Revolver: Issuance and receipt of the revolver.

1. Open the cylinder; use the extractor to eject all of the cartridges in the cylinder. This procedure effectively unloads the revolver.
2. Inspect that the cylinder is empty. Show the security officer that the cylinder is empty. This is verification.
3. Give the officer the revolver. Give the security officer the cartridges. Tell him or her to place the cartridges into the cylinder and close the cylinder, effectively loading the revolver.
4. Instruct the officer to holster the now "loaded" revolver.

Is the procedure complete? Was any step left out? Practice the steps with a fellow security officer or student. Note any difficulties in the procedure and write them down. Practice those procedures with different security officers and note the different interpretations in their responses. Writing procedures is a process.

What if the security officer, in the process of inspecting or manipulating the revolver, points it at another person? Well, the larger class of general instructions for firearms applies. On the handgun protocol, it does say in black and white: "Observe all firearms safety procedures." In the case of firearms, all the rules that apply to firearms apply to the subclass of handguns. What applies to firearms also applies to long guns and handguns, and therefore all the subclasses, like revolvers and pistols.

Assume that there exists the set of elements in the concrete realm that are all the observable elements needed to teach and pass the PSC.1 criteria for private security companies. Call that set of auditable elements = OBSERVABLEPSC01. The concrete and auditable is defined by this example: The student or candidate needs to impact a target seven times placed at 6 m, given a pistol and 10 cartridges of ammunition. The student either hits seven or more times on the target to pass the exam, or the student does not. Impacts on a silhouette or target are verifiable. Those are the verifiable, concrete, observables on the ladder of abstraction.

These elements can be found in a check list of the PSC.1 audit. It is a collection of observable elements that can be physically verified by an internal and/or external auditor. This set of elements OBSERVABLEPSC01 must be demonstrated by the PSC to receive certification under the new PSC.1 standards.

9.2 Resources, Roles, Responsibilities, and Authority:

"Management shall make available resources essential to establish, implement, maintain and improve the QAMS." QAMS is the abbreviation for Quality Assurance Management System. Understanding a QAMS is fundamental to understanding ANSI/ASIS PSC.1. QAMS and PSC.1 all come from a family organized structures or "frameworks" of doing business in an auditable form. Security companies should incorporate the processes outlined in ISO 9001, which is just QAMS, and in doing so also achieve certification in ISO 9001.

As for "to effectively deal with disruptive and undesirable events", this refers to business continuity, or ISO 22,301. That ISO standard specifies requirements to plan, establish, implement, operate, monitor, review, maintain and continually improve a documented management system to prepare for, respond to and recover from disruptive events when they arise. Another related ISO standard that might apply to a security operation is ISO 31,000. Although ISO 31,000 has not been developed with the intention for certification, but it does help management to formalize and conceptualize risk.

So how does a security manager put all of these abstract structures to work for him or her? First and foremost is to have the ability to see how the abstract concepts map or correspond into the concrete. For example, if the actions of corporate security officers are congruent with the vision and mission statement of the company, it could be said that the company is meeting its corporate goals as to its quality management.

Using concepts from set theory and sets can help organize and formalize abstractions. And once these abstractions are categorized and labeled, their mappings into the real world, the world of the concrete, can be studied and understood. One way of doing this is through object-oriented programming (OOP).

OOP is a set of programming languages that have objects (collection of elements, or classes) and methods (how those objects or classes relate to one another). C++, Perl, Python, PHP and the well-known Java and JavaScript are object-oriented programming languages. Where does OOP come into play in understanding how to apply abstract concepts and their applications in the real world? Begin with the concept of "class." A class contains elements. Call it the class or object known as democracy. Is it an abstract class? Yes, "democracy" cannot be seen or felt, but its elements can. International press releases often show photos of people coming out of the ballot stations with their fingers dyed as proof of having cast a vote—this is an element of "democracy" that is tangible.

9.2.2 Procedures for background screening and vetting of all persons

a) Consistency with legal and contractual requirements

In absence of established procedures, take the initiative and establish procedures and documentation.

Legal requirements:

9.2.2 a.1: Where are the company's security operations located? What local and national laws govern those operations at those locations? A subject-matter expert may be needed to advise on the subject as well as an interpreter if foreign languages are involved.

Contractual requirements:

9.2.2 a.2: What are the defined and verifiable limits of the contract? What can the security officers do and not do? A contract with undefined requirements or one that cannot be understood should not be signed. Legal advice from the corporate counsel should be obtained.

Identity verification:

9.2.2. b.1:

Age verification:

9.2.2. b.2:

Personal history verification:

9.2.2. b.3:

The line supervisor needs to communicate with the company's human resources department. The human resources department should verify the candidate's information, including contacting the teachers and all character references provided by the applicant. In some cases, investigators may talk to neighbors and teachers. A clear and traceable series of steps need to be documented to show "linkage." (Linkage is an auditable connection between two objects.)

d) Military and security services records check;

9.2.2.d1: Military service records:

9.2.2.d2: Security service records:

Labor and work history is an important indicator in predicting future work behavior. There is a correlation, as identified in human predictability and human reliability research.

9.2.2.e: Review of possible criminal records.

9.2.2.e1: Criminal records check:

9.2.2.e2: Legal or civil litigation check:

9.2.2.f: Review reports of human rights violations:

9.2.2.g Evaluation for substance abuse: Be specific in your standard, show what it is that you are testing for and to what criteria.

9.2.2.g1: Test for marijuana (THC): 50 ng/ml (or to what criteria?)

9.2.2.g2: Test for cocaine: 300 ng/ml.

9.2.2.g3: Test for methamphetamines, 1000 ng/ml.

Requirements for testing or due diligence can be included by just expanding the paperwork/checklist to add relevant substance abuse tests and corresponding sensitivities. For example, 9.2.2.g4 could be: Test for Methadone 300 ng/ml. Again, these are just suggestions for managers to structure their security program into an auditable framework.

9.2.2.h: Physical and mental evaluation for fitness with assigned activities;

9.2.2.h1: Medical examination for physical fitness:

Blood pressure test, diabetes test, etc. (Do not put "etc." or "etcetera" in audits. Legally that is a loophole.)

9.2.2.h2:

Aerobic fitness/cardiovascular fitness test: For example, run 3.2 km in 12 min; or, run 1.5 miles or 300 m in 1 min (a test that most police departments use to screen candidates).

9.2.2.h3:

Muscular strength and endurance test: For example, the number of pushups in 1 min or 2 min (will depend company's needs to complete the job required).

9.2.2.h4:

Muscular strength and endurance test: Number of sit ups in 1 min or 2 min, etc. (Good stomach muscles help prevent lower back problems and translates into less employee down time.)

9.2.2.h5:

Flexibility test: Consider the "sit and reach test" from the YMCA Fitness Testing and Assessment Manual, 4th edition, 2000—being able to move all joints through their full range of motion is important for good joint function as well as being able to walk, lift, and step normally.

9.2.2.h6:

Body composition test: The simple body mass index (BMI) test is a useful tool to diagnose candidates. It is a measure of body fat based on the height and weight of the candidate. Another body composition test includes just the waist circumference of the candidate. Both tests are helpful indicators of possible cardiovascular disease and health problems.

9.2.2.h7:

Psychological examination: Human resources must understand what the training and operations department needs to determine as suitable. That determination should be passed on to the psychologist to determine what test is most appropriate for selection of personnel (e.g., Kolbe Index, IPIP-NEO Personality Test, Myers-Briggs Type Indicator, MMPI, etc.) Other great indicators of personality and behavior are the candidate's driving record and credit scores. These are indirectly long-term statistical samplings of the candidate's behaviour and are relevant in determining human reliability.

Why is it important to specify the test? Perhaps in the future, there is a problem with employee performance. Given a proper security audit, it may be possible to narrow down the cause. This is part of PDCA cycle of "Plan Do Check and Act" cycle. One must determine if the selection criteria was flawed, and once identified, how to modify it. Good documentation will help in troubleshooting problem areas.

Always consider the costs of personnel selection. Are there ways to cut costs without sacrificing quality? Yes, there is a certain logical sequence to applying these selection criteria. Apply the least expensive and time-consuming tests first, then go on to the more expensive. For example, a company will not invest in a security candidate by starting with a polygraph exam and psychological exam when a series of physical fitness tests might disqualify the candidate early on.

Internal security audits do take time, and yes time is money. They take more time and money if your documentation is not in order. So it is better to start with a clear and easily auditable program. And once your internal audit is completed it is so much easier for third party auditing.

9.2.5 Procurement and Management of Weapons, Hazardous Materials, and Munitions.

9.2.5.a: Compliance Documentation (registrations, certifications, permits):

9.2.5.b: Acquisition: how these weapons are acquired shall be documented, where they were bought, from whom, the quantity, the quality.

9.2.5.c: Secure storage:

This is a very reasonable standard in the "risk reduction" policy. Are there reasonable measures in place to protect company firearms? What are the local standards; does the company meet them? And if no local standards exist, does the company apply the concept of "best practices"?

What is the operating standard or what is the acceptable risk that the company will accept in storing weapons? What is considered reasonable might vary from jurisdiction to jurisdiction. In absence of local standards, will the company accept European standards for wall safes or standards from Underwriters Laboratory (UL), such as UL-140, Class TL-30, Class TRTL-30, or TRTL-60?

Again, the idea is to take those abstract requirements and translate them into something concrete that can be audited against. If an item on the checklist simply reads "Wall safe exists for firearms," that meets the nominal requirement of the standard, but it does not meet a specific standard.

The standard does mention "explosives", but the title of this standard explicitly states PSC, Private Security Companies and not PMCs, Private Military Companies. PMCs probably have access to explosives, whereas most private security companies do not. This is not about clarifying the differences between the two nominal entities. Whether a company is a PMC or PSC, independent of what type of weapons are permitted or not permitted, the idea of traceability should apply.

Looking at section 9.4, Communication: "The organization shall establish, implement, and maintain procedures for: a) communicating with staff and employees," one can borrow informational structure from the ISO 27,001 Information Security standard. Specific elements of the 27,001 standard would have to be mapped into the security operation. Again, it is just a matter of reducing those abstractions down into something that can be exported into company operations so that progress can be audited.

In the PSC.1 section of 9.5.3 Occupational Health and Safety, here again, use the existing framework in ISO 18,001/OHSAS 18,001. ISO 18,001 as a framework for an occupational health and safety management system. It helps design and enact policies, procedures and controls needed for an organization to achieve the best possible working conditions, aligned to internationally recognized best practices.

Another important skill and ability for security auditors is, and always will be, emotional intelligence. Security professionals deal primarily with the human condition and humans have egos. Sometimes these egos are entwined to their work and work environment. An outsider (someone outside of the security company) coming into the security department for an external security audit must be sensitive to possible emotional attachments to a security protocol or procedure. Maybe the protocol or procedure lacks a few key components (or even vital components), but that does not give license to condemn or vehemently criticize. Proceed always with tact and cultural sensitivity. The auditor's job is to assist the company in reaching a better level of quality (Figure 43.8).

There are a lot of tools that exist for the security manager, first-line manager, and security auditor that are "right off the shelf." Sometimes tools have to be developed and deployed internally. However the availability of pre-fabricated frameworks is abundant in the storehouse of ISOs. It is important to take the time to learn their formats and content; ISO 9001, Quality Control Management, ISO 14,001 Environmental standards, ISO 18,001 for Occupational Health and Safety, ISO 22,301 Business Continuity, ISO 27,001 Information Security, ISO 28,000 Security Management Systems for the Supply Chain, ISO 31,000 Risk Management and finally the ANSI/ASIS PSC.1 standard. (Auditors and security consultants might also incorporate the NFPA standards within their evaluations of security.) Working with ISOs, such as ISO 9001, ISO 18,001, ISO 14,001, will enable security professionals to observe the parallels or "mappings" between the standards—the "common" elements or "intersections" between those mentioned standards and PSC.1.

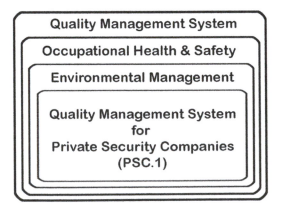

FIGURE 43.8 Perspective of ISO standards in relation to the PSC.1 standard.

Refer website http://www.ifpo.org for further information

End Notes

1. Schnurer E., *Good Fences Aren't Enough* (Somewhere: U.S. News & World Report, August 29, 2014): accessed November 28, 2014. Available: http://www.usnews.com/opinion/blogs/eric-schnurer/2014/08/29/border-fences-cant-stop-ebola-the-islamic-state-or-immigration-crises.

2. Alberts D. S., Stein F. P. and Gartska J. J., *Network Centric Warfare* (Washington, DC: U.S. Department of Defense, 1999): accessed November 28, 2014. Available: http://www.dodccrp.org/files/Alberts_NCW.pdf.

3. *Metcalfe's Law* (Location Unknown: Wikipedia, November 13, 2014): accessed November 28, 2014. Available: http://en.wikipedia.org/wiki/Metcalfe%27s_law.

4. Rafati M., *The Belgian Ministry of Foreign Affairs Digitally Disconnected After Attack* (The Netherlands: Cyberwarzone, May 12, 2014): accessed November 28, 2014. Available: http://cyberwarzone.com/belgian-ministry-foreign-affairs-digitally-disconected-hack/.

5. Russo J. E. and Schoemaker P. J. H., *Managing Overconfidence* (Cambridge, MA: Massachusetts Institute of Technology, Sloan Management Review, Winter 1992.): accessed November 28, 2014, vol. 33, no. 2. Available: http://forum.johnson.cornell.edu/faculty/russo/Managing%20Overconfidence.pdf.

6. ASIS Business Continuity Guideline. *A Practical Guide for Emergency Preparedness, Crisis Management and Disaster Recovery.* Copyright ASIS Internmational 2005, ISBN I-887056-56-4, page 10.

7. Senge P. M., *The Fifth Discipline: The Art & Practice of The Learning Organization* (New York, NY: Random House, January 5, 1999).

8. See note 5 above.

9. Khalsa S., *Forecasting Terrorism: Indicators and Proven Analytic Techniques* (Lanham, MD: Scarecrow Press, Inc., 2004).

10. Goldstein D. G. and Gigerenzer G., *The Recognition Heuristic: How Ignorance Makes Us Smart* (London, UK: Oxford University Press, 1999).

11. Stech, F. J. and Elässer, C., *Midway Revisited: Detecting Deception by Analysis of Competing Hypothesis* (McLean, VA: Stech & Elässer June 2004).

Index

Lightning Source UK Ltd.
Milton Keynes UK
UKOW07f1557170615

253668UK00005B/31/P